Benson John Lossing

Eminent Americans

Benson John Lossing

Eminent Americans

ISBN/EAN: 9783744790284

Printed in Europe, USA, Canada, Australia, Japan

Cover: Foto ©ninafisch / pixelio.de

More available books at **www.hansebooks.com**

EMINENT AMERICANS

COMPRISING

BRIEF BIOGRAPHIES

OF

LEADING STATESMEN, PATRIOTS, ORATORS AND OTHERS, MEN
AND WOMEN, WHO HAVE MADE AMERICAN HISTORY

By BENSON J. LOSSING, LL.D.

Author of "History of the United States," "Field Book of the
Revolution," and "War of 1812," etc.

ILLUSTRATED WITH OVER ONE HUNDRED FINE PORTRAITS
BY LOSSING AND BARRITT

NEW YORK
AMERICAN BOOK EXCHANGE
764 BROADWAY
1881

PREFACE.

> "Lives of great men all remind us
> We may make our lives sublime,
> And, departing, leave behind us
> Foot-prints on the sands of Time."

BIOGRAPHY is History teaching by example. It is the basis of all historical structures. The Chronicles of the nations are composed of the sayings and doings of their men and women. These make up the sum of History.

Sallust says, "I have often heard that Quintus Maximus, Publius Scipio, and other renowned persons of the Roman Commonwealth, used to say that, whenever they beheld the images of their ancestors, they felt their minds vehemently excited to virtue. It could not be the wax, nor the marble, that possessed this power; but the recollections of their great actions kindled a generous flame in their breasts, which could not be quelled till they, also, by Virtue, had acquired equal fame and glory."

It is with the earnest desire of producing precisely such effects upon the minds and hearts of the young people of our country, that this volume has been prepared—that these images have been set up. The Roman youth were excited to great, and generous, and virtuous deeds, by the sight of material objects and the voices of Orators. Our youth have their aspirations for noble achievements awakened and cherished more by the silent yet potent ministration of Books which tell of men worthy to be imitated as examples, or studied as warnings, than by merely sensuous impressions.

The materials for this book have been drawn from the Annals of the United States of America, as Colonies and as a Federal Republic. Such persons have been selected, as examples, who seemed to illustrate by their lives, some special phase in the political, religious, and social life of our country, during its wonderful progress from its earliest settlement until the present time. I have endeavored to present such prominent points of character and deeds, in their lives, as would give the reader a general idea of their relative position in the history of their times; and have also aimed to make the brief sketches so attractive and suggestive, as to excite a desire in the young to know more of these characters and their historical relations, and thus to persuade them to enter upon the pleasant and profitable employment of studying the prominent persons and events of our Republic. If this volume shall achieve that result, the pleasure experienced by the Author in the preparation of it, will be distributed according to his desire.

THE RIDGE, DOVER PLAINS, N. Y.

INDEX.

A

	PAGE
Abbott, Jacob	470
Adams, Samuel	76
Adams, John	87
Adams, John Q.	309
Allerton, Isaac	14
Allison, Francis	47
Alexander, William	106
Allen, Ethan	128
Allston, Washington	262
Ames, Fisher	71
Anderson, Richard C.	299
Armstrong, John	316
Arnold, Benedict	135
Asbury, Francis	195
Ashe, John	99
Ashmun, Jehudi	325
Astor, John Jacob	379
Audubon, John J.	272

B

	PAGE
Bacon, Nathaniel	42
Bainbridge, William	310
Baldwin, Thomas	201
Baldwin, Abraham	256
Ballou, Hosea	318
Banneker, Benjamin	406
Bartram, John	45
Barlow, Joel	117
Bard, Samuel	118
Barney, Joshua	120
Barry, John	121
Barton, William	137
Bayard, James A.	267
Beck, T. Romeyn	409
Belknap, Jeremy	104
Benton, Thomas Hart	448
Biddle, Nicholas	346
Bland, Richard	142
Blennerhassett, Harman	377
Boone, Daniel	192
Boudinot, Elias	133
Boudoin, James	65
Bowditch, Nathaniel	246
Boyleston, Zabdiel	61
Bradford, William	62
Bradford, William	198
Brainerd, David	101
Brant, Joseph	158
Brewster, William	10
Brooks, John	145
Brown, Charles B.	290
Brown, Jacob	338
Brown, James	348
Brown, Moses	371
Bryant, William Cullen	476
Buchanan, James	435
Buel, Jesse	356
Burr, Aaron	253
Burke, Ædanus	258
Burnett, Robert	401
Byrd, William	31

C

	PAGE
Calvert, Leonard	223
Calhoun, John C.	326
Cass, Lewis	464
Canonicus	15
Carroll, John	49
Carroll, Charles	146
Carver, Jonathan	74
Cary, Lott	275
Carey, Matthew	300
Caswell, Richard	96
Channing, William E.	373
Chapin, Edwin Hubbell	487
Chauncey, Isaac	342
Chittenden, Thomas	125
Choate, Rufus	480
Church, Benjamin	12
Claiborne, William C. C.	358
Clarke, George R.	138
Clay, Henry	398
Clinton, DeWitt	257
Clinton, George	330
Colden, Cadwallader	33
Colburn, Zerah	351
Colles, Christopher	235
Cooper, Thomas	239
Cooper, James F.	344
Copley, John S.	52
Cornplanter	231
Coxe, Tench	80
Craik, James	164
Crockett, David	311
Cruger, Henry	266

D

	PAGE
Dana, Francis	92
Davie, William R.	89
Davidson, Lucretia M.	315
Day, Stephen	11
Deane, Silas	79
Dearborn, Henry	328
Decatur, Stephen	343
De Kalb, Baron	291
Dickenson, John	209
Douglas, Stephen Arnold	414
Downing, Andrew J.	375
Drayton, William H.	86
Dunlap, William	337
Dwight, Timothy	107

E

	PAGE
Edwards, Jonathan	177
Eliot, John	17
Ellsworth, Oliver	102
Everett, Edward	420

F

Farragut, David Glascoe	481
Ferguson, Catharine	404
Fillmore, Millard	467
Fitch, John	93
Flint, Timothy	391
Franklin, Benjamin	39
Franklin, William	129
Francis, John W.	431
Francis, John W., Jr.	407
Fulton, Robert	155

G

Gadsden, Christopher	109
Galloway, Joseph	72
Gallatin, Albert	321
Gallaudet, Thomas H	381
Garrison, William Lloyd	471
Gaston, William	350
Gates, Horatio	295
Girard, Stephen	271
Godfrey, Thomas	69
Goodrich, Samuel Griswold	466
Gordon, William	166
Graham, Isabella	332
Gray, William	214
Greene, Nathaniel	59
Greene, Joseph	130
Greenough, Horatio	393
Greeley, Horace	461
Gridley, Richard	122
Grundy, Felix	366

H

Habersham, Joseph	134
Hale, Nathan	212
Halleck, Fitz-Greene	450
Hamilton, Alexander	213
Hancock, John	150
Harnett, Cornelius	83
Harper, James	435
Harrison, Benjamin	103
Harrison, William H	240
Harrington, Jonathan	376
Hawthorne, Nathaniel	426
Hayne, Robert Y	280
Hedding, Elijah	382
Henry, Joseph	477
Henry, Patrick	126
Henderson, Richard	180
Hicks, Elias	208
Holmes, Abiel	329
Hooker, Thomas	26
Hopkins, Samuel	240
Hopkins, Stephen	320
Hopkinson, Francis	57
Hopkinson, Joseph	370
Houston, Samuel	453
Howard, John E	141
Howe, Robert	173
Hull, William	219
Humphreys, David	215
Hutchinson, Thomas	58

I

	PAGE
Inman, Henry	386
Irving, Washington	416
Izard, Ralph	282

J

Jackson, James	131
Jackson, Andrew	244
Jay, John	171
Jefferson, Thomas	123
Johnson, Andrew	469
Johnson, Reverdy	479
Johnson, Richard M	367
Johnson, William	100
Jones, John Paul	95
Jones, David	140
Judson, Adoniram	304
Judson, Ann H	308

K

Kent, James	335
King, Rufus	150
Kinnison, David	403
Kirkland, Samuel	66
Knox, Henry	274
Kosciuszko, Thaddeus	306

L

La Fayette, M. de	287
Lamb, John	263
Langdon, John	154
Laurens, Henry	161
Lawrence, James	352
Lawrence, Abbott	411
Ledyard, John	82
Lee, Ann	68
Lee, Henry	152
Lee, Richard H	186
Lee, Charles	307
Lee, Arthur	234
Lee, Robert Edmund	474
Legarè, Hugh S	308
Leisler, Jacob	64
Lillington, John A	94
Lincoln, Benjamin	298
Lincoln, Abraham	432
Livingston, Robert R	105
Livingston, Edward	174
Livingston, John H	200
Lovel, John	97
Lyman, Phineas	113

M

Macdonough, Thomas	323
Macomb, Alexander	303
M'Intosh, Lachlin	279
M'Kean, Thomas	203
Macon, Nathaniel	312
Madison, James	255
Madison, James	296
Manly, John	114
Marion, Francis	184
Marshall, John	216
Martin, François X	243
Mason, John	28
Mather, Cotton	27
Mather, Increase	48
Meigs, Return J	302
Mercer, Hugh	396
Miantonomoh	20

	PAGE
Mitchill, Samuel L	232
Milnor, James	360
Miller, William	387
Monroe, James	304
Montgomery, Richard	157
Morgan, Daniel	222
Morris, Robert	90
Morris, Gouverneur	202
Morris, George P.	419
Morse, Samuel Finley Breese	460
Motley, John Lothrop	463
Mott, Lucretia	484
Motte, Rebecca	75
Moultrie, William	262
Muhlenberg, Peter	210
Murray, Lindley	63

N

Nelson, Thomas, Jr	111
Newell, Harriet	285
Nott, Eliphalet	429

O

Oglethorpe, James E	51
Olin, Stephen	384
Osceola	357
Otis, James	162
Otis, Harrison G	402

P

Paine, Thomas	228
Paine, Robert Treat	440
Patterson, Robert M	396
Peabody, George	455
Peale, Charles W	176
Peirce, Benjamin	483
Penn, William	24
Perry, Oliver H	348
Percival, James G	413
Peters, Richard	169
Phipps, William	21
Philip, King	38
Philipse, Mary	227
Physic, Philip S	330
Pickens, Andrew	194
Pickering, Timothy	165
Pierce, Benjamin	283
Pierce, Franklin	447
Pike, Zebulon M	191
Pinckney, Charles C	143
Pinckney, Thomas	230
Pinkney, William	237
Pocahontas	16
Polk, James K	388
Pontiac	70
Porter, David	302
Preble, Edward	199
Prentiss, Sargeant S	397
Prescott, William	175
Prescott, William Hickling	454
Putnam, Rufus	182
Putnam, Israel	226

Q

Quincy, Josiah	424
Quincy, Josiah, Jr	187

R

Ramsay, David	167
Randolph, Peyton	84

	PAGE
Randolph, Edmund	170
Randolph, John	292
Red Jacket	264
Reed, Joseph	207
Rittenhouse, David	35
Rivington, James	208
Robinson, Edward	428
Rodgers, John	372
Rogers, Robert	77
Ruggles, Timothy	73
Rumford, Count	269
Rush, Benjamin	78
Rutledge, John	153

S

St. Clair	242
Schoolcraft, Henry R	423
Schuyler, Philip	189
Scott, Winfield	436
Seabury, Samuel	110
Sears, Isaac	251
Sevier, John	331
Seward, William Henry	459
Shelby, Isaac	98
Sherman, Roger	168
Silliman, Benjamin	442
Simms, William Gilmore	452
Slater, Samuel	313
Smith, John	34
Smith, Samuel	324
Sparks, Jared	443
Spencer, Ambrose	302
Spencer, John C	414
Standish, Miles	13
Stark, John	248
Steuben, Baron De	141
Stevens, Ebenezer	148
Stevens, Robert L	415
Stewart, C	439
Stiles, Ezra	49
Story, Joseph	289
Stuart, Gilbert C	114
Stuyvesant, Peter	22
Sullivan, John	347
Sumner, Charles	457
Sumter, Thomas	236
Swain, David L	430

T

Talbot, Silas	211
Taylor, Bayard	473
Taylor, Zachary	353
Telfair, Edward	252
Tennent, William	116
Thacher, William	254
Thomas, Isaiah	149
Thomson, Charles	46
Trumbull, Jonathan	43
Trumbull, John	196
Trumbull, John	259
Tyler, John	426

U

Uncas	37

V

Van Buren, Martin	427
Van Rensselaer, Stephen	260
Vassar, Matthew	445

W

Name	Page
Warren, Mercy	85
Warren, Joseph	190
Warner, Seth	206
Washington, George	55
Washington, Martha	119
Wayland, Francis	418
Wayne, Anthony	286
Weare, Meshech	183
Webster, Noah	224
Webster, Daniel	276
Weems, Mason L.	112
West, Benjamin	20
Wheatley, Philips	249
Wheaton, Henry	334
Wheelock, Eleazer	32
White, William	53
Whitney, Eli	132
Whipple, Abraham	220
Weiser, Conrad	251
Williams, Roger	18
Williamson, Hugh	156
Willett, Marinus	247
Willis, N. P.	422
Wilson, Alexander	181
Wilson, Henry	463
Winslow, Edward	23
Winthrop, John	9
Winthrop, John	44
Wirt, William	218
Witherspoon, John	179
Wolcott, Oliver	238
Wooster, David	42
Woods, Leonard	330
Wool, John E.	438
Wright, Silas	355
Wright, Benjamin	363
Wythe, George	278

JOHN WINTHROP.

THE PILGRIM FATHERS[1] planted the seeds of the Plymouth Colony, amid the December snows, in 1620. Eight years afterward other emigrants, with John Endicott at their head, as governor, founded the colony of the Massachusetts Bay, at Salem. In 1629, John Winthrop, a wealthy Puritan, resolved to convert his large estate into money, and link his fortunes with this new colony. He was chosen to succeed Endicott, as governor, before he left England, and soon after his arrival in June, 1630, he chose the peninsula of Shawmut, on

---

1. In the year 1608, John Robinson, a pious pastor of a flock in the north of England, who would not conform to the rituals of the Established Church, fled, with his people, to Holland, to avoid persecution. They felt that they were only *Pilgrims*, and assumed that name. Toward the close of 1620, about 100 of them, including women and children, arrived on the shores of Cape Cod Bay in the ship May Flower, and planted a colony where the town of Plymouth now stands. They are known as *The Pilgrim Fathers*.

which the city of Boston now stands, for a residence, because pure water gushed from its hills. There he founded the future metropolis of New England.[1]

John Winthrop was born in Groton, Suffolk county, England, on the 12th of June, 1587, and was educated for the profession of the law. Theological studies possessed greater charms for him, and the peculiar seriousness of his mind led him to Puritanism,[2] as he found it at the beginning of King Charles' reign. Because of his many admirable qualities, he was chosen governor under the charter granted in 1629, and was therefore really the *first* governor of Massachusetts, notwithstanding the earlier services of Endicott, as head of the actual settlers.

Winthrop held his first court, composed of deputy-governor Dudley and members of the Council, on the 23d of August, 1630, under a large tree at Charlestown; and the first topic brought under consideration was *a suitable provision for the support of the gospel*. Mr. Winthrop was a man of great benevolence. It was his practice to send his servants among the people at meal-time, on trifling errands, with instructions to report the condition of their tables. When informed of any who appeared to want, he always sent a supply from his own abundance. He was also merciful as a magistrate, for he considered it expedient to temper the severity of law with more lenity in an infant colony than in a settled state. Because of his lenity toward offenders, he was charged, in 1636, of dealing "too remissly in point of justice." The ministers decided that "the safety of the gospel" required more rigor; and, contrary to the motions of his own liberal heart, he was obliged to yield. So zealous were the chief men of the colony in favor of rigorous discipline, that deputy Dudley, a bigot of the strictest stamp, was chosen governor, in place of Winthrop, in 1634; but the latter was re-elected in 1637, and held the office of chief magistrate most of the time, until his death.

Governor Winthrop came to America a wealthy man, but died quite poor. His benevolent heart kept his hand continually open, and he dispensed comforts to the needy, without stint. He regarded all men as equally dear in the eyes of their Maker, yet his early education blinded him to the dignity of true democracy. He regarded it with much disfavor; and when the people of Connecticut asked his advice concerning the organization of a government, he replied, "The best part of a community is always the least, and of that least part the wiser are still less." He had little faith in "the people." Worn out with toils and afflictions, this faithful and upright magistrate entered upon his final rest on the 26th of March, 1649, at the age of sixty-one years.

WILLIAM BREWSTER.

ONE of the noblest of the Pilgrim Fathers, was William Brewster, the spiritual guide of those who landed on Plymouth Rock, in bleak December, 1620. He was born in England in 1560, and was educated at Cambridge. William Davidson, Queen Elizabeth's ambassador to Holland, was his friend and patron in youth. When a wicked policy caused the Queen to disgrace and even destroy innocent men, Davidson, who had been appointed Secretary of State, was a great sufferer. Brewster, with a grateful loyalty, adhered to him as long as

---

1. Boston was so named in honor of John Cotton, minister of Boston, England, who came to America in 1633, and was appointed teacher in the church in Winthrop's capital.
2. Those who would not conform to the rituals of the Established Church of England, and professed great purity of life, as well as of doctrine, were called PURITANS, in derision. It has since become an honorable title.

he could serve him, and then retired among his friends in the North of England. His religious zeal there burned brightly, and his hand and purse were ever open in well-doing. He finally became disgusted with the assumptions and tyranny of the Established Church, and joined a society of separatists, under the pastoral care of John Robinson. Mr. Brewster's house was their Sabbath meeting-place for worship; and when, finally, these non-conformists were obliged to flee from hierarchical persecution, that good Christian attempted to leave friends and country, and follow. He was arrested, with others, and imprisoned at Boston, in Lincolnshire, in 1607; but as soon as he obtained his liberty, he sailed for Holland. His estate had become exhausted, and at Leyden he opened a school for instruction in the English language. He also established a printing-press there, and published several books.

Mr. Brewster was greatly beloved, and was chosen an elder in the church at Leyden, over which his old pastor presided. It was in that capacity that he sailed, with "the youngest and strongest" of Mr. Robinson's flock, in the May Flower, late in 1620. He suffered and rejoiced with the PILGRIMS, in all their strange vicissitudes; and for almost nine years, he was the only regular dispenser of the Word of Life to the Puritans, in the little church at Plymouth. He preached twice every Sunday; but could never be persuaded to administer the sacraments. It was in that church at Plymouth that the largest liberty was first granted to the laity. It was a common practice for a question to be propounded on the Sabbath, and all who felt "gifted" were allowed to speak upon it. This liberty finally became a great annoyance to the ministers, and much difficulty ensued. It had free scope while Elder Brewster officiated, but when Rev. Ralph Smith was settled as pastor over the Plymouth church, he endeavored to check it. Elder Brewster died on the 16th of April, 1644, at the age of eighty-three years.

STEPHEN DAY.

THE first printer who practiced his art within the domain of the United States was Stephen Day, a native of London. The Rev. Jesse Glover, one of the earliest patrons of Harvard College, presented that institution with a font of type, and others contributed money to buy a press. In 1638, Mr. Glover, then in London, engaged Day to accompany him to America, to take charge of the printing-house at Cambridge. Glover died on the voyage, but Day arrived in safety, with his patron's widow and children, and commenced work in January, 1639. His first production was *The Freeman's Oath;* and soon afterward he printed an *Almanac* made by a mariner named Pierce, in which the year begins with March. The first *book*—the first one printed in America—was the *Psalms in Meter*, containing three hundred pages, and was known as *The Bay Psalm Book*. He printed several Almanacs, and also some astronomical calculations by Urian Oakes, then a youth, and afterward President of Harvard College.

Day was an unskilful printer; yet, being the only one in the colony, he was so much esteemed, that the general court of Massachusetts granted him three hundred acres of land, in 1641. He frequently complained that his printing was unprofitable. He continued in the business until the beginning of 1649, when his establishment went into the hands of Samuel Greene, who came to Cambridge with his parents at the age of sixteen years. Greene continued the business until near the close of the century, and many writers have spoken of him as the *first* printer. Day expired at Cambridge, on the 22d of December, 1668, at the age of about fifty-eight years.

BENJAMIN CHURCH.

NEXT to Miles Standish, the warrior-pilgrim of the May Flower, Benjamin Church was the most distinguished military hero in early New England history. He was born at Plymouth, Massachusetts, in 1639, and was instructed in the trade of a carpenter, by his father. He went to Duxbury to reside, and was pursuing his vocation there when King Philip's war broke out.[1] That great chief of the Wampanoags had long kept inviolate the treaty made with the white people by his father, Massasoit; but when provocations multiplied—when he saw spreading settlements reducing his domains, acre by acre, breaking up his hunting grounds, diminishing his fisheries, and menacing his nation with servitude or annihilation,—his patriotism was aroused, and he willingly listened to the hot young warriors around him, who counselled a war of extermination against the English. Philip struck the first blow at Swanzey, thirty-five miles south-west from Plymouth; and for almost a year this dreadful war went on, and extended even to the valley of the Connecticut river. Nearly all of the New England tribes joined Philip in his enterprise. The white people banded, and struck the savages with vigorous blows in all directions. Among their

---

[1] Philip was a son of Massasoit, and he and his brother were named respectively Philip and Alexander, by the white people, in compliment to their bravery. Because, after the death of his father, he became chief sachem of his powerful tribe, he was called *King* Philip.—See page 38.

leaders, Captain Church was the bravest of the brave; and in the Spring of 1676 he completely broke the power of the New England tribes. Almost three thousand Indians had been slain or had bowed in submission, and Philip was a hunted fugitive. He was chased from place to place, and refused to yield. He cleft the head of a warrior who dared to propose submission; and a curse upon the white people was ever upon his lips. At length the "last of the Wampanoags" was compelled to yield to the pressure of circumstances. He went stealthily back to the home of his fathers, at Mount Hope. Soon his wife and son were made prisoners, and his spirit drooped. "Now my heart breaks," said the brave warrior; "I am ready to die." A few days afterward a faithless Indian shot him, in a swamp, and Captain Church, with his own sword, cut off the dead sachem's head. Lacking the magnanimity of a true soldier, the professed Christian leader disfigured the senseless body, then quartered it, and hung it upon trees, declaring, "Forasmuch as he caused many an Englishman's body to lie unburied and rot above the ground, not one of his bones shall be buried." The chieftain's head was carried to Plymouth on a pole, where it was exposed for several years, and his right hand was sent to the governor of Massachusetts. The rude sword of Church which cut off Philip's head is now a cherished relic in the library of the Historical Society of the "Old Bay State."

If we censure Church's want of magnanimity as a soldier, what shall we say of the Christian charity of the Plymouth people in the disposal of King Philip's son. It was a subject for serious consideration. Some of the elders of the church proposed putting him to death; while the more merciful ones proposed to sell him into slavery in Bermuda. The most *profitable* measure appeared the *kindest*, and the innocent child was sold into perpetual bondage.

Captain Church lived many years after the war, at different places in the vicinity of Narraganset Bay, in Rhode Island. His last place of residence was Little Compton, where, on the 17th of January, 1718, he was thrown from a horse. He was very corpulent, and the shock of his fall ruptured a blood vessel, which caused his death in the course of a few hours, at the age of seventy-nine years.

MILES STANDISH.

THE "Hero of New England," as Captain Standish is called, was, like many other heroes and great men, rather diminutive in person. Hubbard, the historian, says, when speaking of him, "A little chimney is soon fired: so was the Plymouth captain, a man of very small stature, yet of a very hot and angry temper." He was born in Lancashire, England, about the year 1584. He was a soldier by profession, and was serving in the Netherlands when Mr. Robinson, with his PILGRIM flock, settled at Leyden. There he joined the Puritans, and came with them to America, in the May Flower. When that vessel anchored in Cape Cod Bay, and it was thought expedient to explore the bleak shore to find a good landing-place, Standish was among the first to volunteer for the service. He was one of those who passed the first Christian Sabbath, after their arrival, in deep snow upon a barren island in Plymouth harbor; and he was the second man who stepped upon Plymouth Rock.

Standish was very serviceable to the English when the Indians showed signs of hostility, and they relied much upon his military skill and personal bravery. Wherever the duties of his profession called him, there he was always found. Two years after the establishment of the Puritans at Plymouth, he was called to protect a new colony at Wissagusset (now Weymouth), who had exasperated the Indians by begging and stealing. They had been sent over by a wealthy London merchant, and most of them were quite unfit for the business of founding a state. The Indians resolved to destroy them; but, through the agency of Massasoit, a firm friend of the English, the conspiracy was revealed to the Plymouth people in time for Captain Standish to march thither with a small company and avert the blow. When he arrived, his anger was fiercely kindled by the insolence of Pecksuot, the chief, and his few followers. Pecksuot sharpened his knife in the presence of Standish, and said, "Though you are a great captain, you are but a little man; and though I be no sachem, yet I am a man of great strength and courage." Standish had the prudence to check his resentment; but the next day, when the chief, and about the same number of his followers as Standish had with him, were in a room with the white people, the captain gave a signal, and five of the savages were slain. Standish snatched Pecksuot's knife from him, and with it slew its owner. When Mr. Robinson (the original pastor of the PILGRIMS, and who remained in Holland) heard of this event, he wrote to the Church of Plymouth "to consider the disposition of their captain, who was of a warm temper. He hoped that the Lord had sent him among them for good, if they used him right; but he doubted whether there was not wanting that tenderness of the life of man, made after God's image, which was meet; and he thought that it would have been happy if they had converted some before they had killed any."

Captain Standish settled in Duxbury, Massachusetts, about 1631; and a place near his residence is still called Captain's Hill. During almost the whole time of his residence in the colony, he was an assistant magistrate. He died at his house in Duxbury, in the year 1656.

ISAAC ALLERTON.

THE *May Flower* passengers may all be considered "distinguished Americans," because they left their birth-land forever, and became founders and citizens of a new empire in this Western World. Of the noble band who signed a constitution of government[1] in the cabin of the May Flower, at Cape Cod, Isaac Allerton was the fifth to append his name to that instrument. He survived the terrors of the first winter in New England,[2] afterward became the agent of the settlers in negotiating the purchase of the new possessions from those of the company in London, who had furnished capital for the enterprise;[3] and, as an enterprising trader, became the founder of the commerce of New England. He established a trading post near the mouth of the Kennebeck, in 1627, and made several business voyages to England. He also established trading posts at Penobscot and Machias. In 1635, he opened a profitable trade with New Haven, New Amsterdam, Virginia, and even with the West Indies. He finally made New Amsterdam (now New York) his chief place of residence, and traded principally in tobacco. In 1643, when the English began to exert a considerable influence in the affairs of New Amsterdam, and a council of eight men represented the people, Mr. Allerton was chosen to fill a seat in that body.

1. The first *written* constitution adopted by a free people.
2. Of the one hundred PILGRIMS only forty survived.
3. Some London merchants formed a partnership with the PILGRIMS, and furnished capital for the enterprise. The service of each emigrant was valued as a capital of ten pounds, and all profits were reserved until the end of seven years. The community system did not work well, and at the end of the seven years, the settlers bought of the merchants their interest in the venture.

Mr. Allerton was accompanied in the May Flower by his wife and four children. His wife died soon after their arrival; and in 1627, he married Fear, a daughter of Elder Brewster, the spiritual guide of the PILGRIM adventurers.[1] She, also, died in 1634. He was again marrried, for we have an account of his shipwreck, *with his wife*, on the coast of Massachusetts, in 1644. The time and place of his death is not known, some asserting that he returned to England, and others that he died in the city of New Amsterdam (New York), in 1659.

CANONICUS.

ONE of the most renowned sachems among the New England tribes was Canonicus, the head of the Narragansets when the PILGRIM FATHERS founded New Plymouth. He regarded the advent of the white men with a jealous fear; and in 1622, feeling strong, with about five thousand fighting men around him, he sent a challenge to Governor Bradford, of the Plymouth colony, notwithstanding Massasoit, the chief sachem of the Wampanoags, was the friend of the English. His token of defiance was a bundle of arrows, tied with a snake skin. Bradford sagaciously filled the skin with powder and ball, and sent it back to Canonicus. The chief had never seen the like before, and he regarded these substances with superstitious awe. They were sent from village to village, and excited so much alarm, that the sachem sued for peace, and made a treaty of friendship, which he never violated; notwithstanding, he often received provocations that would have justified him in scattering all compacts to the winds.

When Roger Williams became an exile from Massachusetts, he found a friend in Canonicus, who gave him all the land in the vicinity of Providence, for a settlement. Williams found more love and generous sentiment in the heart of that forest monarch than among his own countrymen at Boston. When the Pequot war broke out in 1637, Canonicus stood firmly in defence of the English; and a deputation from Massachusetts, who appeared before his island throne opposite Newport, were received with friendly assurances. His palace was a building fifty feet in length, made of upright poles, covered with branches and mats. The royal dinner given to the ambassadors consisted of boiled chestnuts for bread, plenty of venison, and a dessert of boiled pudding made of pounded Indian corn, well filled with whortle-berries. After again assuring the ambassadors of his friendly intentions, he advised the Pequots to bury the hatchet. They refused to listen, and were utterly destroyed by the combined forces of the English, the Narragansets, the Mohegans, and the Niantics.

In 1638, Canonicus began to feel the infirmities of age, and resigned his government into the hands of his nephew, Miantonomoh. That chief was afterward made a prisoner by Uncas, "the last of the Mohegans," and murdered by the consent of the English. The resentment of Canonicus was aroused, and he could hardly be restrained from declaring war against the white people. Prudent counsels prevailed in his cabinet, and peace was maintained. In the beautiful month of June, 1647, this "wise and peaceable prince," as Williams calls him, died at his seat on Conannicut Island, opposite Newport, at the age of eighty-five years.

---

1. The practice of the Puritans of giving their children the names of moral qualities, was exemplified in Brewster's family. His two daughters were named respectively *Fear* and *Love*; and his son's name was *Wrestling*.

POCAHONTAS.

"She was a soft landscape of mild earth,
Where all was harmony and calm quiet,
Luxuriant, budding." BYRON.

SUCH was the sweet little Indian girl, the favorite daughter of the powerful Emperor of the Powhatan Confederacy[1] in Virginia, when the white people laid the foundations of a new empire there. When a site for a settlement was chosen, Captain Smith, the boldest of those early adventurers, penetrated the interior, and was taken prisoner. His captor carried him in triumph from village to village, and then presented him to the Emperor, in his forest palace at Werowocomoco. Smith was condemned to die. With his arms pinioned, and his head upon a huge stone, he was doomed to have his brains dashed out by a blow from a club. When the executioner advanced, Pocahontas, then a girl ten or twelve years of age, leaped from her father's side, where she sat trembling, clasped the head of Smith in her arms, and implored his life.

' How could that stern old king deny
The angel pleading in her eye?
How mock the sweet, imploring grace,
That breathed in beauty from her face,
And to her kneeling action gave
A power to soothe, and still subdue,
Until, though humble as a slave,
To more than queenly sway she grew!"—SIMMS.

The Emperor yielded, and Smith was spared.

---

1. This was a confederacy of more than twenty Indian tribes in the vicinity of the James, York and Potomac rivers. Powhatan was not the family name of the father of Pocahontas, but the title of the emperor, the same as the title of *Pharaoh*, for the Egyptian kings, in the time of the Jewish bondage.

Two years after this event, the Indians formed a conspiracy to exterminate the white people. Again Pocahontas became an angel of deliverance. During a dark and stormy night she left her father's cabin, sped to Jamestown, informed Smith of his danger, and was back to her couch before dawn. It was no wonder that the English regarded the Indian princess with great esteem; and yet, when Smith had left the colony, and indolence and licentiousness had full sway, that gentle girl was ruthlessly torn from her kindred, and held a prisoner on board of an English vessel. Argall, a rough, half-piratical mariner, desirous of extorting advantageous terms of peace from her father, bribed a savage, by the gift of a copper kettle, to betray her into his hands. Powhatan loved his child tenderly, and offered five hundred bushels of corn, and a promise of friendship toward the English, for her ransom. But other bonds, more holy than those of Argall, now detained her. While on the ship, a mutual attachment had budded and blossomed between her and John Rolfe, a fine young Englishman, of good family. With the consent of her father, Pocahontas received Christian baptism, with the title of "the Lady Rebecca," and she and her lover were married.

In 1616, Pocahontas accompanied her husband to England, where she was received at Court with all the distinction due to a princess. But the silly bigot on the throne was highly indignant because one of his *subjects* had dared to marry a *lady of royal blood*, and absurdly apprehended that Rolfe might lay claim "to the crown of Virginia!" Afraid of the royal displeasure, Captain Smith, who was then in England, would not allow her to call him *father*, as she desired to do. She could not comprehend the cause; and her tender, simple heart was greatly grieved by what seemed to be his want of affection for her. She remained in England about a year; and when ready to embark for America with her husband, she was taken sick, and died at Gravesend, in the flowery month of June, 1617, when not quite twenty-two years of age. She left one son, Thomas Rolfe, who afterward became quite a distinguished man in Virginia. His only child was a daughter, and from her some of the leading families in Virginia trace their descent. Among these were the Bollings, Hemmings, Murrays, Guys, Eldridges and Randolphs. The late John Randolph, of Roanoke, boasted of his descent from the Indian princess.

JOHN ELIOT.

GREAT efforts have been made from time to time to Christianize portions of the aboriginals of our country, but none have been more successful than those put forth during the early days of New England settlements, by one who has been justly termed the Apostle to the Indians. John Eliot was born in Essex county, England, in 1604. He was educated at the university of Cambridge, and was engaged in school teaching for several years. He became a gospel minister; and in 1631, arrived at Boston, and commenced ministerial labors there. He was afterward associated with Mr. Wilde at the head of a congregation in Roxbury; and these, with Richard Mather, were appointed, in 1639, to make a new metrical version of the Psalms.

Looking out upon the dusky tribes around him, the heart of Mr. Eliot was troubled by a view of their spiritual destitution, and he resolved to preach the gospel among those heathen neighbors. The twenty tribes known to the English spoke a similar language, and when he had mastered it sufficient to be understood by them, he began his labors. His first sermon was preached to them in the present town of Newton, in October, 1646. He saw blossoms of promise at that first gathering, and very soon fruit appeared, to his great joy. Although violently opposed by the Indian priests, whose "craft was in danger," and also by some of the sachems and chiefs, he was not dismayed, but penetrated the deep wilderness in all directions, relying solely upon his God for protection. Finally, an Indian town was built at Natick, and a house of worship, the first for the use of the Indians ever erected by Protestants in America,[1] was reared there in 1660. Many received the rites of baptism and the Lord's Supper, after being thoroughly instructed in religious doctrines and duties.

Mr. Eliot translated the New Testament into the Indian language, and published it in 1661; and in the course of a few years he established several congregations among these children of the forest, extending even as far as Cape Cod. He obtained unbounded influence over them; and he was also their protector when, during King Philip's war, the Massachusetts people wished to exterminate the Indians, without discrimination. It was estimated that there were five thousand "praying Indians," as the converts were called, among the New England tribes, when Philip raised the hatchet.

When the weight of fourscore years bowed the pious apostle, and he could no longer visit the Indian churches, he persuaded a number of families to send their negro servants to him to be instructed in Gospel truth, and thus he labored for benighted minds, until the last. With the triumphant words, "welcome joy," upon his lips, the venerable and faithful servant died, on the 20th of May, 1690, at the age of eighty-six years.

ROGER WILLIAMS.

THE annunciation of new theories, whether in science, government, religion, or ethics, which clash with prevailing dogmas, is always met with scoffs and frowns, if not with actual persecution. The stand-point of reformers is always in advance of current ideas, and the true value of such men can only be appreciated when their labors have ceased, and they are sleeping with the dead. To such a character we turn when we contemplate Roger Williams, the great champion of toleration, and of private judgment in religious matters. He was born in Wales, in 1599, and was educated at Oxford. He was a minister in the Church of England for a short time, but his independent principles soon led him to non-conformity, and he came to America to indulge in the free exercise of his opinions. He arrived in February, 1631, and in April following, he was chosen assistant minister at Salem. His extreme views concerning entire separation from the Church of England were not palatable to many of his brethren; and his asserted independence of the magistracy in religious matters drew upon him the condemnation of that entire class and their friends. He left Salem and went to Plymouth in 1632; but, on the death of the minister at the former place, he returned there, and took sole charge of the congregation, in 1634. There he proclaimed his peculiar views with more vehemence than ever; and in his excessive zeal for toleration, and individual liberty of thought and action, he became as intolerant as his opposers, without their excuse of care for the stability of the church and civil government. He asserted that an oath ought not to be administered to an unregenerate man; that a Christian ought not to

---

[1] French Jesuits had already established missionary stations on the St. Lawrence, and even on the borders of the great lakes.

Roger Williams

pray with an unregenerate man; that "grace" at table ought to be omitted; and having formed a separate congregation, he even refused to commune with members of his own church who did not separate entirely from all connection with the "polluted New England churches." He finally declared the Massachusetts charter void, because the land had not been purchased from the Indians, and "reviled magistrates." The general court passed a sentence of banishment against him in 1635, and early in January, 1636, he left the colony for the wilderness toward Narraganset Bay, to avoid being seized and sent to England. After severe trials and hardships, he purchased lands from the Indians at the head of Narraganset Bay, and there founded a town, and named it *Providence*. He offered a free asylum to all persecuted people, and many joined him there. Time mellowed his extreme opinions, and he became a pattern of toleration. He also became a Baptist; and when he formed a civil government, it was purely democratic. He, as the head, had no privileges but those which were common to all. He labored zealously for the spiritual and temporal good of the Indians; and in 1643 he went to England to obtain a royal charter. Already other settlements of his friends had been made on Rhode Island.[1] In the spring of 1644, a free charter of incorporation was granted, and these several settlements were united under the title of the *Rhode Island and Providence Planta-*

---

1. The Indian name was *Aquiday*, or *Aquitneck*. It was named Rhode Island because of the red color of its marshy shore, produced by cranberries. The Dutch called it Roodt Eylandt.

tions. He again went to England in 1651, as agent for the colony, where he remained until 1654. On his return he was made president of the colony, in which office he was succeeded, in 1657, by Benedict Arnold.

Roger Williams was an eminent peace-maker between the white people and the Indians, and on two occasions he no doubt saved those who banished him to the wilderness, from utter destruction. While all sects were permitted to enjoy entire freedom within his domains, he was fierce in controversy against the Quakers. In 1672, he held a public dispute with leaders of that sect at Newport, for three days, and one day at Providence, an account of which he afterward published, under the title of "George Fox digged out of his Burrows." A preacher, named Burroughs, was one of the disputants in favor of the principles of Fox.

Roger Williams died at Providence, in April, 1683, aged eighty-four years. His name is cherished as the first founder of a state in the New World, where freedom to worship God according to the dictates of the individual conscience, was made an organic law.

MIANTONOMOH.

ONE of the most renowned of the warriors of the New England Indians, was Miantonomoh, sachem of the Narragansets, and nephew and successor of Canonicus. He took a share in the government of his aged uncle, in 1636, and was the warm friend and benefactor of the first settlers of Rhode Island. He joined Captain Mason against the Pequods in 1637; and the following year he was associated with Uncas, the chief sachem of the Mohegans, in a treaty of peace and friendship with the English at Hartford. The two sachems agreed not to make war upon each other, without first appealing to the English. An occasion soon appeared. Uncas was the aggressor; and by the consent of the governor at Hartford, Miantonomoh, at the head of eight hundred warriors, marched into the Mohegan country. A severe battle ensued on a great plain near Norwich. By stratagem Uncas gained the victory, and Miantonomoh was made a prisoner, with one of his brothers, and two sons of Canonicus. They were sent to Hartford, and the English were asked to decide what should be done with the royal prisoner. The question was referred to an ecclesiastical tribunal, consisting of five of the principal ministers of New England. They decided to hand him over to Uncas for "execution without torture," within the dominions of that sachem. It was an ungenerous and wicked decision, for Miantonomoh had ever been a firm friend of the English, without the selfish incentives that governed Uncas. But just then, a covetous desire to possess the land of Uncas made them willing to secure his favor, even by so foul a procedure. Delighted with the verdict of his Christian allies, the equally savage Mohegan, with a few trusty followers, conducted Miantonomoh to the spot where he was captured, near Norwich, and there a brother of Uncas stepped up behind the unsuspecting victim and cleft his head with a hatchet. The noble Miantonomoh was buried where he was slain; and to this day the locality is called Sachem's Plain. This transaction aroused the fierce ire of the Narragansets against the English, and they had the sympathy of the surrounding tribes. Hatred of the English and of their boasted Christianity, became deep-rooted, and was one of the principal causes which led to the bloody contest known as King Philip's war, about thirty years later. Miantonomoh was about forty-four years of age at the time of his death.

WILLIAM PHIPPS.

"CIRCUMSTANCES make men what they are," is a general truth which few persons of observation will deny. William Phipps illustrated the truth in his life and character, in an eminent degree. He was born in the then far-off wilderness at Pemaquid, now Bristol, in the state of Maine, on the 2d of February, 1651. His father was a gun-smith, and migrated to America, with Winthrop's party, in 1630. William was the tenth of twenty-six children by the same mother. He lived in the wilderness until he was eighteen years of age, without any special aim for life. Then he was apprenticed to a ship carpenter for four years. At the expiration of his minority and servitude he went to Boston, and there, for the first time, studied reading and writing. Charmed with the tales of seamen, among whom his business cast his lot, he resolved to seek his fortunes on the ocean. He left Boston when he was twenty-four years of age, and after many adventures and hardships, he discovered a Spanish wreck on the coast of St. Domingo, and from it fished up pearls, plate, and jewels, to the value of a million and a half of dollars. With this treasure he sailed for England, where he divided the booty so equitably among the seamen, that his own share amounted to only eighty thousand dollars. That was a large fortune for the time; and James the Second was so much charmed by the talent and general character of Phipps, that he knighted him. Three years afterward he returned to Boston, where he took rank in the best society.

In 1690, Sir William Phipps commanded an expedition against Port Royal, in the French territory of Acadie, now Nova Scotia. His expedition comprised eight or nine vessels, and about eight hundred men. He seized Port Royal, brought Acadie into subjection, and obtained sufficient property, by plundering the people, to pay the expenses of the enterprise. This success encouraged the New England colonies to coalesce with New York in efforts to subdue Canada, then held by the French. Sir William commanded a naval expedition against Quebec, which Massachusetts alone fitted out. He sailed from Boston with thirty-four vessels and a thousand men, reached Quebec in safety, and landed his troops; but the strength of the city, and the lack of coöperation on the part of the land troops, caused him to abandon the undertaking and return home. He was soon afterward sent to England to solicit aid in further warfare against the French and Indians. He also asked for the restoration of the old charter of Massachusetts, taken away by Andros.[1] Aid for war was refused; and King William, instead of restoring the old charter, granted a new one, under which Sir William was appointed the first governor, by the king, on the nomination of Increase Mather. He arrived at Boston in May, 1692, and was instrumental in stopping prosecutions for witchcraft, then in fearful activity in the colony.[2] The same year he went to Pemaquid, with four hundred and fifty men, and built a fort there. He was removed from office in 1694, when he went to England, and received positive promises of restoration. But death soon closed his career. He died in London, on the 18th of February, 1695, at the age of forty-four years.

---

1. Edmund Andros was sent to New England, by James the Second, to take away the several charters of the colonies, and consolidate the whole under one government, with himself at the head as the direct representative of royalty. The revolution of 1688, drove James from the throne, and placed William of Orange and his wife, Mary, there. It was to William that Phipps appealed for the restoration of the charters taken away by Andros. The new charter was not so acceptable to the people as the old one.
2. See sketch of Dr Mather.

PETER STUYVESANT.

THE founding of the great commercial city of New York was the work of beaver-hunting Hollanders, at a time when ships from the Zuyder-Zee were in the far-distant waters of the East Indies, and the navies that sailed from the Texel were mistresses of the ocean. Holland then controlled the commerce of the world. A company was chartered to plant trading stations in the region discovered by Henry Hudson,[1] and when settlements were established there, governors were sent to administer political rule. Of the five employed at different times by the company, Peter Stuyvesant was the ablest and the last. He was a son of a clergyman in Friesland, where he was born in 1602, and was educated for the ministry in the High School at Franeker. There he acquired a knowledge of Latin, with which he played the pedant in after life. Liking the military art better than theology, he entered the army, and rose to distinction

---

1. Hudson discovered the Bay of New York and the river bearing his name, at the close of the Summer of 1609. He was then in the service of the Dutch East India Company.

on account of his bravery. His talent commended him to the Dutch West India Company,[1] and he was appointed its first director, or governor, of Curaçoa.

In 1644, Stuyvesant led an expedition against the Portuguese on the island of St. Martin, and lost a leg in an engagement there. He went to Holland for surgical aid, and soon afterward he received the appointment of first director of the province of New Netherland, as the Dutch possessions on the Hudson were called. He arrived at New Amsterdam (now New York) in May, 1647. He found everything in confusion, and the seeds of democracy growing rapidly, because of the tyrannous and dishonest rule of his predecessor. Stuyvesant was an aristocrat, and his profession made him an iron man, as a ruler. He at once commenced much-needed reforms, and declared his honest desire to improve the condition of the people; but he told them frankly that he considered it "treason to petition against one's magistrates, whether there be cause or not." Governed by such sentiments, he ruled vigorously for almost twenty years. He destroyed the power of a growing Swedish colony on the Delaware,[2] settled boundary disputes with the English in Connecticut, and by conciliatory measures made the Indians so friendly, that the New England people believed the silly story that he was leagued with the savages to destroy the Puritans.

When Charles the Second was restored to the throne of his fathers, he gave the territory of New Netherland to his brother James, Duke of York. The duke sent a fleet to take possession.[3] Stuyvesant yielded with great reluctance; and in September, 1664, New Amsterdam was surrendered to the English, and was named New York. Stuyvesant retired to his bouerie or farm, near the East River, where he lived in dignity and quiet until August, 1682, when he died. His wife was Ruth Bayard, a Huguenot. Their remains lie in a vault under St. Mark's Church, in the city of New York.

EDWARD WINSLOW.

ONE of the most accomplished men who came to America in the *May Flower*, was Edward Winslow, a native of Worcestershire, England, where he was born on the 19th of October, 1595. Whilst travelling in Europe, he became acquainted, at Leyden, with the Rev. John Robinson, the pastor of the *Pilgrims* there. He joined that church in 1617, married a young lady there, and made Leyden his place of residence until his departure for America. He was one of the companions of Miles Standish in the search for a landing-place for the *May Flower* passengers; and being a young man of great energy, he became one of the most useful men in the colony. Massasoit became much attached to him; and in 1623, hearing of the severe illness of that sachem, Winslow visited him, and by the skilful use of some medicines, restored him to health, and won his unbounded gratitude. On that occasion, as on many others, the brave young Hobbomac, one of Massasoit's warriors, who lived with the white people, was guide and interpreter. In the following Autumn, Mr. Winslow went to England as an agent for the colony; and the next Spring he returned, and introduced

---

1. This company was formed after the discoveries of Hudson, and was invested with almost vice-regal powers for carrying on trade and making settlements in America and on the coast of Africa.
2. Peter Minuit, an offended director of the Dutch West India Company, went to Sweden and proposed to lead a colony of Swedes to the New World. A *Swedish West India Company* was formed; and in the Spring of 1638, Minuit and a considerable number of settlers located upon the Delaware, on the site of the present New Castle. They called the country New Sweden, and proposed to establish a provincial government, but the more powerful Dutch overthrew all their plans, and the colonists became subjects to Stuyvesant.
3. England claimed all America from Newfoundland to Florida, by virtue of early coast explorations.

the first cattle into New England.[1] He made voyages to England and other places for the benefit of the Plymouth colony, and for private commercial pursuits; and, in 1633, was elected governor. Twice, subsequently, he was elected chief magistrate of the colony, when Bradford declined serving, and always performed his duties with great satisfaction to his constituents. He made many coast voyages, even as far south as Manhattan, for trading purposes; and in 1635, went to England again, when, on a charge of performing illegal clerical services at Plymouth, made by the mendacious Thomas Morton, he was imprisoned four months. There, and during a subsequent visit to his native country, he was active in founding a society for propagating the gospel in New England, which was incorporated in 1649. He was so highly esteemed in his native country, that public employments were thrust upon him, and he never returned to America. He was appointed a commissioner to determine the amount of the restitution to be made to England, by Denmark, for marine spoliations; and in 1655, Cromwell appointed him the first of three commissioners to superintend an expedition against the Spaniards in the West Indies, in which admiral Penn, father of William, was a conspicuous actor. Governor Winslow accompanied the expedition. It failed to accomplish its object; and while the fleet was passing between the islands of St. Domingo and Jamaica, he died of a fever, on the 8th of May, 1655, at the age of sixty years. Mr. Winslow's wife was among those of the *May Flower*, who died during the Winter and Spring of 1621. William White also died at about the same time, and within two months afterward Winslow and White's widow were married. This was the first marriage of Europeans in New England. Mrs. Winslow was not only the first bride, but the mother of the first white child born in New England, her son, Peregrine White, having been born on board the *May Flower* while that vessel lay anchored in Cape Cod Bay.

WILLIAM PENN.

IN glorious contrast with the inhumanity of Spaniards, Frenchmen, and many Englishmen, stands the record on History's tablet of the kindness and justice toward the feeble Indian, of the founder of Pennsylvania.

> "Thou'lt find," said the Quaker, "in me and mine,
> But friends and brothers to thee and to thine,
> Who abuse no power, and admit no line
> 'Twixt the red man and the white."
> And bright was the spot where the Quaker came
> To leave his hat, his drab, and his name,
> That will sweetly sound from the trump of Fame,
> 'Till its final blast shall die.—HANNAH F. GOULD.

William Penn was born in the city of London, on the 14th of October, 1644, and was educated at Oxford. His father was the eminent admiral Penn, a great favorite of royalty. William was remarkable, in early youth, for brilliant talent and unaffected piety. While yet a student he heard one of the new sect of Quakers preach, and, with other students, became deeply impressed with the evangelical truths which they uttered. He, with several others, withdrew from the Established Church, worshipped by themselves, and for non-conformity were expelled from the college. Penn's father sought, in vain, to reclaim him; and when, at length, he refused to take off his hat in the presence of the admiral, and

---

[1]. Horses were not introduced until 1644. The people often rode on bulls. It is said that when John Alden went to be married to Priscilla Mullins, he covered his bull with a handsome cloth. On his return, he seated his bride on the animal's back, and he led him by a rope fastened to a ring in his nose.

even of the king, he was expelled from the parental roof. He was sent to gay France, where he became a polished gentleman after a residence of two years; and on his return he studied law in London until the appearance of the great plague in 1665. He was sent to Ireland in 1666, to manage an estate there belonging to his father, but was soon recalled, because he associated with Quakers. Again expelled from his father's house, he became an itinerant Quaker preacher, made many proselytes, suffered revilings and imprisonments "for conscience sake," and at the age of twenty-four years, wrote his celebrated work, entitled *No Cross, no Crown*, while in prison because of his non-conformity to the Church of England. He was released in 1670, and soon afterward became possessor of the large estates of his father, who died that year. He continued to write and preach in defence of his sect, and went to Holland and Germany, for that purpose, in 1677.

In March, 1681, Penn procured from Charles the Second, a grant of the territory in America which yet bears his name; and two years afterward he visited the colony which he had established there. He founded Philadelphia—city of brotherly love—toward the close of the same year; and within twenty-four months afterward, two thousand settlers were planting their homes there. Penn returned to England in 1684, and through his influence with the king, obtained the release of thirteen hundred Quakers, then in prison. Because of his personal friendship toward James, the successor of Charles (who was driven from the throne by the revolution of 1688, and had his place filled by his daughter, Mary, and William, Prince of Orange), he was suspected of adherence to the fallen monarch, and was imprisoned, and deprived of his proprietary rights. These were restored to him in 1694; and in 1699, he again visited his American colony. He remained in Pennsylvania until 1701, when he hastened to England to oppose a parliamentary proposition to abolish all proprietary governments in America. He never returned. In 1712, he was prostrated by a paralytic disorder. It terminated his life on the 30th of July, 1718, at the age of seventy-four years. Penn was greatly beloved by the Indians; and it is worthy of remark that not a drop of Quaker's blood was ever shed by the savages.

THOMAS HOOKER.

THE true heroes of America are those who, from time to time, have left the comforts of civilized life and planted the seeds of new states deep in the wilderness. Among the remarkable men of that stamp was the Reverend Thomas Hooker, the first minister of Cambridge, Massachusetts, and one of the pioneer settlers in Connecticut. He was born in Leicestershire, England, in 1586, and was educated in Emanuel College, Cambridge. He began his labors as a Christian minister at about the time of the death of James the First, when Archbishop Laud began to harass the non-conformists. In 1630, Mr. Hooker was silenced, because of his non-conformity to the Established Church, and he founded a grammar school at Chelmsford. His influence was great; and falling under the ban of Laud, he was obliged to fly to Holland, where he became an assistant minister to Dr. Ames, both at Delft and Rotterdam. He came to America with the Reverend Mr. Cotton, in 1633, and was made pastor of the church at Cambridge in the Autumn of that year.

In 1636, this "light of the western churches," with other ministers, their families and flocks, in all about one hundred, left the vicinity of Boston for the Connecticut valley, where the English had already planted settlements. It was a toilsome journey through the swamps and forests. They took quite a number of cows with them. These browsed upon the shrubs and grazed in swamp borders, and their milk afforded subsistence for the wanderers. The journey was made in the pleasant month of June, and on the 4th of July they reached the flowery banks of the Connecticut, and received the hearty greetings of welcome of the little band of settlers who were seated on the site of the present city of Hartford. There, in the little meeting-house already built, Mr. Hooker preached when the Sabbath came, and administered the sacrament of the Lord's Supper to all. A greater portion of Mr. Hooker's followers settled at Hartford, while some chose Wethersfield for a residence; and others, from Roxbury, went up the river twenty miles, and founded Springfield.

Mr. Hooker was one of the most powerful preachers of his time, and wrote much and well, on religious subjects. While preaching in the great church of Leicester, before he left England, one of the magistrates of the town sent a fiddler to the church-yard to disturb the worship. Mr. Hooker's powerful voice not only drowned the music, but it attracted the fiddler to the church door. He listened to the great truths uttered, and became converted. Mr. Hooker was a man of great benevolence, and in every sphere of life he was eminently *useful*. He died at Hartford, of an epidemic fever, on the 7th of July, 1647, at the age of sixty-one years.

COTTON MATHER.

SOME of the early New England divines, as well as the magistrates, were exceedingly superstitious, while their piety and general good sense could not be doubted. Cotton Mather, one of the earliest of American-born clergymen, was a prominent specimen of the kind of men alluded to. He was born in Boston, on the 12th of February, 1663, and was educated at Harvard College, where he was graduated at the early age of sixteen years. He was so expert in learning, that before he was nineteen years old, the degree of Master of Arts was conferred upon him, by the college. At the age of twenty-two years, he was ordained a gospel minister, and became the assistant of his father, Increase Mather. Preaching and authorship were the joint professions of his life, and he excelled all others, of his time, in both. He became master of several languages, and was considered a prodigy of learning. He held a fluent pen, yet his writings were not fitted for immortality. They lacked solidity and that true genius which is undying. Many of his productions are already forgotten, and none but his *Magnalia* will probably "live forever." Its extravagances form its chief element of vitality. With all his learning, Dr. Mather was a man of narrow views, a conceited heart, and unsound judgment. He was a firm believer in witchcraft, and probably did more than any other man to promote the spread of that fearful delusion, known in history as Salem Witchcraft[1]. He wrote a book

---

1. A belief in witchcraft was almost universal, at that time. It had produced terrible tragedies on the

on the subject, and stimulated the authorities to prosecute all suspected persons. Several years before, his father had published an account of all the supposed cases of witchcraft in New England, under the title of "Remarkable Providences," which directed public attention to the subject. After the delusion had passed away, Cotton Mather's credulity was exposed by a man named Calef, in a series of letters. Mather sneered at him at first, but when Calef laid his blows on thick and fast, the Doctor called him "a coal from hell," and prosecuted him for slander. The suit was wisely withdrawn.

With all his vagaries and folly, Dr. Mather exhibited much good sense. Dr Franklin has thus illustrated the fact, in a letter to Mr. Mather's son, Samuel, whose house and fine library were consumed at Charlestown during the battle on Breed's Hill, in 1775. "The last time I saw your father was in the beginning of 1724, when I visited him after my first trip to Pennsylvania. He received me in his library; and on my taking leave, showed me a shorter way out of the house through a narrow passage, which was crossed by a beam overhead. We were still talking as I withdrew, he accompanying me behind, and I turning partly towards him, when he said hastily, 'Stoop! stoop!' I did not understand him until I felt my head hit against the beam. He was a man that never missed an occasion of giving instruction, and upon this he said to me, 'You are young, and have the world before you; stoop as you go through it, and you will escape many hard thumps.' This advice, thus beat into my head, has frequently been of use to me; and I often think of it when I see pride mortified, and misfortunes brought upon people by carrying their heads too high."

Cotton Mather married three times, and had fifteen children. He died on the 13th of February, 1728, at the age of sixty-five years.

JOHN MASON.

MILES STANDISH is called *the* "hero of New England" because of priority. There were other men of that olden time who were greater "heroes" than he, when measured by the common standard. John Mason was a greater "hero" than Standish, for he caused the destruction of more Indians than his rival for the palm. He was born in England about the year 1600. He was a soldier by profession, and had practiced his murderous art in that cock-pit of Europe, the Netherlands. In 1630, he came to America, and was one of the original settlers at Dorchester. He went to the Connecticut Valley in 1635, and assisted in founding a settlement at Windsor. The peace of the little colony was soon disturbed by the depredations of the powerful Pequods, whose chief rendezvous was between the Thames and Mystic rivers. They believed the white people to be friendly to their enemies, the Mohegans and Narragansets, and they had resolved to exterminate them. They kidnapped children, stole cattle, and finally made murderous attacks upon the outskirts of the settlement at Saybrook, near the mouth of the Connecticut river. The danger became imminent, and Captain Mason went down to Saybrook, with some followers, to reinforce and command the garrison of the little fort there.

In the Spring of 1637, the settlers in the Connecticut Valley declared war

---

continent of Europe, nearly two hundred years before. Within fifty or sixty years, during the sixteenth century, more than one hundred thousand persons accused of witchcraft, perished in the flames, in Germany alone. The delusion prevailed in Massachusetts for more than six months, in 1692; and during that time, twenty persons suffered death, fifty-five were tortured or frightened into a confession of witchcraft, and over one hundred were imprisoned. The delusion commenced at Danvers, and spread over a great extent of country in the vicinity of Boston.

against the Pequods, and the Plymouth and Massachusetts people promised to assist them. Through the influence of Roger Williams, the Narragansets became allies of the English; and when, late in May, Captain Mason, with eighty white men and seventy Mohegan Indians, anchored his pinnaces near Conannicut Island, he was joined by Miantonomoh, the great chief of the Narragansets, with two hundred warriors. With these, Mason proceeded toward the Pequod country, and was joined, on the way, by the Niantics. Sassacus, a fierce warrior, was the chief sachem of the Pequods. He could summon two thousand braves to the field, and his confidence in his great strength made him less vigilant than a weak leader would have been. He had no intelligence or suspicion of the approach of Mason, from the East. He was first informed of it by the seven survivors of a dreadful massacre. The invaders crept as stealthily along as a panther, and just at dawn, on the 5th of June, 1637, fell upon the chief fort of the Pequods, on the Mystic river. Before sunrise, more than six hundred men, women, and children, had perished by weapons, or by the flames of their own burning wigwams. Only seven escaped to arouse the nation to vengeance. The English, aware of their danger, hastened toward Saybrook; but the power of the Pequods was broken. When, a few days afterward, about one hundred Massachusetts men joined Mason, Sassacus and his followers fled westward, hotly pursued by the English. They took shelter in Sasco swamp, near Fairfield, where, after a severe battle, they all surrendered, except Sassacus and a few others, who fled to the Mohawks for refuge. There the great sachem was treacherously slain. The blow was terrible. A nation had disappeared in a day.[1] The New England tribes were awed; and for forty years afterward the colonists were unmolested by them.

Soon after the war, the governor of Connecticut appointed Mason major-general of all the forces of the colony, which office he filled until his death. He was also a civil magistrate for eighteen consecutive years; and in 1660, he was elected deputy-governor. He retired from public life in 1670; and in 1673, he died at Norwich, at the age of seventy-two years.

BENJAMIN WEST.

"THERE have been more volumes written about this great painter in England," says Lester, "than there have been pages devoted to him in the land of his birth." Here he grew to young manhood, and chose the mother of his children; in sunny Italy he achieved his first triumph in high art, and in England he reigned and died. His birth occurred at Springfield, in Chester county, Pennsylvania, on the 10th of October, 1738. He was the youngest of the nine children of excellent Quaker parents; and at seven years of age, while keeping flies from the sleeping baby of his eldest sister, he sketched her portrait so accurately with black and red ink, that his mother, snatching the paper (which he modestly attempted to conceal) from his hand, exclaimed, "I declare he has made a likeness of little Sally!" His parents encouraged his efforts, and the Indians supplied him with some of the pigments with which they painted their faces. His mother's "indigo bag" furnished him with blue, and from pussy's tail he drew the material for his brushes. Such was the juvenile be-

---

1. Captain Mason wrote a *Brief Memoir of the Pequod War*. It makes one shudder to read his blasphemous allusion to the interposition of God in favor of the English, as if the poor Indian was not an object of the care and love of the Deity! Happily the time is rapidly passing by when men believe that they are doing God service by slaughtering, maiming, or in the least injuring, with vengeful feelings, *any* of his creatures.

ginning of the greatest historical painter of the last century—such were the first buddings of the genius of that boy, who would not ride in company with another, because he aspired to nothing greater than a tailor's shop-board. "Do you really mean to be a tailor?" asked little West. "Indeed I do," replied his boy-companion. "Then you may ride alone," exclaimed the young aspirant, leaping to the ground. "I mean to be a painter, and be the companion of kings and emperors; I'll not ride with one willing to be a tailor!"

At the age of fifteen years, young West had learned the use of proper colors, and was a popular portrait painter. The pursuit of such art was contrary to the discipline of the Quakers. A meeting was called to consult upon the matter. At length one arose and said, "God hath bestowed on this youth a genius for art; shall we question his wisdom? I see the Divine hand in this; we shall do well to sanction the art and encourage this youth." Then the sweet women of the assembly rose up and kissed him. The men, one by one, laid their hands on his head, and thus Benjamin West was solemnly consecrated to the service of the great art. His pictures produced both money and fame, and wealthy men furnished him with means to go to Italy, to study the works of the great masters. There every step was a triumph, and he became the best painter in Italy. He crossed the Alps and went to England. There prejudice and bad taste met him, but his genius overcame both. Among his earliest and best patrons was Archbishop Drummond, who introduced him to the young King, George the Third. His majesty was delighted, and ordered him to paint *The Departure of Regulus*, that noble picture exhibited in the New York Crystal Palace, in 1853. That achievement placed him on the throne of English art. The King, and Reynolds, and West, founded the Royal Academy; and he who, in the face of every obstacle, created a public taste for high art, was properly appointed "Painter to his Majesty." He designed thirty grand pictures, illustrative of The Progress of Revealed Religion, and completed twenty-eight of them, besides a great number of other admirable works. But when insanity clouded the mind of King George, and his libertine son, the Prince of Wales, obtained power, the great painter was neglected. The king of art, who had ruled for five and thirty years, was soon an exile from the court of his excellent friend, and many cherished anticipations of his prime were blighted in his declining years. But when royalty deserted him, the generous people sustained him. He achieved great triumphs in his old age; and finally, on the 11th of March, 1820, when in the eighty-second year of his life, he was laid by the side of Reynolds and Opie in St. Paul's Cathedral.

WILLIAM BYRD.

About half-way between Richmond and Old Jamestown, on the James River, in Virginia, is a fine brick mansion, surrounded by a fertile plantation, known as Westover. It was the residence of Colonel William Byrd, a wealthy cavalier, who came from England during the Protectorate of Oliver Cromwell. He was really the founder of the city of Richmond, at the Falls of the James River. A small fortification had been erected there, as a defense against the Indians, as early as 1645; but about 1680, Colonel Byrd, having received a conditional grant of land at the Falls, sent more than fifty able-bodied men there to make a settlement. He erected a mill and other buildings for the use of their productions, and the settlement was known as *Byrd's Warehouse*. In 1682, Colonel Byrd was a member of the governor's council, and he was much in public employment, until his death. When, after the revocation of the edict of Nantes, a large number of Huguenots, or French Protestants, came to America, three hundred of them were cared for, with parental solicitude, by Colonel Byrd, and they found pleasant homes in the Virginia colony. Many of these were educated men, and in Colonel Byrd they found an agreeable companion. He possessed fine literary and scientific tastes, and had the largest library in America, at that time. In 1723, he was one of the commissioners appointed to establish the boundary line between Virginia and North Carolina. Toward the close of his life he employed his pen on scientific subjects, and was made a member of the London Royal Society. His munificence and style of living were unequalled in the colonies. They were like those of an English nobleman. He died in 1743, at the age of almost eighty years, leaving his homestead, and a splendid fortune, to his son William. He, too, became a public man; and in 1756, was a commissioner to treat with the Indians on the western borders of Virginia. He accompanied the expedition against Fort Duquesne, under Washington's command, in 1758. Being a spendthrift and a gambler, his immense wealth was greatly lessened, at his death. His widow occupied the Westover property at the time of our revolution; and there Benedict Arnold (who was her relative) landed, when he invaded Virginia in the service of his royal purchaser, in 1781. De Chastellux, one of Rochambeau's officers, speaks rapturously of the beauty of Westover, and the pleasures of society there.

ELEAZER WHEELOCK.

THOSE good men who by personal sacrifices and diligent efforts seek to elevate their fellow-beings of low degree, should be remembered and honored. Among those of the past who deserve such reward, is Eleazer Wheelock, the founder of the first school for the Christian education of Indian youths in New England. He was born at Windham, Connecticut, in April, 1711; and in 1733, was graduated at Yale College. Two years afterward he was ordained a gospel minister, and settled as pastor, at Lebanon. There he opened a school for the education of English children; and in 1743, his first Indian pupil was admitted. He was a Mohegan youth of nineteen years, named Samson Occum, who had been converted to Christianity under the preaching of a clergyman at Norwich. Before entering Mr. Wheelock's school, Occum had learned to spell out sentences in the Bible for the edification of his eager dusky listeners. He was anxious to become a spiritual teacher of his tribe. He remained with Mr. Wheelock between four and five years, and afterward became a very successful preacher among the natives on the east end of Long Island. His success with Occum induced Mr. Wheelock to attempt the education of other Indian youths, with special reference to their preparation for missionary labors, believing that they would be more efficient among the savages, than white preachers.[1] In 1762, he had more than twenty Indian youths in his school, the expenses being paid by voluntary subscriptions, small legislative grants, and contributions from the Boston commissioners of the Scotch society for propagating Christian knowledge. A farmer, named Moor, gave a house and some land, adjoining Mr. Wheelock's residence, for the use of the institution, and it became known as Moor's Indian Charity School. To increase its usefulness, it was determined to seek aid in England; and in 1766, Occum and Rev. Mr. Whitaker of Norwich, went thither for that purpose. The money collected by them was put into the hands of trustees, in England, at the head of whom was the Earl of Dartmouth; and its expenditure was intrusted to the Scotch society.

Hoping to be more efficient on the borders of the Indian country, wherein white settlements had not yet been planted, Dr. Wheelock resigned his pastoral charge at Lebanon, and established his school at Hanover, in New Hampshire. He also founded a college there, and named it Dartmouth, in honor of the Earl, notwithstanding that gentleman was opposed to the project, fearing it might interfere with the Indian School.[2] Governor Wentworth gave it a charter, and for nine years Dr. Wheelock labored vigorously at the head of each establishment. The war for Independence seriously affected the prosperity of both enterprises, yet the self-sacrificing founder saw glorious fruit produced by his planting. Among those white missionaries whom he prepared for their work, was the faithful Kirkland, so long a noble laborer among the tribes in the interior of New York. Dr. Wheelock died at Hanover, on the 24th of April, 1779, at the age of sixty-eight years.

---

1. This opinion proved to be erroneous. About one-half of those educated for the ministry returned to their old habits and vices, when they got among their people again. Among Mr. Wheelock's pupils was Brant, the celebrated Mohawk chief.
2. This fact exhibits the modesty of Dr. Wheelock, and at the same time shows that undue deference which all persons formerly rendered to titles and dignities. The college ought to perpetuate the name of Dr. Wheelock, by its own title.

CADWALLADER COLDEN.

THE representatives of royal power, in America, generally regarded the people as their *subjects*, rather than as fellow-citizens, and ruled by despotic power rather than by kindness and conciliation. There were honorable exceptions, and among these was Cadwallader Colden, whose character and public life were truthfully portrayed, more than forty years ago, by John W. Francis, M.D., now [1854] the Nestor of literature and science in New York. Colden was acting governor of New York when the stamp-act riots occurred, and was treated with indignity by a mob, because he was the representative of the king, and at the same time was highly respected by them as a man and valuable citizen.

Cadwallader Colden was born in Duñse, Scotland, on the 17th of February, 1688. He completed his collegiate studies at the university of Edinburgh, in 1705, and after devoting three years to the study of mathematics and medical science, he came to America, where he remained five years, as a practicing physician. He went to Great Britain in 1715, and formed the acquaintance of Halley and other leading men of science; and the following year he married a pretty Scotch girl, returned to America, and settled in the city of New York. Colden soon abandoned his profession, for public employment. He was made surveyor-general of the province, a master in chancery, and finally became one of the governor's council. About the year 1750, he obtained a patent for a large tract of unsettled land near Newburgh, in Orange county, and named his manor, Coldenham. There, after the year 1755, he resided, with his family, most of the time, engaged in agriculture and in literary and scientific pursuits. Many learned essays from his pen enriched the medical and scientific publications of his day; and his *History of the Five Nations of Indians*, is a noble monument in testimony of his careful and judicious researches in that special field of inquiry. Almost all of the scientific men of Europe were his correspondents, and Franklin and other leading Americans were among his intimate epistolary friends. Botany was his favorite study, and he was a constant and valued correspondent of Linnæus, the great master of the science, for a series of years. His voluminous papers are now among the choice treasures of the New York Historical Society.

In 1760, Dr. Colden was appointed lieutenant-governor of the province of New York, and became the acting magistrate, at eighty years of age. He managed public affairs with great prudence during all the trying scenes of the Stamp-Act excitement; and the *Sons of Liberty* respected him, while they defied his delegated power. He was released from office, by Governor Tryon, in 1775, and retired to his country seat, at Flushing, Long Island, where he died on the 28th of September, 1776; a few days before that great conflagration which consumed more than five hundred buildings in the city of New York. Governor Colden was then almost eighty-nine years of age.

JOHN SMITH.

THERE are men whose career appears meteor-like in brilliancy and progress, which nevertheless makes permanent impressions upon the world's history, and beams in the firmament of past events, with steady, planetary lustre. John Smith belongs to the meteor-heroes of our race. He was born at Willoughby, in Lincolnshire, England, in 1559, and in early childhood was distinguished for his daring spirit and love of adventure. At the age of thirteen years, he sold his books and satchel to procure money to pay his way to the sea-shore, for he had resolved to try life on the ocean wave. He was prevented from embarking, and apprenticed to a merchant. Two years afterward he ran away, went to France, and then to the Low Countries, and there studied military tactics. With a portion of his deceased father's estate, young Smith, at the age of seventeen years, went abroad, like a knight-errant, in search of adventures. On a voyage from Marseilles to Naples, a great storm arose. The crew of the vessel were Roman Catholics, who, believing the young *heretic* Englishman to be a Jonah, cast him into the sea to appease the angry waters. He swam to a small island, and there embarked in a French vessel for Alexandria, in Egypt. From thence he went to Italy, and then to Austria, where he entered the imperial army. His valor soon procured him the command of a troop of horse, which, in the war against the Turks, obtained the name of *The Fiery Dragoons*. On one occasion, during a siege, a Turkish officer offered to engage in a duel with any Christian soldier, "to amuse the ladies." The lot fell to Smith. They fought in sight of both armies. Smith cut off his antagonist's head, and carried it in triumph to the Austrian camp; and then fought two other Turkish champions with the same result. He was afterward captured and sold to a Pacha, who sent his prisoner as a present to his sweetheart, to be her slave. Her love was excited, and to insure his safety, she sent Smith to her brother. The Turk treated the captive cruelly. Soon an opportunity for escape was offered, when Smith killed his tyrant, fled into Muscovy, and found his way to Austria. The war had ended, and Smith departed from the Adriatic, with a French sea-captain, for Morocco. He was engaged in a sea-fight near the Canary Islands, with the Spaniards; and then, after a long absence, returned to his native country. His restless spirit now yearned for adventures in the New World, and accompanying the first English expedition which successfully planted a settlement in America, he became the real founder of the Virginia colony. The settlers became jealous of his talent, on the voyage, and, ignorant that he was named in the "sealed box"[1] as one of the Council, they put him in irons, under the plea that he intended to make himself King of Virginia. He was released when his name appeared among the appointed rulers. He possessed great energy, and he not only supported good government by his presence, but saved the colony from destruction. He was rescued from death by Pocahontas, the daughter of the Indian king, while a prisoner among them; and he acquired such influence over the savages, that they were friendly to the English while Smith ruled the colony. He explored the coast from Pamlico Sound to the Delaware river, and constructed a map of the country. An accident caused him to go to England for surgical attendance. Five years afterward he made a trading voyage to America, explored the coast from the Thames to the Penobscot, made a map of the country, and called it New England. Smith offered to accompany the Pilgrim Fathers, to America, in 1620, but on account of his aristocratic notions, his proffered services were declined. He died in London, in 1631, at the age of seventy-two years.

DAVID RITTENHOUSE.

NEAR the banks of the beautiful Wissahiccon, in the vicinity of Germantown, four miles from Philadelphia, lived three hermits a century and a half ago; and near their hiding-places from the world's ken, a mile from the old village where the good count Zinzendorf,[1] the Moravian, labored and reposed, was the birth-place of one whose name is co-extensive with scientific knowledge. It was David Rittenhouse, the eminent mathematician, who was born in Roxborough township, on the 8th of April, 1732. His father was a humble farmer, and David was his chief assistant when his life approached young manhood. The geometrical diagrams which disfigured his implements of labor, the barn doors, and the pig-sty, attested the peculiar workings of his brain while yet a mere lad. These indications of genius would doubtless have been disregarded, and his aspirations remained unsatisfied, had not a feeble body made the abandonment of field labor a stern necessity. David was apprenticed to a clock and mathematical instrument maker, and the pursuit being consonant with his taste, he was eminently successful.

Rittenhouse was a severe student, but on account of his pecuniary wants, he was deprived, in a great degree, of the most valuable sources of information, especially concerning the progress of science in Europe. While Newton and Liebnitz were warmly disputing for the honor of first discoverer of *Fluxions*, Rittenhouse, entirely ignorant of what they had done, became the inventor of that remarkable feature in algebraical analysis. Applying the knowledge which

---

1. The silly King James, instead of making an open appointment of a council for the government of Virginia, placed their names in a sealed box, with directions not to open it until their arrival on the shores of the New World.
1. Zinzendorf was the founder of the *Moravians*, or *United Brethren*, and preached in Germantown, for a while.

he derived from study and reflection, to the mechanic arts, he produced a planetarium, or an exhibition of the movements of the solar system, by machinery. It is a most wonderful piece of mechanism, especially when we consider the fact that the inventor was yet an obscure mechanic in a country village. That work of art is in the possession of the College of New Jersey, at Princeton, it having been purchased on the recommendation of President Witherspoon.[1] It gave him great reputation; and in 1770, he went to Philadelphia, where he pursued his mechanical vocation, and met, daily, members of the Philosophical Society of that city, to whom he had, two years before, communicated the fact that he had calculated, with great exactness, the transit of Venus, which occurred on the 3d of June, 1769. Rittenhouse was one of those whom the Society appointed to observe it. Only three times before, in the whole range of human observations, had mortal vision beheld the orb of Venus pass across the disc of the sun.[2] Upon the exactitude of the performance according to calculations, depended many important astronomical problems, and the hour was looked for-

---

1. When Cornwallis arrived at Princeton, after the severe battle at that place on the morning of the 2d of January, 1777, he saw and admired that work of art, and determined to carry it away with him. The Americans caused him to leave the place too soon to accomplish his purpose. During the same year, Silas Deane, the American commissioner at the French court, actually proposed to present the planetarium to the French king, as a bonus for his good will! The conqueror and the diplomatist were both foiled.

2. See sketch of John Winthrop, LL.D., page 44.

ward to, by philosophers, with intense interest. As the moment approached, according to his own calculations, Rittenhouse became greatly excited. When the discs of the two planets touched, at precisely the expected moment, the philosopher fainted. His highest hopes were realized; and on the 9th of November following he was blessed with the sight of a transit of Mercury.

When Dr. Franklin died, Rittenhouse was chosen President of the American Philosophical Society, to fill his place; and from his own earnings he gave the institution fifteen hundred dollars, on the day of his inauguration. His fame was now world-wide, and many official honors awaited his acceptance. He held the office of treasurer of the state of Pennsylvania, for many years; and in 1792, he was appointed the first Director of the Mint. Failing health compelled him to resign that trust, in 1795; and on the 6th of June, the following year, he died the death of a Christian, at the age of sixty-four years.

UNCAS.

UNLIKE most of the Indian chiefs and sachems who appear conspicuous in our early annals, the line of descent from Uncas comes down almost to our own time, and he has been honored, in preference to all others, with a commemorative monument from the hands of the white man. Uncas was a Pequod, by birth. Rebelling against his chief, Sassacus, he was expelled from the Pequod domain, and by his talent and sagacity soon took the rank and power of a chief among the Mohegans. He became the inveterate enemy of Sassacus; and he was at the head of the Mohegans who accompanied Captain Mason against the Pequods, in 1637. He was always the firm friend of the English; and during that dark period, when King Philip succeeded in arming all the New England tribes against the white people, Uncas remained faithful. He even took up arms against Philip, and with two hundred Mohegans, and a greater number of subjugated Pequods, he marched with Major Talcott to Brookfield and Hadley, and at the latter place assisted in defeating seven hundred of Philip's savage allies.

Like Philip, Uncas was opposed to the preaching of Christianity among his people, preferring to have them believe in the religion of his fathers. Yet he never used coercive measures in opposition; and, finally, he so far yielded, that on one occasion, when the country was suffering from a great drought, he asked a Christian minister to pray for rain. A copious shower fell the next day, and Uncas became like King Agrippa in the presence of Paul—he was almost persuaded to become a Christian. In 1659, Uncas gave a deed to several white people, conveying to them a large tract of land at the head of the Pequod river [the Thames], and there the city of Norwich was founded. The exact period of the death of Uncas is unknown. It is supposed to have occurred about 1683, when he was succeeded by his son Owaneko, or Oneco, who distinguished himself on the side of the English, in King Philip's war. In his old age, Oneco used to go about begging, accompanied by his squaw. As he could not speak English well, Richard Bushnell wrote the following lines for him to present to the benevolent:

"Oneco, King, his queen doth bring to beg a little food,
As they go along their friends among, to try how kind and good;
Some pork, some beef, for their relief; and if you can't spare bread,
She'll thank you for your pudding, as they go a gooding, and carry it on her head."

A neat granite obelisk, about twenty feet in height, has been erected in the city of Norwich, to the memory of Uncas. The foundation stone was laid in

1825, by General Jackson; and in the small cemetery in which it stands, a descendant of Uncas, named Mazeon, was buried in 1827. There are a few of the Mohegan tribe yet living, near Norwich; but soon it may be written upon a tomb-stone, "The last of the Mohegans."

KING PHILIP.

A GENEROUS mind readily appreciates and commends an exhibition of true patriotism, even by an enemy. Those who regard the Indian as without the pale of the sympathies of civilization, are often compelled to yield reluctant admiration of the qualities which make men heroes, sages, and patriots, when exhibited by this *taboo'd* race. No one appears more prominent as a claimant for consideration on account of these qualities, than Metacomet, the last chief of the Wampanoags of Rhode Island, known in history as King Philip. He was one of two sons of Massasoit, the sachem[1] who gave a friendly welcome to the Pilgrim Fathers. They were named, respectively, Alexander and Philip, by governor Winslow, in compliment to their father. Alexander was the eldest, and succeeded his father in authority. He died, and his mantle fell upon Philip, a bold, powerful-minded warrior, whose keen perception had already given him uneasiness respecting the future of his race. He saw, year after year, the encroachments of the white people, yet he faithfully kept the treaty of his father, with them. He even endured insults and gross indignities; and when his hot-blooded warriors gathered around his throne upon Mount Hope, and counselled war, he refused to listen. At length forbearance seemed no longer a virtue, and the hatchet was lifted.

Among the "praying Indians," as Eliot's converts were called, was one who had been educated at Cambridge, and was employed as a teacher. On account of some misdemeanor, he had fled to Philip, and became his secretary. He afterward returned to the white people, and accused Philip of treasonable designs. Because of this charge, he was waylaid and murdered by some of the Wampanoags. Three suspected men were tried, convicted on slender testimony, and hanged. The ire of the Wampanoags was fiercely kindled. Philip was cautious, for he knew his weakness; his young warriors were impetuous, for they counted not the cost of war. The sachem was finally overruled; and remembering the indignities which he had suffered from the English, he trampled solemn treaties under foot, and lighted the flame of war. Messengers were sent to other tribes, and with all the power of Indian eloquence, Philip exhorted his followers to curse the white man, and to swear eternal hostility to the "pale faces." The events which followed have been detailed in our sketch of Captain Church, and need not be repeated here. Metacomet was a patriot of truest stamp, and his general character, measured by the standard of true appreciation, in which all controlling circumstances are considered, bears a favorable comparison with the patriots of other lands, and of more enlightened people. His death occurred in August, 1776, when he was about fifty years of age. During the war, the government of Plymouth offered thirty shillings for every head of an Indian killed in battle. The faithless Wampanoag received that price—"thirty pieces of silver"—for his master's head.

---

1. *Sachem* and *Chief* are distinct characters, yet they are sometimes found in the same person. A *sachem* is the civil head of a tribe; a *chief* is a military leader. Philip was both.

BENJAMIN FRANKLIN.

THE words of Solomon, "Seest thou a man diligent in his business? he shall stand before kings; he shall not stand before mean men," attracted the attention of a Boston tallow-chandler's son, when he was yet in youthhood. That youth was the immortal Benjamin Franklin, who was born on the morning of the 17th of January, 1706, and was christened that afternoon. At the age of eight years he went to a grammar school; but at ten his services were required in his father's business, and his education was neglected. At the age of twelve years he was apprenticed to his brother James, a printer. He made great proficiency in his business, and a love for reading was gratified, often at the expense of half a night's sleep. *The New England Courant*, printed by his brother in 1721, was the third newspaper established in America.[1] Young Franklin wrote several essays for it, which attracted much attention. The author was unknown and unsuspected. At about the same time he read the

---

1. The other two were *The Boston News Letter* and *The Boston Gazette.*

productions of Shaftesbury and Collins, and he became a sceptic in religion, and a powerful disputant, by the use of the Socratic method of argument—asking questions. Because of his scepticism he became unpopular in Boston. This fact, and ill treatment by his brother, determined him to leave the place. He went to New York in a sloop, and from thence to Philadelphia, on foot, where he soon procured employment, as a printer, in the establishment of Mr. Keimer. His intelligence and good conduct attracted the attention of prominent men, among whom was Governor Keith, who advised him to go into business for himself. With promises of aid from the governor, he started for London to buy printing materials. The aid was withheld; and on his arrival, he sought employment for a livelihood. He was now only eighteen years of age. By the practice of the most rigid economy, he saved a greater part of his wages; and his influence among his fellow-workmen, against useless expenses for beer and other things, was beneficial. At night he used his pen; and by a *Dissertation on Liberty*, in which he contended that virtue and vice are nothing more than conventional distinctions, he made the acquaintance of Mandeville and other infidel writers. Franklin always looked back to these early efforts of his pen, in opposition to Christian ethics, with great regret.

Franklin returned to Philadelphia in the Autumn of 1726, as a merchant's clerk; but the death of his employer, the following year, induced him to work, again, for Mr. Keimer. His ingenuity was profitable to his employer, for he engraved devices on type metal, made printer's ink, and in various ways saved money to the establishment. In 1728, he formed a partnership in the printing business with Mr. Meredith, but it was dissolved the following year. He then purchased Keimer's miserably-conducted paper, issued it in a greatly improved style, uttered in it many of those aphorisms which have since become famous, and then laid the foundation of his future usefulness. He married in 1730, lived frugally, and in the course of three or four years began to save money. He opened a small shop for the sale of stationery, to which his pleasant and edifying conversation drew many of the men of literary taste in the town. A literary club was formed, in which questions were discussed which required reference to books. The members brought such as they needed, from time to time, and Franklin conceived the idea of forming a public library. It was popular; and in 1731, the foundation of that noble institution, the Philadelphia Library, was laid.[1] The following year he commenced the publication of *Poor Richard's Almanac*. It was full of sound maxims, and its popularity was so great, that he sold ten thousand copies annually. He continued it until 1757, when the demands of public business upon his time, compelled him to relinquish it.

Franklin's first public employment was undertaken in 1736, when he was appointed clerk of the General Assembly of Pennsylvania. The following year he was appointed Postmaster of Philadelphia. He now began to be one of the most popular men in the province. The fact is demonstrated by the circumstance that, by his personal exertions, he obtained ten thousand names to a voluntary association for the defence of the province, in 1744, when an attempt to procure a militia law had failed. He was chosen a member of the Assembly in 1747, and was regularly re-elected for ten years. Although Franklin was no orator, yet no man possessed greater influence than he, in that body. Yet these public employments did not draw his attention from books and scientific investigations. For a long time he held a theory that the electricity of the scientific

---

1. The association at first consisted of 40 members. The library was first established in the house of Franklin's warm friend, Robert Grace. In 1740, it was placed in the State House. In 1773, it was removed to Carpenter's Hall; and in 1790, the building erected for its use, was completed. The association was incorporated in 1742, as *The Library Company of Philadelphia*.

apparatus and the lightning of the clouds were identical; and in 1752, he demonstrated the truth of his theory by unmistakable experiments.[1] He immediately applied the discovery to a practical use, by showing that pointed iron rods, extending from a distance above the highest part of a house to the ground, would preserve the house from lightning, by conducting it into the earth. The theory and its demonstration were made known in Europe, and Franklin's name became known and venerated throughout the scientific world.

In 1753, Franklin was made deputy postmaster-general of the British colonies in America, and the same year he projected and established the Academy of Sciences of Philadelphia. In 1754, he was one of the colonial delegates who met in Congress at Albany to devise means of defence against the French; and there he submitted a plan of union, similar, in many respects, to our Federal Constitution, but it was rejected by the British government and the colonial assemblies for widely different reasons. Three years afterward, Franklin was sent to England as the agent of Pennsylvania, and was employed in the same capacity by three other colonies. There he associated with the greatest men of the time, and the poor journeyman printer of a few years before, "stood before kings," was caressed by men of learning, was made a member of the Royal Society, and honored with the degree of Doctor of Laws, by the Universities of Edinburgh and Oxford. He returned to America in 1762, and resumed his seat in the Assembly; but two years afterward, the dispute between the colonies and the government having commenced in earnest, he was again sent as agent for Pennsylvania, to England. He remained abroad until 1775, during which time he visited the Continent, and became acquainted with the most learned men in Europe. On the day of his arrival in America, he was elected a member of the Continental Congress; and he was one of the signers of the Declaration of Independence the following year. During the whole period of the revolution he was continually active in a civil capacity at home or abroad. Congress sent him as commissioner to the French court in 1776, and he was one of the most accomplished and adroit diplomatists at Versailles. Finally, when peace was determined upon, Franklin was one of the leading commissioners in forming those treaties with Great Britain and other powers, which secured the independence of the colonies. He was then appointed Minister Plenipotentiary at the French court, and "stood before kings" until, by his own request, another was appointed in his place, and he returned home. He arrived at Philadelphia early in the Autumn of 1785, and was received with the highest republican honors. In 1787, he was a leading man in the convention which formed the Federal Constitution; and the following year he withdrew from public life, being then eighty-two years of age. On the 17th of April, 1790, that great Philosopher, Statesman, and Sage, was undressed for the grave; and beneath a neat marble slab, in the burial-ground of Christ Church, Philadelphia, rest his mortal remains.[2]

---

1. He sent up an iron-pointed kite toward a hovering thunder cloud, and held it by a silken string, attached to the long hempen one. To the silken end was fastened an iron key, and when the cloud passed over, he touched the key with his knuckles, and received a spark. It was a bold but successful experiment.

2. According to his directions, the only inscription on the broad slab is,

BENJAMIN
AND } FRANKLIN.
DEBORAH
1790.

Many years before, he wrote the following epitaph for himself:
"The body of BENJAMIN FRANKLIN, Printer, Like the cover of an old Book, Its contents torn out, (And stripped of its lettering and gilding,) Lies here, food for worms. But the work shall not be lost, For it will (as he believed) appear once more, In a new and more elegant edition, Revised and corrected, by THE AUTHOR."

NATHANIEL BACON.

OFTEN, in men's estimation, success makes effort a virtue, but failure makes it a crime. A successful blow at tyranny is called patriotism; an unsuccessful one is branded as rebellion. Nathaniel Bacon lifted his arm for popular freedom, failed, and history recorded his name among traitors. He was a young man of great boldness and energy of character. His birth-place was in Suffolk county, England, and in London he was educated for the legal profession. He came to America during Cromwell's rule in England, and was soon called to a seat in the council of Governor Berkeley. Thoroughly democratic in his views, Bacon often crossed the official path of the haughty cavalier, as an assertor of popular rights, especially after the restoration of Charles the Second made the Virginia loyalists insolent and tyrannical. The assembly, under the influence of the governor, abridged the liberties of the people, propagated the vipers of intolerance, and imposed heavy fines upon Baptists and Quakers. The people soon learned to despise the name of king, and a strong republican party was formed.

Circumstances soon favored a demonstration of republican strength. Some Indian tribes commenced depredations upon the settlements in the upper part of Virginia, and they finally penetrated as far as Bacon's plantation in the vicinity of Richmond. Berkeley appeared indifferent, and the planters asked the privilege of protecting themselves. The governor refused; when at least five hundred men collected together, chose Bacon for commander, and drove the Indians back to the Potomac. Berkeley was jealous of Bacon, proclaimed him a traitor, and sent troops to pursue and arrest him. The people arose in rebellion, the aristocratic assembly was dissolved and a republican one elected; universal suffrage was restored; Bacon was chosen commander-in-chief of the military, and a commission for him was demanded of the governor. That official was alarmed and promised compliance, not, however, until Bacon, with a large force, approached Jamestown. He was compelled to attest the bravery and loyalty of Bacon; and on the 4th of July, 1676, just a hundred years before the colonies were declared free states, a more liberal and enlightened legislation commenced in Virginia. That day was truly the harbinger of American independence and nationality.

Again the Indians approached, and Bacon proceeded to drive them back. As soon as he had departed, Berkeley treacherously published a proclamation, reversing the proceedings of the assembly, repudiating Bacon's commission, and declaring him a traitor. Back to Jamestown the indignant patriot marched, and lighted a civil war. The governor and adhering loyalists were driven beyond the York river, and the wives of many were detained as hostages for peace. Troops came from England to support Berkeley; and when rumor told of their march up the peninsula, Bacon applied the torch and laid Jamestown in ashes. He then crossed the York to drive the enemies of popular freedom entirely out of the old dominion, but there he met a foe to his life more deadly than royalists or the Indians. The malaria from the low lands infused its poison into his veins, and at the house of Dr. Green, in Gloucester county, the brave republican died, on the 1st of October, 1676, at the age of about thirty-seven years. Berkeley assumed power immediately, and Bacon's followers were terribly persecuted. Twenty were hanged, scores were imprisoned, and much property was confiscated. Because the patriots were unsuccessful, this episode in Virginia history is known as "BACON'S REBELLION."

JONATHAN TRUMBULL.

ONE of the main pillars of support upon which General Washington relied during the War for Independence, was Jonathan Trumbull, then Governor of Connecticut. He was born at Lebanon, Connecticut, on the 21st of June, 1710, and was graduated at Harvard College in 1727. His serious mind turned to theology as a profession, and he commenced its study with the Rev. Solomon Williams, of Lebanon. The death of an older brother, who was engaged in mercantile business with his father, caused Jonathan to change his intentions and become a merchant. When only twenty-three years of age, he was elected a member of the Connecticut Assembly, where he soon became distinguished as one of its most active committee men. In 1766, he was elected lieutenant-governor of the colony, and became ex-officio chief justice of the superior court. He espoused the patriot cause very early; and in 1768, he took the bold step of refusing to take the oath, which enjoined almost unconditional submission to

Parliament, and which a ministerial order required. That step was popular with the people; and the following year he was chosen governor by a very large majority. His influence became almost unbounded throughout New England; and while the Adams's and Hancock were legislating in the Continental Congress, Governor Trumbull was recognized as the great leader in the East. He was an active, self-sacrificing, and reliable man throughout the whole contest; and he had the proud distinction of being the only colonial governor who, at the commencement of the revolution, espoused the republican cause. For fourteen consecutive years he was elected to the chief magistracy of his native State; but when peace returned, and all danger seemed over, he left the helm forever. He declined a reëlection; and at the age of seventy-three years, he retired from public life. In August, 1785, he was seized with a malignant fever, which destroyed his life on the 17th of that month. His son and grandson both filled his chair of office, the latter having been governor in 1849.

The Marquis de Chastellux, who came to America with Rochambeau in 1780, thus speaks of the personal appearance of Governor Trumbull: "He is seventy years old; his whole life is consecrated to business, which he passionately loves, whether important or not; or rather, with respect to him, there is none of the latter description. He has all the simplicity in his dress, all the importance, and even pedantry, becoming the great magistrate of a small republic. He brought to my mind the burgomasters of Holland in the time of the Heinsius's and Barnevelts." He was greatly beloved by Washington; and no name on the pages of our history appears brighter, as a pure patriot and honest man, than that of Jonathan Trumbull.

JOHN WINTHROP.

ONE of the most accomplished scholars of the last century, was John Winthrop, professor of mathematics and natural philosophy in Harvard University. He was born in Boston, in 1715, and was graduated at Harvard when only seventeen years of age. His studies took a wide range, and included theology and medicine, with the natural sciences. When he was appointed Hollis Professor[1] in the university, he was considered the most learned man in America; and his teaching and example gave a powerful impetus to the study of the exact sciences in this country. As early as 1740, he made observations on the transit of Mercury, and published them in the Transactions of the Royal Society of London.

In June, 1761, he went to St. John's, Newfoundland, with his instruments and attendants, to observe the transit of Venus, that point being the most favorable, in America, for such observations. That passage of Venus across the disc of the sun had been looked forward to with great interest, for one hundred and twenty-two years had elapsed since a similar phenomenon had been observed.[2] Mr. Winthrop's observations were accurate, and of the greatest value. They gave his name and that of Harvard College a world-wide reputation. The Royal Society elected him a member of that body; and the University at Edinburgh conferred upon him the degree of LL.D., or Doctor of Laws. He also observed the transit of Venus, in 1769,[3] and the papers which he published on that subject

---

1. A professorship liberally endowed by John Hollis. He founded two professorships in that institution—divinity and mathematics. Mr. Winthrop was professor of mathematics.
2. It cannot be seen with the naked eye. The telescope was first used among moderns early in the 17th century, and the first transit of Venus observed with it, was on the 6th of December, 1631. The next was on the 4th of December, 1639. Again, on the 5th of June, 1761, and the 3d of June, 1769. The next transit will take place on the 8th of December, 1874.
3. See sketch of David Rittenhouse.

procured his admission to membership in the most eminent scientific societies of the world.

In 1767, Dr. Winthrop published his *Cogita de Cometis*, a work of profound research, and of great value to the scientific world. At this time the dispute between the American colonies and Great Britain was assuming much importance, and Dr Winthrop engaged zealously in the cause of the colonists. Notwithstanding he labored intensely in the duties of his professorship, he engaged in all the exciting discussions of the day, and was ever found on the side of human freedom. During all the exciting scenes of the early days of the revolution, around Boston, he was a firm patriot, a wise counsellor, and efficient promoter of the good cause. He held his professorship until his death, which occurred on the 3d of May, 1779, in the sixty-fifth year of his age.

JOHN BARTRAM.

THE men of science in Europe, a hundred years ago, were occasionally startled, as with a meteor flash, by scintillations of great minds in America; and it was a hard question for them to solve how genius could be fostered into vigorous life amid the cool shades of that wilderness. Yet here and there the evidences of such genius intruded upon their stately opinions, and they were compelled to offer the hand of fellowship to American brethren, equal in profundity of knowledge with themselves. Of this class was John Bartram, an eminent botanist, who was born near Darby, in Chester county, Pennsylvania, in the year 1701. He found few helps to education in early life, but study and perseverance overcame a host of difficulties. He seldom sat down to a meal without a book, and he learned the classic languages with great facility. In the study of medicine and surgery he greatly delighted; and drawing his medicines chiefly from the vegetable kingdom, he practiced successfully among the poor of his neighborhood. His avocation was that of a farmer, and his favorite study was botany.

Mr. Bartram was the first American who conceived the plan of establishing a botanic garden for American plants and vegetables. He carried his plan into execution, by devoting about six acres, near Philadelphia, to the purpose. He traversed the country in every direction, from Canada on the north to Florida on the south, in search of new productions, and his garden was enriched and beautified by the results of his explorations. His philosophical knowledge attracted the attention of learned and scientific men, at home and abroad, and with these his intercourse became extensive. He sent many botanical collections to Europe, and their beauty, novelty, and admirable classification, won universal applause. Literary and scientific societies of London, Edinburgh, Stockholm, and other cities, placed his name among those of their honorary members; and finally, George the Third of England appointed him "American Botanist to his Majesty." He held that honorable position until his death, which occurred in September, 1777, when he was in the seventy-sixth year of his age. His zeal in scientific pursuits was unabated till the last. At the age of seventy years, he made a journey in East Florida, to examine and collect the natural productions of that region. His son, William, who accompanied his father in many of these excursions, published, in 1792, an interesting account of their travels through East Florida, the Cherokee country, &c. John Bartram lived and died an exemplary member of the Society of Friends.

CHARLES THOMSON.

OF all the patriots of the Revolution, no man was better acquainted with the men and events of that struggle, than Charles Thomson, who was the permanent Secretary of the Continental Congress for more than fifteen years. He was born in Ireland in 1730, and at the age of eleven years was brought to America in company with three older brothers. Their father died from the effects of sea-sickness, when within sight of the capes of the Delaware. They landed at New Castle, in Delaware, and had no other capital with which to commence life in the New World, than strong and willing hands, and honest hearts. Charles was educated at New London, in Pennsylvania, by Dr. Allison, and became a teacher in the Friend's Academy, at New Castle. He went to Philadelphia, where he enjoyed the friendship of Dr. Franklin and other eminent men. In 1756, he was the secretary for the Delaware Indians, at a great council held with the white people, at Easton; and that tribe adopted him as a son, according to an ancient custom. With all the zeal of an ardent nature, Thomson espoused the republican cause; and when the first Continental Congress met, in Philadelphia, in September, 1774, he was called to the responsible duty of secretary to that body.[1] At about that time, he married Hannah Harrison (the aunt of

---

1. Watson relates that Thomson had just come into Philadelphia, with his bride, and was alighting

President Harrison), whose brother, Benjamin, was one of the signers of the Declaration of Independence. Year after year, Mr. Thomson kept the records of the proceedings of Congress, until the new organization of the government under the Federal Constitution, in 1789. But the demands of public business did not wean him from books, of which he was a great lover. He had a passion for the study of Greek authors, and actually translated the Septuagint from the original into English. He made copious notes of the progress of the Revolution, and after retiring from public life, in 1789, he prepared a History of his own times. But his sense of justice and goodness of heart, would not permit him to publish it; and a short time before he died, he destroyed the manuscript. He gave as a reason, that he was unwilling to blast the reputation of families rising into repute, whose progenitors were proved to be unworthy of the friendship of good men, because of their bad conduct during the war. So the world has lost the most authentic civil history of the struggle for independence, ever produced. Mr. Thomson died on the 16th of August, 1824, when in the ninety-fifth year of his age. He then resided at Lower Merion, Montgomery county, Pennsylvania, where he was buried. In 1838, his nephew removed his remains to Laurel Hill Cemetery, over which is a handsome monument, bearing an appropriate inscription, composed by John F. Watson, Esq., the Annalist.

FRANCIS ALLISON.

THE early instructors of great men ought to have a share in the honors of their pupils, if, as faithful teachers, their instructions have led to such greatness. In that relation to several of the men distinguished in the councils of the nation during our War for Independence, stands Francis Allison. He was born in Ireland in 1705, and completed his education at the University of Glasgow, in Scotland. At the age of thirty years he emigrated to America, and having been ordained a minister in the Presbyterian Church, he was chosen pastor of a flock at New London, in Chester county, Pennsylvania. His Christian zeal made him yearn for more workers in his Master's vineyard, and he opened a free school in which he taught many who expressed themselves desirous of becoming gospel bearers. About the year 1747, he was invited to take charge of an academy in Philadelphia, where he became instructor of many youths, who afterward occupied conspicuous public stations. He had educated Charles Thomson, the secretary of the Continental Congress during the whole of the revolution and several years afterward. In 1755, Dr. Allison was chosen vice-provost of the College in Philadelphia, then just established; and among his earliest pupils, was Francis Hopkinson, one of the signers of the Declaration of Independence. He was professor of moral philosophy; and during these employments he continued his ministerial labors as pastor of the first Presbyterian Church in Philadelphia. Dr. Allison died at Philadelphia, on the 28th of November, 1777, at the age of seventy-two years.

---

from his chaise, when a messenger from the delegates in Carpenter's Hall came to him, and said they wanted him to come and take minutes of their proceedings, as he was an expert at such business. For his first year's service, he received no pay. So Congress informed his wife, that they wished to compensate *her* for the absence of her husband during that time, and wished her to name what kind of a piece of plate she would like to receive. She chose an urn, and that silver vessel is yet in the family.

INCREASE MATHER.

AMONG the most eminent divines and boldest asserters of freedom in New England during the angry discussions between those settlements and the imperial governments in the reign of Charles the Second, was Increase Mather, a native of Dorchester, Massachusetts, where he was born on the 21st of January, 1639. He was an exceedingly precocious child; and at the age of twelve years, entered Harvard College as a student. He graduated with honor in 1656, and the following year entered as a student at Trinity College, Dublin. After an absence of four years, he returned to Boston; and in 1664, was ordained minister of the North Church in that city, which connection he held sixty-two years, a part of the time assisted by his son, Cotton Mather.

Mr. Mather was chosen to fill the presidential chair of Harvard College, after the death of President Oakes, but finally resigned when the faculty required him to live in Cambridge, and thus he separated from his beloved flock in Boston. After the English revolution in 1688,[1] and the expulsion of governor Andros from New England,[2] Mr. Mather went to the court of William and Mary, and by the use of great diplomatic skill, in connection with Sir William Phipps, procured the celebrated charter of 1691, for his native colony. On the assembling of the first legislature, under the new charter, a vote of thanks was adopted by that body, expressive of their appreciation of his faithful public services.

That frightful delusion known as "Salem Witchcraft"[3] prevailed about the time of Mather's return to America, and while his son, Cotton, was fanning the flame, he wrote and spoke against it. Like most people in his day, he believed in the existence of witches,[4] yet his gentle heart and strong common sense utterly condemned the wicked and cruel accusations and prosecutions witnessed almost daily. His pen and tongue were among the most efficient instruments in the final suppression of legal proceedings.

During his presidency of Harvard College, Mr. Mather received the title of Doctor in Divinity from the faculty of that institution. His diploma was the first of the kind issued in America, and he was a worthy recipient of that honor, for his long life was spent in the service of his divine Master, and of his native country. His piety was unaffected, and his benevolence was manifested by his giving one-tenth of all his income to charitable purposes. At the time of his death, which occurred on the 23d of August, 1723, at the age of eighty-four years, he was properly called the Patriarch of New England.

---

1. James, Duke of York, and brother of Charles the Second, succeeded that monarch as King of Great Britain. He was a Roman Catholic, and like all the other Stuart kings, was a bad man. The people rebelled in 1688, and called James' son-in-law, William, Prince of Orange and Nassau, to the throne. He and his wife, Mary, James' daughter, ruled jointly. Their profiles appeared together on the coins, and that fact was the origin of the expression of endearment—

"Cooing and billing,
Like William and Mary on a shilling."

2. Andros has been termed "The Tyrant of New England." When the revolution became known, Andros was seized, at Boston, put on board a vessel, and, with fifty of his political associates, was sent to England, under a charge of mal-administration of public affairs.

3. See sketch of Cotton Mather.

4. We have noticed the effects of this delusion, in a note on page 27. We may add here, that punishments for witchcraft were first sanctioned by the Romish Church a little more than three hundred years ago. Henry the Eighth made the practice of witchcraft a capital offence; and professional "witch hunters" were common in Great Britain. Even the learned Sir Matthew Hale, one of the brightest ornaments of the English judiciary, repeatedly tried and condemned persons accused of witchcraft.

EZRA STILES.

A FEW weeks before the British under Governor Tryon, entered New Haven, in Connecticut, with incendiary intent, a diminutive man of fifty years, with a face beaming with benevolent emotions, and a heart burning with love for his country and his race, was elected President of Yale College. It was Ezra Stiles, a most excellent Christian scholar, who was born at North Haven, on the 15th of December, 1727. He was educated at Yale, where he was graduated in 1742. He possessed a clear intellect, brilliant genius, and remarkable grace in deportment. He became a tutor in the College, and prepared himself for the Christian ministry. Ill health afflicted him, and with it came a state of mental suffering which almost made shipwreck of his character. He doubted the divinity of Christianity, and turned to the law as his chosen profession for life. Thorough investigations of the subject of revealed religion resulted, as usual, in convincing him that the teachings of Jesus proceeded from the great Father of us all. Under this conviction, Mr. Stiles resumed his clerical studies, and became a shining apostle of truth, as pastor of a Congregational society in Newport, Rhode Island, in 1755.

When the storm of the Revolution burst over Narraganset Bay and vicinity, and Rhode Island became a prey to the British invaders, Mr. Stiles' congregation was dispersed, and he preached in various places, until the year 1777, when, on the resignation of Dr. Daggett, he was elected President of Yale College. It was a wise choice, for his fame as a classical and Oriental scholar, and a thorough disciplinarian, had reached to Europe. He already corresponded extensively with leading men of science and learning in the old world, and he has ever been regarded as the most accomplished scholar who has yet filled the presidential chair of "Old Yale." He occupied that important seat until his death, which occurred on the 12th of May, 1795, when he was in the sixty-eighth year of his age. Dr. Stiles left a very interesting manuscript journal, which has never been published. It is in the library of Yale College.

JOHN CARROLL.

IT is a fact worthy of notice, that the Maryland charter, granted by King Charles the First, in 1632, to Lord Baltimore, a Roman Catholic gentleman of fortune and influence, was the first of all the royal patents granted for settlements in America, which guaranteed freedom of thought and worship to *all* who professed a belief in Christ. Then came Baltimore's descendant (Leonard Calvert), with a Roman Catholic colony, and first settled that beautiful country "between North and South Virginia;" (named Maryland, after Henrietta Maria, the Queen of Charles the First,) and to this day, men of that faith have held a controlling influence in the affairs of the colony and state, in civil, military, political, and religious life. One of the most eminent lights of the Roman Catholic Church in Maryland, was John Carroll, a relative of one of the signers of the Declaration of Independence, and for many years a faithful and highly esteemed archbishop, of the archiepiscopal see of Baltimore. He was born on the 8th of January, 1735, at Upper Marlborough, in Maryland, and was remarkable for his docility in childhood, and activity of mind during his earlier years. At the age of thirteen he was sent to the college of St. Omer, in French Flanders, where he remained until he was transferred to the Jesuits' college, at Liege,

six years afterward. He was ordained a Jesuit priest in 1769, renounced all claims to the estate left him by his father, and then became a teacher at St. Omer, and afterward at Liege. In 1773, the Jesuits were expelled from France, and he was obliged to abandon his professorship in the college at Bruges, to which he had been lately appointed, and retire to England. He wrote an able vindication of the Jesuits, but it availed nothing, for he dared not print it, and the manuscript is lost. In England, the accomplished young ecclesiastic became secretary to the Jesuit Fathers there. He also accompanied the son of Lord Stourton (an English nobleman) on a continental tour, as governor, during which time he kept an interesting journal.[1] On his return to England he became a resident in Lord Arundel's family. The quarrel between England and her colonies was now waxing warm, and Mr. Carroll returned to his native country, in 1775. He immediately commenced the duties of his office of priest in his native county.

Mr. Carroll was now called to other duties. Congress was very desirous of winning Canada to the confederation of the American colonies against the

---

[1]. This journal is published in the Biography of Archbishop Carroll, written by his nephew, John Carroll Brent, and published, in Baltimore, in 1843.

mother government, or at least to obtain its neutrality; and for that purpose, appointed Dr. Franklin, Samuel Chase, and Charles Carroll, commissioners to proceed thither, to confer with the leading men there. Father Carroll was invited to accompany them, because his sacred office, his thorough acquaintance with the French language, and his conceded talent, would be of great service. The mission proved unsuccessful, however, and the devoted priest returned to his ministerial labors. Throughout the war, he was attached to the patriot cause, yet he did not neglect his religious duties. His talent and devotion were widely known; and in 1786, he was appointed vicar-general, and took up his residence at Baltimore. At that time his church was in a languishing state in America; but, like Dr. White, of the Protestant Episcopal Church, Mr. Carroll labored assiduously for the growth of his Zion, and may be justly called the Father of the Roman Catholic Church in the United States. He was consecrated a Bishop (the first for the United States) in 1790; and the following year he founded the college at Georgetown. The whole Republic was then but one diocese, under the title of the see of Baltimore. Under his fostering care, and the tolerant principles of our government, the church thrived, and men of every creed regarded Bishop Carroll as one of the best men of the day. Congress, by unanimous vote, invited him to deliver an eulogy on the death of Washington, and that service was admirably performed in St. Peter's church, in Baltimore, on the 22d of February, 1800. In 1808, Baltimore was erected into a metropolitan see. Four suffragan bishops were created, and Dr. Carroll became Archbishop. With every additional duty laid upon him, the venerable prelate's zeal seemed to increase, and he labored faithfully until his death, which occurred on the 3d of December, 1815, at the age of eighty years.

JAMES EDWARD OGLETHORPE.

THE name of Oglethorpe ought to be held in grateful remembrance as one of the noblest of the colonizers of our beautiful land, for he came not hither for personal gain, but for the purpose of perfecting a benevolent scheme which his tender heart and sound judgment had conceived. He was born in Surrey, England, on the 21st of December, 1698. He was educated for the military profession, and became an aide-de-camp to the great Prince Eugene. While a representative in Parliament, in 1728, he was placed upon a committee to inquire into the condition of imprisoned debtors in Great Britain. His benevolent heart was pained at the recitals of woe that fell upon his ears. The virtuous and the good were alike cast into loathsome prisons. A glorious idea was awakened in his mind; and in 1729, he submitted to Parliament a plan for establishing a military colony south of the Savannah river, as a barrier between the Carolinians and the Spaniards in Florida, to be composed of the virtuous debtors then in prison throughout the kingdom. The plan was heartily approved. A royal charter for twenty-one years was granted to a corporation "in trust for the poor," to establish a colony to be called Georgia, in honor of King George the Second, then on the English throne. Oglethorpe was a practical philanthropist; and when sufficient money had been subscribed, and the emigrants were almost ready for departure, he offered to accompany them as governor. He went up the Savannah river early in 1733, and upon Yamacraw Bluff he held a "talk" with some of the Creek chiefs; and there he founded the city of Savannah. In the prosecution of his benevolent enterprise he crossed the ocean several times. His colony rapidly increased, and within eight years twenty-five hundred settlers were sent over by the trustees, at an expense of four hundred thousand dollars. The jealousy of the Spaniards at St. Augustine was aroused, and they menaced the Georgia colony with war. Oglethorpe promptly built forts in the direction of Florida, and by skillful military movements, including some fighting, he kept back the enemy, and secured permanency to his colony.

Oglethorpe took final leave of Georgia in 1743, and in 1745 was promoted to the rank of Brigadier-general in the British army. He was employed, under the Duke of Cumberland, in quelling the Scotch rebellion of 1745; and in 1747, he was promoted to Major-general. When General Gage, who was governor of Massachusetts, and commander-in-chief of the British forces in America, went to England in 1775, the supreme command in this country was offered to Oglethorpe. The merciful conditions upon which, alone, he would accept the appointment did not please the ministry, and general Howe was sent. Oglethorpe died at his seat at Grantham Hall, on the 30th of June, 1785, at the age of eighty-seven years.

JOHN SINGLETON COPLEY.

THE fine arts were but little appreciated and less practiced in America, previous to the revolution; and those artists of American birth who became famous, obtained their laurel-crowns in England. There West and Copley both gained fortune and great fame. The latter was born in Boston in 1738. He possessed a genius for art, and became a pupil of Smibert, a celebrated English portrait painter, who accompanied Dean Berkeley to Rhode Island. Smibert settled in Boston when Berkeley returned to England, where he married and died. Copley was his only student who became proficient; and after his master's death, in 1751, he stood alone in his profession. He painted many full-length portraits, and a lucrative and honorable career was opening before him, when the early storm-clouds of the revolution began to appear. His business waned, and, in 1769, he went to England. This circumstance, and the fact that his father-in-law was one of the consignees of the East India Company's tea, which was destroyed in Boston Harbor in 1773, caused him to be classed among refugee loyalists. He was patronized by Benjamin West, then in the meridian glory of his renown; and in 1770, he was admitted a member of the Royal Academy, then lately established under the auspices of the young king. He visited Boston in 1771, where he remained several months, and then returned to England. In 1774, he went to Italy; and on his return to England in 1776, he there met his wife and children, whom he had left in Boston. They had come with his father-in-law, who was one of the many loyalists who fled to Halifax when Washington drove the British from Boston in the Spring of that year. Copley devoted himself assiduously to portrait painting, for a livelihood, and occasionally produced an historical picture, which attested his fine talent for such composition. On the recommendation of West, he was employed to paint two pictures: one for the House of Lords, the other for the House of Commons. He chose for his subjects, *The Death of Chatham*, and *Charles the First in Parliament*. These established his fame, and he secured a fortune by his profession. His name-sake son, who was born in Boston, in 1772, he educated for the bar. It was a wise choice, for he became as eminent in the profession of the law, as his father had in painting. He was rapidly rising in honor when his father died, suddenly, on the 25th of September, 1815, at the age of seventy-seven years. Twelve years later, the Boston-born son of Copley became Lord Chancellor of England, and was elevated to the peerage, with the title of Lord Lyndhurst.

WILLIAM WHITE.

BECAUSE the Established Church of England was always inseparable from the throne, episcopacy was regarded with jealous fear by the great body of American colonists, and every attempt to establish it in the New World failed, until after the revolution. Episcopal ministers in America could obtain ordination in England and Scotland, only, until 1785, when Dr. Seabury was consecrated a bishop. William White, the son of a sound Philadelphia lawyer, was the second who received that exalted honor in the church, in America. He was born in Philadelphia, on the 4th of April, 1748, and entered the college in that city, at the age of fourteen years. He had serious religious impressions at the age of sixteen years, and these were greatly deepened by the persuasive eloquence of Whitefield, in 1763. Young White was graduated at the age of eighteen, and soon afterward commenced the study of theology. In October, 1770, he embarked for Europe, and with letters to the Bishop of London, he made application to that prelate for deacon's orders. He was successful; and after remaining eighteen months in England, and becoming acquainted with Dr. Johnson, Goldsmith, and other men of letters, he received priest's orders. He was ordained in April, 1772, and in June embarked for America. In the Autumn of that year, he was settled as assistant minister in the parish of Christ Church and St. Peter's, in Philadelphia; and for sixty-four years he was a faithful pastor in the church of his choice. Nor were his pious labors confined to the services of religion alone: he was always foremost in every benevolent work that commended itself to his judgment.

Surveying the disputes between the colonies and Great Britain, with intelligent vision, he early perceived the right; and unlike too many of the episcopal clergymen at that time, he warmly espoused the republican cause. His only sister was the wife of Robert Morris (the patriot and financier), and the outward pressure of circumstances, as well as internal convictions, guided his actions. He did not "beat the ecclesiastical drum" before the Declaration of Independence was promulgated, but on the Sunday following, he ceased officially praying for the king, and soon took the oath of allegiance to the United States. Already he had offered up prayers in the hall of Congress;[1] and when that body, at the close of 1776, convened at Baltimore, he was chosen one of its chaplains.[2] In that capacity he continued to serve until the seat of government was removed to New York. When, again, under the Federal Constitution, the sessions of congress were held in Philadelphia, he acted as chaplain, and his labors in that field of duty ceased only when the seat of government was removed to Washington city, in 1801.

Mr. White was the only episcopal clergyman in Pennsylvania at the close of the revolution, and the church seemed on the verge of dissolution. Yet he labored with increasing zeal. He was called to the rectory of Christ Church and St. Peter's; and in 1783, the University of Pennsylvania gave him its first issued degree of Doctor of Divinity. At about that time he proposed the establishment of an American Episcopal Church, on such a basis, that ministers might be appointed by a convention of clergymen and laymen, without the aid of bishops. The proposition startled many who could not conceive of the existence of "a church without a bishop," but was warmly seconded by those who loved religion for its own sake. The acknowledgment of the independence of the United States, soon afterward, changed the aspect of affairs. Through the exertions of Dr. White, a general convention of delegates from the churches, met in Philadelphia, in October, 1784. He presided; and then and there the broad foundations of the Episcopal Church, in America, were laid. At the request of the American churches, Drs. White and Provost proceeded to England in the Spring of 1786; and on the 4th of February, 1787, they were consecrated bishops, the former for the diocese of Pennsylvania, and the latter for that of New York. From that time, episcopal consecration in the United States was performed at home; and from Bishop White, nearly all of the American prelates, consecrated during his life, received the sacred office. For about thirty years he performed the duties of his episcopate without assistance; but in 1827, the diocese of Pennsylvania becoming very extensive, and as the infirmities of age were pressing hard upon the venerable prelate, an assistant bishop was elected. Yet he continued his labors until the last, as presiding bishop of the church in the United States. In 1835, when the church sent missionaries to China, he prepared instructions for them; and that paper shows that his mental vigor was unimpaired, although the hand that wrote it was eighty-eight years old. It was among the last official labors of his long and useful life. In June, the following year, that devoted patriarch preached his last sermon; and on the 17th of the next month, his spirit ascended to the New Jerusalem. In his writings, and in his example, Bishop White still lives, and the church yet feels his conservative influence.

---

1. It has been erroneously stated that he was the first chaplain of the Continental Congress. That honor belongs to Rev. Jacob Duche.
2. The other was Rev. Patrick Allison, minister of the Presbyterian Church in Baltimore. They were chosen on the 23d of December, 1776.

GEORGE WASHINGTON.

"FIRST IN WAR—FIRST IN PEACE—FIRST IN THE HEARTS OF HIS COUNTRYMEN —was a just sentiment uttered half a century ago by the foster-son[1] of the Great Patriot, when speaking of the character of his noble guardian. And the hand of that son was the first to erect a monumental stone in memory of The Father of his Country, upon which was inscribed: HERE, THE 11TH OF FEBRUARY [O. S.], 1732, GEORGE WASHINGTON WAS BORN. That stone yet lies on the site of his birth-place, in Westmoreland county, Virginia, near the banks of the Potomac. The calendar having been changed,[2] we celebrate his birth-day on the 22d of February.

George Washington was descended from an old and titled family in Lancashire, England, and was the eldest child of his father, by Mary Ball, his second wife. He died when George was little more than ten years of age, and the guidance of the future Leader, through the dangers of youthhood, devolved upon his mother. She was fitted for the service; and during his eventful life, Washington regarded the early training of his mother with the deepest gratitude. He received a common English education, and upon that, a naturally thoughtful and right-conditioned mind, laid the foundation of future greatness. Truth and justice were the cardinal virtues of his character.[3] He was always beloved by his young companions, and was always chosen their leader in military plays. At the age of fourteen years, he wished to enter the navy, but yielded to the discouraging persuasions of his mother; and when he was seventeen years old, he was one of the most accomplished land surveyors in Virginia. In the forest rambles incident to his profession, he learned much of the topography of the country, habits of the Indians, and life in the camp. These were stern but useful lessons of great value in his future life.

Young Washington was appointed one of the adjutants-general of his state at the age of nineteen, but soon resigned his commission to accompany an invalid half-brother to the West Indies. Two years later, when the French began to build forts southward of Lake Erie, he was sent by the royal governor of Virginia, to demand a cessation of such hostile movements. He performed the delicate mission with great credit; and so highly were his services esteemed, that when, in 1755, Braddock came to drive the French from the vicinity of the Ohio, Washington was chosen his principal aid. The young Leader had already

---

1. George Washington Parke Custis, grandson of Mrs. Washington, and adopted son of the distinguished patriot.
2. In consequence of the difference between the old Roman year and the true solar year, of a little more than eleven minutes, the astronomical equinox fell back that amount of time, each annual cycle, toward the beginning of the year. It fell on the 21st of March, at the time of the council of Nice, in 325. Pope Gregory the Thirteenth reformed the calendar in 1582 (when the equinox fell on the 11th of March,) by suppressing ten days in the calendar, and thus restoring the equinox to the 21st of March. The Protestant states of Europe adhered to the old calendar, until 1700; and popular prejudice in England opposed the alterations, until 1752, when the Julian calendar, called *Old Style*, was abolished by Parliament. The retrogression since Gregory's time made it necessary to drop 11 days, instead of ten. Now the difference is about twelve days, so that Washington's birth-day, according to the *New Style*, is on the 23d of February.
3. Young Washington was playing in a field one day with another boy, when he leaped upon an untamed colt belonging to his mother. The frightened animal used such great exertions to get rid of his rider, that he burst a blood vessel and died. George went immediately to his mother, and gave her a truthful relation of all that had happened. This is a noble example for all boys.

been in that wilderness at the head of a military expedition, and performed his duty so well, that he was publicly thanked by the Virginia legislature. Braddock was defeated and killed, and his whole army escaped utter destruction only through the skill and valor of Colonel Washington, in directing their retreat.[1] He continued in active military service most of the time, until the close of 1758, when he resigned his commission, and retired to private life.

At the age of twenty-seven years, Washington married the beautiful Martha Custis, the young widow of a wealthy Virginia planter, and they took up their abode at Mount Vernon, on the banks of the Potomac, an estate left him by his half-brother. There he quietly pursued the business of a farmer until the Spring of 1774, when he was chosen to fill a seat in the Virginia legislature. The storm of the great revolution was then gathering; and toward the close of Summer he was elected a delegate to the first CONTINENTAL CONGRESS, which assembled at Philadelphia, in September. He was a delegate the following year, when the storm burst on Bunker Hill, after the first lightning flash at Lexington; and by the unanimous voice of his compatriots he was chosen commander-in-chief of the army of freemen which had gathered spontaneously around Boston.

For eight long years Washington directed the feeble armies of the revolted colonies, in their struggle for independence.. That was a terrible ordeal through which the people of America passed! During the night of gloom which brooded over the hopes of the patriots from the British invasion of New York, until the capture of Cornwallis, he was the lode-star of their hopes. And when the blessed morning of Peace dawned at Yorktown, and the last hoof of the oppressor had left our shores, Washington was hailed as the Deliverer of his people; and he was regarded by the aspirants for freedom in the eastern hemisphere as the brilliant day-star of promise to future generations.

During all the national perplexities after the return of peace, incident to financial embarrassments and an imperfect system of government, Washington was regarded, still, as the public leader; and when a convention assembled to modify the existing government, he was chosen to preside over their deliberations. And again, when the labors of that convention resulted in the formation of our Federal Constitution, and a president of the United States was to be chosen, according to its provisions, his countrymen, with unanimous voice, called him to the highest place of honor in the gift of a free people.

Washington presided over the affairs of the new Republic for eight years, and those the most eventful in its history. A new government had to be organized without any existing model, and new theories of government were to be put in practice for the first time. The domestic and foreign policy of the country had to be settled by legislation and diplomacy, and many exciting questions had to be met and answered. To guide the ship of state through the rocks and quicksands of all these difficulties required great executive skill and wisdom. Washington possessed both; and he retired from the theatre of public life without the least stain of reproach upon his judgment or his intentions.

The great Patriot and Sage enjoyed the repose of domestic life, at Mount Vernon, in the midst of an affectionate family and the almost daily congratulations of visitors, for almost three years, when the effects of a heavy cold closed his brilliant career, in death. He ascended to the bosom of his God on the 14th of December, 1799, when almost sixty-eight years of age.[2]

---

[1]. Braddock persisted in fighting the Indians according to the military tactics of Europe; and when Washington modestly suggested the policy of adopting the Indian method of warfare, it is said that Braddock haughtily answered, "What! a provincial buskin teach a British general how to fight!"

[2]. See the Frontispiece. On the left, below the portrait, is his birth-place; on the right, his tomb. Liberty and Justice are supporters, in the midst of Plenty, and surmounting Fame is proclaiming his deeds.

FRANCIS HOPKINSON.

THE bud of a keen wit and zealous patriot appeared when, at almost midnight on the 3d of September, 1738, Francis Hopkinson was born in the city of Philadelphia. His father was a fine scholar, and an intimate friend of Dr. Franklin; his mother was a woman of great refinement, and niece of the Bishop of Worcester. They came from England immediately after their marriage, settled in Philadelphia, and died there. When Francis was fourteen years old, his mother was left a widow with a large family of children. She discharged the holy duties of her station with fidelity and success.

Francis Hopkinson was the first scholar and first graduate of the *College of Philadelphia*, of which his father was one of the founders. He was an honor to the institution. The profession of the law was his choice, and he studied in the office of Benjamin Chew, afterward the eminent chief justice of Pennsylvania. He was fond of literary and scientific pursuits, and for the purpose of expanding and strengthening his faculties by contact with eminent men, he went to England, and resided with the Bishop of Worcester, about two years. Soon after his return, in 1768, he married Ann Borden, the accomplished daughter of a wealthy gentleman, the founder of Bordentown, New Jersey; and that became his place of residence. His country was then agitated by the premonitions of the approaching Revolution, and his active mind often found powerful expression through his pen. His first publication, of moment, was a small pamphlet entitled, *A Pretty Story*, which is said to have had great influence on the public mind, in quickening its perceptions of the true relations existing between Great Britain and her colonies. It abounds with fine specimens of imagination, composition, and elegant wit. So in his conversation; it was ever marked by great refinement. He was never known to use a profane word, or utter an expression that would make a lady blush.

When the colonies had drawn the sword and cast away the scabbard, Mr. Hopkinson, who had been an unflinching patriot from the beginning, was chosen a delegate to represent New Jersey in the Continental Congress. In that capacity he signed the *Declaration of Independence*, and soon afterward received the commission of Judge of Admiralty, for Pennsylvania. While in that station he wrote that exceedingly witty poem, entitled *The Battle of the Kegs*.[1]

When the Federal Constitution was before the people, Judge Hopkinson became one of its most zealous and eloquent supporters, with tongue and pen; and in 1790, President Washington appointed him a judge of the United States court, for the district of Pennsylvania, under the new organization of the judiciary. He did not bear the ermine and its honors long, for on the 9th of May, 1791, he was suddenly smitten with epilepsy, which terminated his life in the course of a few hours.

Mr. Hopkinson's genius was versatile. He was proficient in the knowledge of music, mathematics, mechanics, and chemistry. As a satirical writer he has few peers; and he held a front rank as a statesman and jurist. His works, arranged by himself, were published in three volumes, after his death, and are now exceedingly rare.

THOMAS HUTCHINSON.

MANY good men, whose actions have been governed by the purest and loftiest motives, have been made the targets of scorn by partisan writers; and it is difficult, when perusing the pages of history, to judge correctly of the real characters of the prominent men whose actions make up the sum of the record. Thomas Hutchinson, Governor of Massachusetts during some of the most exciting scenes of the early years of the revolutionary struggle, is generally regarded with contempt and indignation by readers of American history, because, like thousands of conscientious men, he chose the royal side in the controversy. He was born in Massachusetts, in 1711, and was graduated at Harvard College in 1727. His father had been a public man, and Thomas studied English constitutional law, with the intention of becoming a statesman. He first embarked in commercial pursuits, however, but did not succeed. For ten consecutive years he was elected a member of the Massachusetts Assembly, and he was Speaker of that body for three years. In 1752, he succeeded his uncle as judge of probate; and from 1749 until 1756, he was a member of the governor's council. In 1758, he was elected lieutenant-governor of the province, and held that office until 1771, when he was appointed governor. In the meanwhile he had held the office of chief justice, after the death of Judge Sewall, in 1760. That office

---

1. A man, named Bushnell, of Connecticut, invented a submarine explosive apparatus, by which ships might be blown up. An ineffectual attempt was made to blow up the *Eagle*, General Howe's flagship, in the harbor of New York, in 1776. In 1778, while the British had possession of Philadelphia, and several of their ships were lying in the Delaware, some Whigs at Bordentown prepared several kegs of powder with a similar machine, and sent them floating down the current of the river, toward the British shipping. They caused great alarm, and in commemoration of that event the *Battle of the Kegs* was written. The author's son, Joseph, wrote the popular national song, *Hail Columbia*.

had been promised to the elder Otis, and the disappointment gave a keener point to the opposition of the younger Otis to the person and administration of Hutchinson, when the dispute between Great Britain and her colonies was progressing. Other things had made Hutchinson unpopular with many of the people. In 1748, he was chiefly instrumental in abolishing the paper currency of the colony, and substituting gold and silver therefor; and he favored the law granting writs of assistance, or general search-warrants for contraband goods, by which no man's house was safe from prying officials. He was also active, with Governor Bernard, in bringing troops to Boston, in 1768, to awe the people; and much of the odium of the massacre in Boston, in March, 1770, was cast upon him.[1] These things created a strong popular feeling against him; and when, in 1772, certain letters which he had written to a former member of Parliament, were sent back from England to Boston by Dr. Franklin, and published, in which he gave advice, in disparagement of popular liberty in America, the people could scarcely be restrained from manifesting their indignation by inflicting personal violence upon him. He was compelled to leave the country in 1774, when he went to England. He died at Brompton, in that realm, on the 3d of June, 1780, at the age of sixty-nine years. However much Governor Hutchinson sinned against our republican faith, his memory deserves to be revered for his faithful labors in the field of historical research. He prepared, with great care, a History of Massachusetts, from the earliest settlements in 1628, until 1760. The first volume was published in 1760, and the second in 1767. He had also prepared much more historical matter concerning the colony; and his unpublished manuscripts were procured for publication in this country, thirty years after his death. His History of Massachusetts is standard authority.

NATHANIEL GREENE.

THIS ablest of Washington's generals was the son of an anchor-smith at Warwick, Rhode Island, where the future hero was born, in 1740. Nathaniel was trained to his father's business, and was taught to love God and his neighbor by his pious Quaker mother. While yet a boy, he acquired some knowledge of Latin; and before his apprenticeship expired, his little earnings, judiciously used, had furnished him with a small library. Contrary to Quaker teachings, he loved the military art, read much of military history with delight, and when the clang of arms came from Lexington and Concord, he went forth to *act* military history, in a nobler cause than warriors usually engage in. At the age of twenty-one years, he had been called to a seat in the Rhode Island legislature; at the age of thirty-five years, he led to Roxbury, after the affair at Lexington, the three regiments which formed the *army of observation*, raised by his State for the defence of the country. The Quakers disowned him, and Washington and his country adopted him. His State had made him a Brigadier; Congress appointed him a Major-general in the Continental army. He was sick during the battle on Long Island, in August, 1776, but was in the engagements at Trenton, Princeton, Brandywine, and Germantown, during the next fifteen months. He was honored with the important office of Quarter-master general in March, 1778, and in June he fought gallantly on the plains of Monmouth. In the Autumn of 1780, he took command of the remnant of the southern army

---

1. A dispute between some of the people and the troops occurred. A large crowd gathered in the streets; the troops were drawn up in line, and after being buffeted with words and missiles, for some time, some of the soldiers fired. Three persons in the crowd were killed. It was made the occasion of great indignation against the troops and government officials.

which had been defeated and dispersed at Camden, under General Gates; and before the close of 1781, he had driven the British from every strong interior position, in the South, and confined them to the cities of Charleston and Savannah. During that year, his famous retreat before Lord Cornwallis, across North Carolina, and the battles at Guilford, Camden, Ninety-Six, and Eutaw Springs, were achieved; and the following year he marched victoriously into Charleston, amid the booming of cannons, the waving of handkerchiefs in fair hands from balconies and windows, and shouts of welcome! from crowds of liberated freemen. At the same hour, the white sails of a British fleet, bearing the last hostile foot from our shores, south of New York, were glistening in the evening sun. And yet the last resting-place, on earth, of this patriot and hero, is unknown to this generation. The grateful Georgians gave him a fine estate in that land of the orange and palm;[1] and while there, in June, 1786, he was overcome by the heat of the sun, fell and expired. His remains were buried in a vault in Savannah, but there is nothing to distinguish them from the common

---

1. In testimony of the grateful appreciation of his services in the South, the Legislature of South Carolina voted him fifty thousand dollars; that of North Carolina, twenty-five thousand dollars; and of Georgia, twenty-four thousand acres of land, in the vicinity of Savannah.

relics of mortality around them. Even the particular vault wherein they were deposited is unknown, and they are lost to humanity forever. His memory, however, shall bloom, ever fresh, in the hearts of his countrymen, and his fame, less perishable than brass or marble, will endure while freedom has a temple or a worshipper. Congress ordered a monument to be erected to his memory at the seat of the Federal Government, but the stone for it is yet in the quarry.[1]

ZABDIEL BOYLSTON.

INOCULATION for the small-pox, so as to ward off the violence of that foul and fatal disease, was first practiced in England, in 1721, by Lady Mary Wortley Montague, whose son had been successfully treated, in that way, at Constantinople. She tried the experiment upon seven capital convicts, and was successful. At about the same time, and while ignorant of the fact of Lady Mary's operations, Doctor Boylston introduced the practice at Boston.[2] He was a man of courage and benevolence; a native of Brookline, Massachusetts, where he was born in 1680. He studied medicine and surgery at Boston, and soon became an eminent practitioner and man of fortune.

Dr. Boylston's attention was first called to the subject of inoculation by Dr. Cotton Mather, who had read an account of its successful practice at Smyrna, in the East. The small-pox was then raging with fearful fatality in Boston; but of all the physicians there, Boylston was the only one who possessed sufficient courage to try the experiment. On the 26th of June, 1721, he inoculated his little son, aged six years, and two servants. He was successful, and began to enlarge the practice. The other physicians opposed him, and in the course of the next month the selectmen of Boston forbade its practice. At that moment six venerable clergymen of the city gave their influence in its favor, and benevolence and good sense triumphed over prejudice and ignorance. In the course of a year he inoculated two hundred and forty-seven persons in Boston; and of two hundred and eighty-six inoculated by himself and physicians in neighboring towns, only *six* died, while of five thousand seven hundred and fifty-nine persons who had the small-pox the natural way, *eight hundred and forty-four* died. Notwithstanding this triumphant vindication of the utility of the practice, Dr. Boylston was mercilessly persecuted by other physicians; and the common people became so exasperated against him, that it was unsafe for him to be seen out after dark. They went so far, at one time, as to parade the streets with halters, declaring their intention to hang him,[3] and those who submitted to his practice were grossly insulted. Dr. Mather and others adhered to him, and he triumphed.

Dr. Boylston went to England in 1725. The fame of his practice preceded him, and he was honored with membership in the Royal Society. When he returned home, prejudice had given way to common sense; and to the end of

---

1. At West Point are two brass cannons, captured from the British, and presented to General Greene. On them is the following inscription: "Taken from the British army, and presented, by order of the United States, in Congress assembled, to Major-general Greene, as a monument of their high sense of the wisdom, fortitude, and military talents which distinguished his command in the Southern Department, and of the eminent services which, amid complicated dangers and difficulties, he performed for his country. October ye 18th, 1783."
2. The safer preventive practice of vaccination, now universally used instead of inoculation, was discovered by Edward Jenner in 1776. Among those who first introduced the new practice into this country, was Doctor Eneas Munson, of Connecticut. He used vaccination in 1782.
3. His alleged offence was the spreading of a loathsome disease throughout the community; and it was also argued that the small-pox being a judgment sent upon the people for their sins, any endeavor to avert the blow would offend God still more!

his days he stood at the head of his profession in America. Bodily infirmity induced him to retire to his patrimonial estate at Brookline, where he engaged in literary and scientific pursuits in connection with agriculture. He had the pleasure of seeing inoculation universally practiced. On the 1st of March, 1766, he said to his friends, "My work in this world is done, and my hopes of futurity are brightening;" and then closed his eyes forever.

WILLIAM BRADFORD.

"THANK God there are no free schools in this province, nor printing press; and I hope we shall not have for these hundred years," said Berkeley, the royal governor of Virginia, in 1671. His hope was almost realized in respect to the press; but in other colonies that mighty worker, then in its childhood, began its labors early. More than thirty years before the utterance of these sentiments, a press had been established at Cambridge, Massachusetts; and sixteen years afterward, William Bradford, who came to America with William Penn, set up a press and printed an Almanac at Philadelphia, or in its immediate vicinity.

Mr. Bradford was a Quaker, and native of Leicestershire, England. He learned the printer's trade in London, and married the daughter of his master, through whom he became acquainted with George Fox, the founder of his sect.[1] The Almanac printed by him was for the year 1687, and was made at Burlington, New Jersey. He printed several controversial pamphlets, and among them was one by George Keith against some of the Quakers of Philadelphia. It was deemed seditious, and Keith and Bradford were arrested and imprisoned, in 1692. They were tried and acquitted; but having incurred the ill-will of the dominant party of Quakers, Bradford took up his residence in New York the following year, where he was appointed government printer, and for a period of about thirty years he was the only practitioner of his art in that province. His first production was a folio volume of laws of the province.

In the Autumn of 1725, Bradford commenced the publication of the first newspaper printed in that colony, which he called *The New York Gazette*. John Peter Zenger, one of his apprentices, became a business competitor in 1726; and in 1733 he, too, published a newspaper, called *The New York Weekly Journal*. Much enmity existed between them, and their respective papers became the organs of the two political parties then existing in New York. Bradford always supported the government party, while Zenger spoke boldly for the people.

Bradford had two sons, Andrew and William, whom he instructed in his art, and made them partners in business. He owned a paper mill at Elizabethtown, New Jersey, in 1728, which is believed to have been the first one established in America. At the age of seventy years, he retired from business, and lived with his son, Andrew, until his death, which occurred on the 23d of May, 1752, when he was ninety-four years of age. He had been printer to the government more than fifty years; and during his long life he had never been seriously sick. At the time of his death, it was announced in his *Gazette*, that "being quite worn out with old age and labor, his lamp of life went out for want of oil."

---

1. Fox promulgated his peculiar tenets about 1650. He boldly condemned sin in high places; and it was while admonishing Justice Bennet, of Derby, that he was first called a *Quaker*, because he told that magistrate to *quake and tremble at the word of the Lord*. Fox came to America in 1670.

LINDLEY MURRAY.

"MURRAY'S GRAMMAR" is as widely known as the English language, and forms a part of the vision of school-days which comes up occasionally before the memory of every educated American. It emanated from an invalid, confined for sixteen years in a sick room. He was the son of an eminent Quaker merchant in the city of New York, but was born at Swetara, near Lancaster, Pennsylvania, in 1745, while his father was engaged in the vocation of a miller, there.

While yet a small boy, Lindley Murray was placed in a school in Philadelphia, where he was thoroughly instructed in the English branches of education, by Ebenezer Kinnersly, a friend and correspondent of Dr. Franklin. He accompanied his father to New York, and was eagerly engaged in the study of the Greek and Latin languages, preparatory to a collegiate course, when failing health compelled him to leave his books. He entered his father's counting-room, but the routine of service there, and the restraints of a stern parent, became exceedingly irksome to him. He thirsted intensely for knowledge to be derived from books; and a punishment which he deemed unmerited, inflicted by his father's hand, was made an excuse for his sudden flight from home. For many weeks he was a close student in a boarding-school at Burlington, New Jersey, before his friends ascertained, by accident, his place of concealment. A reconciliation was effected, and Lindley returned to the drudgery of a merchant's desk.

After much persuasion, young Murray's father permitted him to enter the law office of Benjamin Kissam, as a student, where he enjoyed the fellowship of John Jay, then preparing for that brilliant public career upon which he soon afterward entered. His father gave him a fine law library, and Lindley Murray commenced the practice of his profession, in the city of New York, with promises of great success. He married an amiable woman, and regarded himself as permanently settled for life, when feeble health admonished him to try a change of climate. He went to England, was greatly benefited, and sent for his family; but yearning for his native land, he returned in 1771. When the War for Independence broke out, he acted consistently with the principles and discipline of the Society of Friends, of which he was a valued member, and remained neutral and in retirement, at Islip, Long Island. His father died during the war,[1] and on the return of peace, Lindley went back to the city, resumed the mercantile business, which he abandoned in youth, purchased a beautiful country-seat on the Hudson, and seemed about to take rank with the merchant princes. Again ill-health warned him away from the changeable climate of New York. He went to England, purchased a beautiful estate in Yorkshire, and there gradually sunk into the confirmed invalid's chair. His malady was a disease of the muscles, which finally deprived him of the use of his limbs. For sixteen years he was confined to his room, and it was during that long season of bodily affliction that he produced his popular *English Grammar, English Reader*, and several religious works. At his death, which occurred on the 16th of February, 1826, in the eighty-first year of his age, he left a fund, the interest of which was to be devoted to the diffusion of religious sentiments in America. The Trustees faithfully execute that provision of his will, and have gratuitously distributed many thousands of his "Power of Religion on the Mind." They have just published Dymond's "Inquiry into the Accordance of War with the Principles of Christianity," for the same purpose.

JACOB LEISLER.

THE public life of Jacob Leisler, the first martyr to the democratic faith in America, presents a picture of the active development of republican ideas which had taken root in the New World, and began to germinate, more than half a century before. He was a native of Frankfort, in Germany, and came to America in 1660. He first settled at Fort Orange (Albany), in New Netherland; and about the time when the province passed into the hands of the English, and New Amsterdam became New York, he began commercial life in that city. While on a voyage to Europe, about the year 1675, he was made a prisoner by some Mediterranean pirates, and sold to a Turk, with seven others. He paid a high price for his ransom, and then returned to New York, where he became one of the most successful and influential merchants. In 1683, notwithstanding his well-known Protestant feelings, the Roman Catholic governor Dongan appointed him one of the commissioners of the court of admiralty. He also had command of a militia corps, and was very popular. When, in the Spring of 1689, the dethronement of James the Second was known, and changes took place in the governments of the several colonies, the people of New York immediately appointed a committee of safety, under whose direction Leisler was re-

---

1. Robert Murray, the father of Lindley, owned one of the first three coaches introduced into the city of New York, about ninety years ago. Another, owned by Mr. Beekman, is yet well preserved, and in possession of his descendant, Hon. James W. Beckman. There was much prejudice against coaches, when they were introduced, and Murray called his "a leathern conveniency." His country seat was on land now known as Murray Hill, in the city of New York.

quested to take charge of the fort, in the name of the new sovereigns, William and Mary. Nicholson, the successor of Dongan, fled on board a vessel and departed, and the people consented to Leisler's assuming the powers of governor until a new one should be appointed by the crown. This act offended the magistrates and the aristocracy; and when Governor Sloughter arrived in 1691, Leisler was accused of high treason. His son-in-law, Milborne, who acted as his deputy, was included in the charge. Although Leisler surrendered his authority into the hands of the legally-appointed governor, yet, when he went in person to deliver up the keys of the fort, both he and Milborne were seized and cast into prison by those who had resolved on their destruction. They were tried on a charge of treason, found guilty, and condemned to death. Sloughter felt the injustice of the sentence, and withheld his signature to their death-warrants. He was an inebriate, and at a dinner party, given for the purpose, he became drunk, and while in that state, was induced, unconsciously, to put his name to the fatal instrument. Before he became sober, Leisler and Milborne were suspended upon a gallows on the verge of Beekman's swamp, near the spot where Tammany Hall now [1854] stands. These were the proto-martyrs of liberty in America. Their death lighted an intense flame of party spirit; and the pretence made by their enemies, that Leisler was inimical to the Protestant King and Queen, had not the shadow of a foundation. The fact that in 1689, he purchased a tract on Long Island Sound, in Westchester county, for the persecuted Huguenots (which they named New Rochelle), was a sufficient refutation of the false charge. Leisler's property, which the local government confiscated, was afterward restored to his family.

JAMES BOWDOIN.

FROM the stock of the Huguenots, or French Protestants, who fled from France on the revocation of the edict of Nantes, came many noble men who shine as stars in the firmament of our political and social history. James Bowdoin, the eminent statesman and governor, was of that stock. He was born in Boston on the 18th of August, 1727. His grandfather fled from France in 1685, and came to America by way of Ireland, two years later, and settled at Falmouth (now Portland), in Maine. James was the son of an eminent merchant, and was educated at Harvard College, where he was graduated in 1745. He was remarkable for his application, while a student, and his deportment was always correct. He had just laid the foundation of a good character, when, at the age of twenty-one years, his father died, and left him an ample fortune. Yet that possession did not cause him to fold his hands in idleness. His thirsting mind sought out the pleasant fountains of knowledge; and soon after his marriage, in 1749, he commenced a system of literary and scientific research. He was elected to represent Boston in the General Court, in 1753, where his learning and eloquence soon made him a conspicuous leader. Three years afterward, he was chosen to a seat in the Council, where he was a highly-respected member for many years. When grievances began to be complained of by the colonists, Bowdoin was found upon the side of the people, and for this offence, he was refused a seat in the council, by Governor Bernard, in 1769. Hutchinson, however, allowed him to take a seat at the council board, saying, "His opposition to our measures will be less injurious here than in the house of representatives," to which the people had elected him. He was chosen a delegate to the first Congress in 1774, but the illness of his wife prevented his attendance.

The following year he was chosen president of the council of Massachusetts, and he held that important office most of the time until the adoption of the State Constitution in 1780. He was president of the convention which formed that instrument; and in 1785, when John Hancock resigned the chair of chief magistrate of the State, Bowdoin was chosen to succeed him in office. It was during his administration that the troubles, known as *Shay's Rebellion*, took place in Massachusetts. By his orders, four thousand troops were placed under the command of General Lincoln, to suppress the insurrection; and he was one of the largest contributors to a voluntary subscription of money, which was raised in Boston, within a few hours, to pay the expenses of the troops. He was a member of the Massachusetts convention, called to deliberate on the Federal Constitution, and he gave that instrument his hearty support. Governor Bowdoin was a patron of letters. He subscribed liberally for the restoration of the library of Harvard College, destroyed in 1764; and from 1779 till 1784, he was a fellow of the corporation. In 1780, he was instrumental in founding the American Academy of Arts and Sciences, in Boston; and his fostering care was given to other societies, humane and scientific. The University at Edinburgh conferred upon him the degree of Doctor of Laws, and he was chosen a member of the Royal Societies of London and Dublin. He was a benevolent Christian, in the highest sense of the term; and in all his numerous writings fundamental truths of Christianity were prominently recognized. This eminent man died at Boston, in 1790, at the age of sixty-three years.

SAMUEL KIRKLAND.

"HOW beautiful upon the mountains are the feet of those" who carry the gospel of peace, love, and brotherhood to the dark-minded without the pale of civilization. Peerless among such faithful messengers, was Samuel Kirkland, who, for forty years, labored with untiring zeal among the pagans of central New York. He was born at Norwich, Connecticut, on the 1st of December, 1741, and through life exhibited the indomitable courage, energy, and perseverance of his Scotch lineage. Of his childhood we know very little. In early youth he entered Dr. Wheelock's school at Lebanon, and prepared to be a missionary among the Indians. There he was much beloved—for his gentleness, a quality which endeared him to his fellow-students at Princeton, where he pursued a collegiate course of studies from 1762 until 1764. He left the institution before completing his education, and dwelt with the Seneca Indians from 1764 until 1766. He received his collegiate degree, however, in 1765; and in June, 1766, he was ordained, at Lebanon, as a missionary to the Indians, under the sanction of the Scotch Society for propagating the gospel among the heathen. He entered upon his work in August, and made his residence among the Oneidas at their "council house," a little south-west of Fort Stanwix, now Rome. There he built a house with his own hands, and labored day and night for the good of the poor Indians. Toil and exposure impaired his health, and he sought its restoration by passing the Summer of 1769 with his friends in Connecticut. In the Autumn he married a niece of Dr. Wheelock, and soon afterward he returned to his post of duty in the wilderness, accompanied by his excellent wife, as far as the house of General Herkimer, at the Little Falls of the Mohawk.[1] She remained there a few weeks, until her forest home was made comfortable; and

---

1. Early the following Summer, Mrs. Kirkland started to visit her mother in Connecticut. She proceeded on horseback, but went no further than the house of General Herkimer, where she gave birth to twin sons, in August, 1770. One of these was afterward President Kirkland of Harvard College.

J Kirkland

then they commenced those joint missionary labors, which were exceedingly successful until the preparations of the War for Independence were commenced. Those disturbances deranged their noble plans; and the growing insecurity of forest life caused Mr. Kirkland to fix the residence of his family at Stockbridge, in Western Massachusetts. Yet he did not desert his post, but labored on through all the dark scenes of the seven years' war that ensued, not only for the spiritual benefit of the dusky tribes, but in unceasing endeavors to keep the Six Nations' neutral. He succeeded with the Oneidas, only; the other tribes became active allies of the British, for the influence of Sir William Johnson and his family was greater than that of the missionary.

Mr. Kirkland was chaplain at Fort Schuyler (formerly Fort Stanwix, now Rome, in Oneida county) for some time, and in that capacity he accompanied General Sullivan in his expedition from Wyoming, against the Senecas, in 1778. After that, he was at Fort Schuyler and vicinity, or with his family at Stockbridge, until peace was declared. In subsequent treaties with the Indians, he was very active and useful; and when the field of his labors began again to whiten, under the blessed sun of peace, his family prepared to make their residence in the Indian country. It was never accomplished, for Mrs. Kirkland sickened at the close of 1787, and late in January following, she died. The bereaved missionary left her grave for his harvest field in the wilderness, and toiled

---

1. The Iroquois confederacy in the State of New York. It originally consisted of five tribes, namely, Onondaga, Seneca, Oneida, Mohawk, and Cayuga. These were joined by their kindred in language, the Tuscaroras of North Carolina, in the early part of the last century.

on, year after year, in civil and religious duties. He accompanied a delegation of Senecas to Philadelphia, in 1790, and was rewarded by the conversion to Christianity of the great chief, Cornplanter, with whom he travelled, instructed and convinced. In 1791, he made a census of the Six Nations, and at the same time he succeeded in establishing an institution of learning, which was incorporated in 1793, under the title of *The Hamilton Oneida Academy*. This was the origin of Hamilton College. Mr. Kirkland continued his labors among the Oneidas until his death, which occurred, after a brief illness, at his residence in Paris, Oneida county, on the 28th of February, 1808, in the sixty-seventh year of his age.

ANN LEE.

FOUNDERS of sects become famous by their fruits, whether they be good or evil; and in the consistent, upright character of followers, impostors have obtained canonization as saints. Of such as these was the immortal Ann Lee, the founder, in America, of the sect known as Shaking Quakers. She was born in Manchester, England, about the year 1736. Her father was a blacksmith, and she was taught the trade of cutting fur for hatters. She married young, and had four children, who all died in infancy. At the age of twenty-two years, she became a convert to the doctrines of James Wardley, a Quaker, who preached the holiness of celibacy, and the wickedness of marriage, and whose followers, because of the great agitations of their bodies when religiously exercised, were called Shakers.[1] After nine years of discipline, she opened her mouth as a teacher; and in 1770, while confined in prison as a half-crazed fanatic, she pretended to have had a revelation of great spiritual gifts. She declared that in her dwelt the "Word;" and her followers say, "the man who was called Jesus, and the woman who was called Ann, are verily the two great pillars of the church." She was acknowledged to be a spiritual mother in Israel, and is known by the common appellation of "Mother Ann." She came to New York in 1774, with her brother and a few followers; and in the Spring of 1776, they settled at Niskayuna (now Watervliet, opposite Troy), where the sect still flourishes. Some charged Mother Ann with witchcraft; and vigilant Whigs, knowing that she preached against war in every shape, suspected her of secret correspondence with her countrymen, the British. A charge of high treason was preferred against her, and she was imprisoned in Albany during the Summer of 1776. In the Autumn she was sent as far as Poughkeepsie, with the intention of forwarding her to New York, within the British lines. She remained a prisoner at Poughkeepsie, until some time in 1777, when she was released by Governor Clinton. She then returned to Watervliet. Persecution had awakened sympathy for her, and her followers greatly increased. A wild revival movement in the vicinity, in 1780, poured a flood of converts into her lap, and she deluded the silly creatures with the assertion that she was the "woman clothed with the sun," mentioned in the Apocalypse. She told them that she daily judged the dead of all nations, who came to her, and that no favor could be had, except through a confession of sins to her. She became a *Pontifix Maximus*—a second Pope Joan—and under her directions, the faithful discarded all worldly things, and gave into her hands all their jewels, knee-buckles, money, and other valuables. She excited their fear and admiration by mutterings, groans, and strange

---

1. For a similar reason, George Fox (the founder of the Society of Friends) and his followers were called Quakers. See note on page 62.

gestures; and introduced dancing, whirling, hopping, and other eccentricities, into the ceremonials of pretended worship. Mother Ann declared to her deluded followers that she would not die, but be suddenly translated into heaven like Enoch and Elijah. Notwithstanding she did actually die at Watervliet, on the 8th of September, 1784, her followers believe that it was not real death. In a poetic "Memorial to Mother Ann," written by one of them, occurs the stanza:

> "How much they are mistaken, who think that Mother's dead,
> When through her ministrations so many souls are saved.
> In union with the Father, she is the second Eve,
> Dispensing full salvation to all who do believe."

THOMAS GODFREY.

A PLAIN mechanic was one day replacing a pane of glass in a window on the north side of Arch Street, Philadelphia, opposite a pump, when a girl, after filling her pail with water, placed it on the side walk. The mechanic observed the rays of the sun reflected from the window, into the pail of water. This circumstance produced a train of reflections in a highly mathematical mind, and led to an important discovery. That mechanic was Thomas Godfrey, who was born about a mile from Germantown, in Pennsylvania, in the year 1704.

Godfrey's early education was limited; and at a proper age he was apprenticed to a glazier, in Philadelphia. He entered into the business on his own account in 1725, and was employed in glazing Christ Church and the State House,[1] both of which are yet standing in the old part of Philadelphia. From early boyhood Godfrey exhibited great taste for figures; and, like Rittenhouse, he often exhibited his diagrams in his place of labor. A work on mathematics having fallen into his hands, he soon mastered the science, and then he learned the Latin language, so as to read the works of the best writers upon his favorite subject.

In the Summer of 1729, Godfrey was employed by James Logan to glaze some windows in his library, and there he first saw Newton's Principia. He borrowed the work; and early in 1730, he communicated his invention of the *Quadrant* (an astronomical and nautical instrument, of great value) to that gentleman. His reflections on the Arch Street incident, with the perusal of Newton's work, had resulted in this invention. Mr. Logan took great interest in the matter, and conveyed information of the invention to the Royal Society of London, through his friend, Sir Hans Sloane. That institution rewarded Mr. Godfrey for his ingenuity, by presenting to him a quantity of household furniture, valued at one thousand dollars, but divided the honor of first discoverer equally between him and John Hadley, then vice-president of the institution.

That the sole honor was justly due to Godfrey, there can be no doubt, for the fact appears to be well authenticated, that the first instrument made of brass, from Godfrey's wooden model, was taken by the inventor's brother, captain of a vessel in the West India trade, to the island of Jamaica, and there exhibited to some English naval officers. Among these was a nephew of John Hadley. He purchased the instrument of Captain Godfrey for a large sum of money, and took it to his uncle, in London, who was a mathematical instrument maker. That gentleman made another instrument like it, except a few alterations, and presented it to the Royal Society, with an explanatory paper, as his invention.

---

1. Independence Hall, wherein Congress was assembled when the Declaration of Independence was adopted on the 4th of July, 1776, is in this State House. The exterior of the building has been somewhat changed since then.

That presentation occurred on the 13th of May, 1731, just about the time that Sir Hans Sloane called the attention of the Society to Godfrey's invention. The American inventor, like Columbus, lost the honor of having his name identified with the discovery, and the instrument is known as *Hadley's Quadrant*. Mr. Godfrey died in Philadelphia, in December, 1749, at the age of forty-five years.

PONTIAC.

SAVAGE and treacherous as he is, the native Indian, in his forest home, has many generous and noble qualities, such as we have been taught to admire when displayed by Roman warrior or Greek law-giver. Pontiac, the great chief of the Ottawa tribe a hundred years ago, possessed these in an eminent degree; and had his natural endowments been nurtured under the warm sun of civilization, no doubt his name would have been high among the great ones of earth. But he was forest born, and forest bred, and history speaks of him only as a great chief, filled with deadly hatred of the white man, and renowned for bloody deeds and bloodier intentions.

Pontiac, when he first became known to the white man, was ruler of the whole north-west portion of our present domain. Where Cleveland now stands in its pride, Major Rogers first met the great chief, one bright morning in the Autumn of 1760. He informed Pontiac that the English had taken Canada from the French, and then made a treaty of friendship with him. Though Pontiac had been the fast friend of the French during the war just ended, he now appeared upon the field of history, for the first time, in the full strength of mature manhood. He was doubtless sincere in his treaty with the English, but the non-fulfilment of their promises, and the influence of French emissaries, soon made him trample all compacts beneath his feet. He did more, far more than any North American Indian ever effected before or since. He confederated all the Indian tribes of the North-west to utterly exterminate the English, or drive them from all their posts on the great lakes, and in the country around the head waters of the Ohio. Like Philip of Mount Hope, Pontiac viewed the approach of white settlements with jealousy and alarm. He saw, in the future, visions of the displacement, perhaps destruction, of his race, by the pale-faces; and he determined to strike a blow for life and country. So adroitly were his plans matured, that the commanders of the western forts had no suspicion of his conspiracy until it was ripe, and the first blow had been struck. Early in the Summer of 1763, within a fortnight, all of the posts in possession of the English, west of Oswego, fell into his hands, except Niagara, Fort Pitt, and Detroit. Early the following Spring, Colonel Bradstreet penetrated the country to Detroit, with a strong force. The Indians were speedily subdued, their power was broken, and the hostile tribes sent their chiefs to ask for pardon and peace. The haughty Pontiac refused to bow. He went to the country of the *Illinois* tribe, where he was basely murdered, in 1769, by a Peoria Indian, who was bribed by an English trader to do the deed, for a barrel of rum. The place of his murder was at Cahokia, on the east side of the Mississippi, a little below St. Louis. A great man fell, when Pontiac died. He was the greatest of all chiefs known to the white men, and deserved a better fate. It is said that during his operations in 1763, he appointed a commissary, and even issued bills of credit, which passed current among the French inhabitants of the North-west. When he died, he wore a uniform presented to him by Montcalm, who esteemed him highly. Pontiac was an actor in the last scene in the drama of the French and Indian War.

FISHER AMES.

"HAPPILY he did not need the smart of guilt to make him virtuous, nor the regret of folly to make him wise," were the words uttered by one who knew Fisher Ames well, and appreciated his noble character. He was a son of Dr. Ames, a physician and a wit,[1] of Dedham, Massachusetts, where he was born on the 9th of April, 1756. He was a delicate child; and so precocious was he in the acquirement of knowledge, that at six years of age he commenced the study of Latin. At the age of twelve he was admitted to Harvard College, where he was graduated in 1774. That was a year of great gloom in Massachusetts, and indeed throughout the whole country; and as young Ames' mother was poor, and the times made a choice of business difficult, he taught a common school for awhile. He read and studied incessantly, and, finally, prepared for the profession of the law, under William Tudor, in Boston. He commenced its

---

1. He kept a public-house at Dedham, and on one occasion, the colonial judges having, as he thought, decided a case against him unlawfully, he sketched their honors upon a sign-board in front of his tavern, in their full-bottomed wigs, tippling, with their backs to an open volume, labelled "Province Law." The Boston authorities sent some officers to Dedham, to remove the sign. The doctor was prepared for them; and when they arrived, they found nothing hanging but a board, on which was inscribed, "A wicked and adulterous generation seeketh for a sign, but no sign shall be given them."

practice at Dedham, in 1781, and soon stood at the head of the bar in his native district. From early youth he had exhibited rare oratorical powers. These powers now had fine opportunities for expansion, and with pen and tongue Fisher Ames soon attracted the attention of all classes of his countrymen. He was a member of the convention for ratifying the Federal Constitution, in 1788, and there his eloquence gained him the heartiest applause. He was elected a member of the Massachusetts Legislature the same year, and in 1789, he was the first representative of his district, in the Federal Congress. There he was the chief speaker in all important debates. It is said that on one occasion,[1] in 1796, his eloquence was so powerful, that a member, opposed to him, moved that the question on which he had spoken should be postponed until the next day, "that they should not act under the influence of an excitement of which their calm judgment might not approve." John Adams bluntly said, in allusion to that speech, "there was n't a dry eye in the house, except some of the jackasses that occasioned the necessity of the oratory."

Mr. Ames was the author of the "Address of the House of Representatives," to President Washington, on his signifying his intention to withdraw from office. At about the same time, his own feeble health compelled him to decline a re-election, and he retired partially from public life. He was a member of the council of his State for some years; and in 1800, he pronounced a eulogy on Washington, before the State Legislature. He was chosen President of Harvard College, in 1805, but he declined the honor. His powers of life gradually failed for several years; and on the 4th of July, 1808, his pulse ceased to beat, at the age of fifty years. In the old church-yard at Dedham is a plain white monument, on which is the simple inscription—FISHER AMES. Mr. Ames was a fluent and voluminous writer, and his collected productions are among the choicest things in our literature.

JOSEPH GALLOWAY.

AMONG the eminent loyalists of Pennsylvania, who adhered to the patriot cause until the war had fairly begun, Joseph Galloway was, perhaps, the most distinguished. He was born in Maryland, in 1730, and early in life he went to Philadelphia to practice law, in which profession he soon took a high rank. He obtained a beautiful wife and a considerable fortune by marrying the daughter of Lawrence Growdon, who was Speaker of the Assembly of Pennsylvania, for many years. Mr. Galloway was a member of that body in 1764, and his sympathies, as manifested by his words and actions, were always on the side of the people. So well convinced were the people of his staunch republicanism, that he was elected a member of the first Continental Congress in 1774, and was a very active participant in the debates in that body. He submitted a plan of union between Great Britain and the colonies, by which the latter might be comparatively independent, with a president at their head, appointed by the king. His plan was not adopted; and when the Congress agreed upon a non-importation, non-consumption, and non-exportation scheme, called the *American Association*, Mr. Galloway signed it. He was never in favor of a political separation from Great Britain, yet he was always in favor of the most stringent measures for compelling the government to redress the grievances of the colonists. In 1775, he began to show signs of wavering, by earnestly asking to be excused

---

1. Speech on Jay's Treaty.

from serving as a delegate in the Continental Congress; and in 1776, when the question of independence began to be agitated, he abandoned the Whigs, and became one of the most violent and proscriptive Loyalists. Afraid to remain in Philadelphia, he joined the royal army in New York, where he remained until early in the Summer of 1788, when he went to England, accompanied by his only daughter.[1] In 1779, he was summoned before parliament to testify concerning the state of affairs in America. He was severe upon General Howe and other British officers, in relation to their stupid management. He kept up an extensive correspondence with the Loyalists, in America, during the remainder of the war, and wrote several pamphlets on subjects connected with the hostilities. Mr. Galloway's large estates in Pennsylvania were confiscated; and when a commission was appointed, in London, for prosecuting the claims of the Loyalists, he was made a member of the board for Delaware and Pennsylvania. A large part of his property was afterward restored to his daughter, and is still in possession of his descendants. Mr. Galloway never returned to America. He died in England, in September, 1803, at the age of seventy-three years. During the war, all the Whig writers took delight in making him a target for their wit and scorn. Trumbull, in his *McFingall*, gave him many hard hits; and Philip Freneau, and other poets, scorched him severely.

TIMOTHY RUGGLES.

THERE were many able men who stood in opposition to the British government in the first revolutionary movements of the American colonies, but who timidly receded when the quarrel became fierce, and the government uttered its menacing thunders. Timothy Ruggles, of Massachusetts, was of that class. He was born at Rochester, in that province, in 1711, and was graduated at Harvard in 1732. He became a lawyer; and at the age of twenty-five years, he was an influential member of the General Assembly. He rose rapidly in his profession, and was often called to measure forensic weapons with the Otises, father and son. He was fond of military life, and held the commission of colonel in the provincial forces under Sir William Johnson. At the battle at Lake George, in 1755, he was second in command to Johnson;[2] and was active in the campaigns of the two years following, under Amherst, when he held the commission of Brigadier-general. He also served with distinction, under that officer, in 1759–'60, in his expedition against Quebec and Montreal. In 1762, he was appointed chief justice of the common pleas, and was Speaker of the Assembly at the same time. In 1763, he made Hardwick his residence, where he practiced his profession. The storm of the Revolution soon began to lower; and when, in the Autumn of 1765, a congress of delegates, from the different provinces, to consider the grievances of the people, was held at New York, General Ruggles was a delegate thereto, from Massachusetts, and was chosen president of the convention. He was unwilling to go as far as his colleagues, and refused his coöperation in the proceedings of the congress, for which he was

---

1. It is supposed that Galloway's departure from Philadelphia was hastened by the discovery that his daughter was about to marry Judge Griffin, a firm Whig, and afterward President of the Continental Congress.
2. For his good conduct in that campaign, he was rewarded with the almost sinecure office of Surveyor-general of the king's forests. It was a lucrative office, with very little labor.

greatly censured. From that time he ranked among the royalists, and in 1774, was made a councillor, and accepted the office. That act made him very obnoxious to the patriots, and he was compelled to leave the country, and take refuge under royal military rule, in Boston. His large estates were confiscated, and he became a refugee, when the British were driven from Boston, by Washington, in the Spring of 1776. He afterward returned to the vicinity of New York, and organized a corps of about three hundred loyalists, but seems not to have performed much active service. In 1779, he went to Nova Scotia, where he resided until his death, which occurred in 1798, when he was eighty-seven years of age. General Ruggles was a scholar, but rude in manners and speech. He has many descendants in Nova Scotia.

JONATHAN CARVER.

THE earliest American-born traveller, of note, was Jonathan Carver, who first saw the light of life in Connecticut, in 1732. He was educated for the medical profession, but chose the military art as a vocation, and led a company of Connecticut provincials in some of the expeditions against the French in northern New York, from 1756 to 1759. He served with reputation until the peace in 1763, and soon afterward he formed the bold resolution to explore the continent of America from Lake Superior to the Pacific Ocean. He also hoped thereby to be instrumental in finding the long-sought north-west passage to India.

Mr. Carver left Michillimackinac in the Autumn of 1766. That was the most westerly of the British military posts. Bearing a few gifts for the Indians, he penetrated the present Minnesota Territory to the head waters of the St. Pierre, more than a thousand miles from the point of his departure. He was foiled in his grand design; and after spending some time on the northern and eastern shores of Lake Superior, exploring its bays and tributaries, carefully observing the productions of nature and the habits of the Indians, he returned to the settlements, and laid his papers before the governor of Massachusetts, at Boston. He had been absent about two years, and had travelled over seven thousand miles.

Having carefully arranged his journals and charts, Mr. Carver went to England for the purpose of publishing them. He petitioned the king for a reimbursement of funds which he had spent in the service of the government, in these explorations, but his claims were deferred. He received permission, however, to publish his papers, and he sold them to a bookseller. Just as they were ready for the press, he was ordered to deliver all his charts and papers into the hands of the Commissioners of Plantations, and he was compelled to re-purchase them from the bookseller. Ten years elapsed before he was allowed to lay them before the public. In disappointment and poverty, he became a lottery clerk; and finally, in 1779, his necessities induced him to sell his name to a historical compilation, published in folio, and entitled *The New Universal Traveller.* This act caused the loss of his clerkship, and many professed friends abandoned him. He died in the suburbs of London, in extreme want, in 1780, at the age of only forty-eight years. Such is sometimes the fate of genius. An edition of his travels was published in Boston in 1797.

REBECCA MOTTE.

THE fortitude, courage, and unfaltering patriotism of the women of the Revolution, were remarkably and universally displayed. Everywhere—in every province, they were actors as well as sufferers; and many a scheme of British aggression was frustrated by the sisters, wives, and daughters of those who were in the camp or field. South Carolina presents many such bright examples, but none appear more brilliant than Rebecca Motte, whose unwavering courage and fidelity, as well as sacrifices, attest her ardent patriotism. She was the youngest daughter of Robert Brewton, who emigrated to America in 1733, and married, at Charleston, an accomplished young lady, a native of Ireland. He made Charleston his residence, and there Rebecca was born on the 28th of June, 1738. At the age of twenty, she married Jacob Motte, a descendant of one of the Huguenot families of South Carolina. He owned a fine plantation near the banks of the Congaree, and there Mrs. Motte, the mother of six children, and a widow, resided during the War for Independence.

After the fall of Charleston, in 1780, the British commander sought to hold military possession of South Carolina, by establishing fortified camps in the interior. The fine mansion of Mrs. Motte was taken possession of, fortified for the purpose, and named Fort Motte. The garrison was commanded by Major McPherson, in May, 1781, when Marion and Lee appeared and commenced a siege. Mrs. Motte had been driven from her mansion by the British, and had taken up her abode in her farm-house, whither her mother[1] (who resided with her) had carried a beautiful bow and bundle of arrows, presented to her son by an East India captain. Having but one cannon, the Americans could make but little impression on the British works. Lee's fertile mind conceived the idea of dislodging the enemy by burning the mansion, that act to be effected by hurling ignited combustibles upon the dry roof, by means of arrows. He suggested the plan to Mrs. Motte. She heartily approved of it, notwithstanding it involved the destruction of her property; and she presented Lee with the East India bow and arrows, for the service. The hoped-for result was accomplished; and after the British had surrendered, Mrs. Motte regaled the officers of both armies with a sumptuous dinner. One of her daughters married General Thomas Pinckney, one of the most valuable officers of the South. Mrs. Motte lived, greatly beloved by all, until the year 1815, when she died, at the age of seventy-seven years. "Her children" (and children's children) "rise up and call her blessed."

SAMUEL ADAMS.

"SUCH is the obstinacy and inflexible disposition of the man, that he can never be conciliated by any office or gift whatever," was the unintentional eulogium of Samuel Adams, by the royal governor, Hutchinson, when asked why he did not purchase the patriot by offers of place and money. The eulogium was just, for a more inflexible patriot never bared his arm for conflict, than that scion of the old Puritan stock of Boston. He was born in that city on the 27th of September, 1722, and in 1740, was graduated at Harvard College. His ideas of popular rights seem to have had an early growth, for in 1743, when he received the degree of Master of Arts, he proposed for discussion the question, "Is it lawful to resist the supreme magistrate, if the commonwealth cannot otherwise be preserved?" He maintained the affirmative, with great vigor. His pen was early employed in political discussion, and the soundness of his judgment, and purity of his thoughts, made him very popular, even before public affairs called his patriotism into activity. His earliest public office was that of tax-gatherer, by which he became personally acquainted with all classes of people. In 1765, he was chosen a member of the Massachusetts Assembly. He was also clerk of that body, and for almost ten years he swayed a powerful influence in the Colonial Assembly, as a leading and bold representative of the republican party among the people. Step by step, inch by inch, Samuel Adams fought the enemies of popular liberty during the dark hours which preceded the bursting of the storm of the Revolution; and he was the most active of the patriots of Boston in exciting the people to acts like that of the destruction of the cargoes of tea, in 1773. When royal government was repudiated, in 1774, he was chosen a member of the provincial council; and when General Gage sent his secretary to dissolve the assembly, just previous to that popular congress, he found the door of the legislative chamber locked, and the key was in Samuel Adams' pocket. Adams

---

1. Mrs. Brewton was remarkable for her boldness in the presence of danger, and for her keen wit. While in Charleston, when the British had possession of that city, her society was courted by the *elite* among the conquerors, notwithstanding she often made them feel the keenness of her sarcasm. On going into the city, an officer inquired, "What news from the country?" "All nature smiles," she replied, "for everything is Greene, down to Monk's Corner." General Greene had just taken possession of the State down to that point. Just before the siege of Fort Motte, a young British subaltern insulted the family, by giving the names of different American officers to pine saplings, and then cutting off their tops with his sword. After their surrender, Mrs. Brewton requested him to amuse her again, in that way, and expressed her regret that the loss of his sword would deny her the privilege. Colonel Moncrief occupied Governor Rutledge's house, in Charleston. Passing it with a British officer, Mrs. Brewton took a piece of a crape flounce accidentally torn from her dress, and tied it to the front railing, observing that the house and friends of the governor ought to mourn for his absence. She was arrested, and sent to Philadelphia a few hours afterward.

was chosen a delegate to the Continental Congress, in 1774, and there he was an exceedingly useful public servant for several years. He was an earnest advocate of the resolution which declared the colonies "free and independent states;" and when some members faltered through fear of failure, the stern Puritan exclaimed, "I should advise persisting in our struggle for liberty, though it were revealed from heaven that nine hundred and ninety-nine were to perish, and only one of a thousand were to survive, and retain his liberty! One such free man must possess more virtue, and enjoy more happiness, than a thousand slaves; and let him propagate his like, and transmit to them what he hath so nobly preserved." Such was the temper of the man who originated the idea of a Colonial Congress, in 1765, and was the earliest advocate of a Continental Congress, in 1774. He affixed his signature to the Declaration of Independence in 1776; and in 1781, he retired from Congress, but not from public life. He was a leading member of the Massachusetts convention to form a state constitution; and in 1789, he was chosen lieutenant-governor of his native State. In 1794, he was elected governor, as the successor of John Hancock, and was annually re-elected, until 1797, when the infirmities of old age compelled him to retire from public life. On the morning of the 2d of October, 1803, that noble patriot expired, in the city of his birth, at the age of eighty-two years.

ROBERT ROGERS.

THE French and Indian war developed much military genius among the American colonists, which was afterward brought into requisition by the demands of the revolutionary contest. It did not always take its place on the side of republicanism, as in the case of Ruggles and many others. Major Robert Rogers, the bold commander of a corps of Rangers, and a companion-in-arms with Putnam and Stark, was another example of defection to the cause of freedom in America. He was a native of Dunbarton, in New Hampshire, and having entered the military service in 1755, became an eminent commander of a corps which performed signal services as scouts, and executors of small but important enterprises, when not engaged with the main army. After the peace in 1763, he returned to his native place, and received the half-pay of a regular British officer of his rank, until the War for Independence broke out. In 1766, he was made governor of Michillimackinac, in the far North-west, where he had confronted the confederates of Pontiac, a few years before. He was accused of a design to plunder his own fort, and was sent in irons to Montreal. After his release he went to England, was presented to the king, and met with royal favor; but extravagant habits led him into debt, and he was cast into prison. He finally returned to America, and when the revolutionary contest began, the color of his politics was doubtful. His movements, toward the close of 1775, gave reason to suspect him of being a spy; and in June, 1776, Washington had him arrested, at South Amboy, and brought to New York, where he professed great friendship for his native country. He was released on parole, by Congress, and directed to return to New Hampshire, which he did. He soon afterward boldly espoused the royal cause, raised a corps, which he called the *Queen's Rangers*, and was with Howe, in Westchester, previous to the battle at White Plains. He soon afterward left his corps in command of Lieutenant-colonel Simcoe, and went to England. By an act of his native State, he was banished, and never returned to America. When, and where he died, is not on History's record. He was a brave soldier; but, according to his own confession, his half-pay from the crown made him an adherent of royalty.

BENJAMIN RUSH.

MANY faithful practitioners of the medical art have justly borne the honorable title given to St. Luke, of "beloved physician;" but none have better deserved it than Dr. Rush of Philadelphia. He was born at Byberry, about twelve miles north-east from that city, on the 24th of December, 1745. When six years of age, death deprived him of his father, and his mother placed him under the care of his maternal uncle, Dr. Finley, who was at the head of an academy in Maryland. Desirous of giving him a classical education, his mother sold her little estate in the country, engaged in trade in Philadelphia, with success, and in 1759, was able to place him in college at Princeton, where he was graduated at the close of 1760. The medical profession was his choice; and he studied the science under the eminent Doctors Redman and Shippen, until 1766, when he went to Edinburgh to complete his scientific studies there. In the Summer of 1768, he went to Paris; and in the Autumn he returned home, bearing the diploma of Doctor of Medicine, which he had received at Edinburgh. He immediately commenced practice in Philadelphia, and never was success more brilliant. His skill, polished manners, intelligence, and kind attentions to the poor, made him popular with all classes, and he soon found himself possessed of a very lucrative practice.

In 1769, Dr. Rush was appointed professor of chemistry in the Medical College of Philadelphia, yet his professional duties did not occupy his whole time. He espoused the patriot cause immediately after his return home, and his pen became a powerful instrument in arousing the people to energetic action in favor of popular freedom. He declined a proffered seat in the Continental Congress in 1775; but when, the following year, some of the Pennsylvania delegates were opposed to independence, and withdrew, he consented to take the seat of one of them, and his name was affixed to the great Declaration, in August. The following year, Congress appointed him physician-general of the middle department; and from that time he declined all public employment, until 1787, when he was a member of the Pennsylvania convention which ratified the Federal Constitution. In 1789, he was made professor of the theory and practice of medicine in the Medical College of Philadelphia; and in 1796, he was made professor of the practice of medicine in the Medical College of Pennsylvania. He held his three professorships until his death. His lectures were of the highest order, and students from all parts of the United States flocked to Philadelphia, to attend them. Dr. Rush was also connected with the United States mint, for many years.

When, in 1793, the yellow fever appeared in Philadelphia, of most malignant type, and many alarmed physicians fled, Dr. Rush remained at the post of duty, with a few faithful students, and was instrumental in saving scores of lives. Some of his pupils died, and he was violently attacked by the disease, yet he did not remit his labors, when he could leave his bed. For his fidelity in that trying hour he was greatly beloved. Nor did his usefulness end with his life. The impress of his mind and energy is upon several institutions; and the general appreciation of his character was manifested by his being made honorary member of many literary and scientific societies, at home and abroad.[1] In all stations he exhibited the character of a consistent Christian, and his principles remained unscathed amid all the infidelity which French writers had infused into the minds of men in high places, toward the close of the last century. That great and good man died peacefully at Philadelphia, on the 19th of April, 1813, when in the sixty-eighth year of his age. That event was the disappearance of a bright star from the social firmament.

SILAS DEANE.

THE first diplomatic agent employed by the Continental Congress, in Europe, was Silas Deane, a native of Groton, Connecticut. The date of his birth is unknown. He was graduated at Yale College in 1758, and being an active patriot, was chosen a delegate to the first Continental Congress, in 1774. Early in 1776, he was sent by that body, as a political and commercial agent, to the court of France, to sound the cabinet of Louis the Sixteenth on the subject of granting military supplies to the revolted colonies. The French King, willing to injure England, listened to Deane's overtures with eager ears, and he obtained noble verbal promises. In the Autumn of 1776, when the colonies had been declared independent, Dr. Franklin and Arthur Lee were appointed commissioners, with Mr. Deane, to negotiate treaties with foreign powers. They met at

---

1. He founded the Philadelphia Dispensary, in 1786; and he was also one of the principal founders of Dickinson College, at Carlisle, Pennsylvania. He was president of the American Society for the abolition of slavery; of the Philadelphia Medical Society; vice-president of the Philadelphia Bible Society; and one of the vice-presidents of the American Philosophical Society.

Paris, in December of that year, but it was soon discovered by Deane's colleagues, that his appointment was an injudicious one. He exceeded his instructions concerning the employment of engineers for the continental army, and he was profuse in his promises of offices of high rank, to induce French gentlemen to go to America.

Influenced by Deane's promises, many French officers came over, and Congress became very much embarrassed by their applications for commissions. Deane was recalled in the Autumn of 1777, and John Adams was appointed in his place. Deane arrived at Philadelphia the following Spring, in company with Mr. Gerard, the first minister sent hither by France, after the treaty of amity between the two governments, in February, 1778. He was called upon to explain his official course abroad, before the assembled Congress, but he did not entirely acquit himself of the suspicion that he had misapplied the public funds, while in office, and he evaded thorough scrutiny by pleading that his vouchers were left among his papers, in Europe. In order to mislead public opinion, he published an address, in which he arraigned members of Congress and those in charge of the operations of the office for foreign affairs, at Philadelphia. Thomas Paine was at the head of that office, and in his reply to Deane, he revealed some secrets concerning transactions with the French government, and was requested to resign. In 1784, Deane published another address to the people of the United States, complaining of ill treatment by the government. Very little attention was paid to his complaints, and he soon afterward went to England. He died in extreme poverty at Deal, in England, in 1789, at the age of about fifty years.

TENCH COXE.

AS we survey the labors of useful men, we are often compelled to regret the paucity of their personal history, left on record. We admire their deeds, and wish to know more of the men, but Time has drawn the veil of oblivion, even over the traditions of their private life. Such is the case in relation to Tench Coxe, one of the most indefatigable of the public-spirited men of our country, and to whom the Cotton interest, especially, is vastly indebted, for he labored long, assiduously, and efficiently, in its behalf. He was a grandson of Dr. Daniel Coxe, physician to the Queen of Charles the Second, and of Queen Anne, of England, who became one of the principal proprietors of the soil of West Jersey. His son, William Coxe, married the daughter of Tench Francis, attorney-general of the province of Pennsylvania, and these were the parents of Tench Coxe, who was born in Philadelphia, on the 22d of May, 1755. His chief distinction is that of a lucid and powerful advocate of the cultivation of cotton in the United States, and of other industrial pursuits. He says that as early as 1785, when he was but thirty years of age, he "felt pleasing convictions that the United States, in its extensive regions south of Anne Arundel and Talbot counties, Maryland, would certainly become a great cotton producing country." He made these suggestions public at that time; and after the convention at Annapolis, in 1786, called to consider the business and general interests of the new Republic, the matter received considerable attention. While the convention that framed the Federal Constitution was in session in Philadelphia, in 1787, Mr. Coxe delivered an admirable address on his favorite theme, before a large number of gentlemen who had assembled in that city, for the purpose of establishing a society for the encouragment of manufactures and the useful arts. That address thoroughly awakened the public mind. Before that time, not a

TENCH COXE.

bale of cotton had ever been exported from the United States to any country, and no planter had adopted its cultivation as a "crop." What a change has taken place within less than seventy years! That then neglected article has now become a staple of several of the States of our Union, and the source of great national wealth.

From 1787, until the death of Mr. Coxe, on the 17th of July, 1824, there was never any important movement in favor of the introduction and promotion of manufactures, in which his name did not appear prominent. In 1794, he published a large octavo volume, which contained what he had previously written on the subject of the growth of cotton, and cognate topics. At that time he was commissioner of the revenue at Philadelphia, and his whole time was devoted to the investigation of the subjects of national industry and national prosperity. In 1806, he published an essay on naval power and the encouragement of manufactures. The following year he published a memoir on the culture and manufacture of cotton, and this was followed by other similar productions, at various times, until his death, when at the age of sixty-eight years. Tench Coxe is regarded by those who appreciate his usefulness, as a national benefactor.

JOHN LEDYARD.

THE world has never produced a more indefatigable traveller and explorer, than John Ledyard, the eldest son of a sea captain, who resided at Groton, Connecticut. There John was born in 1751. His father died while he was yet a lad; and after his mother had married again, he was taken into the family of his grandfather, at Hartford, and treated as a son. His guardian died, when John was about eighteen years of age, and he entered Dartmouth College as a divinity student. He became dissatisfied, and resolved to leave the institution. He had already been a wanderer among the Five Nations in New York for three months, and had tasted the pleasures of exciting travel. Having no money to pay travelling expenses to Hartford, he constructed a canoe, laid in "sea stores" contributed by kind friends, and all alone he made a perilous voyage down the winding Connecticut and its numerous rapids, to Hartford, a distance of one hundred and forty miles. This first adventure revealed the spirit within. He soon made his way to New London, and shipped as a common sailor, for Gibraltar. There he joined the army, but being released, he made his way back by way of the Barbary coast and the West Indies, in 1771. He then sailed from New York to England, where he entered the navy, and as corporal of marines, accompanied Captain Cook in his third and last great voyage. Ever brave and resolute, young Ledyard became the favorite of his commander, and he was frequently intrusted with little enterprises, which required skill and courage. He was with Cook when he was killed by the people of the Sandwich Islands, in 1778. After visiting the shores of Kamschatka, the expedition returned to England, and Ledyard came to America. He arrived after an absence of eight years, and took lodgings under his mother's roof at Southold, Long Island, without being recognized by her, for some hours. The war of the Revolution was then in progress, and Ledyard could not consistently remain among the enemies of his country, so he crossed over to Connecticut, joined his friends at Hartford, and there wrote an account of the voyage with Captain Cook.

Ledyard now planned a voyage to the north-west coast of America, but received very little encouragement. He sailed for Cadiz, thence to L'Orient, and going to Paris, he had an interview there with Mr. Jefferson and La Fayette. They approved of his projected voyage, for commercial purposes, to the north-west coast, and Paul Jones, then in Paris, entered heartily into the scheme. The plan failed, however, and Ledyard conceived the bold project of making a journey by land, through the Russian dominions, to Behring's Straits, by way of Kamschatka, and thus reach the north-west coast. He went to London, and Sir Joseph Banks and other scientific gentlemen contributed funds to aid him in his enterprise. He proceeded to Hamburg, thence to Copenhagen and Stockholm; and without a companion he traversed the country north of the Gulf of Bothnia, under the Arctic circle, and made his way to St. Petersburg. There he procured a passport from the Empress Catharine, and started for Siberia, over the Ural Mountains. After dreadful hardships, which few men could have endured, he reached Yakutsk, on the great Lena river, six thousand miles eastward of St. Petersburg. He pushed on further to the Kamschatkan Sea, but finding much ice, he returned to Yakutsk, to await the opening of Spring. There, for reasons unknown to him, he was suspected of being a spy, and was seized by two Russian soldiers, in the name of the Empress. In the depth of Winter he was conveyed through the north of Tartary, by the way of Moscow, to the confines of Poland, and there his conductors wished him a pleasant journey, and told him he would be hanged if he entered the Russian dominions again. Ragged and penniless, he made his way to Konigsberg, where a correspondent of Sir Joseph Banks gave him five guineas, with which he proceeded to England. There he found a project on foot, for exploring the interior of Africa. Ledyard at once engaged, with enthusiasm, in the enterprise. When one of the managers of the association, which had been formed for the purpose, asked Ledyard how soon he would be ready to start, he promptly replied, "To-morrow morning." After writing to his mother, he sailed from London, in June, 1788, reached Cairo on the 19th of August, and then prepared to penetrate the interior. He joined a caravan for Sennaar, and was on the point of departure, with high hopes, when he was attacked by a bilious fever, which terminated his life on the 17th of January, 1789, at the age of thirty-seven years. Ledyard was a fluent and even elegant writer. He was a man of keen observation, and his notes of travel, truthful in the extreme, exhibited tales of romantic interest, such as the brain of the most expert writer of fiction could never have conceived. His narrative of Captain Cook's voyage, published at Hartford, in 1783, is full of exciting interest. From his papers in the possession of his relative, Dr. Isaac Ledyard, Mr. Sparks, the historian, compiled an interesting life of the traveller, and published it in 1828.

CORNELIUS HARNETT.

ONE of the chief master spirits of the Revolution, in North Carolina, was Cornelius Harnett, of Wilmington. He was born in England in 1723, and came to America in early life. He was a man of wealth and distinction before the disputes, which led to the Revolution, commenced; and he was among the earliest of the Southern patriots to denounce the Stamp Act and kindred measures. In 1770 and 1771, he represented the borough of Wilmington in the colonial legislature, and was chairman of the most important committees of that body. In conjunction with Robert Howe (afterward a general in the Revolution) and Judge Maurice Moore, Mr. Harnett was appointed by the Assembly to draw up a remonstrance against the appointment of commissioners, by the royal governor, to run the southern boundary of the province, and he was then known as one of the firmest Whigs[1] in all the South. Josiah Quincy, the young and ardent patriot of Boston, visited Mr. Harnett in 1773, and after describing the pleasures of a visit spent with him and Robert Howe, he spoke of Harnett's unflinching integrity, and called him "the Samuel Adams of North Carolina." Toward the close of that year, Mr. Harnett was made chairman of the committee of correspondence, of Wilmington District, and, throughout the revolution, as it gathered and burst over the country. When a provincial congress was called, in 1775, he was then the representative of his old constituents; and in that Congress at Halifax, on the Roanoke, in 1776, from which issued the first official voice in favor of the independence of the colonies, Cornelius Harnett was a bold leader, and with his own hand drew up those noble instructions to the North Carolina delegates in the Continental Congress. When, in the Spring of 1776, Sir Henry Clinton appeared at Cape Fear, with a British fleet, Harnett and Howe were honored with an exemption from the terms of a general pardon, because, like John Hancock and Samuel Adams, they were considered arch-rebels. When, on the 26th of July,

---

1. The terms *Whig* and *Tory* were copied from the political vocabulary of Great Britain, where they originated in the time of Charles the Second. The term *Whig* denoted the opposers of government, and that of *Tory* its adherents. In that relation to public affairs, they were first used in America, about the year 1770. The Republicans were called *Whigs*, the Loyalists, *Tories*.

1776, the Declaration of Independence arrived at Halifax, Harnett read it to the people, who, when he had finished it, took him upon their shoulders, and bore him in triumph through the town. In the Autumn, he drafted a State Constitution and Bill of Rights. When, under that constitution, Richard Caswell was made governor of the new State, Harnett was one of his council. He was afterward a member of the Continental Congress, and his name is attached to the *Articles of Confederation*.[1] When, in 1780 and 1781, the British took possession of the country around the Cape Fear, Harnett was made a prisoner, and died while a captive. Upon a slab of brown stone, at the head of his grave in St. James' church-yard, Wilmington, is the simple inscription—"CORNELIUS HARNETT. Died 1781, aged fifty-eight years."

PEYTON RANDOLPH.

THE chroniclers of ancient dynasties are often foiled in their researches concerning early kings, and when they have lost the clue of regular descent, or find it leading back into the domains of mere myth, they conveniently conclude that the first monarch of the line was begotten by a god. We have no such difficulty in this great republican empire of the West, for dynasties change with men, and eyes are yet undimmed which saw the first chief magistrate of this free nation. He was a Virginian—a native of the State called "the mother of presidents"—and his name was Peyton Randolph. He was born in the year 1723, and was a descendant of one of the oldest of the aristocratic families of Virginia who boast of having the royal blood of Powhatan[2] in their veins.

According to a then prevailing custom, young Randolph was sent to England to be educated. He was graduated at Oxford, with honor, and received the degree of Master of Arts. He commenced the study of law on his return home; and so rapid was his success in his profession, that he was made attorney-general of the colony of Virginia, in 1756, when thirty-three years of age. At that time, the French and Indian War was progressing, and the Indians, incited by the French, were desolating the Virginia frontier. Narratives of these outrages aroused the indignation of Mr. Randolph, and collecting a hundred men, he led them to the borders of the Indian country, and taught the savages some terrible retributory lessons. Toward the close of that contest, Mr. Randolph was elected to a seat in the Virginia Legislature, and he often presided over that body. There his influence was very great, and as the storm of the Revolution came on apace, his voice was ever heard on the side of freedom.

Mr. Randolph was elected a delegate to the first Continental Congress, which assembled in Carpenter's Hall, Philadelphia, on the 5th of September, 1774. Charles Thomson recorded on that day: "The Congress proceeded to the choice of a President, when the Hon. Peyton Randolph, Esq., was unanimously elected." This vote made him really the *first President of the United States*, for then and there our Union had its birth. He was again chosen President when another Congress met at the same place, in May following, but feeble health compelled him to resign the office, fourteen days afterward, when John Hancock was chosen to fill his place. Mr. Randolph resumed his seat in Congress early the following Autumn; and on the 22d of October, 1775, he died at Philadelphia, from the effects of apoplexy, in the fifty-third year of his age.

---

1. These formed a constitution of government for the United States, until 1789, when the present Federal Constitution went into operation, as a substitute.
2. See sketch of Pocahontas.

MERCY WARREN.

JAMES OTIS was a noble actor in the earlier scenes of the Revolution, and his beloved sister, Mercy, equally patriotic in her more limited sphere, was a faithful recorder of those acts, and of the subsequent events which led to the founding of our republic. She was the third child of Colonel Otis, of Barnstable, Massachusetts, and was born there on the 25th of September, 1728. As eldest daughter, much of her childhood and youth was spent in domestic employments, and her leisure was devoted to reading and study. Her opportunities for education were limited, but she found a never-failing source of instruction in the conversation and the library of Rev. Jonathan Russell, the parish minister. There she read Raleigh's *History of the World*, and that gave her a taste for such practical and important knowledge. Her gifted brother, James, was also her aid and adviser in literary pursuits; and so great was the attachment between them, that when the insanity which clouded his intellect, at the last, was manifested by ravings, her voice, alone, could calm his spirit. At the age of twenty-six years, Miss Otis became the wife of James Warren, a merchant of Plymouth, and a man of congenial mind and temper. Her life passed happily in alternate employments in domestic duties, in needle-work, and in the use of the pen in prose and poetry, until the gathering storm of the Revolution disturbed the repose of all families. Her brother was then uttering his noble thoughts in the senate; and she too, fired with patriotic ardor, labored with her pen, in the great cause. She was in correspondence with most of the controlling spirits of that day, and her political opinions were consulted by many who gave them vital action in the council and the field. Her roof was always a free shelter to patriots of every condition, and there D'Estaing and other French officers spent many pleasant and instructive hours. In 1775, was published her satirical drama, in two acts, entitled *The Group*, in which she introduced many of the leading Tory characters of the day. It had a powerful effect at the time. She early conceived the idea of preparing a faithful chronicle of the war, and for that purpose she kept a journal, from the commencement to the end. After the war, her poetical pieces were collected into a volume, dedicated to General Washington. It contained her tragedies, *The Sack of Rome*, and *The Ladies of Castile*. The first was so much esteemed, that John Adams, then United States minister in London, expressed a desire to have it performed upon the stage in that city, "before crowded houses, for the honor of America." Her *History of the Revolution* was published at Boston, in three volumes, in 1805, though completed several years before. She was then seventy-eight years of age, and yet possessed much of the personal grace and vivacity of mind, mentioned by Rochefoucault, who visited her seven years before. The preface, written at that time, shows remarkable mental vigor. Her earnest prayer always was, to be spared the loss of her mental faculties, while she lived, and the boon was vouchsafed. When, on the 19th of October, 1814, her spirit took its flight, her reason was unclouded, though its earthly tenement was almost eighty-eight years of age.

WILLIAM HENRY DRAYTON.

ONE of the most brilliant and promising young men of South Carolina, when the revolutionary contest began, was Judge Drayton, a scion of one of the oldest and best distinguished cavalier families of the South. He was a nephew of Governor Bull, and was born in September, 1742. For about eleven years he was a student at Windsor and Oxford, in England; and on his return to South Carolina, he prepared for the profession of the law. He went to England again in 1771, and there published the discussions between the friends and opponents of the government, in Charleston. He was introduced at court, and being fully impressed with the belief that Great Britain would speedily redress the grievances of the colonists, he accepted the appointment of a seat in the royal governor's council. Being soon undeceived, he opposed government measures with great energy, and was finally dismissed for his contumacy.

In September, 1774, Mr. Drayton published a pamphlet, addressed to the Continental Congress, in which the grievances of the Americans were clearly stated, and an able Bill of Rights presented. He yet held the position of one of his majesty's justices, to which he had been appointed in 1771, and was the only native-born citizen who had ever been honored with that office. He retained his position until the Spring of 1775, when the royal judges made their last circuit. During the following Summer he labored manfully in the cause of freedom, as President of the Provincial Congress of South Carolina; and in the Autumn, when the British sloops of war, *Tamar* and *Cherokee*, menaced Charleston with bombardment, because of the rebellious movements of its citizens, he was appointed, by the committee of safety, to the command of the armed ship, *Prosper*, employed to oppose them. Commodore Drayton returned their fire promptly several times, and thus actual hostilities at the South commenced.

In March, 1776, Judge Drayton was chosen chief justice of the then revolted colony of South Carolina, by the unanimous voice of his Whig countrymen; and his admirable charge to the grand jury, delivered a month afterward, was hailed throughout the land as one of the noblest expressions of patriotic public sentiment yet uttered. It placed the author in the same honorable position as John Hancock and Samuel Adams, of Massachusetts, who were denounced as archtraitors. From that time, until the close of his career, he was regarded as one of the chief leaders of the rebellion in the South, and yet he found time to chronicle, in minute detail, the preliminary and current events of the great struggle. He became a member of the Continental Congress, and died suddenly while in the discharge of his legislative duties, in Philadelphia, on the 3d of September, 1779, at the age of thirty-seven years. "*A Memoir of the American Revolution, from its commencement to the year* 1776," prepared by Judge Drayton, was revised and published by his son, Governor John Drayton, in 1821.

JOHN ADAMS.

IN our Republic, where offices and titles are not hereditary, it is seldom that father and son both occupy the same post of honor; and it is still more rare, in any country, for both to be equally distinguished for talent and usefulness, as in the case of the elder and younger Adams. They both occupied important diplomatic stations, and both became chief magistrate of the United States. John Adams, the elder, was born at Braintree, Massachusetts, on the 30th of October, 1735, and was a lineal descendant of one who fled to America, to avoid the persecutions of Laud, during the reign of Charles the First. His maternal ancestor was John Alden, of the May Flower, and thus he was an inheritor of a love of freedom. He received a primary education at a common school in Braintree, and there he was prepared for a scholarship in Harvard College, where he was graduated at the age of twenty years. The law was his chosen profession; and under Mr. Putnam, of Worcester, he made rapid progress, not only in that study, but in the acquirement of general information, for he there had the free use of an extensive library, belonging to Mr. Gridley, the attorney-general of Massachusetts. The value of such a fountain of knowledge, to him, was soon apparent; and when, in 1758, he commenced the practice of law at Braintree, he gave ample assurance of speedy eminence, both as a professional and a public man. He was admitted as a barrister, in 1761, and at the same time took part with Otis and others in denunciations of Writs of Assistance. When the tempest raised in America by the Stamp Act was at its height, Mr. Adams wrote and published his famous *Essay on the Canon and Feudal Law*, which at once placed him high the public esteem.

Mr. Adams married in 1766, and soon afterward made Boston his place of residence. There he took front rank with the political agitators, and was one of the most prudent, yet decided of the popular leaders.[1] In 1770, he was elected to a seat in the Massachusetts Assembly; and in 1774, he was chosen one of five to represent that province in the First Continental Congress. He was again elected to the same office in 1775, and nominated George Washington for the important station of commander-in-chief of the armies of the United States. On

---

1. His popularity was put to the severest test in 1770, when Captain Preston, and some of his soldiers who had fired upon a mob and killed three people [see note on page 59], were tried for murder. Adams, in the face of greatly-excited public opinion, consented, as a lawyer, to defend Preston, and he was acquitted. The faith of the people, in Adams, was so unwavering, that this seeming treason to their cause did not lesson his character in their esteem.

John Adams

the 6th of May, 1776, he offered a resolution, in Congress, equivalent to a declaration of independence, and when that subject assumed a more definite form, soon afterward, he was one of the ablest advocates of the measure. His signature was affixed to the great instrument which declared the colonies "free and independent States." Mr. Adams labored on assiduously in Congress,[1] until appointed, by that body, to fill the place of Silas Deane at the French court. Franklin had done all the necessary diplomatic work, and Mr. Adams returned in 1779. He then assisted in framing a state constitution for Massachusetts, and while thus employed, was appointed a minister plenipotentiary to negotiate a peace, and form a commercial treaty, with Great Britain. He was very active while abroad, and at one time was intrusted with no less than six missions.[2] In 1781, he was associated with Franklin, Jay, and Laurens, in various negotiations, and was the first of the American commissioners who signed the definitive treaty of peace, with Great Britain, in 1783. He was the first United States minister to the British court, and did not return home until 1788. He was elected the first vice-president of the United States, under the Federal

---

1. In the course of the eighteen months preceding his departure for Europe, Mr. Adams had been on ninety different committees, and was chairman of *twenty-five* of them.
2. To treat for peace with Great Britain; to make a commercial treaty with Great Britain; to negotiate the same with the States General of Holland; the same with the Prince of Orange; to pledge the faith of the United States to the Armed Neutrality; and to negotiate a loan of ten millions of dollars.

Constitution, in 1789, and in 1796, he was elevated to the presidential chair. At the close of his term, in 1801, he retired from public life, but lived to see his son occupy the chair of chief magistrate, twenty-four years afterward. In 1824, he was chosen president of the Massachusetts convention for revising the state constitution, which he assisted in forming forty-five years before, but he declined the honor. His powers of life were then failing; and on the 4th of July, 1826, he expired, with the words "Independence forever!" upon his lips, in the ninety-second year of his age.[1]

WILLIAM RICHARDSON DAVIE.

WHEN the first thunder-peal of the Revolution rolled over the South, hundreds of her gallant sons seized their arms, and rushed to the field; and many, who were living in obscurity, then burst the chrysalis of comparative insignificance and became honored leaders of the popular mind. Among these was William Richardson Davie. He was born at Egremont, near White Haven, England, on the 20th of June, 1756. His father brought him to America when he was a small child, and on his return, left him with his maternal uncle, Rev. William Richardson, of South Carolina. At a proper age, he was placed under the care of Dr. Witherspoon, of the College of New Jersey, at Princeton, where he was graduated in 1776, a few weeks before Washington and his broken army passed through there, in their flight toward the Delaware.

Young Davie returned to North Carolina, full of patriotic fire, and resolved on becoming a soldier. He could not then obtain a commission, so he went to Salisbury and studied law, supposing the war would not continue many months. But as the clouds thickened, young Davie became restive, and he induced a popular friend to raise a troop of dragoons, of which the fledgling hero was made lieutenant. They marched toward Charleston, and the command devolving on Lieutenant Davie, he procured the attachment of his corps to the legion of Count Pulaski. In that capacity he fought at Stono Ferry, in June, 1779, where he was so badly wounded that he was confined for five months in a hospital.

In 1780, Davie was placed at the head of a legionary corps, with a commission of major from the governor of North Carolina. He spent the last shilling of a bequest made by his lately-deceased uncle and guardian, in equipping this corps, and then went to the field to oppose the progress of the British troops toward the interior of the Carolinas. He nobly aided Sumter in his operations in the vicinity of the Catawba, early in August, and was hastening to join the army of Gates, when it was defeated and dispersed near Camden. He was afterward with Rutherford at Ramsour's Mills, and nobly confronted the enemy at Charlotte, after a brilliant display of courage and skill at Wahab's Plantation. For his services during that campaign, he was rewarded with the commission of colonel commandant of the cavalry of North Carolina.

When Greene took command of the southern army, he appointed Colonel Davie his commissary-general. In all the important operations which followed, Davie was exceedingly efficient; and at the trying hour at Ninety-Six, in the Summer of 1781, Greene sent Colonel Davie to present the condition of his army to the legislature of North Carolina. He performed the service well; and prospects

---

1. Mr. Adams and Mr. Jefferson both expired on the same day, and at almost the same hour. They were both on the committee that framed the Declaration of Independence; both voted for that instrument just fifty years before; both signed it; both had been foreign ministers; and both had been President of the Republic they had helped to establish. The coincidence of their deaths was therefore quite remarkable.

of peace appearing in the Autumn, he left the army, married a daughter of General Allen Jones, in 1783, and in the town of Halifax, on the Roanoke, commenced the practice of law. In that pursuit he soon became eminent, and was chosen a delegate to the convention which framed the Federal Constitution. In 1797, he was commissioned a major-general of militia, and the next year, he was appointed a brigadier in the army of the United States. In 1798, he was elected governor of the State of North Carolina, and was soon afterward appointed, by President Adams, an associate envoy extraordinary to France, with Ellsworth and Murray. After his return, he went to reside at Tivoli, a beautiful estate on the Catawba river, in South Carolina. His wife died in 1803, and he remained in retirement until his death, which occurred at Tivoli, in December, 1820, when he was in the sixty-fourth year of his age. General Davie was one of the founders of the North Carolina University, at Chapel Hill. He was chiefly instrumental in procuring the erection of the buildings for that institution; and, as grand master of the masonic fraternity, he laid the corner-stone.

ROBERT MORRIS.

IT is an often demonstrated truth, that "money is the sinew of war." It was eminently so during the revolutionary struggle, when its strength and usefulness in the cause of freedom, were controlled by Robert Morris, a wealthy and influential merchant of Philadelphia. He was born in Lancashire, England, in January, 1733. His father was a Liverpool merchant extensively engaged in the American trade, who came to America in 1744, and settled on the eastern shore of Chesapeake Bay. His son, Robert, with his grandmother, followed in 1746, and was placed in a school in Philadelphia, where an inefficient teacher wasted his time and patience.[1] In 1749, young Morris was placed in the counting-room of Charles Willing, of Philadelphia; and on the death of his employer, in 1754, he entered into a partnership with that gentleman's son, which continued thirty-nine years. That firm soon became the most wealthy and extensive among the importers of Philadelphia, and consequently they were the heaviest losers by the non-importation agreements,[2] which gave such a deadly blow at the infant commerce of the colonies, after the passage of the Stamp Act. Yet they patriotically joined the league, and made the sacrifice for the good of the cause of right.

In November, 1775, Mr. Morris was elected to a seat in the Continental Congress,[3] where his exceeding great usefulness was soon discovered. Its appreciation was manifested by placing him upon committees, having in charge the "ways and means" for carrying on the war. In the Spring of 1776, he was chosen, by Congress, a special commissioner to negotiate bills of exchange, and to take other measures to procure money for government. At that time, no man's credit, in America, for wealth and honor, stood higher than that of Robert Morris. He was again elected to Congress after the Declaration of Independence

---

1. On one occasion Robert's father censured him for his tardiness in learning. His reply and excuse were, "Why, sir, I have learned all that the master could teach me."
2. One of the measures adopted by the colonists to compel Great Britain to do them justice, was that of American merchants everywhere agreeing not to import any more goods from the mother country, until all obnoxious acts should be repealed. These leagues, recommended by the Continental Congress in 1774, and generally subscribed to, had a powerful effect on Parliament, for in the Lower House (Commons) the mercantile interest had a potential representation.
3. When the news of the battle of Lexington reached Philadelphia, Mr. Morris and some friends, members of the St. George's Society, were celebrating their anniversary. There the subject was discussed, and Morris and a few others, by solemn vow, dedicated themselves to the cause of the Revolution.

had been adopted, and being favorable to that measure, he signed the document, with most of the others, on the second day of August following. Toward the close of that year, when the half-naked, half-famished American army were about to cease the struggle, in despair, he evinced his faith in the success of the conflict, and his own warm patriotism, by loaning for the government, on his own responsibility, ten thousand dollars.[1] It gave food and clothing to the gallant little band under Washington, who achieved the noble victory at Trenton, and a new and powerful impetus was thereby given to the Revolution.

Mr. Morris was continually active in the great cause during the whole of the war. He fitted out many privateers. Some were lost, others were successful in bringing him rich prizes; and at the return of peace he estimated that his losses and gains were about equal. In May, 1781 about the gloomiest period of the struggle, Mr. Morris submitted to Congress a plan for a National Bank. It was approved, and the Bank of North America, with Robert Morris as its soul, was established, and became a very efficient fiscal agent. He was assisted by Gouverneur Morris; and through the active agency, in financial matters, of these gentlemen, much of the success which resulted in the capture of Cornwallis,

---

1. "I want money," said Morris to a Quaker friend, "for the use of the army." "What security canst thou give?" asked the lender. "My note and my honor," responded Morris. "Robert, thou shalt have it," was the prompt reply.

at Yorktown, must be attributed.[1] During that year Mr. Morris accepted the office of Financial Agent (Secretary of the Treasury) of the United States. After the war, he was twice a member of the Pennsylvania Legislature, and he was one of the framers of the Federal Constitution. He was a senator in the first Congress convened under that instrument; and Washington appointed him his first Secretary of the Treasury. He declined the office, and named Alexander Hamilton as more capable, than himself, to perform the duties. At the close of his senatorial term, Mr. Morris retired from public life, not so rich in money, by half, as when he entered the arena. Soon the remainder of his large fortune was lost by speculations in wild land, in the western part of the State of New York, afterward purchased by an association known as *The Holland Land Company*. On the 8th of May, 1806, Robert Morris, the great Financier of the Revolution, died in comparative poverty, at the age of a little more than seventy-three years.

FRANCIS DANA.

MASSACHUSETTS is pre-eminent among the States in the production of distinguished men. Prominent among those of whom she may be justly proud, is the name of Francis Dana, who was born at Charlestown, near Boston, in August, 1742. He was educated at Harvard University, and chose the law as his profession. In the midst of the confusion and distress incident to the closing of the port of Boston, by parliamentary decree, in 1774,[2] Mr. Dana went to England, and passed a year with his brother, a clergyman, at Wroxeter. He returned to America at the close of 1775, took an active part, as a patriot, in the exciting political proceedings of the time, and in the Autumn of 1776, was elected a delegate to the Continental Congress. In that important station he remained until November, 1779, when he accompanied John Adams to Paris, as Secretary of Legation.

Toward the close of 1780, Congress appointed Mr. Dana minister plenipotentiary at the court of Russia. The Empress Catherine would not openly receive him, for fear of offending England, but he was allowed to remain in St. Petersburg until the close of the war, when he returned home, and was immediately chosen a delegate to the Congress of 1784. Mr. Dana was an efficient advocate of the Federal Constitution, in the Massachusetts convention, and exerted great influence in the political affairs of his State. President Adams appreciated his worth, and offered him the office of envoy extraordinary to France, with Messrs. Marshall and Pinckney, in 1797. He declined the honor, and Elbridge Gerry, one of the signers of the Declaration of Independence, accepted it. Mr. Dana had then held the important office of chief justice of Massachusetts, for five years, to which he had been appointed by President Washington. He retained his seat on the bench until 1806, when he retired to private life, but not to a life of inaction. He was a thorough Federalist; and during the exciting political period, from the election of Jefferson in 1800, until his death, his pen was often busy. Judge Dana died at his residence in Cambridge, near Boston, on the 25th of April, 1811, at the age of sixty-eight years.

---

1. The Bank of North America did not go into operation until December, 1781. Yet Morris, on his own personal responsibility, was acting as efficiently as the bank could then have done, in providing funds for the American army under Washington, in making its successful expedition into Virginia.

2. In consequence of the destruction of two cargoes of tea in Boston Harbor, in December, 1773, and other rebellious movements, the British parliament ordered the port of that city to be closed, and all its public offices to be removed. This blow at the business of that thriving town, was a retaliatory measure, and produced great irritation throughout the colonies.

JOHN FITCH.

THE records of human inventions are full of instances of originators being deprived of the honors and emoluments due to them. John Fitch, an early applicant of steam power to the propulsion of boats, is a remarkable instance of that kind. . He was born between Hartford and Windsor,[1] in Connecticut, on the 21st of January, 1743. At the age of eight years, he was taken from school, and put to labor on a farm; after which he had but one month in each year to devote to study under instruction. But most of the leisure moments of childhood were employed with his books; and at the age of eleven years, he planted and raised some potatoes, for the express purpose of purchasing a complete Geography. His health was naturally feeble, and he appears to have been overworked on the farm. He ran away from home, and was afterward apprenticed to a clock-maker. He learned the business imperfectly, and abandoned it at his majority, for that of a brass-founder. He married a young lady, in 1767, but incompatibility of temper and views caused them to separate at the end of two years. They had two children, but a reconciliation never took place, and the cloud always deeply shadowed his path of life.

Mr. Fitch was a silversmith in Trenton, New Jersey, when the British army entered it, and destroyed his shop and contents, in the Winter of 1776, because he was engaged in repairing American arms. He joined the army, and was with Washington at Valley Forge. There he heard some officers speak of the fertility of Kentucky. He procured the appointment of deputy surveyor, and in the Spring of 1780, set out on foot, for that untraversed wilderness beyond the Alleghanies. He returned to Philadelphia the following year, the owner of sixteen hundred acres of fine land in the Ohio Valley, and filled with dreams of future opulence. Again he started for the great West, and while descending the Ohio, with some others, in the Spring of 1782, he was made a prisoner by the Indians, where Marietta now stands. He was redeemed from captivity, at Detroit, by a British officer, went to Canada, and returning to Pennsylvania, he constructed a map of the Western Country. He now conceived the idea of "gaining a force by steam;" and in August, 1785, he presented the subject to the Continental Congress, and asked for aid to try experiments in applying the power to the propulsion of vessels, by means of wheels or paddles. At about this time, Mr. Rumsey, of Virginia, had conceived a similar idea, and Mr. Fitch, disappointed and exasperated by what he deemed the stupidity of Congress, went from State to State, in search of aid, but without success. He engaged in a bitter controversy with Rumsey, in relation to priority of invention; and in the meanwhile, new claimants appeared. Yet all seemed to have distinct plans, with identical aim—the moving of a boat by means of steam-power. Fitch and Rumsey procured protective statutes from different State legislatures. The former organized a stock company, to carry out his designs, in 1786, but little was effected by it. The State of Pennsylvania refused to lend him one hundred and fifty pounds, to procure an engine from England. With another mechanic, he succeeded in constructing an engine and boat; and on the 1st of May, 1789, the *first steamboat* was seen moving upon the waters of the Delaware. The boat went at the rate of eight miles an hour, and yet there was not confidence enough in the project, to sustain the persevering inventor. To him success was as "clear as any problem in Euclid;" and in a letter to Franklin, he expressed his full belief that "*steamboats would answer for sea voyages, as well as inland naviga-*

---

1. The house in which he was born stood upon the dividing line of those towns, and it is said that his birth occurred in the Windsor portion of the dwelling.

tion." Despairing of gaining funds to perfect his invention, in America, Fitch went to France and England, in 1792; but, disappointed and almost penniless, he returned home, and retired to Kentucky. He found a good deal of his land occupied; and in 1797, he commenced ejectment suits. Soon after this his mind and body began to give way under the pressure of long-continued excitements, and, though temperate through life, he determined to shorten his days by the excessive use of spirituous liquors. He foretold the time of his death by a mathematical calculation, and on the 2d of July, 1798, he died at Bardstown, Kentucky, and was buried there. Had his countrymen appreciated his inventions, and sustained his efforts, the glory awarded to Fulton would doubtless have been due to John Fitch, full twenty years earlier than the success of the former established his own fame.

JOHN ALEXANDER LILLINGTON.

THE Cape Fear region of North Carolina abounded with true Republicans, when the party lines between Whigs and Tories were distinctly drawn, just before the war of the Revolution was lighted up. John A. Lillington was one of the truest stamp. He was the son of a British military officer, who was a member of the royal council of Barbadoes, in 1698. His son John, captivated by the glowing accounts given of North Carolina, emigrated thither, and settled within the present limits of New Hanover county; and in 1734, built a fine mansion there, which he called *Lillington Hall*. It stands on the north branch of the Cape Fear river, about thirty miles from Wilmington. The proprietor inherited the military tastes of his father; and when the notes of preparation for the Revolution were heard all over the land, his skill was brought into requisition. He was also a member of the Wilmington committee of safety in 1775; and when the Scotch Highlanders and others in the vicinity of Cross Creek (Fayetteville), took up arms for the king, under Donald McDonald, in the Winter of 1776, Colonel Lillington commanded one of the provincial corps which marched against, and defeated them, at Moore's Creek, under the general command of Colonel Caswell. It was the initial battle of the Revolution in the South, and the victory was hailed with delight. Colonel Lillington was made a brigadier; and from that time, until the approach of Gates, in 1780, he was active in the council and field. Both he and his son joined the army of Gates, and participated in the disgrace of defeat at Camden.

General Lillington remained in service until the close of the war, when he withdrew from public life, and sought repose in the bosom of his family at *Lillington Hall*. There appears to be no record of the birth or death of General Lillington. The slab over his grave, near his mansion, has an appropriate inscription, but it bears no date, except that of his battle at Moore's Creek. It tells us, however, that "To intellectual powers of a high order, he united incorruptible integrity, devoted and self-sacrificing patriotism." Tradition avers, that he possessed a frame of Herculean proportions and strength, and that, in his generous kindness to all around him, must we find the reason of the salvation of *Lillington Hall* from the flames, when all others in the neighborhood were desolated. The *Tories* loved him for his goodness of heart; the *Whigs* revered him for his stern patriotism.

JOHN PAUL JONES.

SOMEWHERE, in the great city of Paris, rest the remains of one of the bravest naval commanders known in history, but, like the sepulchre of General Greene, its identity is lost to this generation, and the reproach of that oblivion rests upon the government of the United States. John Paul Jones is *the* naval hero of the elder war for American independence; and, like many of the patriots of that struggle, whom we delight to honor, he was born beyond the Atlantic. His birth occurred on the 6th of July, 1747, at Arbigland, on the Frith of Solway, Scotland. At the age of twelve years he was apprenticed to a ship-master in the Virginia trade. In 1766, he became mate of a Jamaica "slaver" (as vessels engaged in the importation of negroes, from Africa, were called), and two years afterward, while on his way to Scotland, in another vessel, he became master by the death of the two chief officers. In that position he was retained, though only twenty-one years of age. On the death of his mother, in 1773, he settled in Virginia.[1] When the Revolution broke out, he offered his services to

---

[1]. He went there to take charge of some property belonging to a deceased brother. His original name was John Paul, but, for reasons not known, he added the name of Jones, after settling in Virginia.

Congress, and received the commission of a lieutenant in the navy, near the close of 1775. He soon afterward became commander of a vessel, with which he took sixteen prizes. In 1777, he was ordered to Paris, to arrange some naval operations with the American commissioners there; and in the Spring of 1778, he was spreading universal alarm along the coasts of Scotland, by his bold exploits. At Whitehaven, he captured two forts with thirty cannon; and at another time, almost succeeded in making the Earl of Selkirk, at Kirkcudbright, a prisoner. After a very successful cruise in the British waters, he returned to Brest, with two hundred prisoners of war and much booty. At the close of the Summer of 1779, he made another cruise, with a little squadron, his flag-ship being the *Bonhomme Richard;* and on the evening of the 23d of September, he had an engagement with the *Serapis* and *Countess of Scarborough,* two strong English vessels that were convoying the Baltic merchant fleet. He had already captured thirteen vessels during the cruise, and boldly attacked these. It was one of the most desperate sea-fights that ever occurred. At one time the *Richard* and *Serapis* were side by side, lashed together, and thus poured broadsides into each other, while with pike, cutlass, and pistol, the combatants fought hand to hand upon both vessels. After a conflict of two hours, the British vessel surrendered; but Jones' flag-ship was so shattered, that, sixteen hours after the victory, it went beneath the deep waters of Bridlington Bay. This victory gave Jones great *eclat,* both in America and Europe. King Louis of France presented him with an elegant gold-mounted sword, with appropriate emblems and motto upon its blade; and Congress then voted special thanks to the victor, and had a gold medal struck in his honor, and presented to him, eight years afterward. Captain Jones returned to Philadelphia, in 1781; and when peace was established, he went to Europe as agent for the recovery of prize money. He returned to America in 1787, and the following year he was solicited to join the Russian navy, with the commission of rear-admiral. He served against the Turks, in the Black Sea, for awhile, but disliking the position, he retired to Paris, on a pension from the Empress Catharine, in 1789. There he resided most of the time, until his death, which occurred on the 18th of July, 1792, a few days before the arrival of a commission for him, from President Washington, to treat with Algiers. Though the minute circumstances of his death have been related, and the French National Assembly noticed it by an eulogistic resolution —though it is said that his body was placed in a leaden coffin to be conveyed to the United States, if asked for, yet "the place of his sepulchre is not known unto this day."

RICHARD CASWELL.

THE first victory of republican troops in North Carolina, was won by those under the command of a lawyer in the prime of life; and the first incumbent of the chair of chief magistrate of that State, after it became a sovereign commonwealth by the act of the people, was that same lawyer, Richard Caswell. He was a native of Maryland, where he was born on the 3d of August, 1729. In 1746, he went to North Carolina, where, through influential letters of introduction, he found employment in one of the public offices. He became deputy-surveyor of the colony; and in 1753, was made clerk of the county court of Orange. He studied law with William Heritage (his second father-in-law), obtained a license, and practiced with great success. He was chosen a member of the Colonial Assembly from Johnston county, in 1754, and continued to represent that district until 1771. During the last two years of his legislative duties in the Colonial Assembly, he was Speaker, and at the same time he held the office of colonel of the militia of his county. In that capacity he commanded the right wing of Governor Tryon's forces at the battle of the Allamance, his regard for law and order causing him to condemn the rebellious movements of the Regulators.[1] He was one of the delegates of North Carolina, in the Continental Congress, in 1774, and was re-elected the following year; but being chosen treasurer of the southern district of his State, he resigned his seat in the Autumn, and returned home.

In February, 1776, Colonel Caswell was the commander of the provincial forces who defeated the Scotch Loyalists in a battle upon Moore's Creek, in New Hanover county, North Carolina; and in April following, the Provincial Congress gave him the commission of a brigadier, for the district of Newbern. He was chosen president of the Provincial Council, which framed a constitution for the State, in the Autumn of 1776, and was elected the first governor under that instrument. During the stormy period of the three succeeding years, he held that office, performed his duty with rare faithfulness and ability, and refused compensation for his services. He led the troops of North Carolina, under Gates, in 1780, and was a participant in the disastrous defeat of the Americans at Camden. From 1782 to 1784, he was Speaker of the State Senate, and controller-general. Then he was again elected governor of the State. He filled that office until 1786, when he became ineligible, according to the provisions of the constitution. The following year, he was chosen a delegate to the convention which formed the Federal Constitution in the city of Philadelphia; and when the General Assembly of his State met, he was chosen Speaker of the Senate. But his course on earth was nearly finished. Domestic bereavements had clouded his life with melancholy; and while presiding in the Senate, on the 5th of November, 1787, he was prostrated by paralysis. He lingered in almost insensibility, until the tenth, when he expired, in the sixtieth year of his age.

JOHN LOVELL.

"THE Master" of many of the leading men of the War for Independence, in New England, was John Lovell, a descendant of one of the first settlers in the Massachusetts colony. He was born in 1708, and was graduated at Harvard College, at the age of twenty years. He succeeded Jeremiah Gridley as assistant in the South Grammar School of Boston, and in 1738, was placed at its head, where he exercised pedagogue authority for almost forty years. He wrote several political and theological pamphlets; and in 1743, he delivered a funeral oration, on the death of Peter Faneuil, the founder of Faneuil Hall, which was published. Unlike a great proportion of his earlier pupils, Master Lovell was a Loyalist, and left Boston, with other refugees, when the British were driven from that city in March, 1776. He died in Halifax, Nova Scotia, in 1778, at the age of seventy years.

---

1. The people of the interior of North Carolina, were chiefly of Scotch-Irish descent, and thoroughly imbued with independence of spirit. They warmly sympathized with their brethren of the sea-board in opposing the Stamp Act; and in 1771, an association of the principal inhabitants of Orange and adjacent counties, was formed to resist the growing rapacity of office holders, and regulate the political affairs of their section. They called themselves *Regulators*. Tryon, then governor of the colony, led an armed force against them, and in May, 1771, they had a bloody skirmish on the Allamance Creek. The *Regulators* were overpowered, and six of the prisoners then captured, were hung at Hillsborough. There, really, the *first blood* of the Revolution was shed.

ISAAC SHELBY.

IF being a hero in two wars, with a long interval of useful service in civil life, should command the reverence of posterity, surely Isaac Shelby, of Kentucky, may worthily make claim to such reverential regard. He was born a few miles from Hagerstown, Maryland, on the 11th of December, 1750, and inherited from his Welsh ancestors that courage and perseverance for which he was so distinguished. He became a professional surveyor; and, at the age of twenty-one years, he settled in Western Virginia. He was with his father, Evan Shelby, in the battle at Point Pleasant, in 1774, and was afterward employed by Henderson and others, as a surveyor, in Kentucky. In July, 1776, he was appointed to the command of a company of minute-men, by the Virginia committee of safety; and the following year, Governor Patrick Henry appointed him commissary of supplies. In 1778, he was attached to the Continental commissary department; and in the Spring of 1779, he was elected to a seat in the Virginia Legislature, from Washington county. Governor Jefferson gave him the commission of major, in the Autumn of that year, about which time he was engaged in defining the boundary line between Virginia and North Carolina, which placed his residence in the latter State. A new county of *Sullivan* was formed, and Governor Caswell appointed him colonel of that district. He took very little part in military affairs, until the Summer of 1780, when Charleston fell into the hands of the British, and the subjugation of the whole South seemed inevitable. Colonel Shelby was then locating lands for himself, in Kentucky. His country needed his services, and they were freely given. He hastened home, raised a corps of three hundred mounted riflemen, crossed the mountains, and joined Colonel McDowell, on the Broad River. He was very active in that vicinity; and with Colonels Campbell, Sevier, and other brave officers and soldiers, he fought the decisive and successful battle, with Major Ferguson, on King's Mountain, in October, 1780. He suggested to General Greene that expedition which resulted so brilliantly for Morgan, and his country, at the Cowpens. In the campaign of 1781, Shelby was under the command of Marion, for awhile; and the following year, he was elected to a seat in the North Carolina Legislature. He afterward made Kentucky his residence, and was one of the framers of its constitution, in 1792. He was elected the first governor of the new State, and after an interval of comparative repose, he was again the incumbent of that important office, in 1812. Another war with Great Britain was then impending. The fire of 1776 still warmed his bosom, and he called his countrymen to arms, when the proclamation of war went forth. Henry Clay presented him with a sword, voted by the legislature of North Carolina for his gallantry at King's Mountain, thirty-two years before, and with that weapon he marched at the head of four thousand Kentucky volunteers, toward the Canada frontier, in 1813, though the snows of threescore and three Summers were upon his head. He fought gallantly upon the Thames, in Canada; and for his valor there, Congress honored him with a gold medal. President Monroe appointed him Secretary of War, in 1817, but he declined the honor, for he coveted the repose which old age demands. His last public act was the holding of a treaty with the Chickasaw Indians, in 1818, with General Jackson for his colleague. His sands of life were now nearly exhausted. In February, 1820, he was prostrated by paralysis, yet he lived, somewhat disabled, until the 18th of July, 1826, when apoplexy terminated his life. He was then almost seventy-six years of age.

JOHN ASHE.

THE resistance to official oppression in some of the interior counties of North Carolina, in 1771, known as *the Regulator movement*, was not viewed, by many good men, as a legitimate part of the general opposition to government measures, then rampant throughout the colonies; and some who were the most earnest in denouncing the Stamp Act,[1] zealously assisted Governor Tryon, in his measures for suppressing these insurgents. Of these, John Ashe was conspicuous. He was born in England, in 1721, and at the age of six years, he accompanied his father to America, and grew to manhood near the banks of the Cape Fear river, in North Carolina. He was a representative in the Colonial Assembly for several years, and from 1762 to 1765, he was Speaker of that body. He

---

1. In order to raise a revenue from the American colonies, to replenish the exhausted treasury of England after the French and Indian War, the Parliament decreed that every "piece of paper, parchment, or vellum," on which any legal instrument was written, should bear the government stamp, to make it valid, for which certain prices were to be paid, according to the character of the instrument. The Americans justly regarded it as a scheme to tax them, indirectly, without their consent, and they resisted. The country was greatly excited, and the colonies were on the eve of rebellion, when the obnoxious act was repealed. It became a law in 1765, and was repealed in 1766.

warmly opposed the Stamp Act, and, with Hugh Waddell and others, he exercised his authority as colonel of the militia of his county, and led an armed force to Wilmington, to compel the stamp distributer[1] to resign. He commanded a part of the troops in Governor Tryon's expedition against the *Regulators*, in 1771. On one occasion, during that expedition, while he was out reconnoitring, he was caught by some of the insurgents, tied to a tree, and severely whipped. He afterward became convinced of the justice of the seemingly rebellious movement, and was one of the most zealous of the revolutionary patriots of the South. In the Colonial Assembly, he advocated republicanism; and as a member of the Provincial Congress, and of the committee of safety at Wilmington, he was exceedingly active. He first suggested a Provincial Congress; and at the head of five hundred men, he destroyed Fort Johnson, in 1775. For this he was denounced as an arch-rebel, but the republicans were more numerous than adherents of the crown, and he was unharmed. With eloquent words and energetic acts, he aroused the whole country around Wilmington, early in 1776; and he also raised and equipped a regiment. He was made a brigadier, and was active in his section until he joined Lincoln on the Savannah, in the Autumn of 1778, with regiments from Halifax, Wilmington, Newbern, and Edenton. With these he pursued the British down the right bank of the Savannah, from Augusta, early in 1779, but in a battle at Brier Creek, was defeated, with great loss. He then returned home; and when the British took possession of Wilmington, in 1781, General Ashe was made a prisoner, and his family suffered much. During his captivity he was attacked by the small-pox. While sick, he was released on parole, but died while accompanying his family to a place of quiet, in October, 1781, at the age of sixty years.

WILLIAM JOHNSON.

ONE of the "baronial halls" yet in existence in the United States, is that of Sir William Johnson, at Johnstown, a few miles north of the Mohawk river. Its first proprietor, William Johnson, was a native of Ireland, where he was born about the year 1714. He was a nephew of Sir Peter Warren, a distinguished naval commander in the British service. Sir Peter married Miss Watts, of New York, and purchased an extensive tract of land upon the Mohawk. When about twenty years of age, young Johnson came to America to look after his uncle's possessions in the wilderness. He learned the Indian language, and soon acquired a great influence, especially over the Mohawk tribes, within whose domains he resided. He built a large stone mansion on the Mohawk, near the present village of Amsterdam, called it Fort Johnson, and resided there twenty years before he built Johnson Hall, above alluded to. He was shrewd, cunning, and licentious. Many of the half-breed warriors of the Mohawks, who took sides against the Republicans in the War for Independence, were his children, for he had numerous Indian concubines, among whom was a sister of the famous Mohawk chief, Joseph Brant. He also had a white wife, the pretty daughter of a German emigrant, by whom he had a son and two daughters.[2]

---

1. Men were appointed in all the colonies to sell the stamps, or stamped paper. The office was so obnoxious to the people, that none were allowed to exercise it.
2. In those days, emigrants were often sold to service, by their own consent, to pay their passage-money to America. The girl alluded to had been purchased by a man named Phillips, in the Mohawk Valley. She attracted the attention of Johnson; the sequel was told to a neighbor by Phillips himself: "Johnson, that tammed Irishman, came todder day and offered me five pounds for her, threatening to

In 1755, Johnson was intrusted with the command of the provincial troops of New York, in an expedition against the French and Indians on Lake Champlain. He had a severe battle with them at the head of Lake George, in which he was early wounded, and the command devolved on General Lyman. The provincials were victorious, and Johnson received the honors of knighthood, and five thousand pounds sterling, because of the victory. He was also appointed superintendent of Indian affairs, with a handsome salary, and continued to hold his military commission. In 1759, he was again in the field; and his superior officer (Prideaux) being killed in an attack upon Fort Niagara, he became commander-in-chief, and was successful. Such was now his influence over the Indians, that when Lord Amherst was at Oswego, in 1760, preparing to proceed against Montreal, Sir William furnished him with a thousand Iroquois warriors. He died at Johnson Hall, on the 11th of July, 1774, at the age of about sixty years. He had commenced a powerful opposition to the republican movements in the Mohawk Valley, and the mantle of his influence fell upon his son, Sir John Johnson, who succeeded to his title, office, and estates

DAVID BRAINERD.

TO leave the endearments of home and the pleasures of civilized life, and spend the strength of manhood among pagans, with the sole aim of doing good to the needy, is true heroism—an exhibition of chivalry, worthy of the honors of knighthood. Prominent on the list of such self-sacrificing champions, is the name of David Brainerd, eminent as a missionary among the Indians of our land. He was born at East Haddam, Connecticut, on the 20th of April, 1718. In 1739, he entered Yale College, as a student; and in 1743, he was expelled from that institution, first, because he had disobeyed orders, in attending prohibited meetings of those who were attached to the preaching of Whitefield and Tennant, and secondly, because he indiscreetly questioned the piety of one of the tutors, and would not acknowledge his error. He then commenced theological studies, with a view of becoming a missionary, for he ardently desired to be a teacher of the poor Indians, in the knowledge of the gospel. At the age of twenty-five years he began his labors among the Stockbridge Indians, in the vicinity of Kinderhook, New York. He lived in a wigwam, slept on straw, and ate boiled corn, hasty-pudding, and samp. Though feeble in body, and often ill, he persevered; and when, in 1744, his "flock" agreed to go to Stockbridge, he went with his glad tidings to the Delaware Indians. He continued in the vicinity of Easton nearly a year, during which time he visited the tribes on the Susquehannah in the Wyoming Valley and vicinity. Then he returned, and took up his abode among the New Jersey Indians at Crosswicks, where he was remarkably successful. In less than a year, he baptized seventy-seven converts, and the whole tribe became thoroughly reformed in their morals. His health gradually gave way, and he was compelled to leave the field of duty, where his heart lingered. He went to Boston in July, 1747, and returning to Northampton, he took up his abode with Jonathan Edwards. In the family of that great and good man his flower of life faded, and when the leaves began to fall in Autumn, he fell, like an apple early ripe, into the lap of the grave. His spirit went from earth on the 9th of October, 1747, when he was only twenty-nine years of age.

horsewhip me and steal her, if I would not sell. I tot five pounds pether as a flogging, took it, and he's got the gal."

OLIVER ELLSWORTH.

NEVER was the harmony between private and public virtue more complete, than that exhibited in the character and career of one of the most beloved of New England patriots and jurists, Oliver Ellsworth. He was born at Windsor, the point of earliest settlement in Connecticut, on the 29th of April, 1745. His father was a respectable farmer, and with the strong common sense of his class, he prepared Oliver for the stern duties of life, by habits of labor, application, and frugality. His mental superiority was early discovered, and his father alternated the lad's daily life, between vigorous physical labors, and studies preparatory to a collegiate course of education. He entered Yale College at the age of seventeen years, but greater advantages appearing at Princeton, he completed his studies there, where he was graduated in 1766. His talents were not brilliant, and precocity did not show blossoms of promise as precursors of the fruit of disappointment. Slowly but strongly his intellect unfolded, while he labored with unceasing energy upon a rough farm, where his toil was sweetened by the sympathies of a charming wife, one of the Wolcott family. His evenings were devoted to the study of the law, and at the age of about twenty-five, he commenced its practice in the vicinity of Hartford. His ambition soared not to place and honor, and the farmer-lawyer, at that time, gave but little promise of being a chief justice of the United States. The electric spark of vitality to his latent greatness and loftier aspirations was communicated by a stranger, in court, whom Ellsworth heard remark, and inquire, after one of his forensic efforts, "Who is that young man? He speaks well." Young Ellsworth pondered these words, and bright visions of fame broke upon his mind.

Increase of legal business induced Ellsworth to make Hartford his residence, and there he received the appointment of State's Attorney. As the quarrel with Great Britain progressed, he was always found on the side of the people. He even went to the field with the militia of his State, when the war broke out. In 1777, he was chosen a delegate to the Continental Congress, and in 1780, took a seat in the council of his native State. He continued a member of that body until 1784, when he was appointed a judge of the superior court of Connecticut. Judge Ellsworth was a warm friend of the Federal Constitution, did much toward effecting its ratification, in his State, and in 1789, was elected the first representative of Connecticut in the Senate of the United States. There he became greatly distinguished for his legislative qualities, stern integrity, and faithful devotion to the public interest. For seven years he served his country nobly in the national councils. In the Spring of 1796, he was appointed chief justice of the United States. He was now in the full prime of life, and his mind in its utmost vigor. He bore the ermine with majesty, and cast it off in unsullied purity when, toward the close of 1799, President Adams appointed him, with Davie and Murray, an ambassador to the French court, at the head of which was the youthful Bonaparte. After negotiating a treaty for which they were sent, Judge Ellsworth visited other parts of the Continent, and England. While lingering in Great Britain for the benefit of the health of himself and an invalid son, he resigned the office of chief justice. He returned home early in 1801, and was immediately elected to the council of his State. His health was now becoming impaired by a distressing internal disease; and when, in May, 1807, he was appointed chief justice of Connecticut, he declined the office, for he was conscious that his death was near. Six months afterward, his prophecy was fulfilled. He died on the 26th of November, 1807, at the age of sixty-two years.

BENJAMIN HARRISON.

"WE are about to take a very dangerous step, but we confide in you, and are ready to support you in every measure you shall think proper to adopt," were the significant words of the constituents of Benjamin Harrison, as he was about to proceed to take his seat in the Continental Congress, at Philadelphia, in 1774, as a delegate from Virginia. They were the words of men who knew their servant well, and allowed no shadow of distrust to cloud their hopes. He was a patriot of the truest stamp. The exact time of his birth is not certainly known. It occurred at Berkeley, the seat of his father, on the James River, a few miles above the residence of Colonel Byrd, at Westover. He was educated at the college of William and Mary, at Williamsburg, but on account of the sudden death of his father,[1] and some difficulty with one of the professors, he was not graduated, and never took his degree. In 1764, young Harrison was elected a member of the Virginia House of Burgesses, where he soon became an influential leader. He was chosen Speaker of that body, and when the Stamp Act excitement shook royal power in Virginia, the governor tried to win him to the support of government, by offering him a seat in his council. Harrison re-

---

1. The venerable man and two of his four daughters were killed by lightning, in his house, at Berkeley, during a terrible thunder-storm.

jected the offer, boldly avowed his republican principles, and from that time became identified with the revolutionary party in Virginia. He was one of the representatives of Virginia in the first Continental Congress, when his relative, Peyton Randolph, was chosen its president. In the Autumn of 1775, he was one of a committee of Congress who visited the American army at Cambridge, to devise plans for the future, with Washington; and the following year he warmly supported, and affixed his signature to, the Declaration of Independence. He was a member of the *Foreign Committee* until its dissolution in 1777, and at that time he returned to Virginia, and took his seat in the House of Burgesses. He was chosen speaker, and held that station until 1782, when he was elected governor of Virginia. As military lieutenant of his county, he was very active in endeavors to capture Arnold, the traitor, and with Nelson, kept the militia disciplined and vigilant, until the great victory at Yorktown. Mr. Harrison served as governor, two terms, and then retired to private life. He was again brought into the public service by being chosen governor, in 1791. On the day after the election, he invited a party of friends to dine with him. He had recently recovered from a severe attack of gout in the stomach; indulgence on that occasion invited its return, and the day following was his last on earth. He died in April, 1791. William Henry Harrison, the ninth President of the United States, was his son.

JEREMY BELKNAP.

AMONG the writers of New England, Jeremy Belknap, D.D., holds a high rank. He was a descendant of one of the early inhabitants of Boston, and was born in that city on the 4th of June, 1744. He was prepared for college in the grammar school of the celebrated John Lovell, and was graduated at Harvard, in 1762. While a lad, he was remarkable for the beauty and chasteness of his compositions, and his friends saw in him the germ of an elegant writer. He was equally fluent and correct in his conversation; and the profession of a gospel minister being consonant with his seriousness of thought, he applied himself to the study of theology. In 1767, he was ordained pastor of the church at Dover, New Hampshire, where he passed twenty years of his ministerial life, in the enjoyment of the cordial esteem of men of every class. He wrote considerable in favor of the colonies, before the war, but took very little part in public affairs during the Revolution. Toward the close of his labors in Dover, he wrote a history of New Hampshire, in two large volumes, which gained him great reputation as an accurate chronicler. In 1787, Dr. Belknap was called to the pastoral charge of a congregational church in Boston, and there he spent the remainder of his years, a faithful minister and an assiduous student. The fields of literature had great charms for him, and in pursuit of the pleasures to be found therein, he spent much time. The last literary labor of his life was an American Biography, in which he exhibited much patient research and careful analysis. He did not live to complete it, for, in June, 1798, he was suddenly prostrated by paralysis of the whole system, and died on the 20th of that month, at the age of fifty-four years. He experienced the "privilege" for which he aspired, as expressed in the following lines, found among his papers:

> "When faith and patience, hope and love,
> Have made us meet for heaven above,
> How blest the privilege to rise,
> Snatched, in a moment, to the skies!
> Unconscious to resign our breath,
> Nor taste the bitterness of death."

ROBERT R. LIVINGSTON.

VERY few of the American settlers were descendants of aristocratic families, except the cavaliers of Virginia, and as a general rule, they were staunch republicans when the great political question of right and power was to be decided between the colonists and Great Britain. Robert Livingston, the first of the name who emigrated to America, was a lineal descendant of the Earl of Livingstone,[1] of Scotland. From him descended the family of that name so numerous at the period of the Revolution, and since, and who were all remarkable for their unflinching patriotism during the great struggle. Robert R. Livingston was a great grandson of the first "lord of the manor."[2] To the careful research and accurate pen of John W. Francis, M.D., we are indebted for a record of the chief events of his life. He was born in the city of New York, in 1747, and was educated at King's (now Columbia) College, where he was graduated in 1764. He studied law under the guidance of William Smith, chief justice of New York, and became an eminent practitioner of that profession.

---

1. He was hereditary governor of Linlithgow Castle, in which Mary, Queen of Scots, was born, and his daughter was one of the four ladies who accompanied that unfortunate Queen to France.
2. The Manor of Livingston, in Columbia county, New York. It was one of those manorial estates, established under the *patroon* privileges of the Dutch rule in that province. See note 1, page 260.

His zeal for popular liberty was thoroughly awakened during the excitement incident to the Stamp Act, and he was an early participant in those movements which resulted in revolution. The brave General Montgomery, who fell at Quebec, had married his sister, and that event intensified his devotion to the republican cause. In 1776, he was elected a member of the Continental Congress, at the same time holding the office of delegate in the Provincial Congress of New York. He was appointed one of the committee to draft a Declaration of Independence, but, being called to duties at home, before the final vote was taken, his name does not appear upon that instrument.

Mr. Livingston was made Secretary of Foreign Affairs (Secretary of State) when the new organization of government, under the Articles of Confederation, was completed; and performed the duties of that station with rare ability, until 1783, when he was appointed Chancellor of the State of New York. He was a warm supporter of the Federal Constitution, in the New York convention held at Poughkeepsie in 1788, to consider it; and on the 30th of April, the following year, he administered the oath of office to Washington, the first President of the United States. In 1801, Mr. Jefferson appointed him resident minister at the court of Napoleon, and he successfully negotiated the purchase of Louisiana, from the French, for fifteen millions of dollars. By his enlightened patronage of Robert Fulton, in his experiments in steam navigation, he conferred a lasting benefit on mankind, and his name will always be honorably associated with that inventor, and the wonderful results of those experiments. Chancellor Livingston died at his seat, at Clermont, in Columbia county, on the 26th of February, 1813, in the sixty-sixth years of his age. "His person," says Dr. Francis, who knew him intimately, "was tall and commanding, and of patrician dignity. Gentle and courteous in his manners, pure and upright in his morals, his benefactions to the poor were numerous and unostentatious. In his life, he was without reproach—in death, victorious over its terrors."

WILLIAM ALEXANDER.

ONLY one, of all the American officers of the Revolution, bore a title of nobility by descent of patent, and his was disputed and denied. That officer was William Alexander, who claimed the title of Earl of Stirling. He was the son of James Alexander, of Scotland, who took refuge in America, in 1716, after a warm participation in the cause of the son of James the Second, "pretender" to the rightful heirship of the throne of England. William was born in the city of New York, in 1726. His mother was the widow of David Provoost, a bold smuggler in the early part of the last century, and well known by the name of "Ready Money Provoost." Young Alexander joined the army in the French and Indian war, and was secretary to General Shirley. He accompanied that officer to England, in 1755, and there made the acquaintance of some of the leading men of the realm. By their advice, he instituted proceedings to obtain the title of Earl of Stirling, to which his father was heir-presumptive when he left Scotland. Although he did not obtain a legal recognition of the title, his right to it was generally conceded, and from that time he was addressed as Earl of Stirling. He returned to America in 1761, married the daughter of Philip Livingston (sister of Governor Livingston, of New Jersey), and built a fine mansion, on his estate, at Baskenridge. He was a member of the New Jersey Provincial Council for a number of years; and when the choice between republicanism and royalty had to be made, he was found on the side of the people.

In 1775, the Provincial Convention of New Jersey appointed him colonel of the first regiment of militia, and in March, 1776, Congress gave him the commission of a brigadier. General Lee left him in command at New York in April, and in August, he fought valiantly in the battle near Brooklyn, and was made prisoner. He was exchanged; and in February following, Congress made him a major-general. He performed active and varied services until the Summer of 1781, when he was ordered to the command of the northern army, with his head-quarters at Albany. An invasion from Canada was then expected. Indeed it was commenced under St. Leger, but the vigorous preparations of Stirling intimidated him, and the scheme was abandoned. Late in the Autumn, he took command in New Jersey, and had jurisdiction and general supervision of military affairs, in that State and in New York, to Fishkill above the Hudson Highlands. Lord Stirling was again in command at Albany, in 1782, where he died, on the 15th of January, 1783, in the fifty-seventh year of his age. It is a singular fact, that during the War for Independence, Lord Stirling had command, at different times, of every brigade of the American army, except those of South Carolina and Georgia.

TIMOTHY DWIGHT.

TWENTY days after the Declaration of Independence was adopted by the Continental Congress, a young man, twenty four years of age, addressed the students of Yale College on the subject of the future of the States then just declared "free and independent," in language truly prophetic.[1] That young prophet was Timothy Dwight, a grandson of the celebrated Jonathan Edwards, and many years the honored president of that ancient institution of learning. He was born at Northampton, Massachusetts, on the 14th of May, 1752. He was educated at Yale College, where he was graduated in 1769. From that period, until 1771, he taught a grammar school, in New Haven, and at the same time he devoted eight hours each day to severe study. At the age of nineteen years he was chosen a tutor in Yale College, and performed the duties of his station with great satisfaction for six years. It was while he was engaged in that vocation that he delivered the address above alluded to. He took his second degree in 1772, and, on that occasion, he delivered a learned dissertation on the history, eloquence, and poetry of the Bible. At about that time he commenced his sacred epic, *The Conquest of Canaan*, and finished it at the age of twenty-two years. Severe application and want of bodily exercise now seriously affected his health, but it was speedily restored by a change of habits, and sickness was a stranger to him during the next forty years.[2]

Mr. Dwight married in the Spring of 1777; and in June following, he was licensed to preach the gospel. In September, he withdrew from the college, was appointed chaplain to General Parson's brigade, and joined the Continental

---

1. After speaking of the establishment of a republican government, having for its basis the virtue and intelligence of the people, he referred to the necessary influence which such a government would have on the general advancement of mankind. He spoke of the yet undeveloped resources of the soil and mines, the organization of new States, the vast increase of population; and then referred to the condition of that portion of the Continent under Spanish rule, from which during the last twenty years, we have received such vast accessions of territory. After speaking of the vices and degradation of the people, he says, "*the moment our interest demands it, these extensive regions will be our own;* the present race of inhabitants will either be entirely exterminated, or revive to the native human dignity, by the generous and beneficent influence of just laws and rational freedom."

2. He was always afflicted with a painful disease of the eyes, caused by his intense use of them in study too soon after recovering from the small-pox.

Army, at West Point, on the Hudson. There he wrote several patriotic songs, of which the one commencing,

"Columbia! Columbia! to glory arise,
The queen of the world, and the child of the skies,"

was the most celebrated. That, too, like his address the year before, was truly prophetic. On receiving the news of his father's death, he left the army, settled at the homestead in Northampton, and with filial regard cherished his aged mother, for several years. He preached occasionally in the neighboring towns, and superintended a school at Hadley. In 1781, he was elected a member of the Massachusetts legislature, but he soon abandoned civil employment for that of clerical duties. He was ordained pastor of a church at Greenfield, near Fairfield, Connecticut, where he opened an academy, and labored industriously in the cause of religion and education, for twelve years. The building in which he taught school, on "Greenfield Hill," is yet [1854] standing. In 1785, his *Conquest of Canaan* was first published, three thousand subscribers for it having been obtained. In 1794, another poem, called *Greenfield Hill*, was published, and increased his fame as an epic poet. Higher and more arduous duties now awaited him. On the death of Dr. Stiles, in 1795, he was chosen President of Yale College, and for ten years performed the duties and received the emoluments of Professor of Theology, in that institution, by annual appointment, when the office became permanent. In 1800, he completed his revision of Watts' Psalms and Hymns, to which he added thirty-nine of his own; and in 1809, he published almost two hundred of his most important sermons, in five volumes. From 1805 until 1815, he spent his college vacations in travelling through New England and the State of New York, taking full notes of what he saw and heard. These formed the basis of his published *Travels*, in four volumes. After suffering for nearly a year from an acute disease, he died, on the 11th of January, 1817, at the age of almost sixty-five years. Dr. Dwight was the author of a great many published discourses and pamphlets on various subjects, chiefly of a theological and philosophical character.

CHRISTOPHER GADSDEN.

TORIES, or those who adhered to Great Britain when the War for Independence commenced, were very numerous in South Carolina, and it required greater courage on the part of the Whigs, or opposers of government, to avow their principles, than in communities where such loyalists were exceptions. Bold among the boldest, was Christopher Gadsden in denouncing British oppression, even as early as the period of the Stamp Act.[1] He was a native of Charleston, South Carolina, where he was born in 1724. He was sent "home," as England was called, to be educated, and remained several years with his relatives in the west of England. He returned to Charleston at the age of sixteen years, and was soon afterward apprenticed to a merchant in Philadelphia, where he remained till he was twenty-one years of age. He then went to England; and on the death of the purser of the vessel in which he returned, he was appointed to fill his place. He retained that situation two years, and then engaged in mercantile business in Charleston.

Gadsden's father owned a large property in Charleston, but lost it all in play with Lord Anson, a celebrated admiral in the British navy, who visited that city in 1733. That portion of the town still bears the name of Ansonborough. Christopher was successful, purchased all the property that once belonged to his father, and lived in the "Anson house," as it was called, till his death. Henry Laurens was his nearest neighbor and dearest friend, and they always acted shoulder to shoulder as unflinching patriots. Gadsden was appointed a delegate to the Congress which assembled at New York in 1765, in consequence of the passage of the Stamp Act; and from that period, through all the storms of the Revolution, until the fall of Charleston, in 1780, he was regarded as the most reliable of the patriot leaders, both civil and military. He was chosen a delegate to the first Continental Congress, in 1774; and in that body, urged an immediate attack upon General Gage at Boston, before he should be reinforced by fresh troops from Great Britain. He was considered rash, but the measure was only delayed a few months.

In 1775, Mr. Gadsden was elected senior colonel of three regiments raised at Charleston, and was subsequently made a brigadier. He was active at the time of the attack on Charleston, in 1776; and two years afterward he gave his efficient aid in forming a republican constitution for his native State. He resigned his military commission in 1779, and was lieutenant-governor of the State,

---

1. Under a wide-spreading live oak, a little north of the residence of Mr. Gadsden, the patriots used to assemble during the Summer and Autumn of 1765, and even the next Summer, after the Stamp Act was repealed, to discuss the political question of the day. From that circumstance, the green oak, like the famous Boston elm, was called *Liberty Tree*. Under that tree, Gadsden boldly warned the people, in 1776, not to rejoice too much, for the repeal was only a *show* of justice.

when Charleston was captured by Sir Henry Clinton, in May, 1780. A few weeks after the capitulation, he was treacherously taken from his bed at night, and, with others, was conveyed on board prison ships, in violation of the solemn stipulations contained in the articles of capitulation. They were taken to St. Augustine; and because the venerable patriot would not submit to indignities at the hands of Governor Tonyn, he was cast into a loathsome prison, where he remained until exchanged in June, 1781, eleven months afterward. From St. Augustine he sailed to Philadelphia, with other prisoners. On his return to Charleston, he was elected a member of the State legislature, where, notwithstanding his bad treatment, he generously opposed the confiscation of the property of the Loyalists. He was elected governor of his State, in 1782, but declined the honor. He remained in private life until his death, on the 28th of August, 1805, at the age of eighty-one years.

SAMUEL SEABURY.

THE first Protestant Bishop, in the United States, was the son of a Congregational minister who preached at Groton, Connecticut, and afterward became an episcopal clergyman at New London. That son, Samuel Seabury, was born at New London, in 1728; was graduated at Yale College, in 1751, and was ordained a priest, in London, England, in 1753. He had previously commenced a course of medical study, in Scotland, but circumstances caused him to choose the ministry as a profession, and he studied theology, in London. On his return to America, he was settled in the ministry at New Brunswick, New Jersey, for a little while, and then he complied with a call to Jamaica, Long Island, where he remained from 1757 until the close of 1766. From Jamaica he went to West Chester, in Westchester county, New York, and there he was settled when the war of the Revolution broke out. Like many of his clerical brethren, he adhered to the crown; and in consequence of his signing a protest against the measures of the Whigs, he became very obnoxious to the republican party.

In the Autumn of 1775, a party of horsemen, led by Isaac Sears, of New York, came from Connecticut, entered the city at noon-day, destroyed the printing-press of James Rivington (the editor of the Royal Gazette), carried off his types, to the tune of Yankee Doodle, and made bullets of them. On their way back to Connecticut, they seized Mr. Seabury, conveyed him to New Haven, kept him a prisoner there, for some time, and then paroled him to Long Island. He had kept a school at West Chester, for some time. That was broken up, and his church was converted into a hospital. Finding no peace within the limits of his parole, he fled to the arms of the British in New York, after they had taken possession of that city in the Autumn of 1776. He served as a chaplain to Colonel Fanning's corps of Loyalists, toward the close of the Revolution, and when peace came, he returned to his native town. In 1784, at the request of his clerical and lay brethren in the East, Mr. Seabury went to London, to seek episcopal consecration. Some difficulties prevented the accomplishment of his wishes, and he went to Scotland, where, on the 4th of November, of that year, he was consecrated a Bishop, by three non-juring prelates of the Scottish Church.[1] He presided over the diocese of Connecticut and Rhode Island, with great dig-

---

1. Those who regarded the deposition of James the Second, in 1688, as illegal, and refused to swear allegiance to the new sovereigns, William and Mary, his successors. Among these were several Scotch Bishops, who were deprived of their sees, in 1690. The Scotch Episcopal Church has always differed from that of England, in ecclesiastical matters, and its ministers have been called Non-Jurors, even until now.

nity and energy, for about twelve years, when he was called to give an account of his stewardship to his heavenly Master. He was buried at New London, where he expired, and over his grave is a plain, elevated slab, upon which it is recorded that he died on the 25th of February, 1798, in the sixty-eighth year of his age. The piety and benevolence of Bishop Seabury endeared him to all, of whatever name or creed, for he was a true Christian.

THOMAS NELSON, JR.

SELF-SACRIFICING patriotism was frequently exhibited during the revolutionary struggle, and oftentimes private property was cheerfully given for the public good. Everywhere, personal ease and family endearments were abandoned for the hardships of public life. Thomas Nelson, jr., of Yorktown, Virginia, was of that class of patriots. He was born at Yorktown, on the 26th of December, 1738. According to the common practice among the wealthy, in Virginia, at that time, he was sent to England to be educated, where he remained until 1761, when he returned home. He watched the progress of difficulties between Great Britain and her colonies with lively interest, and his sympathies were always with the latter. He first appeared in public life, in 1774, when he was elected a member of the House of Burgesses, of Virginia, and he was one of eighty-nine members of that assembly who, when dissolved by the royal governor (Dunmore), met at the Raleigh tavern, organized, and appointed delegates to the first Continental Congress. He was a member of a provincial convention held in the Spring of 1775, in which Patrick Henry uttered those sublime words, "*Give me liberty or give me death!*" and was one of the boldest patriots therein. He there first proposed the organization of the militia of the colony, for the defence of its liberties, and he was appointed to the command of a regiment after such organization was effected. He was elected to a seat in the Continental Congress, in 1775, and the following year he signed the Declaration of Independence. In 1777, severe and protracted illness compelled him to resign his seat and return home. By activity in military life, for awhile, Mr. Nelson's health was improved, and he was again elected a delegate to Congress, in 1779. But ill health compelled him to resign in April following. When British depredators by land and sea menaced that portion of the country, General Nelson, at the head of the militia of Lower Virginia, was active in its defence. In 1781, he succeeded Jefferson, as governor of the State; and in both civil and military capacities, he was exceedingly active and efficient. He even pledged his private fortune as security for the State, in order to raise funds to keep the militia in the field; and the combined French and American armies found him a powerful auxiliary in the siege of Yorktown, in the Autumn of 1781. During that siege, his own fine mansion, situated within the enemy's lines, was occupied by British officers. He observed that in the storm of balls which the besiegers were pouring upon the town and the British works, his own house was spared. He begged the cannoniers not to regard his property with favor, and actually directed a piece himself, so that the balls would fall upon his mansion. It had the effect to drive the officers from that strong retreat, and no doubt hastened the surrender of Cornwallis. A month after the surrender, General Nelson heeded the warnings of declining health, and retired to private life. The remainder of his days were spent in quiet, alternately at his mansion in Yorktown, and upon his estate at Offley. He died at the former place on the 4th of January, 1789, in the fifty-third year of his age.

MASON L. WEEMS.

IT is a singular fact that Dr. Weems, the earliest biographer of Washington and Marion, a man extensively known in the world of letters, and who occupied a large place in the public attention, while he lived, should be almost without a record in his country's annals. I have never met with a notice of the time and place of his birth. He received a good plain education, studied the science of medicine, as a life avocation, but became a preacher of the Gospel, in communion with the Protestant Episcopal Church, in Virginia. He officiated, for awhile, in Pohick church, a few miles from Mount Vernon, of which Washington was vestryman previous to the Revolution, and who was also one of Weems' parishioners afterward. Mr. Weems was a man of very considerable attainments as a scholar, physician, and divine; and his philanthropy and benevolence were unbounded. He used wit and humor freely; and his eccentricities and sometimes singular conduct, lessened the esteem of people for his character as a clergyman. He wrote lives of Washington, Penn, Franklin, and Marion, when an increasing family, and the operations of benevolence, made heavy drafts upon his income. He also became an agent for the sale of a quarto Bible, published by the eminent Mathew Carey, of Philadelphia, at the commencement of the present century, in which business he was wonderfully successful. He always preached, when invited, during his travels, and harangued people at public gatherings at courts and fairs, where he offered his Bibles, and other good books, for sale. His fund of anecdote was inexhaustible; and after giving a promiscuous audience the highest entertainment of fun, he found them in good mood to purchase his books. In his vocation, he accomplished a vast amount of good; and a large family and numerous friends lamented his death with the most earnest grief. He died at Beaufort, South Carolina, on the 23d of May, 1825, at an advanced age.

PHINEAS LYMAN.

ASSURANCE, supported by titled influence, often wears an epaulette and a star, while true merit is rewarded with faint praise and an honorable scar. Such a lesson of life did experience teach Phineas Lyman, a brave officer of provincial troops, during the French and Indian war. He was born in Durham, Connecticut, in the year 1716. He was one of the Berkeleyan scholars in Yale,[1] and received his first degree in 1738. The following year he was appointed a tutor in that institution, in which avocation he was engaged for three years, at the same time he was studying the theory of law. He commenced its practice at Suffield, in 1743, and he soon arose to the front rank at the bar of Hampshire county. He was elected a member of the Colonial Assembly, in 1750, and in 1753, was chosen to a seat in the council. At the age of thirty-nine years, he was appointed major-general of the Connecticut forces, and took the field in the Spring of 1755. He concentrated between five and six thousand troops on the upper waters of the Hudson, built Fort Edward, and there awaited the arrival of his commander-in-chief, General William Johnson, who was to lead the provincials against the French on Lake Champlain. The fortress was first called Fort Lyman, in honor of the Connecticut general, but its name was changed in deference to a scion of royalty. In the severe battle with the French and Indians, near the head of Lake George, in September of that year, General Lyman bore the most conspicuous part, and yet Johnson, jealous of his merits, withheld praise. Through the agency of titled friends at court, Johnson received the patent of a baronet, and twenty thousand dollars to support its dignity, as a reward for a victory won chiefly through the skill and bravery of General Lyman. The patriotic hero did not allow personal considerations to stand in the way of public duty, and he served with distinction during the whole war. He was the commander of the expedition which captured Havana, in 1762; and after the peace in 1763, he went to England, as agent of a company called *The Military Adventurers*—soldiers of the war—who asked for an appropriation of land for a colony in the Mississippi and Yazoo country. The same company had purchased an extensive tract of land on the Susquehannah, and General Lyman was intrusted with the management of matters connected with that purchase. Deluded month after month by idle promises from the changing ministry, in England, he at length came back, after wasting eleven years abroad, and almost losing his mind. He returned in 1774, and at about that time, a tract of land having been granted, in the Mississippi and Yazoo country, he went thither, with his oldest son. Both died in "West Florida," in 1775, and the following year, his wife and all her family, except her second son, went thither. She soon died; and a few years afterward, difficulties with the Spaniards caused the whole company of settlers, near Natchez, to fly for their safety across the country, a thousand miles, to Savannah. The history of General Lyman's family is a melancholy one. He died at the age of fifty-nine years, a victim of ingratitude and injustice.

---

1. From Bishop Berkeley, who was a patron of Yale College. He endowed a professorship known as the Berkeleyan.

JOHN MANLEY.

THE naval operations of the United States during the Revolution were far more extensive and important than is generally supposed, especially in the privateer department. It is asserted, by good authority, that the number of vessels captured by American cruisers, during the war, was eight hundred and three; and that the value of merchandise obtained, amounted to over eleven millions of dollars. Among the earlier- and most intrepid of the naval commanders of that period, was John Manley, who received his commission from Washington, at Cambridge, on the 24th of October, 1775,[1] and was put in command of the schooner LEE, with instructions to cruise in Massachusetts Bay. He made a great many captures, and his services became the theme of eulogium throughout the whole country. Among his prizes was an ordnance brig, which contained heavy guns, mortars, and intrenching tools, of great value to the army then besieging the British, in Boston. When Congress organized a navy, the services of Captain Manley were appreciated, and he was raised to the command of the *Hancock*, thirty-two guns. He cruised with success, but on the desertion of a colleague, while engaged with the *Rainbow* (afterward the flag-ship of Admiral Collier, in the Autumn of 1777, when on our coast with a small fleet), he was made a prisoner, on the 8th of July, 1777. Manley suffered a long and rigorous confinement in the *Rainbow*, and at Halifax, and his services were lost to the country for almost the entire remainder of the war. He was released in 1782, and the frigate, *Hague*, was placed under his command. While cruising in the West Indies, he was chased by a British seventy-four, and driven on a sand bank. Three other ships of the line attacked him, but after sustaining their heavy fire for four days, he got his vessel off, hoisted the continental flag, fired thirteen guns as a parting salute, and escaped. On his return to Boston, he was tried on some charges made against him by one of his officers, and his reputation was under a partial cloud, for a time. He died in Boston on the 12th of February, 1793, at the age of fifty-nine years, and was buried with military honors.

GILBERT CHARLES STUART.

IN the beautiful region of Rhode Island, at a place called Narraganset, the handsome wife of a Scotch snuff-maker gave birth to a son, who became the most distinguished portrait-painter in America. His father's name was Stuart, and his loyalty to the young claimant of the English throne,[2] made him add Charles to the name of Gilbert, given to his boy. Gilbert Charles Stuart was born in 1754, and at a very early age manifested great energy of character and a decided talent for art. At the age of thirteen years he practised drawing likenesses with black-lead pencil, and at the age of eighteen he commenced a course of instruction, in painting, under an amateur artist, named Alexander. He was pleased with the lad, took him with him on a tour in the Southern States,

---

1. Washington caused six vessels to be fitted out for the purpose of cruising on the New England coast. These were very efficient. They made many prizes, from which the American army, early in 1776, was quite well supplied with cannon, mortars, balls, ammunition, and stores. The siege of Boston and expulsion of the British therefrom, could not have been accomplished without those supplies from captured British vessels. Toward the close of 1775, the Continental Congress adopted measures for organizing and employing a navy.

2. Charles Edward Stuart, a grandson of James the Second, who was driven from the throne in 1688. His son made an effort to gain the throne of his father, in 1716. The efforts of his grandson were put forth in 1745, but after the great battle at Culloden, he became a fugitive.

and finally invited him to go to Scotland with him. Mr. Alexander died soon after his arrival at Edinburgh, and left his pupil in the care of Sir George Chambers. He, too, died, and young Stuart returned to Newport, as a competent portrait-painter. The late Dr. Benjamin Waterhouse was Stuart's intimate friend, through life; and in the Winter of 1773-'4, they practiced the drawing of the human figure from life, by procuring a muscular blacksmith for a model. This was the first "Life School of Design," in America, and Stuart and his friend Waterhouse were the only students.

The troubles of the Revolution affected Stuart's business, and in the Autumn of 1775, he went to England. Being a skilful musician, as well as painter, Stuart gained a subsistence by practicing both arts.[1] His friend Waterhouse was then in London, perfecting his medical studies, and he procured Stuart some sitters, but his eccentric habits were a continual bar to permanent prosperity. After two years' residence there, he became acquainted with West, and found in him a friend and benefactor. In the studio of that great artist he became an industrious pupil, and there he first became acquainted with Trumbull. In 1781, he set up an easel for himself, had continual and highly-remunerative employment, and might have become the successor of Reynolds, as the first portrait-painter in Great Britain, had not intemperate habits, which were increasing

[1]. While in extreme poverty, in London, Stuart was attracted by the sound of an organ in an open church. He went in, ascertained that several persons were exhibiting their skill as candidates for organist, and boldly asked permission to enter the lists. It was granted, and the young stranger was chosen at a salary quite sufficient to meet his wants.

in proportion to his prosperity, thwarted the aspirations of his genius. He went to Dublin, where he was courted for his wit and conviviality, and finally returned to America, in 1793. His fame had preceded him, and his studio in New York was thronged with sitters and admirers. Filled with an ardent desire to paint a portrait of Washington, he visited Philadelphia, and there he produced that great picture of the Patriot, which is regarded as the perfect model for all correct likenesses of the revered Father of his Country. Stuart was so pleased with Pennsylvania, while residing in Philadelphia and at Germantown, that he contemplated purchasing a farm at Pottsgrove, and making that his permanent residence. His irregular habits, as usual, interfered with his plans, and we find him in Washington City, after the removal of the seat of government thither. In 1805, he settled in Boston, where he continued in the practice of his profession, until his death, which occurred in July, 1828, at the age of seventy-four years. The original portrait of Washington, from his pencil, is the property of the Boston Athenæum. His last work is a head of John Quincy Adams, intended for a full-length portrait of that statesman.

WILLIAM TENNENT.

MEN sometimes become more distinguished by their connection with remarkable circumstances, than for any achievements of their own, and their real fine gold of character is lost in the glitter of extraneous events. At this day, that powerful preacher and indefatigable servant of Christ, William Tennent, is better known to the world "as a man who lay in a trance," than as a laborer for the good of his fellow-men. He was born in Ireland, on the 3d of June, 1705, and came to America when in the fourteenth year of his age. Under the care of his brother, Gilbert, he studied theology so ardently, at New Brunswick, in New Jersey, that his health gave way, his body became emaciated, and one morning, while conversing with his brother, in Latin, on the state of his soul, he fainted, and seemed to expire. He was prepared for burial, and the funeral procession was about to move, when his physician, who had been absent, returned, and thought he discovered indications of lingering life. But his body was cold and stiff, and his brother insisted upon his burial. The funeral, however, was postponed for awhile, and just as they were about to start again for the grave, Mr. Tennent opened his eyes, gave a groan, and again appeared lifeless. He revived, slowly recovered, but for a long time he was totally ignorant of every past transaction of his life. Suddenly his faculties began to resume their functions, and in 1733, he was ordained a minister of the church at Freehold, New Jersey. That church, and the house in which he lived, are yet [1854] standing. He never forgot the scenes of that cataleptic state in which he lay when his friends thought him dead. He seemed to have been wafted to a region of ineffable glory, where he heard things unutterable. He was accompanied by a heavenly conductor, and on asking permission to join the happy throng of beings before him, the guide tapped him upon the shoulder, and said, "You must return to earth." That was the moment when he opened his eyes, and saw his brother disputing with the doctor. Although he had been insensible for three days, the time did not seem to him more than twenty minutes. After a life of great usefulness as pastor of the flock at Freehold, for forty-three years, the storm of the Revolution disturbed him, and with his family, he went to reside with his son, in South Carolina. On his journey from Charleston to the interior, when about fifty miles from the sea-board, he sickened and died. Elias Boudinot was his executor, but he could never discover any trace of Tennent's papers. His death occurred on the 8th of March, 1777.

JOEL BARLOW.

OF Barlow, the youngest of the triad of American poets during the struggle for independence,[1] it might have frequently been said,

> "The Minstrel Boy to the war has gone,
> In the ranks of death you'll find him,"

for during his vacations at Yale College, he would shoulder his musket, offer himself as a volunteer, at the nearest camp, and fight bravely when opportunity occurred. Joel Barlow was the youngest of the ten children of a respectable farmer, and was born at Reading, in Connecticut, in the year 1754. He was graduated at Yale, in 1778, when he bore a slight scar, received in the battle at White Plains two years before. Four of his brothers were in the Continental army, and his whole being was thoroughly imbued with republican principles. He married a sister of Abraham Baldwin, a distinguished statesman of Connecticut, and in 1783, he settled at Westford, and commenced the publication of a paper, called *The Mercury*. Although, at the close of his collegiate course, he had studied theology six weeks, and was licensed to preach, he preferred the profession of the law; and in 1785, he was regularly admitted to the bar, as a practitioner. His poetic talents were now widely known and appreciated; and that same year, at the request of several congregational ministers, he prepared and published a revised edition of Watts' poetic version of the Psalms,[2] and added to them a collection of hymns, several of them from his own pen. In 1787, he published his most ambitious poem hitherto attempted, entitled, "*Vision of Columbus*," which was dedicated to Louis the Sixteenth of France, and was republished in London and Paris, with applause from the critics. With Trumbull, Humphreys, Dwight, and others, he published a satirical poem, called *The Anarchiad*. Others soon followed; when, becoming enamored with the principles of the French Revolution, he went to Paris, was honored by the gift of citizenship, made France his home for many years, and by successful commercial pursuits, he amassed a large fortune. During the worst of the Revolution (whose horrid scenes disgusted him), he travelled over portions of the Continent, and in Piedmont he wrote his celebrated poem, called *Hasty Pudding*. On his return to Paris, in 1795, Washington appointed him consul at Algiers, with power to negotiate a treaty with that government, and those of Tunis and Tripoli. After an absence of seventeen years, he returned to America, with his fortune, and built an elegant mansion on the east branch of the Potomac, near Washington city, which he afterward called "Kalorama." He enlarged his original "*Vision of Columbus*," and in 1807, it was published under the title of *The Columbiad*, in a splendid quarto volume, richly illustrated, and inscribed to his friend, Robert Fulton. In 1811, he commenced the preparation of a *History of the United States*, when President Madison appointed him minister plenipotentiary to the French government. The following year, the Duke of Bassano invited him to a conference with Napoleon, at Wilna, in Poland. The call was urgent, and he travelled thither, night and day, without rest. The fatigue and exposure brought on a disease of the lungs, which terminated his life at Zarnowica, near Cracow, on the 4th of December, 1812, when in the sixty-eighth year of his age.

---

1. John Trumbull, David Humphreys, and Joel Barlow.
2. On one occasion Mr. Barlow met Oliver Arnold, a cousin of the traitor, in a book-store in New Haven, and asked him for a specimen of his talent for making extempore rhymes. Oliver at once said, in allusion to Barlow's version of the Psalms:

> "You've proved yourself a sinful cre'tur;
> You've murdered Watts and spoiled the meter;
> You've tried the word of God to alter,
> And for your pains deserve a halter."

SAMUEL BARD.

THE medical profession in the United States has included many of our noblest citizens, distinguished alike for their patriotism, learning, and benevolence. Samuel Bard, who adorned the profession by the exercise of all these qualities, was the son of an eminent physician, in Philadelphia, where he was born on the 1st of April, 1742. His early moral and intellectual training was thorough, and the associations of his childhood and youth were favorable to the development of his genius. While residing a short time in the family of Doctor Cadwallader Colden, he acquired a taste for botany, under the teachings of an accomplished daughter of that gentleman. A genius for drawing and painting enabled him to make beautiful copies of plants, some of which are yet in his family. He was graduated at Columbia College, in 1761, and the same year he went to Europe, to obtain a thorough medical education. He was absent in France, England, and Scotland, five years; and such was his skill in botany, that he obtained the annual medal given by Professor Hope, at Edinburgh, for the best collection of plants, in 1765. He there received his degree, returned home, entered into partnership with his father, and in 1768, married his beautiful cousin, Mary Bard. He made New York his residence the same year, and there he formed and executed the plan of founding the Medical School of New York, where degrees were conferred in 1769. He delivered a course of chemical lectures in 1774, but the breaking out of the Revolution deranged all his plans for the improvement of his profession. His father was then residing at Hyde Park, in Dutchess county, New York, and thither he took his family, for safety. By special permission of the British commander, he went to New York, in 1777, and engaged anew in his business. But his old friends, who were chiefly Whigs, had all fled, and he did not obtain practice sufficient to pay his expenses. He returned to the country, and remained there until the British evacuated the city in the Autumn of 1783, when he again resumed his practice there. He did not remain long. Four of his children died by prevailing scarlatina, and at the same time the health of his wife began to fail. He withdrew from business to attend upon her; and at her recovery, in 1784, he again commenced the practice of his profession, in New York. He was very successful, and with his own means, he liquidated all the debts of his father, which misfortune had burdened him with. Having acquired a competency, he resolved to retire from active business, and for that purpose he formed a partnership with the late Dr. David Hosack, on the 1st of January, 1796. This connection continued four years, when Dr. Bard withdrew wholly from the practice of his profession, and left the extensive business in the hands of his skilful young partner. At his beautiful seat, near the residence of his father at Hyde Park, he sat down in the retirement of private life; but when, three years afterward, the yellow fever appeared in New York, he yielded to the calls of duty, and was "the beloved physician" of the rich and poor during that trying time. He finally took the disease himself, but the careful nursing of his wife, and his own skilful prescriptions, carried him safely through. Then again he left the field of active duty as a physician, never to return to it. In 1813, he was elected president of the College of Physicians and Surgeons, of New York, and held that office until his death, which occurred on the 24th of March, 1821, at the age of seventy-nine years. His disease was pleurisy. He and his wife had often expressed a desire to both die at the same time. The privilege was vouchsafed to them. The faithful wife died the day preceding the death of her husband, of the same disease, and they were buried in one grave.

MARTHA WASHINGTON.

THE reflected glory of Washington's character gave distinction to all who were connected with him by domestic ties or the bonds of consanguinity. There were many matrons of his day, equally noble and virtuous as she who bore him, yet "Mary, the mother of Washington," appears the most illustrious of them all. Beauty, accomplishments and noble worth belonged to Martha Dandridge as a maiden, and Martha Custis as a wife and mother, but her crowning glory in the world's esteem is the fact that she was the bosom companion of the Father of his Country. Martha Dandridge was born in New Kent county, Virginia, in May, 1732, about three months later than her illustrious husband. In 1749, she married Daniel Parke Custis, of New Kent, one of the wealthiest planters of Eastern Virginia, and settled, with her husband, on the banks of the Pamunkey river, where she bore four children. Her husband died when she was about twenty-five years of age, leaving her with two surviving children and a large fortune in lands and money.[1] She became acquainted with Colonel Washington, in 1758, when his greatness was fast unfolding; and on the 6th of January, 1759, they were married. By the bequest of his half-brother, Lawrence Washington, he owned the beautiful estate of Mount Vernon, on the Potomac, and

---

1. He left her thirty thousand pounds sterling (about $148,000) in certificates of deposits in the Bank of England. These were in an iron chest, yet in the possession of her only surviving grand-child, George Washington Parke Custis, Esq., of Arlington House, Virginia.

there they made their home during the remainder of their lives. Occasionally, during the War for Independence, Mrs. Washington visited her husband in camp, and shared his honors, his anxieties, and his hopes. Almost at the very hour of his great victory at Yorktown, her only son, who was Washington's aid, expired a few miles distant from the scene of carnage; and with the shout of triumph, that filled his mother's heart with joy, came a stern messenger with tidings that poured it full of woe.[1]

While her husband was President of the United States, Mrs. Washington presided with dignity over the executive mansion, both in New York and Philadelphia; but the quiet of domestic life had more charms for her than the pomp of place, and she rejoiced greatly when both sat down again, at Mount Vernon, to enjoy the repose which declining age coveted. But that pleasant dream of life soon vanished, for her companion was taken away by death a little more than two years afterward. When she was certified of the departure of his spirit, she said, "'Tis well; all is now over; I shall soon follow him; I have no more trials to pass through." In less than thirty months afterward the stricken widow was laid in the tomb, at the age of almost seventy-one years. In marble sarcophigi their remains now lie together, at Mount Vernon—that Mecca of many pilgrims.

JOSHUA BARNEY.

SEVERAL of the naval commanders who won glory for themselves and country during the war with England in 1812–'15, commenced their nautical career, and learned their earliest nautical lessons, during the War of the Revolution. In that earlier naval school, Joshua Barney was educated for his profession. He was born in the city of Baltimore, on the 6th of July, 1759. He made several sea voyages while yet a lad, and at the beginning of the War for Independence, he entered the sloop, *Hornet*, as master's mate, and accompanied the fleet of Commodore Hopkins to the West India seas, in 1775. He was at the capture of New Providence,[2] and for his bravery there was promoted to a lieutenantcy. After being made prisoner and released three different times, he assisted in conquering a valuable prize, in the Autumn of 1779, which was taken into Philadelphia. The following year he married the daughter of alderman Bedford of that city, spent the honey-moon with his bride, and then repaired to Baltimore to resume his naval duties. He was soon afterward made a prisoner, and sent to England, where he escaped from a cruel confinement and returned to America. In 1782, he was placed in command of the *Hyder Ally*, of sixteen guns, belonging to the State of Pennsylvania. In April, of that year, he captured the British ship, *General Monk*, after an action of twenty-six minutes. This vessel was bought by the United States, and in September, it sailed for France, with Barney as commander, who bore dispatches for Dr. Franklin, at Paris. In that vessel he brought back the French loan to the United States in chests of gold and barrels of silver. Peace soon came, and he left the service, for awhile.

---

1. Mr. Custis died at Eltham, about thirty-five miles from Yorktown, from the effects of camp fever. Washington hastened thither as soon as public affairs at camp would allow him. Mrs. Washington and Dr. Craik were already there. The latter informed the chief, that his beloved step-son had just expired, on his arrival. He wept like a child; and when he recovered himself, he said to the weeping mother, "I adopt his two younger children as my own, from this hour." These were the present proprietor of Arlington House, and the late Eleanor Parke Custis, wife of Major Lawrence Lewis, the favorite nephew of Washington.

2. One of the Bahama Islands. They took possession of the town now called Nassau, and made the governor prisoner. He was afterward exchanged for Lord Stirling, who was made prisoner at the battle near Brecklin, at the close of August, 1776.

In 1796, Captain Barney went to France, with Mr. Monroe, as the bearer of the American flag to the National Convention. He there accepted an invitation to take command of a French squadron, but resigned his commission in 1800, and returned to America. Commodore Barney was among the most efficient commanders in service, when the United States declared war against England, in 1812; and the following year, he had charge of a flotilla in the Chesapeake Bay for the protection of the coast. When the British invaded Maryland, and pressed forward toward Washington city, near the close of the Summer of 1814, Barney abandoned his flotilla, and with his marines, engaged in a battle with the enemy at Bladensburg, where he was wounded in the thigh by a musket ball, which was never extracted. In May, 1815, he was sent on a mission to Europe, and on his return in the ensuing Autumn, he retired to private life, after having been in service forty-one years, and fought twenty-six battles and one duel. He visited Kentucky, in 1817, and started to emigrate thither the following year. When about to embark on the Ohio, at Pittsburg he was taken ill, and died there on the 1st of December, 1818, at the age of fifty-nine years.

JOHN BARRY.

"THE first commodore in the American Navy," was *not* the brave John Barry, as is generally asserted. Yet he was in active service as commander, about as early as Esek Hopkins, to whom that honor, conferred by Congress, properly belongs. Barry was a native of Wexford, in Ireland, where he was born in 1745. He was educated for the sea, and at the age of fifteen years he came to America, and was employed as commander in the merchant service, until the Revolution commenced. When, in February, 1776, Commodore Hopkins sailed with a small squadron against the fleet of Dunmore, then committing depredations on the Virginia coast, Barry left the Delaware, in the *Lexington*, of sixteen guns, to clear the Virginia waters of the numerous small cruisers of the enemy which infested them. He performed that service well; and prior to the promulgation of the Declaration of Independence, he was promoted to the frigate, *Effingham*. Circumstances prevented his departure in that vessel from the Delaware, and at the head of a volunteer company, under the command of General Cadwalader, he assisted in some of the operations which resulted in the capture of the Hessians at Trenton, near the close of 1776. He was with the army during the succeeding Winter; and when, the next Autumn, the British took possession of Philadelphia, he went up the Delaware with the *Effingham*, and endeavored to save her, at the same time indignantly refusing an offered bribe to employ her in the king's service. He greatly annoyed the British shipping in the Delaware, by secret night enterprises in small boats. In September, 1778, his sphere of usefulness was enlarged by being appointed to the command of the *Raleigh*, of thirty-two guns, in which he sailed from Boston. He fell in with a British fleet, and after a severe action of many hours, he was compelled to run his vessel ashore, upon a barren island. He had terribly handled his antagonists, and but for the treachery of one of his men, he would have burned the *Raleigh*, and deprived the enemy of all advantage. A court-martial honorably acquitted him of all blame.

Early in 1781, Captain Barry took command of the frigate *Alliance*, and in that vessel he conveyed to L'Orient, Colonel John Laurens, a special ambassador to the court of France. In May he had an engagement with two English vessels, in which he was severely wounded. He was victorious, and his antagonists became prizes. In the Autumn, Captain Barry conveyed La Fayette and Count Noailles to France, in the *Alliance*, and then he cruised successfully among the West India islands, until March, 1782, when he encountered a British squadron. His skill, coolness, and bravery, were eminently displayed in that engagement. He fought chiefly in defence of the American sloop-of-war, Luzerne, which was conveying a large amount of specie. It was saved, and contributed to found the Bank of North America,[1] the first institution of the kind in the United States. After the close of the war, Captain Barry continued in the service, and he was efficient in protecting our commerce from the depredations of French vessels, when war between France and the United States commenced on the ocean, in 1797. Captain Barry died at Philadelphia, on the 13th of September, 1803, at the age of fifty-eight years.

RICHARD GRIDLEY.

VERY few Americans directed their attention to military engineering, previous to the Revolution, and therefore those French engineers who proffered their services to the Continental Congress, were eagerly accepted and commissioned. At the opening of the war, near Boston, in 1775, Richard Gridley was the only efficient American engineer in the army. He was a native of Boston, where he was born in 1711. His brother, Jeremy, was the able attorney-general of Massachusetts, who defended the Writs of Assistance,[2] and other government measures, against the patriotic attacks of James Otis, and his compatriots. We have no record of the early life of Richard. His first appearance before posterity was as an engineer in the provincial army, sent to capture the strong fortress of Louisburg, on Cape Breton, in 1745. After that event, he entered the regular army, and in 1755, he was lieutenant-colonel of infantry, and chief engineer. He accompanied General Winslow, in that capacity, to Albany, in the Summer of 1756, preparatory to an expedition against Crown Point, on Lake Champlain. He proceeded to erect fortifications at the head of Lake George. The expedition failed, through the tardiness of Lord Loudon. In 1758, Colonel Gridley served under General Amherst, and was with Wolfe, at Quebec. When the War for Independence began at Lexington and Concord, the patriotism and skill of Colonel Gridley caused his appointment of chief engineer of the army that soon gathered around Boston; and under his directions, all the fortifications erected during the Summer of 1775, and Winter of 1776, in that vicinity, were constructed. Up to that time he had received the half-pay of a British officer, and possessed Magdalen Island as a gift for his services under Wolfe. He was wounded in the battle on Breed's ["Bunker's"] Hill, yet not so as to disable him. In September, 1775, Congress gave him the commission of a major-general, and made him commander-in-chief of the Continental artillery, to which office Colonel Henry Knox succeeded in November following. After the British left Boston, in March, 1776, General Gridley was engaged in throwing up fortifications at several points about the Harbor. He died at Stoughton, Massachusetts, on the 21st of June, 1796, in the eighty-fifth year of his age.

---

1. See sketch of Robert Morris.
2. General search-warrants, which allowed the officers of the king to break open any citizen's store or dwelling to search for contraband merchandise. It opened a way to many abuses, and the people violently opposed the measure. This was among the first of those government measures which drove the Americans into rebellion.

THOMAS JEFFERSON.

THE only material memorials of the author of the Declaration of Independence, in our country, are a dilapidated granite obelisk over his neglected grave at Monticello;[1] a bronze statue in front of the President's House at Washington city, erected by private munificence; a fine statue upon a monument to Washington, erected by the State of Virginia, at Richmond, and a few busts. The nation has quarried no stone for his monument, nor is it requisite. The DECLARATION OF INDEPENDENCE, written on parchment, and preserved in the memory of generations, is a nobler monument than can be wrought from brass or marble.

Thomas Jefferson was born at Shadwell, Albemarle county, Virginia, on the 13th of April, 1743. He was of Welsh descent. When his father died, his mother was left with Thomas and another son, and six little daughters. They

---

[1]. It is within an enclosed family burial-ground, just in the edge of the forest which covers the western portion of Monticello. Visitors, with Vandal hand, have so broken off pieces of the obelisk, to carry away with them, that it now presents a sad appearance. To preserve the marble tablet, on which is the following inscription, written by Jefferson himself, the present [1855] proprietor has removed it to his house:
"Here lies buried, THOMAS JEFFERSON, Author of the Declaration of American Independence; of the Statute of Virginia for Religious Freedom; and Father of the University of Virginia."

were blessed with a handsome estate, and that portion of it called Monticello (little mountain), near the then hamlet of Charlottesville, fell to Thomas when he reached his majority. He was a student in William and Mary College, at Williamsburg, about two years, and then commenced the study of law with George Wythe, afterward Chancellor of Virginia. While yet a student, in 1765, he heard Patrick Henry's famous speech against the Stamp Act, and it lighted a flame of patriotism in young Jefferson's soul that burned brighter and brighter until the hour of fearless action arrived. In 1767, he commenced the practice of law; and in 1769, he first appeared in public life as a member of the Virginia Assembly. He was one of the most active workers in that body, until called to more influential duties as member of the Continental Congress, in 1775. He was always remarkable for his ready pen; and as a member of the committee of correspondence, and by pamphlets and newspaper paragraphs, from 1773, until the culmination of public sentiment in the Declaration of Independence, he labored intensely and potentially.[1] When Richard Henry Lee's resolution in favor of independence was under consideration, early in the Summer of 1776, and a committee of five were appointed to prepare a preamble in the form of a Declaration, Mr. Jefferson, the youngest of the committee, was chosen to make the draft, chiefly because of his facile use of the pen in elegant and appropriate expressions of sentiment. At his lodgings, in the house of Mrs. Clymer, in Philadelphia, that famous document was written, and after some modifications, it was adopted on the 4th of July, 1776. The author's name is appended to it, with fifty-five others. Soon afterward, Mr. Jefferson resigned his seat in Congress, and became a leading actor in the civil events of the Revolution in Virginia, from that time until the peace in 1783. He assisted in revising the laws of Virginia; and in June, 1779, he was elected governor of the State, as successor of Patrick Henry. From about the beginning of that year, until the close of 1780, the British and German troops, captured at Saratoga, were quartered in his vicinity, and he greatly endeared himself to them by his uniform kindness. During his administration, Arnold, the traitor, invaded Virginia, and Cornwallis and his active officers overran portions of the State along the James river, from Richmond to its mouth. The fiery Tarleton attempted the capture of Governor Jefferson, in June, 1781, and almost succeeded.[2] It was a most trying time for Virginia, and Jefferson, sagaciously perceiving that a military man was needed in the executive office, declined a re-election, and was succeeded by General Nelson, of Yorktown.

Mr. Jefferson now sought the retirement of private life, to indulge in the genial pursuits of literature and science.[3] He was not permitted to find happiness in repose there. His wife died, and his heart was terribly smitten. Then came a call from his countrymen to represent them abroad, and at the close of 1782, he departed for Philadelphia, to sail for France, to assist the American commissioners in their negotiations for peace with England. Intelligence of the accomplishment of that duty reached him before his departure, and he returned home. He was at Annapolis when Washington resigned his commission, in December, 1783, and the Address of President Mifflin to the chief was from Mr. Jefferson's pen. In 1784, he went to France, as associate diplomatist with Franklin and Adams, and the same year he wrote his essay on a money-unit, to which we are mainly indebted for our convenient coins. He succeeded Dr. Franklin as minister at the French court, in 1785; and on his return to America,

---

1. His pamphlet entitled "A Summary View of the Rights of British America," was so much admired, that Edmund Burke caused it to be reprinted in London, with a few alterations.
2. Jefferson was advised of the approach of Tarleton, when he was within half a mile of his house, and escaped by fleeing to the dark recesses of Carter's Mountain, lying southward of Monticello. Tarleton captured some members of the Virginia Legislature, then in session at Charlottesville.
3. His *Notes on Virginia* is the most important of the various productions of his pen.

in 1789, before he reached his home at Monticello, he received from Washington the appointment of Secretary of State. He resigned that office in 1793, and became the head of the republican party, in opposition to Washington's administration. In the Autumn of 1796, he was chosen vice-president of the United States, and in the Spring of 1801, he took his seat as chief magistrate of the nation. After eight years of faithful service in that exalted office, he retired forever, from public life. With untiring perseverance he succeeded in establishing that yet flourishing institution, the *University of Virginia;* and until the last, his life was spent in pursuits of public utility. The latter years of his life were clouded by pecuniary embarrassment. He sold his library to the Federal Government, in 1815, consisting of six thousand volumes, for twenty-four thousand dollars. He survived that great sacrifice eleven years, and then his spirit took its flight, while his countrymen were celebrating the fiftieth anniversary of the independence of the United States. He died on the 4th of July, 1826, at the age of eighty-three years.[1]

THOMAS CHITTENDEN.

THERE are crises in the history of States, sometimes occurring in their infancy, at other times in their maturity, when the concentration of influence in one man has made him instrumental in conferring great benefits upon the public. Thomas Chittenden, the first governor of the independent State of Vermont, was an illustration of this fact. He was born at East Guilford, Connecticut, on the 6th of January, 1729; received only the meagre rudiments of an English education, then furnished by the common schools, and married at the early age of twenty years. Then he made his residence at Salisbury; and his natural abilities, combined with a pleasing person and address, soon made him popular. He was chosen commander of a militia regiment, and for several years he represented his district in the legislature of Connecticut. Unlearned as he was, he became a leading man; and by performing the duties of a justice of the peace for Litchfield county, for several years, he became acquainted with the laws and the proper manner of administering them. Agriculture was his delight, and every day spared from his official duties was devoted to a personal engagement in the affairs of his farm. His family had a rapid growth, and he emigrated to the borders of the Onion river,[2] in 1774, on what was known as the *New Hampshire Grants*, on the east side of Lake Champlain, for the purpose of laying the foundations of a fortune for his children. There, separated by an almost trackless wilderness from his early friends, he opened many fertile acres to the blessed sunlight, and invited settlers to come and form the nucleus of a State. Soon, political agitations disturbed his repose; and, in 1775, he was appointed one of a committee to visit the Continental Congress at Philadelphia, and ask political advice. The threatening aspect of affairs in the North, toward the close of the Summer of 1776, caused the settlers to flee southward, and Mr. Chittenden took up his abode in Arlington, in the present Bennington county, where he was made president of the committee of safety. He warmly espoused the cause of the people of the New Hampshire Grants, in their controversy with New York.[3]

---

1. See sketch of John Adams.
2. The Indian name of this river was *Ouinooske*. His location was in the present town of Williston, Vermont, south-east from Burlington.
3. The State of New York claimed jurisdiction over the present territory of Vermont, then known as the New Hampshire Grants, and a very warm dispute arose. Bloodshed was often threatened, but the matter was finally settled by a purchase of the claims of New York for $30,000.

He was one of the committee who drafted a declaration of the independence of Vermont,[1] adopted on the 15th of January, 1777. He also assisted in the formation of a State constitution, in July, 1777, and was elected the first governor under it. That office he held until his death, with the exception of one year. When, in 1780, the British authorities in Canada supposed the people of Vermont to be royally inclined (because they would not join the confederation of States), and appointed a commission to confer with the dissatisfied colonists, Governor Chittenden was chosen one of the committee on the part of the Vermont people. That whole matter was so adroitly managed by Chittenden, Allen, and others, for three years, that the authorities of both Canada and the United States were deceived. They thus secured Vermont from easy British invasion until peace was sure, when that State became a member of the great confederacy. The course of the Vermont leaders, though highly patriotic, was regarded with suspicion, until the mask was removed. At the close of the war, Governor Chittenden returned to Williston, with his family, where he passed the remainder of his days. He resigned the office of governor in the Summer of 1797, and on the 25th of August, of that year, he died, in the sixty-ninth year of his age.

PATRICK HENRY.

"GIVE me Liberty, or give me Death!" were the burning words which fell from the lips of Patrick Henry, at the beginning of the War for Independence, and aroused the Continent to more vigorous and united action.[2] He was the son of a Virginia planter in Hanover county, and was born on the 29th of May, 1736. At the age of ten years he was taken from school, and commenced the study of Latin in his father's house. He had some taste for mathematics, but a love of idleness, as manifested by his frequent hunting and fishing excursions, for sport, and utter aversion to mental labor, gave prophecies of a useless life. At twenty-one years of age, he engaged in trade, but neglect of business soon brought bankruptcy. He had married at eighteen, and passed most of his time in idleness at the tavern of his father-in-law, in Hanover, where he often served customers at the bar. As a last resort, he studied law diligently for six weeks, obtained a license to practice, but he was twenty-seven years of age before he was known to himself or others, except as a lazy pettifogger. Then he was employed in the celebrated *Parsons' cause*,[3] and in the old Hanover courthouse, with his father on the bench as judge, and more than twenty of the most learned men in the colony before him, his genius as an orator and advocate beamed forth in that awful splendor, so eloquently described by Wirt. From that period he rose rapidly to the head of his profession. In 1764, he made Louisa county his residence, and his fame was greatly heightened by a noble defence of the right of suffrage, which, as a lawyer, he made before the House of Burgesses, that year. In 1765, he was elected to a seat in that house, and during that memorable session, he made his great speech against the Stamp

---

1. Partly owing to the troubles with New York, Vermont would not join the confederacy in 1777, but, at a convention at Westminster, it was declared an independent State. It was admitted into the Union in February, 1791.
2. In the Virginia convention, held in St. John's church at Richmond, in March, 1775. It was one of the most powerful speeches ever made by the great orator, and ended with the words quoted above. They were afterward placed on flags, and adopted as a motto under many circumstances.
3. This was a contest between the clergy and the State legislature, on the question of an annual stipend claimed by the former. A decision of the court had left nothing undetermined but the amount of damage. Henry's eloquence electrified judge, jury, and people. The jury brought in a verdict of one *penny damages*, and the people took Henry upon their shoulders, and carried him in triumph about the court-house yard.

Act.[1] In 1769, he was admitted to the bar of the general court, and was recognized as a leader, in legal and political matters, until the Revolution broke out. He was a member of the first Continental Congress, in 1774, and gave the first impulse to its business;[2] and when, in 1775, Governor Dunmore attempted to rob the colony of gunpowder, by having it conveyed on board a British war-vessel, Patrick Henry, at the head of resolute armed patriots, compelled him to pay its value in money. In 1776, Henry was elected the first republican governor of Virginia, and was reëlected three successive years, when he was succeeded by Thomas Jefferson. During the whole struggle, he was one of the most efficient public officers of the State; and in 1784, he was again chosen governor.

Patrick Henry was a consistent advocate of State Rights, and was ever jealous of any infringement upon them. For that reason, he was opposed to the Fed-

---

1. He had introduced a series of resolutions, highly tinctured with rebellious doctrines, and supported them with his wonderful eloquence. The house was greatly excited; and when, at length, he alluded to tyrants, and said, "Cæsar had his Brutus, Charles the First his Cromwell, and George the Third—" there was a cry of "Treason! treason!" He paused a moment, and then said, "may profit by their example. If that be Treason, make the most of it."
2. When all was doubt and hesitation at the opening of the session, and no one seemed ready to take the first step, a plain man, dressed in ministers' grey, arose and proposed action. "Who is it? who is it?" asked several members; "Patrick Henry," replied the soft voice of his colleague, Peyton Randolph,

eral Constitution, and in the Virginia convention, called in 1788, to consider it, he opposed its ratification with all the power of his great eloquence. He finally acquiesced, when it became the organic law of the Republic, and used all his efforts to give it a fair trial and make it successful. Washington nominated him for the office of Secretary of State, in 1795, but Mr. Henry declined it. In 1799, President Adams appointed him an envoy to France, with Ellsworth and Murray, but feeble health and advanced age compelled him to decline an office he would have been pleased to accept. A few weeks afterward, his disease became alarmingly active, and he expired at his seat, at Red Hill, in Charlotte county, on the 6th of June, 1799, at the age of almost sixty-three years. Governor Henry was twice married. By his first wife he had six children, and nine by the second. His widow married the late Judge Winston, and died in Halifax county, Virginia, in February, 1831.

ETHAN ALLEN.

THE name of *Green Mountain Boys* is always associated with ideas of personal valor and unflinching patriotism; and Ethan Allen has ever been regarded as the impersonation of the proverbial independence of character, of the early settlers along the eastern shores of Lake Champlain. He was born in Litchfield county, Connecticut, near the borders of New York, and at an early age emigrated to the region above alluded to, known as the *New Hampshire Grants*, now Vermont. At about the year 1770, a violent controversy arose between the settlers of this tract and the civil authorities of New York, respecting territorial claims. Ethan Allen took an active part in the controversy, and became a leader of the *Green Mountain Boys*, as the settlers were called, against the alleged usurpations of the New York government.[1] The latter finally declared Allen and his associates to be outlaws, offered fifty pounds colonial currency for his apprehension,[2] and contemplated an armed invasion of the territory. Allen believed himself in the right, and boldly maintained his position, until a common danger alarmed all the colonies, and made them unite as brethren for common defence. When the news of the affair at Lexington reached those remote settlers, they were electrified with zeal for the maintenance of freedom; and in less than thirty days afterward, we find Colonel Allen and some of his Green Mountain boys and Massachusetts militia, in concert with Colonel Benedict Arnold and some Connecticut men, wresting the strong fortresses of Ticonderoga and Crown Point from the British.[3] Early in the following Autumn, Colonel Allen was sent to Canada, to ascertain the temper of the people there; and in an attempt, with Colonel Brown, to capture Montreal, with a small force, he was made a prisoner, put in irons on board a vessel, and sent to England, with the assurance that he would be hanged. Great crowds flocked to see him, on his arrival, for the fame of his exploits had reached England. His grotesque garb attracted great attention. He was regarded almost as a strange wild beast of the forest, and for more than a year he was kept a close prisoner.

In January, 1776, Colonel Allen was sent, in a frigate, to Halifax, where he

---
1. See Note 3, p. 125.
2. He came very near being captured by a party of New Yorkers, while on a visit to his friends in Salisbury. They intended to seize him, and convey him to the jail at Poughkeepsie.
3. When Allen thundered at the door of the commander of the garrison of Ticonderoga, after the soldiers were subdued, and that affrighted official asked by what authority he demanded a surrender, the colonel's reply was, "By the Great Jehovah and the Continental Congress!" It was on the morning of the day when Congress was to assemble at Philadelphia.

remained in jail until the following October, when he was conveyed to New York, then the British head-quarters. There he was kept, part of the time on parole on Long Island, and part of the time in the Provost and other prisons in New York, until May, 1778, when he was exchanged for Colonel Campbell of the British army. His health had suffered much during his imprisonment, yet he repaired to head-quarters, and offered his services to Washington, when his strength should be restored. He arrived at Bennington, his place of residence, on the evening of the last day of May, and he was welcomed by booming cannons and the huzzas of the people. The civil authorities of the now independent State of Vermont commissioned him major-general of the State militia, but an opportunity for the exercise of his bravery and military skill did not again occur. He was active, with Governor Chittenden and others, in the adroit political game played by Vermont with the authorities of the United States and of Canada; and his patriotism ever burned pure, even at a time when General Clinton wrote to Lord George Germain, "There is every reason to suppose that Ethan Allen has quitted the rebel cause." General Allen continued active in public affairs after the war, until his death, which occurred suddenly at Colchester, on the 13th of February, 1789, when he was about sixty years of age. Colonel Allen was the author of several political pamphlets; a theological work, entitled Oracles of Reason, and a Narrative of his Observations during his captivity.[1]

WILLIAM FRANKLIN.

IT is worthy of note, that one of the most distinguished Loyalists during the War for Independence, was the only son of one of the noblest Patriots in that struggle. That Loyalist was William, the first-born child of Benjamin Franklin. He was born in Philadelphia, in 1731, and was carefully educated by his father, for professional life. He was postmaster of the city of Philadelphia; clerk of the Assembly for awhile; and entered the provincial army as captain, early in the French and Indian war. He was warmly commended for his services at Ticonderoga. After the war, he went to England with his father, and in Scotland he became acquainted with the Earl of Bute, who, for almost ten years, had great influence in the councils of George the Third. In 1763, William Franklin was appointed governor of New Jersey, and was very popular for a time. Like all other royal governors, he soon assumed undue personal dignity, and quarrelled with the legislature. He was a thorough monarchist in principle, and when the disputes between the colonists and the imperial government commenced in earnest, he did not hesitate in taking sides with the crown, in opposition to his distinguished father. At the beginning of 1774, all intercourse between father and son was suspended, and as the political troubles thickened, the breach widened. Month after month the breach between the governor and the New Jersey Assembly also widened; and finally a Provincial Congress at Trenton assumed political authority, and royal government ceased in that province. A State Constitution was adopted in July, 1776, and William Livingston became

---

1. The stern integrity and truthfulness of Colonel Allen were well illustrated on one occasion, when he was prosecuted for the payment of a note for sixty pounds, given to a man in Boston. It was sent to Vermont for collection, but it was inconvenient for him to pay it then, and he was sued. The trial came on, and his lawyer, in order to postpone the matter, denied the genuineness of the signature. To prove it, it would be necessary to send to Boston for a witness. Allen was in a remote part of the court-room, when the lawyer denied the signature. With long strides Allen rushed through the crowd, and, standing before his advocate, he said, in angry tone, "Mr——, I did not hire you to come here and lie. That is a true note—I signed it—I 'll swear to it—and I 'll pay it. I want no shuffling—I want time. What I employed you for was to get this business put over to the next court, not to come here and lie and juggle about it." The time was given, and Allen paid the note.

Franklin's successor, by the choice of the people. The Whigs went still further. Franklin was declared to be an enemy of his country, and was sent, a prisoner, to East Windsor, Connecticut. He was kept under the eye of Governor Trumbull, until 1778, when he was exchanged, released, and took refuge with the British army in New York. There he was secretly active in fomenting discontents among the people, wherever he could make an impression. He was president of the Board of Loyalists, who had their head-quarters near Oyster Bay, Long Island, but went to England before the close of the contest. In the picture of the *Reception of the American Loyalists by Great Britain, in* 1783, painted by Benjamin West, Governor Franklin appears at the head of a group of figures. After an estrangement of ten years, he solicited and obtained a reconciliation with his father. Although Dr. Franklin accepted the olive branch thus filially held out, and proposed "mutually to forget" the past, he seems to have remembered the estrangement, when he made his will, for, after making a comparatively small bequest to William, he remarks, "The part he acted against me in the late war, which is of public notoriety, will account for my leaving him no more of an estate he endeavored to deprive me of." Governor Franklin continued in England until his death, and enjoyed a pension, from the British government, of four thousand dollars a year. He died in November, 1813, at the age of about eighty-two years. His wife died of grief, while he was a prisoner, in 1778, and a monumental tablet was erected to her memory in St. Paul's church, New York city.

JOSEPH GREEN.

IN the same year when Dr. Franklin first saw the light, a genuine wit and poet was born in the same city of Boston. His name was Joseph Green. He was first instructed in the South Grammar School, and then entered Harvard College, where he was graduated in 1726. He became an accomplished scholar, and man of business; and by successful mercantile life, for a few years, he acquired a competent fortune. Generous, polite, elegant in deportment, and exceedingly popular with all classes, Mr. Green might have acquired almost any mark of public distinction, but he loved private life, and could never be prevailed upon to accept office. He took very little part in politics, yet when Hutchinson left the government of Massachusetts, he was one of those who signed a complimentary address to that functionary. This act offended the republicans, and the royal party claimed him; but when, in 1774, Massachusetts was deprived of her charter, and a number of counsellors were appointed by mandamus, Green refused to serve, and sent his resignation to General Gage. Yet the tendencies of Mr. Green were so decidedly loyal, that he was included in the act of banishment, of 1778. He had been absent from Boston about three years already, and he never returned to his native country. He died in London, on the 11th of December, 1780, at the age of seventy-four years. Mr. Green's poetry was generally humorous. He wrote a burlesque on a psalm written by his fellow wit, Doctor Byles. Also a burlesque on the Free Masons, and a "Lamentation on Mr. Old Tenor" (paper money), which gained him great applause. He was a member of a club of sentimentalists, who published several pamphlets; and he attacked the administration of Governor Belcher, exposed its anti-republican tendencies, and ridiculed the chief magistrate by putting his speeches into rhyme. Mr. Green was a Loyalist of the milder stamp, and was governed by a pure heart and clear head in his choice of government.

JAMES JACKSON.

WHEN the British army was about to leave Savannah, in July, 1782, General Wayne, then in command in Georgia, chose an accomplished young man of twenty-five, whose valor was the theme for praise in the Southern army, to receive the keys of the city from a committee of British officers. That young officer was Major James Jackson, a native of Devonshire, England, where he was born on the 21st of September, 1757. He came to America, with his father, in 1772, and studied law in Savannah. He loved his adopted country, and in 1776, shouldered his musket, and was active in repelling an invading force that menaced Savannah. In 1778, he was appointed brigade major of the Georgia militia, and was wounded in a skirmish on the Ogeechee, in which General Scriven was killed. At the close of that year he participated in the unsuccessful defence of Savannah; and when it fell into the hands of Colonel Campbell, he was among those who fled into South Carolina and joined Moultrie's brigade. His appearance was so wretched and suspicious, during that flight, that he was arrested by some Whigs, and tried and condemned as a spy. They were about to hang him, when a gentleman of reputation, from Georgia, recognized him, and saved his life. He was active in the siege of Savannah by Lincoln and D'Estaing, in October, 1779, and in 1780, he was in the battle at Blackstocks under Colonel Elijah Clarke, of Georgia. General Andrew Pickens made him his brigade major, in 1781, and his fluent speech expressing his ardent patriotism, infused new zeal into that corps. He was at the siege of Augusta, in June, 1781, and when the Americans took possession, Jackson was left in command of the garrison. Subsequently he performed more active and arduous services, as commander of a legionary corps; and at Ebenezer, on the Savannah, he joined General Wayne, and was the right arm of his force until the evacuation of the Georgia capital, in 1782. As some reward for his patriotic services during the war, the legislature gave him a house and lot in Savannah. He married in 1785, and the next year was commissioned brigadier-general of the State militia. In 1788, he was elected governor of Georgia, but modestly declined the honor on account of his youth and inexperience, being then only little more than thirty years of age. He was one of the first representatives of Georgia in Congress, after the organization of the Federal Government; and from 1792 to 1795, was a member of the United States Senate. In the meanwhile he was promoted to major-general, and never failed in the faithful performance of his duties, civil and military. The State Constitution of Georgia, framed in 1798, was chiefly the work of his brain and hand. From that year until 1801, he was governor of the State, when he was again chosen United States' senator. He held that office until his death, which occurred at Washington city, on the 19th of March, 1806, at the age of forty-nine years. His mortal remains lie beneath a neat monument in the Congressional burial-ground, upon which is an inscription, written by his personal friend and admirer, John Randolph, of Roanoke. Governor Jackson made many powerful enemies in the South, because of his successful exposures of stupendous land frauds, but his course increased the zeal and number of his friends. There never lived a truer patriot or more honest man, than General James Jackson.

ELI WHITNEY.

EVERY labor-saving machine is a gain to humanity; and every inventor of such machine is a public benefactor. High on the list of such worthies is the name of Eli Whitney, the inventor of a machine for cleaning cotton to prepare it for the bale, known by the technical term of *gin*. He was born at Westborough, Massachusetts, on the 8th of December, 1763. His mechanical genius was early manifested; and while yet a mere child, he constructed many things with great skill. He entered Yale College in 1789, and was graduated in 1792. He then engaged to go to Georgia as a private tutor in a family, and on his way, he fell in with the widow of General Greene, who was returning to Savannah, with her family. On his arrival, he found himself without occupation and with very little money, for the person with whom he had made an engagement had hired another preceptor. Mrs. Greene had become much interested in young Whitney, and at once invited him to make her house his home, to pursue what studies he pleased. He commenced the study of law, but his mind was much on mechanics. Several distinguished visitors at the house of Mrs. Greene, from the interior, on one occasion, expressed their regret that there was not some machine for cleaning the green seed cotton,[1] as its culture, with such aid, would

---

1. This labor was then performed chiefly by female servants. To separate one pound of clean staple cotton from the seeds was considered a good day's work for one person.

be very profitable at the South. The great mechanical genius of young Whitney was known to Mrs. Greene, and she said, "Apply to my young friend here, he can make anything." Although he had never yet looked upon a cotton seed, his mind began to plan. He procured a small quantity of uncleaned cotton, and with such rude tools as a plantation afforded, he went to work and constructed a machine, under the kind auspices of Mrs. Greene and Phineas Miller, who became her husband. The machine was examined with delight, for it would do the work of months in a single day. With it, one man could do the work of a thousand. It opened a way to immense wealth to the Southern planters. Great excitement prevailed; and when the people found that they could not see the great invention until it was patented, they broke open the building in which it stood, carried it away, and soon many similar machines were in use. Whitney went to his native State, patented his invention, and in partnership with Mr. Miller, commenced the manufacture of machines for Georgia. Before he could secure a patent, it was in common use;[1] and to complete his misfortunes, his shop with all its contents, and his papers, were consumed. He was made a bankrupt; and the inventor of the *cotton gin*, which has been worth hundreds of millions of dollars to the people of the South, never received a sufficient amount of money from it, to reimburse his actual outlays and losses. He was treated with the utmost unfairness by some southern legislatures, as well as by individuals; and everywhere among those who were profiting immensely by the invention, his rights were denied. Even Congress denied his application to extend his patent. Disappointed, and disgusted with the injustice of his fellow-men, Mr. Whitney turned his attention to other pursuits. He commenced the manufacture of fire-arms, in 1798, for the United States. But misfortune seemed to be uniformly his lot in life, except in his choice of the excellent Henrietta, daughter of Pierpont Edwards, for his wife. After great sufferings from disease, he died near New Haven, on the 8th of January, 1825, at the age of fifty-nine years.

ELIAS BOUDINOT.

THE American Bible Society, whose labors have accomplished a vast amount of good, in the dissemination of the Holy Scriptures, was established in 1816; and Elias Boudinot, one of its founders, and a warm patriot of the Revolution, was its first president. He was born in Philadelphia, on the 2d of May, 1740. He inherited a love of freedom and religious devotion from his Huguenot ancestors, and when the colonists began to question the right of Great Britain to tax them without their consent, he took a stand for his countrymen. He had received a classical education, studied law with Richard Stockton, one of the signers of the Declaration of Independence, and married that patriot's sister. Boudinot practiced his profession in New Jersey, and soon rose to distinction. In 1777, he was appointed commissary-general of prisoners, by Congress, and the same year he was elected to a seat in the Continental Congress. In November, 1782, he was elected president of that body, and in that capacity he signed the preliminary treaty of peace with Great Britain. At the close of the war he resumed the profession of the law, but was again called into public life in 1789,

---

1. On one occasion, when suits for the infringement of the patent in Georgia were commenced, Mr. Miller wrote, "The jurymen at Augusta have come to an understanding among themselves, that they will never give a cause in our favor, let the merits of the case be as they may."

by an election to a seat in Congress, under the Federal Constitution. He was a member of the House of Representatives six years, when Washington appointed him Director of the Mint, on the death of Rittenhouse. He held that position until 1805, when he retired from public life, and made his residence the remainder of his days, at Burlington, New Jersey. In 1812, he was elected a member of the American Board of Commissioners for Foreign Missions, to which he made a donation of five thousand dollars; and when he was elected president of the American Bible Society, in 1816, he gave that institution ten thousand dollars. He was a trustee of the College at Princeton for many years, and there founded a cabinet of natural history, at a cost of three thousand dollars. His whole life was one of usefulness; and at his death, he bequeathed a great portion of a large fortune to institutions and trustees, for charitable purposes. The remainder of his estate he left to the General Assembly of the Presbyterian Church, of which he was a member. He died at Burlington, on the 24th of October, 1821, at the age of eighty-one years.

JOSEPH HABERSHAM.

GEORGIA may boast of many noble patriots, but she had none, in the War for Independence, of truer stamp, than Joseph Habersham, the son of a merchant of Savannah, where he was born in 1750. He was one of the earliest advocates of popular rights in the Georgia capital, and, with other young men, acted, as well as spoke, against unjust royal rule. Early in the Summer of 1775, a letter from Sir James Wright, the royal governor of Georgia, to General Gage, was intercepted by the vigilant Whigs of Charleston, who had seized the mails. It contained a request for that officer to send some troops to Savannah, to suppress the rising rebellion there. The letter was sent to the committee of safety at Savannah, and aroused the fiercest indignation of the Whigs. At about that time, a British vessel arrived at the mouth of the Savannah, with many thousand pounds of powder. It was determined to seize the vessel and secure the powder, for the use of the patriots. On the night of the 10th of July, thirty volunteers under young Habersham (then holding the commission of colonel) and Commodore Bowen, captured the vessel, placed the powder, under guard, in the magazine at Savannah, and sent five thousand pounds of the ammunition, to General Washington at Boston. In January, 1776, Colonel Habersham was a member of the Georgia Assembly; and on the 18th of that month, he led a party of volunteers, to the capture of Governor Wright. They paroled him a prisoner in his own house, from which, on a stormy night in February, he escaped, made his way to the British ship, *Scarborough*, and went to England. Thus Colonel Habersham put an end to royal rule, in Georgia. He was active in the council and field, during the whole war, and held the commission of lieutenant-colonel in the Continental army. In 1785, he was chosen a member of Congress, to represent the Savannah district; and in 1795, President Washington appointed him Postmaster-general of the United States. He resigned that office in the year 1800, and two years afterward, was made president of the Branch Bank of the United States, at Savannah. He filled that office with distinguished ability until a short time before his death, which occurred in November, 1815, at the age of sixty-five years.

BENEDICT ARNOLD.

"WE accept the treason, but despise the traitor," was the practical expression of British sentiment when Arnold, one of the bravest of the American generals, was purchased with British gold, and attempted to betray the liberties of his country. He was a native of Norwich, Connecticut, where he was born on the 3d of January, 1740. He was a descendant of Benedict Arnold, one of the early governors of Rhode Island, and was blessed with a mother who, according to her epitaph, was "A pattern of patience, piety, and virtue." But he was a wayward, disobedient, and unscrupulous boy; cruel in his tastes and wicked in his practices.[1] He was bred to the business of an apothecary, at Norwich, under the brothers Lathrop, who were so pleased with him as a young man of genius, that they gave him two thousand dollars to commence business with. From 1763 to 1767, he combined the business of bookseller and druggist, in New Haven, when he commenced trading voyages to the West Indies, and

---

1. While yet a mere youth, he attempted *murder.* A young Frenchman was an accepted suitor of Arnold's sis'er. The young tyrant (for Arnold was always a despot among his play-fellows) disliked him, and when he could not persuade his sister to discard him, he declared he would shoot the Frenchman if he ever entered the house again. The opportunity soon occurred, and Arnold discharged a loaded pistol at him, as he escaped through a window. The young man left the place forever, and Hannah Arnold lived the life of a maiden. Arnold and the Frenchman afterward met at Honduras, and fought a duel. The Frenchman was severely wounded.

horse dealing in Canada. He was in command of a volunteer company, in New Haven, when the war broke out, with whom he marched to Cambridge, and joined the army under Washington. Then commenced his career as the bravest of the brave. His first bold exploit had been in connection with Ethan Allen in the capture of Ticonderoga, in May, 1775. In September following he started from Cambridge for Quebec, by way of the Kennebeck and the wilderness beyond its head waters, in command of an expedition; and after an unsuccessful attempt to take the capital of Canada, he joined Montgomery, and participated in the disastrous siege of that walled town on the last day of the year. There he was severely wounded in the leg, but escaping up the St. Lawrence, held command of the broken army until the arrival of General Wooster in April following. Arnold retired to Montreal, then to St. Johns, and left Canada altogether, in June, 1776. During the Summer and Autumn of that year, he was active in naval command on Lake Champlain. He assisted in repelling the invasion of Connecticut, by Tryon, in April, 1777; and during the latter part of that Summer, he was with General Schuyler, in his preparations for opposing the attempt of Burgoyne to penetrate beyond Fort Edward, or Saratoga.

While the American army was encamped at the mouth of the Mohawk, Arnold marched up that stream, and relieved the beleagured garrison of Fort Schuyler (or Stanwix), on the site of the present village of Rome.[1] He was in the battles at Stillwater; and despite the jealous efforts of Gates to cripple his movements, his intrepidity and personal example were chiefly instrumental in securing the victory over Burgoyne, for which the commanding general received the thanks of Congress and a gold medal, while Arnold was not even mentioned in the official despatches from Saratoga. This was one of the first affronts that planted seeds of treason in his mind. He was again severely wounded at Saratoga, and suffered much for many months When, in the Spring of 1778, the British evacuated Philadelphia, Arnold was appointed military governor there, because of his incapacity for active field service, on account of his wounds. There he lived extravagantly, married the beautiful daughter of Edward Shippen, a leading Tory of Philadelphia, and commenced a system of fraud, peculation, and oppression, which caused him to be tried for sundry offences by a court-martial, ordered by Congress. He was found guilty on some of the charges, and delicately reprimanded by Washington. Indignant and deeply in debt, he brooded upon revenge on one hand, and pecuniary relief on the other. He opened a correspondence with the accomplished Major André, adjutant-general of the British army, and after procuring the command of the fortresses at West Point, on the Hudson, and vicinity, he arranged, with André, a plan for betraying them into the hands of Sir Henry Clinton, the British commander at New York. His price for his perfidy was fifty thousand dollars and a brigadier's commission in the British army. After a personal negotiation with Arnold, André was captured,[2] the treason became known, but the traitor had fled to his new friends in New York. He soon afterward went on a marauding expedition into Virginia,[3] and then on the New England coast, near his birth-place, everywhere exhibiting the most cruel spite toward the Americans whom he had sought to injure beyond measure. The war ended, and he went to England. There he

1. While Burgoyne penetrated the State from the North, St. Leger, with Tories and Indians, attempted to take Fort Schuyler, and then sweep the Mohawk Valley.
2. Andre was hanged as a spy, at Tappan, on the west side of the Hudson, in October, 1780. He had been drawn into that position by the villany of Arnold, and could the traitor have been caught, Andre would have been saved.
3. In a skirmish between Richmond and Petersburg, some Americans were made prisoners. One of them was asked by Arnold, what his countrymen would do with him, if they should catch him. The young man promptly replied, "Bury the leg that was wounded at Quebec and Saratoga, with military honors, and hang the rest of you." Great efforts were made to capture the traitor, while he was in Virginia. That was the chief object of La Fayette's expedition to that State.

was everywhere shunned as a serpent, and he made his abode in St. Johns, New Brunswick, from 1786 until 1793. He went to the West Indies, in 1794, and from thence to England. He died in Gloucester Place, London, on the 14th of June, 1801, at the age of sixty-one years. Just three years afterward, his wife died at the same place, aged forty-three.[1]

WILLIAM BARTON.

*"What hath the gray-haired prisoner done?
Hath murder stained his hand with gore?
Ah, no! his crime's a fouler one—
God made the old man poor!"*

THUS indignantly did the gifted pen of Whittier refer to the brave Colonel Barton, in his noble protest against imprisonment for debt. Barton was a worthy scion of old Rhode Island stock, and was born in Providence in 1750. Of his early life we know nothing, but when the War for Independence appealed to the patriotism and romance of the young men of America, we find him among the most daring of those who gave the British great annoyance after they had taken possession of Rhode Island, in 1776, and were encamped at Newport and vicinity. Young Barton had passed through the several grades of office, until the opening of 1777, when we find him holding the commission of lieutenant-colonel of militia, and performing good service in preparations for driving the British from Rhode Island. General Prescott, an arrogant, tyrannical man, was the commander-in-chief of the enemy there, and the people suffered much at his hands.[2] They devised various schemes to get rid of him, but all failed until a plan, conceived by Colonel Barton, was successfully carried out. Prescott's head-quarters were at the house of a Quaker, five miles north of Newport. On a sultry night in July, 1777, Barton, with a few trusty followers, crossed Narraganset Bay from Warwick Point, in whale boats, directly through a British fleet, and landed in a sheltered cove a short distance from Prescott's quarters. They proceeded stealthily in two divisions, and secured the sentinel and the outside doors of the house. Then Barton boldly entered, with four strong men and a negro, and proceeded to Prescott's room on the second floor. It was now about midnight. The door was locked on the inside. There was no time for parley. The negro, stepping back a few paces, used his head as a battering-ram, and the door flew open. Prescott, supposing the intruders to be robbers, sprang from his bed and seized his gold watch. The next moment Barton's hand was laid on his shoulder, and he was admonished that he was a prisoner, and must be silent. Without giving him time to dress, he was conveyed to one of the whale-boats, and the whole party returned to Warwick Point, undiscovered by the sentinels of the fleet. Prescott's mouth was kept shut by a pistol at each ear. The prisoner first spoke after landing, and said, "Sir, you have made a bold push to-night." Barton coolly replied, "We have been fortunate." At sunrise the captive was in Providence, and in the course of a few days he was sent to the head-quarters of Washington, in New Jersey.[3] For this brave

---

1. Their son, James Robertson Arnold, born at West Point, became a distinguished officer in the British army. He passed through all the grades of office, from lieutenant. On the accession of Queen Victoria, he was made one of her aids-de-camp, and rose to the rank of major-general, with the badge of a Knight of the Royal Hanoverian Guelphic Order.
2. This was the same Prescott who commanded at Montreal, in 1775, and treated Colonel Ethan Allen so cruelly when he was made prisoner.
3. Prescott's haughty demeanor was not laid aside in his captivity. On his way to New Jersey, he

service, Congress presented their thanks and an elegant sword, to lieutenant-colonel Barton, and in December following, he was promoted to the rank and pay of colonel in the Continental army. He was also rewarded by a grant of land, in Vermont. In the action at Butt's Hill, near Bristol Ferry, in August, 1778, Colonel Barton was so badly wounded, that he was disabled for the remainder of the war. In after years, the land in Vermont proved to be an unfortunate gift. By the transfer of some of it he became entangled in the meshes of the law, and was imprisoned for debt, in Vermont, for many years, in his old age.

> "For this he shares a felon's cell,
> The fittest earthly type of hell!
> For this, the boon for which he poured
> His young blood on the invader's sword,
> And counted light the fearful cost—
> His blood-gained liberty is lost."

When La Fayette was "our nation's guest," in 1825, he heard of the situation of his old companion-in-arms, paid the debt and set him at liberty! It was a significant rebuke, not only to the Shylock who demanded the "pound of flesh," but to the American people. Colonel Barton died at Providence, in 1831, at the age of eighty-four years.

GEORGE ROGERS CLARKE.

ONE of the most interesting episodes in the history of our country, is that which relates to the conquest of the region long known as the Northwestern Territory,[1] from the motley masters of the soil—English, French, and Indians. The chief actor in those events, was George Rogers Clarke, a hardy Virginia borderer, whose youth was spent in those physical pursuits which give vigor to the frame and activity to the mind. He was born in Albemarle county, Virginia, on the 19th of November, 1752, and first appeared in history as an adventurer beyond the Alleghanies, in 1772. He had been engaged in the business of land-surveyor, for some time and that year he went down the Ohio, in a canoe, as far as the mouth of the Great Kanawha, in company with Rev. David Jones, then on his way to preach the gospel to the western tribes.[2] He was captain of a company in Dunmore's army, which marched against the Indians on the Ohio and its tributaries, in 1774.[3] Ever since his trip in 1772, he ardently desired an opportunity to explore those deep wildernesses in the great vallies; and in 1775, he accompanied some armed settlers to Kentucky, as their commander. During that and the following year, he traversed a great extent of country south of the Ohio, studied the character of the Indians, and made himself master of many secrets which aided in his future success. He beheld a beautiful country, inviting immigration, but the pathway to it was made dan-

---

and his escort dined at the tavern of Captain Alden, at Lebanon, Connecticut. The common dish of corn and beans was set before him. He supposed the act to be an intentional insult, and strewing the *succotash* on the floor, exclaimed, "Do you treat me with the food of hogs." Captain Alden hated the tyrant, and for this act he horsewhipped him. After Prescott was exchanged for General Charles Lee, and was again in command on Rhode Island, he treated a gentleman, who called upon him on business, with much discourtesy. He said in excuse, "He looked so much like a cursed Connecticut man that horsewhipped me, that I could not endure his presence."

1. It embraced the present States of Ohio, Indiana, Illinois, Michigan, and Wisconsin.
2. See sketch of David Jones.
3. The Shawnees and other tribes had committed many depredations on the Virginia frontier for several years, and in 1774, Lord Dunmore, then governor of that province, led quite a large force against them. A severe battle was fought at Point Pleasant, at the mouth of the great Kanawha; and at Chillicothe, Dunmore made a treaty of peace and friendship with them.

gerous by the enemies of the colonists, who sallied forth from the British posts at Detroit, Kaskaskia, and Vincennes, with Indian allies. Convinced of the necessity of possessing these posts, Clarke submitted the plan of an expedition against them, to the Virginia legislature, and early in the Spring of 1778, he was at the Falls of the Ohio (now Louisville), with four companies of soldiers. There he was joined by Simon Kenton, another bold pioneer. He marched through the wilderness toward those important posts, and at the close of Summer all but Detroit were in his possession.

Clarke was now promoted to colonel, and was instructed to pacify the western tribes, if possible, and bring them into friendly relations with the Americans. While thus engaged, he was informed of the re-capture of Vincennes. With his usual energy, and followed by less than two hundred men, he traversed the drowned lands of Illinois, through deep morasses and snow-floods, in February, 1779; and on the 19th of that month, appeared before Vincennes. To the astonished garrison, it seemed as if those rough Kentuckians had dropped from the clouds, for the whole country was inundated. The fort was speedily surrendered, and commander Hamilton (governor of Detroit), and several others, were sent to Virginia as prisoners. Colonel Clarke also captured a quantity of goods, under convoy from Detroit, valued at $50,000; and having sufficiently garrisoned Vincennes and the other posts, he proceeded to build Fort Jefferson, on the western bank of the Mississippi, below the Ohio.

When Arnold invaded Virginia, in 1781, Colonel Clarke joined the forces under the Baron Steuben, and performed signal service until the traitor had departed. He was promoted to the rank of brigadier, the same year, and went beyond the mountains again, hoping to organize an expedition against Detroit. His scheme failed, and, for awhile, Clarke was in command of a post at the Falls of the Ohio. In the Autumn of 1782, he penetrated the Indian country between the Ohio and the Lakes, with a thousand men, and chastised the tribes severely for their marauding excursions into Kentucky, and awed them into comparatively peaceful relations. For these deeds, John Randolph afterward called Clarke the "American Hannibal, who, by the reduction of those military posts in the wilderness, obtained the lakes for the northern boundary of our Union, at the peace in 1783." Clarke made Kentucky his future home; and during Washington's administration, when Genet, the French minister, attempted to organize a force in the West, against the Spaniards, Clarke accepted from him the commission of major-general in the armies of France. The project was abandoned, and the hero of the north-west never appeared in public life afterward. He died near Louisville, Kentucky, in February, 1818, at the age of sixty-six years.

DAVID JONES.

THE ministers of the "church militant" frequently performed double service in the righteous cause of truth, during the War for Independence, for they had both spiritual and temporal enemies to contend with. Among these, the Rev. David Jones was one of the most faithful soldiers in both kinds of warfare. He was born in New Castle county, Delaware, on the 12th of May, 1736, and, as his name imports, was of Welsh descent. He was educated for the gospel ministry under the Rev. Isaac Eaton, at Hopewell, New Jersey, and for many years was pastor of the Upper (Baptist) Freehold church. Impressed with a desire to carry the gospel to the heathen of the wilderness, he proceeded to visit the Indians in the Ohio and Illinois country, in 1772. On his way down the Ohio river, he was accompanied by the brave George Rogers Clarke, whose valor gave the region, afterward known as the North-western Territory, to the struggling colonists, toward the close of the Revolution. Mr. Jones' mission was unsuccessful, and he returned to his charge at Freehold. Because of his zealous espousal of the republican cause, he became very obnoxious to the Tories, who were numerous in Monmouth county. Believing his life to be in danger, he left New Jersey, settled in Chester county, in Pennsylvania, and in the Spring of 1775, took charge of the Great Valley Baptist church. He soon afterward preached a sermon before Colonel Davie's regiment, on the occasion of a Continental Fast, which was published, and produced a salutary effect. It was entitled, *Defensive War in a Just Cause, Sinless.* In 1776, Mr. Jones was appointed chaplain to Colonel St. Clair's regiment, and proceeded with it to the Northern Department. He was on duty at Ticonderoga, when the British approached, after the defeat of Arnold on the Lake below, and there preached a characteristic sermon to the soldiers, which was afterward published. He served through two campaigns under General Gates, and was chaplain to General Wayne's brigade in the Autumn of 1777. He was with that officer at the Paoli Massacre,[1] where he narrowly escaped death, but lived to make an address at the erection of a monument there, over the remains of his slaughtered comrades, forty years afterward. He was in the battles at Brandywine and Germantown, suffered at White Marsh and Valley Forge, and continued with Wayne in all his varied duties from the battle at Monmouth in June, 1778, until the surrender of Cornwallis, at Yorktown, in October, 1781. Such was his activity as a soldier, that General Howe offered a reward for him, while the British held possession of Philadelphia; and on one occasion, a detachment of soldiers were sent to the Great Valley to capture him.[2] At the close of the war, he returned to his farm, and resumed his ministerial labors.

When General Wayne took command of the army in the North-western Territory, in 1794, Mr. Jones was appointed his chaplain, and accompanied him to the field; and when, again, in 1812, a war between the United States and Great Britain commenced, the patriotic chaplain of the old conflict entered the army, and served under Generals Brown and Wilkinson, until the close of the contest. He was then *seventy-six years of age*. When peace came, he again put on the armor of the gospel, and continued his warfare with the enemy of souls until the last. His latest public act was the delivery of the dedicatory address on laying the corner-stone of the Paoli Monument, in 1817. On the 5th of February, 1820, this distinguished servant of God and of the Republic, died in peace, in the eighty-fourth year of his age, and was buried in the Great Valley churchyard, in sight of the pleasant little village of Valley Forge.

JOHN EAGAR HOWARD.

MARYLAND may boast of many lovely sons, but she cherishes the memory of none more warmly than that of John Eagar Howard. He was born in Baltimore county, on the 4th of June, 1752. He was a very young man when the War for Independence commenced, and entered eagerly into the plans of the republicans. He became a soldier in 1776, and commanded a company of militia in the service known as The Flying Camps, under General Hugh Mercer. In that capacity he served at White Plains, in the Autumn of that year; and when, in December, 1776, that corps was disbanded, he accepted the commission of major in one of the Continental battalions of his native State. Then commenced his useful military career. In the Spring of 1777, he joined the army under Washington, at Middlebrook, in New Jersey, but returned home in June, on account of the death of his father. He again joined the army, a few days after the battle on the Brandywine, in September; distinguished himself for cool courage in the engagement at Germantown; and afterward wrote a graphic account of the whole affair. He was also at the battle on the plains of Monmouth the following year; and in June, 1779, he was commissioned a lieutenant-colonel in the 5th Maryland regiment, "to take rank from the 11th day of May, 1778." In 1780, he went to the field of duty, in the South, when De Kalb

---

1. Near the Paoli Tavern, in Chester county, Pennsylvania, General Wayne was surprised a few nights after the battle on the Brandywine, by General Grey of the British army, and a large number of his command were slain. That event is known in history as the Paoli Massacre.
2. While reconnoitring alone one night, Chaplain Jones saw a dragoon dismount, and enter a house for refreshments. Mr. Jones boldly approached, seized the horseman's pistols, and going into the house, claimed the owner as his prisoner. The unarmed dragoon was compelled to obey his captor's orders, to mount and ride into the American camp. The event produced great merriment, and Wayne laughed immoderately at the idea of a British dragoon being captured by his chaplain.

marched thither with Maryland and Delaware troops, with the vain hope of aiding the besieged Lincoln, at Charleston. He served under Gates until after the disastrous battle near Camden, in August, and his corps formed a part of the Southern army, under General Greene, at the close of that year. In January following, he won unfading laurels by his skill and bravery at the Cowpens, under Morgan, and received a vote of thanks and a silver medal from Congress. At Guilford, a month afterward, he greatly distinguished himself when Greene and Cornwallis contended for the mastery. There he was wounded, returned home, and did not engage in active military services afterward. When peace came, the intrepid soldier was conquered by the charms of Margaret, daughter of Chief Justice Chew, around whose house, at Germantown, he had battled manfully, and they were married. He sought the pleasures of domestic life, but in the Autumn of 1788, he was drawn from his retirement, to fill the chair of chief magistrate of his native State. He held that office three years. In 1794, he declined the proffered commission of major-general of militia, and the following year he also declined the office of Secretary of War, to which President Washington invited him. He was then a member of the Maryland Senate; and in 1796, he was chosen to a seat in the Senate of the United States, where he served until 1803. Then he retired from public life forever; yet when, in 1814, the British made hostile demonstrations against Baltimore, the old veteran, unmindful of the weight of threescore years, prepared to take the field. The battle at North Point rendered such a step unnecessary, and he sat down in the midst of an affectionate family, to enjoy thirteen years more of his earthly pilgrimage. His wife was taken from him, by death, early in 1827; and on the 12th of October, of that year, he followed her to the spirit land, at the age of seventy-five years. Honor, wealth, and the ardent love of friends, were his lot in life; and few men ever went down to the grave more truly beloved and lamented, than John Eagar Howard.

RICHARD BLAND.

AMONG the galaxy of patriots who composed the real strength of the Virginia House of Burgesses, in 1774, no one was more beloved and reverenced, than Richard Bland, who was born early in the last century. He was a member of the colonial legislature of Virginia many years, and a leader of the popular branch, or House of Burgesses. Although a true republican, he was not prepared, at the moment, to stand by Patrick Henry in his denunciations of British tyranny, in 1765, yet he did not flinch, soon afterward, when duty demanded bold action. He was one of the committee to prepare a remonstrance with parliament, in 1768; and in 1773, he was one of the first general committee of correspondence, proposed by Dabney Carr. He was chosen a delegate to the first Continental Congress in 1774, but declined the appointment the following year, because, as he said, he was "an old man, almost deprived of sight." Francis Lightfoot Lee, who signed the Declaration of Independence the following year, was appointed in his place; and three years afterward, the aged patriot went to his final rest. Mr. Wirt speaks of him as "one of the most enlightened men in the colony; a man of finished education, and of the most unbending habits of application. His perfect mastery of every fact connected with the settlement and progress of the colony, had given him the name of the Virginia Antiquary. He was a politician of the first class, a profound logician, and was also considered as the first writer in the colony."

CHARLES COTESWORTH PINCKNEY.

"MILLIONS for defence, but not one cent for tribute," were the noble words uttered by Charles Cotesworth Pinckney when, as an ambassador to the French government, some unaccredited agents demanded a loan from the United States, as a prerequisite to a treaty which he had been sent to negotiate. That sentiment expressed the national standard of independent integrity, ever maintained in our intercourse with foreign nations.[1] The author of it was born in Charleston, South Carolina, on the 25th of February, 1746. His father was chief justice of South Carolina, and held a high social position there. At the age of seven years Charles, with his brother Thomas, were taken to England by their father, to be educated. He was first at Westminster, then at Oxford, and when his collegiate course was completed, he studied law in the Temple. On his return to Charleston, in 1769, he commenced a successful professional career, and at the same time became an active participator in the popular movements against the imperial government. He had taken a part against the Stamp Act, in England, and he was a full-fledged patriot on his arrival home. When, in 1775, Christopher Gadsden became colonel of a regiment raised by the Provin-

---

[1]. Jackson's instructions to foreign ministers were, "Ask nothing but what is right, and submit to nothing that is wrong."

cial Congress, Pinckney received the appointment of captain of one of its companies, and he went up into North Carolina, as far as Newbern, on recruiting service. He was active in the defence of his native city the following year, and remained in service until the fall of Charleston, in 1780. He accompanied General Robert Howe in his unfortunate expedition to Florida, in 1778, and assisted in the repulse of Prevost, from Charleston, the following year.[1] When, early in 1780, the British fleet, bearing General Clinton and an invading army, appeared off Charleston, Pinckney, now holding the commission of colonel, was appointed to the command of the garrison at Fort Moultrie, in the harbor. When the city and its defences finally yielded to superior numbers, and were surrendered, Colonel Pinckney was made a prisoner. He suffered much from sickness and ill-treatment during a captivity of almost two years, and was not allowed to participate in the struggle in the field during that time. In February, 1782, he was exchanged, and was soon afterward breveted brigadier-general. On the return of peace he resumed the practice of his profession, and was a member of the convention which framed the Federal Constitution, in 1787. He declined a proffered seat in Washington's Cabinet, but in 1796, he accepted the appointment of minister to the French Republic, then controlled by a Directory.[2] It was while in the midst of personal peril there, that he uttered the noble sentiment just quoted. When war with France seemed inevitable, in 1797, and Washington was chosen commander-in-chief, Pinckney was appointed the second major-general in the army.[3] He retired from active life at about the year 1800, and for a quarter of a century lived in elegant ease, though taking much interest in the progress of public affairs. He found exquisite enjoyment in the bosom of his family and the companionship of books, until the latest hours of his long life. He died on the 16th of August, 1825, in the eightieth year of his age.

BARON DE STEUBEN.

MUCH of the success of the Continental army in its more skillful achievements, during the greater portion of the War for Independence, was due to the science and valor of several foreign officers engaged in its service; and the names of La Fayette, Steuben, De Kalb, Pulaski, Koskiusczko, and Du Portail, will ever be held in grateful remembrance by the American people. To Frederick William Augustus, Baron de Steuben, the army was indebted for that superior discipline displayed on the plains of Monmouth, and afterward. He had been an aid-de-camp of Frederick the Great of Prussia; and the Prince Margrave, of Baden, in whose service he afterward engaged, gave him the commission of lieutenant-general, and decorated him with the Order of Fidelity, as a special mark of favor. He received titles and emoluments from other monarchs, and splendid offers for the future, but he left them all, came to America to help a struggling young people in their efforts to be free, and joined the Continental army, as a volunteer, at Valley Forge. Congress appointed him inspector-general, with the rank and pay of major-general, in May, 1778, and his thorough

---

1. General Prevost marched from Savannah, with a strong British force, to attack Charleston, in 1779, and appeared before the city. The rapid approach of General Lincoln caused him to retreat suddenly by way of the numerous islands along the shore from Charleston to Savannah.
2. The Directory was the executive power of the French government, after the Revolution, and was established in 1795. It consisted of five persons elected for four years, and ruled in connection with two representative Chambers, called respectively *The Council of Ancients*, and *The Council of Five Hundred*.
3. One of his aids, George Washington Parke Custis, of Arlington House, Virginia, died in 1856. He was the father-in-law of Robert E. Lee.

discipline prepared the Americans for more efficient action in future. As a volunteer, he fought at Monmouth; and his services throughout the war were of the greatest benefit. He was active in Virginia from the invasion of Arnold, in January, 1781, until the capture of Cornwallis, in October following. At the siege of Yorktown, his skill and valor were particularly conspicuous, for he fought bravely and well in the trenches there.[1] At the close of the war, he remained in America. The State of New Jersey gave him a small farm; that of New York presented him with sixteen thousand acres of wild land, in Oneida county; and the Federal government granted him a pension of twenty-five hundred dollars a year. He took up his abode on his New York domain, gave one-tenth of the whole to his aids (North and Walker) and servants, and parcelled the remainder among twenty or thirty tenants. He built himself a log hut on the site of the present Steubenville, New York; and there the once courted companion of kings and nobles—the ornament of gay courts—lived in chosen obscurity, during the Summer months. His Winters were spent in the best society in the city of New York. He died suddenly of apoplexy, at his log-built residence, on the 28th of November, 1795, at the age of sixty-four years. His neighbors buried him in his garden; but afterward, according to his written request, he was wrapped in his military cloak, placed in a plain coffin, and buried in the woods near by. When a public road passed over the spot, his remains were taken up and buried a third time, in the town of Steuben, a few miles from Trenton Falls. There a plain monument, erected in 1826, covers his grave.[2]

JOHN BROOKS.

FROM many a district school-house in our favored land have issued youths of humble origin, who, by their virtues and attainments, have adorned society, and honored their country. John Brooks, one of the most eminent chief magistrates of Massachusetts, was a graduate of one of those "colleges for the people," and his boyhood and early youth were spent in the obscure labors of a farm. He was born at Medford, in 1752. At the age of fourteen years he was apprenticed to Dr. Simon Tufts, and his fellow-student in medicine was Benjamin Thompson, afterward the celebrated Count Rumford. He always evinced a fondness for military exercises, and organized the village boys into train-bands, with himself as commander. He commenced the practice of medicine at Reading, and then, in 1774, he took command of a company of minute-men. With these, he assisted in annoying the British forces in their retreat from Concord, on the 19th of April, 1775, and soon afterward he was commissioned a major in the army that gathered around Boston. He assisted Prescott in throwing up the redoubt on Breed's Hill, but was absent on duty during the battle the next day. He remained with the Continental army at Boston until the following year, and then participated in the battles on Long Island and at White Plains. He was with Arnold in his expedition against St. Leger, at Fort Schuyler, on the Mohawk, in 1777, and bore the commission of lieutenant-colonel. At the

---

1. On one occasion, when a bomb-shell was about to burst, the Baron leapt into a ditch, followed by Wayne, who fell on him. "Ah, my dear fellow," said the Baron, "I know you are always good at covering a retreat."
2. General William North, one of his aids, erected a mural monument to the memory of Steuben, in a German church in Nassau Street, New York. It is now in the church edifice of that congregation, in Forsyth Street. General North was United States senator, and was twice Speaker of the New York Assembly. He passed the latter years of his life in New London, Connecticut, but died in the city of New York, on the 4th of January, 1836, at the age of eighty-three years.

battles at Saratoga, in September and October following, he performed signal services at the head of a regiment, and he is a conspicuous person in Trumbull's picture of the Surrender of Burgoyne. At the battle of Monmouth he was acting adjutant-general; and during the whole war he was a most valuable officer, especially while assistant inspector, under Baron Steuben. Washington always had the greatest confidence in his integrity and patriotism; and in the crisis at Newburgh, in the Spring of 1783, when sedition and mutiny appeared rife, the commander-in-chief made Brooks his special confidant.[1]

At the close of the war, Colonel Brooks, poor in purse but rich in character, resumed the practice of his profession, at the same time he held the office of major-general of militia. He was a zealous friend of the Federal Constitution, and received local offices under it, from the hands of Washington. When war with England was declared in 1812, General Brooks was appointed adjutant-general of Massachusetts, by Governor Strong; and in 1816, he succeeded that gentleman as chief magistrate of his native State. For seven consecutive years he performed the duties of governor with dignity and fidelity; but declined a reëlection in 1823, and retired to private life. He continued to evince much interest in societies to which he belonged, especially that of the Massachusetts Medical Society, of which he was president. Admiring his abilities as a statesman, the Faculty of Harvard University conferred upon him the honorary degree of Doctor of Laws. Governor Brooks died on the 1st of March, 1825, at the age of about seventy-three years.

CHARLES CARROLL.

THE last survivor of the glorious company of those who signed the Declaration of Independence, was Charles Carroll, who, to enable the British ministers to identify him as an arch-rebel, and not mistake his cousin of the same name, added "of Carrollton" to his signature on that great instrument. He was of Irish descent,[2] and was born at Annapolis, in Maryland, on the 20th of September, 1737. His father was a Roman Catholic gentleman of large fortune, and sent Charles to the Jesuits' College at St. Omer, in France, when he was eight years of age. There he remained six years, when he was transferred to another seminary of learning at Rheims. He was graduated at the College of Louis the Grande at the age of seventeen years. He then commenced the study of law at Bourges, remained there a year, then went to Paris and studied until 1757, and finally completed his professional education in London. After an absence of twenty-two years, he returned to Maryland, in 1765, a finished scholar and well-bred gentleman. He found his countrymen in a state of high excitement on account of the Stamp Act, and at once espoused the popular cause with great zeal. He held a fluent and powerful pen; and as early as 1771, Mr. Carroll was known throughout the colonies as an able advocate of popular liberty.

---

1. The remnant of the Continental army, stationed at Newburgh in 1783, became much discontented by the prospect of being soon disbanded without being paid the amount of arrears due, or any provision for the future being made for them. An anonymous writer (afterward acknowledged to be Major Armstrong), called a meeting of the officers to adopt measures to compel Congress to make a satisfactory arrangement, or else to take redress in their own hands. Washington took immediate steps to prevent the convention, and called a meeting, himself, of the officers. It resulted in a noble exhibition of patriotism on the part of the great body, and the army was saved the disgrace of a mutiny, after so much suffering in the glorious cause.

2. His grandfather, Daniel Carroll, was a native of Littemourna, in Ireland. He was a clerk in the office of Lord Powis, and under the patronage of the third Lord Baltimore, principal proprietor of Maryland, he emigrated to that colony in the reign of James II.

Charles Carroll of Carrollton

In 1772, he engaged in an anonymous newspaper discussion with the secretary of the colony, in which he opposed the assumed right of the British government to tax the colonies without their consent. The unknown writer was thanked by the Legislature, through the public prints, for his noble defence of popular rights. When the author became known, he was at once regarded as the favorite of the people.

Mr. Carroll early perceived, and fearlessly expressed the necessity of a resort to arms, and he was among the most zealous advocates for the political independence of the colonies, even before that question assumed a tangible form in the public mind. He was chosen a member of the first committee of safety, at Annapolis, and in 1775, took his seat in the Provincial Congress. The Maryland convention had steadily opposed the sentiment of independence which was taking hold of the public mind, and that fact accounts for the delay in sending Mr. Carroll to the Continental Congress. He visited Philadelphia early in 1776, and Congress appointed him one of a committee, with Dr. Franklin and Samuel Chase, to visit Canada on a political mission.[1] Soon after his return, the views of the Maryland convention having changed, he was elected to a seat in the Continental Congress, too late to *vote* for independence, on the 4th of July, but

---

1. See sketch of Archbishop Carroll.

in time to affix his signature to the instrument on the 2d of August.[1] Ten days afterward he was appointed a member of the Board of War, and held that position during the remainder of his service in Congress. He assisted in framing a constitution for his native State, in 1776, and in 1778, he left the national council to take a more active part in the public affairs of Maryland. He was a member of the Maryland Senate, in 1781, and in 1788, he was elected one of the first senators from that State in the Federal Congress. There he remained two years, when he again took his seat in his State Senate, and retained it for ten consecutive years. He then retired from public life, at the age of sixty-four years, and in the quiet seclusion of a happy home he watched with interest the progress of his beloved country for more than thirty years longer. When Adams and Jefferson died, in 1826, Mr. Carroll was left alone on earth, in the relation which he bore to his fifty-five colleagues who signed the Declaration of Independence. He lived on, six years longer, an object of the highest veneration; and finally, on the 14th of November, 1832, his spirit passed peacefully and calmly from earth, when he was in the ninety-sixth year of his age.

EBENEZER STEVENS.

MANY of the meritorious officers of the artillery service in the War for Independence have not found that prominence in history which they deserve. Among those thus overlooked was General Stevens, who, from the earliest until the latest period of the contest, was one of the most efficient and patriotic soldiers of the time. He was born in Boston, in 1752, and at an early age became thoroughly imbued with the principles of the *Sons of Liberty*.[2] He was one of those who "made Boston Harbor a tea-pot,"[3] in December, 1773, when fearing unpleasant consequences, he withdrew to Rhode Island. He went with the Rhode Island Army of Observation to Roxbury, under General Greene, in 1775, and his skill in the artillery and engineering department was such, that early in December of that year, Washington directed him to raise two companies of artillery in Massachusetts and Rhode Island, and proceed to join Montgomery in his attack on Quebec. The commission was speedily executed by the young soldier, and after great fatigue in dragging cannons through snow and over rough hills, the little expedition reached Three Rivers on the St. Lawrence, and heard of the disastrous blow given to the Americans, at Quebec. Stevens returned to St. John's on the Sorel, and rendered efficient service in the Northern Department during 1776. He was in command of the artillery at Ticonderoga, in 1777, and shared in the mortifications of St. Clair's retreat before Burgoyne, in July. He joined General Schuyler at Fort Edward, and was so distinguished as the commander of the artillery in the battles which resulted in the capture of Burgoyne, that Trumbull, in his picture of that scene, introduced Captain Stevens in a con-

---

1. Mr. Carroll was elected on the 4th of July, and took his seat on the 18th of the same month. He affixed his signature to the Declaration, with most of the others, a little more than a fortnight afterward. See sketch of John Carroll.

2. During the excitement incident to the Stamp Act, the patriotic opposers of the measure formed associations for the purpose in the different colonies, and styled themselves *Sons of Liberty*. In like manner a large association of ladies was formed in Boston, who pledged themselves not to use tea, while an obnoxious duty was upon it, and called themselves *Daughters of Liberty*. A full account of these associations will be found in Lossing's *Pictorial Field Book of the Revolution*.

3. The people of Boston and other sea-ports resolved that cargoes of tea, which the East India Company had sent to consignees in America, should not be landed so long as an impost duty was levied on the article. An attempt to land two cargoes in Boston caused a large company, some of them in the disguise of Mohawk Indians, to go on board of the vessels on a moonlight night, in December, 1773, and break open and cast into the waters of the harbor, all the chests of the obnoxious article.

spicuous position. He continued in command of the artillery, at Albany, until the Autumn of 1778, when he became attached to Colonel Lamb's regiment, in the New York line. He was made lieutenant-colonel, by brevet, in April, 1778. For the contemplated invasion of Canada, La Fayette selected him as the chief of his artillery; and early in 1781, he accompanied the Marquis into Virginia, to oppose Arnold. General Knox, the commander-in-chief of the artillery, had the highest confidence in his excellence, and invested him with full powers, in the Autumn of 1781, to collect and forward artillery munitions for the siege of Yorktown. In the decisive actions which resulted in the capture of Cornwallis and his army, Colonel Stevens was eminently efficient; and in Trumbull's picture of that event, he is seen mounted, at the head of his regiment. From that time until the close of the war, he was with Colonel Lamb at West Point and vicinity; and when peace came, he commenced mercantile life in the city of New York. He accepted office in the military corps of his adopted State, and rose to the rank of major-general, commanding the division of artillery of the State of New York. In 1800, he superintended the construction of the fortifications on Governor's Island, in the harbor of New York. He held the office of major-general of artillery when another war with England occurred, in 1812, and he was called into the service of the United States, in defence of the city of his adoption. He was senior major-general until the return of peace, in 1815. For many years he was among the most distinguished merchants of the commercial metropolis, and died at the green old age of about seventy-one years, on the 2d of September, 1823.

ISAIAH THOMAS.

PRINTING, "the art preservative of all arts," has been represented, at all times in its history, by men eminent for their intellectual greatness and extensive social and political influence. Philosophers, statesmen, and theologians, of the highest order of genius, have been fellows of the craft. Eminent among the best was Isaiah Thomas, the historian of the art. He was born in Boston, in 1749, and at six years of age, being the son of a poor widow, he was placed in charge of Zechariah Fowle, a ballad and pamphlet printer, to learn the great art. After an apprenticeship of eleven years, he went to Nova Scotia, where he worked for a Dutch printer, awhile. There, as well as in the other colonies, the Stamp Act was just beginning to create much opposition to the imperial government, and young Thomas, who had been nurtured in the Boston school of politics, took a prominent part against the measure. He was threatened with arrest, but the repeal of the act lulled the storm, and in 1767, he returned to New England. He afterward went to Wilmington, North Carolina, and also to Charleston, in search of employment, but without success. Disappointed and poor he returned to Boston, in 1770, and formed a business partnership with his old master. It continued only three months, when Thomas purchased the printing establishment of Fowle, on credit, worked industriously and well, and in March following he issued the first number of "*The Massachusetts Spy*;" a weekly political and commercial Paper; open to all Parties, but influenced by None." It gave the ministerial party a great deal of uneasiness, and vain efforts were made to control or destroy it.[2] When the British held martial

---

1. Fowle & Thomas had issued a tri-weekly paper with this name the previous year, but it did not continue long. The new weekly paper was printed on a larger sheet than any yet published in Boston.
2. An article against the government, which appeared in the *Spy* toward the close of 1771, caused Governor Hutchinson to order Thomas before the council, to answer. The bold printer refused com-

rule in Boston, in 1775, Thomas took his establishment to Worcester, and fourteen days after the skirmishes at Lexington and Concord, he commenced the publication of the *Spy*, there. He continued in Worcester after the war, and was blessed with prosperity. He formed a partnership, in 1788, and opened a printing-house and book-store in Boston, under the firm of Thomas and Andrews. They planted similar establishments in other places, to the number of eight; and in 1791, they published a fine folio edition of the Bible. By industry and economy, Thomas amassed a handsome fortune, and was an honored citizen of his adopted town. He was one of the principal founders of the Antiquarian Society at Worcester, and was its president and chief patron. In 1810, he printed and published his *History of Printing in America*, in two octavo volumes, which has ever been a standard work on the subject. He lived more than twenty years afterward, the Patriarch of the Press. His death occurred at Worcester on the 4th of April, 1831, when he was eighty-two years of age.

RUFUS KING.

ALMOST every young man of talent, at the commencement of the War for Independence, engaged in the public service, civil or military, and oftentimes in both. Young men of every profession and from every class became soldiers, as volunteers or levies, or took part in the public councils. These were schools of the highest practical importance to those who were to be participants in the founding of the new republican confederation. Among the worthiest and most active of these, was Rufus King, son of an eminent merchant of Scarborough, Maine. He was born in the year 1755, and received a good preparatory education under Samuel Moody, of Byfield. He entered Harvard College, in 1773, and remained there until the students were dispersed when the American army gathered around Boston. Young King resumed classical studies with his old teacher in the Autumn of 1775. He returned to college in 1777, and was graduated with great reputation as a classical scholar and expert orator. He studied law under Judge Parsons, at Newburyport, after having served as aid to General Glover, for a short time, in Sullivan's expedition against the British on Rhode Island, in the Summer of 1778. In 1780, he was admitted to the bar, and his first effort, as a pleader, was as adverse counsel to his eminent law-tutor. It was an effort of great power, and opened at once the high road to proud distinction in his profession. The people appreciated his talent; and in 1784, he was elected to a seat in the legislature of Massachusetts. He was chosen a representative of Massachusetts, in Congress, the same year; and in 1785, he introduced a resolution, in that body, to prohibit slavery in the territories north-west of the Ohio river. In 1787, he was chosen a delegate to the Federal Convention, and there he was one of the most efficient and zealous friends of the constitution framed by that body. In the Massachusetts convention called to consider that instrument, he nobly advocated its high claims to support. He soon afterward made New York city his residence, for there he had married Miss Alsop, daughter of one of the delegates in the first Continental Congress; and there was a wider field for his extraordinary mental powers. He was chosen a member of the State Legislature, in 1789, and in the Summer

---

pliance; and the attorney-general tried, but in vain, to have him indicted by the grand jury. Such resistance was made to these measures, that the government at length deemed it prudent to cease efforts to silence his seditious voice.

of that year, he and General Schuyler were elected the first senators in Congress, from New York. On the promulgation of the treaty made by Jay, with the British government, in 1794, there was much excitement, and King and Hamilton warmly defended it, in a series of papers signed *Camillus*, all of which, except the first ten, were written by the former. In the United States Senate, he was one of the most brilliant of its orators, and his influence was everywhere potential.

In the Spring of 1796, President Washington appointed Mr. King minister plenipotentiary to Great Britain, where he continued to represent his country with great dignity and ability during the whole of Mr. Adams' administration, and the first two years of Mr. Jefferson's. During his sojourn in London, he successfully adjusted many difficulties between his own government and that of Great Britain, and he possessed the warmest personal esteem of the first men in Europe. After his return home, in 1803, he retired to his farm, on Long Island, and remained in comparative repose until aroused to action by the events immediately preceding the war declared in 1812. While at the court of Great Britain, he had made unwearied efforts to induce that government to abandon its unjust and offensive system of impressing seamen into the naval service, and he took an active part in public affairs during the first year of the war. He was elected to the United States Senate, for six years, in 1813, and in 1820, he was reëlected for the same length of time. Hoping to be useful to his country in the adjustment of some foreign relations, Mr. King accepted the appointment of minister to Great Britain, from Mr. Adams, in 1825, and took up his residence in London. Severe illness during the voyage disabled him for active duties, and after being absent about a year, he returned home. His health gradually failed, and on the 29th of April, 1827, he died at his seat, near Jamaica, Long Island, at the age of seventy-two years.

HENRY LEE.

THE right arm of the Southern army, under General Greene, was the legion of lieutenant-colonel Henry Lee, and its commander was one of the most useful officers throughout the war. He was born in Virginia, on the 29th of January, 1756. His early education was intrusted to a private tutor under his father's roof, and his collegiate studies were at Princeton, under the guidance of the patriotic Dr. Witherspoon. There he was graduated in 1774; and two years afterward, when only twenty years of age, he was appointed, on the nomination of Patrick Henry, to the command of one of the six companies of cavalry raised by his native State for the Continental service. These were at first under the general command of the accomplished Colonel Theodoric Bland.[1] In 1777, Lee's corps was placed under the immediate command of Washington, and it soon acquired a high character for discipline and bravery. Its leader was promoted to major, with the command of a separate corps of cavalry; and with this legion he performed many daring exploits. In July, 1779, he captured a British fort, at Paulus's Hook (now Jersey City), for which Congress gave him thanks and a gold medal. He was at Tappan when André was tried and condemned, in the Autumn of 1780; and from his corps Washington selected the brave Sergeant Champe to attempt the seizure of Arnold, in New York, so as to punish the really guilty, and let the involuntary spy go free.[2]

Lee was promoted to lieutenant-colonel, in November, 1780, and early in 1781, he joined the army under Greene, in the Carolinas. In connection with Marion, and other Southern partisans, he performed efficient service for many months, in the region of the Santee and its tributaries. He was active in Greene's famous retreat before Cornwallis, from the Yadkin to the Virginia shores of the Dan, and in the battles at Guilford, Augusta, Ninety-Six, and Eutaw Springs, the services of his legion were of vast importance, for Lee was always in the front of success as well as of danger. Soon after the latter battle, he left the field, returned to Virginia, and married a daughter of Philip Ludwell Lee, of Stratford. He bore to civil life the assurance of his Southern commander, that his services had been greater than those of any one man attached to the army.

Mr. Lee resided with his father-in-law, and in 1786, was elected to a seat in

---

1. He was a native of Virginia, qualified himself for the practice of medicine, but cast it aside for the duties of a soldier, when the war broke out. He performed many brilliant services with his corps of dragoons, and he was in command of the British and German captives, taken at Saratoga, while on their march to, and residence in Virginia. In 1780, he was elected to a seat in Congress. He was opposed to the Federal Constitution, but acquiesced in the will of the majority, and represented his district in the Federal Congress. He died at New York, in June, 1790, while attending a session of Congress, at the age of forty-eight years.

2. Washington was anxious to save Andre, and made great efforts to secure the person of Arnold. Sergeant Champe went to the British in New York, as a deserter, enlisted in Arnold's corps, and just as his scheme for seizing the traitor and conveying him across the Hudson, on a dark night, was perfected, that corps embarked for Virginia, with Champe. He afterward deserted, and joined Lee's legion in North Carolina.

the Continental Congress, where he served his constituency faithfully until the adoption of the Federal Constitution. In 1791, he succeeded Beverly Randolph as governor of Virginia, and held that office three consecutive years. When, in 1794, resistance to excise laws was made in Western Pennsylvania, and the speck of civil war, known as *The Whiskey Insurrection*, appeared, Washington appointed Governor Lee to the command of the troops sent to quell the rebellion. He performed his duty well, but made many bitter enemies among the contemners of the law. In 1799, he was a member of the Federal Congress, and was chosen by that body to pronounce a funeral oration, on the death of Washington, in the hall of the House of Representatives. He retired to private life, in 1801, and for many years was much annoyed by pecuniary embarrassments. It was while restrained within the limits of Spottsylvania county, by his creditors, in 1809, that he wrote his interesting *Memoirs of the War in the Southern Department of the United States.* He was active in attempts to quell a political mob, in Baltimore, in 1814, and was so severely wounded, that he never recovered. Towards the close of 1817, he went to the West Indies, for his health, but found no sensible relief. On his return the following Spring, he stopped to visit a daughter of General Greene, on Cumberland Island, on the coast of Georgia, and there he expired on the 25th of March, 1818, at the age of sixty-two years.

JOHN RUTLEDGE.

LIKE Governor Trumbull in New England, John Rutledge was the soul of patriotic activity in South Carolina, during the darkest period of the Revolution, whether in civil authority or as general director of military movements. He was a native of Ireland, and came to America with his father, Doctor John Rutledge, in 1735. After receiving the best education that could be obtained in Charleston, he went to London, and prepared for the profession of the law, at the Temple.[1] In 1761, he returned to Charleston, became an active and highly esteemed member of his profession, and stood shoulder to shoulder with Gadsden, Laurens, and others, in defence of popular rights. He was chosen one of the representatives of his adopted State, in the first Continental Congress, with his brother, Edward, as one of his colleagues. When, in the Spring of 1776, the civil government of South Carolina was revised, and a temporary State Constitution was framed, Rutledge was appointed president of the State, and commander-in-chief of its military. Under his efficient administration, Charleston was prepared for the attack made in June, by Clinton and Parker, and the enemy was repulsed. His patriotism was never doubted, yet, like many others of the aristocracy, he had not entire faith in the wisdom and integrity of the people. When, therefore, in 1778, a permanent constitution for South Carolina was adopted, he refused his assent, because he thought it too democratic. His prejudice yielded, however, and in 1779, he was chosen governor under it, and was invested with temporary dictatorial powers by the legislature. He took the field at the head of the militia, and managed both civil and military affairs with great skill and energy, until after the fall of Charleston, in 1780.[2] When Greene, aided by the southern partisan leaders, drove the British from the interior, to

---

1. This was the most celebrated place for law students in London. The building or buildings were so called, because they formerly belonged to the Knights Templars. They are designated as the Inner and the Middle Temple. The original Temple-hall, or house of the Templars, was erected in 1572; and Temple-bar was built just one hundred years afterward.
2. Charleston was besieged in the Spring of 1780, by a combined land and naval force, under General Sir Henry Clinton and Admiral Arbuthnot. It was defended by Lincoln, with a feeble force, for nearly three months. On the 12th of May, 1780, it was surrendered to the British.

the sea-board, in 1781, Rutledge convened a legislative assembly at Jacksonborough, and thoroughly re-established civil government. After the war he was made judge of the Court of Chancery. He was a member of the convention that framed the constitution of the United States; and in 1789, was elevated to the bench of the Supreme Court of the Republic, as associate justice. He was appointed chief justice of South Carolina, in 1791; and in 1796, he was called to the duties of chief justice of the United States. In every official station he displayed equal energy and sterling integrity; and while yet bearing the robes of the highest judicial office in the Republic, he was summoned from earth. His death occurred in July, 1800, when he was about seventy years of age.

JOHN LANGDON.

"YOUR head will be a button for a gallows rope," said Secretary Atkinson to young John Langdon, toward the close of 1774, after he and others, among whom was the future General Sullivan, had seized the fort at Portsmouth, and carried off a hundred barrels of powder, and a quantity of small arms, before Governor Wentworth even suspected such a daring enterprise.[1] That brave hero and future statesman was born in the town of Portsmouth, New Hampshire, in 1740. He was educated at a public grammar school, prepared himself for mercantile life, and prosecuted business upon the sea until the great ocean of public feeling began to be agitated by the tempest of the Revolution. Then he espoused the republican cause, and his first overt act of rebellion and treason was the seizure of the powder and arms, above alluded to. In January, 1775, he was chosen a delegate to the Continental Congress. There he remained until 1776, when affairs in his own State demanded his presence there. He also served as a volunteer in some military expeditions. In 1777, he was Speaker of the New Hampshire Assembly; and when Burgoyne was approaching the Hudson with his invading army, and the whole North and East were in commotion, Langdon offered to loan the State three thousand hard dollars, and the avails of his silver plate and some West India goods, to equip men for the army under Gates, remarking that if the American cause should triumph, he would get his pay, if not, his property would be of no value to him. He did more, for, with many members of the New Hampshire legislature, he served as a volunteer in the battles at Saratoga, which resulted in the capture of Burgoyne. Mr. Langdon was president of the New Hampshire convention that framed the State Constitution, in 1779; and the same year he was appointed Continental agent to contract for building some ships for the service of Congress. He was again elected to a seat in Congress, in 1783, and in March, 1785, he was chosen chief magistrate of his native State. He represented New Hampshire (with Nicholas Gilman) in the convention which framed the Federal Constitution, was its zealous supporter, and after serving another term as governor, or president of his State, was chosen to a seat in the United States Senate, where he served about ten years. He was afterward an active member of the State Legislature, and was governor of the State almost four years. He retired into private life, in 1812, whither he carried the most profound respect of his countrymen. That venerable patriot died at his birth-place, on the 18th of September, 1819, at the age of seventy-eight years.

---

1. Atkinson was Langdon's personal friend, and was in earnest. The crowd present assured Langdon that they would protect him at all hazards. Atkinson advised him to flee from the country, but the young patriot remained, and in all the trying scenes that soon followed he was nobly sustained by his fellow-citizens.

ROBERT FULTON.

THE genius of Fulton was of no ordinary mold. It began to unfold in less than ten years after his birth, which occurred at Little Britain, Lancaster county, Pennsylvania, in 1765. His parents were industrious and virtuous natives of Ireland, in easy but not affluent circumstances, and Protestants in religious faith. His early education was meagre, but application in after life supplied all deficiencies. At the age of seventeen years he was painting landscapes and portraits in Philadelphia, and educating his mechanical faculties by observations in the workshops of that capitol. Pleased with his love of art, his friends sent him to London, at the age of twenty-one years, to receive instruction in painting, from the eminent Benjamin West. He formed one of that artist's family for several years; and then, for a season, he resided in Devonshire, and enjoyed the society of the Duke of Bridgewater and Earl of Stanhope,[1] whose tastes for mechanics developed and encouraged those of Fulton.

Internal navigation by canals, and improvements in machinery, now engrossed his attention, and having heard of Fitch's experiments in the application of

---

1. Stanhope was the inventor of the printing press, known by his name, and which was in general use until succeeded by the invention of Andrew Ramage.

steam to the propulsion of boats, a new and glorious vision filled his mind with its splendors. He abandoned the profession of a painter, and became a civil engineer. In the Summer of 1797, he entered the family of Joel Barlow, in Paris, and there, for seven years, he assiduously pursued the study of the natural sciences and of modern languages. There he became acquainted with the wealthy and influential Robert R. Livingston. That gentleman fired the zeal of Fulton, by representing the immense advantages to be derived from the use of steam in navigating the inland waters of the United States. Wealth, talent, and genius joined hands, and Fulton and Livingston navigated the Seine, by a steam-boat, in 1803. They came to America, and in 1807, the steamer *Clermont*, Fulton's experiment boat, made a voyage from New York to Albany, one hundred and fifty miles, in thirty-six hours, against wind and tide! His triumph was complete and his fame was secured.

Fulton received his first patent in 1809, and for several years he was engaged in the perfection of steam-boat machinery, and in the improvement and construction of submarine explosive machines, called *Torpedoes*, to be used for blowing up vessels of war. He was successful in the construction of submarine batteries; and his great heart was delighted, in 1814, by the appropriation by Congress of three hundred and twenty thousand dollars, for the construction of a steam ship-of-war, under his directions. The *Fulton* was launched in July of that year; and he who saw in her another triumph of his own genius and skill, was marching onward in the pathway of renown to great emoluments, when he was suddenly laid in the grave. He died on the 24th of February, 1815, at the age of fifty years. Six steam-boats were then afloat on the Hudson, and the honor of first crossing the ocean by steam power was just within his grasp, for he was building a vessel, designed for a voyage to St. Petersburg, in Russia.

HUGH WILLIAMSON.

ONE of the most distinguished of the adopted sons of North Carolina, both for his intellectual acquirements, and his varied public services, was Hugh Williamson, a native of Nottingham, Pennsylvania, where he was born on the 5th of December, 1735, the eldest of ten children. He was educated at the University of Pennsylvania, where he was graduated in 1757, and then prepared himself for the gospel ministry. He was licensed to preach, but ill health compelled him to abandon that vocation, and in 1760, he was appointed Professor of Mathematics, in the institution where he was educated. He resigned his professorship in 1764, and went to Edinburgh to study the science of medicine. He pursued the same studies, for awhile, at Utrecht; and in 1772, he returned to Philadelphia, and commenced the successful practice of his profession. He took much interest in the subject of popular education, and near the close of 1773, he sailed from Boston for England, with Dr. Ewing, to solicit aid for an academy at Newark, in Delaware. The vessel in which they sailed conveyed the first intelligence to Europe of the destruction of tea in Boston Harbor. As Dr. Williamson saw the occurrence, he was summoned before the Privy Council, in February, 1774, to give information on the subject. He gave a lucid account of the public feeling in America, and assured the Council that a persistance in enforcing parliamentary measures offensive to the colonists, would result in civil war. Soon after this he went to Holland and the Low Countries, and remained on the Continent until intelligence of the Declaration of Independence by the Continental Congress reached him, when he sailed for America. Off the capes of the Delaware the vessel was captured by a British cruiser, but Dr. Williamson escaped in an open boat, with some important despatches.

In 1777, Dr. Williamson went to Charleston, and with a younger brother engaged in mercantile speculations. To avoid capture, he ordered his vessel, which he had laden with merchandise for Baltimore, to proceed to Edenton, North Carolina, where he disposed of the cargo, and settled as a practising physician. The following year, he served as surgeon under Colonel Richard Caswell, and was at the head of the medical staff of that officer in the disastrous battle at Camden, in August, 1780. He was permitted to attend his wounded countrymen within the British lines, and was instrumental in relieving much suffering. He resumed his profession, at Edenton, when peace was promised; and in 1782, he represented that district in the North Carolina legislature. He was elected to Congress, in 1784, where he represented his adopted State for three years; and in 1787, he was a member of the convention that framed the Federal Constitution. That instrument was not regarded with favor, in North Carolina, and because of his zealous advocacy of it, Dr. Williamson lost much of his popularity, for awhile. The cloud soon passed away, and from 1790 until 1792, he represented the Edenton district in the Federal Congress. He then retired to private life, and devoted himself to literary pursuits, making the city of New York, (where he married his wife in 1789), his place of residence. His most important production was a *History of North Carolina*, in two volumes, published in 1812. Two years afterward, he was associated with Dewitt Clinton in establishing the Literary and Philosophical Society of New York; and he was active in social life until the last. Dr. Williamson died suddenly, while taking an evening ride, on the 22d of May, 1819, at the age of eighty-four years.

RICHARD MONTGOMERY.

IN September, 1759, the accomplished General Wolfe perished in the arms of victory on the Plains of Abraham, at Quebec, at the early age of thirty-two years. Near him, when he fell, was a handsome young soldier, ten years his junior, who, a little more than sixteen years later, was the commanding general in a siege of the same city, and also perished in the midst of his troops. That young soldier was Richard Montgomery, who was born in the north of Ireland, in 1736, and entered the British army at the age of twenty years. After the conquest of Canada, he was in the campaign against Havana, under General Lyman; and at the peace in 1763, he took up his residence in New York. He finally left his regiment, returned to England, and made unsuccessful attempts to purchase a majority. He sold his commission in 1772, came to America, and purchased a beautiful estate on the Hudson, in Dutchess county, New York. He soon afterward married a daughter of Robert Livingston. It was a happy union, but those dreams of long years of domestic peace were soon disturbed by the gathering tempest of the Revolution. Montgomery, with all the ardor of the people of his birth-land, espoused the patriot cause, joined the army under General Schuyler, destined for the invasion of Canada, and was second in command, in the Autumn of 1775, bearing the commission of a brigadier. Illness of the chief devolved the whole duty of leadership upon Montgomery, and he went on successfully until St. John, Chambly, and Montreal, were in his power. Congress gave him the commission of major-general, and amid the snows of December, he pressed forward to join Arnold in an assault upon Quebec. For three weeks he besieged that city; and early on the morning of the 31st of December, while snow was fast falling, an attempt was made to take the town by storm. Montgomery was killed while loading a division along the shores of the St. Lawrence, beneath the precipitous Cape Diamond. Arnold was also wounded at another point of attack, and the great object of the expedition failed. For forty years the remains of Montgomery rested within the walls of Quebec. At the request of his widow, in 1818, they were disinterred, conveyed to New York, and placed beneath a mural monument, erected by order of Congress, on the external wall of the front of St. Paul's church, in that city. Millions of people, passing along Broadway, have looked upon that monument, the memorial of one whose praises were spoken in Parliament by the great Chatham and Burke, and of whom Lord North said, "Curse on his virtues; they have undone his country." He was in the fortieth year of his age when he fell.[1]

JOSEPH BRANT.

THAYENDANEGEA, one of the most renowned of the warriors of the Six Nations of Indians in the State of New York, was a Mohawk of the pure native blood. His father was an Onondaga chief, and Thayendanegea (which signifies a *bundle of sticks*, or *strength*), was born on the banks of the Ohio, in 1742. There his father died, and his mother returned to the Mohawk Valley with her two children—this son, and a sister who became a concubine of Sir William Johnson. She married a Mohawk, whom the white people called Barent, which, in abbreviation, was pronounced Brant. Sir William Johnson placed the boy in Dr. Wheelock's school, at Lebanon, in Connecticut, where he was named Joseph, and was educated for the Christian ministry among his own people. Sir William employed him as secretary and agent in public affairs, with the Indians, and his missionary labors never extended much beyond the services of an interpreter for Mr. Kirkland and others. He was much employed in that business from 1762 to 1765. Under the stronger influence of Johnson and his family, Brant resisted the importunities of Mr. Kirkland to remain neutral when the war of the Revolution approached, and he took an active part with the British and Tories. In 1775, he left the Mohawk Valley, went to Canada, and finally to England, where he attracted great attention, and found free access to the nobility. The Earl of Warwick caused Romney, the eminent painter, to make a portrait of him, for his collection, from which the prints of the great chief have been made. Throughout the Revolution, he was engaged in predatory warfare, chiefly on the border settlements of New York and Pennsylvania, with the Johnsons and Butlers; and he was generally known as Captain Brant, though he held a colonel's commission, from the king. Brant again visited England, in 1783, to make arrangements for the benefit of the Mohawks, who had left their ancient country, and had settled on the Grand River, west of Lake Ontario, in Upper Canada. The territory given them by the government embraced six miles on both sides of the river from its mouth to its source. There Brant was the head of the nation until his death. He translated a part of the New Testament into the Mohawk language, and labored much for the spiritual and temporal welfare of his ruined people. There he died on the 24th of November, 1807, at the age of sixty-five years. One of his sons was a British officer on the Niagara frontier, in the war of 1812; and a daughter married W. J. Kerr, Esq., of Niagara, in 1824.

---

1. The inscription on his monument says that he was thirty-seven years old. This is a mistake.

JOHN HANCOCK.

EVERY American reader is familiar with the name and the bold, clerkly signature of the president of the Continental Congress, in 1776.[1] With a hand as firm as his heart, he affixed that signature to the Declaration of Independence, saying, "The British ministry can read that name without spectacles; let them double their reward."[2] He was born at Braintree, Massachusetts, in 1737, and at an early age was left to the care of a paternal uncle, a wealthy merchant of Boston, who cherished his future heir with great affection. At a proper age, John was placed in Harvard College, where he was graduated in 1754, when only seventeen years old. He then entered his uncle's counting-room as clerk; and such was his integrity and capacity, that in 1761, he was sent to England on a business mission. There he saw the coronation of George the Third, and

---

1. The fac-simile above given is a third smaller than the original. It was reduced to accommodate it to the page.
2. This was in reference to a large reward that had been offered for the apprehension of John Hancock and Samuel Adams, early in 1775, they being considered arch-rebels,

became acquainted with some of the leading men in London. When he was twenty-six years of age, his uncle died, and left him a large fortune—the largest in New England—and he became not only one of the most eminent of the Boston merchants, but a leader in the best society of Massachusetts. Fond of popularity and the excitements of public life, he entered the arena of politics, and became a leader of the republican party in New England. He represented Boston in the General Assembly, in 1766, and was much esteemed by those noble colleagues, Otis, Cushing, and the Adamses. He stood shoulder to shoulder with those patriots in resistance to the obnoxious measures of parliament, which succeeded the Stamp Act;[1] and one of the earliest of the popular outbreaks in Boston was in consequence of the seizure of one of Mr. Hancock's vessels by the officers of the customs.[2] He was an abettor of the tea-riot, in 1773; and in March following, he boldly delivered the annual oration, in commemoration of the "Boston massacre."[3] The same year he was chosen president of the Provincial Congress of Massachusetts, and also a delegate to the Continental Congress, which convened in Philadelphia, in September. He was a member of that body the following year, and on the resignation of its president, Peyton Randolph, Mr. Hancock was chosen to fill that exalted seat. He performed his arduous duties with dignity and fidelity; and when, in July, 1776, the Declaration of Independence was adopted, it was sent forth to the world with the names of only President Hancock and Secretary Thomson attached.[4]

Mr. Hancock's health became impaired, in 1777, by the ravages of gout, a disease hereditary in the family, and he resigned his seat in Congress, and returned home, with a hope and desire for happiness in the repose of domestic life.[5] But his fellow-citizens soon sought his aid in the preparation of a constitution for the new republican State of Massachusetts. He assisted them with cheerfulness, and he was honored by an election to the chief magistracy of the commonwealth under its new organization. He held the office five consecutive years, and then declined a reëlection. In 1787, he was again elected governor, and held that position, by the annual choice of the people, until his death, which occurred on the 8th of October, 1793, at the age of fifty-six years. From the first appearance of Mr. Hancock in public life, until his death, a period of about thirty years, no man was more popular in New England. He did not possess extraordinary talent, but was endowed with great tact, a clear perception of human character and the secret of its control, and made a liberal and judicious use of his large fortune in acts of benevolence, and for public good. He was beloved by all his cotemporaries for his courtesy and kindness of heart, and his enemies were only those who foolishly allowed political differences to engender ill-will in their own hearts.

---

1. In 1767, Mr. Hancock was elected a member of the executive council, but the governor rejected him. He was again and again elected, and as often rejected. At last the governor, who knew his character well, and feared his popularity, admitted him to a seat. Previous to his first election to the council, the governor, hoping to win him to the cause of the crown, presented him with a lieutenant's commission. Mr. Hancock perceived the bribe in the proffered honor, and tore up the commission in the presence of the people.

2. His sloop *Liberty* was seized by the officers of customs, under a charge of concealing contraband goods. The people turned out, beat the officers, burned the government boat, and drove the officials to the fort in the harbor, for safety.

3. See notes on pages 59 and 87. For several years a public oration was pronounced on the anniversary of the event alluded to.

4. The other signatures were attached to the document on the 2d of August following, when the Declaration was duly engrossed on parchment.

5. When, in 1778, General Sullivan prepared to attack the British on Rhode Island, and called upon the New England militia for aid, Mr. Hancock took the field, for a short time, as commander of those of his own State. He was a participator in the stirring events near Bristol Ferry, at the northern end of Rhode Island, in August, 1778.

HENRY LAURENS.

THE descendants of the Huguenots, or French Protestant refugees, who fled to America toward the close of the seventeenth century, were all faithful to the principles of their ancestors when the War for Independence was kindling, and almost to a man were found on the side of the republicans. Of these, Henry Laurens, of South Carolina, was one of the most active and uncompromising patriots of that period. He was born in Charleston, in 1724, became a successful merchant, and in 1770, retired from business with a large fortune. He had already taken part in the political movements in the province, and when he went to England, in 1771, for the pleasure of change, he there heartily espoused the patriot cause, in the disputes then growing warmer and warmer. He even justified the people of Boston, in the destruction of the tea, in 1773, for he persisted in regarding it in its political aspect only; and in the British metropolis he was looked upon as a rebel, though he had not yet committed an overt act of rebellion. Mr. Laurens returned to Charleston, in 1774, and presided over the first Provincial Congress, held in that city in January, 1775. When the Congress appointed a council of safety to act in its stead, Mr. Laurens was chosen president of that body. It was an office equivalent to that of governor, and consequently he may be regarded as the first republican chief magistrate of South Carolina. When a temporary constitution for the new State was framed in 1776, he was made vice-president under it; and the following year he was elected to a seat in the Continental Congress. He was chosen its president, in November, 1777, but resigned the office in December, 1778. In 1779, Congress appointed him minister plenipotentiary to Holland, to negotiate a commercial treaty with that power, but he did not sail for Europe until the Summer of 1780. The vessel that conveyed him was captured by a British frigate. Mr. Laurens cast his papers into the sea, but as they did not sink immediately, they were recovered, and disclosed the fact that Holland had already been in secret negotiation with the revolted colonies. That discovery led to a declaration of war by Great Britain against Holland. Laurens was taken to London, and imprisoned in the Tower about fourteen months, under a charge of high treason. For some time he was not allowed the solace of conversation, books, pen, ink, paper, or the receipt of letters. That rigor was abated, yet his confinement made terrible inroads upon his constitution. At length public sentiment expressed its displeasure because of his treatment, and the ministry, fearing retaliation on the part of the Americans, desired an excuse to release him. One of his friends was instructed to say, that he should be pardoned, if he would write a note to Lord North, and express his sorrow for what he had done. "Pardon!" exclaimed Laurens indignantly. "I have done nothing to require a pardon, and I will never subscribe to my own infamy and the dishonor of my children." He could never be induced to make the least concessions; and finally, when public clamor for his release became too vehement to be longer disregarded, the ministry had him admitted to bail[1] on security procured by themselves, and he was discharged

---

1. In that ceremony, when the words of the recognizance, "Our Sovereign Lord the King," were read, Mr. Laurens immediately said, "Not *my* sovereign!" On another occasion, when he was requested to write to his son, John, then on a mission to France, and advise him to leave that country, Mr. Laurens replied, "My son is of age, and has a will of his own; if I should write to him in the terms you request, it would have no effect, he would only conclude that confinement and persuasion had softened me. I know him to be a man of honor. He loves me dearly, and would lay down his life to save mine; but I am sure he would not sacrifice his honor to save mine, and I applaud him." That son was worthy of such a father. He was sent to France to solicit a loan. He was assured by Vergennes, the French minister, that his king had every disposition to favor the Americans. Young Laurens withdrew to the opposite side of the room, and said, with emphasis, "*Furor*, sir! The respect which I owe to my country will not admit the term. Say that the obligation is mutual, and I cheerfully subscribe to the obligation. But as the last argument I shall offer to your excellency, the sword which I now wear in defence of

before the allotted time of trial. Lord Shelburne was then premier, and he solicited Mr. Laurens to remain in Europe, and assist in the pending negotiations for peace. Laurens complied; and in November, 1782, he signed the preliminary treaty between the United States and Great Britain. Soon after that event, he returned home, suffering much from the effects of his rigorous confinement. His constitution was shattered beyond recovery, and he steadily refused the honors of official station frequently offered him by his grateful countrymen. His health gradually failed, and on the 8th of December, 1792, he expired, when almost sixty-nine years of age. The following remarkable injunction, expressed in his Will, was literally complied with: "I solemnly enjoin it on my son, as an indispensable duty, that as soon as he conveniently can after my decease, he cause my body to be wrapped in twelve yards of tow-cloth, and burnt until it be entirely consumed, and then, collecting my bones, deposit them wherever he he may think proper."

JAMES OTIS.

"OTIS was a flame of fire. With a promptitude of classical allusions, a depth of research, a rapid summary of historical events and dates, a profusion of legal authorities, a prophetic glance of his eyes into futurity, and a rapid torrent of impetuous eloquence, he hurried away all before him. American Independence was then and there born." Such was the expressed estimate of the power and influence of James Otis, by John Adams, when writing of that early patriot's great speech against Writs of Assistance,[1] before the General Court of Massachusetts. He was the son of Colonel James Otis, of Barnstable, and was born there on the 5th of February, 1725. He was educated at Harvard College, where he was graduated in 1743. Choosing the law for a profession, he studied it under the eminent Jeremy Gridley, and commenced its practice at Plymouth when he was twenty-one years of age. Two years afterward, he went to Boston to reside, where his talent and integrity soon raised him to a front rank in his profession. It was in 1761 that he made the powerful speech above alluded to, on which occasion he was opposed by his law-tutor, Mr. Gridley, then attorney-general of the province. "Every man of an immense crowded assembly," wrote John Adams, "appeared to go away, as I did, ready to take up arms against Writs of Assistance." The following year Mr. Otis was elected to a seat in the Massachusetts General Assembly, and he became the head and front of opposition to aggressive ministerial measures, in New England. In the Colonial Congress of delegates at New York, in 1765, gathered in consequence of the passage of the Stamp Act, Mr. Otis was an efficient member; and the same year he wrote and published, in pamphlet form, a powerful vindication of the rights of the colonies. It was re-published in London, and awakened the ire of ministers to such a degree that they threatened the author with arrest on a charge of

---

France, as well as my own country, unless the succor I solicit is immediately accorded, I may be compelled, within a short time, to draw against France as a British subject. I must now inform your excellency that my next memorial will be presented to his majesty, in person." This bold reply had great effect upon Vergennes, for he most dreaded a *reconciliation* between the United States and Great Britain. True to his promise, Laurens attended at the audience chamber of the king, the next day, and presented his memorial, in person, to his majesty. It was handed to Count Segur, and on the following day Laurens was officially informed that the required aid should be given. The succor came, and in the Autumn, by the assistance of French funds, and French soldiers and seamen, Cornwallis was captured, and the death blow to British power in America was given. That noble young man was killed in a skirmish on the banks of the Combahee, at the close of hostilities, in August, 1782, when he was only twenty-nine years of age. He had been Washington's aid, and that chief loved him as a child. Greene wrote, "The State will feel his loss."

1. See note 2, page 122.

sedition. For several years, Mr. Otis held the office of judge advocate. Becoming disgusted with the continually developing government schemes to enslave the colonies, he determined to dissolve all personal connection with the crown party, and resigned that lucrative office, in 1767.

Mr. Otis was sometimes unnecessarily caustic in the use of his tongue and pen. In the Summer of 1769, he published some severe strictures upon the conduct of the commissioners of customs, and early in September, he had a personal affray with one of them, named Robinson, and others. Robinson struck Otis a severe blow on the head, with a bludgeon, from the effects of which he never recovered. His brain was injured and his reason was dethroned. A jury, in a civil suit against the ruffian, awarded a verdict of ten thousand dollars, damages. Otis had lucid intervals, and during one of them, he magnanimously forgave his destroyer when he craved the boon, and generously refused to receive a dollar of the sum awarded to him. For many years afterward the patriot lived on, with his great intellect in ruins, a comparatively useless man and a deep grief to his relatives.[1] None loved him more devotedly, or grieved more

---

[1] The following anecdote is related of Mr. Otis as illustrative of his ready use of Latin even during moments of mental aberration. Men and boys, heartless and thoughtless, would sometimes make themselves merry at his expense when he was seen in the streets afflicted with lunacy. On one occasion he was passing a crockery store, when a young man, who had a knowledge of Latin, sprinkled some water upon him from a sprinkling-pot with which he was wetting the floor of the second story, at the same time saying, *Pluit tantum, nescio quantum, Scis ne tu?* "It rains so much, I know not how much. Do you know?" Otis immediately picked up a missile, and, hurling it through the window of the crockery

bitterly, than his gifted sister, Mercy Warren, and to her hand and voice his occasionally turbulent spirit lent a quick and willing obedience. When, at times, the cloud was lifted from his reason, he talked calmly of death, and often expressed a desire to die by a stroke of lightning. His wish was gratified. On the 23d of May, 1783, he stood leaning on his cane, in the door of a friend's house at Andover, watching the sublime spectacle of a hovering thunder-cloud, when suddenly a bolt leaped from it like a swift messenger from God to his spirit, and killed him instantly.[1]

All through the great struggle for independence, to which his eloquence had excited his countrymen, James Otis was like a blasted pine on the mountains— like a stranded wreck in the midst of the billows. It was just as the sunlight of peace burst upon his disenthralled country, that his spirit departed for the realm of unclouded intelligence.

JAMES CRAIK.

OF the family physician of the great Washington, and the companion-in-arms of that beloved Leader in his earlier military career, there are but few records left, and these cluster like parasites around the huge proportions of the biography of the Father of his country. Dr. Craik was a native of Scotland, and settled in Virginia, while yet quite a youth. He accompanied lieutenant-colonel Washington in his expedition against the French and Indians in Western Pennsylvania, in 1754, and was a surgeon in one of the provincial corps, under Braddock, the following year. He dressed that officer's fatal wounds on the night of the battle of the Monongahela, and stood by Colonel Washington when he read the impressive funeral service of the Church of England, over the body of the fallen commander. Fifteen years afterward, while Dr. Craik was exploring some wild lands near the mouth of the Great Kenhawa, he met a venerable chief, who said, that in the battle when Braddock was killed, he fired his rifle at Washington fifteen times, but could not hit him! His young warriors did the same, with a like result, and all believed that the Great Spirit specially protected the young hero.

Dr. Craik served in his professional capacity during portions of the War for Independence; and at the siege of Yorktown, he was director-general of the hospital there. He accompanied Washington to the death-bed side of Mr. Custis —one of the children of Mrs. Washington; and at the close of the war, he settled near Mount Vernon, by invitation of the Chief, and became his family physician. When the good Patriot was suddenly prostrated by the disease which terminated his life, a servant was dispatched, in great haste, for Dr. Craik. With all the attention of a dear friend, and the skill of a good physician, he watched his noble patient until the last. He lived to take an interest in another war for independence, but died in the midst of its tumult. It was on the 6th day of February, 1814, when the spirit of the family physician of Washington left earth for the world of light and immortality. He was then in the eighty-fourth year of his age.

---

store, it smashing everything in its way, exclaimed, *Fregi tot, nescio quot, Scis ne tu?* "I have broken so many, I know not how many. Do you know?"

1. Honorable Thomas Dawes wrote a commemorative ode, in which he thus referred to the manner of Otis' death :
"Hark! the deep thunders echo 'round the skies!
On wings of flame the eternal errand flies;
One chosen, charitable bolt is sped,
And Otis mingles with the glorious dead."

TIMOTHY PICKERING.

> 'Through Salem strait, without delay,
> The bold battalion took its way;
> Marched o'er a bridge, in open sight
> Of several Yankees armed for fight;
> Then, without loss of time or men,
> Veer'd 'round for Boston, back again,
> And found so well their projects thrive,
> That every soul got back alive."

THUS wrote Trumbull, in his *McFingal*,[1] concerning an event at Marblehead, in Massachusetts, in which Colonel Timothy Pickering, one of the most useful of the military and civil officers of the Republic in its earlier days, was chief actor. Pickering was a native of the ancient town of Salem, in Essex county, Massachusetts, where he was born on the 17th of July, 1745. He entered Harvard College, as a student, at the age of fourteen years, and was graduated at nineteen, with the usual college honors. He studied law, and entered upon its practice at the moment when the tempest of popular indignation, raised by the Stamp Act, was sweeping over the land. He entered the arena of political discussion, and was at once the avowed champion of popular freedom. For several years he was register of Salem, and colonel of the Essex militia; and when, in 1774, the people of Salem resolved to address General Gage on the subject of the Boston Port-Bill, Colonel Pickering was chosen to prepare it, and present it in person to the governor.[2] A few months afterward, he had the honor of making the first resistance to the invasion of the province by British troops. He was informed that a body of them had landed at Marblehead, for the purpose of marching through Salem to seize some American stores in the interior. It was Sunday, the 25th of February, 1775. The ministers of the churches dismissed their congregations. The men gathered at the call of Colonel Pickering, and when the invaders approached the Salem drawbridge, these minute-men boldly confronted them. Perceiving prudence to be the better part of valor, the British marched back to Marblehead, and returned to Boston. This was the event alluded to by the poet.

Early in the Spring of 1775, Colonel Pickering was chosen judge of the Court of Common Pleas, of Essex; and when, on the 19th of April, intelligence of the skirmish at Lexington reached him, he hastened, at the head of his regiment, to intercept the invaders. After that he exercised the duties of his judgeship, until the Autumn of 1776, when, at the head of seven hundred Essex men, he joined the army under Washington, near New York, and was with him in his memorable retreat across the Jerseys, toward the close of that year. He continued with the chief until the Winter of 1777–'8, when he was appointed, by Congress, a member of the Board of War. In the battles at Brandywine and Germantown, he had acted as adjutant-general, and his military skill and experience, commended him highly to his commander and the national council. In 1780, he succeeded General Greene in the important office of quartermaster-general. He performed the duties of that office efficiently until the close of the war, and then he made Philadelphia his residence. Difficulties soon afterward occurred among the Connecticut and Pennsylvania people, in the Wyoming Valley, and Mr. Pickering was appointed by his adopted State, to attempt a settlement of the

---

1. See sketch of John Trumbull, the poet.
2. For the purpose of punishing the people of Boston for the destruction of the cargoes of tea, in 1773, parliament decreed that the port of that city should be closed—that no vessels should enter or clear there, and that the Custom House and other public offices should be removed to Salem. The act took effect on the 1st of June, 1774. Great distress ensued. The people of Marblehead gave the Bostonians free use of their docks, and in the Address alluded to in the text, the people of Salem refused to receive any favors at the expense of their neighbors of Boston.

troubles. There he suffered personal ill-treatment, his life was endangered, and he finally returned to Philadelphia. In 1790, he was a member of the convention to revise the constitution of Pennsylvania; and the following year Washington appointed him Postmaster-general, as successor to Mr. Osgood. He continued in that office until the resignation of General Knox, almost four years afterward, when he succeeded that officer as Secretary of War. The same year he was appointed Secretary of State, and held the position until 1800, when Mr. Adams removed him for political causes. Mr. Pickering was then fifty-five years of age, poor in purse, but rich in integrity. He built a log cabin for his family on some of his wild land in Pennsylvania, and commenced the arduous task of clearing it for cultivation. Generous friends purchased the tract at a liberal price, and he returned to his native State, out of debt and possessing a moderate competence. The legislature of Massachusetts chose him to represent that State in the United States Senate, in 1803; and, in 1805, he was reëlected for six years. He was a member of the Board of War, of Massachusetts, in 1812, and, in 1814, he was elected a member of the United States House of Representatives. Old age now began to demand repose, and he retired from public life, in 1817. He was permitted to live about twelve years longer; and on the 29th of January, 1829, he died at Salem, when almost eighty-four years of age.

WILLIAM GORDON.

THE most faithful and impartial History of the American Revolution, by a cotemporary author, was written by William Gordon, an English independent clergyman, who was in America during the struggle of the colonists for civil and political freedom. He was born in Hertfordshire, England, about the year 1740, and at an early age was pastor of an Independent congregation at Ipswich, where his faithfulness in reproving Sabbath-breakers, made him many enemies, and gave him an uneasy place. He became successor to Dr. Jennings, as pastor of a church at Wapping, and was so much beloved, that he might have passed his life pleasantly there. But he had long yearned to make America his home, and, in 1770, he sailed for Boston. For about a year he preached in one of the churches at Roxbury; and in July, 1772, he was chosen its pastor. He was a republican, and soon became identified with the popular party, in Massachusetts, in opposition to the crown. When the Provincial Congress of that colony was formed, in 1774, Dr. Gordon was chosen its chaplain, and he continued a faithful adherent to the patriot cause. After the promulgation of the Declaration of Independence, in 1776, he conceived the idea of writing a history of the progressing struggle, and he kept full notes during the entire war. When it was ended, he was allowed free access to public records, and to the papers of Washington, Greene, Gates, and other distinguished officers. In 1786, he returned to his native country, completed his history, and published it in London, in 1788. It was soon afterward re-published in New York, in three volumes. The work is now very scarce. The author received about fifteen hundred dollars for his service in its preparation. In 1793, he was settled as a pastor at St. Neots, in Huntingdonshire, but his unpopularity as a preacher, on account of evidently failing intellect, caused his friends to persuade him to resign. He afterward made his residence at Ipswich, where he preached a few occasional sermons. Soon his memory became a blank, he sunk into imbecility, and thus remained, until his death, on the 19th of October, 1807, when about seventy-seven years of age.

DAVID RAMSAY.

THE authors of our country are indebted to Dr. David Ramsay, of South Carolina, one of the earliest historians of the War for Independence, for the first suggestions and efforts in relation to a copyright law.[1] He was born of Irish parents, in Lancaster county, Pennsylvania, on the 2d of April, 1749, and at a suitable age was placed in the College at Princeton, New Jersey. There he was graduated in 1765, and after performing the duties of tutor in a private family in Maryland for about two years, he commenced the study of medicine, in Philadelphia. In 1772, he entered upon its practice there, but, at the solicitation of friends, he made the city of Charleston his residence, the following year. There he soon took a front rank as a physician and scholar, and being an ardent patriot, he became a political leader by the side of Gadsden, Laurens, and others. His pen and tongue were ever busy in the good cause; and he also attended

---

[1]. Soon after the assembling of the first Federal Congress, under the new Constitution, in 1789, Dr. Ramsay sent in a petition, asking for the passage of a law for securing to him and his heirs the exclusive right to vend and dispose of his books, respectively entitled, *The History of the Revolution in South Carolina*, and *A History of the American Revolution*. A bill for that purpose was framed and discussed. Finally, in August, it was "postponed until the next Congress." A similar bill was introduced in January, 1790, and on the 30th of April following, the first copyright law recorded on the statute books of Congress, was passed.

the republican army as a surgeon much of the time until after the siege of Savannah, in which he participated.

Dr. Ramsay was an efficient member of the Council of Safety, and also of the Legislative Assembly of South Carolina, and became a distinguished object of British and Tory hatred. He was in Charleston during the memorable siege in 1780; and when it fell into the hands of the British, he was made a captive, and with many other eminent citizens, suffered banishment to, and imprisonment at, St. Augustine, in Florida. After an absence of eleven months, he returned, resumed his seat in the legislature at Jacksonborough, in the early part of 1782, and therein, after all his sufferings, he was one of the most earnest advocates of leniency toward the Tories. He was elected a member of Congress that same year, and continued to represent his adopted State, in that body, until after the close of the war. He was again elected to Congress, in 1785, and in November, 1786, he was chosen its president, *pro tempore*, during the protracted absence of President Hancock. His first historical work, mentioned in his petition referred to in the note on the preceding page, was published in 1785, and his *History of the American Revolution* was issued in 1790. He now declined all official stations and honors, and devoted himself to his profession, and to literary pursuits. He wrote a life of Washington, and published it in 1801; and in 1808, he published a *History of South Carolina*.[1] He then wrote a History of the United States; and he continued the employment of all of his leisure hours in the preparation of a series of historical works, intended to illustrate the state of society, literature, religion, and form of government of the United States of America, by a general historical view of the world. These he did not live to complete, according to his original intention, yet they were sufficiently perfect to warrant their publication, in twelve octavo volumes, in 1819. His *History of the United States* was brought down to the treaty of Ghent, in 1814, by the reverend Samuel Stanhope Smith, and other literary gentlemen, and published in three octavo volumes, in 1817. In the midst of his useful and unwearied labors,[2] literary and professional, Dr. Ramsay was snatched from earth. He was shot by a maniac, near his residence, and on the 8th of May, 1815, his labors and his mortal life closed forever, when he was little more than sixty-six years of age.

ROGER SHERMAN.

IT is said that "Love laughs at locksmiths." So true Genius laughs at impediments, and gathers strength for conquests in proportion to the severity of its conflicts. The life of Roger Sherman, a humble shoe-maker, illustrates the fact. He was born in Newton, Massachusetts, on the 19th of April, 1722. While Roger was an infant, his parents removed to Stonington, where they resided until the death of his father, in 1741. Roger was then nineteen years of age. He had been apprenticed to a shoemaker, but now the necessities of his mother required him to take charge of a small farm that her husband had left. They sold the estate in 1744, and went to reside in New Milford, Connecticut, where Roger's elder brother had married and settled. The journey was performed on foot by Roger, and he carried his "kit" of shoemaker's tools, on his back. There he worked industriously at his trade, and at the same time he applied himself assiduously to study, for his early education was exceedingly

---

1. This was an extension of a work, published in 1796, entitled, "A sketch of the soil, climate, weather and diseases of South Carolina."
2. Dr. Ramsay seldom slept more than four hours of the twenty-four, each day.

limited. He learned rapidly, for his mind was quick, comprehensive, and logical, and at his bench he acquired a vast amount of knowledge from books.[1] After awhile, he became a partner of his brother, in mercantile business, and employed his now more numerous leisure hours in the study of the law, but without a tutor or guide. He soon became proficient in the requisite knowledge, and at the close of 1754, he was admitted to the bar. His talents at once drew public attention toward him, and in 1755, he was elected to a seat in the General Assembly of Connecticut. He was appointed a justice of the peace the same year; and after a law-practice of about five years, he received the appointment of judge of the court for Litchfield county. He made his residence in New Haven, in 1761, where he received the same official honors and emoluments. He was also chosen treasurer of Yale College; and that institution conferred upon him the honorary degree of Master of Arts. In 1766, he was elected to the State Senate, and he fearlessly took part with the people in their opposition to the Stamp Act. He was a leading patriot in Connecticut, until the commencement of the Revolution; and all through that struggle he was ever at his post of duty, for he regarded eternal vigilance as the price of liberty. He was elected a delegate for Connecticut in the first Continental Congress, in 1774, and he held a seat there during a greater portion of the war. He advocated independence, and signed the great Declaration. In 1783, he assisted in the revision of the laws of Connecticut, and he was a representative of that State in the convention that framed the Federal Constitution. In his State convention called to act upon it, he ably advocated its ratification, and for two years after the organization of our present government, he represented Connecticut in the Federal Congress. He was then promoted to a seat in the Senate of the United States, and occupied that honorable position at the time of his death, which occurred on the 23d of July, 1793, when in the seventy-third year of his age. He then held the office of mayor of New Haven, having been the first chosen to that post of duty, after the borough was organized as a city.

RICHARD PETERS.

THE first Secretary of War, of the United States, was Richard Peters, an eminent jurist and agriculturist of Pennsylvania. He was born near Philadelphia, on the 22d of August, 1744, and was educated at the college in that city, where he was graduated in 1764. He had acquired a thorough knowledge of the Greek and Latin languages, and spoke the French and German fluently. He chose the profession of law as a pursuit, and his knowledge of the German language was of essential service to him in the management of property cases in the interior of Pennsylvania. He was distinguished for wit and humor, and when he accompanied a delegation to confer with some of the Six Nations of Indians, his vivacity so pleased the children of the forest, that he was formally adopted as a son, by the Senecas. At the opening of the Revolution he appeared in the field as captain of a company of volunteers; and when, in June, 1776, a Board of War was appointed by Congress, Mr. Peters was chosen its Secretary, and thus became the first incumbent of that office, now one of the cabinet bureaus. He held that position until 1781, and performed the duties of his sta-

---

1. He always had an open book by his side, on the bench, and read at intervals, when his eyes were not required upon his work. He thus acquired a fair knowledge of mathematics, and before he was twenty-one years of age he made astronomical calculations for an Almanac published in New York.

tion with great ability.¹ He was succeeded by General Lincoln, and retired with the expressed thanks of Congress. He was then elected a member of that body, and was a representative of his State therein for several years. On the organization of the Federal Government, in 1789, Mr. Peters declined a fiscal office tendered to him by Washington, but accepted that of judge of the United States District Court of Pennsylvania. He bore the ermine with great honor to himself and country, for thirty-six years, and was always zealous in the promotion of the material interests of his State. In the construction of public works of utility he was always foremost; and to him the country is indebted for the use of gypsum in agriculture, and the introduction of clover. The subject of farming occupied much of his attention, and he was one of the founders, and for a long time president of the Philadelphia Agricultural Society. Judge Peters died at Blockley, near Philadelphia, on the 21st of August, 1828, at the age of eighty-four years.

EDMUND RANDOLPH.

AMONG the most important members of the convention which framed the Constitution of the United States, was Edmund Randolph, the only son of John Randolph, attorney-general of Virginia. Of his birth and youthful career History bears no record. He was quite a young man when the Revolution commenced, and was one of Washington's aids, at Cambridge, in 1775. He left the army in November following, and returned to Virginia, on account of the death of his relative, Peyton Randolph, president of the Continental Congress. Four years later he was elected a member of that body, and represented his native State there until March, 1782. He succeeded Patrick Henry as governor of Virginia, in 1786, and it was chiefly through his agency that Washington was persuaded to represent that State in the Federal Convention, in 1787. Randolph was very active in that convention, but, like Patrick Henry, he was so jealous of State Rights, that he declined to affix his name to the Constitution, desiring to be free to act upon it afterward, as his judgment or the opinions of his constituents might dictate.² When the time came to act, his desire for union overcame his narrower scruples; and in the Virginia State Convention he eloquently advocated the adoption of the Federal Constitution. Washington made him the first attorney-general of the United States, under that compact; and in 1794, Randolph succeeded Mr. Jefferson as Secretary of State. He resigned that office in August, 1795, and turned his attention to his embarrassed private affairs. His resignation was in consequence of some misunderstanding with the administration; and in the Autumn of that year he published a *Vindication*. He then withdrew from public life, and never again entered the arena. He died in Frederick county, Virginia, on the 12th of September, 1813.

---

1. Next to Robert Morris, Mr. Peters was one of the most efficient men of the Revolution, in providing the "ways and means" of carrying on the war. In the Summer of 1781, Washington prepared to attack the British in New York, and was expecting the aid of Count De Grasse, with his squadron of French ships of war. He received notice that De Grasse's aid could not be given. Washington was greatly disappointed, but instantly he conceived the expedition to Virginia, which resulted in the capture of Cornwallis. Peters and Morris were then both in Washington's camp, on the Hudson. At the moment when he conceived the Virginia expedition, he turned to Peters, and said, "What can you do for me?" "With money, everything—without it, nothing," Peters replied, at the same time casting an anxious look toward Morris, the great financier. "Let me know the sum you desire," said Morris. Before noon Washington had completed his plans and estimates. Morris promised the money, and raised it upon his individual security.

2. He endeavored to procure a vote in the convention, authorizing amendments to be submitted by the State conventions, and to be finally decided on by another general convention. This proposition was rejected.

JOHN JAY.

AMONG the many tnousands of the Huguenots of France who fled to England and America toward the close of the seventeenth century, to escape fiery persecutions, was Augustus Jay, a young merchant. He landed at Charleston, in South Carolina, but soon proceeded northward, and settled in the city of New York. There he married the daughter of Balthazar Bayard, one of the refugees who came with the New Rochelle colony.[1] These were the grand-parents of John Jay, the venerated American patriot and statesman. He was born in the city of New York, on the 12th of December, 1745. At eight years of age he was placed in a boarding school at New Rochelle, and at fourteen he entered King's (now Columbia) College, as a student. He was an apt scholar, and gave early promises of his subsequent brilliant career. He was graduated in 1764, bearing the highest honors of the college, and commenced the study of law under Benjamin Kissam. He was admitted to the bar in 1768, and ascended rapidly to eminence in his profession. In 1774, he was married to the daughter of that sturdy patriot, William Livingston (afterward governor of New Jersey), and entered the political field, with great ardor, as the champion of popular

---

1. See sketch of Jacob Leisler.

rights. He was one of the most prominent members of the New York committee of correspondence, in the Spring of 1774, and in September following, he took a seat in the first Continental Congress. He was the youngest member of that body, being less than twenty-nine years of age, and he was the latest survivor. His genius as a statesman was exhibited in the *Address to the People of Great Britain*, put forth by Congress. Jefferson, ignorant of its authorship, said, "It is the production of the finest pen in America." From that time Mr. Jay was identified with most of the important civil measures in his native State; and he also performed much duty in the Continental Congress, until the Summer of 1776, when all his energies were devoted to public business in New York. With tongue, pen, and hand, he was indefatigable; and as a member of the convention at Kingston, in the Spring of 1777, he was chosen to draft a State Constitution. Under that instrument he was appointed chief justice of New York, and held his first term at Kingston, in September, 1777. He was an efficient member of the Council of Safety, appointed to act in place of the legislature, when not in session. In the Autumn of 1778, he was again elected to Congress, and three days after taking his seat there, he was chosen its president. He filled the chair with dignity and vigor, until September, 1779, when he was appointed minister to Spain to obtain the acknowledgment of the independence of the United States, to form a treaty of alliance, and to borrow money. We cannot even refer to his numerous and efficient diplomatic services from that time until 1782, when he was appointed one of the commissioners for negotiating a peace with Great Britain. In all of them he exhibited consummate skill and statesmanship; and to his vigilance we are indebted for advantages obtained by the treaty, of which the artful French minister attempted to deprive us. He signed the preliminary treaty, in November, 1782, with Adams, Franklin, and Laurens, and the following year he affixed his signature to the definitive treaty.

Mr. Jay returned to the United States, in July, 1784, and immediately entered upon the duties of chief of the foreign department of the government, to which he was chosen before his arrival. He occupied that station until the new organization of government under the Federal Constitution, when he was appointed the first chief justice of the United States. He was a zealous advocate of the Constitution, with his pen,[1] and in the verbal debates in the State convention called to consider it. In 1794, Mr. Jay was appointed an envoy extraordinary to negotiate a commercial treaty, and settle some disputes between the United States and Great Britain. The treaty was not satisfactory to a great portion of his countrymen, and as it also offended France and the "French party" here, intense excitement prevailed throughout the country. Yet he was sustained, and on his return home, in 1795, he found the office of governor of his native State awaiting him. He was chief magistrate of New York until 1801, when he withdrew from public life to enjoy repose at his beautiful seat at Bedford, in Westchester county, although he was then only fifty-six years of age. He succeeded Elias Boudinot as president of the American Bible Society, and he was a generous patron of every moral and religious enterprise. Greatly beloved by all his friends, and respected for his many virtues by his political enemies, that patriarch of the Republic went peacefully to his rest, on the 17th of May, 1829, in the eighty-fourth year of his age.

---

1. He was a colleague with Madison and Hamilton, in writing the series of papers known, in the collected form, as *The Federalist*. In that labor he was interrupted, for some time, on account of a severe wound in the head, from a stone, hurled during a riot in New York, known as *The Doctors' Mob*.

ROBERT HOWE.

BECAUSE of the excess of their patriotic zeal, Samuel Adams and John Hancock, of Massachusetts, were denounced as arch-rebels, and were excluded from the offered advantages of a general amnesty. In like manner, Sir Henry Clinton denounced Robert Howe and Cornelius Harnett, of the Cape Fear region, in North Carolina, in the Spring of 1776, and they were honored with the ban of outlawry because of their patriotism. Howe was born in Brunswick, North Carolina, but, strange to say, history bears no record of his private life, and both it and tradition are silent respecting the time of his birth and his death. When Josiah Quincy was in Wilmington, in 1773, he made the acquaintance of Mr. Howe, and said in a letter, descriptive of an evening spent in political discussion: "Robert Howe, Esq., Harnett, and myself, made the social triumvirate of the evening." So bitter were the Tories against Howe, that his property was several times injured; and when Clinton appeared in the Cape Fear region, early in 1776, he sent Cornwallis, with nine hundred men, to indulge his petty spite by ravaging that patriot's plantation, near old Brunswick village.

Howe was appointed colonel of the first North Carolina regiment, in 1775, and in December of that year, he joined Woodford, of Virginia, at Norfolk, in opposition to Governor Dunmore and his motley army.[1] For his gallantry there, Congress appointed him a brigadier in the Continental army, and ordered him to Virginia. He was with the army, at the North, during portions of 1776 and 1777; and in the Spring of 1778, he was promoted to major-general, and placed in chief command of the Southern army. At his head-quarters at Savannah, he planned a campaign against the British and Tories in Florida, in the Summer of 1778. It failed in its execution; and at the close of that year, he was driven from Savannah, by a British force under lieutenant-colonel Campbell. These reverses caused him to be censured unjustly;[2] and when General Lincoln took command of the Southern army, Howe attached himself to that of the northern department, the following year. He coöperated with Wayne in his attack upon Stony Point, on the Hudson, in 1779. He was on duty in the vicinity of West Point and the Hudson Highlands from that time until near the close of the war. Washington appointed him, in two instances, to discharge the important duty of quelling a mutiny, first in the New Jersey line, and then in that of Pennsylvania. He always had the unbounded confidence of the commander-in-chief. Though always a very useful officer, Howe never became distinguished for any great achievement. Like the actions of General Heath and many others, his line of duty lay in the *useful* rather than the *brilliant*—their military history is an epic, not an epigram.

---

1. Dunmore, the royal governor of Virginia, having been driven from Williamsburg, by the people, commenced a depredatory warfare upon the coast of that State. His force consisted of Tory refugees and negroes, yet, with the aid of some British ships, he succeeded in burning Norfolk, on the 1st of January, 1776.

2. Among those who raised their voice against General Howe, was Christopher Gadsden, of Charleston. Howe required him to deny or retract. Gadsden would do neither, and a duel ensued. All the damage sustained by the parties, in the fight, was a scratch upon Gadsden's ear, by Howe's ball. Major Andre wrote a humorous account of the duel, in eighteen stanzas, to the tune of *Yankee Doodle.* He concludes by saying:

> "Such honor did they both display,
> They highly were commended,
> And thus, in short, this gallant fray,
> Without mischance, was ended.
>
> No fresh dispute, we may suppose,
> Will e'er by them be started;
> And now the chiefs, no longer foes,
> Shook hands, and so they parted."

EDWARD LIVINGSTON.

THE Livingston family in America, an off-shoot of a stock noted among the Scotch nobility of Queen Mary's time,[1] has always been remarkable for fine specimens of talent, public spirit, and genuine patriotism. Among the later members, Edward Livingston appears conspicuous as a statesman and jurist. He was truly "to the manor born," for his birth occurred at Clermont, Columbia county, New York, on the feudal estate known as *Livingston's Manor*, in the year 1764. He was at school in Kingston, Ulster county, when that village was burned by the British, in 1777, and two years afterward he entered Princeton College, and pursued his studies in the midst of alarms and interruptions incident to the war then in progress. He graduated, in 1781, with only three others. Two of these were associated with him, thirteen years afterward, as members of the House of Representatives, at Washington. He studied law under Chancellor Lansing, at Albany, and was admitted to the bar in 1785.

Mr. Livingston was called into public life, in 1794, by being elected a representative of the counties of New York, Queen's, and Richmond, in the Federal Congress, where he soon became a distinguished leader of the Republican party.

---

1. See sketch of Robert R. Livingston.

He maintained a seat there until 1801, when he declined a reëlection, and resumed the practice of his profession. President Jefferson soon afterward appointed him United States Attorney for the District of New York. He had filled the office with great ability, until the yellow fever broke out in the city of New York, in 1803, when he was called to the performance of holier duties. Thousands fled, but Edward Livingston remained amid the pestilence, to visit the sick and bury the dead. He was finally smitten by the destroyer, but his useful life was spared. His public and private business had suffered greatly, and the unfaithfulness of some of those unto whom he had entrusted the performance of public duties, placed upon his shoulders almost crushing pecuniary responsibilities. He resigned his office, took up his residence in New Orleans, and by assiduous attention to his profession, was enabled to liquidate every debt, with interest.

When the British attempted the invasion of Louisiana, in 1814, Mr. Livingston offered his services to General Jackson, and they were accepted; and his pen wrote the noble defence of Jackson, when that officer was unjustly arraigned before the civil tribunal for alleged military tyranny. Mr. Livingston was the principal of a commission appointed to codify the laws of Louisiana; and he is the sole author of the penal code of that State, adopted in 1824. On the very night when the last page of manuscript was prepared for the press, a fire consumed the whole, and he was two years engaged in reproducing it. That work is his noblest and most enduring monument.

Mr. Livingston was chosen a delegate to the Federal Congress, in 1823; and in 1829, the legislature of Louisiana appointed him United States Senator. He became one of the brightest ornaments of that higher house, but after serving two sessions, he was called to the cabinet of President Jackson, as Secretary of State. In 1833, he was appointed minister to France, an office held, thirty years before, by his distinguished brother, Robert R. Livingston. His health failed soon after his arrival in Paris, and he returned to America, not, however, until he had satisfied his countrymen that he was fully competent to perform any duty to which they might call him. He was with his relatives in Redhook, Dutchess county, New York, when, on a bright morning in May (23d), 1837, the spirit of this laborious public servant departed for the land of rest.

WILLIAM PRESCOTT.

HISTORIANS have disputed concerning the chief command at the earliest regular battle of the Revolution, known as that of "Bunker's Hill," some awarding that honor to General Israel Putnam, and others to Colonel William Prescott. Documentary evidence is conclusive in favor of the claim of Prescott, and its justice is not questioned at the present day. He was born in Goshen, Massachusetts, in 1726. Of his early life we have no reliable record. His father was for some years a member of the Massachusetts council. We first find a notice of William's public life, in his commission of lieutenant, under General Winslow, in the expedition against Cape Breton, in 1758. There he was distinguished for his bravery. On his return, he left the service, and settled at Pepperell, as the inheritor of a large estate. He took quite an active part in the popular movements while the Revolution was ripening, and had command of a regiment of minute-men, in the Spring of 1775. The events at Lexington and Concord called him to the field, and he was very active in assisting General Ward in the organization of the impromptu army that gathered around Boston, in May and June following. Confidant in his military skill, General Ward selected Colonel Prescott to fortify and garrison Bunker's Hill, and on the evening of the 16th of June, 1775, he crossed Charlestown Neck, for that purpose, with a thousand men, and intrenching tools, after an impressive prayer in their behalf was offered up on the green at Cambridge, by President Langdon, of Harvard College. Breed's Hill being nearer Boston, Prescott proceeded to fortify that, and at early dawn the next morning, the British in the city and on the shipping in the harbor,[1] were astonished and alarmed by the apparition of a strong redoubt, almost finished, in a position which commanded their most impressible points. In the action that ensued, the following day—the memorable 17th of June—Prescott was chief commander. Putnam was on Bunker's Hill, urging forward reinforcements, and General Warren was in the redoubt, as volunteer. Though driven from the Charlestown peninsula, the gallant colonel wished to attack the conquerors the next day, but was overruled by prudent counsellors.

Colonel Prescott continued under the command of Washington until after the battle at White Plains, in the Autumn of the following year; and he served as a volunteer under Gates, until the surrender of Burgoyne, in October, 1777. After the war, he represented his district in the State legislature, and he was acting magistrate of Pepperell from 1786 until his death. That event occurred on the 13th of October, 1795, when he was about sixty-nine years of age.

CHARLES WILSON PEALE.

"PRAY tell me, Mr. Hesselius," said a saddler's apprentice—a handsome young man of twenty—to an eminent portrait-painter in Annapolis, Maryland, as he stood before him with a good specimen of his mechanical skill —"pray tell me how you mix such beautiful tints for your canvas." That saddler's apprentice was Charles Wilson Peale, afterward one of the most eminent painters in our country. He was born at Charlestown, Maryland, in 1741, and in Annapolis he successively learned the trades of saddler, watch-maker, silversmith, and carver. From the day when he asked Hesselius that important question, his artist life began, for the generous painter cordially complied with his wishes. Peale studied the art and practised his mechanical trade, until an opportunity offered for him to go to England and place himself under the tutorship of the great West. He remained with that famous artist during the years 1770, and 1771, when he returned to America, and practiced his art, as a portrait-painter, without a rival for fifteen years. When the Revolution broke out, he joined the army, and was at the head of a company in the battles at Trenton, Brandywine, Germantown, and Monmouth. While at Valley Forge, in the Winter of 1777-'8, he conceived the grand design of making a gallery of portraits of all the distinguished actors in the Revolution, American and foreign, and commenced the task with vigor.[1] In the Spring of 1778, when the army moved, he gathered up his art materials, and, at the head of his company, he fought gallantly at Monmouth. He had commenced a full-length portrait of Washington,

---

[1]. One of the vessels, named *Falcon*, anchored within short cannon shot of Breed's Hill, was commanded by Captain Linzee, of the British navy. It is a singular fact in the curious history of coincidences, that William H. Prescott, the eminent historian, and grandson of Colonel William Prescott, married a grand-daughter of Captain Linzee. The swords used by Colonel Prescott and Captain Linzee, at the time of the battle on Breed's Hill, are crossed in a conspicuous place in the library of the Historian.

[1]. He also painted many in miniature, some of which I have seen in the possession of his son, at Washington city.

at Valley Forge; after the Monmouth battle, he had another sitting, and at Princeton he completed it.[1] Mr. Peale paid much attention to the preservation of animals after death, and possessed a decided antiquarian taste. After the war, he opened a picture gallery, for exhibition, in Philadelphia, and then established a museum of Natural History and miscellaneous curiosities. He also practiced dentistry, invented machinery, and in various ways was one of the most active and industrious of men. He lectured on Natural History, and was a zealous supporter of the Philadelphia Academy of Fine Arts. He lived temperately and frugally, and practiced his art in colors when past eighty years of age.[2] He died in February, 1827, at the age of almost eighty-six years. His son, Rembrandt Peale, a worthy successor of his father in the line of art. is yet [1855] living, in Philadelphia, at the age of seventy-six years.

JONATHAN EDWARDS.

THE most acute metaphysician and sound theologian which our country has yet produced, was Jonathan Edwards, who was born at East Windsor, Connecticut, on the 5th of October, 1703. The remarkable analytical powers of his mind were developed in early childhood, and at the age of ten years he read with delight the profound essay of Locke on the Human Understanding. A few days before the completion of his thirteenth year, he entered Yale College, as a student, and was graduated there before he was seventeen years of age. He remained in that then infant institution for two years longer, in the eager study of theology, preparatory to the assumption of the Christian ministry as his profession. He received a license to preach, in the Summer of 1722, and almost immediately afterward, he was selected by several New England ministers to preach to a small body of Presbyterians in the city of New York. In 1724, he was appointed a tutor in Yale College, where he remained until called to a pastoral charge in Northampton, Massachusetts, in the Summer of 1726. There he was ordained as a colleague with his grandfather, the Rev. Solomon Stoddard, who, for more than fifty years, had been the pastor of the Congregational church in that town. That continued to be the home-field of labor, of Mr. Edwards, for twenty-three years, when an increasing dislike of his pure church discipline alienated his people from him, and, in June, 1750, he was dismissed by an ecclesiastical council.[3]

In 1751, Mr. Edwards was appointed a missionary to the Stockbridge Indians, in Berkshire county, Massachusetts, and in that field he labored for about six years. His duties being comparatively light, he devoted much of his time to theological and metaphysical studies, and in that comparative retirement he wrote his great work on *The Freedom of the Will*, which has been considered by

---

1. That portrait, having Nassau Hall, at Princeton, for a back-ground, is in the gallery of the National Institute, at Washington city. When the Americans, under Washington, drove the British out of Nassau Hall, on the morning of the 2d of January, 1777, they sent a cannon ball into the building, which destroyed a portrait of King George. Washington presented the college with a sum of money, because of the damage done to the building. The Faculty employed Peale to paint a full-length portrait of the great Patriot, and placed it in the frame occupied by that of the king, where it yet remains.
2. I have seen a full-length portrait of himself, which he painted at the age of eighty. In October, 1854, all of his paintings remaining in the museum at Philadelphia, were sold at auction. Many of them were purchased by the City Council, and now decorate the walls of Independence Hall.
3. Mr. Edwards had been informed of immoralities in which many of the young people of his congregation indulged, and he thought the matter ought to be inquired into. The church readily favored his views, but when it was found that the accused persons belonged to some of the wealthiest and most influential families in the place, it was impossible to proceed with the inquiry. The conscientious pastor did not swerve from duty, but the failure of his attempt to correct the morals of the young people, strengthened their hands. For six years before his dismissal he fought the enemy manfully.

Jonathan Edwards

the most learned men in Europe and America, to be one of the greatest efforts of the human mind. In 1754, a severe illness, and the troubles incident to the French and Indian war, then progressing, interrupted his labors, and, beyond the efforts of his pen, his field of usefulness was very limited. It was soon enlarged. In the Autumn of 1757, his son-in-law, Rev. Aaron Burr, president of the college of New Jersey, at Princeton, died, and Mr. Edwards was invited by the Trustees of that institution to take his place. He was formally elected president, toward the close of September, 1757. He reluctantly accepted the call, for he knew there were more delights to himself in the quiet pursuits in which he was engaged, than in the duties of such official station, and he regarded his labors with his pen as more useful than any others in which he might engage at that time of life. He was inaugurated in February, 1758. Five weeks afterward, that great and good man was laid in the grave. The smallpox was prevalent in Princeton at the time of his arrival, and a skilful physician was brought from Philadelphia to inoculate[1] President Edwards and his family. He seemed to do well, but when all danger appeared to be over, a secondary fever supervened, his throat became so obstructed that medicines could not be swallowed, and the disease, gathering increased strength, terminated his life on the 22d of March, 1758, when he was in the fifty-fifth year of his age. The

---

1. See Note 2, page 61.

published theological writings of President Edwards are voluminous, and are ranked among the most valuable uninspired contributions to religious literature, of any age.

JOHN WITHERSPOON.

IN the family circle, the temple of worship, the hall of learning, and the forum of legislation, few men ever performed their whole duty more faithfully than did John Witherspoon, of New Jersey, in whose veins ran the blood of the great Scottish reformer, John Knox. He was born in the parish of Yester, near Edinburgh, Scotland, on the 5th of February, 1722. His father was a Scottish minister, and the loveliness of his mind and temper was transmitted to his son. He educated the intellectual and moral faculties of that promising boy with the greatest care, for he designed him for that gospel ministry which he afterward adorned. At the age of fourteen years he was placed in the University of Edinburgh, where he became a close student, especially of sacred literature. He went through a regular course of theological studies, and at the age of twenty-two he was graduated, with a license to preach. He accepted a call to Beith, in the west of Scotland; and in 1745, while, with some others, he was gazing upon the battle of Falkirk, where the troops of the Scotch Pretender to the throne of England[1] were victorious, he was made a prisoner, and was confined in the castle of Doune, for some time. He afterward took charge of a parish in Paisley; and the fame of his learning and piety caused him to receive invitations to settle in Dundee, Dublin, and Rotterdam in Holland. In 1766, the trustees of the College of New Jersey, at Princeton, invited him to accept the presidency of that institution, and through the influence of Richard Stockton (afterward Witherspoon's colleague in the Continental Congress), then in Scotland, he was persuaded to accept the office. He came to America, in 1768, was inaugurated in August of that year, and under his efficient administration the affairs of the college prospered wonderfully. Its usefulness had been greatly impaired by party feuds; these were soon healed, and that seminary, which seemed past resuscitation, was becoming one of the most flourishing in the land, when the blight of the Revolution fell upon it. Its pupils were then scattered, its doors were closed, and early in 1776, Doctor Witherspoon employed his talents and influence in another field of usefulness. He assisted in forming a republican constitution for New Jersey, and in June he was elected to a seat in the Continental Congress, where he nobly advocated independence, and signed his name to the Declaration thereof.[2] He was a faithful member of Congress until 1782, and took a conspicuous part in military and financial matters. In 1783, he endeavored to revive the prostrated College at Princeton, and found an efficient co-worker in his son-in-law, Vice-President Smith. Contrary to the dictates of his own judgment, Dr. Witherspoon went to Great Britain for pecuniary aid to the institution, and he collected scarcely enough to pay the expenses of the journey. He came back with a heavy heart but determined purpose, and labored on faithfully in the pulpit and in the college, while his powers of life remained active. About two years before his death he lost his eye-sight, yet he maintained his place in his pulpit with unabated zeal, until a few weeks before his departure. His useful life closed on the 10th of November, 1794, at the age of almost seventy-three years.

1. Charles Edward, grandson of James the Second, who was dethroned in 1688.
2. In the course of debate on the subject of Independence, John Dickenson, of Pennsylvania, ventured to assert that the people were not "ripe for a declaration of independence." Doctor Witherspoon warmly observed, "In my judgment, sir, we are not only ripe, but rotting."

RICHARD HENDERSON.

ALTHOUGH Daniel Boone may be considered the first thorough explorer of the wilderness of Kentucky, and James Harrod built the first log-house in all that beautiful land, yet Colonel Richard Henderson must be regarded, *politically*, as the father of that commonwealth. He was a native of Virginia. He was born in Hanover county, on the 20th of April, 1735. His father emigrated to Granville county, North Carolina, in 1745, and being appointed sheriff of that district, Richard had an opportunity of learning many useful lessons in matters pertaining to law. He prepared himself for the legal profession, arose rapidly to the highest rank, accumulated a competent fortune, and, when the insurrectionary movements in that section of the county, known as *the Regulator War*,[1] occurred, he was a judge of the superior court. As such, he was driven from the bench at Hillsborough, by the Regulators, in the Autumn of 1771, and the courts of justice, in that region, were closed. He was an ambitious and ostentatious man. By extensive speculations, at about this time, he had become somewhat embarrassed in pecuniary affairs, and had gained the ill-will of the common people. Bold, ardent, and adventurous, he resolved to go beyond the mountains, and there, in the beautiful country traversed by Boone, he commenced a scheme of land speculation, in 1774, more extensive than any known in the history of our country. He formed a company, of which he was chosen president, and by a treaty held at Wataga with the heads of the Cherokee nation, he purchased the whole land lying between the Cumberland river and mountains, and the Kentucky river, which comprised more than one-half of the present State of Kentucky. Henderson took possession of the country in the name of the company, in the Spring of 1775. Governor Martin, of North Carolina, proclaimed the purchase to be illegal. The legislature of Virginia did the same, but Judge Henderson paid no regard to their fulminations against him, and proceeded to establish a proprietary government, in imitation of the old colonies. Its capital was Boonesborough, and its title was TRANSYLVANIA. Under a large elm tree near Boone's fort, the first legislature of the new State met on the 23d of May, 1775.[2] The session was opened with prayer by the Rev. John Lythe; and Colonel Henderson in his verbal "message" as president, expressed the very essence of republican government, when he said, "If any doubts remain among you, with respect to the force and efficiency of whatever laws you now or hereafter make, be pleased to consider that all power is originally in the people; make it their interest, therefore, by impartial and beneficent laws, and you may be sure of their inclination to see them enforced."

The State of TRANSYLVANIA as an independent republic did not long exist, for Virginia and Carolina took efficient means to destroy it. The treaty with the Cherokees, and the purchase of their lands, were declared null. Yet they did not deprive the company of all advantages. North Carolina and Virginia each granted to them two hundred thousand acres. Relinquishing all political claims, Judge Henderson opened a land office on the site of Nashville, in 1779, for the sale of this legally-granted domain. The following Summer he returned to Granville county, and sought repose in the bosom of his family. Old difficulties were forgotten, for the great question of independence was then in process

---

1. See note on page 97; also sketch of John Ashe.
2. It was composed of Squire Boone, Daniel Boone, William Coke, Samuel Henderson, Richard Moore, Richard Calloway, Thomas Slaughter, John Lythe, Valentine Hammond, James Douglas, James Harrod, Nathan Hammond, Isaac Hite, Azariah Davis, John Todd, Alexander S. Dandridge, John Floyd, and Samuel Wood. Thomas Slaughter was chosen chairman, Mathew Jewett clerk, and John Lythe chaplain.

of solution by the whole people of the newly-proclaimed Union. Judge Henderson did not take part in public affairs, but lived on in quiet until the 30th of January, 1785, when he died at the age of fifty years. Henderson county, Kentucky, was named in his honor.

ALEXANDER WILSON.

WE may justly claim Alexander Wilson as an American, though born in North Britain, for here the genius which has made him world-renowned, as The American Ornithologist, was developed, and cultivated, and bore fruit. He was born in Paisley, Scotland, and in a grammar school, in that large town, he acquired a rudimental knowledge of the classics. His father designed him for the clerical profession, but the expansive mind of the youth would not allow him to be a sectarian, and the scheme was abandoned. From earliest boyhood he loved the fields and the sky; and he regarded the towering mountains and grand old forests as the most appropriate temples wherein man should worship the Creator of all. Pecuniary misfortune compelled his father to suspend Alexander's literary pursuits, on which he had entered with enthusiasm, and finally the necessity of learning some mechanical trade seemed imperative. The ardent youth could not brook the idea of having his powers confined to such a narrow sphere, for he felt a great soul stirring within; yet he reverently bent his inclinations to his father's wishes. Every leisure moment, however, was employed in study, and in the midst of his mechanical employment, he composed articles, in prose and verse, which attracted public attention, before he was nineteen years of age. He soon became the life of a select literary circle, yet his daily avocations, so repugnant to his nature, burdened his spirit with gloom. He saw no chance for expansion in his native country; and in 1794, he embarked for America, to profit by the free air and as free institutions. For more than a dozen years afterward he was engaged in the humble but honorable employment of a district school teacher. His lot seemed a hard one, but he found consolation in poetry, music, and his favorite study of birds. The latter became a passion with him, and he had the good fortune, at length, to form an acquaintance with William Bartram, of Philadelphia, the celebrated American Botanist.[1] From him he obtained a standard work on ornithology, the perusal of which was the commencement of a new era in Wilson's life. He found the work quite inaccurate in many particulars concerning the birds of the United States, and he formed the idea of making a complete system of American Ornithology. He at once applied himself successfully to the study of drawing and coloring from nature. At about this time, he became clerk to a bookseller in Philadelphia, with a liberal salary, and to him he disclosed his scheme of a work on American birds. Mr. Bradford was delighted with the idea, and at once gave Wilson every facility for preparing that magnificent work, *The American Ornithology*, in seven volumes, which appeared in 1808. Every portion of our country, from the Atlantic to the Mississippi, and from the St. Lawrence to the Gulf of Mexico, was traversed by Wilson, all alone, with the sublime ardor of a man conscious of performing a great work. His splendid volumes at once attracted the earnest attention of the learned in both hemispheres, and fame and fortune awaited him. But he did not live long to enjoy either. The hardships and privations to which he had been exposed, impaired a never rugged constitution, and on the 23d of August, 1813, he died, peacefully, at Philadelphia, when at the age of about forty years.

RUFUS PUTNAM.

THE name of Putnam is suggestive of bold daring border exploits, and true patriotism, notwithstanding of the eighty males of that name, living in America, in 1740, only two (Israel and Rufus) appear conspicuous in our country's annals. Rufus was born at Sutton, Worcester county, Massachusetts, on the 9th of April, 1738. On the death of his father, in 1745, he went to live with his maternal grandfather, in Danvers, where he attended a district school for two years. His mother married again, and Rufus lived with her until his stepfather died, in 1753. That illiterate man denied the lad all opportunities for education. At the age of sixteen he was apprenticed to a mill-wright. At that time the French and Indian war was kindling brightly, and the campaign of Braddock, and the bold exploits of his kinsman, Israel, warmed a martial spirit within him. At the age of nineteen years he entered the provincial army as a private soldier; and he mentions, in his journal, the note-worthy fact, that the captain of his company[1] prayed with the men every night and morning during the campaign. He remained in service until 1761, when he resumed his em-

---

1. Captain Ebenezer Learned, who was a colonel in the army under General Gates at the capture of

ployments of mill-building and farming. Having acquired a knowledge of surveying, he practiced it successfully for several years before the clarion of the Revolution called him again to the field. He was one of the military land company, who sent General Lyman to England, in 1763;[1] and 1773, he accompanied Colonel Israel Putnam and others to the "Yazoo country."

Mr. Putnam joined the revolutionary army at Cambridge, in 1775, and there his knowledge of surveying was brought into requisition. He assisted efficiently in the construction of those works on Dorchester Heights, which caused the British to prepare for leaving Boston. After that, he was employed elsewhere in the engineering department; and in August, 1776, he was appointed by Congress, an engineer, with the rank of colonel. In February, 1778, he succeeded Colonel Greaton in command of troops in the northern department, and during the remainder of the war he was actively connected with the engineering corps of the army. On the 8th of January, 1783, he was commissioned a brigadier-general in the Continental army, but peace was now exchanging the olive branch for the laurel and the palm, and he soon afterward retired to his farm.

From 1783 to 1788, he was engaged in organizing a company for emigrating to and settling in the Ohio country, and thither he went, as the general agent, in the Spring of 1788. He was accompanied by about forty settlers. They pitched their tents at the mouth of the Muskingum river, formed a settlement there, and called it Marietta. Suspecting hostility on the part of the neighboring Indians, he built a fort near by, and called it *Campus Martius*. That year they planted one hundred and thirty acres of corn. This was the beginning of that tide of emigration to Ohio which soon flowed so deep and broad; and General Putnam lived to see a flourishing State organized, and having, at the time of his death, seventy counties, and three-quarters of a million of inhabitants. In 1789, President Washington appointed him judge of the supreme court of the *North-west Territory*; and, in 1792, he was appointed a brigadier, under General Wayne. In 1796, he was made surveyor-general of the United States, and held that office until after the accession of Mr. Jefferson to the presidency. He was a member of the convention that framed a constitution for the State of Ohio, in 1802, and this was his last public service of much moment. He made Marietta his residence, and enjoyed the repose of private life until the first day of May, 1824 when he died. No individual did more for securing the benefits to be derived from the conquests of George Rogers Clarke north of the Ohio,[2] than General Rufus Putnam, and he has been justly styled the FATHER OF OHIO.

MESHECH WEARE.

"HE dared to love his country and be poor," was the epigramatic encomium bestowed upon Meshech Weare, the first republican governor of New Hampshire, by one who knew and estimated his worth. He was not possessed of brilliant genius, superior intellect, nor extraordinary abilities of any kind, but exhibited a happy combination of good sense, stern integrity, pure heart, and clear intelligence. He was precisely the man for the place and times in which his lot was cast. Mr. Weare was a native of Hampton, New Hampshire, where he was born in 1714. He was educated at Harvard College, where he was graduated in 1735. In the disputes between Governor Wentworth and the

---

1. See sketch of General Lyman.   2. See sketch of George Rogers Clarke.

Colonial Assembly, Mr. Weare, (for a number of years a member of that body), was always found on the side of the people. In 1752, he was chosen Speaker of the house. When, in 1754, delegates from the several colonies assembled at Albany to discuss plans for mutual defence, and to consider the expediency of a political union, Mr. Weare represented New Hampshire in that body, and warmly approved a plan of confederation, proposed by Dr. Franklin. And when, ten years later, the disputes between the colonies and Great Britain grew warm, Mr. Weare was a staunch supporter of all republican measures.

In January, 1776, a hastily-prepared Constitution went into operation in New Hampshire, and Mr. Weare was chosen to an office equivalent to that of governor of the embryo State. He was also appointed chief justice of the supreme court; and in such high estimation was he held by his fellow-citizens, that they virtually invested him with dictatorial prerogatives, for he wielded the powers of the highest offices in their gift, legislative, executive, and judicial. In 1779, a new Constitution was framed by a convention, of which John Langdon was president, but the people rejected it. Again, in 1784, a convention framed a Constitution, and it was accepted. Again, Meshech Weare, the faithful servant of the people, was elected chief magistrate, but the duties of public life, combining with the decay of age, had now produced great feebleness in his vital powers, and before the expiration of the year, he was compelled to resign the office which he had held with so much dignity for nine years. He retired to private life, a worn out public servant, and died at Hampton Falls, on the 15th of January, 1786, at the age of seventy-two years. His voluminous papers, comprised in several large manuscript volumes, are now in the custody of the New York Historical Society.

FRANCIS MARION.

THERE is scarcely a plantation within thirty miles of the banks of the Congaree and Santee, from Columbia to the sea, that has not some local tradition of the presence of Marion, the great partisan leader in South Carolina during the Revolution. He was a descendant of one of the Huguenots who fled from France toward the close of the seventeenth century, and was born at Winyaw, near Georgetown, South Carolina, in 1732. His infancy gave no promise of mature life, much less of greatness in achievements; for, according to Weems, he was as "small as a New England lobster, at his birth, and might have been put into a quart pot." His education was very limited, and, except a few months at sea, while a youth, his life was spent in agricultural pursuits, until his twenty-seventh year. Then the hostilities of the Indians on the western frontiers called the young men of the Carolinas to arms, and Marion became a soldier, with Moultrie and others, who afterward fought nobly for freedom. In the wild Cherokee country he obtained great applause for his bravery; and when the Revolution broke out, he was offered a captain's commission, which he accepted. He was successful in the recruiting service, early in 1776; and during the attack on Charleston, in the Summer of that year, he fought bravely under Moultrie, in the Palmeto fort, in the harbor. He was afterward engaged in the contest at Savannah, and was in Charleston while the siege of that city, by the British, in the Spring of 1789, was progressing. Disabled by an accident,[1]

---

1. Marion was dining with some friends at a house in Tradd Street, Charleston, when, on an attempt being made to cause him to drink wine contrary to his practice and desire, he leaped from a window, and sprained his ankle. The Americans yet kept the country toward the Santee, open, and Marion was conveyed to his home.

he left the city before its surrender, and made his way home, where he remained until just before the defeat of Gates near Camden, in August following. Then, notwithstanding he was quite lame, he mounted his horse, collected a score of volunteers, and offered his services to Gates. They were not readily accepted by that proud general, because of the uncouth appearance of the men.[1] Soon afterward, being called to the command of the militia of the Williamsburg District, in the vicinity of the Black and Pedee rivers, he formed his famous *Brigade*, with which he performed such wondrous feats during the remainder of the war. I need not stop to detail his exp!oits during the two years succeeding the formation of his brigade, for they are, or ought to be, familiar to every American reader, young or old. Suffice it to say, that to *Marion's Brigade*, more than to any other corps in the South, the credit of the expulsion of the British from the Carolinas and Georgia, is due; and General Greene regarded him as his strong right arm, especially after the siege of Ninety-Six, in the Summer of 1781.

---

[1]. According to Colonel Williams, they must have appeared worse than Falstaff's "ragged regiment."

Just before the war, Marion had occupied a seat in the legislature of South Carolina, and early in 1782, when that body was reorganized by Governor Rutledge, he was again elected to the Senate. Circumstances soon called him from the council to the field, and he did not relinquish his sword until the British evacuated Charleston toward the close of 1782, and the sun of peace arose. Then he disbanded his Brigade, and retired to his farm near Eutaw Springs, on the Santee. There all was utter desolation; and at the age of fifty, he commenced the world anew, as a planter, with scarcely money enough to purchase utensils for his laborers. An almost sinecure office—commander of Fort Johnson, in Charleston harbor—was created for him, and the emoluments were of essential service to the veteran. At length a Desdemonia, enamored of the hero because of his exploits, offered him her hand and fortune, through the kind mediation of friends. She was a Huguenot maiden of forty years, comely and rich. The hitherto invincible soldier was conquered, and his home at Pond Bluff was made happy during the remainder of his life, by a loving wife and the means for dispensing a generous hospitality to his friends. He enjoyed these pleasures for about ten years, alternating them occasionally with legislative duties, and then went to his rest, without having a child to perpetuate his name or blood. He died on the 29th of February, 1795, at the age of about sixty-three years, and was buried in the church-yard at Belle Isle, where a neat marble slab denotes the resting-place of his remains.

RICHARD HENRY LEE.

IN the midst of the doubt, and dread, and hesitation, which for twenty days had brooded over the Continental Congress, after the first step had been taken in the direction of political independence of Great Britain, a clear, musical voice was heard uttering a resolution, "That these united colonies are, and of right ought to be, free and independent States; that they are absolved from all allegiance to the British Crown; and that all political connection between them and the State of Great Britain is, and ought to be, totally dissolved." It was the voice of Richard Henry Lee, a delegate from Virginia. He was a scion of one of the early cavalier families of that State, and was born at Stratford, in Westmoreland county, on the 20th of January, 1732. According to the fashion of that time, his father sent him to England to be educated. He was in a school at Wakefield, in Yorkshire, for several years, where he was a thoughtful student, and lover of ancient classic and historical literature. At the age of nineteen years he returned to Virginia, and his time was spent in athletic exercises and study. He formed a military corps among his youthful companions, was elected to the chief command, and first appears in history at the council called at Alexandria, by Braddock, in 1755.[1] There young Lee appeared and offered the services of himself and volunteers, in the proposed expedition against the French and Indians on the Ohio. The proud Braddock refused to accept the services of these plain young provincials, and the deeply-mortified Lee returned home with his troops. Then was planted in his bosom the first seeds of hatred and disgust of the insolence of British officials, and it germinated and bore abundant fruit twenty years afterward.

---

1. General Braddock called a council of colonial governors, at Alexandria, on the Potomac, to consult upon a campaign against the French and Indians. Several of those magistrates, with Admiral Keppel, met there, arranged satisfactory plans, and Braddock started on his unfortunate march toward the

In 1757, Governor Dinwiddie appointed Mr. Lee a justice of the peace. At about the same time he was elected to a seat in the House of Burgesses of Virginia, though only twenty-five years of age. He was extremely diffident, but at times his zeal would master his bashfulness, and then those powers of oratory, afterward so conspicuous in the Continental Congress, would beam out in wondrous splendor. He was one of the earliest opposers of the Stamp Act, and was the first man in Virginia to stand forth in public as its avowed opponent. From that time until the war broke out, he was a leader among the patriots in his State; and long before the idea became general, he spoke of the necessity of *independence.* He was a member of the first Continental Congress, in 1774, and while in that body he was always upon the most important committees. In June, 1776, he fearlessly offered the resolution above quoted, and took upon himself the fearful responsibility of being branded by the imperial government as an arch-traitor.[1] After considerable debate, that resolution was made the special order of the day for the 2d of July following,[2] and a committee of five were appointed to draw up a preamble or declaration, in accordance with it. On the day when the resolution to appoint a committee was proposed, Mr. Lee was summoned, by express, to his home in Virginia, on account of illness in his family, and for that reason he was not a member of that committee. He afterward affixed his signature to the Declaration, and thus became one of the immortal Fifty-Six. He was active in Congress, in the Virginia Assembly, or in the field at the head of militia, until the close of the war. In 1783, he was again elected to Congress, and was chosen president of that body. He was opposed to the Federal Constitution, because he reverenced State rights; but, like Patrick Henry, he yielded cheerful acquiescence when it became the organic law of the Republic. He was chosen the first United States Senator, from Virginia, under it, and held that office until the infirmities of premature age compelled him to retire to private life, at his beautiful seat at Chantilly, in his native county. He was greatly beloved by his relatives, friends, and the whole people, and he was sincerely mourned by the nation, at his death. Mr. Lee went to his rest on the 19th of June, 1794, when in the sixty-third year of his age.

JOSIAH QUINCY, JR.

"LET me tell you one very serious truth, in which we are all agreed; your countrymen must seal their cause with their blood." So wrote a young man of thirty, from London, toward the close of 1774. He was Josiah Quincy, junior, grandson of Judge Edmund Quincy, and the child of a wealthy Boston merchant. He was born in Braintree, Massachusetts, on the 23d of February, 1744. Eagerness for knowledge, and assiduity in study, marked his whole collegiate career in Harvard University; and when he was graduated, in 1763, he entered upon the study of the law, under Oxenbridge Thacher, of Boston, with equal eagerness. After two years' close study, he was admitted to the bar, and was soon regarded as one of the most promising young men in the profession. His attention was soon drawn to the agitation of the political waters of his

---

1. At that time, a son of Mr. Lee was at school at St. Bees, in England. One day, while standing near his tutor, a gentleman asked, "What boy is this?" The professor replied, "He is the son of Richard Henry Lee, of America." The gentleman put his hand upon the boy's head, and said, "We shall yet see your father's head upon Tower Hill." The boy promptly answered, "You may have it when you can get it." That boy was the late Ludwell Lee, Esq., of Virginia.
2. The resolution was adopted on the 2d of July, but the Declaration was debated until the 4th, and then agreed to.

country, and as early as 1767, he began to write political essays in favor of popular liberty. From that time, Otis and Quincy were the boldest denunciators of the oppressive measures of Great Britain.[1] He was the colleague of John Adams in defending Captain Preston and others after the "Boston Massacre," in 1770, and eloquently pleaded their cause.[2] During the three years of comparative quiet, after that event, he pursued his avocations in the law with great assiduity; but early in 1773, a pulmonary disease compelled him to seek relief in a warmer climate. He visited Charleston and several places in North Carolina, everywhere mingling with the most ardent friends of freedom.[3] On his return home he was active in the movements which resulted in the destruction of tea in Boston Harbor.[4] He wrote several powerful papers, the most important of which was signed "Marchmont Nedham." He also published, in 1774, severe strictures on the Boston Port Bill,[5] which included *Thoughts on Civil Society and a Standing Army.*

For the double purpose of seeking renewed health and to serve his country in the dark hour of its trial, he secretly embarked for London, in September, 1774, and at once obtained interviews with the ministry and the leading men of both parties. He attended the debates in parliament, took full notes of all current political events, and kept his friends in America advised of all important movements in which they were concerned. He became thoroughly convinced of the necessity for his countrymen to prepare for war, and in less than two months after his arrival in England, he expressed the sentiment quoted at the opening of this memoir. After becoming thoroughly acquainted with the dispositions and intentions of the king and his ministers, and hopeless of reconciliation, Mr. Quincy resolved to return home, and, if his health would permit, to arouse his countrymen to immediate and powerful action. He embarked for Boston, in March, 1775, with a heart big with revolution, and a brain teeming with noble ideas and dreams of the glorious future of his beloved country. He had said to Dr. Franklin, on parting, "New England alone can hold out for ages against Great Britain, and, if they were firm and united, in seven years they would conquer them." But Providence did not permit him to realize any of his aspirations, nor again to set his feet upon his native shores. He was blessed with the sight of his dear land, but before the vessel reached the port of Gloucester, the tooth of consumption destroyed the thread of life, and he expired. It was on the 26th of April, 1775, when he was about thirty-one years of age. His son, then a little child, has erected a noble monument to the memory of his father, by writing and publishing a record of his life.

---

1. In 1768, he asked, "Shall we hesitate a moment in preferring death to a miserable existence in bondage?" And, in 1770, he boldly said, "I wish to see my countrymen break off—*off forever!*—all social intercourse with those whose commerce contaminates, whose luxuries poison, whose avarice is insatiable, and whose unnatural oppressions are not to be borne."
2. See note on page 87.
3. See sketches of Harnett and Howe.
4. On the day when the destruction of the tea occurred, a great concourse of people were assembled at the "Old South Meeting-house," and were harangued by young Quincy. "It is not, Mr. Moderator," he said, "the spirit that vapors within these walls, that must stand us in stead.' The exertions of this day will call forth events which will make a very different spirit necessary for our salvation. Whoever supposes that shouts and hosannahs will terminate the trials of this day, entertains a childish fancy. He must be grossly ignorant of the importance and value of the prize for which we contend; we must be equally ignorant of the power of those who have combined against us. We must be blind to that malice, inveteracy and insatiable revenge which actuate our enemies, public and private, abroad and in our bosoms, to hope that we shall end this controversy without the sharpest, the sharpest conflicts—to flatter ourselves that popular resolves, popular harangues, popular acclamations, and popular vapor, will vanquish our foes. Let us consider the issue. Let us look to the end. Let us weigh and consider before we advance to those measures which must bring on the most trying and terrible struggle this country ever saw." When he concluded, the question was put whether the people would allow the tea to be landed. As with one voice, the multitude said, No! At twilight, a voice in the church gallery shouted, "Boston harbor a tea-pot to-night!" A man disguised as an Indian gave a war-whoop, and the people rushed to the wharf. A pale moon was shining upon the snow. In a short time three hundred and forty-two chests of tea were broke open, and their contents were cast into the water.
5. See note 2, page 165.

PHILIP SCHUYLER.

PURE patriotism, unselfish benevolence, unflinching integrity, and unwavering public and private virtue, were the marked characteristics of Philip Schuyler, a grandson of the valiant mayor of Albany, in 1690, when the scouts of Frontenac alarmed all the border settlers of New York, and French and Indians laid Schenectada in ashes. Philip was born at Albany, on the 22d of November, 1733. He was the oldest child of his parents, and by the law of primogeniture, he inherited his father's real estate. That parent died while Philip was young, and he was left to the care of his mother. With that noble generosity which marked his career through life, he divided the estate, to which he was entitled, equally with his brothers and sisters. At the age of twenty-two years, he entered the provincial army, and commanded a company under Sir William Johnson, at Fort Edward and Lake George. He continued in the service until 1758, and accompanied the young Lord Howe, as colonel of a regiment, in the expedition against Ticonderoga and Crown Point. When that nobleman was killed,

Colonel Schuyler conveyed his body to Albany, for interment.[1] After the peace in 1763, he was quite active in several civil capacities; and as member of the Colonial Assembly of New York, he was marked for his devotion to the cause of the colonists. He was a member of the second Continental Congress, in 1775, and was appointed by that body the third of the four major-generals, under Washington, commissioned for the command of the American army. He took command of the Northern Department, and started with a considerable force to invade Canada, in the Autumn of 1775. He sickened on Lake Champlain, placed the chief command in the hands of his lieutenant, General Montgomery, and returned to Albany. During the following year he was active among the Six Nations of Indians, and also in perfecting the discipline of his Division of the army. In March, 1777, he was superseded by General Gates, without any good reason, but was reinstated in May following. In June, Burgoyne penetrated the northern frontier, and General Schuyler was active in preparations to check his invasion. At the moment when all was ready to strike a decisive blow, Gates was again placed in command, and unfairly received the laurels of conquest. Schuyler's love for his country was stronger than his resentment, and as a simple citizen he aided the Americans greatly in the accomplishment of the victory over Burgoyne, at Saratoga. He demanded and obtained a trial before a court of inquiry, and received a highly flattering verdict. Washington then urged him to accept military command, but he preferred to aid his country in a less public but not less efficient way. He was a member of Congress under the first confederation, and after the ratification of the Federal Constitution, the legislature of New York chose General Schuyler, with Rufus King, to represent that commonwealth in the Senate of the United States. He served until 1791, when he was elected to the Senate of his native State. He was again chosen United States Senator, in place of Aaron Burr, in 1797, but did not retain his seat long, for his health was failing. In 1803, his wife, the companion of all his joys and sorrows, died; and, in July, 1804, his spirit was terribly smitten by the murder of his accomplished son-in-law, Alexander Hamilton, by the duellist's hand.[2]

JOSEPH WARREN.

"NOT all the havoc and devastation they have made has wounded me like the death of Warren," wrote the wife of John Adams three weeks after the battle of Bunker Hill. "We want him in the Senate; we want him in his profession; we want him in the field. We mourn for the citizen, the senator, the physician, and the warrior." The death of Joseph Warren was indeed a severe blow to the patriot cause. He was the son of a Massachusetts farmer, and was born in Roxbury, near Boston, in 1740. He was graduated at Harvard College, in 1759, and then commenced the study of medicine. Soon after commencing its practice, he took a prominent place in the profession, in Boston; and he had few superiors, when inclination called him to participate in the political movements of the day. Patriotism was a ruling emotion of his heart, and he never lacked boldness to express his opinions freely. He was one of the earliest members of the association, in Boston, known as *Sons of Liberty;* and from 1768 until the fierce kindling of war on Breed's Hill, he was extremely efficient in

---

1. As an example for his men, Lord Howe had his hair cut short, that it might not become wet and produce colds in the region of the neck. Many years after the interment of his remains at Albany, they were removed, and it was found that his hair had grown several inches, and was smooth and glossy.
2. See sketch of Alexander Hamilton.

fostering a spirit of rational liberty and independence among the people. His suggestive mind planned many daring schemes in secret caucus, and he was ever ready to lead in the execution of any measures for resisting the encroachments of imperial power. He delivered the first annual oration on the subject of the "Boston Massacre," in 1771; and, in 1775, he solicited the honor of performing the perilous service again, because some British officers had menaced the life of any one who should attempt it. The "Old South" was crowded, and the aisles, stairs, and pulpit, were filled with British soldiers, full armed. The intrepid young orator entered by a window, spoke fearlessly, in the presence of those bayonets which seemed alive with threats, of the early struggles of the colonies of New England, and then, in sorrowful tones and deep pathos of expression, told of the wrongs and oppressions under which they were then suffering. Even the soldiers wept; and thus the young hero, firm in the faith that "resistance to tyrants is obedience to God," triumphed, and fearlessly bearded the lion in his den. From that day Gage regarded him as a dangerous man.

When John Hancock went to the Continental Congress, Warren was chosen to fill his place as president of the Massachusetts Provincial Assembly. He held that position when the skirmishes at Lexington and Concord occurred; and before and after the events of that day, he was very active, secret and open. Four days before the battle of Bunker's Hill, he was commissioned a major-general. He hastened to Breed's Hill, on the memorable 17th of June, 1775, and toward the close of the action, placed himself under Colonel Prescott, as a volunteer. When the Americans were compelled to retreat, Warren and Prescott were the last men to leave the redoubt. He had proceeded but a short way toward Bunker's Hill, where Putnam was trying to rally the fugitives, when a musket ball passed through his head, and killed him instantly. He was left on the field. His body was recognised the next day by his intimate acquaintance, Dr. Jeffries, of the British army, and it was buried where it fell. After the British left Boston, in the Spring of 1776, it was taken up, carried to the city, and interred with masonic and military honors, beneath St. Paul's church. Almost upon the spot where he fell, the great Bunker Hill monument now stands, a memorial alike for the noble Warren, and of the deeds which consecrated that eminence. Congress expressed its sorrow by resolutions, and its gratitude by ordering that his "eldest son be educated at the expense of the United States." Congress also ordered a monument to be erected. It yet remains to be done.

ZEBULON MONTGOMERY PIKE.

ONE of the earliest explorers of the wilderness around the head waters of the Mississippi, now known as the Minnesota Territory, was the brave Pike, who died in the hour of victory near York, in Upper Canada, with the captured British flag under his head. He was the son of an officer in the United States army, and was born at Lamberton, New Jersey, on the 5th of January, 1779. He entered the army while yet a mere boy, and his whole life was devoted to the military profession. He was early subjected to athletic exercises, and he grew to manhood with a frame of uncommon vigor. His education was neglected, but by his own exertions he mastered the Latin, French, and Spanish languages. Love of study was a characteristic of his early youth, and he read with avidity the few books that fell in his way. Soon after the purchase of Louisiana from the French, in 1803, the United States government determined to explore that vast and mostly unknown territory. Under the enlightened direction of President Jefferson, Captains Lewis and Clarke were sent to explore the Missouri to its source, and young Pike was commissioned to make a similar exploration in search of the sources of the Mississippi. He left St. Louis, in August, 1805, with twenty men, and made a most wonderful journey, during eight months and twenty days, an account of which was published in an octavo volume.[1] Soon after his return, General Wilkinson selected Pike to command another expedition in the interior of Louisiana, in the direction of Northern Mexico. After great sufferings, he returned, in the Summer of 1807, and received the thanks of Congress. Passing through several promotions, in military rank, he reached that of colonel of infantry, in 1810. He was stationed on the northern frontier at the commencement of the war with Great Britain, in 1812, and early the following year he was promoted to brigadier. In the Spring of 1813, he was chosen, by General Dearborn, to command the land troops in an expedition against York (now Toronto), the capital of Upper Canada. He sailed from Sackett's Harbor, in a squadron under Commodore Chauncey, on the 25th of April, and on the 27th he landed, with seventeen hundred men, in the face of a galling fire from a large force of British and Indians. Pike pressed forward, and the British fled to their fortifications, while the Indians scattered in all directions. The general led his troops in person, and after capturing a battery, he rushed forward toward the main works. The British fired their magazine, and a terrible explosion took place. A heavy stone struck the breast of the brave leader, and wounded him mortally. He was conveyed to the commodore's ship, in a dying condition. While on the way, there was a shout, and one of his attendants said, "The British union jack is coming down, and the stars are going up!" Pike could not speak, but sighed heavily, and then smiled. He lingered a few hours on ship-board; and when the British flag was brought to him, he signified his desire to have it placed under his head. It was done, and a moment afterward the hero died. He was only a little more than thirty-four years of age. His name and memory is perpetuated, not only in his country's annals, but by the titles of ten counties and twenty-eight townships and villages, chiefly in the Western country.

DANIEL BOONE.

FEW men of such humble pretensions occupy so large a space in history, as Daniel Boone. His heroism as an explorer, pioneer, settler, and patriotic defender of the soil he had won by his courage in the path of the discoverer, partakes so largely of the spirit of chivalry and true romance, that we incontinently look upon him with a sentiment of hero-worship. Daniel Boone was born in Berks county, Pennsylvania, in 1734. His parents were from Bradninch, near Exeter, England; and while Daniel was a small boy, they left Pennsylvania, and settled near the banks of the Yadkin, in North Carolina. At that time the region beyond the Blue Ridge was an unknown wilderness to the white people, for none had ventured thither, as far as is known, until about the year 1750. It was almost twenty years later than this, when Boone was approaching the prime of life, that he first penetrated the great Valley of the Mississippi, in company with others. He had already, as a bold hunter, been within the eastern verge of the present Kentucky, but now he took a long "hunt," of

---

[1]. Lieutenant Pike did not discover the true source of the Mississippi. That achievement was reserved for Henry R. Schoolcraft, who, in 1832, discovered the chief fountain of the Father of Waters to be Itaska Lake, in latitude 47 deg., 13 min., 35 sec., north, and that its whole majestic course is within the territory of the United States.

about three years. He had made himself familiar with the wilderness; and, in 1773, in company with other families, he started with his own to make a settlement on the *Kain-tuck-ee* river. The hostile Indians compelled them to fall back, and Boone resided on the Clerich river until 1775, when he went forward and planted the settlement of Boonesborough, in the present Madison county, Kentucky.[1] There he built a log fort, and in the course of three or four years, several other settlers joined him. His wife and daughters were the first white women ever seen upon the banks of the Kentucky river. He became a great annoyance to the Indians; and while at the Blue Licks, on the Licking river, in February, 1778, engaged with others in making salt, he was captured by some Shawnee warriors from the Ohio country, and taken to Chillicothe. The Indians became attached to him, and he was adopted into a family as a son. A ransom of five hundred dollars was offered for him, but the Indians refused it. He at length escaped (in July following his capture) when he ascertained that a large body of Indians were preparing to march against Boonesborough. They attacked that station three times before the middle of September, but were repulsed.

---

1. On the 14th of July, 1776, one of Boone's daughters, and two other girls, were seized by the Indians, while they were in a boat, near Boonesborough, and carried away. Their screams alarmed the people at the fort, and Boone and others started in pursuit. It was then just at sunset. They came up with the kidnappers on the 16th, about forty miles from Boonesborough, rescued the girls, and conveyed them safely back to their home.

During Boone's captivity, his wife and children had returned to the house of her father, on the Yadkin, where the pioneer visited them in 1779, and remained with them for many months. He returned to Kentucky, in 1780, with his family, and assisted Colonel Clarke in his operations against the Indians in the Illinois country. He was a very active partisan in that far-off region beyond the Alleghanies until the close of the war. From that time, until 1798, he resided alternately in Kentucky and in Western Virginia. He had seen that "wilderness blossom as the rose;" and in less than twenty years from the time when he built his fort at Boonesborough, he saw Kentucky honored as a sovereign State of an independent union of republics. Yet he was doomed to lose all personal advantages in the growth of the new State. Neglecting to comply with new land laws, of whose details he was probably ignorant, he lost his title to lands which he had discovered and subdued; and the region which so recently seemed all his own, now filled with half a million of his fellow-citizens, afforded him no home in fee simple! Indignant at what he considered base ingratitude, he shouldered his rifle, left Kentucky forever, and, with some followers, plunged into the interminable forests of the present Missouri, beyond the Mississippi river. They settled upon the Little Osage, in 1799, and the following year, Boone and his companions explored the head waters of the Arkansas. A long time afterward, when he was almost eighty years of age, he trapped beavers on the Great Osage. Soon after his return from that "hunt," he sent a memorial to the legislature of Kentucky, setting forth that he owned not an acre of land on the face of the earth, had nowhere to lay his head, and asked a confirmation of title to lands given him in Louisiana, by the Spanish governor, before that territory was ceded to the United States. Congress secured two thousand acres to him, and so his old age was made comparatively happy by the prospect of a grave in the bosom of his own soil. The brave old hero died in Missouri, on the 26th of September, 1820, at the age of almost ninety years. His remains now lie beside those of his wife, in a cemetery at Frankfort, Kentucky.

ANDREW PICKENS.

CELTIC blood flowed in the veins of very many of the sages and soldiers who laid the foundations of our Republic. In those of Pickens, the eminent partisan soldier of South Carolina, it was unmixed, for his parents were both natives of that portion of Ireland where there had been no infusion of the English or Scotch element. He was born in Paxton parish, Dauphin county, Pennsylvania, on the 19th of September, 1739, and while he was yet a child, his parents emigrated to the Waxhaw settlement, in the upper part of South Carolina. His first military lessons, in actual service, were received while serving as a volunteer under lieutenant-colonel Grant, against the Cherokees, in 1761, having for his companions, Marion and Moultrie. He was a warm republican; and when the war of the Revolution was kindled, he took the field as captain of militia. His zeal, courage, and skill, immediately attracted attention, and he arose rapidly to the rank of brigadier-general. In the region watered by the Savannah, in both Georgia and South Carolina, General Pickens performed very important services during the war, especially in the year 1781. He completely humbled the Cherokees and the Creeks; broke the power of the Tories in the upper country around Augusta; and was distinguished for bravery at the Cowpens, the siege of Augusta, and at Eutaw Springs. He and Marion commanded the militia of South Carolina in the latter engagement, and in the early part of the conflict,

Pickens was severely wounded by a musket ball. From the close of the war until 1794, he was continually in public life, chiefly as a legislator, and then he was elected to a seat in the House of Representatives of the United States. He was also appointed one of the two major-generals of the militia of his State; and in 1796, he declined a reëlection to Congress, but took a seat in the legislature of South Carolina. He held that position until 1801, at the same time often acting as commissioner to treat with the Indians. Washington had also solicited him to accept the command of a brigade of light troops to act under Wayne against the tribes of the North-west, but he declined the honor. He retired to private life, in 1801, and there he remained in the peaceful repose of a planter, in Pendleton District, South Carolina, until 1812, when he accepted a seat in his State legislature. He declined the proffered office of governor the following year, and again sought repose in the bosom of his family. There he went to his final rest, on the 17th of August, 1817, at the age of seventy-eight years. General Pickens married Rebecca Calhoun, in 1765. They lived together fifty years. She was aunt of the late John C. Calhoun; and at the time of her marriage was considered one of the most beautiful young ladies in the South. Her nuptials were attended by a great number of relatives and friends, and "Rebecca Calhoun's wedding" became an epoch in the social history of the district, from which old people used to reckon. The remains of husband and wife lie together in the grave-yard of the "old stone meeting-house," in Pendleton.

FRANCIS ASBURY.

PERHAPS no Christian minister, since the settlement of America, has travelled as extensively, and labored as untiringly in the face of every kind of obstacle, as Francis Asbury, the senior Bishop of the Methodist Church[1] in the United States. He was born near Birmingham, England, on the 20th of August, 1745, and came to America, in 1771, at the age of twenty-six years, as a preacher of the gospel in the simplicity of the new sect. Two years afterward, the first annual conference of the American Methodists was held at Philadelphia. The converts under the preaching of John and Charles Wesley had widened the circle of the denomination greatly, and at that conference there were ten preachers, representing a membership of about eleven hundred. Mr. Asbury continued to travel and preach continually from that time until 1784, when Dr. Coke, whom Mr. Wesley had appointed a presbyter of the church in England, and missionary to America, consecrated him a superintendent or Bishop of the Methodist Episcopal Church in the United States. With the zeal of an ancient apostle, he entered upon the discharge of his great duties, and visited and organized churches, and planted others, in all parts of the republic. In 1790, he crossed the great mountains, and held a conference five miles from the present Lexington. It was the first general assemblage of the Methodists in the wilderness of the West. That conference then numbered only twelve preachers. They were "indifferently clad," said Bishop Asbury, "with emaciated bodies, and subject to hard fare, but, I hope, rich in faith."

---

1. This sect was founded, in 1729, by John Wesley and a minister named Morgan. Their doctrine is the same as that of the Church of England, but they discarded most of its rituals. They adhere to the Episcopal form of church government, though varying somewhat from the Church of England in its administration. The name, as applied to a religious sect, is older than the organization of Wesley or others. It was given to two kinds of Popish Doctors of Divinity, in France, about the middle of the seventeenth century, who violently opposed the Huguenots. In England, it was applied to those church members who were evangelical in their views, and zealous in their preaching. Methodism has been well defined by an English writer, as "Christianity in earnest."

From the time of his consecration until his death, a period of thirty-two years, Bishop Asbury travelled yearly through every State in the increasing Union, and kept in efficient action the great machinery of the travelling connection. In the exercise of his episcopal office, he ordained not less, probably, than three thousand preachers, and uttered seventeen thousand sermons. After spending fifty-five years in the ministry (forty-five in America), that faithful servant of Christ was called to his rest, at the house of his old friend, George Arnold, in Virginia, on the 31st of March, 1816, in the seventy-first year of his age. His remains, by order of the General Conference, were taken to Baltimore, and deposited in a vault prepared for the purpose under the recess of the pulpit of the Methodist Church in Eutaw Street.

JOHN TRUMBULL.

THE name of Trumbull, the painter,[1] like Trumbull, the magistrate, will ever be associated with the noblest chapter of American history, because his pencil illustrated its noblest events. The painter was the youngest son of the magistrate, and was born at Lebanon, Connecticut, on the 6th of June, 1756. After receiving an excellent education at Lebanon, he entered Harvard College, where he remained about a year, and was graduated in 1772. He had early felt the inspirations of art and the aspirations of genius; and during much of his college years at Harvard, he was studying books on the subject of drawing and painting, or was engaged in copying some pictures there. He painted his first original picture—*The Battle of Cannæ*—soon after leaving college, and resolved to devote his life to art, when the gathering storm of the Revolution diverted him from that pursuit, and caused him to exchange his pencil for a sword. His father wished him to become a clergyman, but the *church* militant had not for him the charms of martial life, and he became adjutant of the first Connecticut regiment, which was stationed at Roxbury, in the Summer of 1775. A drawing which he made of the enemy's works, by request of Washington, so pleased the commander-in-chief, that he made the young painter his aid-de-camp, in August. He was promoted to major of brigade, in the Autumn, and in that capacity he attracted the attention of adjutant-general Gates. He was appointed, by Gates, adjutant-general of the Northern Department, with the title of Colonel, in June, 1776, and accompanied that officer to Ticonderoga. He did not receive his commission from Congress until the following Spring, and then it was dated in September. The young soldier was offended, and returned the commission with a spicy letter tendering his resignation. Then ended his military career, and he went to Boston to resume the study of art. In 1780, he sailed for London, to place himself under the instruction of Benjamin West. The great painter received him kindly, and Trumbull was pursuing his studies quietly, when, late in the year, he was arrested as a rebel, and cast into prison on a charge of treason. West immediately interceded for him, before the king, and received the royal assurance that the young painter's *life* should be spared. After an imprisonment of eight months, he was admitted to bail on condition that he should quit the country immediately. West and Copley became his sureties. He went to Amsterdam, and then embarked for America, but the ship was compelled to

---

1. The great painter was a lineal descendant of Rev. John Robinson, the "father of the Pilgrims." His mother's name was Faith Robinson, and was the fifth in descent from the minister at Delft. While at the house of J. G. W. Trumbull, Esq., at Norwich, Connecticut, in 1849, the writer was shown a silver cup, bearing the initials of the Rev. Mr. Robinson, which was brought to America, in 1621, and has been

put back, and he did not reach home until the beginning of 1782. He visited the army on the Hudson, toward Autumn, but peace soon came. His father then urged him to pursue the profession of the law, but the Artist would not listen; and, in November, 1783, he again went to England, and resumed his studies, under West, with great zeal, industry, and success. He was so successful in the treatment of *Priam bearing back to his Palace the body of Hector*, in 1785, that he matured a plan for producing a series of historical paintings, representing events in the American Revolution. Before the close of 1786, he had produced his *Battle of Bunker Hill* and *Death of Montgomery*. These were engraved. Then followed his superb painting *The Sortie of the Garrison of Gibraltar*, which he sold for twenty-five hundred dollars. He came to America, in 1789, and painted as many of the portraits of the signers of the Declaration as were then present in Congress. In 1791 and 1792, he was chiefly employed in painting heads for his four great national pictures, now in the Rotunda of the capitol, at Washington city, namely, *Signers of the Declaration of Independence, Surrender of Burgoyne, Surrender of Cornwallis, Washington Surrendering his Commission.* He then went to England as private secretary to Mr. Jay. He went to Paris and engaged in commercial pursuits, for awhile; and, in August, 1796, he was appointed fifth commissioner to carry out the designs of one article of Jay's treaty with Great Britain. His duties did not end until 1804, when he returned to the United States, and resumed his pencil at New York. Lacking encouragement, he again went to England, and remained there until 1815, when he returned to New York. The following year he received a commission from our government to paint the four pictures above alluded to. He was engaged seven years on them. He was chosen president of the American Academy of Arts, in 1817, and was annually elected to that office for many years. Finding no purchasers for his collection of paintings, he presented them to Yale College, and they are all in New Haven, in a building erected for the purpose, called *The Trumbull Gallery*. The venerable artist, soldier, and patriot, died in the city of New York, on the 10th of November, 1843, in the eighty-eighth year of his age.

WILLIAM BRADFORD.

"PITIFUL it was to see the heavy care of these poor women—what weeping and crying on every side; some for their husbands carried away on the ship; others not knowing what should become of them and their little ones; others melted in tears, seeing their poor little ones hanging about them, crying for fear and quaking with cold." So wrote William Bradford, describing the scene on the sea-shore of England when a company of conscientious Puritans were endeavoring to escape to Holland from their persecutors at home. While they were embarking on a Dutch ship, a troop of mounted men appeared, seized those on shore, a part of them women and a part of them men, while others on the vessel were carried away, the captain of the ship fearing arrest also. So families were parted for awhile, but they were finally united in Holland, then the only place in Europe where religious and political freedom was tolerated. Bradford was then only nineteen years of age. He was born in Austerfield, Yorkshire, England, in March, 1588. His father left him a comfortable estate, but, joining the persecuted Puritans, he resolved to flee with some of them to Holland. He made two unsuccessful attempts, but finally joined his brethren in the Netherlands. Bradford had suffered imprisonment, for being a dissenter, in Boston, Lincolnshire.

In Amsterdam he learned the art of silk-dyeing, and when, at the age of twenty-one, he came into possession of his patrimony, he engaged, but without success, in commerce. Bradford was one of Mr. Robinson's congregation, and was a zealous promoter of the project of making a settlement in America. With Elder Brewster and others, he formed one of the "Pilgrims" who sailed in the *Mayflower*, and he was one of the foremost in energy and good judgment in selecting a place to land on the shores of Cape Cod Bay, amid the snows of December, 1620. Before this was accomplished, his young wife fell into the sea and was drowned.

On the death of Governor Carver in April, 1621, Bradford was chosen to fill his official place, and was annually re-elected so long as he lived, excepting five years, between 1633 and 1645. Among his first and most important acts as governor, he cultivated the friendship of the Indians, especially the great chief Massasoit, who ruled a large domain in the vicinity of Plymouth, the town founded by the "Pilgrims." It was wise as well as just policy, and Bradford was rewarded for his kindness to the sachem by being forewarned by him of a conspiracy of barbarians for destroying the colony.

The account of the first interview between Bradford and Massasoit presents points of picturesque and romantic interest. The old sachem had sent a message to the governor, expressing a desire to meet him and his people. He was invited to Plymouth. Late in March, 1621, he appeared on the top of a hill with sixty of his best men. Edward Winslow was sent out with Massasoit's messenger, as Bradford's representative, carrying as a present to the forest monarch, three knives, a copper chain with a jewel attached, an earring, "a pot of strong water," plenty of biscuit, and some butter brought from the *Mayflower*. After a brief interview, Winslow remained as a hostage, while Massasoit and twenty unarmed followers went forward and met Miles Standish and six musketeers at a brook which divided the parties. Massasoit and his escort were conducted to an unfinished building, where they were seated on a rug and cushions. Governor Bradford came "with drum and trumpet after him" and a few musketeers. After cordial salutations and bountiful feasting, a treaty was concluded by which it was agreed that the parties should be friends, and that they should give mutual protection against enemies.

Governor Bradford was very energetic in promoting the welfare of the colony and in defending it against evils. He wrote a history of Plymouth Colony from 1602 to 1647, which remained in manuscript, having a place in the library of the old South Church, Boston. When the British army retreated from that city in the spring of 1776, one of the officers carried this manuscript away to Halifax. It was recovered eighty years afterward, and was published by the Massachusetts Historical Society in 1856. Governor Bradford died May 9, 1657.

EDWARD PREBLE.

THE sons of revolutionary fathers often inherited the courage and patriotism of their ancestors; indeed, the contrary was the exception to a rule, and true philosophy has a reason for it. The father of Edward Preble, one of the most distinguished of our naval commanders, was the honorable Jedediah Preble, of the ancient town of Falmouth (now Portland), Maine. He was a brigadier under the government of the Massachusetts colony, one of the first commanders of the army at Cambridge, in 1775, and a civilian of eminence when the Revolution had fairly commenced. Edward was born at the homestead, on the 15th of August, 1761, and received an academic education at Newbury. In early childhood he was noted for great resolution, and a love of athletic exercises. Like many lads of that seaport, he had a great desire for ocean life, and he made a voyage to Europe, in a privateer, in 1778. The following year he became a midshipman in one of the Massachusetts vessels, and was captured during the second cruise. Through the influence of Colonel Tyng, a friend of young Preble's father, the young man was released at New York, while the remainder of the crew were sent to England. He now entered as first lieutenant, on board the sloop of war, *Winthrop*, in which he continued during the remainder of the contest, and performed many deeds of valor. After the war, Preble was a shipmaster in many successive voyages, but stood ready for public service when his country should call him to duty.

When, in 1798, our hostile relations with France made it necessary to prepare our little navy for service, Preble was one of the five first-lieutenants, appointed by Congress. In the Winter of 1798–'9, he made two cruises, and the following Spring he commanded the *Essex*, under a captain's commission. In the year

1800, he was sent to convoy our merchantmen from the East India seas. He was afterward appointed to the command of the *Adams*, on the Mediterranean station, but ill-health soon compelled him to leave the service, for awhile. In 1803, he was placed in command of the frigate *Constitution*, and with the *Philadelphia* and several smaller vessels, he proceeded to the Mediterranean to humble the Algerine pirates who infested those waters. The principal powers engaged in that system of commercial robbery were those of Algiers, Tunis, Morocco, and Tripoli, known as the Barbary States. Preble first brought the Emperor of Morocco to terms, and then appeared before Tripoli, with his squadron. There he lost the *Philadelphia*, which struck upon a rock in the harbor, was captured by the Tripolitans, and the officers and crew were made prisoners.[1] Preble was soon afterward relieved by his senior, Commodore Barron. The value of his gallant services on the African coast was recognized by a vote of Congress, conferring upon him the thanks of the nation, and an elegant medal. These were presented to him, on his return home, by the President of the United States. On leaving his squadron, his officers expressed their esteem in a highly complimentary address. His services were soon afterward lost to his country, at a moment when they were needed more than ever. His health gave way toward the close of 1806, and on the 25th of August, 1807, he died, when in the forty-sixth year of his age. He was buried in his native town, with military honors.

JOHN H. LIVINGSTON.

THE friend and earliest biographer of President Livingston says of him, "He was a man whose praise is in all the churches; first in her councils—first in her honors—first in her affections." He was born at Poughkeepsie, Dutchess county, New York, on the 30th of May, 1746.[2] He received parental instruction, only, until his seventh year, when he was placed under other tutors, among whom was the father of the late Chancellor Kent. At the age of twelve years, he entered Yale College, as a student, and was graduated in 1762, when only sixteen. The profession of the law opened a brilliant future for him, and he commenced its study under Bartholomew Crannel, of Poughkeepsie. His habitual seriousness was deepened into strong religious convictions, by hearing a sermon from the lips of the eminent Whitefield, and he resolved to abandon the law, and become a minister of the gospel. He accordingly went to Holland, in 1766, to prosecute theological studies in the University of Utrecht, and there he remained until 1770, and acquired the degree of Doctor of Divinity. He returned to America the same year, and became pastor of the Dutch Reformed Church in the city of New York. Through his influence, internal dissensions, which had prevailed for some time, were healed; the two parties formed a union, and, in 1772, the Dutch churches became independent of the classis of Amsterdam; a result for which he had labored while in Holland.

When the Revolution broke out, all was confusion in New York, and Dr. Livingston went to reside at Kingston, in October, 1775, where, a month afterward, he was married to Sarah, daughter of Philip Livingston. Until the British took possession of the city of New York, the following year, Dr. Livingston went

---

1. See sketches of Bainbridge and Decatur.
2. The house in which he was born was in possession of the family of his only child, the late Colonel Henry A. Livingston until about 1880. When the British went up the Hudson, in 1777, to burn Kingston, they fired a heavy round shot at this mansion, because its proprietor was a staunch Whig. It passed into the building, and the ball was preserved by the family. The house stands on the margin of the river. It was built in 1714, the year when the father of Dr. Livingston was born.

down frequently, and preached to the remnant of his flock, who were compelled to remain.[1] He officiated ministerially at Albany and Livingston's Manor; and, in 1781, he took up his abode at his father's mansion, in Poughkeepsie, and occupied the pulpit of the Dutch Church there, for about two years. When the British left New York, Dr. Livingston resumed his pastoral charge there, and the following year he was chosen, by the first convention, Professor of Theology. He performed his new duties, with those of his ministerial services, with great zeal, in New York and its immediate vicinity, until 1810, when, on the removal of Queen's College (the theological school in which he was professor) to New Brunswick, in New Jersey, he was chosen its president. His inaugural address is a model of its kind, full of learning and the purest Christian spirit. In 1813, he completed a version of the Psalms and Hymns used in the church, pursuant to the request of the general Synod, and that collection is now the standard book throughout that denomination. As the college under his charge did not flourish as a *literary* institution, an effort was commenced, in 1815, to make it a Theological Seminary, exclusively. That measure was carried into effect, and from that time, until the present, it has held that character. Its name has been changed to *Rutger's College*, in honor of a distinguished citizen of New York who nobly patronised it.

---

1. Dr. Livingston administered the Lord's Supper in the Middle Dutch Church (now [1855] the city Post Office), in June, 1776, the last until the British left the city, in November, 1783.

Dr. Livingston's health began to fail many years before his death, yet he labored on and hoped on, until the last. Finally, in January, 1825, he was attacked with acute pain, but was soon relieved. On the evening of the 28th he prayed fervently, in his family, and went to bed in usual health. When his grandson called him to arise for breakfast the next morning, the spirit of the good man had departed to the bosom of his God whom he so dearly loved and so faithfully served. He was then in the seventy-ninth year of his age.

GOUVERNEUR MORRIS.

THE preparation of the Constitution of the United States in the form adopted by the convention, in 1787, and ratified by a majority of the States, the following year, was the work of the accomplished scholar and statesman, Gouverneur Morris, brother of Lewis, one of the signers of the Declaration of Independence. He was born at Morrisania, on the Westchester shore of the Harlem River, New York, on the 31st of January, 1752. The death of his father left him to the care of his mother at the age of twelve years. He was graduated at King's (now Columbia) College, in the city of New York, in May, 1768, at the age of sixteen years, and his oration on that occasion, on the subject of *Wit and Beauty*, made a marked sensation among the polished circles of the day. He studied law under William Smith, the historian of New York, and afterward chief justice of the province, and was licensed to practice, in the Autumn of 1771. He was not yet twenty years of age, yet he had already engaged in political discussions of the day, especially upon financial subjects, and had attracted the attention of many leading men. He continued much before the public in speech and in print, until 1775, when he was elected to a seat in the New York Provincial Congress. There he made a most favorable impression, and was soon an acknowledged leader, although then only twenty-three years of age. He was one of the committee of correspondence for the city of New York, and his pen was continually busy for the patriot cause. In the Summer of 1776, he was sent as special agent to the Continental Congress, on the subject of payment to troops; and in the Autumn of the following year, he was elected to a seat in that body. He was placed on a committee to confer with General Washington on the subject of a new organization of the Continental army, and he spent nearly three months in the camp at Valley Forge. From the moment of presenting his credentials, Mr. Morris was one of the most active and highly esteemed members of Congress; and finally, when the government was newly organized, in 1781, under the Articles of Confederation, he was made assistant financial agent with his great namesake of Philadelphia. He was now a permanent resident of that city, where, by an accident, he lost a leg.[1] He remained there until 1786, when he purchased the paternal estate at Morrisania from a Tory brother, and soon afterward made it his abode. He was a delegate from Pennsylvania in the convention that framed the Federal Constitution, and when the various articles had been thoroughly discussed and agreed upon, the task of putting the whole instrument into proper form and language was entrusted to Mr. Morris. The following year he went to Paris, and resided there until early in 1790, when, having received from President Washington the appointment of

---

1. He was thrown from a carriage in the streets of Philadelphia, and the bones of one of his legs were so much shattered, that amputation became necessary. He always wore a rough stick, as a substitute, and would never consent to have a handsome leg made.

private agent to transact important business with the British ministry, he went to London. After accomplishing his business, he made a brief tour on the Continent. Early in 1792, he received intelligence of his appointment as minister plenipotentiary to the French court, and that important station he filled until the Autumn of 1794, when he made another Continental tour, chiefly for the purpose of gathering information for the benefit of himself and country. He finally returned to America in the Autumn of 1798, and retired to private life at Morrisania, after an absence of ten years, during which time he had been engaged in the most arduous public and private duties. He was soon afterward elected to fill a vacancy in the United States Senate, and held a seat there from May, 1800, until March, 1803. He travelled most of the remainder of 1803, in the United States and Canada. His thoughts were ever active on the subject of the internal improvement of his native State. He was among the earliest to appreciate Jesse Hawley's plan for connecting the waters of Lake Erie and the Hudson, by a canal, and was one of the most ardent friends of the project. He did not live to see it consummated, for death suddenly terminated his career, on the 6th of November, 1816, in the sixty-fifth year of his age. Mr. Morris was a fine writer, and his pen wielded an extensive influence during half a century.

THOMAS M'KEAN.

AMONG the numerous men of note, in Pennsylvania, who received an academic education under Francis Allison,[1] was the eminent Chief Justice M'Kean, of that State. He was born in Chester county, Pennsylvania, on the 19th of March, 1734. He studied law with his relative, David Finney, at New Castle, in Delaware; and during his student life, he was clerk of the prothonotary Court of Common Pleas, for that county. He was admitted to practice before he was twenty-one years of age, and his upward course in his profession was rapid and highly honorable. In 1756, he was appointed deputy of the attorney-general, to prosecute in the county of Sussex, and the following year he was admitted to the bar of the Supreme Court of Pennsylvania. He was appointed clerk of the assembly of Delaware, at about the same time; and that body, in 1762, appointed him a colleague, with Cæsar Rodney, to revise and print the laws of the province enacted during the preceding ten years. That same year he was chosen a member of the Delaware Assembly,[2] and then he commenced his distinguished political career, in earnest, which continued for almost half a century. He was annually reëlected to the Assembly for seventeen years, against his continually expressed desire to leave public life, and even while, for six years of the time, he was a resident of the city of Philadelphia. This was an extraordinary proof of his ability and fidelity.[3]

In 1764, the legislature appointed him one of three trustees of the provincial loan office, and he performed the duties of that station until 1772. He was a delegate to the "Stamp Act Congress" held in New York, in 1765, and was

---

[1]. See sketch of Francis Allison.
[2]. The present State of Delaware, which William Penn obtained by grant and purchase, in 1682, and annexed to his province of Pennsylvania, was originally known as *The Territories*, comprising the three counties : New Castle, Kent, and Sussex. Penn gave the people of Pennsylvania a new and more liberal charter, in 1701, but the people of *The Territories* preferred a separate and independent government. A compromise was effected. The Delaware counties were allowed a distinct and independent assembly, under the same governor and council as Pennsylvania. Such was the political condition of the two commonwealths, until finally separated in 1776.
[3]. When he finally positively declined a re-election, in 1777, the people insisted that he should name some of the best men in Delaware, for their representatives. He did so, and all were elected.

one of the most energetic friends of popular liberty in that assembly. In 1771, he was appointed collector of the customs at New Castle, and was a commissioner of the revenue. In the Autumn of 1772, he was chosen Speaker of the Assembly. He was a delegate for his adopted province in the first Continental Congress, in 1774; and he was a member of the national council from that time until the return of peace, in 1783. As such he advocated independence, and signed the great Declaration. He was one of the committee appointed to draw up the Articles of Confederation; and while acting as a senator in Congress, and president of the newly-organized State of Delaware, he was also distinguished as a soldier, in New Jersey, with the commission of colonel. In July, 1777, he was commissioned chief justice of Pennsylvania, and held that exalted office for twenty years. It was a position of great responsibility, but Judge M'Kean was equal to the task he had assumed. He was president of Congress, in 1781; and, in 1787, he was a member of the Pennsylvania convention which ratified the Federal Constitution. He was its earnest advocate, and was extremely influential in procuring its ratification, by Pennsylvania. In 1789, Judge M'Kean assisted in amending the constitution of his native State; and ten years afterward, at the end of a warm party contest, he was elected governor of Pennsylvania. He was rather violent in his party zeal, and his course as chief magistrate created the most bitter animosity against him. His political enemies tried to impeach him, but his stern integrity never allowed him to deviate from the strict line of duty, and they found no true basis for their attempts to degrade him. For nine years he governed Pennsylvania with firmness, ability, and great discretion, and then retired from public life. Only once again did he appear in a popular assembly. It was in Independence Hall, in 1814, when the safety of Philadelphia seemed in jeopardy from the British. He presided, and reminded the people that there were then only two parties, "our country and its invaders." The venerable patriot went down into the grave, on the 24th of June, 1817, when past the eighty-third year of his age.

THOMAS BALDWIN.

ONE of the most eminent lights of the Baptist Church, in America, was the Reverend Thomas Baldwin, D.D., who was born at Bozrah,[1] Connecticut, on the 23d of December, 1753. His early education was very limited, yet his ardent aspirations for knowledge overcame many obstacles in his way. When he was sixteen years of age his parents went to Canaan, then a frontier town in New Hampshire, to reside, and there his youth was spent in the laborious vocation of a blacksmith, the business of his step-father. He was frequently called upon to read sermons to the people on the Sabbath, when the minister was absent, he being the only young man in the place capable of performing such service. Only a few books could then be obtained, yet so thoroughly did he study all that fell in his way, that, when arrived at manhood, he possessed a stock of miscellaneous knowledge much greater than that of most young men of his time, out of cities.

Young Baldwin was married to Ruth Huntington, of Norwich, in 1775, and

---

1. The origin of this name is a little amusing. A plain man, who lived where Fitchville now is, was not remarkable for quoting Scripture correctly. On one occasion, in quoting the sentence from Isaiah, "Who is this that cometh from Edom, with dyed garments from Bozrah," &c., he stated that the *Prophet Bozrah* said thus and so. He was ever afterward called the Prophet, and his place was named Bozrah. When the town was incorporated, that name was given to it.

soon afterward became a member of the Baptist Church. He was ordained for the Christian ministry, in the Summer of 1783; and at about the same time he was elected to a seat in the Connecticut legislature. Never was a man more devoted to his calling, than was this eminent young servant of Christ. He soon declined political office, because it interfered with his ministerial labors. Like Paul, his own hands ministered to his necessities, for, during the first seven years of his pastoral labors, his salary did not amount to forty dollars a year. Yet he travelled on horseback over a large district of country.

The fame of Mr. Baldwin, as a zealous preacher, was soon in all the churches; and, in November, 1790, he was installed pastor of the Second Baptist Church, in Boston. The change from the ruder society of the frontier, to the more refined of the metropolis, was very great, yet his services were most acceptable, from the beginning. His fervid and persuasive eloquence captivated all hearts, and remarkable revivals occurred under his preaching. Within the space of two years [1803–1805], over two hundred communicants were added to his congregation.

In 1803, the Faculty of Union College, New York, conferred the degree of Doctor of Divinity, upon Mr. Baldwin; and the same year he commenced the publication of the *American Baptist Magazine*. He was its sole editor until 1817, and senior editor until his death. It was a powerful auxiliary in his hands, in promoting the growth of the Baptist Church in this country; and, for a long time, it was the only publication issued by that denomination on this side the Atlantic.

Although eminent as a preacher and editor, Dr. Baldwin is more widely known to the reading world as an author. The number of his published works is thirty-four, a large proportion of which consists of sermons, printed by special request. His writings on Baptism have always been regarded as expressing the opinions of the standard authorities of his denomination. Dr. Baldwin was a zealous friend of institutions of learning, especially of those fostered by the Baptist Church; and during his long life, until his steps began to totter, he was an active laborer. He literally "died in harness," for he expired at Waterville, Maine, on the day after preaching two instructive sermons at Hallowell. His departure was on the 29th of August, 1825, at the age of seventy-two years. Temperate and regular in his habits, his old age was like a sunny landscape just at evening, suffused with golden light.

SETH WARNER.

AMONG the *Green Mountain Boys* of the last century, the man next to Ethan Allen in their esteem, for daring courage, unflinching patriotism, and pleasant companionship, was Seth Warner, a native of Woodbury, Connecticut, where he was born at about the year 1744. We have no reliable records of his early life, except that he was fond of athletic sports and the excitements of the chase. He took up his abode at Bennington, in the present Vermont, in 1773, and was famous throughout that whole region as a deer and bear hunter. In the controversy with the authorities of Vermont, he was one of the leaders of the people; and in March, 1774, the legislature of New York passed an act of outlawry against him. He was with Ethan Allen at the capture of Ticonderoga, in May, 1775, and commanded the little force that took possession of Crown Point immediately afterward. He received a colonel's commission from Congress, raised a regiment of *Green Mountain Boys*,[1] and joined the army in Canada, under General Montgomery; but on the approach of Winter, they were discharged. He had been of great service after the capture of Ethan Allen, at Montreal, and on the 1st of November, had repulsed a considerable British force, under Governor Carleton, which attempted to land at Longueuil for the purpose of driving the invading Americans back to Lake Champlain. The following Spring, Warner raised another regiment, marched toward Quebec, and was very serviceable in the final retreat of the Americans from Canada. In all the operations in the vicinity of Lake Champlain, in 1776, Colonel Warner was an efficient participator; and he was at Ticonderoga, in the Summer of 1777, when Burgoyne compelled the Americans to abandon that post. He commanded a part of St. Clair's troops in that retreat, and gallantly fought the pursuing enemy at Hubbardton, on the 7th of July. Defeated in that engagement, he made a successful retreat to Manchester, and on the 16th of August following, he was with the gallant Stark in the engagement known as the Battle of Bennington. He then joined General Gates on the Hudson, assisted in humbling Burgoyne, and participated in the glory of his defeat and capture. He engaged very little in public life, after that event, because his health was greatly impaired by a complication of disorders. He lingered on until 1785, when death ended his sufferings. He died at his birth-place, at the age of about forty-one years. Grateful for his services, his adopted State granted a valuable tract of land to his widow and children.

---

1. See sketch of Ethan Allen.

JOSEPH REED.

"I AM not worth purchasing, but, such as I am, the King of Great Britain is not rich enough to do it," are the noble words attributed by tradition to Joseph Reed, of Pennsylvania, and uttered when a bribe was offered for his influence in favor of Great Britain, in 1778. He was born at Trenton, New Jersey, on the 27th of August, 1741. His father soon afterward made Philadelphia his residence, for several years. Joseph was designed for the profession of the law, and was educated in the college at Princeton, where he was graduated in 1757, with a Bachelor's degree, at the early age of sixteen years. He first studied law with Richard Stockton, and completed his legal education in the Temple, in London. On his return home, he made Philadelphia his residence, entered warmly into political life, and was one of the committee of correspondence in his adopted city, in 1774. He was chosen president of the first popular convention in Pennsylvania; and, in 1775, he accompanied Washington to Cambridge as his aid and secretary. He remained with the chief during that campaign, and the following year, when Gates was appointed to the command in the Northern Department. Mr. Reed was then appointed adjutant-general of the American army, with the rank of colonel. He performed efficient service in the battle near Brooklyn, in August, 1776, especially in the management of the admirable retreat of the Americans. In the Spring of 1777, he was appointed a brigadier, in command of cavalry, but declined the honor, yet he remained attached to the army until after the battle at Germantown, in the Autumn of 1777. He was soon afterward elected to a seat in Congress, and was a member of that body when, in the Spring of 1778, commissioners came from England to negotiate a peace on the basis of the submission of the colonists to the crown. It was to the agent of one of these commissioners that he is said to have addressed the words above quoted.[1] The fact became known, and Congress refused further intercourse with the commissioners. In 1778, General Reed was chosen president of the newly-organized commonwealth of Pennsylvania, and filled that station with great ability until October, 1781, when he retired from public life, and resumed the practice of the law. Like all dutiful men, he was the target for unmeasured abuse from his political opponents; but when time dissipated the clouds of party rancor, all men beheld in Joseph Reed a patriot and an honest man. His health became impaired in 1784, and he went to England to seek its restoration, but without beneficial results.[2] He died on the 4th of March, 1785, at the age of forty-four years.

---

1. The agent chosen was Mrs. Ferguson, a native of Pennsylvania, whose husband was a relative of Adam Ferguson, the secretary of the commission. She was a woman of superior attainments, and loved her country. She was a passive, rather than an active agent in the matter. In her account of her interview with Mr. Reed, she says his words were, "My influence is but small, but were it as great as Governor Johnstone [the commissioner who approached General Reed, through Mrs. Ferguson] would insinuate, the King of Great Britain has nothing within his gift that would tempt me." Alluding to this, Trumbull, in his "M'Fingall," says:

> "Behold, at Britain's utmost shifts,
> Comes Johnstone, loaded with like gifts,
> To venture through the Whiggish tribe,
> To cuddle, wheedle, coax, and bribe;
> And call to aid his desp'rate mission,
> His petticoated politician;
> While Venus, joined to act the farce,
> Strolls forth embassadress of Mars."

2. Mr. Reed married a daughter of Dennis de Berdt, a London merchant, in 1770. Though in delicate health, she was active in her sphere of duty in relation to public events. She was at the head of an association of ladies, formed in Philadelphia in 1780, to furnish clothing for the army. No less than twenty-two hundred ladies joined the association, and contributed by their money and needles to the comfort of the soldiers.

JAMES RIVINGTON.

PERHAPS one of the most acute and successful political gamesters in this country, was James Rivington, "the king's printer," in New York, during a greater portion of the War for Independence. He was a native of London, well-educated, courtly in deportment, and a general favorite among his acquaintances. He was a bookseller in London, but failing in business, he came to America, in 1760, and opened a book-store in Philadelphia. The following year he opened another at the foot of Wall Street, New York; and, in 1762, he established a third, in Boston. His partner in the latter died three years afterward, and it was closed. In the course of a few years he again failed in business, but settling his affairs satisfactorily, he resumed it in New York, and thereafter confined his operations to that city. He commenced printing books, in 1772; and, in the Spring of the following year, he published the first number of his *Royal Gazetteer*, a weekly newspaper. It was conducted with considerable fairness, but after the hostilities in Massachusetts, in the Spring of 1775, he took strong ground against the Whigs, and excited their fiercest indignation. Their ire took tangible shape in November of that year, when Isaac Sears (a leader of the Sons of Liberty ten years before), at the head of a troop of Connecticut militia, marched into the city at noon-day, destroyed Rivington's press, and carried off his type to the tune of Yankee Doodle. Rivington soon afterward went to England, but returned in the Autumn of 1776, when the British had taken possession of New York. Early in 1777, he resumed the publication of his paper, and from that time till the close of the war, he dealt hard and unscrupulous blows upon the patriots, from Washington and Congress down to the most obscure official. And yet, toward the close of the conflict, while his press was the vehicle of the coarsest abuse of Washington and his friends, it is a well-attested fact that Rivington was secretly furnishing the American commander-in-chief valuable information concerning the movements and plans of the enemy within the city. Such was the case from early in 1781, until the evacuation of the city by the British near the close of 1783.[1] This fact accounts for the otherwise inexplicable circumstance, that Rivington, the arch-loyalist, was allowed to remain while thousands of less offending Tories were compelled to flee to Nova Scotia. Rivington sagaciously perceived the inevitable result of the conflict, and thus made a peace-offering to the Americans. His business declined after the war, and he lived in comparative poverty for many years, simply because he would not relinquish his expensive mode of living.[2] He died in July, 1802, when at the age of about seventy-eight years.

---

1. By means of books which he printed, he performed his treason without suspicion. He wrote his information upon thin paper, and bound those billets in the covers of books which he adroitly managed to sell to persons employed by Washington to buy of him, but who were ignorant of the transaction. Washington removed the covers, and found the desired information. Referring to the change in the tone of Rivington's paper, at the close of the war, Philip Freneau, the vigorous epic and lyric poet of the Revolution, wrote, in the editor's name:

"You know I was zealous for George's command,
But since he disgraced it, and left us behind,
If I thought him an angel I've altered my mind.
On the very same day that his army went hence,
I ceased to tell lies for the sake of his pence;
And what was the reason—the true one is best,
I worship no sun that declines to the west."

2. Referring to this, Freneau wrote:

"Long life and low spirits were never my choice,
As long as I live I intend to rejoice;
When life is worn out, and no wine 's to be had,
'Tis time enough then to be serious and sad,
'Tis time enough then to reflect and repent,
When our liquor is gone, and our money is spent."

JOHN DICKENSON.

THE "Letters of a Farmer of Pennsylvania to the Inhabitants of the British Colonies," published in the *Pennsylvania Chronicle*, during the Summer and Autumn of 1767, had a powerful influence on the American mind, in preparing it for the great struggle for freedom, even then impending. The author was John Dickenson, a native of Maryland, where he was born, on the 13th of November, 1732. His father was first judge of the Court of Common Pleas, in Delaware, and being wealthy, his son had every advantage of social position and pecuniary ease, at the beginning of life. He was well educated by private tutors, and then went to England and studied law in the Temple, for three years. He first appeared in public life as a member of the Pennsylvania Assembly, in 1764, where the readiness of his pen attracted general attention. He was also a member of the Stamp Act Congress, in 1765. He soon afterward commenced writing political essays; and during the whole conflict, which commenced in earnest in 1775, his pen was always active and efficient. His *Letters of a Pennsylvania Farmer*, above alluded to, were published in London, by Dr. Franklin, in 1768, and the following year they were translated into French, and published at Paris.[1]

---

1. The people of Boston passed a vote of thanks to Mr. Dickenson for those Letters, and the Society of Fort St. David, of Philadelphia, presented him with an address in "a box of heart of oak."

Mr. Dickenson was a member of the first Continental Congress, in 1774, and his pen was instrumental in the preparation of two of the State papers put forth by that body. He wrote the Declaration of the Congress of 1775, setting forth the causes and the necessity for war; yet he steadily opposed the idea of political independence, for he hoped for a reconciliation. For that reason, he was intentionally absent from Congress on the 4th of July, 1776, for he was unwilling to vote on the subject of independence, contrary to the expressed wishes of his constituents. In the Autumn of 1777, President M'Kean, of Delaware, commissioned him a brigadier-general, but his military career was short. He was again elected to Congress, in 1779, and there, as before, his pen was employed in the preparation of important State papers. In 1780, he took his seat, as a member, in the Delaware Assembly; and, in 1782, he was elected president or governor of Pennsylvania. He held that office until October, 1785. He was one of the most accomplished and efficient members of the convention that framed the Federal Constitution; and over the signature of *Fabius* he published nine ably-written letters in its defence. In 1792, he assisted in forming a Constitution for Delaware; and, in 1797, he published another series of political letters over the signature of *Fabius*. At about that time he retired from public life, and the remainder of his days were passed in the enjoyment of domestic and social happiness, at Wilmington, where he died on the 14th of February, 1808, at the age of seventy-five years. Dickenson College, at Carlisle, Pennsylvania, is a noble monument to perpetuate his memory. It is now [1854] under the control of the Baltimore and Philadelphia conferences of the Methodist Episcopal Church.

PETER MUHLENBERG.

SPIRITUAL and temporal warfare was the lot of many Gospel ministers, during the War for Independence. Of those who wielded weapons manfully, in both fields of conflict, was John Peter Gabriel Muhlenberg, who generally wrote his name with the John and Gabriel omitted. He was a native of Trappe, a village in Montgomery county, Pennsylvania, where he was born on the 1st of October, 1746. He was the son of Dr. Melchoir Muhlenberg (the founder of the Lutheran Church in America), and the daughter of Conrad Weiser, the great Pennsylvania Indian agent. Peter was educated for the ministry, partly in this country, and partly in Europe. He was ordained in 1768, and commenced his pastoral labors in Western New Jersey the following year. He was called to the charge of a congregation in Virginia, in 1771, and it being necessary to obtain ordination from an English Bishop, before he could enter upon his duties there, he went to London for the purpose, at the beginning of the following year. He and Mr. (afterward Bishop) White were ordained at the same time. On his return, he became minister of the parish of Woodstock, Virginia, and was soon an acknowledged leading spirit of that section among those who opposed British aggressions. He was chairman of the committee of safety in that county, in 1774, and was elected to a seat in the House of Burgesses. At the close of 1775, he was appointed colonel of a Virginia regiment, and, relinquishing his pastoral duties,[1] he joined the army, and was in the battle at Charleston, in

---

1. In concluding his farewell sermon, he quoted the language of Holy Writ, which declares that there is "a time for all things," and added, with a trumpet voice, "there is a time to fight, and that time has now come!" Then laying aside his gown, he stood before his flock in the full uniform of a Virginia colonel. He then ordered the drums to be beaten at the church door for recruits, and almost three hundred men, chiefly of his congregation, were enrolled under his banner, that day.

June, 1776. Congress commissioned him a brigadier, in February, 1777, and he was ordered to take charge of all the Virginia Continental troops. He joined the army, under Washington, at Middlebrook, in May, and was with the chief in all his movements from that time until 1779—Brandywine, Germantown, White Marsh, Valley Forge, and Monmouth. He was with Wayne at the capture of Stony Point, in July, 1779, and was very active afterward, in Virginia, until the capture of Cornwallis, in the Autumn of 1781. He was a brave participator in that last great battle of the Revolution. At the close of the war he was promoted to major-general, and removed to Pennsylvania. He never resumed his ministerial labors, but served his native State in several civil offices. He was a member of the first and third Congress, after the organization of the Federal Government, and was also a United States Senator, in 1801. He was appointed supervisor of the revenue of Pennsylvania the same year; and, in 1802, he was made collector of the port of Philadelphia. In that office he remained until his death, which occurred at his country seat, near Philadelphia, on the 1st of October, 1807, when he was precisely sixty-one years of age. His remains lie buried in the burial-ground at Trappe, near the church wherein he was baptized.

SILAS TALBOT.

THE exigencies of the public service during the War for Independence oftentimes made officers amphibious—called to duty on land and water—as in the case of Arnold, Drayton, and others. Silas Talbot was of this class, and one of the bravest and most devoted. His memory has been rescued from oblivion by an accomplished writer of our day (H. T. Tuckerman, Esq.), who, with infinite pains, has grouped the chief incidents of his checkered life into a miniature volume. Our hero was a lineal descendant of Sir Richard de Talbot of the time of William the Conqueror, and seems to have inherited the martial taste of his illustrious ancestor. He was a native of Rhode Island, but little is known of his early life. He was a young man when the war broke out, and he entered heartily into the contest. He then resided in Providence, where he had married, in 1772, and built himself a house, with his own earnings. Early in 1775, he had organized a little company of volunteers; and, in June following, the State gave him the commission of captain in one of its regiments. He joined the camp at Roxbury, was active during that campaign, and accompanied the army to New York, in the Spring of 1776. There he performed some daring exploits against the British shipping in the harbor, which elicited the thanks of Congress, and procured him a major's commission. In the Autumn of 1777, he was in the memorable siege of Fort Mifflin, on the Delaware, where he was twice badly wounded. The following year we find Major Talbot busily engaged in furnishing boats for General Sullivan to transport his troops across the channel at the upper end of Rhode Island; and from that time, until the evacuation of the Island, by the British, he was active in all military and naval events, in that vicinity. In the Autumn of 1779, he was commissioned a captain in the navy, and he afterward made as successful cruises, as he had already during his six months of naval command previous to the date of his commission. He was captured by a small British fleet, in 1780, and suffered the horrors of the Jersey prison-ship,[1] and the Provost jail, at New York, for several months. He was

---

1. This was an old hulk, moored where the Brooklyn Navy Yard now is, and used as a prison for captured American seamen. Soldiers were also immured there. Several thousands perished of famine

finally taken to England, and exchanged at the close of 1781. After the war, he purchased a portion of the forfeited estate of Sir William Johnson's heirs, on the Mohawk, and retired to private life. In 1794, when a new organization of the navy took place, Captain Talbot was called into the public service; and he superintended the construction of the *Constitution*, which became his flag-ship, in 1799, while on a cruise in the West Indies, with the afterward renowned commander of the same ship (Hull), as his lieutenant. Talbot remained in active service until 1801, when he resigned his commission, took up his abode in the city of New York, and lived in retirement until his death, on the 30th of June, 1813. His remains were buried under Trinity Church.

NATHAN HALE.

ONE of the earliest martyrs in the cause of popular liberty, in America, was Captain Nathan Hale, whose fate, and that of Major Andrè, history may properly parallel. He was a son of Richard Hale, of Coventry, Connecticut, and was born in that town, twenty miles from Hartford, about the year 1754. He was graduated at Yale College, with distinguished approbation, in 1773, when the tempest of the Revolution was gathering force. Fired with zeal for liberty, he joined the Connecticut troops that hastened to Boston after the skirmishes at Lexington and Concord, and was with Captain (afterward Colonel) Knowlton in the battle on Breed's Hill. He continued with the army under the immediate command of Washington, until the following year, and participated in the battle near Brooklyn, and the retreat of the American army, from Long Island. At that time Knowlton was in command of a regiment, called *Congress' Own*, that assumed a sort of body-guardianship to the commander-in-chief, and young Hale held a captain's commission in it. While the American army were upon Harlem Heights, and the great body of the British were yet on Long Island (in the vicinity of Brooklyn, and of the present Astoria), Washington was very anxious to ascertain the exact condition of the enemy's forces. He applied to Colonel Knowlton for a judicious person to go as a spy into the British camp. Captain Hale volunteered for the service, and bearing instructions from Washington, he crossed Long Island Sound from the Connecticut shore, visited the British camps, made notes and sketches, unsuspected, and was about to embark from Huntington, to Connecticut, when he was discovered and exposed, it is said, by a Tory relative, and was made a prisoner. He was taken to Sir William Howe's head-quarters at Turtle Bay, confined in Beekman's green-house in the garden, until morning, and then, without the form of a regular trial, was handed over to Cunningham, the brutal provost-marshal in New York, for execution as a spy. That wretch would not allow him to have the company of a clergyman, nor the use of a Bible; and he even destroyed the letters which the victim had written to his mother and sisters during the night. Amid cruel jeers he was hanged, like a dog, upon an apple tree, and his body was buried in a grave beneath its shadow. He suffered death in accordance with the stern laws of war, but his treatment, from the hour of his capture until his death, was disgraceful to the British commander. Hale's last words were, "I only regret that I have not more lives to give to my country."[1] A beautiful monument has been erected to his memory in his native town.

---

and disease in that loathsome prison. The Provost Jail was also a place of horrors. It was in Liberty Street, near Nassau Street.

1. A full account of Hale's capture and death may be found in Onderdonk's *Revolutionary Incidents on Long Island*, and in Lossing's *Pictorial Field-Book of the Revolution*.

ALEXANDER HAMILTON.

AROUND the name of Hamilton, the pure patriot, the brave soldier, the accomplished statesman, and acute financier, there is a halo which brightens with the lapse of years, for he was peerless among his fellows. He was a native of the island of Nevis, in the West Indies, and was descended from a Scotch father and a French mother. He was born on the 11th of January, 1757. He received a fair education in childhood, and at the age of twelve years he became a clerk in the mercantile house of Nicholas Cruger, at St. Croix. Every leisure moment he devoted to study; and while yet a mere youth, a production of his pen gave such evidence of great genius, that the friends of his widowed mother provided means for sending him to New York to be thoroughly educated. At the age of sixteen years he accompanied his mother to the United States, and entered King's (now Columbia) College as a student, where he remained about three years. The contest of words, with Great Britain, was then raging, and gave scope to his thoughts and topics for his pen. When only seventeen years of age he appeared as a speaker at public meetings, and he assisted the Sons of Liberty in carrying off British cannon from the battery of Fort George, at the foot of Broadway, in 1775. He entered the army as captain of an artillery company, raised chiefly by himself, and performed good service at White Plains, Trenton, and Princeton. His pen was as active as his sword, and many articles, attributed to more mature and eminent men, were the offspring of his brain.

He attracted the special attention of Washington, and in March, 1777, the commander-in-chief appointed him his aid-de-camp, with the rank of lieutenant-colonel. During the remainder of the war, until the capture of Cornwallis in the Autumn of 1781, he was Washington's chief secretary, and was also the leader of a corps of light infantry, under La Fayette, at the siege of Yorktown. After that event he left the army, and, in 1782, was admitted to practice at the bar of the Supreme Court of the State of New York. He was a member of Congress during that year, but declined a reëlection. He had married a daughter of General Philip Schuyler, in 1780, and he looked to his profession for the support of his family. He rose to distinction very rapidly, yet in the midst of his extensive business, he found time to employ his pen upon subjects of national importance. He was a member of the convention that framed the Federal Constitution, and in connection with Madison and Jay, wrote the series of articles in favor of that instrument, known as *The Federalist.* Of the eighty-five numbers, Hamilton wrote fifty-four. He was also a member of the State convention, held at Poughkeepsie in 1788, that ratified the Constitution. When, in 1789, the new government was organized, Washington, on the earnest recommendation of Robert Morris, placed Mr. Hamilton at the head of the Treasury. It was a wise choice, for financial difficulties were more formidable than any others in the way of the administration, and no man was more capable of bringing order out of confusion, than Mr. Hamilton. His consummate skill soon regulated money matters; but while he was improving the fiscal condition of the government, he was injuring his own. He accordingly resigned his office, in 1795, and turned his attention to his profession. When a provisional army was raised, in 1798, Washington accepted the commission of commander-in-chief, only on condition that Hamilton should be his associate, and second in command. This was Hamilton's last public service. In the Winter of 1804, he became involved in a political dispute with Colonel Aaron Burr, which resulted in a duel in July following. They met at Hoboken, and upon the same spot where his son was killed in a duel a few years previously, Hamilton was mortally wounded, and died the next day, July 12th, 1804, at the age of little more than forty-seven years. His wife survived him, in widowhood, fifty years. She died on the 9th of November, 1854, at the age of ninety-seven years and three months. The voluminous papers of General Hamilton were purchased by Congress, and after being arranged by his son, John C. Hamilton, they were published in seven octavo volumes, in 1841.

WILLIAM GRAY.

THE successful and honorable merchant is one of the most valuable integrals of a nation's strength, for he is the factor of the nation's labor and capital. One of the most eminent in this profession was William Gray. He was born in Lynn, Massachusetts, in 1751, and when quite a small boy, was apprenticed to a merchant in Salem. He finished his commercial education with Richard Derby,[1] of that port; and such was his character for enterprise and strict integrity during his apprenticeship, that when, soon after its close, he commenced

---

1. After the skirmishes at Lexington and Concord, on the 19th of April, 1775, the Provincial Congress of Massachusetts, in session at Watertown, with Joseph Warren at its head, prepared a full and elaborate statement of the affair, with an Address to the People of Great Britain. Richard Derby (the master of young Gray) was employed to carry these documents to England, and place them in the hands of Dr. Franklin, in London. He arrived there on the 29th of May, and the Address and Statement were published in the London papers. This was the first information the British public had of the affair.

business for himself, he had the entire confidence and good-will of the whole community. Prosperity waited upon him in all his transactions, and in less than twenty-five years after he commenced business, he was taxed as the wealthiest man in Salem, notwithstanding some of the largest fortunes in the United States belonged to men of that town. His enterprise and industry was wonderful; and at one time he had more than sixty sail of square-rigged vessels on the ocean. For more than fifty years he arose at dawn, and was ready for the business of the day before others had finished their last nap. Although he had millions of dollars afloat on the sea of business, he was careful of small expenditures—those leaks which endanger the ship—and his whole life was a lesson of prudent economy, without penuriousness.

Mr. Gray was a democrat, and his sincerity was evinced by the fact that during the embargo, he took sides with Jefferson, notwithstanding all New England was in a blaze against the president, and it was an injury to the amount of tens of thousands of dollars to the great merchant's business. In the midst of the commercial distress, he removed to Boston, and having pleased the people while a State Senator, he was chosen lieutenant-governor of the Commonwealth. He used his immense riches for the wants of government, and never took advantages of the exigencies of the times, to speculate in government securities. After the war of 1812–'15, he engaged largely in business again, but he lost often and heavily. Yet he died a rich man, honored and beloved for his virtues, on the 4th of November, 1825, at the age of about seventy-four years.

DAVID HUMPHREYS.

IT is inscribed upon a neat granite monument, in a cemetery at New Haven, Connecticut, that "David Humphreys, doctor of laws, member of the Academy of Sciences of Philadelphia, Massachusetts, and Connecticut, of the Bath [Agricultural Society] and of the Royal Society of London," was "a distinguished historian and poet; a model and a patron of science, and of the ornamental and useful arts." He was born in Derby, Connecticut, in 1753, and was graduated at Yale College, in 1771. A few months afterward, he went to reside, as a tutor, in the family of Colonel Philipse,[1] of the Philipse Manor, on the Hudson. How long he remained in that capacity we have no record, and we lose sight of the future "historian and poet" until the war of the Revolution began, when we find him at the head of a company of Connecticut militia. He afterward joined the Continental army, with a captain's commission, and was under the immediate command of General Putnam until 1778, when that officer made him one of his aids, with the rank of major. He held that commission until the Autumn of 1780, when he was promoted to the office of aid to Washington, with the rank of colonel. He remained in the military family of the commander-in-chief until the close of the war. For his valor at Yorktown, where Cornwallis was captured, Congress honored him with a vote of thanks, and the present of an elegant sword.

In May, 1784, Colonel Humphreys was appointed secretary to the commission for negotiating treaties with foreign powers, and with his friend Kosciuszko, accompanied Mr. Jefferson to Paris. He returned in 1786, and was elected to a seat in the Connecticut legislature. He was appointed to the command of a regiment raised for the western service, but was not called to the field; and from

---

1. Brother of Mary Philipse, wife of Colonel Roger Morris. See page 227.

1786 till 1788, he resided at Hartford, where, with Trumbull, Barlow, and Hopkins, he wrote the *Anarchiad*. By invitation of Washington, Colonel Humphreys resided in the family of the great Patriot from 1788 until appointed by his illustrious friend minister to Portugal, in 1790. He went thither in 1791, and returned in 1794. He was soon afterward appointed minister to Spain, and took up his abode at Madrid, early in 1795. While there he negotiated treaties with Tripoli and Algiers, and was successful in all his diplomatic duties. He was succeeded in office by General Thomas Pinckney, in 1802, and then returned home. The year previously, he sent a flock of one hundred merino sheep to America, the first ever seen in this country, and the cultivation of this valuable stock was his chief employment during the latter years of his life. He took command of the militia of Connecticut, in 1812, but was not in actual service. Being blessed with ample pecuniary means,[1] he lived in elegant retirement until his sudden death, which was caused by an organic disease of the heart. That event occurred on the 21st of February, 1818, when he was sixty-five years of age.

Colonel Humphreys wrote much in prose and verse. In 1782, he published quite a long poetical address to the armies of the United States. He wrote a number of smaller poems, a tragedy, and several political tracts; and, in 1788, he wrote a Life of General Putnam, from narratives uttered by the old hero's lips, carefully written out.

JOHN MARSHALL.

THE long-honored patriot, and eminent chief justice of the United States, John Marshall, was born at Germantown, in Fauquier county, Virginia, on the 24th of September, 1755, and was the oldest of fifteen children by the same mother. He received some classical instruction in early youth, and from childhood he evinced a taste for literature and general knowledge. He became physically vigorous by field sports, and his solitary meditations were generally amid the wildest natural scenery. When Dunmore invaded Lower Virginia, in 1775, young Marshall was appointed lieutenant in the "minute battalion," and, with his father, performed good service in the battle at the Great Bridge, near the Dismal Swamp. In July, the following year, he was attached to the Virginia Continental line, with the same commission; and, early in 1777, he joined the army under Washington. He was in the battles of Brandywine and Germantown, suffered at Valley Forge, and fought at Monmouth in the Summer of 1778, as commander of a Virginia company. He remained in service until early in 1780, when he turned his attention to the study of the law. He attended the lectures of Mr. Wythe (afterward chancellor of Virginia), and toward the close of Summer was admitted to practice. A few months afterward, Virginia was invaded by Arnold, and Marshall again joined the army in defence of his native State. There being a redundancy of officers, he soon resigned his commission, but he had no opportunity to practice his profession until after the capture of Cornwallis, in the Autumn of 1781. He then soon rose to distinction as a lawyer; and, in the Spring of 1782, he was elected to a seat in the Virginia legislature. In the Autumn of that year he was chosen a member of the executive council.

In January, 1783, Mr. Marshall married a daughter of the treasurer of Virginia, and they lived together about fifty years. He resigned his seat at the

---

1. In 1797, Colonel Humphreys married the daughter of a very wealthy English merchant, of Lisbon.

council board, in 1784, and immediately afterward (though a resident of Richmond) he was chosen to represent his native county in the legislature. He represented Henrico county, in 1787. In the Virginia convention called to consider the Federal Constitution, Mr. Marshall was one of the most zealous and effective supporters of that instrument. He served in the Virginia legislature until 1792, when he again devoted his whole time to his profession. He was a member of the Virginia House of Delegates, in 1795, and nobly defended Jay's memorable treaty.[1] His speech, on that occasion, made a profound impression in America and Europe. Soon afterward, he was sent as one of three envoys extraordinary to the government of France. On his return, he was elected to a seat in the Federal Congress. Within three weeks after entering upon his duties there, he was called upon to announce, in that body, the death of Washington! His words, on that occasion, were few but deeply impressive. His career in the national legislature was short, for, in 1800, he was chosen first Secretary of War, and then Secretary of State; and, in January, 1801, he was appointed chief justice of the Supreme Court of the United States. From that time he discarded party politics, and in his lofty station he performed his exalted duties with great dignity and unsuspected integrity, during the remainder of his life. He was

---

1. See sketch of John Jay.

not unmindful of the claims of his native State, and as his residence was at its capital, he frequently assisted in public duties. This eminent jurist died at Philadelphia, on the 6th of July, 1835, in the eightieth year of his age. Two days before his death he enjoined his friends to place only a plain slab over the graves of himself and wife, and he wrote the simple inscription himself.[1] Judge Marshall's *Life of Washington*, published in 1805, and revised and republished in 1832, is a standard work.

WILLIAM WIRT.

IT has been well observed that "it is the peculiar felicity of our republican institutions, that they throw no impediment in the career of merit, but the competition of rival abilities." Hundreds of the leading men in our Republic have illustrated the truth of this sentiment, and none more so than the accomplished William Wirt. He was born at Bladensburg, in Maryland, on the 18th of November, 1772, and was left a poor orphan at an early age. His paternal uncle took charge of him, and at the age of seven years he was placed in a school at Georgetown, in the District of Columbia. From his eleventh until his fifteenth year he was at the same school in Montgomery county, continuously, where he was taught the Latin and Greek languages, and some natural philosophy. He there had the advantages of a good library, and improved it; and as early as his thirteenth year, he commenced authorship with promise. Young Wirt was a tutor in the family of the late Ninian Edwards, governor of Illinois, for about eighteen months. After a brief residence at the South, on account of ill-health, he commenced the study of law at Montgomery Court-house, and was licensed to practice, in the Autumn of 1792. He commenced his professional career, the same year, at Culpepper Court-house, in Virginia, and soon became eminent. With vigorous body and intellect, pleasing person and manners, he became a favorite, and married the daughter of an accomplished gentleman (the intimate friend of Jefferson, Madison, and Monroe) residing near Charlottesville. His wife died in 1799, and in deep distress Wirt left the scenes of his late happy life, went to Richmond, and was clerk of the House of Delegates during three sessions. There he was greatly esteemed for his talents and social accomplishments, and he received the appointment, in 1802, of chancellor of the eastern district of Virginia. In the Autumn of that year he married an accomplished young lady of Richmond, and soon resumed the practice of the law. In 1803–'4, he wrote his beautiful essays under the name of *The British Spy*, and at about the same time he took up his abode in Norfolk. He returned to Richmond, in 1806, and the following year he was engaged in the trial of Aaron Burr, for treason. His great speech on that occasion was warmly applauded. He was a member of the Virginia legislature, in 1808, and from that time until after the war, he

---

1. Their graves are in the plain cemetery on Shoccoe Hill, Richmond, and the inscription is as follows: "JOHN MARSHALL, son of THOMAS and MARY MARSHALL, was born on the 24th of September, 1755; intermarried with MARY WILLIS AMBLER, the 3d of January, 1783; departed this life the 6th day of July, 1835." Judge Marshall was an exceedingly plain man, in person and habits. He always carried his own marketing home in his hands. On one occasion, a young housekeeper was swearing lustily because he could not hire a person to carry his turkey home for him. A plain man standing by, offered to perform the service, and when they arrived at the door, the young man asked, "What shall I pay you?" "Oh, nothing," replied the old man, "you are welcome; it was on my way, and no trouble." "Who is that polite old gentleman who brought home my turkey for me?" inquired the young man of a bystander. "That," he replied, "is John Marshall, chief justice of the United States." The astonished young man exclaimed, "Why did he bring home my turkey?" "To give you a severe reprimand," replied the other, "and to learn you to attend to your own business." The lesson was never forgotten.

pursued his profession successfully. In the Winter of 1817-'18, he removed to Washington city, having received, from Mr. Monroe, the appointment of Attorney-general of the United States. He held that office through three presidential terms, and at the end of Mr. Adams' administration, he made Baltimore his residence. In 1832, he was nominated by the Anti-Masonic party for President of the United States, but received the majority of the electoral votes in only one State—Vermont. During 1833 he was engaged in founding a colony of Germans, in Florida. It proved a failure. In January following he attended the Supreme Court at Washington, and his feebleness of health was then very much increased by hearing of the death of his eldest daughter. A severe cold hastened the progress of his disease, and on the 18th of February, 1834, he expired, at the age of sixty-three years. His *Life of Patrick Henry* is the most brilliant of the published productions of his pen.

WILLIAM HULL.

"I CAN wait," said the great and good Lavater, when an enemy assailed his character. Many injured men have been compelled to wait, and finally to go into the grave without the solace of vindication; yet posterity, more just than cotemporaries, usually render a righteous judgment. General William Hull, a brave patriot of the Revolution, waited many long years for a vindication of his character from the imputations of cowardice, and even of treason, uttered by a judicial verdict and the prejudices of public opinion. Long after he fell asleep in death, his vindication was made complete. He was a native of Derby, Connecticut, where he was born on the 24th of June, 1753. He acquired physical vigor while a youth, by farm labor, and at the age of fifteen years he entered Yale College, as a student. He was graduated with usual honors, in 1772. His parents designed him for the ministry, but on leaving college he became tutor of a school, for awhile, then reluctantly began the study of Divinity, and finally became a student in the Law School at Litchfield, Connecticut. He was successful, and was admitted to the bar, in 1775. He was soon afterward elected captain of a militia company, and joined the army under Washington, at Cambridge. He continued with Washington during the siege of Boston, and the subsequent operations in the vicinity of New York and in New Jersey. He acted as field officer in the battle at Trenton, and soon afterward Washington promoted him to major in a Massachusetts regiment. He behaved bravely in the battle at Princeton. In the following May he marched some recruits to Ticonderoga, and was active during the Summer and Autumn of that year, until Burgoyne was humbled at Saratoga. In the battles on that occasion, he was particularly distinguished. He suffered at Valley Forge, fought at Monmouth, and in the Autumn was in command of a regiment, first at Poughkeepsie, and then at White Plains. He was at the capture of Stony Point, in the Summer of 1779, and he was soon afterward promoted to the rank of lieutenant-colonel. His services now became multifarious, and until the close of the war, he was regarded by General Washington as one of his most useful officers.

When, after the treaty of peace, in 1783, the British still retained possession of several frontier forts, in violation of the stipulations of that treaty, Colonel Hull was sent to Quebec, by the United States government, to make a formal demand upon the governor-general of Canada for their immediate surrender. On his return, he made his residence at Newton, Massachusetts; and, in 1786, he was one of General Lincoln's volunteer aids in quelling the insurrection known as *Shay's Rebellion.* He was also very active in civil affairs. In 1793, he was appointed a commissioner to make arrangements with the British government to hold a treaty with the Western Indians. He visited England and France, in 1798, and soon after his return, was honored with the office of judge of the court of Common Pleas, and the commission of major-general in the militia of Massachusetts. He was also elected a State Senator, and was employed in various public duties until 1805, when Congress appointed him governor of the Michigan Territory. He held that office when war was declared against Great Britain, in 1812, at which time he was at the head of an army, marching to crush the power of hostile Indians. He was immediately commissioned one of the four brigadiers to assist General Dearborn, the commander-in-chief. In the comparatively weak fort at Detroit, he was invested by a strong force of British and Indians; and, to save his command from almost certain destruction, he surrendered the fort, his army of two thousand men, and the Territory, to the enemy. For this he was tried for treason and cowardice, and being unable to produce certain official testimony which subsequently vindicated his character, he was found guilty of the latter, and sentenced to be shot. The President of the United States, "in consideration of his age and revolutionary services," pardoned him, but a cloud was upon his fame and honor. He published a vindicatory memoir, in 1824, which changed public opinion in his favor. Yet he did not live long to enjoy the effects of that change. He died at Newton, on the 29th of November, 1825, at the age of seventy-two years. A Memoir of General Hull, by his daughter and grandson, was published in 1848. It fully vindicates the character of the injured patriot, by documentary evidence.

ABRAHAM WHIPPLE.

"YOU, Abraham Whipple, on the 17th of June, 1772, burned his majesty's vessel, the Gaspé, and I will hang you at the yard arm.
"JAMES WALLACE."

"To SIR JAMES WALLACE:
"SIR,—Always catch a man before you hang him.
"ABRAHAM WHIPPLE."

Such was the correspondence between two opposing naval commanders in Narraganset Bay, in the Summer of 1775. Whipple was a native of Providence, situated at the head of that bay, where he was born in 1733. He received very little education, and from earliest youth his life was spent chiefly upon the ocean. He was in the merchant service for many years, and at the age of twenty-seven he was commander of a privateer named *The Game Cock.* During a single cruise, in 1760, he took twenty-three French prizes. When the colonists and the mother government quarrelled, Captain Whipple espoused the cause of his countrymen, and was among those who committed the first overt act of rebellion, in New England, in the burning of the British armed schooner, Gaspé, above alluded to.[1] Captain Whipple sailed on a trading voyage to the West Indies soon afterward, and did not return until 1774.

---

1. The Gaspe was stationed in Narraganset Bay to enforce the revenue laws. While chasing an American vessel up the bay, it ran aground on a sandy shoal. Captain Whipple and a number of seamen went down the bay on the night of the 17th of June, boarded the schooner, captured the commander and crew, and then burned the vessel. Notwithstanding a commission was appointed to investigate the affair, and a large reward was offered for the perpetrators, their names were not made known until war with Great Britain had actually commenced.

In the Spring of 1775, Sir James Wallace, in command of the British frigate *Rose*, blockaded Narraganset Bay. The legislature of Rhode Island fitted out two vessels for the purpose of driving the intruder away. These were under the general command of Whipple, and he soon expelled Wallace from the Rhode Island waters. In this business Whipple had the honor of firing the first gun in the naval service of the Revolution.[1] In the Autumn following, Captain Whipple was ordered on a cruise to the Bermudas, to seize powder, but was unsuccessful. In December, he received a commander's commission, from Congress; and, in February, 1776, he sailed on a cruise in the squadron of Commodore Hopkins, the naval commander-in-chief. From that time until the fall of Charleston, in May, 1780, he was in active service. There he was in command of quite a strong, but inadequate naval force, all of which remaining above water,[2] became spoils for the victors. For two years and seven months he remained a prisoner on parole, in Pennsylvania, when he was exchanged. He left the service, in 1782, and was allowed to go almost entirely unrequited to a citizen's

---

1. A British vessel had been captured at Machias earlier than this, but no authority had been given for the act. Whipple was the first to act *legally*.
2. Whipple sunk several of his vessels to prevent British ships from going up the Cooper river channel.

duty. He took command of a merchant ship, and had the honor of first unfurling the American flag in the river Thames, at London. He was elected to a seat in the Rhode Island legislature, in 1786. On the formation of the Ohio company, he emigrated to the wilderness, in company with General Rufus Putnam, and was among the founders of Marietta. He was then fifty-five years of age. The threatening savages that hung around this settlement until the peace negotiated with the Indians, in 1795, called into action the great resources of his genius, and he was of essential service to the colony. After that treaty of peace, he moved to a small farm on the banks of the Muskingum, where he struggled on in poverty until 1811, when Congress granted him the half-pay of a naval captain.[1] His future years were thus made to him seasons of ease and absence from care. They were few, however, for he was seventy-eight years of age when tardy justice awarded its benefits. Commodore Whipple died near Marietta, on the 29th of May, 1819, at the age of eighty-five years. Over his grave, at Marietta, is a neat stone, bearing an appropriate inscription.

DANIEL MORGAN.

"All people said old Morgan never feared—they thought old Morgan never prayed—they did not know—old Morgan was often miserably afraid." So talked that "thunderbolt of war"—the "brave Morgan, who never knew fear," as the chronicler said—to his children and neighbors when they sat and listened to his thrilling stories of the campaigns for freedom.[2] He was of Welsh descent, and was born in Pennsylvania, in the year 1736. His family were in humble circumstances, and his education was only such as could be acquired at an ordinary country school, at that time. At the age of seventeen he wandered into Virginia, and there became a wagoner for one of the wealthy planters in Frederick county. He owned a team when Braddock marched to the fatal field of the Monongahela, and he accompanied that expedition as a bearer of supplies. For alleged insult to a British officer, he received five hundred lashes almost without flinching. A few days afterward the officer became convinced of the injustice of the charge, and apologized to young Morgan, in the presence of the whole regiment. His love for British officers was never very ardent afterward; and when they became his foes on the field, the remembrance of that degrading punishment gave strength to his arm and keenness to his blade.

In 1756, Morgan was commissioned an ensign in the provincial army, because of his military skill and service in the former campaign, and then he first became acquainted with Washington. From that time until the Revolution commenced, he was much in service against the Indians; and tradition tells a hundred tales of his great daring. In 1774, he owned a fine farm in Frederick county, and that year he was in Dunmore's expedition beyond the Alleghanies. In May, 1775, Congress appointed him a captain, and in less than a week thereafter, ninety-six men—the nucleus of his celebrated rifle corps—were enrolled under his banner, and were on their way to Boston. He led the van of Arnold's wonderful expedition from the Kennebeck to the St. Lawrence, in the Autumn

---

1. In the year 1800, the veteran sailor was permitted to breathe the salt air of the ocean once again. Some enterprising men at Marietta built a square-rigged vessel there, named it *St. Clair*, and, loading it with pork and flour, sent it to Havana. Commodore Whipple was appointed its commander, and he performed the voyage successfully. He thus had the honor of navigating the first vessel that ever sailed from the Ohio to the Gulf.

2. He said that before the assault on Quebec, where Montgomery was killed, he knelt by the side of a cannon and prayed fervently; and when, at the Cowpens, he was compelled to fight the superior force of Tarleton, he went aside, before the battle, and prayed earnestly for his country, his army, and himself, and then, in his rough way, cheered on his men,

of 1775; and in the siege of Quebec, he led the forlorn hope of Arnold's division. When Arnold was wounded there, Morgan took command, fought desperately, and was made prisoner.[1] When exchanged, he was commissioned a colonel in the Continental army, and from that time Washington considered Morgan's rifle corps the right arm of his forces. He was the chief instrument in the capture of Burgoyne, in the Autumn of 1777; and because of his brilliant achievements on that occasion, his neighbors called his fine estate "Saratoga." He received the commission of brigadier, and was one of the most active officers in the Southern campaigns. His military glory culminated when, on the 17th of January, 1781, he defeated the British, under Tarleton, at the Cowpens, west of the Broad river, in South Carolina. For that achievement Congress awarded him the thanks of the nation, and a gold medal. In consequence of the infirm state of his health, he then left the service, and retired to his farm, where he devoted himself to agricultural pursuits. Washington desired him to be placed at the head of the expedition against the Western Indians, in 1791, but St. Clair was chosen. In 1794, he commanded the troops in Western Pennsylvania, designed to secure the power over the whiskey insurgents, obtained by General Lee. He was elected to Congress the same year, where he served two sessions. He removed to Winchester, Virginia, in the year 1800, where, after confinement to his house and bed by extreme debility, he expired, on the 6th of July, 1802, in the sixty-sixth year of his age. His remains rest beneath a marble slab, appropriately inscribed, in the Presbyterian grave-yard at Winchester.

LEONARD CALVERT.

ALTHOUGH George Calvert, who was created Lord Baltimore by James the First of England, was the founder of Maryland, yet the chief honor is due to his younger son, Leonard, because he led the first colony thither, planted it, and laid the broad foundations of that commonwealth, in social and political institutions. He was born about the year 1606, when his father was clerk of the Privy Council under the patronage of Robert Cecil, James' Secretary of State His father died in April, 1632, just before his patent for Maryland had possessed the seals of office. He was succeeded by his eldest son, Cecil. The charter was completed in June, 1632, and Leonard Calvert, with about two hundred persons of good families, all of the Roman Catholic faith, reached Old Point Comfort, near the entrance to Chesapeake Bay, in February, 1634. He was appointed governor of the colony which he was sent to plant. As they passed up the bay, and entered the broad Potomac, Calvert fired a cannon, erected a cross, and took possession of the country "in the name of the Saviour of the world and of the king of England." At the mouth of a creek on the north side of the Potomac, the settlers pitched their tents, founded a town which they called St. Mary's, named the creek St. George, and there began the noble business of building up a free State in the wilderness. They dealt justly with the natives, and prospered. To every emigrant, fifty acres of land, in fee, were granted; and, according to the terms of the charter, every person who professed a belief in the Trinity, of whatever sect, Protestant or Roman Catholic, was allowed full privilege to worship as he pleased. This toleration was a noble feature in that first charter of Maryland, and is very properly regarded with pride by the descendants of those early colonists.

---

1. While a prisoner, he was urged to accept the commission of a colonel in the British army, but he indignantly refused it.

Governor Calvert built himself a commodious house at St. Mary's, and was managing the affairs of the province with prudence and energy, when the civil war in England, which resulted in the death of King Charles and the exaltation of Oliver Cromwell to the seat of chief magistrate of the realm, disturbed the repose of all the Anglo-American colonies. Lord Baltimore was deprived of his proprietary rights, and Governor Calvert was superseded by a Protestant appointed by the Parliament. He then retired to Virginia. In 1646, after an absence of almost two years, he returned, with a military force, and recovered possession of the province. In April, 1647, he issued a general pardon, proceeded to St. Mary's to firmly reëstablish good government there, and sat down in the midst of an affectionate and loyal people, to enjoy coveted repose. A longer and more profound rest was near, for, on the 9th of June following, he died, at the age of about forty-one years.

NOAH WEBSTER.

"HE taught millions to read, but not one to sin," was the glorious and comprehensive eulogy awarded to the memory of Noah Webster, the great lexicographer. He was maternally descended from William Bradford, the second governor of the Plymouth colony, and paternally from John Webster, who was governor of Connecticut, in 1656. He was born in West Hartford, Connecticut, on the 16th of October, 1758, at the very time when Washington was leading his brave Virginians to the capture of Fort du Quesne. He acquired his early education at a district school, and at the age of sixteen years entered the freshman class in Yale College. The murmurs of the storm of the Revolution were then becoming louder and louder, and, during the four years of his collegiate course, his studies were frequently interrupted by the disturbances of current events. In the Autumn of 1777, he joined the army of volunteers that flocked from New England to the camp of Gates, and he participated in the capture of Burgoyne and his army. He then resumed his studies, and was graduated in 1778. He commenced life as teacher of a district school in Hartford, with one dollar in his pocket, but a noble capital of industry, a good education, and an indomitable will. He studied law during leisure hours, and was admitted to practice, in 1781. Finding little to do in his profession, he went to Goshen, in New York, and there opened a high school, which he called *The Farmer's Hall Academy*.

While studying law, Mr. Webster perceived the many defects in the English language, and in resolving to improve it, he formed the great purpose of his life, the compilation of a *Dictionary*. He first prepared an elementary work, which he submitted to several members of the Congress, in 1783, and then published it, at Hartford. It was soon followed by two others, and the whole comprised a spelling-book, an English grammar, and a reader. At least twenty millions of Webster's Spelling-book have already [1854] been sold in the United States, and the sale is still great. After the Revolution, Mr. Webster wrote essays on several national subjects, and he coöperated with Dr. Ramsay in procuring a copyright law for the protection of American authors. He ably supported the Federal Constitution, with his pen; and he established a daily newspaper in the city of New York, devoted to the administration of President Washington. After engaging in other newspaper enterprises in that city, he removed to New Haven, in 1798, and there commenced the preparation of his first Dictionary. It was published in 1806, and in the Preface, he publicly announced that he had now

entered upon the great work of his life. That was at a time when a growing family and slender pecuniary means appeared great obstacles; but he possessed an iron will, and his spirit was undaunted. He toiled on in the midst of many discouragements; and, in 1812, he made his abode at Amherst, Massachusetts, where his family expenses were less. He returned to New Haven, in 1822, and the Faculty of Yale College then conferred upon him the degree of Doctor of Civil Law. He was yet engaged in his great labor, and, in pursuit of his object, he went to Europe in 1824, and spent a year in the collection of materials. His mighty task was completed in 1827; and, in 1828, his *American Dictionary*, the greatest work of its kind ever undertaken, was published. It was soon afterward republished in England, and at once took an exalted position in the world of letters, and gave its author great renown. An enlarged edition, carefully revised by the author, was published in 1841; and so he left it, a precious legacy to his country and mankind. During the long years in which Dr. Webster was engaged on his Dictionary he was no recluse, but was a practicing lawyer, an agriculturist, a legislator, and an academician. His old age, after a life of great activity, was serene, for the pure light of Christianity rested in beauty upon the good man's path. When his physician told him he must die, he replied, "I am ready;" and on the 28th of May, 1843, he went quietly to his rest, in the eighty-fifth year of his age. His Dictionary is rapidly approaching the position of highest authority, especially among men of purest taste and most comprehensive knowledge.

ISRAEL PUTNAM.

FULL of romance and stirring interest was the career of General Putnam, the hero of two wars, of whom Dr. Ladd said, "He seems to have been almost obscured amidst the glare of succeeding worthies; but his early and gallant services entitle him to everlasting remembrance." And the same pen wrote—

> "Hail, Putnam! hail, thou venerable name,
> Though dark oblivion threats thy mighty fame,
> It threats in vain—for long shalt thou be known,
> Who first in virtue and in battle shone."

Israel Putnam was born at Salem, Massachusetts, on the 7th of January, 1718. He was descended from one of the first settlers of that ancient New England town. His education was neglected, and he grew to manhood with a vigorous but uncultivated mind. He delighted in athletic exercises, and generally bore the palm among his fellows. At the age of twenty-one years he commenced the life of a farmer, in Pomfret, Connecticut,[1] where he "pursued the even tenor of his way" until 1755, when he was appointed to the command of a company of Connecticut troops, destined for the war with the French and Indians on the northern frontier. He performed essential service under General Johnson at Lake George and vicinity during that campaign; and the following year he had command of a corps of Rangers, and bore the commission of a captain in the provincial army. He had many stirring adventures in the neighborhood of Lake Champlain. In August, 1758 (then bearing a major's commission), he was near the present Whitehall, at the head of the lake, watching the movements of the enemy, and had a severe encounter with the French and Indians, in the forest. Putnam was finally made prisoner, and the savages tied him to a tree, and prepared to roast him alive. A shower of rain and the interposition of a French officer, saved his life, and he was taken to the head-quarters of the enemy at Ticonderoga. From thence he was sent, a prisoner, to Montreal, in Canada, where, through the kindness of Colonel Peter Schuyler, of Albany (who was also a prisoner), he was humanely treated. The following Spring he was exchanged, and returned home. He joined the army again, soon afterward, and was promoted to lieutenant-colonel. He was a bold and efficient leader during the remainder of the war, and then he returned to his plow and the repose and obscurity of domestic life in rural seclusion.

Colonel Putnam was an active friend of the people when disputes with government commenced ten years before war was kindled; and when the intelligence of bloodshed at Lexington reached him, while plowing in the field, he had no political scruples to settle, but, unyoking his oxen, he started, with his gun and rusty sword, for Boston. He soon returned to Connecticut, raised a regiment, and hastened back to Cambridge, then the head-quarters of a motley host that had hurried thither from the hills and valleys of New England. When, six weeks afterward, Washington was appointed commander-in-chief of the Continental army, Putnam was chosen to be one of four major-generals created on that occasion. He performed bravely on Bunker's Hill before his commission reached him, and from that time, throughout the whole struggle until the close of 1779, General Putnam was a faithful and greatly-esteemed leader. His ser-

---

1. During one night, a wolf that had been depredating in the neighborhood for some time, killed seventy of his fine sheep and goats. It was ascertained to be a she-wolf, and Putnam and his neighbors turned out to hunt and destroy her. She was driven into a rocky cave, and at ten o'clock at night, Putnam, with a rope fastened to his leg, descended into the den with a gun and torch, and sought out and boldly shot the depredator. Then giving a concerted signal, he was drawn up by the rope. He again descended, seized the dead wolf by the ears, and was again drawn up amid the cheers of his companions, who were waiting in exultation, in the moonlight above.

vices were too numerous to be detailed here—they are all recorded in our country's annals, and remembered by every student of our history. At West Point, on the Hudson, his military career was concluded. Late in 1779, he set out to visit his family in Connecticut, and on the way he suffered a partial paralysis of his system, which impaired both his mind and body. At his home in Brooklyn, Connecticut, he remained an invalid the remainder of his days. With Christian resignation,[1] and the fortitude of a courageous man, he bore his afflictions for more than ten years, and then, at the close of the beautiful budding month of May (29th), 1790, the veteran hero died, at the age of seventy-two years. His *Memoir*, prepared by Colonel David Humphreys, from narratives uttered by the patriot's own lips, was first published, by order of the State Society of the Cincinnati of Connecticut, in 1788, and afterward published in Humphrey's collected writings, in 1790. A neat monument, bearing an epitaph, is over his grave in Brooklyn, Connecticut.

MARY PHILIPSE.

THE beautiful and accomplished American girl of twenty-six Summers, who won the first love of Washington just when his greatness was dawning, is worthy of the historic embalmer's care, for she forms a part of the story of the great central figure in the group of American worthies of the past generations. Mary Philipse was the daughter of the Honorable Frederick Philipse, Speaker of the New York Colonial Assembly, and one of the early great landholders on the Hudson river, in Westchester county. She was born at the more modern manor-house of the family, in the present village of Yonkers,[2] on the 3d of July, 1730. Of her early life we have no record except the testimony which her accomplishments bore concerning her careful education. Her sister was the wife of Colonel Beverly Robinson, of New York, and there Miss Philipse was residing when she made the acquaintance of Washington, above alluded to. It was in the memorable year, 1756, when the whole country was excited by the current events of the French and Indian war. Washington was a Virginia colonel, twenty-four years of age, and had won his first bright laurels at the Great Meadows and the field of Monongahela. On account of difficulties concerning rank, he visited the commander-in-chief, Governor Shirley, at Boston, and it was while on his way thither, on horseback, that he stopped at the house of Colonel Robinson, in New York. There he saw the beautiful Mary Philipse, and his young heart was touched by her charms. He left her with reluctance and went on to Boston. On his return, he was again the willing guest of Colonel Robinson, and he lingered there, in the society of Mary, as long as duty would allow. It is believed that he offered her his hand, but a rival bore off the prize. That rival was Colonel Roger Morris, Washington's companion-in-arms on the bloody field of Monongahela, and one of Braddock's aids, on that occasion. Roger and Mary were married, in 1758, and lived in great happiness until the storm of the Revolution desolated their home. Colonel Morris then espoused the cause of the king; and when the American army, under Washington, was encamped on

---

1. General Putnam was a professing Christian and member of the Congregational Church at Brooklyn. It is said that after the war he arose in the congregation and apologized for swearing pretty severely on Bunker's Hill, when he could not induce the timid militia to follow him to reinforce Prescott in the assailed redoubt on Breed's Hill. "It was almost enough to make an angel swear," he said, "to see the cowards refuse to secure a victory so nearly won."

2. That old manor-house, over a century and a quarter old, is yet standing (1881) and is well preserved in its original form and condition. It is used for public purposes by the municipality of Yonkers.

Harlem Heights, in the Autumn of 1776, his beautiful mansion, overlooking the Harlem river, became the head-quarters of the commander-in-chief. Both Colonel Morris and his wife were included in the act of attainder, passed by the New York legislature, in 1778. It is believed that she, and her sister Mrs. Inglis, were the only females who were attainted of treason during the struggle. A large portion of their real property was restored to their children, of whom John Jacob Astor purchased it, in 1809, for one hundred thousand dollars, and afterward sold it to the State of New York for half a million.[1] Colonel Morris died in England, in 1794, at the age of sixty-seven years, and his wife lived a widow thirty-one years afterward. She died, in 1825, at the age of ninety-six, and was buried by the side of her husband, near Saviour-gate church, York, where their son, Henry Gage Morris, of the royal army, erected a monument to their memory.

THOMAS PAINE.

FEW men have ever received so large a share of the odium of common public opinion (which Hood defined as "the average prejudice of mankind") as Thomas Paine, whose pen was almost as powerful in support of the republican cause in the early years of the Revolution, as was the sword of Washington; because it gave vitality to that latent national sentiment which formed the necessary basis of support to the civil and military power then just evoked by the political exigencies of the American people. He was a native of Thetford, England, where he was born, in 1737. He was bred to the business of stay-maker, carried on by his father, but his mind could not long be chained to the narrow employment of fashioning whale-bone and buckram for the boddices of ladies. He sought and obtained an interview with Dr. Franklin, when that statesman first went to England as agent for Pennsylvania, and by his advice Paine came to America, in 1774, and at once employed his powerful pen in the cause of the aroused colonies. Many of his articles appeared in Pennsylvania papers, over the signature of *Common Sense;* and at the beginning of 1776, he wrote a pamphlet, at the suggestion of Dr. Rush, bearing that expressive title. It was the earliest and most powerful public appeal in favor of the independence of the colonies, and did more, probably, than any other instrumentality, to fix that idea firmly in the minds of the people. Within a hundred days after its appearance, almost every provincial assembly had spoken in favor of independence.[2] Paine also commenced a series of papers called *The Crisis,* the first number of which was written in the camp of Washington, near the Delaware, at the close of 1776. They were issued at intervals, during the war. In the Spring of 1777, Paine was appointed, by Congress, Secretary to the Committee on Foreign Affairs, with a salary of seventy dollars a month. It was a position of great trust and responsibility, and he performed the duties satisfactorily until 1779, when, in a public dispute with Silas Deane, he revealed some secrets of his bureau, and was threatened with dismissal. He at once resigned his office, but remained a firm friend to his adopted country. After the war, he used his pen for a livelihood; and in 1790, he visited his native country. There he wrote his *Rights of Man,* which

---

1. This purchase was necessary to quiet the occupants of the land in their possession, for they had purchased from the commissioners under the confiscation act.
2. So highly was that essay esteemed, that the legislature of Pennsylvania voted the author twenty-five hundred dollars. Washington regarded it as his most powerful aid. In a letter to Joseph Reed, he said, "By private letters which I have lately received from Virginia, I find that *Common Sense* is working a powerful change there in the minds of many men."

offended the government, and he went to Paris on the eve of the French Revolution. He participated in the opening scenes of that struggle, was made a member of the National Assembly, and finally, having offended the Jacobins, he was imprisoned and sentenced to the guillotine. While in prison, he wrote the chief portions of his *Age of Reason*. He escaped death by a seeming accident.[1] In 1802, he returned to America, and resided a part of the time upon a farm at New Rochelle, presented to him by the State of New York, for his revolutionary services. Paine became very intemperate, and fell low in the social scale, not only on account of his beastly habits, but because of his blasphemous tirade against Christianity. His *Age of Reason* is a coarse and vindictive assault upon revealed religion, exhibiting neither sound logic nor honest argument. The corruptions of Christianity as he saw them in France and England, at that time, afford extenuating apologies for his vindictiveness. Had Thomas Paine lived at this day, he would never have written his *Age of Reason* and other libels upon God and humanity. As a patriot of truest stamp, his memory ought to be revered—as an enemy to that religion on which man's dearest hopes are centered, he is to be pitied and condemned.

Mr. Paine died in New York, in 1809. Jarvis, the painter, took an impression of his face in plaster, after his death. That impression is now in possession of the New York Historical Society. His friend and admirer, William Cobbett,

---

1. He was saved by a singular providence. Every night an officer passed along the rows of cells in the prison, and with a piece of chalk marked the doors from which prisoners were to be taken to the scaffold. Paine's door happened to be open at the time, and it was marked on the inside, when it was closed for the night the fatal sign was not visible, and he escaped. .

had his bones exhumed, and conveyed to England; and in 1839, his friends in political and religious sentiment erected a beautiful monument to his memory over his emptied grave, near New Rochelle, on which is inscribed, beneath a medallion bust, "THOMAS PAINE, AUTHOR OF COMMON SENSE."

THOMAS PINCKNEY.

WE have already considered the career of Charles Cotesworth Pinckney, one of the noblest of South Carolina's many noble sons. He had an accomplished brother, four years his junior, who bore a conspicuous part in the great struggle for independence, and honored the diplomacy of his country. Thomas Pinckney was born at Charleston, on the 23d of October, 1750, and at the age of three years was taken to England, with his brother Charles, to be educated. There he grew to manhood, chose his life-pursuit, acquired the proper preparatory knowledge, and, after an absence of twenty years, returned to his native land. In early boyhood he felt a martial spirit stirring within him. It grew with his growth, and his studies were almost exclusively military, on his arrival home. He became a thorough tactician in theory, and, on the organization of a military force in his native city, he was intrusted with the command of a company. He was a rigid disciplinarian, yet his men all loved him. He soon rose to the rank of major, and was very active in recruiting and disciplining the militia, until the arrival of General Lincoln, in 1779, as commander-in-chief of the Southern army. Lincoln appointed Major Pinckney one of his aids, and in that capacity he was engaged in the siege of Savannah, in the Autumn of that year. Several months previously, he had gained great applause for his gallantry in the battle at Stono Ferry, just below Charleston. He was not among the captives at Charleston, in May, 1780; and when Gates took command of the Southern army, Pinckney was appointed his aid. He fought gallantly at the battle near Camden, in August, and there had his leg badly shattered by a musket ball. He could not retreat, and was made a prisoner and sent to New York. His wound disabled him during the rest of the war, and he remained in private life until 1787, when he was elected to succeed General Moultrie as governor of South Carolina. He displayed statesmanship of the highest order; and, in 1792, President Washington appointed him minister plenipotentiary to the British court. He managed the complicated and important affairs of his mission with great skill. Toward the close of 1794, Mr. Pinckney was appointed minister to Spain, and took up his residence at Madrid the following year. He soon afterward concluded a treaty with the Spanish court, by which the free navigation of the Mississippi was secured to the people of the United States. He returned home the following year, to attend to his domestic affairs, and remained in private life until the proclamation of war with Great Britain, in 1812, called many a veteran hero to the field. President Madison appointed General Pinckney to the command of the Southern Department, and it was under his directions that General Jackson successfully prosecuted the war with the Indians. His forecast and generosity opened to Jackson that military career which he pursued so gloriously. General Pinckney resigned his commission on the return of peace, and he resumed his favorite employment—scientific agriculture. He lived more than thirteen years after the peace of 1815. After a long illness, he died, on the 2d of November, 1828, when a little more than seventy-eight years of age. General Pinckney married a daughter of Rebecca Motte, the patriotic widow of the Congaree, whose portrait and memoir may be found in another part of this work.

CORNPLANTER.

CENTENARY honors crowned *Ga-nio-di-eugh*, or the Cornplanter, a chief of the *Seneca* nation, who, for seventy-five years, held a conspicuous place in the history of his race, as one of the bravest and most eloquent of its warriors. He is supposed to have been born about the year 1735; and he first appears on the page of history as the leader of a war party of the Senecas when that nation was in alliance with the French against the English. He was a participator in the bloody battle in which General Braddock was killed. He was a native of Conewaugus, in the Genesee Valley, and a half-breed, his father having been a white man from the Mohawk region.[1] Cornplanter was a war-chief of his tribe when the Revolution began. Being in the full vigor of manhood, active and brave, he was one of the most distinguished of the dusky leaders who spread destruction over the white frontier settlements in New York, and in the Valley of Wyoming. In the bloody forays at Cherry Valley and Wyoming, Cornplanter was conspicuous; and during the invasion of the Seneca country, by Sullivan, in 1779, and the fearful vengeance therefor inflicted by the Indians afterward, Cornplanter was a chief leader of his people.[2] He was the most inveterate and active foe of the Americans during the whole war, but after the treaty of peace he became the fast friend of the United States. He was chiefly instrumental in the pacification treaty at Fort Stanwix, in 1784, when Red Jacket opposed him with his wonderful eloquence. At the close of the treaty the brave chief said significantly, "I thank the Great Spirit for this opportunity of smoking the pipe of friendship and love. May we plant our own vines, be the fathers of our children, and maintain them." He was also conspicuous in treaties in Ohio, which gave offence to his nation. Hoping to exalt himself upon the ruins of Cornplanter, Red Jacket fostered the discontent, and the life of the former was placed in jeopardy. He repaired to Philadelphia and applied to President Washington for counsel and relief. Cornplanter laid a most touching appeal for himself and his nation, before the President. The reply was kind, but Washington could not go behind treaties. Relief, however, was promised, and Cornplanter went back, a happier man.

During the troubles with the Indians in the north-west, until Wayne's victory in 1794, Cornplanter remained neutral; and he was at the council held in the Seneca country to treat with Thomas Morris respecting portions of the territory afterward known as the *Holland Land Purchase*. During the years of repose which followed, Cornplanter was assiduous in endeavors to improve the moral character of his nation. He made great efforts to stay the progress of intemperance; and he was the first and most eloquent of temperance lecturers in America.[3] He readily assumed many of the habits and pursuits of the white men; and having failed to become chief sachem of his nation, through the in-

---

1. In his own language, he said, "When I was a child I played with the butterfly, the grasshopper, and the frog. . . . The Indian boys took notice of my skin being different in color from theirs, and spoke about it. I inquired of my mother the cause, and she told me that my father lived in Albany. I still ate my victuals out of a bark dish. I grew up to be a young man, and married me a wife, and I had no kettle or gun. I then knew where my father lived, and went to see him, and found he was a white man and spoke the English language. He gave me victuals while I was at his house, but when I started to return home, he gave me no provision to eat on the way. He gave me neither kettle nor gun."
2. Cornplanter made his father a prisoner, at Fort Plain, but shielded him from all harm, and sent him to a place of safety.
3. While speaking upon this subject, in 1822, Cornplanter said, "The Great Spirit first made the world, next the flying animals, and found all things good and prosperous. He is immortal and everlasting. After finishing the flying animals, he came down to earth, and there stood. Then he made different kinds of trees, and woods of all sorts, and people of every kind. He made the Spring and other seasons, and the weather suitable for planting. These he *did* make. *But stills to make whiskey to give to the Indians he* DID NOT *make*. . . . The Great Spirit has ordered me to stop drinking, and He wishes me to inform the people that they should quit drinking intoxicating drinks."

trigues of Red Jacket, he retired to a large tract of land on the Alleghany river, which the legislature had presented to him, and there cultivated a farm in obscurity during the remainder of his long life. When Rev. Timothy Alden visited him, in 1816, he was the owner of sixteen hundred acres of fine bottom land. He was a professing Christian,[1] though very superstitious. There the old chief lived on in quiet obscurity, until he had passed his hundredth year. He died at his residence on the 7th of March, 1836, with a confused notion of being happy in the Christian's heaven, or in the elysian fields, pictures of which came down upon the tide of memory from his early youth.

SAMUEL L. MITCHILL.

"AMONG those," says Knapp, "who did not gain all the laurels at home, that he should have had, while he was honored by almost every intelligent court, and every learned society abroad, was Doctor Mitchill." He was a native of North Hempstead, Queen's county, Long Island, where he was born of Quaker parents, on the 20th of August, 1764. He was educated by private tutors, supplied chiefly by his maternal uncle, Dr. Samuel Latham, whose name he bore. That gentleman saw and admired the budding of his genius. Young Mitchill soon became an excellent classical scholar. Nature wooed him; and so enamored was he of her beauties and hidden wealth, that he became her devotee while a lad, and was a philosopher when only twenty years of age.

Young Mitchill chose the medical profession as a life-pursuit, and commenced study with his uncle. In 1780, he was placed under the instructions of Dr. Samuel Bard, and after a little more than three years, he went to Edinburgh, in Scotland, then the seat of science, in Great Britain. There he had Thomas Addis Emmet and Sir James M'Intosh for his class-mates and friends; and when he left the institution, he bore its highest honors. The fame of his acquirements preceded him, and when he returned home he was received into the first intellectual circles in New York. The Faculty of Columbia College gave him the degree of Master of Arts. For awhile he turned his attention to constitutional law, with the intention of engaging in legislative duties. In 1788, he was one of the commissioners who treated with the heads of the Six Nations, at Fort Stanwix (now Rome), and obtained from them the cession of Western New York. In the meanwhile he practiced his profession, and was indefatigable in his study of the natural sciences. In 1790, he was elected to a seat in the New York Legislative Assembly; and, in 1792, he was chosen Professor of Chemistry, Natural Sciences, and Agriculture, in Columbia College. He was then considered the best naturalist and practical chemist, in America. In 1796, he made his famous report of a mineralogical survey of the State of New York; and the following year he commenced the publication of the *Medical Repository*, of which he was chief editor for sixteen years. He was the founder (and a long time president) of the Lyceum of Natural History, of New York; and he took a great interest in the New York Historical Society, and kindred institutions. He was a special and efficient friend to domestic manufactures and agriculture, and was the first, in this country, to apply the science of chemistry to the practical pursuit of the latter avocation. As a legislator he was wise, full of forecast, and possessed great boldness and perseverance.[2] For his efforts in behalf of

---

1. See sketch of Samuel Kirkland.
2. He was a member of the New York legislature, in 1798, when Chancellor Livingston applied for the exclusive right of navigating the waters of the Hudson river with boats propelled "by fire or

steam navigation on the Hudson, his name should be associated with that of Fulton, Barlow, and Livingston.¹

For about twenty years, Dr. Mitchill acted as one of the physicians of the New York Hospital. Notwithstanding his immense labors in the field of scientific research, and his voluminous publications upon almost every variety of subjects, he found time to mingle in political strife, and share in the labors and honors of official station. He represented the city of New York, in Congress, six consecutive years, and was afterward United States Senator. He was possessed of vast and varied knowledge; and yet, because he sometimes advanced

---

steam." With his usual forecast, Dr. Mitchill perceived the feasibility of the project, and presented a bill accordingly. Everybody ridiculed him. The elder portion of the legislature considered the whole matter too absurd to be seriously entertained, while the younger members, when they desired a little fun, would call up Dr. Mitchill's "hot water bill," and bandy jokes without stint. Yet the Doctor persevered, procured the passage of his bill, and had the pleasure of laughing at his persecutors, a few years afterward.

1. After preparing the sketches of these three men, printed on preceding pages, I was furnished with evidence from the correspondence of Barlow (in possession of one of his descendants, who intended to arrange them for the press), that Fulton was far more indebted to that friend for pecuniary aid and general encouragement, than to any one else. When Livingston first met Fulton in France, he was dubious concerning the feasibility of his scheme, while Barlow was sanguine, and was doing all in his power to assist Fulton. When experiments had furnished actual demonstration, and Livingston could no longer doubt, then he lent his wealth and influence to Fulton. Barlow was Fulton's *benefactor*; Livingston was his *business partner* and friend.

opinions of which the world had not yet dreamed, he was sneered at by the sciolist, and ridiculed by shallow upstarts in science. He was thoroughly appreciated in Europe, where almost every literary and scientific institution thought it an honor to enrol his name upon its list of members. Dr. Mitchill died at his residence, in New York City, on the 7th of September, 1831, in the sixty-seventh year of his age.

ARTHUR LEE.

DURING the early years of the War for Independence, and for many months before the flame broke forth in Massachusetts, the American patriots were much indebted to secret observers of political men and things in Europe, who kept the former continually and accurately informed of passing events. One of the most efficient of these observers was Arthur Lee, of Virginia, brother of Richard Henry Lee, author of the resolution proposing independence for the United States of America. He was born at Stratford, in Westmoreland county, Virginia, on the 20th of December, 1740. He was educated in the Edinburgh University, where he studied the science of medicine, for some time. On his return, he commenced its practice at Williamsburg, then the capital, and centre of fashion, of Virginia. In 1766, while the Americans were yet greatly excited concerning the Stamp Act, he went to London, and commenced the study of the law, in the Temple. There he formed a close intimacy with Sir William Jones, (the eminent Oriental scholar), and many other men of note. During all the agitations from that period until the beginning of the war, Dr. Lee kept the Americans informed, chiefly through his brother, Richard Henry, of the plans and measures of the ministry, and was of essential service to the cause of popular liberty in America. He wrote much for the press in favor of the colonies; and, in 1775, he was accredited agent of Virginia, in England. In the Summer of that year, he presented the second petition of the American Congress to the king; and, in the Autumn of 1776, he was appointed a commissioner of the United States at the French court, as colleague of Dr. Franklin and Silas Deane. He held that position until 1779, when Franklin was appointed sole minister. In the meanwhile, Dr. Lee had been appointed a special commissioner to Spain to solicit a loan; and in the same capacity, and for the same purpose, he visited the capital of Prussia, but the king, unwilling to offend Great Britain, would not openly receive him.[1] Dr. Lee returned to America, in 1780, when Silas Deane was laboring to blacken his character.[2] The people believed in their hitherto faithful friend, and, early in 1781, Dr. Lee was elected to a seat in the House of Burgesses, of Virginia. That body sent him to Congress, where he held a seat until 1785. In 1784, he was appointed one of the commissioners to treat with the representatives of the Six Nations of Indians, at Fort Schuyler (now Rome), and soon afterward he was called to a seat at the Treasury Board. Early in 1790, he was admitted to the bar of the Supreme Court of the United States, but his earthly career was almost closed. He purchased a farm near Urbana, on the Rappahannock, and there he died, on the 14th of December, 1792, at the age of almost fifty-two years.

---

1. Dr. Lee was successful in his mission to both Spain and Prussia. Although the King of Prussia would not receive him openly, he had continual correspondence with the court, and his brother William was a resident agent of the United States there. While in Berlin, his papers were stolen, and he charged the British minister with the theft. The king ordered an investigation, and they were soon secretly returned. At the request of the Prussian monarch, the British minister was recalled. Dr. Lee received warm assurances of friendship from the king, and obtained favors for the United States.
2. See sketch of Deane.

CHRISTOPHER COLLES.

IN that superb Offering of Intellect to Worth and Genius, the *Knickerbocker Gallery*,[1] published at the close of 1854, Dr. John W. Francis has given an exceedingly interesting sketch of Christopher Colles, a name but little known to this generation, while the influence of his genius is everywhere felt in the great pulsating arteries of our national enterprise, for it was in the highest degree suggestive. This kindly embalming by an appreciating hand, has saved a name deserving of honor from that forgetfulness which the world too often indulges toward genius in linsey-woolsey.

Mr. Colles was born in Ireland about the year 1757. Under the care and instructions of Richard Pocoeke, the celebrated Oriental traveller, he acquired much scientific knowledge and considerable expertness in the use of different languages. His patron died in 1765, and Colles came to America soon afterward. He first appeared in public here as a lecturer on canal navigation, at about the year 1772; and he is unquestionably the first man who suggested, and called public attention to the importance of a navigable water-communication between the Hudson river and the Lakes. He presented a memorial on the subject to the New York State legislature, in the Autumn of 1784, and in April following, a favorable report was made. Colles actually made a survey of the Mohawk, and the country to Wood creek, by which a water-communication with Oneida and Ontario lakes might be effected. The results of that tour were published in a pamphlet, in 1785. More than ten years before, Colles had matured a plan for supplying the city of New York with wholesome water, and steps were taken for the purpose, when the Revolution interfered. Year after year he was engaged in his favorite projects. In 1797, his name appeared among applicants for a contract to supply the city of New York with water; and it was unquestionably his fertile mind that conceived the idea, then first put forth, of obtaining water from Westchester county. The *Bronx*, instead of the *Croton*, was the proposed fountain of supply. In 1808, he published an interesting pamphlet on canals.

In 1789, Mr. Colles published a series of sectional Road Maps, for the use of travellers in New York, New Jersey, Pennsylvania, Maryland, and Virginia; and, in 1794, he issued the first number of "The Geographical Ledger." But these undertakings were far from profitable to him, and he eked out a comfortable subsistence by land-surveying and itinerant public instruction in the various branches of practical science. He also constructed band-boxes for a living, when he made New York his permanent residence, and frequently assisted almanac makers in their calculations. He manufactured painters' colors, and proof-glasses to test the quality of liquors. Finally "we find our ubiquitous philosopher in good quarters and in wholesome employment," says Dr. Francis, as actuary of the American Academy of Fine Arts. He also made profitable exhibitions of a telescope and microscope of his own construction, and had a marine telegraph on the Government House at the Bowling-green. These humble employments did not lessen him in the esteem of the eminent men of that time, who knew and admired the profundity of his acquirements; and De Witt Clinton always regarded him as among the most prominent and efficient promoters of internal improvements. Dr. Mitchill was his warm friend; Jarvis thought it an honor to paint his portrait;[2] and Dr. Hosack commemorated him

---

[1]. A volume composed of contributions from the surviving writers for *The Knickerbocker Magazine*, and embellished with their portraits. It was prepared as a testimonial of esteem for Lewis Gaylord Clarke, the editor of the *Magazine*, and for his benefit the profits of the work were devoted. The above sketch is the substance of Dr. Francis' Memoir of Colles.
[2]. That picture is in the possession of the New York Historical Society.

in his Life of Clinton. And finally, in the great celebration which took place in New York, in November, 1825, when the waters of Erie were united with the Atlantic, "the effigy of Colles was borne with appropriate dignity among the emblems of that vast procession." He had then been in the grave four years, having gone to his rest in the Autumn of 1821. Of all the people of that great city where the inanimate effigy of Colles was so soon to be honored, only *two* besides the officiating clergyman followed his body to the grave! These honored two were Dr. Francis and John Pintard. The Rev. Dr. Creighton (who declined the bishopric of New York, in 1852), officiated on the occasion, and the remains of Christopher Colles were deposited in the Episcopal burial-ground in Hudson Street. No memorial marks the spot, and the place of his grave is doubtless forgotten!

THOMAS SUMTER.

THE "South Carolina Game-Cock," as Sumter was called, was, next to Marion, the most useful of all the southern partisans during the latter part of the Revolution. Of his early life and habits we have no reliable record, and the place of his birth is unknown. That event occurred, as some circumstances indicate, about the year 1734. His name first appears in public as lieutenant-colonel of a regiment of riflemen, in March, 1776, and he appears to have been in Charleston until within a few days before its surrender to the British, in May, 1780. He was not among the prisoners, and was doubtless in the vicinity of the Catawba, at that time, arousing his countrymen to action. He was in the field early in the Summer of 1780, and was actively engaged in partisan warfare with the British and Tories, when Gates approached Camden, in August. At the close of July he had attacked the British post at Rocky Mount, on the Catawba; and, early in August, he fought a severe battle with the British and Loyalists at Hanging Rock. Immediately after the defeat of Gates, Sumter was attacked by Tarleton, near the mouth of the Fishing Creek, and his little band was utterly routed and dispersed. With a few survivors and new volunteers, he hastened across the Broad River, ranged the districts upon its western banks, and, in November, defeated Colonel Wemyss, who attacked his camp at the Fish Dam Ford, in Chester district. Twelve days afterward, he defeated Tarleton in an engagement at Blackstocks, on the Tyger river; but, being severely wounded, he proceeded immediately to North Carolina, where he remained until his wounds were healed.

Early in February, 1781, Sumter again took the field, and while Greene was retreating before Lord Cornwallis, he was aiding Marion, Pickens, and others, in humbling the garrisons of the enemy on the borders of the low country. He continued in active service during the whole campaign of 1781, and did much toward humbling the British posts near Charleston; but ill-health compelled him to leave the army before the close of the war. He was for a long time a member of the House of Representatives of the United States, and also of the Senate in the earlier years of the Republic. Finally, when he retired from public life, he took up his abode near Bradford Springs, on the High Hills of Santee (now Statesburg), South Carolina. There he lived until he had almost reached centenary honors. He died there, on the 1st of June, 1832, when in the ninety-eighth year of his age. When the writer visited that region, in 1849, the house and plantation of General Sumter were owned by a mulatto named Ellison, a man greatly esteemed. He had purchased the freedom of himself and family in early life, and was then the owner of a large estate in land, and about sixty

WILLIAM PINKNEY.

ONE of the most profound and brilliant of the orators and statesmen of his age, was the equally-renowned diplomatist, William Pinkney, of Maryland. He was born at Annapolis, on the 17th of March, 1764. Although his father was a staunch loyalist, William, as soon as he reached young manhood toward the close of the Revolution, warmly espoused the cause of the patriots. He possessed great strength of mind, but his early education was sadly neglected. By severe study he soon made amends, and took front rank among his more fortunate companions. He first studied the science of medicine, but, regarding the law with more favor, not only as more agreeable to his inclinations but as more promising in personal distinctions, he abandoned the former, and devoted his energies to the latter. He was admitted to the bar at the age of twenty-two years, and soon afterward he commenced the practice of his profession in Harford county, Maryland, where, in 1789, he married a sister of (afterward) Commodore Rodgers.

In 1792, Mr. Pinkney was elected to a seat in the executive council of Maryland; and, in 1795, was chosen a delegate to the State legislature. The following year, President Washington appointed him one of the commissioners under the provisions of Jay's treaty, and he proceeded to England. He performed his arduous and varied duties with great ability and success. Soon after his return to America, in 1805, he removed to Baltimore, and was immediately appointed attorney-general of Maryland. The following year he was again sent to England to treat concerning the impressment of American seamen into the British service, and other matters which finally resulted in war. After remaining in Europe several years, he returned in 1811, and became one of the most ardent supporters of Mr. Madison's administration. He was chosen a member of the Maryland Senate, and toward the close of 1811, President Madison appointed him attorney-general of the United States. He went to the field in defence of his native State, in 1814, and fought the British bravely at Bladensburg. He was soon afterward elected to Congress; and, in 1816, he was appointed minister to the court of St. Petersburg. There he remained until 1820, when he returned home, and was immediately chosen to a seat in the United States Senate. In that body, and in the Supreme Court of the United States, he labored intensely until the close of 1821, when his health suddenly gave way. He died on the 25th of February, 1822, in the fifty-ninth year of his age.

OLIVER WOLCOTT.

HENRY WOLCOTT was one of the earliest and most active settlers in the Connecticut Valley, whither he went from Dorchester, near Boston, in 1736, and made his residence at Windsor. There, on the 26th of November, 1726, his distinguished descendant, Oliver Wolcott, was born. At the age of seventeen years he entered Yale College, as a student, and left it in 1747, bearing the usual college honors. The contest with the French and Indians, known as *King George's War*, was then in progress, and young Wolcott obtained a captain's commission, raised a company, and joined the provincial army. Peace soon came, but he held his commission, and arose regularly to the rank of major-general. At the close of the war he studied medicine, and when about to commence its practice, he was appointed sheriff of Litchfield county, Connecticut, where he resided. He was distinguished for his early advocacy of the cause of the colonists in the dispute with Great Britain, and was a member of the council of his native State from 1774 until 1786. In the meanwhile he was a member of the Continental Congress, chief justice of Litchfield county, and judge of probate, of that district. As a member of Congress, he signed the Declaration of Independence; and he was also appointed, by that body, one of the commissioners of Indian affairs for the northern department. As umpire and active participator in the matter of dispute between Connecticut and Pennsylvania, concerning the Wyoming Valley, Judge Wolcott performed an important service, in procuring a settlement.

At home Judge Wolcott was very active in recruiting men for the continental service,[1] and he was in command of a body of troops in the army of Gates, at Saratoga, when Burgoyne was captured. In 1786, he was elected lieutenant-

---

1. When, in July, 1776, the American soldiers pulled down and broke in pieces the leaden equestrian statue of George the Third, which stood in the Bowling-green at the foot of Broadway, New York, a greater portion of it was sent to Governor Wolcott, at Litchfield, to be converted into bullets. This service was performed by a son and two daughters of Governor Wolcott, Mr. and Miss Marvin, and Mrs. Hench. According to an account-current of the cartridges made from that statue, found among the papers of Governor Wolcott, it appears that it furnished materials for forty-two thousand bullets. Referring to this matter, Ebenezer Hazard, in a letter to Gates, said, "His [the king's] troops will probably have melted majesty fired at them."

governor of Connecticut, and was annually reëlected to that office for ten years, when he was chosen chief magistrate. He was again chosen governor, in 1797, and was an incumbent of the chair of State at the time of his death, which occurred on the 1st of December, of that year, when he was in the seventy-second year of his age. Inflexible integrity, sterling virtue, and exalted piety, were the prominent traits of Governor Wolcott's character. He was also a bright example as a patriot and Christian.

THOMAS COOPER.

POLITICAL as well as religious persecutions in Europe have, from time to time, driven many valuable men to this country for their own preservation and for our special benefit. Few of these have held a more prominent place in the public esteem than Dr. Thomas Cooper, for many years president of the College of South Carolina. He was a native of England, where he was born in 1759. He was graduated at Oxford University at the age of eighteen years. Bearing in his hand the honors of that institution, and in his heart the glowing enthusiasm of a liberal soul, he entered boldly and fearlessly upon the sea of politics, with a democratic idea as his guiding star. When the French Revolution blazed forth, young Cooper attached himself to the party in England that hailed the event with delight, and he soon became a marked man by friends and foes. When the atrocities of the so-called Republican party, in France, chilled the blood of even its warm friends in England, and enthusiasm began to cool, Cooper found his country an uncomfortable and perhaps a dangerous place to domicil in; and, in 1794, he came to America, with his friend Dr. Priestly, and other reformers. He resided awhile in New York city, then in Philadelphia, and became first a judge of a court of common pleas in Pennsylvania, and then professor of chemistry in Dickenson College, at Carlisle, in that State. He was a great student, yet, unlike many great students, he was a dispenser as well as a recipient of knowledge. His attainments were multifarious and extraordinary; and he wrote and published works on Law, Medical Jurisprudence, and Political Economy. He translated Justinian and Broussais; and he was a habitual writer upon current politics, always in favor of the Republican party. He efficiently sustained the administrations of Jefferson, Madison, and Monroe. Jefferson offered him the Professorship of Chemistry in the University of Virginia, but he declined it. He subsequently filled the same chair in the College of South Carolina, where his lectures were of the highest order, not only on account of their scientific instructions, but for their beauty as specimens of English composition. He finally became president of that institution, yet, with all his wealth of knowledge and peculiar powers of impartation, the institution did not flourish to that degree which the accomplishments of its head taught its friends to expect. The reason may be found in the fact that Dr. Cooper was an avowed unbeliever in revealed religion, and Christian parents would not intrust their children to his care. He was the more dangerous in this respect, because his manners were captivating, and his opposition to Christianity was so courteous, that no one was repelled by a shock such as the writings of Paine and others give to the soul which had hitherto dwelt in an atmosphere of belief. Dr. Cooper was an esteemed resident of Columbia, South Carolina, for about twenty years, and died there, while in the performance of his duties as president of the college, on the 11th of May, 1839, in the eightieth year of his age.

SAMUEL HOPKINS.

FEW theologians of our country have exerted a wider special influence than Samuel Hopkins, a descendant of Governor Hopkins, of Connecticut, and the chief of the Calvinistic sect of Christians known as *Hopkinsians*. He was born in Waterbury, Connecticut, on the 17th of September, 1721, and in the excellent society of that town his youth was spent, and the labors of a farm were his occupation. He was graduated at Yale College, in 1741, and that year he heard both Whitefield and Gilbert Tennant preach. Their sermons made a deep impression upon his mind, and almost unsettled his reason. He remained a recluse in his father's house for several months, and then went to Northampton to study divinity under Jonathan Edwards. He was ordained a Christian minister at Great Barrington, Massachusetts, on the 28th of December, 1743. There he remained until 1769, when he was dismissed by an ecclesiastical council. He went to Newport, Rhode Island, in 1770, where he preached for awhile, but new views concerning vital religion, which he had put forth, displeased many of his hearers, and, at a meeting, they resolved not to give him a call as a pastor. He prepared to leave them, and preached a farewell sermon. That discourse so interested and impressed the people, that they urged him to remain and become their pastor. He complied, and the connection was severed only by his death thirty-three years afterward. When the British took possession of Rhode Island, in 1776, Mr. Hopkins retired, with his family, to Great Barrington, and preached at Newburyport, Canterbury, and Stamford. After the evacuation of Rhode Island, by the British, in 1780, he returned to Newport, but his flock were so scattered and impoverished, that they could not give him a stated salary. Yet he declined invitations to preach elsewhere to more favored congregations; and during the remainder of his life he continued a faithful pastor there, and subsisted upon the weekly contributions of his friends. He was deprived of the use of his limbs, by paralysis, in 1799, but so far recovered as to be able to preach again. He died on the 20th of December, 1803, at the age of eighty-two years. Dr. Hopkins was an inefficient preacher. His pen, and not his tongue, was the chief utterer of those sentiments which have made his name famous as a Calvinistic theologian.[1]

WILLIAM HENRY HARRISON.

ON the banks of the James River, in Charles City county, Virginia, is a plain mansion, around which is spread the beautiful estate of *Berkeley*, the birth-place of a signer of the Declaration of Independence, and of one of the Presidents of the United States. The former was Benjamin Harrison, whose career we have already sketched. The latter was his son, William Henry Harrison, whose life we will now consider. He was born on the 9th of February, 1773. At a suitable age he was placed in Hampden Sydney College, where he was graduated; and then, under the supervision of his guardian (Robert Morris), in Philadelphia, prepared himself for the practice of the medical art. At about that time an

---

1. Dr. Hopkins not only embraced the whole Calvinistic doctrine of "total depravity" and "predestination and election," but added thereto some extraordinary views concerning the origin and nature of sin, quite incompatible with reason or common sense. Yet many embraced his doctrines; and his two volumes of sermons have been extensively read and admired by those who have a taste for such metaphysical disquisitions.

WILLIAM HENRY HARRISON.

army was gathering to chastise the hostile Indians in the North-west. Young Harrison's military genius was stirred within him, and having obtained an ensign's commission from President Washington, he joined the army at the age of nineteen years. He was promoted to a lieutenancy, in 1792; and, in 1794, he followed Wayne to conflicts with the North-western tribes, where he greatly distinguished himself. He was appointed secretary of the North-western Territory, in 1797, and resigned his military commission. Two years afterward, when only twenty-six years of age, he was elected the first delegate to Congress from the Territory.[1] On the erection of Indiana into a separate territorial government, in 1801, Harrison was appointed its chief magistrate, and he was continued in that office, by consecutive reappointments, until 1813,[2] when the war with Great Britain called him to a more important sphere of action. He had already exhibited his military skill in the battle with the Indians at Tippecanoe, in the Autumn of 1811. He was commissioned a major-general in the Kentucky militia, by brevet, early in 1812. After the surrender of General Hull, at Detroit, he was appointed major-general in the army of the United States, and intrusted with the command of the North-western division. He was one of the best officers in that war; but, after achieving the battle of the Thames,

---

1. It included the present States of Ohio, Indiana, Illinois, and Michigan. General St. Clair was then governor of the Territory.
2. He had also held the office of commissioner of Indian affairs, in that Territory, and had concluded no less than thirteen important treaties with the different tribes.

and other victories in the lake country, his military services were concluded. He resigned his commission, in 1814, in consequence of a misunderstanding with the Secretary of War, and retired to his farm at North Bend, Ohio. He served as commissioner in negotiating Indian treaties; and the voice of a grateful people afterward called him to represent them in the legislature of Ohio, and of the nation. He was elected to the Senate of the United States, in 1824. In 1828, he was appointed minister to Colombia, one of the South American Republics. He was recalled, by President Jackson, on account of some differences of opinion respecting diplomatic events in that region, when he returned home, and again sought the repose of private life. There he remained about ten years, when he was called forth to receive from the American people the highest honor in their gift—the chief magistracy of the Republic. He was elected President of the United States by an immense majority, and was inaugurated on the 4th of March, 1841. For more than twenty days he bore the unceasing clamors for office, with which the ears of a new president are always assailed; and then his slender constitution, pressed by the weight of almost threescore and ten years, suddenly gave way. The excitements of his new station increased a slight disease caused by a cold, and on the 4th of April—just one month after the inauguration pageant at the presidential mansion,—the honored occupant was a corpse. He was succeeded in office by the vice-president, John Tyler.

ARTHUR ST. CLAIR.

THERE were brave soldiers, full of confidence in themselves and their companions-in-arms, during the War for Independence, who lacked skill as leaders, and failed in winning that fame to which their courage entitled them. Arthur St. Clair was of that number. He was an officer of acknowledged bravery and prudence, yet he was far from being an expert military leader. He was born at Edinburgh, in Scotland, in 1734, and was a lieutenant in the army under Wolfe, in the campaign against Canada, in 1759. He remained in America, after the peace, and was placed in command of Fort Ligonier, in Westmoreland county, Pennsylvania. He also received a grant of a thousand acres of land in that then wilderness, and resided there until the beginning of the Revolution. He was appointed to the command of a battalion of Pennsylvania militia, in January, 1776, and received from Congress the commission of colonel. He raised a regiment, proceeded to the northern department to operate against Canada, and, in August, was promoted to brigadier-general. He behaved with great bravery and skill in the battles at Trenton and Princeton; and, in February, 1777, he was commissioned a major-general. He was placed in command of Ticonderoga the following Summer. The post was weak in many ways, and when, in July, Burgoyne, with a powerful army, approached and took an advantageous position, St. Clair abandoned it, and retreated toward the Hudson, where Schuyler was preparing to meet the invaders. That retreat proved a disastrous one in the loss of men and munitions. A court of inquiry honorably acquitted him; and, in 1780, he was ordered to Rhode Island. Circumstances prevented his taking command there; and, in 1781, when the allied American and French armies proceeded to attack Cornwallis, at Yorktown, in Virginia, he remained in Philadelphia, with a considerable force, to protect Congress. He obtained permission to join the main army, and arrived at Yorktown during the siege. After the capture of the British army there, he proceeded to join General

Greene, in the South, and on his way he drove the British from Wilmington, North Carolina.

General St. Clair was a member of the executive council of Pennsylvania, in 1783, and was elected to Congress three years afterward. He was president of that body, early in 1787. Upon the erection of the North-western Territory into a government, in 1788, he was appointed its governor, and held that office until 1802, when Ohio was admitted into the Union as a sovereign State.

St. Clair commanded an army against the Miami Indians, in 1791; and, in the Autumn of that year, was defeated with the loss of almost seven hundred men. He was then suffering from severe illness, yet bore himself bravely. Public censure was loud and ungenerous, but a committee of the House of Representatives acquitted him of all blame. When he retired from public life, in 1802, he was an old man, and almost ruined in fortune. He resided in dreary loneliness near Laurel Hill, Westmoreland county, and for a long time vainly petitioned Congress to allow certain claims. He finally obtained a pension of sixty dollars a month, and his last days were made comfortable. He died on the 31st of August, 1818, at the age of eighty-four years. His remains rest in the graveyard of the Presbyterian Church, at Greensburg, and over it the Masonic fraternity placed a handsome monument, in 1832.

FRANCOIS XAVIER MARTIN.

PERHAPS one of the most learned jurists and erudite scholars that ever adorned the profession of the law, in this country, was François Xavier Martin, better known to the general reader as the accomplished Historian of North Carolina.[1] He was born at Marseilles, in France, on the 17th of March, 1762. At the age of twenty years he came to America. The war of the Revolution was then just drawing to a close, and he took up his residence at Newbern, in North Carolina, and prepared himself for the profession of the law. On his first appearance at the bar, he gave evidence of that acuteness which marked his whole career, in whatever station in life he was called to act. His practice became extensive and lucrative, and he soon took a high social position in his adopted State. In 1806, he was called to represent Newbern district in the House of Commons of North Carolina. Soon after the close of his duties therein, President Madison (in 1809) appointed him United States Judge of the Mississippi Territory, and he made his residence at Natchez. On the 1st of February, 1815, he was elevated by Governor Claiborne to the bench of the Supreme Court of Louisiana, as one of the associate judges. He held that office for twenty-two years, when, in January, 1837, he became chief justice of the State, on the death of Judge Mathews. Chief Justice Martin remained at the head of the Supreme Court of Louisiana until the adoption of the present constitution of that State, in the Autumn of 1845, when he retired to private life. He was then in the eighty-fourth year of his age. Judge Martin lived but a little more than a year after his retirement. He died on the 10th of December, 1846. No man ever left an official station with fewer stains of sins of omission or commission upon his garment, than Judge Martin, for through his long life not a syllable in disparagement of his honesty and integrity was ever uttered. His memory is cherished with the deepest affection by the members of his profession, and by the community in which he lived.

---

1. His History of North Carolina, including the story of its discovery, settlement, and progress of colonization, until the beginning of the Revolution, was commenced in 1791, but was not published until 1829, when it was issued from a New Orleans press, in two octavo volumes.

ANDREW JACKSON.

"ASK nothing but what is right—submit to nothing wrong," was Andrew Jackson's great political maxim; and it was an abiding principle in his character from his earliest youth until the close of his life. That noble principle was the key to his great success in whatever he undertook, and is worthy of adoption by every young man when he sets out upon the perilous voyage of active life. Jackson's parents were from the north of Ireland, and were among the early Scotch-Irish settlers in the upper part of South Carolina, in the vicinity of Waxhaw Creek. Jackson's father lived north of the dividing line between North and South Carolina, in Mecklenburg county, and there Andrew was born on the 15th of March, 1767. His father died five days afterward, and a month later, his mother took up her abode in South Carolina, near the meeting-house of the Waxhaw settlement. He received a fair education, for his mother designed him for the Christian ministry. But his studies were interrupted by the tumults of the on-coming Revolution, and soon after the fall of Charleston, the Waxhaw settlement became a terrible scene of blood, in the massacre of Buford's regiment by the fiery Tarleton.[1] Every element of the lion in young Jackson's nature was aroused by this event, and, boy as he was, not yet fourteen years of age, he joined the patriot army and went to the field. One of his brothers was killed at Stono, and himself and another brother were made captives, in 1781. The widow was soon bereaved of all her family, but Andrew; and after making a journey of mercy to Charleston, to relieve sick prisoners, she fell by the wayside; and 'the place of her sepulchre is not known unto this day.' Left alone at a critical period of life, with some property at his disposal, young Jackson commenced a career that promised certain destruction. He suddenly reformed, studied law, and was licensed to practice, in 1786. He was soon afterward appointed solicitor of the Western District of Tennessee, and journeying over the mountains, he commenced, in that then wilderness, that remarkable career as attorney, judge, legislator, and military commander, which on contemplation assumes the features of the wildest romance, viewed from any point of appreciation. His lonely journeyings, his collisions with the Indians, his difficulties with gamblers and fraudulent creditors and land speculators, and his wonderful personal triumphs in hours of greatest danger, make the record of his life one of rare interest and instruction.

In 1790, Jackson made his residence at Nashville, and there he married an accomplished woman, who had been divorced from her husband. In 1795, he assisted in forming a State Constitution for Tennessee, and was elected the first representative, in Congress, of the new State. In the Autumn of 1797, he took a seat in the United States Senate, to which he had been chosen, and was a conspicuous supporter of the democratic party. He did not remain long at Washington. Soon after leaving the Senate, he was appointed judge of the Supreme Court of his State. He resigned that office, in 1804, and retired to his beautiful estate near Nashville. There he was visited by Aaron Burr, in 1805, and entered warmly into his schemes for invading Mexico. When Burr's intentions were suspected, Jackson refused further intercourse with him until he should prove the purity of his intentions. For many years Jackson was chief military commander in his section; and when war against Great Britain was proclaimed,

---

1. Tarleton gave no quarter, and about one hundred and fifty men, ready to surrender to superior numbers, were killed or cruelly maimed. The wounded and the dying were taken into the Waxhaw meeting-house, and there the mother of Jackson, and other women, attended them. Under the roof of that sacred edifice, young Jackson first saw the demon of war in its most horrid form, and all that misery and British power and oppression, were ever afterward associated in his mind.

in 1812, he longed for employment in the field. He was called to duty in 1813. Early the following year he was made a major-general, and from that time until his great victory at New Orleans, on the 8th of January, 1815, his name was identified with every military movement in the South, whether against the hostile Indians, Britons, or Spaniards. In 1818, he engaged successfully in a campaign against the Seminoles and other Southern Indians, and, at the same time, he taught the Spanish authorities in Florida some useful lessons, and hastened the cession of that territory to the United States.

In 1821, President Monroe appointed General Jackson governor of Florida; and, in 1823, he offered him the station of resident minister in Mexico. He declined the honor, but accepted a seat in the United States Senate, to which the legislature of Tennessee had elected him. He was one of the four candidates for President of the United States, in 1824, but was unsuccessful. He was elevated to that exalted station, in 1828, by a large majority, and was reëlected, in 1832. His administration of eight years was marked by great energy; and never were the affairs of the Republic, in its domestic and foreign relations, more prosperous than at the close of his term of office. In the Spring of 1837, he retired from public life forever, and sought repose after a long and laborious career, devoted to the service of his country. He lived quietly at his residence near Nashville, called *The Hermitage*, until on a calm Sunday, the 8th of June, 1845, his spirit went home. He was then a little more than seventy-eight years of age. The memory of that great and good man is revered by his countrymen, next to that of Washington, and to him has been awarded the first equestrian statue in bronze ever erected in this country. It is colossal, and occupies a conspicuous place in President's Square, Washington city, where it was reared in 1852.

NATHANIEL BOWDITCH.

THE practical man who, in any degree, lightens the burden of human labor, is eminently a public benefactor. Such was Nathaniel Bowditch, who, by navigators, has been aptly termed *The Great Pilot*. He was the son of a poor ship-master, of Salem, where Nathaniel was born on the 26th of March, 1773. His education was acquired at a district school; and at the age of thirteen years he was apprenticed to a ship-chandler. He performed his duties faithfully until manhood, and during his whole apprenticeship he employed every leisure moment in reading and study. Mathematics was his favorite study, and it became the medium of his greatest public services.

At the age of twenty-two years young Bowditch went on a voyage to the East Indies, as captain's clerk, and his naturally strong mind was engaged chiefly on the subject of navigation, while at sea. The result of his reflections, observations, and calculations, was the publication, in 1802, of the well-known nautical work, entitled the *New American Practical Navigator*.[1] For nine years he was himself a practical navigator, and during that time he rose gradually from captain's clerk to master. He left the sea, in 1804, and became president of a Marine Insurance Company, at Salem. That office he held for almost twenty years. Two years before, while his ship lay wind-bound in Boston Harbor, Captain Bowditch went to Cambridge to listen to the commencement exercises at Harvard College, and while standing in the crowded aisle, he heard his own name announced, by the president, as the recipient of the degree of Master of Arts. It was to him the proudest day of his life. He was then about twenty-nine years of age.

In 1806, Mr. Bowditch published an admirable chart of the harbors of Salem, Beverly, Marblehead, and Manchester. In 1816, he received the degree of Doctor of Laws, from Harvard College; and was elected a member of the Royal Society of London, in 1818. He contributed many valuable papers to scientific publications, but the great work of his life was the translation and annotation of Laplace's *Mecanique Celeste*. He published it at his own expense entirely, remarking that he would rather spend a thousand dollars a year, in that way, than to ride in his carriage. It was a task of great labor and expense, and consists of five large volumes. The first was published in 1829, the second in 1832, and the third in 1834. He read the last proof sheets of the fourth volume only a few days before his death. The revision of the fifth was left to other hands. Dr. Bowditch died on the 16th of March, 1838; and his last words were "Lord, now lettest thou thy servant depart in peace, according to thy word." He was a man of great literary and scientific attainments, and was proficient in the

---

[1]. The origin of that work shows how comparatively insignificant events will result in great benefits. On the day previous to his sailing on his last voyage, he was called upon by Edmund N. Blunt, then a noted publisher of charts and nautical books, at Newburyport, and requested to continue the corrections which he had previously commenced on Moore's book on navigation, then in common use. In performance of his promise to do so, he detected so many and important errors, that he resolved to prepare an entire new work. That work was his *Practical Navigator*.

Latin, Greek, French, Italian, Spanish, Portuguese, and German languages. He was not ambitious for public life, yet he twice occupied a seat in the executive council of Governor Strong, of Massachusetts. His memory is sweet for his life was pure.

MARINUS WILLETT.

NO member of the associated *Sons of Liberty*, in New York, exceeded Marinus Willett in devotion to republican principles, and in boldness of action when called to their support. He was born at Jamaica, Long Island, on the 10th of August, 1740. He was one of thirteen children, and lived to survive them all. The French and Indian war was burning fiercely in northern New York when he approached young manhood. His military passion was fired, and, before he was eighteen years of age, he entered the provincial army with a second lieutenant's commission, under the command of Colonel Oliver Delancy.[1] He shared in the misery of Abercrombie's defeat at Ticonderoga, in 1758; and immediately afterward he accompanied Colonel Bradstreet in his successful expedition against Fort Frontenac (now Kingston, Upper Canada), at the foot of Lake Ontario. Fatigue and exposure impaired his health, and he left the service soon afterward. When, a few years later, the Stamp Act spread a deep and ominous murmur over the land, Mr. Willett had chosen his banner, and from that time until the organization of an army of patriots to fight for liberty, he was one of the boldest supporters of his country's rights, by word and deed.

When British troops in New York were ordered to Boston, after the skirmish at Lexington, they attempted to carry off a large quantity of spare arms, in addition to their own. Willett resolved to prevent it, and, though opposed by the mayor and other Whigs, he led a body of citizens, captured the baggage-wagons containing them, and took them back to the city. These arms were afterward used by the first regiment raised by the State of New York. Willett was appointed second captain of a company in Colonel M'Dougal's regiment, and accompanied Montgomery in his northern expedition. After the capture of St. John's, on the Sorel, he escorted prisoners taken at Chambly, to Ticonderoga, and then was placed in command of St. John's. He held that post until January, 1776. In November of that year he was appointed lieutenant-colonel; and, at the opening of the campaign of 1777, he was placed in command of Fort Constitution, on the Hudson, opposite West Point. In May he was ordered to Fort Stanwix, or Schuyler (now Rome), where he performed signal services. He was left in command of the fort, and remained there until the Summer of 1778, when he joined the army under Washington, and was at the battle of Monmouth. He accompanied Sullivan in his campaign against the Indians in 1779, and was actively engaged in the Mohawk Valley, in 1780, 1781, and 1782. At the close of the war he returned to civil pursuits. Washington highly esteemed him; and, in 1792, he was sent by the President to treat with the Creek Indians at the South. The same year he was appointed a brigadier-general in the army intended to act against the North-western Indians. He declined the appointment, for he was opposed to the expedition. He was for some time sheriff of New York, and was elected mayor of the city, in 1807. He was chosen elector of president and

---

1. It may be interesting to the young to know the style of a military dress at that time. Willett thus describes his own uniform: A green coat trimmed with silver twist, white under-clothes, and black gaiters; also a cocked hat, with a large black cockade of silk ribbon, together with a silver button and loop.

vice-president, in 1824, and was made president of the Electoral College. Colonel Willett died in the city of New York, on the 23d of August, 1830, in the ninety-first year of his age.

JOHN STARK.

"BOYS! there's the enemy. They *must be beat*, or Molly Stark must sleep a widow this night! Forward, boys! March!" Such were the vigorous words of a hero of two wars, the gallant General Stark, as he led his corps of Green Mountain Boys to attack the Hessians and Tories, near Bennington. He was an unpolished soldier, who had learned the art of desultory warfare in service against the French and Indians in northern New York. He was the son of a Scotchman, and was born at Londonderry (now the city of Manchester), New Hampshire, on the 28th of August, 1728. His early childhood was spent in the midst of the wild scenery of his birth-place, and in youth he was remarkable for expertness in trapping the beaver and otter, and in hunting the bear and deer. Just before the breaking out of the French and Indian war, he penetrated the forests far northward, and was captured by some St. Francis Indians. He suffered dreadfully for a long time, and then was ransomed at a great price. This circumstance gave him good cause for leading a company of Rangers against these very Indians and their sometimes equally savage French allies, four years afterward. He became a captain, under Major Rogers, in 1756, and in that school he was taught those lessons which he practiced so usefully twenty years later.

When intelligence reached the valleys of the North, that blood had been shed at Lexington, Stark led the train-bands of his district to Cambridge, and was commissioned a colonel, with eight hundred men under his banner. With these he fought bravely in the battle of Bunker's Hill. He went to New York after the British evacuated Boston, in the Spring of 1776. Then, at the head of a brigade in the northern department, under Gates, he performed essential service in the vicinity of Lake Champlain; and near the close of the year, he commanded the right wing of Sullivan's column in the battle at Trenton. He shared in the honors at Princeton; but, being overlooked by Congress when promotions were made, he resigned his commission and retired from the army. But when the invader approached from the North, his own State called him to the field, in command of its brave sons; and on the Walloomscoik, a few miles from Bennington, he won that decisive battle which gave him world-wide renown. Then it was that he made the rough but effective speech above quoted, that indicated the alternative of death or victory. Congress was no longer tardy in acknowledging his services, for he had given that crippling blow to Burgoyne, which insured to Gates' army a comparatively easy victory. The national legislature gave him grateful thanks, and a brigadier's commission in the Continental army. He joined Gates at Saratoga, and shared in the honors of that great victory. In 1779, he was on duty on Rhode Island, and the following year he fought the British and Hessians at Springfield, in New Jersey. In the Autumn of 1780, he was one of the board of officers that tried and condemned the unfortunate Major André; and until the last scenes of the war, he was in active service. When he sheathed his sword, he left the arena of public life forever, though he lived almost forty years afterward. General Stark died on the 8th of May, 1822, at the age of almost ninety-four years. Near his birth-place, on the east side of the Merrimac, is a granite shaft, bearing the simple inscription, MAJOR-GENERAL STARK. His eulogium is daily uttered by our free institutions—his epitaph is in the memory of his deeds.

PHILLIS WHEATLEY.

> " 'Twas mercy brought me from my pagan land,
> Taught my benighted soul to understand
> That there 's a God—that there 's a Saviour too;
> Once I redemption neither sought nor knew."

SO felt the heart, and so recorded the pen of a child of Africa, who, by her talent and virtue, honored her race and challenged the kindly regard of many of the good and great of our country. The lady of a respectable citizen of Boston, named Wheatley, went to the slave-market, in that city, in 1761, to purchase a child-negress, that she might rear her to be a faithful nurse in the old age of her mistress. She saw many plump children, but one of delicate frame, modest demeanor, and clad in nothing but a piece of dirty carpet wrapped about her, attracted her attention, and Mrs. Wheatley took her home in her chaise, and gave her the name of Phillis. The child seemed to be about seven years of age, and exhibited remarkable intelligence, and apt imitative powers. Mrs. Wheatley's daughter taught the child to read and write, and her progress was wonderful. She appeared to have very little recollection of her birth-place, but remembered seeing her mother pour out water before the sun at its rising. With the development of her intellectual faculties her moral nature kept pace; and she was greatly beloved by all who knew her for her amiability and perfect docility. She soon attracted the attention of men of learning; and as Phillis read books with great avidity, they supplied her. Piety was a ruling sentiment in her character, and tears born of gratitude to God and her kind mistress, often moistened her eyes. As she grew to womanhood her thoughts found expression through her pen, sometimes in prose but more frequently in verse; and she was often an invited guest in the families of the rich and learned, in Boston. Her mistress treated her as a child, and was extremely proud of her.[1]

At the age of about sixteen years (1770) Phillis became a member of the "Old South Church," then under the charge of Dr. Sewall; and it was at about this time that she wrote the poem from which the above is an extract. Earlier than this she had written poems, remarkable for both vigor of thought and pathos in expression. Her memory, in some particulars, appears to have been extremely defective. If she composed a poem, in the night, and did not write it down, it would be gone from her, forever, in the morning. Her kind mistress gave her a light and writing materials at her bed-side, that she might lose nothing, and in cold weather a fire was always made in her room, at night. In the Summer of 1773, her health gave way, and a sea-voyage was recommended. She accompanied a son of Mr. Wheatley, to England, and there she was cordially received by Lady Huntingdon, Lord Dartmouth, and other people of distinction. While there, her poems, which had been collected and dedicated to the Countess of Huntingdon, were published, and attracted great attention. The book was embellished with a portrait of her, from which our picture was copied. She was persuaded to remain in London until the return of the court, so as to be presented to the king, but, hearing of the declining health of her mistress, she hastened home. That kind friend was soon laid in the grave, and Phillis grieved as deeply as any of her children. Mr. Wheatley died soon afterward, and then his excellent daughter was laid by the side of her parents. Phillis was left destitute, and the sun of her earthly happiness went down. A highly-intelligent colored man, of Boston, named Peters, offered himself in marriage to the poor orphan, and was accepted. He proved utterly unworthy of the excellent creature he had wedded, and her lot became a bitter one, indeed. She and her husband went to the interior of the State, to live, for awhile, and then returned to Boston. Misfortune seems to have expelled her muse, for we have no production of her pen bearing a later date than those in her volume published in 1773, except a poetical epistle to General Washington, in 1775,[2] and a few scraps written at about that time. A few years of misery shattered the golden bowl of her life, and, in a filthy apartment, in an obscure part of Boston, that gifted wife and mother, whose youth had been passed in ease and even luxury, was allowed to perish, alone! Her spirit took wing on the 5th of December, 1794, when she was about forty-one years of age.

---

1. On one occasion, Phillis was from home on a visit, and, as the weather was inclement, her mistress sent one of her slaves, with a chaise, after her. Prince took his seat beside Phillis. As they drew up to the house, and their mistress saw them, the good woman indignantly exclaimed, "Do but look at the saucy varlet—if he has not the impudence to sit upon the same seat with Phillis!" And she severely reprimanded Prince for forgetting the dignity of Phillis.

2. Phillis' letter was dated the 26th of October, 1775. Washington answered it on the 28th of February, 1776, as follows. His letter was written at his head-quarters, at Cambridge:

"MISS PHILLIS,—Your favor of the 26th of October did not reach my hands till the middle of December. Time enough, you will say, to have given an answer ere this. Granted. But a variety of important occurrences, continually interposing to distract the mind and withdraw the attention, I hope will apologize for the delay, and plead my excuse for the seeming, but not real neglect. I thank you most sincerely for your polite notice of me in the elegant lines you inclosed; and however undeserving I may be of such encomium and panegyric, the style and manner exhibit a striking proof of your poetical talents; in honor of which, and as a tribute justly due to you, I would have published the poem, had I not been apprehensive that, while I only meant to give the world this new instance of your genius, I might have incurred the imputation of vanity. This, and nothing else, determined me not to give it a place in the public prints. If you should ever come to Cambridge, or near head-quarters, I shall be happy to see a person so favored by the Muses, and to whom nature has been so liberal and beneficent in her dispensations. I am, with great respect, your obedient, humble servant,

"GEO. WASHINGTON."

CONRAD WEISER.

ONE of the most noted agents of communication between the white men and the Indians, was Conrad Weiser, a native of Germany, who came to America in early life, and settled, with his father, in the present Schoharie county, New York, in 1713. They left England, in 1712, and were seventeen months on their voyage! Young Weiser became a great favorite with the Iroquois Indians in the Schoharie and Mohawk Valleys, with whom he spent much of his life. Late in 1714, the elder Weiser, and about thirty other families, who had settled in Schoharie, becoming dissatisfied by attempts to tax them, set out for Tulpehocken, in Pennsylvania, by way of the Susquehanna river, and settled there. But young Weiser was enamored of the free life of the savage. He was naturalized by them, and became thoroughly versed in the languages of the whole Six Nations, as the Iroquois confederacy in New York were called. He became confidential interpreter and special messenger for the province of Pennsylvania among the Indians, and assisted in many important treaties. The governor of Virginia commissioned him to visit the grand council at Onondaga, in 1737, and, with only a Dutchman and three Indians, he traversed the trackless forest for five hundred miles, for that purpose. He went on a similar mission from Philadelphia to Shamokin (Sunbury), in 1744. At Reading he established an Indian agency and trading-house. When the French on the frontier made hostile demonstrations, in 1755, he was commissioned a colonel of a volunteer regiment from Berks county; and, in 1758, he attended the great gathering of the Indian chiefs in council with white commissioners, at Easton. Such was the affection of the Indians for Weiser, that for many years after his death they were in the habit of visiting his grave and strewing flowers thereon. Mr. Weiser's daughter married Henry Melchoir Muhlenburg, D.D., the founder of the Lutheran Church, in America.

ISAAC SEARS.

FEW men have occupied so large a space in the public attention, of whom so little is known, as Isaac Sears, one of the great leaders of the *Sons of Liberty*, in New York, previous to the occupation of that city by the British, in 1776. So generally was he regarded as the bold leader in popular outbreaks, that he acquired the name of *King* Sears, by which title he is better known than by his commercial one of captain. Of him, a Loyalist writer in Rivington's *Gazette* wrote, exultingly, when the New York Assembly yielded to ministerial requirements:

> "And so, my good masters, I find it no joke,
> For YORK has stepp'd forward and thrown off the yoke
> Of Congress, committees, and even *King Sears*,
> Who shows you good nature by showing his ears."

Isaac Sears was lineally descended from one of the earlier settlers in Massachusetts, who came from Colchester, England, in 1630. He was born at Norwalk, Connecticut, in 1729. Of his youth and early manhood we know little, except that he was a mariner. He first appeared in public life as a prominent member of the association called *Sons of Liberty*, in 1765, when he was a successful merchant in the city of New York, and a sea-captain of note. He was the chairman of the first Committee of Correspondence appointed by the citizens of New York, in 1765, and had for his colleagues John Lamb, Gershom Mott, William Wiley, and Thomas Robinson. At a later period, he was wounded in an affray with some soldiers; and in every enterprise against the schemes of government officials he was an acknowledged leader. Early in the Summer of 1775, he assisted Lamb, Willett, M'Dougal, and others, in seizing some British stores at Turtle Bay (46th Street, and East River, New York); and in August following, he led a party of citizens to assist Captain Lamb in removing British cannons from the battery of Fort George, at the foot of Broadway, while the *Asia* vessel of war was hurling round shot at them and the town.[1] In the Autumn of that year he led a party of mounted militia-men from Connecticut, who destroyed Rivington's printing-press, and carried off his type, at midday.[2]

Although Captain Sears continued to be an active Whig during the remainder of the Revolution, we do not find his name in connection with any important event. When peace came, his business and fortune were gone; and, in 1785, he made a voyage to China, as a supercargo, being a partner with others in a commercial venture. Captain Sears was very ill with fever, on his arrival at Canton, and died there, on the 28th of October, 1785, at the age of almost fifty-seven years. He was buried upon French Island, and his fellow-voyagers placed a slab, with a suitable inscription upon it, over his grave.

EDWARD TELFAIR.

MANY of the leading men in Georgia, at the time of the breaking out of the Revolution, were of Scotch descent, and, unlike the settlers from the same stock, in Eastern North Carolina, they were generally adherents to the patriot cause. Edward Telfair was born in Scotland, in 1735, and received an English education at the grammar school of Kirkcudbright, on the domain of the Earl of Selkirk.[3] He came to America when twenty-three years of age, and resided some time in Virginia, as agent of a commercial house. From thence he went to Halifax, on the Roanoke; and, in 1766, made his residence in Savannah. He was one of the earliest and most efficient promoters of the rebellion there, and was one of the leading members of the committee of safety, in 1774. With a few others he broke open the provincial magazine and secured the powder for the use of the patriots; and he also assisted in the seizure of the royal governor, Sir James Wright.[4] In 1778 he was elected to a seat in the Continental Congress; and on the 24th of July of that year he signed the ratification of the *Articles of Confederation*. He continued a member of that body until 1783, when he was appointed a commissioner to conclude a treaty with the Cherokee chiefs, by which the boundary line between their nation and Georgia was determined. He was governor of Georgia, first in 1786, and then from 1790 to 1793. He had the honor of entertaining President Washington, when he visited Georgia, in 1791, at his family seat, near Augusta. Governor Telfair died at Savannah, on the 19th of September, 1807, in the seventy-second year of his age. He was buried with military honors.

---

1. One of the buildings injured by that cannonade was the tavern of Samuel Fraunce, commonly known by the name of *Black Sam*, on account of his dark complexion. It was the same building in which Washington had his final parting with his officers, at the close of the war, and for many years has been known as the Broad Street Hotel. It is on the corner of Pearl and Broad Streets. In allusion to the event, Philip Freneau wrote, in his *Petition of Hugh Gaine*:

"At first we supposed it was only a sham,
'Till he drove a round ball through the roof of Black Sam."

Two of the cannons removed at that time by Alexander Hamilton and some of his college associates, might be seen at the entrance-gate to the grounds of Columbia College until 1855.
2. See sketch of Rivington, and also of Bishop Seabury.
3. See sketch of John Paul Jones.   4. See sketch of Joseph Habersham.

AARON BURR.

IN this country, where character alone is the accepted standard of respectability, and where the shield of class does not avert the odium of public opinion from the openly immoral man, let his birth and attainments be ever so exalted, there is necessarily a public virtue which no aspirant for honor dare neglect. In this sentiment is grounded our dearest hopes for the future of our Republic; and however melancholy in itself the spectacle of such a character as that of Aaron Burr may appear to the eye of the Christian and Patriot, the detestation in which it is held is a confirmation of faith in that public virtue. Burr was undoubtedly a patriot, and possessed many noble traits of character, but over all was spread the foul slime of libertinism; and he who might have shined among the bright stars of our country's glory, is, in a degree, a "lost pleiad,"

"—— Damned to everlasting fame."

Aaron Burr was the son of the pious President Burr, of the College at Princeton, and the daughter of the eminent Jonathan Edwards. He was born at Newark, New Jersey, on the 5th of February, 1756, and before he was three years of age he lost both his parents. He was a wayward boy, yet full of intellectual promise. At twelve years of age he entered Princeton College, and left it in 1772, a ripe scholar for one of his years, and the recipient of academic honors. He resolved to make the law his profession, but before he could engage in its practice, the storm of the Revolution burst upon the country, and he joined the Continental army, at Cambridge. Full of adventurous spirit, he volunteered to accompany Arnold through the wilderness, to Quebec. There he was made one of Montgomery's aids, and was with that officer when he fell. Soon after that he entered the military family of General Washington, from which he was expelled in consequence of some immoral conduct which disgusted the commander-in-chief. Burr was commissioned a lieutenant-colonel, in 1777, and continued in active service until 1779, when failing health compelled him to resign his office. He had already acquired an unenviable character for expertness in intrigue; and his hostility to Washington was always bitter and uncompromising.

Burr commenced the practice of law, at Albany, in 1782, and soon afterward removed to the city of New York, where he became distinguished in his profession. He was appointed attorney-general of the State, in 1789; and from 1791 to 1797, he was a member of the United States Senate, and an influential republican leader, in that body. His winning manners gave him wonderful influence. The power of his fascinations over the other sex was almost unbounded and he used it for the basest purposes. As a politician he was artful and intriguing; and he managed so adroitly for himself, that he received for the office of President of the United States, in 1800, the same number of votes as Mr. Jefferson, the head and founder of the Republican party. Congress decided in favor of Jefferson, after thirty-six ballotings, and Burr was declared Vice-President, according to usage in the early days of the Republic.

Burr was the bitter enemy of all Federalists; and, in 1804, he managed to draw Alexander Hamilton into a duel, which became the terrible result of a political quarrel. Burr murdered Hamilton,[1] and ever afterward society put the mark of Cain upon him. Two years afterwards he was engaged in forming an expedition in the western country, professedly to invade Mexico. It was suspected that Burr intended to attempt a severance of the Western from the Eastern States, and make himself president of the former. He was arrested on a charge of high treason, tried at Richmond, in Virginia, in 1807, and acquitted. He passed the remainder of his life in comparative obscurity and almost total neglect. Profligate and unscrupulous until the last, that wretched man, whose libertinism had carried desolation into many households, went down into the grave,

"Unwept, unhonored, and unsung;"

a warning to all. He died on Staten Island, near New York, on the 14th of September, 1836, at the age of eighty years.

JAMES THACHER.

ONE of the latest survivors of the medical staff of the Continental army, was James Thacher, M.D., whose interesting *Journal*, kept during the entire war, was published in 1827, and is regarded as standard authority in relation to matters of which it treats. James Thacher was born at Barnstable, Massachusetts, in 1754. He studied medicine in his native town, under Dr. Abner Hersey, and was prepared to enter upon the practice of his profession, "at the

---

1. The friends of both parties endeavored, in vain, to settle the dispute without recourse to arms, but Burr seemed resolved on taking the life of Hamilton. He exacted such concessions and humiliating terms of compromise, as he knew no man of honor would agree to. Hamilton fired his pistol in the air, while Burr, with fatal aim, sent a bullet with the errand of death. It was a foul murder.

precise time," he says, when he found his country "about to be involved in all the horrors of a civil war." In July, 1775, when only twenty-one years of age, he went to the Massachusetts Provincial Congress, at Watertown, and solicited the appointment of assistant hospital surgeon, at Cambridge. With nine others he received the coveted appointment, and he continued in active duty in the hospital and camp until the capture of Cornwallis, at Yorktown. It was under his directions that the general inoculation of the American army for the small-pox was performed, at its encampment in the Hudson Highlands, opposite West Point, in the Spring of 1781. In his *Journal*, Dr. Thacher says, "All the soldiers, with the women and children, who have not had the small-pox, are now under inoculation.[1] . . . . Of five hundred who have been inoculated here, four only have died."[2] He then mentions the interesting medical fact, that an extract of butternut, made by boiling down the inner bark of that tree, was very successfully substituted for the usual doses of calomel and jalap employed to reduce the system. He found it to be more efficacious and less dangerous than the mineral drug. He adds, concerning remedies found on our soil, "The butternut is the only cathartic deserving of confidence which we have yet discovered."

Dr. Thacher made his profession his life-vocation, after the war; and he enjoyed the honors and veneration due to a faithful patriot in that struggle, for more than sixty years after the eventful scenes at Yorktown. He wrote several medical works, and also a *History of Plymouth*. His *Medical Biography* is a work of much value. Through life he indulged an antiquarian taste; and during his long residence in the elder town of New England, he was a warm friend of the Pilgrim Society there. He died at Plymouth, on the 24th of May, 1844, at the age of ninety years.

JAMES MADISON, D.D.

THE first Bishop of the Protestant Episcopal Church in Virginia, was James Madison, a native of Rockingham county, in that State, and for many years president of William and Mary College. He was born near Port Republic, on the 27th of August, 1749. His early education was acquired at an academy in Maryland; and, in 1768, he entered William and Mary College, as a student. He was graduated in 1772, and in addition to other collegiate honors, he received the gold medal assigned by Lord Botetourt as a prize for the encouragement of classical literature. On leaving the college, young Madison commenced the study of law under the afterward celebrated Chancellor Wythe, and was admitted to the bar, but he felt called to the gospel ministry, and prepared himself for its duties. He visited England, and received priest's orders; and on his return, in 1773, he was chosen Professor of Mathematics in William and Mary College. When only twenty-eight years of age (1777), he was chosen president of that institution, and then again visited England to become better instructed in those acquirements which his station demanded. He returned in 1778, and then "commenced that long career of usefulness, which entitles him to be considered as one of the greatest benefactors of Virginia." In 1784, he resigned his Professorship of Mathematics, and became Professor of Natural and Moral Philosophy, and International Law. These and the presidency he retained until his death.

Until 1776, the Church of England had been the established religion in Virginia. That year the Virginia Assembly repealed all laws requiring conformity

---

1. See note 2, page 61.
2. There was also a partial inoculation of the troops stationed at Morristown, in New Jersey.

thereto. There had never been a resident Bishop in Virginia. At a convention held in Richmond, in 1785, presided over by Dr. Madison, the subject of a resident Bishop was considered; and the following year Rev. Dr. Griffith was requested to proceed to England, with White and Provost, and receive consecration. Circumstances prevented his going; and, in 1790, Dr. Madison was elected to fill the episcopate. He was consecrated at Lambeth, in September of that year. Bishop Madison made his first episcopal visitation in 1792. Although he labored with as much energy in the cause of his church, as a naturally feeble constitution and his college duties would allow, it continually declined, and became almost extinct. Many beautiful church edifices, built before the Revolution, are now melancholy monuments of the decay of episcopacy in Virginia. The Protestant Episcopal Church there was finally revived under the evangelical labors of Bishop Moore, and is now in a flourishing condition.

Bishop Madison continued to discharge the duties of his offices in William and Mary College after his occupation in the episcopal field was almost ended. He died on the 6th of March, 1812, at the age of about sixty-two years. Bishop Madison was an eminently literary man, and devout Christian professor. His remains are beneath a marble monument in the Chapel Hall of the Institution he so much loved and cherished.

ABRAHAM BALDWIN.

WE have but slight records on the page of history of Abraham Baldwin, a brother-in-law of Joel Barlow, and, in many respects, one of the most useful of men. He was a native of Connecticut, but became an honored and much-beloved adopted citizen of the State of Georgia. He was born in 1754, and was graduated at Yale College at the age of about eighteen years. From 1775 until 1779, he was a tutor in that institution, and was one of the most eminent of the classical and mathematical scholars of that day. While teaching, he studied law, was admitted to practice, and then removed to Savannah. There he was admitted to the Georgia bar, and took an exalted position at once. Within three months after his arrival in Georgia, he was elected a member of the State legislature. Being an ardent friend of education, he originated a plan for a university, drew up a charter by which it should be endowed with forty thousand acres of land, and with the aid of John Milledge, procured the sanction of the legislature. The college, known as the University of Georgia, was located at Athens, and Josiah Meigs was appointed its first president.

Mr. Baldwin was elected to a seat in Congress, in 1786, and the following year he was chosen to represent Georgia, with Colonel William Few as his colleague, in the convention that framed the Federal Constitution. He was continued a member of Congress for ten years after the organization of the new government, when, in 1799, he and his friend Milledge were chosen United States Senators. He occupied that exalted position until his death, which occurred at Washington city, on the 4th of March, 1807, when he was about fifty-three years of age. His remains were placed by the side of those of his friend, General James Jackson, in the Congressional burying-ground. Mr. Baldwin was never married. His father died in 1787, and left six orphan children, half-brothers and sisters of Abraham. With the tenderness of a father he studied their welfare, and used his ample fortune in educating them all. They enjoyed his protection and aid until all were established for themselves in life-pursuits. A truly *good* man was lost to earth, when Abraham Baldwin died.

DEWITT CLINTON.

THERE are men whose forecast reaches far in advance of their generation, and whose sagacity works wonders for posterity. These are laughed at as idle dreamers by the many, and venerated as philosophers and prophets by the few. Such was Dewitt Clinton, a son of James Clinton, a useful brigadier-general of the Revolution, who was born at Little Britain, in Orange county, New York, on the 2d of March, 1769. He graduated at Columbia College, in 1786, became a lawyer, then private Secretary to his uncle, George Clinton, the first Republican governor of New York, and then a State Senator, in 1799. Even at this early period of his public life, his efforts were directed to the elevation of his fellow-men. Throughout his long political career he was the earnest and steadfast friend of education, and the rights of man. His powerful mind was brought to bear with great vigor upon the subject of legislative aid in furtherance of popular education, and also the abolition of human slavery in the State of New York. In 1801, he was appointed to a seat in the Senate of the United States, and was annually elected mayor of the city of New York, from 1803 to 1815, except in 1807 and 1810. Some of the noblest institutions for the promotion of art, literature, science, and benevolence, in that city, were founded under his auspices.[1]

---

[1]. The chief of these were the New York Historical Society, the Academy of Arts, and the Orphan Asylum. See sketch of Isabella Graham.

He was an unsuccessful candidate for the office of President of the United States, in 1812; and, in 1815, he withdrew from public life.

Mr. Clinton was one of the earliest and most efficient supporters of Jesse Hawley's magnificent scheme for uniting Lake Erie with the Hudson river by a canal, first promulgated by that gentleman, in 1807; and, in 1817, Mr. Clinton having been called from his retirement into public life again, was chiefly instrumental in procuring the passage of a law for constructing the great Erie Canal, at an estimated cost of five millions of dollars. He was elected governor of his State, and for three years, while holding that office, he brought all his official influence to bear in favor of two grand projects—the establishment of a literature fund, and the construction of the canal. A strong party was arrayed against him, and many denounced the scheme of making a canal three hundred and sixty-three miles in length, as that of an insane mind. He and his friends persevered; and, in 1825, that great work was completed. The event was celebrated throughout the State by orations, processions, bonfires, and illuminations, and soon the madman was extolled as a wise benefactor. He was again elected governor of his State, by an overwhelming majority. In 1826, he declined the honor of ambassador to England, offered him by President Adams, and was reëlected governor. He now strongly urged a change in the State Constitution (since effected), so as to allow universal suffrage at elections. While in the midst of his popularity and usefulness, he died suddenly, at Albany, on the 11th of February, 1828, at the age of fifty-nine years. Mr. Clinton was a fine writer, a good speaker, and an industrious seeker after knowledge of every kind. Some of his essays and addresses are choice specimens of composition, embodying deep thought and clear logic. His enduring monument is the Erie Canal, whose bosom has borne sufficient food to appease the hunger of the whole earth, and poured millions of treasure into the coffers of the State.

ÆDANUS BURKE.

THE honest heart, jolly wit, and varied accomplishments of Judge Burke, of South Carolina, are matters of historic record, and cannot be forgotten. He was a native of Galway, Ireland, where he was born about the year 1743. At the commencement of the American Revolution, he came to fight for liberty, for he was a democrat of truest stamp. His heart was filled with the sentiment, "Where liberty dwells, there is my country." He made his abode in Charleston, and was active in the early military events in that vicinity. He was a lawyer by profession, and considering his services more valuable in civil than in military affairs, the provincial legislature appointed him a judge of the Supreme Court of the newly-organized State, in 1778. When Charleston fell, and the South lay prostrate at the feet of British power, in 1780, Judge Burke took a commission in the army. He resumed the judicial office when the Republicans regained the State, early in 1782. He was opposed to the Federal Constitution, because he feared consolidated power, yet he served as the first United States Senator from South Carolina, under that instrument. His Federalist friends told him that he had been sent to see that the corruptions and abuses which he had predicted should not be practiced. He had already made his name conspicuous by his published essay against some of the aristocratic features of the Cincinnati Society; and while in Congress he was the favorite friend of Aaron Burr. He afterward became Chancellor of the State of North Carolina. Wit, humor, and conviviality, were his distinguishing social characteristics. The former were ever visible whether he was on the bench or in the drawing-room; while the latter finally became such a habit that he was its slave. He lived a bachelor, and was the soul of every dinner-party, whether abroad or at his own house. Inebriation finally clouded his intellect, and at length his body became excessively dropsical. On one occasion, when his physician had "tapped" him, and while the water was flowing freely, the judge coolly observed, "I wonder where all that water can come from, as I am sure that I never drank as much since I arrived at years of discretion." On being assured by one of his friends that he would be better after the operation, he replied, "Nothing in my house is better after being *tapped.*" His levity continued until his last moments, and he died as "the fool dieth" because he had "lived as the fool liveth." He was one of many sad examples which young men of talent should study as warnings. He died at Charleston, on the 30th of March, 1802, at the age of fifty-nine years, and was buried in the grave-yard of the Episcopal Church, near Jacksonborough.[1]

JOHN TRUMBULL.

THE name of Trumbull is identified with the history of New England, in various ways. We have already given sketches of the *governor* and the *artist*, of that name; we will now consider Trumbull the *poet.* He was born in Watertown, New Haven county, Connecticut, on the 24th of April, 1750. He was an only son, delicate in physical constitution, and a favorite of his accomplished mother. He was an exceedingly precocious child, and at the age of seven years was considered qualified to enter Yale College, as a student. There he was graduated, in 1767, with the degree of Bachelor of Arts, and remained a student three years longer. He turned his attention chiefly to polite literature, as well as the Greek and Latin classics, and became a most accomplished scholar. He and Timothy Dwight became intimate friends, and the bond of mutual attachment was severed only by death. They were co-essayists, in 1769; and, in 1771, they were both appointed tutors in the college. The following year young Trumbull published the first part of a poem entitled *The Progress of Dulness.* He selected the law as his profession, and devoted much of his leisure time to its study. He was admitted to the bar in 1773, but immediately afterward went to Boston, and placed himself under the instruction of John Adams. He commenced the practice of law at Hartford, in 1781, and soon became distinguished for legal acumen and forensic eloquence. During his residence in Boston, he had conceived the idea of a satirical poem, in which the British and Tories should figure conspicuously; and, in 1782, his *M'Fingal* was completed, and published at Hartford. He was soon afterward associated with Humphreys, Barlow, and Dr. Lemuel Hopkins, in the production of a work which they styled *The Anarchiad.* It contained bold satire, and exerted considerable influence on the popular taste.

In 1789, Mr. Trumbull was appointed State Attorney for the county of Hartford; and, in 1792, he represented that district in the Connecticut legislature. His health failed; and, in 1795, he resigned his office, and declined all public business. Toward the close of 1798, a severe illness formed the crisis of his

---

1. Many anecdotes are preserved concerning Judge Burke's absent-mindedness. It was the custom for the judges in Charleston, during the sessions, to leave their gowns at a dry-goods store near the court-house, when they went to their meals. The owner of this store was Miss Van Rhyn, a middle-aged maiden lady, who carefully hung the judicial robes upon pegs where her own clothing was suspended. On one occasion, Judge Burke took down his robe (as he supposed) hastily, went with it under his arm, and proceeded to array himself preparatory to the opening of the court. He found much difficulty in getting it on, when all at once he exclaimed, before an audience uproarious with laughter, "Before God, I have got into Miss Van Rhyn's petticoat!"

nervous excitement, and after that his health was much better. He was again elected to a seat in the State legislature, in May, 1800, and the following year he was appointed a judge of the Superior Court of Connecticut. From that time he abandoned party politics, as inconsistent with judicial duties. In 1808, he was appointed judge of the Supreme Court of Errors. In 1820, he revised his works, and they were published in Hartford, in handsome style, by S. G. Goodrich, now [1854] American consul at Paris. He received a handsome compensation for them. He and his wife afterward went to Detroit, and made their abode with a son-in-law. There Judge Trumbull died, on the 10th of May, 1831, at the age of eighty-one years.

STEPHEN VAN RENSSELAER.

FIFTH in lineal descent from Killian Van Rensselaer, the earliest and best known of the American *Patroons*,[1] was Stephen Van Rensselaer, one of the best men of his time, in the highest sense of that term. He was born at the manor-house, near Albany, New York, on the 1st of November, 1764. He was the eldest son, and inherited the immense manorial estates of his father, known as the *Patroon Lands*. That parent died when Stephen was quite young, and the boy and the estate were placed under the supervision of guardians, one of whom was Philip Livingston, his maternal grandfather. Born to a princely fortune and highest social station in the New World, young Van Rensselaer was educated accordingly. He was a student in the college at Princeton, for some time, and completed his education at Harvard University, where he was graduated in 1782. The War for Independence had just closed when he attained his majority, but the conflicts of opinion respecting the establishment of a new government had yet to be waged. In these discussions Mr. Van Rensselaer took a decided and active part, and he was repeatedly elected to a seat in the New York Assembly. He was a warm supporter of the Federal Constitution, and battled manfully for it and the administration of Washington, side by side with Hamilton, Jay, and Madison. In 1795, he was elected lieutenant-governor of his native State, when John Jay was chief magistrate, and he held that station six years. His friends predicted for him, a brilliant official career, but the defeat of the Federal party, in 1800, and the continued ascendency of the Republican, closed his way to distinction through the mazes of political warfare.

When war was declared against Great Britain, in 1812, Mr. Van Rensselaer, bearing the commission of a major-general, was placed, by Governor Tompkins, in command of the New York militia, destined for the defence of the northern frontier. Those were a part of his troops, under General Solomon Van Rensselaer, who assisted in the battle at Queenstown. After the war, General Van Rensselaer was elected to a seat in the Federal Congress, where he served his country during several consecutive sessions. By his casting-vote in the delegation of New York, he gave the presidency of the United States to John Quincy Adams. With that session closed the political life of Stephen Van Rensselaer, but he still labored on and hoped on in the higher sphere of duty of a benevolent Christian. Like his Master whom he loved, he was ever "meek and lowly," and "went

---

1. To encourage the emigration of an agricultural population to New Netherland (as New York was originally called), the Dutch West India Company, under whose auspices the province was founded, granted to certain persons who should lead or send a certain number of families to make a settlement in America, large tracts of land with specified social and political privileges. Among the directors of the company who availed themselves of the offer, was Killian Van Rensselaer, who became the proprietor of Rensselaerwick, a territory in the vicinity of Albany about forty-eight miles long, and twenty-four wide. It was established in 1637, and the proprietor was called a *Patroon*, or patron; a name derived from the civil law of Rome, which was given to owners of large landed estates.

about doing good." Frugal in personal expenditures, he was lavish, yet discriminating, in his numerous benefactions. He did not wait for Misery to call at his door; he sought out the children of Want. To the poor and the ignorant he was a blessing. In 1824, he founded a seminary for the purpose of "qualifying teachers for instructing the children of farmers and mechanics in the application of experimental chemistry, philosophy, and natural history, to agriculture, domestic economy, the arts, and manufactures." He liberally endowed it, and the "*Rensselaer School*" is a perpetual hymn to the memory and praise of its benefactor. In the cause of the Bible, Temperance, and every social and moral reform, Mr. Van Rensselaer's time and money were freely given; and in these labors he continued until death. He was an early and efficient friend of internal improvements, and, on the death of Dewitt Clinton, he was appointed president of the Board of Canal Commissioners. He held that station during the remainder of his life. That "good citizen and honest man" died on the 26th of January, 1840, in the seventy-fifth year of his age.

WASHINGTON ALLSTON.

NO man ever possessed a more exquisite appreciation of the Beautiful, than Washington Allston, one of the most gifted of painters, and yet no man ever kept the Beautiful in more severe subordination to the Good and True, in the productions of both his pencil and pen. That appreciation made him shrink from frequent efforts in the higher department of his art, for he felt the impuissance of his hand in the delineations of the glorious visions of his genius. It has been well observed by Professor Shedd, that Allston accomplished so little, because he thought so much. This gifted painter and poet was born in South Carolina, in 1780, and was educated at Harvard College, where he was graduated in the year 1800. His genius for art was early developed; and, in 1801, he went to Europe, to study the works of the best masters there. He remained abroad eight years, and enjoyed the friendship of the most distinguished poets and painters of England and the Continent. In painting, West, Reynolds, and Fuseli were his instructors; and Wordsworth, Southey, and Coleridge, were his chief literary companions. No private American ever made a better or more lasting impression abroad, than Washington Allston. As a colorist, he was styled the American Titian. A small volume of his poems was issued in London, in 1813; and in later productions of his pen, he exhibited a power in writing elegant prose, surpassed by few. But he is chiefly known to the world as a painter, and as such posterity will speak of him. His chief works are *The Dead Man restored to Life by Elijah; Elijah in the Desert; Jacob's Dream; The Angel liberating Peter from Prison; Saul and the Witch of Endor; Uriel in the Sun; Gabriel setting the Guard of the Heavenly Host; Spalatro's Vision of the Bloody Hand; Anne Page*, and several exquisite smaller works. He was engaged on his greatest work—*Belshazzar's Feast*—when his final sickness fell upon him, and he was not permitted to finish it. It exhibits great powers of intellect and taste; and, as far as it is completed, it presents the embodiment of the highest conceptions of true genius. Most of his life was spent at Cambridge, Massachusetts, where he was educated; and there the "painter-poet and the poet-painter" left earth for the sphere of Intelligence and Beauty, on the 9th of July, 1843, when in the sixty-fourth year of his age.

WILLIAM MOULTRIE.

SEVERAL of those who, during the War for Independence, acted its history, have since written its history, and the truths of those great events can never be obscured by the fictions of posterity. Among those who have played that two-fold part in the drama recorded in our annals, is William Moultrie, whose valor won the honor of having the fort he defended bear his name. He was a native of South Carolina, where he was born, in 1730. He was descended from one of that Huguenot company of which Marion's ancestor was a member, and inherited the patient endurance, courage, and love of liberty of that persecuted people. History first notices him as a subaltern in an expedition against the Cherokee Indians, in 1760, under the command of Governor Littleton. He was also prominent in subsequent expeditions against that unhappy people. He was active in civil affairs before the Revolution; and, when the hour for decision in that matter came, he was found in the ranks of the patriots as a military officer. When, early in the Summer of 1776, a strong land and naval force menaced Charleston, Moultrie, bearing the commission of a colonel, took command of Fort Sullivan, in the harbor, and bravely defended it while cannons on British war-vessels were pouring an incessant storm of iron upon it.[1] For that gallant defence he was promoted to a brigadier, and the fort was named *Moultrie*, in his honor.[2] From that time until the fall of Charleston, in 1780, General Moultrie was one of the most efficient of the Southern officers, on the field of action, or as a disciplinarian in camp. After the surrender of Charleston, he was kept a prisoner in the vicinity, for awhile, and was then paroled to Philadelphia, where he remained until the close of hostilities, in 1782. After his return home he was chosen governor of his native State, and was repeatedly reëlected to that office. His integrity as a statesman and public officer was a bright example; his disinterestedness was beyond all praise. His fellow-citizens honored him with truest reverence, and his intimate acquaintances loved him for his many private virtues. The infirmities of age at length admonished him to retire to private life; and in domestic repose he prepared his *Memoirs* of the Revolution in the South, which were published in two octavo volumes, in 1802. Like a bright sun setting without an obscuring cloud, the hero and sage descended peacefully to his final rest, on the 27th of September, 1805, at the age of seventy-five years.

JOHN LAMB.

THE *Sons of Liberty* in New York were distinguished for their loyalty to republican principles, their zeal in the promotion of popular freedom, and their boldness in every hour of difficulty and danger. Among the most fearless of those early patriots was John Lamb, son of an eminent optician and mathematical instrument maker. He was born in the city of New York, on the 1st of January, 1735. He received a good common education, and learned the business of his father. He abandoned it in 1760, and became an extensive wine merchant. Through all the exciting times until the kindling of the War for Independence, Mr. Lamb was extensively engaged in the liquor trade, and, at the same time, was one of the most active politicians of the day, after the passage of the Stamp Act had aroused the American people. He spoke French and German fluently, was a good scholar, and was exceedingly expert in the use of his tongue and pen. These he devoted to the public good. On one occasion, in 1769, when an inflammatory hand-bill had called "the betrayed inhabitants to the fields,"[3] Lamb harangued the multitude in seditious words. He was taken before the Legislative Assembly to testify concerning the authorship of the hand-bill, but was soon discharged.[4] This event intensified his zeal, and he continued

---

1. During the action, a cannon ball cut the American flag-staff, and the banner fell outside of the fort. Sergeant William Jasper, of Moultrie's regiment, immediately leaped down from the parapet, picked up the flag while the balls were falling thick and fast, coolly fastened it to a sponge staff, and unfurled it again over the bastion of the fort. For this daring feat, Governor Rutledge presented Jasper with his own sword, the next day, and offered him a lieutenant's commission. The young hero modestly refused it, saying, "I can neither read nor write; I am not fit to keep officers' company; I am only a sergeant."
2. On the day when the enemy departed from Charleston, Mrs. Bernard Elliott (a niece of Mrs. Rebecca Motte), presented General Moultrie's regiment with a pair of elegant silk colors, wrought by the ladies of Charleston. These were afterward planted upon the fortifications at Savannah, when Lincoln and D'Estaing besieged that city, in October, 1779. Both the young officers who bore them were killed. Sergeant Jasper was there, and, seizing one of them, he mounted a bastion, when he, too, was killed by a bullet. These flags were surrendered at Charleston, in 1780, and were afterward trophies in the Tower of London.
3. The ground now occupied by the City Hall and its surrounding Park was called "the fields." There a "Liberty Pole" was erected, and there the popular assemblages were held.
4. The hand-bill was written by Alexander MacDougall, afterward a general in the Continental army.

to be an accepted political leader until 1775, when he entered the artillery service of the army, with the commission of captain. He accompanied Montgomery to Quebec at the close of that year. He was severely wounded there, in the cheek, by a grape-shot, and was made prisoner. Soon after that he was promoted to major, and appointed to the command of the artillery in the Northern Department, but was not exchanged, and allowed to enter the service again, until early in 1777, when Congress gave him the commission of lieutenant-colonel, under the immediate command of General Knox. We cannot here even enumerate his multifarious duties, as commander of artillery, during the remainder of the war. It is sufficient to say that he was everywhere brave and skilful, and shared in the dangers and honors of the final victory at Yorktown. He was as warm a politician after the war as before it, and served his fellow-citizens faithfully in the legislature of his native State. After the organization of the federal government, Washington appointed him collector of customs at the port of New York, and he held that office until his death, on the 31st of May, 1800, at the age of sixty-five years. Then a patriot of truest stamp was lost to the world.

RED JACKET.

THE renowned Seneca warrior and orator, *Sa-go-ye-wa-thee*, the Red Jacket,[1] was born about the year 1750, near the spot where the city of Buffalo now stands, that being the chief place of residence of the Seneca leaders. Tradition alone has preserved a few facts concerning his youth. He was always remarkably swift-footed, and was often employed as a courier among his own people. He took part with the British and Tories during the Revolution, but was more noted for his power as an orator in arousing the Senecas to action, than as a leader upon the war-path. Brant, whom Red Jacket's ambition greatly annoyed, even charged him with cowardice during Sullivan's campaign in the Seneca country, in 1779, and always spoke of Red Jacket with mingled feelings of hatred and contempt, as a traitor and dishonest man.[2] The celebrated Seneca first appears in history in the record of Sullivan's campaign, and then in an unfavorable light. After that we have no trace of him until 1784, when he appeared at the great treaty at Fort Stanwix (now Rome), where, by certain concessions of territory by the Six Nations, they were brought under the protection of the United States. There the eloquence of Red Jacket beamed forth in great splendor; and there, too, the voice of the eloquent Cornplanter[3] was heard. Red Jacket was prominent at a council held at the mouth of the Detroit river, in 1786. After that there were many disputes and heart-burnings between the white people and the Indians of Western New York, concerning land titles, and Red Jacket was always the eloquent defender of the rights of his people. At all treaties and councils he was the chief orator. He frequently visited the seat

---

1. This name was given him from the circumstance that a British officer, toward the close of the Revolution, gave him a richly-embroidered scarlet jacket, which he took great pleasure in wearing. Others were presented to him, as one was worn out; and even as late as the treaty at Canandaigua, in 1794, Captain Parish, one of the United States' interpreters, gave him one. The red jacket became his distinctive dress, and procured him the name by which he is best known.
2. Thomas Morris says that Red Jacket was called the cow-killer from the circumstance that, having on one occasion during the Revolution, aroused his people to fight, was found, during the engagement, in a place of safety, cutting up a cow that he had killed, which belonged to another Indian. When Cornplanter, Brant, and Red Jacket, were at Morris' table, one day, Cornplanter told the story, as if another Indian had committed the act. The narrator and Brant laughed heartily, and Red Jacket endeavored to join them, but was evidently very much embarrassed.
3. See sketch of Cornplanter.

of our national government, in behalf of his race, and was always treated with the utmost respect.[1]

Unlike Cornplanter, Red Jacket's paganism never yielded to the gentle influences of Christianity, and he was the most inveterate enemy to all missionary efforts among the Senecas. He had become a slave to strong drink, and he attributed the prevalence of the vice among his people to the missionaries, who, he said, sold liquor to the Indians, and cheated them of property. On the breaking out of the war, in 1812, the Senecas, under the leadership of Red Jacket, declared themselves neutral, but they soon became allies of the United States, and engaged in hostilities on the Canada frontier. Red Jacket was in the bloody battle at Chippewa, and behaved well, but he seems to have been constitutionally a coward, and was always far braver in council than in the field. Yet this cowardice in battle, though well known to the nation, did not lessen their affection for him, nor materially weaken his influence as head Chief of the Senecas.

Red Jacket had a large family of children, some of whom, like their mother, became professing Christians.[2] Eleven of them died of that terrible disease, the *consumption*, one after another, and Red Jacket felt his bereavement to be the chastisement of the Great Spirit for his habitual drunkenness. On being asked about his family, by a lady who once knew them, the chief said, sorrowfully, "Red

---

[1]. On one occasion, Washington presented a large silver medal to Red Jacket, bearing the representation of a white man and an Indian shaking hands, and the names of Washington and Red Jacket engraved upon it.

[2]. His second wife became a professed Christian, in 1826. She is represented as a woman of remarkable personal dignity and superiority of mind. Her conversion alienated her husband for several months, and he resided some distance from her. He finally thought better of it, asked and obtained her forgiveness, and they lived in perfect harmony afterward.

Jacket was once a great man, and in favor with the Great Spirit. He was a lofty pine among the smaller trees of the forest. But after years of glory he degraded himself by drinking the fire-water of the white man. *The Great Spirit has looked upon him in anger, and his lightning has stripped the pine of its branches!*"

The influence of Christianity and civilization upon the Seneca nation disturbed the repose of Red Jacket, during the latter part of his life. These influences, working with a general disgust produced by his excessive intemperance, alienated his people; and, in 1827, he was formally deposed.[1] It was a dreadful blow to the proud chief, and he went to Washington city to invoke the aid of government in his behalf. He returned with good advice in his memory, obtained a grand council, and was restored to authority. But his days were almost numbered. He soon afterward became imbecile, and, in a journey to the Atlantic sea-board, he permitted himself to be exhibited in museums, for money! At last the greatest of all Indian orators was called away. He died on the 20th of January, 1830, at the age of about eighty years. Over his grave, Henry Placide, the comedian, placed an inscribed slab of marble, in 1839.

HENRY CRUGER.

ONE of the chief grievances of which the American colonists complained was the fact that they were compelled to suffer *taxation*, without enjoying the privilege of *representation*, and were thus, practically, the victims of tyranny. Yet they *were* represented by a few, in the British parliament, when the quarrel which resulted in dismemberment was progressing, but of that few, only one was a native of the western world. It was Henry Cruger, who was born in the city of New York, in 1739. On arriving at manhood, he joined his father, who had established himself as a merchant in the American trade, at Bristol, England. The elder Cruger was highly esteemed, and became mayor of Bristol; an honor afterward bestowed upon his son. It is worthy of remark here, that father and son, belonging to another branch of the Cruger family, were, at about the same time, successively honored with the mayoralty of the city of New York.

In 1774, Henry Cruger was elected to a seat in Parliament, as representative of the city of Bristol, having for his colleague the afterward eminent Edmund Burke. That then fledgling statesman was introduced at the hustings by Mr. Cruger, and delivered an address at the conclusion, which elicited warm applause. It is reported that a gentleman present exclaimed, "I say ditto to Mr. Burke." That laconic sentence became a "bye-word," and was erroneously attributed to Mr. Cruger. The speeches of Mr. Cruger, in Parliament, were marked by sound common sense and great logical force; and on all occasions he urged the necessity of a conciliatory course toward the Americans. Like Lord Chatham, he deprecated a severance of the colonies from the British realm; but, in 1780, when the continuance of union became impossible, he declared that "the American war should be put an end to, at all events, in order to do which the independency must be allowed, and the thirteen provinces treated as free States." His course pleased his constituents, who, on various occasions, testified their warmest approbation. After the war, he returned to his native city, and was elected a member of the Senate of the State of New York. He died in the city

---

1. The act of deposition, written in the Seneca language, was signed by twenty-six chief men of "";

of New York, on the 24th of April, 1827, at the age of eighty-eight years. His brother, John Harris Cruger, who was in the British military service previous to the Revolution, adhered to the crown, and was in command of a corps of Loyalists at the South. He held the commission of a lieutenant-colonel, and commanded the garrison at Fort Ninety-Six when it was besieged by General Greene. Colonel Cruger was a son-in-law of Colonel Oliver Delancey. He died in London, in 1807, at the age of sixty-nine years. His wife died at Chelsea, England, in 1822, at the age of seventy-eight years.

JAMES A. BAYARD.

WHEN, in 1814, the American and British governments resolved to close an unprofitable and fratricidal war, by a treaty of peace, the most accomplished statesmen in the Union were chosen commissioners, to meet those of Great Britain, at Ghent, in Belgium, to negotiate. On that commission was James A. Bayard, an eminent statesman of Delaware. He was born in the city of Philadelphia, on the 28th of July, 1767. At a very early age he became an orphan, and was adopted by an affectionate uncle, who took special care to have him thoroughly educated. His studies were completed in the College at Princeton, New Jersey, where he was graduated with the highest honors, in 1784, at the age of seventeen years. He chose the profession of law, studied it with great assiduity, under General Joseph Reed and Jared Ingersoll, and was admitted to the bar, in August, 1787. He was married in 1795, and the following year he was a successful Federal candidate for a seat in Congress, where he first appeared in May, 1797. There he was noted for his industry, integrity, and consistency; and during his services as a member of the House of Representatives, from 1797 until 1804, no man was more highly esteemed for talents and personal worth than Mr. Bayard.

When, in the Winter of 1801, the choice between Jefferson and Burr, the Republican candidates for President of the United States, devolved upon the House of Representatives, and Mr. Bayard and three other Federal members held the choice in their own hands, his colleagues submitted the matter to his judgment, and he fortunately gave the office to Jefferson. A few days afterward President Adams appointed Mr. Bayard minister plenipotentiary to France, but he patriotically declined it for political reasons. In 1804, he was elected to a seat in the United States Senate, to fill a vacancy; and, in February, 1805, he was reëlected for the full term of six years. In that body, also, he was an esteemed leader; and, in 1811, the legislature of Delaware again elected him United States Senator, for another full term. He opposed the declaration of war against Great Britain, in 1812, but, when a majority in Congress gave sanction to the measure, he cheerfully acquiesced, and, it is said, actually labored with his own hands in the erection of defences at Wilmington, where he resided. In 1813, the Emperor of Russia offered his mediation between the United States and Great Britain, and Mr. Bayard and Albert Gallatin were sent to St. Petersburg to negotiate. There they remained six months, when, hearing nothing from England, they proceeded to Amsterdam. They arrived in that city in March, 1814. There they were informed that England would not accept the mediation of Russia, but was ready to treat for peace with the United States. They were also informed that Messrs. Adams, Clay, and Russell, had been added to the commission. All finally met with the British commissioners at Ghent, in August, 1814, where they remained until the 24th of December following, when a treaty was agreed upon and signed.[1] Fourteen days afterward, Mr. Bayard left Ghent for Paris; and on the 4th of March, 1815, while in that city, he was seized with a fatal, but lingering disease. He waited there until duty should call him to London to negotiate a treaty of commerce, with which service the commission had been charged. Greatly debilitated, he reached England at the middle of May, where he was met by a commission, appointing him minister to Russia. Feeling that death was now rapidly approaching, he declined the honor, and hastened home. He arrived at Wilmington on the 1st of August, where his family received him with mingled tears of joy and grief, after an absence of more than two years. Five days afterward he departed to that distant land beyond the grave, from which there is no return. He died on the 6th of August, 1815, when a little more than forty-eight years of age.

ELIAS HICKS.

THE Society of Friends, commonly called Quakers, having but one accepted standard of faith and discipline, were remarkable for their unity until about 1825, when Elias Hicks, a distinguished and influential preacher, boldly enunciated Unitarian doctrines. This produced much dissatisfaction, and the hitherto united and peaceful society exhibited two parties, styled respectively *Orthodox*, or Trinitarians, and *Hicksites*, or Unitarians, and was agitated by much and violent party feelings. The breach widened, and finally a separation took place. The two parties assumed distinct organizations, and the Unitarians, being in the majority, generally took possession of the meeting-houses, and compelled the Orthodox to erect new ones. The breach still continues.

Elias Hicks was born in Hempstead, Long Island, on the 19th of March, 1748. Of his early life we have no record, except that it was passed in the quiet pursuits of a farmer. He was married in January, 1771, and at about that period was acknowledged a member of the Society of Friends. Four years afterward he first appeared as a minister; and for fifty-three years he was a teacher among his brethren. During that time he travelled extensively throughout the United States and Upper Canada; and at the age of eighty years he visited his brethren and sisters in New Jersey, Pennsylvania, Maryland, Ohio, and Indiana, like Paul, "confirming them in the faith.". Soon after his return home, his wife died, and the following Summer he visited the northern and western parts of the State of New York, everywhere preaching with great clearness and power. The writer heard him at that time, and remembers well how logically he set forth the doctrine which he had espoused and then ably advocated. His labors ceased six months afterward. On the 4th of February, 1830, he wrote a long and interesting letter to a Western friend, and immediately afterward his whole right side was smitten with paralysis. He died on the 27th of the same month, aged eighty-two years. During his ministry, he travelled almost ten thousand miles, and delivered at least one thousand discourses.[2]

---

1. Bayard's colleagues were John Quincy Adams, Henry Clay, Jonathan Russell, and Albert Gallatin. Those of Great Britain were Lord Gambier, Henry Goulbourn, and William Adams.
2. An anecdote is told which illustrates his conscientiousness. He was informed by his son-in-law that a man who owed them both had become a bankrupt, "but," said the son, "he has secured thee and me." "Has he secured all?" inquired the old man. On receiving a reply in the negative, he said, "That is not right;" and he insisted upon the creditors placing him and his son-in-law on the same footing with others.

COUNT RUMFORD.

BY industry, perseverance, and integrity, working in harmony with genius and a truly benevolent spirit, Benjamin Thompson, a humble New Hampshire schoolmaster, became a "Count of the Holy Roman Empire," and a companion of kings and philosophers. He was born at Woburn, Massachusetts, on the 28th of March, 1753. His widowed mother was in comfortable circumstances, and the common school furnished him with an elementary education. He was a merchant's clerk, at Salem, for awhile, and then commenced the study of medical science in his native town. He attended lectures at Cambridge, in 1771, and employed a portion of his time in teaching schools, first at Wilmington, and then at Bradford. He was finally invited to take charge of a school at Rumford (now Concord), in New Hampshire. The fame of his philosophical experiments already made preceded him, and his handsome face, noble person, and grace of manners, made him a favorite. Before he was twenty years of age, he was the husband of a young and wealthy widow, daughter of Rev. Timothy Walker, minister of the town. His talent and this connection gave him high social position, at once, and he found leisure to pursue scientific investigations. Thus he was employed when the storms of the Revolution began to gather darkly. The time came when he must make public choice of party—be active, or suffer suspicion. With conscientious motives, he declined to act with the

Whigs. His neutrality was construed as opposition, and he was finally compelled to fly, for personal safety, to the protection of the British, in Boston, leaving behind him all he held most dear on earth—mother, wife, child, friends, and fortune. That persecution, under Providence, led to his greatness.

Mr. Thompson remained in Boston until the Spring of 1776, when General Howe sent him to England with important despatches for the British ministry concerning the evacuation of the New England capital. The ministry appreciated his worth, and scientific men sought his acquaintance. He was offered public employment, and accepted it; and in less than four years after he landed in England, a homeless exile, he was made Under-Secretary of State. In 1782, he was in America a short time, but could not see his family. The following year he went to Germany, bearing letters of introduction from eminent men in England. He was introduced to the Elector of Bavaria, who at once offered him honorable employment in his service. He repaired to England to ask permission to accept it, received the favor, and was knighted by the king. Soon after his return to Munich he entered upon public service, and the "Yankee schoolmaster," like Joseph, became the second man in the kingdom. The Elector made him Lieutenant-General; Commander-in-chief of the Staff; Minister of War; Member of the Council of State; a Knight of Poland; Member of the Academy of Sciences in three cities; Commander-in-chief of the General Staff; Superintendent of the Police of Bavaria, and Chief of the Regency during the sovereign's compulsory absence, in 1796. He accomplished great civil and military reforms, in Bavaria; and during his ten years' service, he produced such salutary changes in the condition of the people, that he won the unbounded love and admiration of all classes.[1] When, in 1796, Munich was assailed by an Austrian army, Sir Benjamin Thompson commanded the Bavarian troops, and he conducted the defence so successfully that he won the highest praises throughout Europe. The Bavarian monarch attested his appreciation of his great services, by creating him a Count of the Holy Roman Empire. He chose the name of the birth-place of his wife and child for his title, and henceforth he was known as Count of Rumford.

In 1792, Sir Benjamin had heard of the death of his wife. He had soon afterward visited England, on account of ill-health, where he remained some time, engaged in scientific pursuits. From there, in 1794, he wrote to his daughter, the infant he left behind, to join him. She did so, early in 1796. She was then a charming girl of twenty years, and, with a father's pride, he conveyed her to Munich, introduced her at court, and placed her at the head of his household. Ill health again compelled him to travel, and he went to England, bearing the highly honorable commission of Bavarian minister at the court of St. James. He could not be received, as such, for the laws of English citizenship would not allow it. At about that time he received an invitation from the American government to visit his native land. Circumstances prevented his compliance, and he again went to Munich, where he remained until the death of the Elector, in 1799, when he quitted Bavaria forever. He went to Paris, married the widow of the celebrated Lavoisier, and at a beautiful villa at Auteil, near Paris, he passed the remainder of his days in literary and scientific pursuits, and in the society of the most learned men in Europe. There he died, on the 21st of August, 1814, in the sixty-second year of his age. His daughter inherited his

---

1. He established a military workhouse at Manheim, and, by stringent, yet benevolent regulations, he almost totally abolished vagrancy and mendicity from Munich, which had ever been noted for these nuisances. In the exercise of his good taste and enterprise, he greatly adorned and beautified Munich. A barren waste near the city was converted into a charming park for the enjoyment of the people, and there pleasure-gardens bloomed. To express their gratitude for these various reformatory efforts, the nobility and other principal inhabitants of Munich erected a handsome monument, with appropriate inscriptions upon it, commemorative of his deeds, within the beautiful pleasure-grounds he had given them.

large fortune, and the title of Countess of Rumford.[1] After many vicissitudes in Europe, she returned to her native land, and died at Concord, on the 2d of December, 1852, at the age of seventy years.[2] The death of Count Rumford, says Professor Renwick, deprived "mankind of one of its eminent benefactors, and science of one of its brightest ornaments."

STEPHEN GIRARD.

IT is honorable to be wealthy, when wealth is honorably acquired, and when it is used for laudable or noble purposes. One of the most eminent possessors of great riches, among the comparatively few in this country, was Stephen Girard of Philadelphia, where the memory of his opulence is perpetuated by a college bearing his name. He was a native of France, and was born near Bordeaux, on the 24th of May, 1750. He was the child of a peasant, and the only school in which he was educated was the great world of active life. When about eleven years of age he left his native country, and sailed as a cabin-boy for the West Indies. He afterward went to New York, and spent several years in voyages between that port and the West Indies and New Orleans, as cabin-boy, seaman, mate, and finally as master. Having saved some money, he opened a small shop in Philadelphia, in 1769, and the next year he married the beautiful daughter of a caulker. His own asperity of temper made their connubial life unhappy. She became insane, in 1790, and died in the Philadelphia hospital, in 1815, leaving no children.

After his marriage, Girard occasionally sailed to the West Indies, as master of his own vessel. On one occasion he was captured, and, after awhile, returned home poor. After the war of the Revolution, he and his brother carried on a profitable trade with St. Domingo; and on their dissolution of partnership, Stephen continued the business on his own account. While two of his vessels were there, in 1804, the great revolt of the negroes, which resulted in the massacre of the white people, took place. Many planters who sent their valuables on board his vessels never lived to claim them, for whole families were destroyed. A large sum of money was thus placed in his possession and never called for. He afterward engaged extensively and successfully in the East India trade; and, in 1812, he opened his own private bank, in Philadelphia, with a capital of one million two hundred thousand dollars. When the new United States Bank was started, in 1816, he subscribed for stock to the amount of over three millions of

---

1. In addition to ample provisions for his mother, Count Rumford gave the American Academy of Arts and Sciences five thousand dollars, in 1796, and also very liberally endowed a professorship in Harvard University. The Rumford Professorship in that institution was established in 1816.
2. The residence of Miss Sarah Thompson, Countess of Rumford, was a beautiful villa on the banks of the Merrimac, south of the village of Concord. A gentleman of the highest respectability, who was intimately acquainted with that lady, informs me that it was her firm belief that her father did not die in France, as is supposed. She related that on hearing of the death of her father, she repaired to Autenil, but the servants could not show his grave, and their conduct appeared mysterious. She afterward went to England, and lived in a house that belonged to her father, at Brompton, and which was bequeathed to her in his Will. An adjoining landholder soon afterward claimed the property, and took legal steps to eject her. Without solicitation on her part, one of the most distinguished lawyers in London espoused her cause, secured a verdict in her favor, and refused any compensation. Fourteen years after the reported death of her father, the Countess, while repairing her house, was looking out of a window upon a neighboring dwelling, when she *plainly saw the Count at a window*. He immediately stepped back, out of sight. When she recovered from her surprise, she rushed to the street, and hastened toward the house where she saw her father. At that moment he *stepped into a coach*, and she never saw him afterward. The Countess fully believed that he had probably become entangled in some political coil in France, found it necessary to retire from the world, had his death reported, and lived *incognito* in London, and sometimes at Brompton. She believed that he had kept a vigilant eye over her welfare, and that he employed and paid the eminent London barrister, who managed her suit at Brompton. She died in the belief that her father was yet alive, in 1852, when she so distinctly saw him at Brompton.

dollars, which immensely augmented in value. The capital of his own bank finally reached four millions of dollars. In all his pecuniary transactions, Mr. Girard was successful, if accumulation is the test of success. He left behind a fortune of about nine millions of dollars, a very small portion of which was bequeathed to his relatives. Few of them received more than ten thousand dollars each, except a favorite niece, to whom he gave sixty thousand dollars. The city of Philadelphia, in trust, was his chief legatee. He left two millions of dollars, "or more if necessary," to build and endow a college for the education and maintenance of "poor male orphan children," to be "received between the ages of six and ten, and to be bound out between the ages of fourteen and eighteen, to suitable occupations, as those of agriculture, navigation, arts, mechanical trades, and manufactures."[1] Mr. Girard died in Philadelphia, of influenza, on the 26th of December, 1831, in the eighty-second year of his age.

JOHN JAMES AUDUBON.

BARON CUVIER, the great naturalist, paid a just tribute of praise to Audubon's work, *The Birds of America*, when he said, "It is the most gigantic and most magnificent monument that has ever been erected to Nature." The man who reared it possessed genius of the highest order, and his name and deeds will be remembered as long as the Bird of Washington soars in the firmament, or the swallow twitters in the barn.

John James Audubon was born in New Orleans, on the 4th of May, 1780, of French parents in opulent circumstances. From infantile years he was ever delighted with the song and plumage of birds; and his educated father fostered that taste which afterward led him to fame, by describing the habits of the tenants of the woods, and explaining the peculiarities of different species. At the age of fifteen years young Audubon was sent to Paris to complete his education. There he enjoyed instruction in art, for two years, under the celebrated David. When about eighteen years of age he returned to America, and soon afterward his father gave him a farm on the banks of the Schuylkill, at the mouth of Perkioming creek, not far from Philadelphia. His time was chiefly spent in forest roamings, with his gun and drawing materials. The study of birds had become a passion, and the endearments of a home, presided over by a young wife, could not keep him from the woods, whither he went at early dawn, and returned wet with the evening dews.

In 1809, Mr. Audubon went to Louisville, Kentucky, to reside, where he remained about two years in a mercantile connection, but spending most of his time in the woods. There, in March, 1810, he first saw Wilson, the great ornithologist.[2] A few months afterward he moved further up the Ohio to the verge of the wilderness, and then commenced in earnest that nomadic life in the prosecution of his great study, which marked him as a true hero. With gun, knapsack, and drawing materials, he traversed the dark forests and pestiferous fens, sleeping

---

1. Mr. Girard has been much censured because he directed, in his Will, "that no ecclesiastic, missionary, or minister, of any sect whatsoever, shall ever hold or exercise any station or duty whatever in said college; nor shall any such person ever be admitted, for any purpose, or as a visitor, within the premises appropriated to the purpose of said college." Mr. Girard immediately explained, by averring that he "did not mean to cast any reflection upon any sect or person whatever." In view of the clashing doctrines of various sects, he desired "to keep the tender minds of the orphans" free from those excitements. He required the instructors to teach the purest morality, in all its forms, and summed up his object by saying that he wished the pupils, when they left the college, to adopt "at the same time, such religious tenets as their matured reason may enable them to prefer."
2. See sketch of Wilson.

beneath the broad canopy of heaven, procuring food with his rifle, and cooking it when hunger demanded appeasement, and undergoing, day after day, the greatest fatigues and privations. For months and years he thus wandered, from the shores of the Gulf of Mexico to the rocky coasts of Labrador, studying and preserving, with no other motive than the gratification of a great controlling passion. It was not until after an interview with Charles Lucien Bonaparte, the eminent ornithologist, in 1824, that Audubon experienced a desire for fame, and thought of publishing the results of his labors. Thus far his mature life had been devoted to the worship of Nature in one of its most beautiful and interesting forms, and the devotee was entirely lost to himself in the excess of his emotions. Now a new world opened before him. He made another tour of eighteen months' duration; and, in 1826, he sailed for England to make arrangements for publishing some of his drawings and descriptive notices. The portraits of birds were of life size, and their exhibition produced a great sensation among artists and literary men, in Great Britain. He was received with enthusiasm, especially at Edinburgh, where true genius has always been appreciated, and there he made an arrangement for the engraving of his pictures. Subscriptions to his work, amounting to about eighty thousand dollars, were speedily obtained, and

Audubon personally superintended the engravings. He was most cordially received in Paris, in 1829; and the following year he was again traversing the wilds of his native country. Toward the close of 1830, the first volume of his great work was issued. The monarchs of France and England headed his subscription list. The second volume appeared in 1834, and within the next three years, the work was completed in four magnificent volumes, containing over a thousand figures. In 1839, Mr. Audubon made his residence on the banks of the Hudson, near the city of New York, and there his family have ever since resided. In 1844, he completed and published his great work, in seven imperial octavo volumes, the engravings having been carefully reduced.

Not contented with the accomplishment of such a vast undertaking, Mr. Audubon, at the age of sixty-five years, again went to the fields, forests, swamps, and mountains, with his two sons, to explore another department of natural history. After immense toil and continual hardships, he returned full freighted with drawings and descriptions of *The Quadrupeds of America*, equal, in every respect, to those of his other work. These were published under his immediate supervision, and with the completion of that work his great labors ceased. He lived in repose at his residence near Fort Washington, until the 27th of January, 1851, when, at the age of seventy-one years, he went to his final rest. Then a brilliant star went out from the firmament of genius.

HENRY KNOX.

THE founder and chief of the artillery service in the Continental army was Henry Knox, a young bookseller in Boston (his native city), when the War for Independence was kindled at Lexington and Concord. He was born on the 25th of July, 1750, and while a mere youth, his feelings were zealously enlisted in favor of popular freedom, by the political discussions elicited by the Stamp Act and succeeding parliamentary measures. He was known and marked as a *rebel* at the time of the tea-riot; and when Lucy, the accomplished daughter of Thomas Flucker, secretary of the province, gave him her heart and hand, her friends regarded her as a ruined girl. How different the result from the anticipation! Some of these, who adhered to the royal cause, and were afterward broken in fortune, thought it an honor to enjoy the friendship of Lucy Knox, who, during the time of the first presidency, stood in the front rank of social position.

After the skirmishes at Lexington and Concord, young Knox escaped from Boston, accompanied by his wife, who carried his sword concealed in her petticoat. He entered the army at Cambridge, fought gallantly as a volunteer at the battle of Bunker Hill, then entered the engineer service with the commission of lieutenant-colonel, and superseded Gridley as commander. In the Autumn of 1775, he was directed, at his own suggestion, to organize an artillery corps; and the army at Boston being without heavy guns, he was sent, in November, to transport thither the cannons and ammunition from the captured fortresses of Ticonderoga and Crown Point. After great fatigue and hardships, he arrived at Cambridge, at the close of the year, with forty-two sled loads of munitions of war.[1] These were used effectively, a few weeks later, in driving the British from Boston. In December, 1776, Congress resolved to "appoint a brigadier-

---

1. These consisted of eight brass and six iron mortars, two iron howitzers, thirteen brass and twenty-six iron cannons, twenty-three hundred pounds of lead, and one barrel of flints.

general of artillery," and Colonel Knox received the commission. From that time until the final great action at Yorktown, in 1781, General Knox was in constant and efficient service, and most of the time under the immediate command of Washington. He was always influential in council and active in duty.

After the capture of Cornwallis, Knox was promoted to major-general, and remained in service until the close of the war. He was in command of the remnant of the Continental army which marched into and took possession of the city of New York, when the British evacuated it in November, 1783. He succeeded General Lincoln as Secretary of War under the old Confederation; and on the organization of the new government, in 1789, President Washington called him to the same office, in his cabinet. He resigned that office in 1794. On the organization of a provisional army, in 1798, to repel expected French invasion, General Knox was appointed to a command, but he was never called from his retirement at Thomaston, Maine, to the field of military duty. There he lived in dignified repose after a successful and honorable career, until the Autumn of 1806, when, on the 25th of October, he died suddenly, in the fifty-seventh year of his age. His death was caused by the lodgment of a chicken bone in his throat, while at dinner.

To the benevolent and patriotic emotions of General Knox is due the immortal honor of having suggested that truly noble institution, the *Society of the Cincinnati*.[1]

LOTT CARY.

"NOT many wise men, after the flesh, not many mighty, not many noble, are called" to the great work of human redemption, spiritual and social. The authors of great reforms, the real founders of kingdoms, the great benefactors of mankind, have generally been men who were nurtured and reared among the warm sympathies of the common people, and their origin, like that of Lott Cary, has often been in the most profound depths of obscurity. That faithful servant of God and of his own people, was of African descent, and born a slave, near Charles City Court-house, in Virginia, on the plantation of William Christian. In 1804, he was hired out as a common laborer in the city of Richmond, where he became intemperate, and was very profane. Three years afterward deep religious impressions changed his habits and thoughts, and he became a member of the Baptist Church. He could not read, but, procuring a New Testament, and applying himself faithfully, he acquired a knowledge of the alphabet and words, and finally succeeded in learning to both read and write. His industry and fidelity in a tobacco factory, enabled him, with a little friendly aid, to purchase himself and two half-orphan children, in 1813, for eight hundred and fifty dollars. He soon became an itinerant preacher on the plantations in the vicinity of Richmond, and labored with the most earnest zeal for the spiritual good of his race. In 1821, the American Colonization Society sent its first band of emigrants to Africa, and Lott Cary volunteered to leave a salary of several hundred dollars a year, to accompany those people to a field where he felt that he might be of vast service to his benighted nation. He participated in all the hardships and dangers of that little colony, yet he persevered, and became one

---

[1]. This was an association composed of the officers of the Continental army, organized for the purposes of mutual friendship and mutual relief. Although every one of the original members are gone down into the grave, the Society continues, because the membership is hereditary. The eldest male descendant of the original member is entitled to the privileges of membership. There was a General Society, and auxiliary State Societies. Washington was the first president of the General Society, and Knox was the first secretary. There are several State Societies in existence.

of the founders of the now flourishing republic of Liberia, on the western coast of Africa.[1] He became health-inspector and physician of the colony, having received some instruction in the healing art, from Dr. Ayres; and, in 1824, he had more than a hundred patients. As early as 1815, he assisted in forming an African Missionary Society, in Richmond; and in Africa he performed its work as well as he could. Through his agency, a school was established about seventy miles from Monrovia. In September, 1826, he was appointed vice-agent of the colony; and when, in 1828, Mr. Ashmun, the agent of the Society, was compelled to withdraw on account of ill-health, he cheerfully and confidently left the entire control of affairs in Mr. Cary's hands. He managed well, as chief of a colony of twelve hundred freemen, for about six months, when, on account of a difficulty with the natives, he prepared for a military expedition against them. While making cartridges, an explosion took place, which killed the venerated Cary and seven others, on the 8th of November, 1828. His death was a great loss to the colony and to the cause of the gospel triumphs in dark Africa.

DANIEL WEBSTER.

AS early as 1813, during the first months of his long membership in the National Legislature, the speeches of Daniel Webster marked him as a peerless man, and drew from a Southern member the expression, "The North has not his equal, nor the South his superior." That high preëminence in statesmanship he held until his death.

Daniel Webster was born in Salisbury, New Hampshire, on the 18th of January, 1782, and was descended from the hardy yeomanry of New England. His father was a thrifty farmer, and he taught all of his sons to labor industriously with their hands. As Daniel emerged from childhood to youth, and his physical frame became strong and hardy, he labored in the fields during the Summer, and attended a district school, two miles from his home, in the Winter.[2] The remarkable tenacity of his memory was exhibited at a very early age, and at fourteen he could repeat several entire volumes of poetry. At about that time he entered the Phillips Academy, at Exeter,[3] New Hampshire, then under the charge of Dr. Abbott. After studying the classics, for awhile, under Dr. Woods, of Boscawen, New Hampshire, he entered Dartmouth College, at Hanover,[4] at the age of fifteen years. There he pursued his studies with industry and earnestness, yet with no special promises of future greatness. He was graduated with high honor, chose law as a profession, and completed a course of legal studies under Christopher Gore, of Boston, afterward governor of Massachusetts. He was admitted to the Suffolk bar, in 1805, but preferring the country, he first established himself at Boscawen, and afterward at Portsmouth, New Hampshire. He made his residence at the latter place, in 1807, and that year he was admitted to practice in the Supreme Court of New Hampshire. There he became noted

---

1. He said in a letter, in 1823, after he had been in several battles with the hostile natives, "There never has been a minute, no, not when the balls were flying around my head, when I could wish myself again in America."
2. The teacher at that time was Benjamin Tappan, a native of East Kingston, New Hampshire, where he was born in 1767. He was educated at the Exeter Academy, and at the solicitation of Webster's father, went to Salisbury, and took charge of the district school. Master Tappan survived his distinguished pupil a few months. He died on the 9th of February, 1853, at the age of almost eighty-six years.
3. There are two academies bearing the same name—one at Exeter, founded by Honorable John Phillips; the other at Andover, Massachusetts, founded by Honorable Samuel Phillips.
4. See sketch of Eleazer Wheelock.

as one of the soundest lawyers in the State; and during his nine years' residence in Portsmouth, he made constitutional law a special study.

Mr. Webster first appeared in public life, in 1813, when he took his seat in the House of Representatives at Washington, at the extra session of the thirteenth Congress. It was a most propitious moment for a mind like Webster's to grapple with the questions of State policy, for those of the gravest character were to be then discussed. It was soon after war was declared against Great Britain, and the two great political parties, Federalists and Republicans, were violently opposed. Henry Clay was Speaker of the Lower House, and he immediately placed the new member upon the very important Committee on Foreign Affairs. He made his first speech on the 11th of June, 1813, which at once raised him to the front rank as a debater. His series of speeches, at that time, took the country by surprise, and he became the acknowledged leader of the Federal party in New England, in and out of Congress. He was reëlected to a seat in the House of Representatives, in 1814, by a large majority. At the close of the term he resumed the practice of his profession; and, in 1816, he removed to Boston, because it afforded a wider field for his expanding legal business. In 1817, he retired from Congress, and the following year he was employed in the great Dartmouth College case, in which difficult constitutional questions were involved. His efforts in that trial placed him at the head of constitutional lawyers in New England, a position which he always held.

In 1821, Mr. Webster assisted in the revision of the Constitution of Massachusetts, and he was elected a representative of Boston, in Congress, the following year. An almost unanimous vote reëlected him, in 1824. He was chosen United States Senator, in 1826, but did not take his seat until the Autumn of 1828, on account of severe domestic affliction. In that body he held a front rank for twelve consecutive years. Probably the greatest contest in eloquence, logic, and statesmanship, ever exhibited in the Senate of the United States, was that between Webster and Hayne, of South Carolina, in 1830. Mr. Webster supported President Jackson against the nullifiers of the South, in 1832; but the fiscal policy of Jackson and Van Buren was always opposed by him. In 1839, he made a brief tour through portions of Great Britain and France, and returned in time to take an active part in the election canvass which resulted in the choice of General Harrison for chief magistrate of the Republic. The new president made Mr. Webster his Secretary of State, and he was retained in the cabinet of President Tyler. In 1842, he negotiated the important treaty concerning the north-eastern boundary of the United States, known as the Ashburton treaty. In May, the following year, Mr. Webster retired to private life, but his constituents would not suffer him to enjoy coveted repose. He was again sent to the Senate of the United States, in 1845, where he opposed the war with Mexico, but sustained the administration after hostilities had commenced, by voting supplies. In 1850, he offended many of his northern friends by his course in favor of the Compromise Act, in which the Fugitive Slave law was embodied. On the death of President Taylor, Mr. Fillmore, his successor, called Mr. Webster to his cabinet as Secretary of State, and he held that responsible office, until his death, which occurred at the mansion on his fine estate at Marshfield, on the 24th of October, 1852, when at the age of almost seventy-one years.

GEORGE WYTHE.

IT is often a great misfortune for a young man to be master of wealth, actual or in expectation, at the moment of reaching his majority, for it too frequently causes noble resolves, aspiring energies, and rugged will, born of the necessity for effort, to die within him, and his manhood becomes dwarfed by idleness or dissipation. Such was the dangerous position in which George Wythe, one of Virginia's most distinguished sons, found himself, at the age of twenty years. He was born in Elizabeth county, in 1726, of wealthy parents, and received an excellent education. His father died while the son was a child, and his training devolved upon his accomplished mother. Promises of great moral and intellectual excellences appeared when his youth gave place to young manhood, but at that moment his mother died, and he was left master of a large fortune, and his own actions. He embarked at once upon the dangerous sea of unlawful pleasure, and for ten years of the morning of life, he had no higher aspirations than personal gratification. Then, at the age of thirty years, he was suddenly reformed. He forsook unprofitable companions, turned to books, became a close student, prepared himself for the practice of the law, and, in 1757, was admitted to the bar. Genius at once beamed out in all his efforts, and he arose rapidly to eminence in his profession. Honor was an every-day virtue with him, and he was never engaged in an unrighteous cause.

For several years preceding the Revolution, Mr. Wythe was a member of the Virginia House of Burgesses; and during the Stamp Act excitement he stood shoulder to shoulder with Henry, Lee, Randolph, and other Republicans. He was elected a delegate to the Continental Congress, in 1775, and the following year he affixed his signature, in confirmation of his vote, to the Declaration of Independence. During the Autumn of that year, he was associated with Thomas Jefferson and Edmund Randolph, in codifying the laws of Virginia, to make them conformable to the newly-organized republican government. The following year he was Speaker of the Virginia Assembly; and he was appointed the first high chancellor of the State, when the new judiciary was organized. That office he held during the remainder of his life, a period of more than twenty years.

Chancellor Wythe was Professor of Law in William and Mary College, for awhile, and was the legal instructor of Presidents Madison and Monroe, and Chief Justice Marshall. He was a member of the convention, in 1786, out of which grew that of 1787, in which was formed the Federal Constitution; and in the Virginia State Convention that ratified it, he was its advocate. Under that instrument he was twice chosen United States Senator. Notwithstanding his public duties were multifarious and arduous, he taught a private school, for a long time, where instruction was free to those who chose to attend. A negro boy belonging to him having exhibited fine mental powers, he taught him Latin, and was preparing to give him a thorough classical education, when both the chancellor and the boy died, after partaking of some food in which poison had evidently been introduced. A near relative, accused of the crime, was tried and acquitted. Chancellor Wythe died on the 8th of June, 1800, in the eighty-first year of his age.

LACHLIN M'INTOSH.

THE compliment of being "the handsomest man in Georgia," at the commencement of the Revolution, was bestowed upon Lachlin M'Intosh, a native of Scotland. He was born near Inverness, in 1727, and was a son of the head of the Borlam branch of the clan M'Intosh, who, when Lachlin was nine years of age, came to America with General Oglethorpe. He accompanied that gentleman in an expedition against the Spaniards, in Florida, was made prisoner and sent to St. Augustine, where he died; and Lachlin, at the age of thirteen years, was left to the care of an excellent mother. The newly-settled province afforded small means for acquiring an education, and Mrs. M'Intosh was unable to send her son to Scotland, for the purpose. His naturally strong mind, excited by a love for knowledge, overcame, as usual, all difficulties. Just as he approached manhood, he went to Charleston, where his fine personal appearance, and the remembrance of his father's military services in Georgia, procured him many warm friends. Among these was the noble John Laurens, and he entered that gentleman's counting-room as under clerk. Disliking the inaction of commercial life within doors, he left the business, returned to his paternal estate and the bosom of his family, on the Alatamaha, married a charming girl from his native country, and commenced the business of a land-surveyor. Success attended his efforts; and, inheriting the military taste of his father, he made himself familiar with military tactics, and thus was prepared for the part he was called upon to act in the War for Independence. He was a leading patriot in his section of Georgia; and when the war broke out, he entered the army, received the commission of colonel, and was exceedingly active in the early military movements in that extreme Southern State. He was commissioned a brigadier, in 1776, and a rivalry between himself and Button Gwinnett, one of the signers of the Declaration of Independence, resulted in a fierce quarrel, which ended in a duel. The challenge was given by Gwinnett. Both were wounded; Gwinnett mortally. M'Intosh was tried for murder, and acquitted; but the trouble did not end there. The feud spread among the respective friends of the parties, and, at one time, threatened serious consequences to the Republican cause at the South. To allay the bitter feeling, M'Intosh patriotically consented to accept a station at the North, and Washington appointed him commander-in-chief in the Western department, with his head-quarters at Pittsburg.

Early in 1778, General M'Intosh decended the Ohio with a considerable force, erected a fort thirty miles below Pittsburg, and after considerable delay, he marched toward the Sandusky towns in the interior of Ohio, to chastise the hostile Indians. The expedition accomplished but little, except the building of another fort near the present village of Bolivia, which M'Intosh named Laurens, in honor of his old employer, then president of Congress. He returned to Georgia, in 1779, and was second in command to Lincoln at the siege of Savannah, in October of that year. He remained with Lincoln during the following Winter and Spring, and was made a prisoner, with the rest of the Southern army, on the surrender of Charleston, in May, 1780. After his release, he went, with his family, to Virginia, where he remained until the close of the war. Then he returned to Georgia, a poor man, for his little estate was almost wasted. He lived in retirement and comparative poverty, in Savannah, until 1806, when he died, at the age of seventy-nine years.

ROBERT Y. HAYNE.

THE names of Daniel Webster and Robert Y. Hayne will ever be associated in the legislative annals of the Republic, because their great debate in the United States Senate, in 1830, was one of the most remarkable for logic and eloquence which ever occurred in that body. Hayne was more than nine years the junior of his powerful New England antagonist, having been born on the 10th of November, 1791, near Charleston, South Carolina. His education was obtained at a grammar-school in Charleston, and at the age of seventeen years he commenced the study of law under the direction of the since eminent jurist and statesman, Langdon Cheves. He had not yet reached his majority, when the clouds of impending war between the United States and Great Britain gathered darkly. Having secured his admission to the bar, he volunteered his services, early in 1812, for the military defence of the sea-board, and entered the army as lieutenant. He arose rapidly to the rank of major-general of his State militia, and was considered one of the best disciplinarians in the South. On receiving an honorable discharge, General Hayne retired to Charleston, and commenced the practice of law as a means of procuring a livelihood. At about that time, Mr. Cheves had accepted a seat in Congress, and Mr. Hayne had the advantage of securing much of his practice. Before he was twenty-two years of age his business was very extensive; and from that time until his death, his practice was probably greater and more lucrative than that of any lawyer in South Carolina.

Mr. Hayne first appeared as a legislator, in 1814, when he was elected to a seat in the South Carolina Assembly. There he was distinguished for his eloquence,[1] and his firm support of President Madison's administration, in its war

---

1. Mr. Hayne's first effort at oratory was an oration on the 4th of July, 1812, at Fort Moultrie, which won for him great applause, and gave promise of his future brilliancy as a public speaker. It is worthy

measures. In 1818, he was chosen Speaker of the Assembly; and the same year he received the appointment of attorney-general for the State. In every duty to which he was called, young Hayne acquitted himself nobly; and the moment he had reached an eligible age, he was elected to a seat in the Senate of the United States, where, for ten years, he represented South Carolina with rare ability. He was an ever-vigilant watchman upon the citadel of State Rights, and as a member of the famous "Union and State Rights Convention," held toward the close of 1832, he was chairman of the committee of twenty-one who reported the "ordinance of nullification," which alarmed the country, and called forth President Jackson's puissant proclamation. Like his great coadjutor, Mr. Calhoun, General Hayne was sincere and honest in the support of his views, and always commanded the highest respect of his political opponents.

About a fortnight after the adoption of the celebrated "ordinance," General Hayne was chosen governor of the State, and a few days after President Jackson's proclamation reached him, he issued a counter-manifesto, full of defiance. Civil war seemed inevitable, but the compromise measures proposed by Mr. Clay, and adopted by Congress early in 1833, averted the menaced evil. Governor Hayne filled the executive chair, with great energy, until 1834; and, on

of remark, that his election to the South Carolina Assembly, at the head of thirty-one candidates, by a larger vote than any individual had ever received, in a contested election, in Charleston, was an evidence of his great popularity. He was then not twenty-three years of age.

retiring from that exalted office, he was elected mayor of Charleston. His attention was now specially turned to the great subject of internal improvements; and, in 1837, he was elected president of the "Charleston, Louisville, and Cincinnati Rail Road Company." He held that office until his death, which occurred at Ashville, North Carolina, on the 24th of September, 1841, when in the fiftieth year of his age. Governor Hayne may be ranked among the purest-minded men of his age.

RALPH IZARD.

IN the year 1844, a daughter of Ralph Izard, one of the noblest of the sons of South Carolina, published a brief memoir of him, attached to a volume of his correspondence, and accompanied by a portrait, under which is the appropriate motto, "An honest man's the noblest work of God." Ralph Izard was entitled to that motto, for few men have passed the ordeal of public life with more honor and purity than he. He was born in 1742, at the family-estate called *The Elms*, about seventeen miles from Charleston, South Carolina, and at a very early age was sent to England to be educated. He pursued preparatory studies at Hackney, and completed his education at Christ College, Cambridge. On arriving at his majority, he returned to America, took possession of his ample fortune left by his father, and, having no taste for the professions, he divided his time between literary and agricultural pursuits, and the pleasures of fashionable life. He passed much of his time, in early life, with James De Lancey, then lieutenant-governor of the province of New York, and married his niece, a daughter of Peter De Lancey, of Westchester county, in 1767. In 1771, they went to London, and occupied a pleasant house there, for some time, in the enjoyment of the best intellectual society of the metropolis. His ample fortune allowed the indulgence of a fine taste, and books, painting, and music, were his chief delight. Yet he possessed a thoroughly republican spirit, and refused offers to be presented to court, because etiquette would compel him to bow the knee to the king and queen. He watched the course of political events with great interest; and finally, in 1774, the excitement in London on the subject of American affairs so troubled him, that he went to the Continent with his wife, and travelled many months. But everywhere the apparition of his bleeding and beloved country followed him, and he resolved to return home and engage in the impending conflicts. He returned to England, and there used all his efforts to enlighten the ministry concerning the temper of his countrymen, but to little purpose.

War commenced, and, finding it difficult to return to America, he went to France, in 1777, when Congress appointed him commissioner to the Tuscan court. Circumstances prevented his presenting himself to the Duke of Tuscany, for a long time, and he asked permission of Congress to resign his commission and return home. In the meanwhile the false representations of Silas Deane had induced Congress to recal him. That body afterward made ample amends for the injustice. He remained in Paris until 1780, and in the meanwhile had served his country efficiently in many ways, officially and unofficially. On one occasion he pledged his whole estate as security for funds needed by Commodore Gillon, who had been sent from South Carolina to Europe, to purchase frigates.

On his return to America, in 1780, Mr. Izard immediately repaired to the head-quarters of Washington, and was there when the treason of Arnold was discovered. It is evident from his correspondence that he was chiefly instrumental in procuring the appointment of General Greene to the command of the Southern army, toward the close of that year. For that service he received the thanks of the governor of South Carolina. Early in 1781, he was elected to a seat in the Continental Congress, where he remained until peace was established. Then he was joined by his family, whom he had left in France, and he retired to his estate to enjoy the repose of domestic life. His countrymen would not allow him to be inactive, and he was chosen the first United States Senator from South Carolina, for the full term of six years, during which time he was a firm supporter of the administration of President Washington. In 1795, he took final leave of public life, and once more sought repose, with the pleasant anticipations of many years of earthly happiness. But two years afterward he was suddenly prostrated by paralysis. His intellect was mercifully spared, and he lived in comparative comfort until the 30th of May, 1804, when he expired, at the age of sixty-two years. A tablet was placed to his memory in the parish church of St. James, Goose Creek, near his paternal seat—*The Elms.*

BENJAMIN PIERCE.

THE career of Benjamin Pierce, the father of the fourteenth President of the United States, affords a noble example of true manhood in private and public life, which the young men of our Republic ought to study and imitate. It is an example of perseverance in well-doing for self, friends, and country, being rewarded by a conscience void of offence, a long life, and the love and honor of fellow-men. In these lies hidden the priceless pearl of earthly happiness.

Benjamin Pierce was descended from ancestors who settled at Plymouth, Massachusetts, three years after the *Pilgrim Fathers* first landed on that snowy beach.[1] He was the seventh of ten children, and was born in Chelmsford, Massachusetts, on Christmas day, 1757. He was left fatherless at the age of six years, and was placed under the guardianship of a paternal uncle. His opportunities for education were small, but the lad, possessing a naturally vigorous intellect, improved those opportunities with parsimonious assiduity. His body was invigorated by farm-labor; and when, at the age of seventeen years, the first gun of the Revolution at Lexington echoed among the New England hills, and he armed for the battle-fields of freedom, young Pierce was fitted, morally and physically, for a soldier of truest stamp. He hastened to Lexington, pushed on to Cambridge, and six days after the retreat of the British troops from Concord, he was enrolled in Captain Ford's company as a regular soldier. He fought bravely on Breed's Hill seven weeks afterward; was faithful in camp and on guard until the British were driven from Boston, in the Spring of 1776; followed the fortunes of Washington during the ensuing campaigns of that year, and was orderly sergeant of his company, before he was twenty years of age, in the glorious conflicts which resulted in the capture of Burgoyne at Saratoga, in the Autumn of 1777. His valor there won for him the commission of ensign. The young man who bore that commission and the American flag, in the hottest of the fight, was killed. Young Pierce rushed forward, seized the banner, and

---

1. The facts in this brief sketch of the life of Governor Pierce are gleaned from a well-written biography, from the pen of the Honorable C. E. Potter, editor of *The Farmer's Monthly Visitor*, published at Manchester, New Hampshire. It appears in the number for July, 1852, accompanied by an accurate portrait of Governor Pierce.

bore it triumphantly to the American lines, amid the shouts of his companions. He remained in service during the whole war, and reached the rank of captain. When the American troops entered the city of New York, in the Autumn of 1783, Captain Pierce commanded the detachment sent to take possession of the military works at Brooklyn. This was the concluding act of his services in the Continental army, and a few weeks afterward he returned to Chelmsford, after an absence of almost nine years.

The war left young Pierce as it found him, a true patriot, but penniless, for the Continental paper-money, in which he had been paid, had become worthless. Yet he was rich in the glorious experience of endurance under hardships; and entering the service of a large landholder, it was not long before he owned a small tract of land in the southern part of Hillsborough, New Hampshire, whereon he built a log-hut, and commenced a clearing, in the Spring of 1786. He was unmarried, and lived alone. Labor sweetened his coarse food and deepened his slumbers. He cultivated social relations with the scattered population around him; and, in the Autumn of 1786, the governor of New Hampshire appointed him brigade-major of his district. In blooming May, the following year, he married. Fifteen months afterward death took his companion from him, and he was left with an infant daughter, the wife and widow of General John M'Neil. He married again in 1789, and the union continued almost fifty years.[1] At about the same time he was elected to a seat in the New Hampshire legislature, and was promoted to the command of a regiment. When, in 1798, Congress authorized the raising of a provisional army, in expectation of war with France, Colonel Pierce was offered the same commission in the regular service, but he declined it. In 1803, he was elected to the council of his State, and retained that office by reëlection until 1809, when he was appointed sheriff of the county of Hillsborough. The governor had already commissioned him a brigadier-general of the militia, in which position he acquitted himself with great dignity and honor.

General Pierce held the office of sheriff until 1813, when he was again made a member of the council. After five years' service there, he was again elected sheriff; and no man ever performed official duties in a manner more acceptable to the public than he. In 1827, he was chosen governor of New Hampshire; and, in 1829, he was again called to the same station. Three years afterward he held his last public office. It was in the Autumn of 1832, when he was chosen, by the democratic party, a presidential elector. When the duties of that office were ended, he sought repose upon his farm at Hillsborough, after having been engaged in the public service almost continually for fifty-five years. A partial paralysis of the system prostrated him, in 1837, but he was not confined to his room until November, 1838. From that time he suffered intensely until mercifully relieved by death, on the 1st of April, 1839, in the eighty-second year of his age.

We cannot too reverently cherish the remembrance of such men. Not one of them are now on the shores of Time.[2]

> "Oh! honored be each silvery hair!
> Each furrow trenched by toil and care!
> And sacred each old bending form
> That braved oppression's battle storm."

---

1. His second wife, mother of President Pierce, died in December, 1838, a few months before the departure of her honored husband.

2. It was estimated that at the close of 1854, not more than one thousand of the two hundred and thirty thousand of the Continental soldiers, and the fifty-six thousand militia, who bore arms during the war, remained among us. The last survivors, Lemuel Cook and William Hutchings, died in 1862.

HARRIET NEWELL.

To be a martyr in any cause requires the truest elements of heroism. To forsake country, friends, and the enjoyments of civilization at the bidding of an emotion born of a great principle, to do good for others, is an act of heroism of which those whom the world delights to honor as its great heroes, have very little appreciation. But such is the heroism which makes faithful Christian missionaries, moved by an emotion of highest benevolence to do good to the souls and bodies of men. Of the "noble army of martyrs," she who was ever known in girlhood as "sweet little Hatty Atwood," became a bright example of faith and self-denial. She performed no important service on the missionary field of action; indeed, she had barely entered upon its verge and heard the cry of the heathen for help, when she was called to another sphere of life. But she was one of the earliest, purest, most lovely of those who went from America to India, bearing to the dark chambers of paganism there, the candle of the Lord God Omnipotent. Her example is her glory.

Harriet Atwood was born in Haverhill, Massachusetts, on the 10th of October, 1793. She was blessed with a sweet disposition, and was always a favorite with her playmates. Studious and thoughtful from early childhood, her mind was naturally imbued with an abiding sense of the good and the true, which form the basis of sound religious character. At the age of thirteen years, while at the academy in Bradford, Massachusetts, she became more deeply impressed with the importance of religious things, than ever. She withdrew from the company of frivolous persons, read religious books and her Bible much of her leisure time; and, in 1809, when not yet sixteen years of age, she made an open profession of Christianity. In the Winter of 1811, she became acquainted with Mr. Newell, her future husband. He was preparing for missionary service in India, and in April following, he asked her companionship as wife and co-worker in the distant land to which he was going. The conflicts of that young spirit with the allurements of home, friends, and personal ease, was severe but short. She consented; and, with the blessings of her widowed mother, she was married, in February, 1812, and the same month sailed with Mr. and Mrs. Judson, and others, for India. On account of hostilities then progressing between the United States and England, this little band of soldiers, under the banner of the Prince of Peace, were not permitted to remain at Calcutta, so they took their departure for the Isle of France. They reached it after a voyage of great peril, toward the close of Summer. A few weeks afterward Mrs. Newell gave birth to a daughter. The delicate flower was plucked from its equally delicate stem, by the Angel of Death, five days after it had expanded in the atmosphere of earth, and its spirit was exhaled as sweet incense to Heaven. The mother soon followed. Hereditary consumption was the canker at the root of life, and on the 30th of November, 1812, that lovely Christian's head was pillowed upon the bosom of mother earth. She was then only nineteen years of age. Her widowed mother, who wept over her at parting, lived on in humble resignation for more than forty years. She died in Boston, in July, 1853, at the age of eighty-four years.

ANTHONY WAYNE.

THE fearless courage and desperate energy of General Anthony Wayne obtained for him, among his countrymen, the title of "Mad Anthony;" and some of his exploits entitle him to the distinction. He was born in Easttown, Chester county, Pennsylvania, on the 1st of January, 1745. He was educated with considerable care, in Philadelphia, became proficient in mathematics, and commenced the business of surveying, in his native town, at the age of about eighteen years. Skill and popularity in his profession soon established his reputation permanently; and, in 1765, when only twenty years of age, he was sent by a company of gentlemen to locate lands for them in Nova Scotia. They made him superintendent of the settlement, but after remaining there about two years, he returned home, married, and resumed his business of surveyor, in his native county. His talent attracted general attention; and, in 1773, he was elected to a seat in the Pennsylvania Assembly. He continued in that service until 1775, when he left the council for the field, having been appointed colonel in the Continental army. He accompanied General Thomas to Canada, in the Spring of 1776, and at the close of service there, he was promoted to brigadier. After a year of active service, he was engaged efficiently with the commander-in-chief in the battles at Brandywine,[1] Germantown, and Monmouth, in all of which his skill and valor were conspicuous. In 1779, he made a night attack upon the strong fortress at Stony Point, on the Hudson, and the entire garrison were made prisoners. It was one of the most brilliant achievements of the war, and Congress rewarded him with its thanks, and a gold medal. It made him the most

---

1. While encamped near the Paoli tavern, in Chester county, Pennsylvania, after the battle at Brandywine, his command was attacked at midnight, by a strong force of British and Hessians, under General Grey, and many of them were killed. Over the spot where they were buried, a neat marble monument stands. See sketch of the Reverend David Jones.

popular man in the army, below the commander-in-chief, and his praises were spoken in every part of the land.

In 1781, General Wayne proceeded, with the Pennsylvania line, to Virginia, and there coöperated with La Fayette and Baron Steuben against Arnold, the traitor, who had invaded that State. Wayne's retreat at Jamestown, when almost surrounded by the British troops, was one of the most masterly performances ever accomplished. In the siege of Yorktown, he performed many deeds of great valor, and after participating in the joy of the great victory there, he proceeded southward, to prosecute the war in Georgia. He kept the British within their lines at Savannah until they were compelled to evacuate the State, and then Wayne, in triumph, took possession of the capital. For his great services there, the legislature of Georgia made him a present of a valuable farm. On retiring from the army, he took up his abode in his native county. In 1788, he was a member of the Pennsylvania convention, called to consider the Federal Constitution, and was its earnest advocate. In 1792, he was appointed to succeed St. Clair in the command of troops in the Ohio country, and after prosecuting war against the Indians, with great vigor, he gained a decided victory over them, in August, 1794. A year afterward he concluded a treaty of peace with the North-western tribes, at Greenville, and thus terminated the war. On his return home, he was seized with gout, and died in a hut at Presque Isle (now Erie, Pennsylvania), in December, 1796, at the age of fifty-one years. According to his request, he was buried under the flag-staff of the fort on the shore of Lake Erie. In 1809, his son, Isaac, had his body removed to Radnor church-yard, Delaware county, Pennsylvania, and over it the Pennsylvania Society of the Cincinnati erected a handsome marble monument, with suitable inscriptions, the same year.

MARQUIS DE LA FAYETTE.

THOSE cosmopolitan lovers of liberty, who came from Europe to assist the colonists in their struggles for freedom and independence, are so identified with the founders of our Republic, that each deserves a noble cenotaph to his memory. In an especial manner ought Americans to reverence the name and deeds of La Fayette, who, fifty years after the contest in which he had aided us had closed, came to behold the glorious superstructure of free institutions which had been reared upon the consecrated foundation that he had helped to plant.

Gilbert Mottier,[1] Marquis de La Fayette, was a native of France, where he was born on the 6th of September, 1757. He belonged to one of the most ancient of the modern French nobility, and received an education compatible with his station. When a little more than seventeen years of age he married the Countess de Noailles, daughter of the Duc de Noailles, a beautiful young lady about his own age, and the possessor of an immense fortune. In the Summer of 1776, he was stationed, with the military corps to which he belonged, near the town of Mentz. He was an officer in the French army, though only eighteen years of age. At a dinner-party, where the Duke of Gloucester, brother of the King of England, was the guest on the occasion, he heard of the struggles of the far-off American colonies, and their noble Declaration of Independence. He heard, with indignation, of the employment of German troops and other strong

---

1. In the *Biographie des Hommes* his name is written Marie-Paul-Joseph-Roch-Yves-Gilbert-Mottiers de la Fayette.

measures employed by England to enslave that struggling people, and his young soul burned with a desire to aid them. He left the army, returned to Paris, offered his services to the American commissioners, fitted out a vessel at his own expense, and, with Baron de Kalb and other European officers, sailed for America. They arrived at Georgetown, South Carolina, in April, 1777, and La Fayette hastened, by land, to Philadelphia. Congress, after some hesitation, accepted his services, and he entered the army under Washington, as a volunteer, but bearing the honorary title of major-general, conferred upon him by the national legislature, in July. His first battle was on the Brandywine, where he was severely wounded in the knee, and was nursed, for some time, by the Moravian sisters at Bethlehem, in Pennsylvania. He was in the battle at Monmouth, the following Summer, and was active in Rhode Island.

In October, 1778, La Fayette obtained leave to return to France, and Congress ordered the American minister in Paris to present him an elegant sword, in the name of the United States of America. There he remained until the Spring of 1780, when he returned with the joyful intelligence of the on-coming of a French army and navy to assist the struggling colonists. He was in active and continual service here until the capture of Cornwallis and his army, at Yorktown, in the Autumn of 1781. In that achievement he performed a gallant part, as well as in the events in Virginia, immediately preceding. Soon after the capitulation at Yorktown, he returned to France, and, by his own exertions, was raising a large army there for service in America, when intelligence of peace reached him. In 1784, he visited America, and was every where received with the greatest enthusiasm by his old companions-in-arms. With the blessing of a free people, he again returned to his native country, and from that time until the death of Washington, those two great men were in affectionate correspondence.

La Fayette took an active part in the politics of France, when the great Revolution there approached. He was an active member of the Legislative Assembly, where, amidst the intense radicalism of the theoretical democrats, he was a fervent but conservative advocate of republicanism. Because of his moderation he was suspected, and he fled from France to avoid the fate of many good men who lost their heads during the Reign of Terror. He did not entirely escape, but was seized and kept a prisoner in a dungeon at Olmutz, in Germany, during three years, where he endured great personal suffering. After his release, he lived in comparative retirement with his devoted wife (on whom his misfortunes had fallen heavily) until 1814, when the first downfall of Napoleon, whom he hated, brought him again into public life. In 1815, he was a member of the Chamber of Deputies, and in that assembly he offered the resolution for the appointment of a committee to demand the abdication of the Emperor. He was again a member of the Chamber of Deputies, in 1818. Six years afterward he was invited to visit the United States as the guest of the nation; and, in 1824, the American frigate *Brandywine* (so named in his honor) conveyed him to our shores. His journey through the different States was a continual ovation, and every where the surviving soldiers of the Revolution flocked to greet the "dear Marquis." In the Republican movements in France, in 1830, which dethroned Charles the Tenth, La Fayette took a conspicuous part, and, nobly refusing the chief magistracy of his nation, which the people and the legislature offered him, he indicated the head of Louis Philippe, of the Orleans family, as the proper one for the French crown. Afterward that ungrateful monarch treated La Fayette with coldness and disdain. In 1834, that venerated patriot of two hemispheres went to his rest, at the age of seventy-seven years.

JOSEPH STORY.

"WHATEVER subject he touched was touched with a master's hand and spirit. He employed his eloquence to adorn his learning, and his learning to give solid weight to his eloquence. He was always instructive and interesting, and rarely without producing an instantaneous conviction. A lofty ambition of excellence, that stirring spirit which breathes the breath of Heaven, and pants for immortality, sustained his genius in its perilous course." These were the beautiful words of Judge Story when speaking of a noble companion in profession who had just passed from earth, and they may, with earnest truth, be applied to the now departed jurist himself.

Joseph Story was born at Marblehead, Massachusetts, on the 18th of September, 1779. He pursued academic studies under the Rev. Dr. Harris (afterward president of Columbia College, New York), and entered Harvard University, as a student, in 1795. He was graduated there in 1798, studied law, was admitted to the bar, in 1801, and made Salem his place of residence and professional practice. His fine talent was speedily appreciated, and he soon possessed an extensive and lucrative practice. He was often opposed to the most eminent lawyers of the day, who were Federalists, he having become attached to the Democratic party at the commencement of his professional career. In 1805, he was chosen to represent Salem in the Massachusetts legislature, and was annually reëlected to that station until 1811, when he was appointed a judge of the Supreme Court of the United States. In the meanwhile (1809–10) he had served a few months in the Federal Congress, as representative of the district in which he resided. During that brief congressional career, he was distinguished for his talent and energy, especially in his efforts to obtain a repeal of the famous Embargo Act. Mr. Jefferson regarded Mr. Story as the chief instrument in procuring the repeal of that act, so obnoxious in its operations upon the commerce and manufactures of New England.[1]

Mr. Story was only thirty-two years of age when President Madison made him an associate justice of the Supreme Court of the United States, and from that time he discarded party politics, and labored incessantly to become eminently useful as a jurist. He was a worthy coadjutor of the illustrious Marshall, and in commercial and constitutional law he had no peer upon the bench of the Federal judiciary. In 1820, Judge Story was a member of the convention that revised the constitution of Massachusetts, and distinguished himself by eloquent expressions of the most liberal sentiments. In 1829, Mr. Nathan Dane founded a Law School in connection with Harvard University, on the express condition that Judge Story should consent to become its first professor. The eminent jurist acquiesced, and became greatly interested in the important duties of instruction to which his position called him. Indeed, he was so impressed with the importance of the labor, and so enamored with its pleasures, that he contemplated a resignation of his seat on the bench in order that he might apply all his time and energies to the school.

Judge Story wrote much and well. The most important of his productions are *Commentaries on the Law of Bailments*; *Commentaries on the Constitution of the United States*, three volumes, 1833; an abridgment of the same; *Commentaries on the Conflict of Laws*, 1834; *Commentaries on Equity Jurisprudence*, in two volumes; a treatise on the *Science of Pleading in Courts of Equity*, 1838; on the *Law of Agency*, 1839; on the *Law of Partnership*, 1841; on the *Law of Bills of Exchange*, 1843; and on the *Law of Promissory Notes*, 1845. To the *Encyclopædia Americana*, and the *North America Review*, he contributed many valuable papers; and he delivered many addresses upon various important subjects. Judge Story died at Cambridge, Massachusetts, on the 10th of September, 1845, at the age of sixty-six years.

CHARLES BROCKDEN BROWN.

A GENTLE spirit, full of angelic sweetness, passed from earth to heaven when that of Charles Brockden Brown put off its mortality. He was born of Quaker parents, in Philadelphia, on the 17th of January, 1771. His body was always frail, but his mind was vigorous and his soul ever hopeful. He was dearly loved in the home where he was nurtured, carefully tutored in the rudiments of education, and at the age of ten was placed under the charge of a teacher named Proud, whose instruction he enjoyed for five years. Young Brown was wonderfully precocious, and he made remarkable progress in the study of the Latin, Greek, and French languages, and mathematics. Like Watts, his thoughts "came in numbers," and before he was fifteen years of age, he had actually commenced three epic poems. Young Brown's friends wished him to be a lawyer, and he commenced legal studies. They were not congenial to his

---

[1]. Mr. Story's course offended Mr. Jefferson, for the Embargo was one of the favorite measures of the President. He called Mr. Story a "pseudo-republican."

taste, and he resolved to devote his life to literature. With young men of corresponding tastes he associated for mutual improvement in studying and in composition. His health was feeble, and he made long pedestrian journeys into the country in quest of invigoration. But it came not.

In 1793, young Brown visited an intimate friend in New York, where he formed the acquaintance of several literary young men. For some time he resided alternately in New York and Philadelphia, carefully preparing his mind to become a public writer. He chose the Novel as the best medium through which to convey his peculiar views of humanity to the world; and, in 1798, when twenty-seven years of age, his *Wieland* appeared, and at once established his reputation as an author of highest rank. The following year he established a monthly magazine in New York; and, in 1800, he published three novels—*Arthur Mervyn*, *Ormond*, and *Edgar Huntley*. *Clara Howard* was published in 1801; and, in 1804, his last novel, entitled *Jane Talbot*, was first issued in England, and afterward in Philadelphia. That year he married the daughter of a Presbyterian clergyman, in New York, and immediately removed to Philadelphia, where he afterward assumed editorial control of *The Literary Magazine* and *The American Register*. These were ably conducted by him until failing health compelled him to lay aside his pen, and, in the bosom of an affectionate family, surrounded by dear friends, to prepare for death, which the unmistakable symptoms of consumption were heralding. That disease was rapidly developed during 1809, and in February, the following year, he expired.

BARON DE KALB.

UPON the green in front of the Presbyterian Church in Camden, South Carolina, is a neat marble monument erected to the memory of one of the brave foreigners who fought for liberty in America, and thereby gained the imperishable dignity of citizenship, in spite of the conventional restrictions which impose the necessity of native birth or fealty oath, to make men such. That officer was Baron de Kalb, Knight of the Royal Order of Military Merit, and a native of Alsace, a German province ceded to France. He was educated in the art of war in the French army, and came to America, with La Fayette, in the Spring of 1777. He offered his services to the Continental Congress, and on the 15th of September following, that body commissioned him a major-general in the regular army. He had been in America before, having been sent hither, about 1762, as a secret agent of the French government, to ascertain the state of the Anglo-American colonies. Although travelling in disguise, he excited suspicion. On one occasion he was arrested, but was immediately released, as nothing justified his detention. It was through De Kalb that La Fayette gained an introduction to the American commissioners in Paris, and, with the young marquis, the veteran soldier left the honors and emoluments of a brigadier in the French service, and joined the fortunes of a people in rebellion against one of the great powers of the earth.

De Kalb was active in the events near Philadelphia during the Autumn preceding the memorable Winter encampment at Valley Forge. The following year he was in command in New Jersey. While at Morristown, in the Spring of 1780, he was placed at the head of the Maryland line, and with these, and the Delaware Continental troops, he marched southward, in April, to reinforce General Lincoln, then besieged in Charleston. He was too late; and General

Gates being sent soon afterward to take command of the troops in the South, De Kalb became subordinate to that officer. Gates reached De Kalb's camp, on the Deep river, at the close of July, 1780, and pressed forward to confront Cornwallis, at Camden. Seven miles north of that village, the two armies unexpectedly met, at midnight; and in the severe battle which occurred the following morning [August 16], De Kalb was mortally wounded, and the Americans were utterly defeated and routed. He fell, scarred with eleven wounds, while trying to rally the scattering Americans. He died at Camden, three days afterward, was buried where his monument now stands, and an ornamental tree was planted at the head of his grave. The corner-stone of that monument was laid in 1825, by his friend and companion-in-arms, La Fayette. On the 14th of October, 1780, Congress ordered a monument to be erected to his memory in the city of Annapolis, Maryland, but that duty, like justice to his widow and heirs, has been delayed until now.[1]

JOHN RANDOLPH.

SEVENTH in descent from Pocahontas, the beloved daughter of the great Emperor of the Powhatans, was John Randolph, who usually made the suffix, "of Roanoke," to his name. He was the son of a respectable planter in Chesterfield county, three miles from Petersburg, Virginia, where he was born on the 2d of June, 1773. It was through his paternal grandmother, Jane Bolling, that the blood of Pocahontas was transmitted to him. He lost his father while he was an infant, and his mother afterward married Judge St. George Tucker. His health was always delicate, and until he entered the college at Princeton, after a residence in Bermuda for a year, his studies were irregular. His mother died in 1788, and then he entered Columbia College, in the city of New York. There he remained until 1790, when he returned to Virginia, and completed his education in William and Mary College. In 1793, he went to Philadelphia to study law with his uncle, Edmund Randolph, then attorney-general of the United States. He made but little progress in preparing for the profession, and never entered upon its practice. He delighted in the British classics, and read a great deal, but for some time after reaching his majority, he had no fixed intentions concerning a life-employment.

Mr. Randolph's first appearance in public life was in 1799, when he was elected to a seat in Congress. He had already displayed great powers of eloquence in the peculiar line of satire or denunciation, and just before his election, he was brought into antagonism with Patrick Henry, on the subject of the Alien and Sedition laws. When he commenced a reply to a speech by Henry, a gentleman remarked, "Come, colonel, let us go—it is not worth while to listen to that boy." "Stay, my friend," replied Henry, "there's an old man's head on that boy's shoulders." Congress was a field particularly suited to his capacities, and for thirty years (with the exception of three intervals of two years each), he was a member of the House of Representatives. During that time he was a representative of Virginia in the Senate of the United States for about two years.

---

1. In 1819, 1820, and 1821, the surviving heirs of Baron de Kalb petitioned Congress for the payment of alleged arrears due the general at his death, and also for certain indemnities, but the claim was disallowed. Simeon de Witt Bloodgood, Esq., brought the matter to the attention of Congress, in 1836, but without success. On the 15th of December, 1854, the House of Representatives voted an appropriation of sixty-six thousand dollars to the heirs of Baron de Kalb, and on the 19th of January following, the Senate voted in favor of the appropriation; so, at last, tardy justice will have reached the family of the hero.

He was seized with a paroxism of insanity, in 1811, after many months of moodiness, irascibility, and suspicions of his best friends; and he had returns of this malady several times during his life. He strenuously opposed the war with Great Britain, in 1812. Up to 1806, he had been a consistent member of the Republican party; then his views changed, and he became an opponent of Madison, more bitter than any Federalist of New England. His political course, after the war, was erratic, and he delighted to be in the minority, because it gave him special opportunities for vituperation. He favored the claims of Mr. Crawford for the Presidency of the United States, in 1824; but, in 1828, he was the warm friend of General Jackson, and his ardent supporter for the same office.

In 1822, Mr. Randolph made a voyage to England for the benefit of his health, where his political fame and strange personal appearance created quite a sensation. He made another voyage thither, in 1824, but his health was too much impaired to receive any permanent benefit. From that time the current of his public career was often interrupted by sickness. In 1829, he was a member of the Virginia convention, called to revise the constitution of that State; and, in 1830, President Jackson appointed him minister to Russia. He accepted the station, on condition that he might spend the Winter in the south of Europe, if his health should require it. He reached St. Petersburg in September, but his stay was short. Soon after his reception by the Emperor, the rigors of approaching Winter compelled him to leave the region of the Neva. He arrived in London, in December, where he made a characteristic speech at the Lord Mayor's dinner. He remained in England until the Autumn of the following year, when he returned home in a state of extreme exhaustion. He rallied, and his constituents again elected him to Congress. But he did not take his seat there. Disease was busy with its fingers of decay. Consumption was making terrible breaches in the citadel of life; and on the 23d of May, 1833, he died in a hotel in Philadelphia, while on his way to New York to embark for Europe, for the benefit of his health. Mr. Randolph was a strange compound of opposing qualities. He was brilliant without sound sense; morose and irascible with a kindly heart toward friends; an apparently gloomy fatalist—almost an Atheist at times —yet overflowing, frequently, with pious thoughts and sentiments.[1] He was a famous but not a great man.

JOSIAH BARTLETT.

FEW men have been more faithful in the performance of public duties, or more honest and honorable in their private relations, than Josiah Bartlett, one of the two members of the medical profession, in New Hampshire, who signed the Declaration of Independence. He was descended from an ancient Norman family, some of whom became quite distinguished in English history. He was born at Amesbury, Massachusetts, in November, 1729. He was a maternal relative of Daniel Webster, and, like that statesman, he arose to eminence by the force of his own character, under Providence, without the factitious aid of wealth or family influence. He lacked a collegiate education, but having acquired a knowledge of Greek and Latin in the family of a relative, he was prepared for the study of medicine, his chosen profession. He commenced its practice at Kingston, New Hampshire, was skilful, and soon acquired a moderate fortune.

Although an unbending republican in principle, Dr. Bartlett was greatly esteemed by the royal governor, Benning Wentworth, and received from him a magistrate's commission, and the command of a regiment of militia. In 1765, he was chosen a representative in the New Hampshire legislature, and there he became popular by his staunch advocacy of the cause of the colonists in their opposition to the Stamp Act. Wentworth attempted to win him to the side of the crown, by tempting bribes, but he rejected every overture. In 1774, he was a member of the general Committee of Safety. The appointment of that committee alarmed the governor. He dissolved the Assembly; but the members, with Dr. Bartlett at their head, reassembled, and, like those of Virginia, appointed delegates to the Continental Congress. One of these was Dr. Bartlett. Wentworth soon afterward took away his magistrate's and military commissions; but the governor, in turn, was speedily deprived of his office, and became a fugitive. Dr. Bartlett was reëlected to Congress, in 1775, and was one of the committee chosen to devise a plan for a confederation of the States. He earnestly supported the proposition for independence, and was the first man to sign it, after John Hancock.

Dr. Bartlett remained in Congress until 1778, when he obtained leave to re-

---

1. It is said that on one occasion he ascended a lofty spur of the Blue Ridge, at dawn, and from that magnificent observatory saw the sun rise. As its light burst in beauty and glory over the vast panorama before him, he turned to his servant and said, with deep emotion, "Tom, if any body says there is no God, tell them they lie!" Thus he expressed the deep sense which his soul felt of the presence of a Great Creator.

turn home and superintend his deranged private affairs. He did not again resume his seat in that body, for the following year he was appointed chief justice of the Court of Common Pleas of his native State. He was afterward raised to the bench of the Superior Court; and was very active in favor of the Federal Constitution. The legislature elected him first United States Senator, under the new government, but he declined the honor, having been previously chosen president, or governor of New Hampshire. That office he held, by successive election, until 1794, when he retired to private life, and sought needful repose, after serving his country faithfully full thirty years. That repose upon which he entered was but the prelude to a far longer one, near at hand. He died on the 19th of May, 1795, in the sixty-sixth year of his age.

HORATIO GATES.

TWO of the general officers of the Continental army were natives of England. These were Horatio Gates and Charles Lee, and both bear the just odium of being jealous of Washington, and aspiring to supplant him. Gates was born about the year 1728, and came to America as a subaltern in General Braddock's army, in 1755. He remained in Virginia, and paid much attention to military tactics. Being known as a good disciplinarian, he was chosen, by Congress, adjutant-general of the Continental army, when it was organized, in June, 1775; and he performed efficient service in his department, under Washington, until June, 1776, when he was appointed to the chief command of the Northern Department, with the commission of major-general. In the Autumn of that year he joined the main army in New Jersey, with a detachment of his command. The following Summer he superseded General Schuyler, who had been placed in command of the Northern forces, a few weeks before, and gained all the honor of the capture of Burgoyne and his troops, at Saratoga, in October, when the real praise was due to Schuyler, Arnold, and others. In that whole affair Gates exhibited a want of magnanimity unbecoming a patriot and soldier. During the ensuing Winter he entered into a conspiracy, with others, to disparage Washington, and secure for himself the office of commander-in-chief. He used his power as President of the Board of War, for that purpose, but the scheme utterly failed. While the conspirators were thus busy, Washington and his army were suffering dreadfully at Valley Forge. From that time until appointed to the command of the Southern army, in the Spring of 1780, his military services were of little account.

When the news of Lincoln's misfortunes at Charleston reached Congress, that body, without consulting Washington, appointed Gates to the command in the South, foolishly supposing his name, as "the conqueror of Burgoyne," would have the effect to rally the people.[1] Washington would have named Greene, and all would have been well. Gates and his secretary overtook De Kalb and the army at Deep River, in July, and marched forward to meet Cornwallis at Camden. His excessive vanity brought great misfortune. He was so sure of a victory, that he made no provision for a retreat; and when that movement became necessary, it assumed the character of a rout. Marching at midnight in a deep sandy road, the advanced guards of the two armies met a few miles north of Camden, without being aware of each other's approach. A fight in the

---

1. General Charles Lee, who knew Gates well, said to him, on his departure, "Take care that you do not exchange Northern laurels for Southern willows." There was prophecy in the warning.

dark ensued, and the following morning a severe battle took place. The Americans were defeated and fled in great confusion. Gates, almost unattended, hastened toward Charlotte. He tried to rally his fugitive troops in that vicinity, but failed. General Greene was soon afterward appointed to succeed him, and then commenced that series of brilliant movements which finally resulted in driving the British to the sea-board. A committee of Congress, appointed to scrutinize Gates' conduct, acquitted him of blame, and the national legislature sanctioned the verdict. He remained on his farm in Virginia until 1782, when he was reinstated in his military command in the main army, but active services were no longer needed. At the close of the contest he retired to his estate, where he remained until 1790, when he made his permanent abode upon Manhattan Island, near New York city. Two years later he was a member of the legislature of New York, where he served one term. He died at his residence, near the corner of the present Twenty-Third Street and Second Avenue, in New York, on the 10th of April, 1806, at the age of seventy-eight years. General Gates possessed many excellent qualities, but he was deficient in the necessary qualifications for a successful commander, and his vanity generally misled his judgment. He was a gentleman in his manners, humane and benevolent, but he lacked intellectual cultivation and true magnanimity.

JAMES MADISON.

WITHIN site of Blue Ridge, in Virginia, lived three Presidents of the United States, whose public career commenced in the Revolutionary times, and whose political faith was the same throughout a long series of years. These were Thomas Jefferson, James Monroe, and James Madison. The latter was born at the house of his maternal grandmother, on the banks of the Rappahannock, in Virginia, on the 16th of March, 1751. His parents resided in Orange county, and there, during a long life, the eminent statesman lived. After completing his preparatory studies, he was sent to the college at Princeton, New Jersey, then under the charge of Dr. Witherspoon, for his parents knew the atmosphere of the lower country at Williamsburg to be uncongenial for persons from the mountain regions. He left Princeton, in the Spring of 1773, with health much impaired by intense stud[1] and immediately entered upon a course of reading preparatory for the practice of the law, which he had chosen for a profession. Political affairs attracted his attention, and he was diverted from law to public employments. In the Spring of 1776, he was a member of the convention which formed the first Constitution for the new free State of Virginia; and the same year he was elected a member of the State legislature. He lost the suffrages of his constituents the following year, because, it was alleged, that he would not "treat" the people to liquor, and could not make a speech! The legislature named him a member of the executive council, in which office he served until 1779, when he was elected to membership in the Continental Congress. He took his seat there in March, 1780, and for three years he was one of the most reliable men in that body.[2]

Mr. Madison was again a member of the Virginia Assembly, from 1784 to 1786, where he was the champion of every wise and liberal policy, especially in

---

1. While at Princeton, he slept only three hours of the twenty-four, for months together.
2. He was the author of the able Instructions to Mr. Jay, when he went as minister to Spain; also of the Address of the States, at the end of the war, on the subject of the financial affairs of the confederacy.

religious matters. He advocated the separation of Kentucky from Virginia; opposed the introduction of paper money; supported the laws codified by Jefferson, Wythe, and Pendleton; and was the author of the resolution which led to the convention at Annapolis, in 1786, and the more important constitutional convention, in 1787. He was a member of the convention that formed the Federal Constitution, and he kept a faithful record of all the proceedings of that body, day after day.[1] After the labors of the convention were over, he joined with Hamilton and Jay in the publication of a series of essays in support of it.[2] These, in collected form, are known as *The Federalist*. In the Virginia convention called to consider the constitution, Mr. Madison was chiefly instrumental in procuring its ratification, in spite of the fears of many, and the eloquence of Patrick Henry. He was one of the first representatives of Virginia in the Federal Congress, and occupied a seat there until 1797. He was opposed to the financial policy of Hamilton, and to some of the most important measures of Washington's administration, yet this difference of opinion did not produce a personal alienation of those patriots.[3] His republicanism was of the conservative stamp, yet Mr. Jefferson esteemed him so highly that he chose him for his Sec-

---

[1] His interesting papers were purchased by Congress, after his death, for the sum of thirty thousand dollars.
[2] See sketches of Hamilton and Jay.
[3] Mr. Madison was opposed to the Alien and Sedition laws, enacted at the beginning of John Adams' administration; and it became known, after his death, that he was the author of the famous Resolutions on that topic, adopted in the convention of Virginia, held in 1798.

retary of State, in 1801. That station he filled with rare ability during the whole eight years of Jefferson's administration, and then he was elected President of the United States. It was a period of great interest in the history of our Republic, for a serious quarrel was then pending between the governments of the United States and Great Britain. In the third year of his administration the quarrel resulted in war, which continued from 1812 until 1815.

After serving eight years as chief magistrate of the Republic, Mr. Madison, in March, 1817, returned to his paternal estate of *Montpelier*, where he remained in retirement until his death, which occurred almost twenty years afterward. He never left his native county but once after returning from Washington, except to visit Charlottesville, occasionally, in the performance of his duties as visitor and rector of the University of Virginia. He made a journey to Richmond, in 1829, to attend a convention called to revise the Virginia Constitution. He had married an accomplished widow, in Philadelphia, in 1794, and with her, his books, friends, and in agricultural pursuits, he passed the evening of his days in great happiness. At length, at the age of eighty-five years, on a beautiful morning in June (28th), 1836, the venerable statesman went peacefully to his rest.

BENJAMIN LINCOLN.

THE first Secretary of War after the struggle for independence had resulted successfully for the colonists, in the capture of Cornwallis and his army, was Benjamin Lincoln, one of the most accomplished soldiers of the contest, then almost ended. He was born at Hingham, Massachusetts, on the 3d of February, 1733. He was trained to the business of a farmer, and had very few educational advantages. Until past forty years of age he pursued the quiet, unpretending life of a plain agriculturist, occasionally holding the office of justice of the peace, sometimes representing his district in the colonial legislature, and, when the tempest of the Revolution was about to burst forth, he was colonel of the militia of his county, under a commission from Governor Hutchinson. At the close of 1774, the Provincial Congress of Massachusetts appointed him major-general of militia, and being an excellent disciplinarian, he was actively employed until the close of 1776, in training recruits for the Continental service. With quite a large body of Massachusetts levies, he joined Washington, at Morristown, in February, 1777. On the 19th of that month, Congress appointed him one of five major-generals. During the ensuing Summer and Autumn he was active in collecting troops and otherwise assisting in the operations which resulted in the capture of Burgoyne and his army, at Saratoga. In the battle of the 7th of October, at Saratoga, he was severely wounded, and was detained from active service until 1778, when he joined the army under Washington. In September of that year, he was appointed to supersede General Howe, in command of the Southern Army, and arrived at Charleston, in December. He was chiefly engaged during the following season in keeping the British below the Savannah river. On the arrival of a French fleet and army, under D'Estaing, off the Georgia coast, early in September, Lincoln marched toward Savannah, to cooperate with them in besieging the British army, then strongly intrenched in that city. After a siege and assault, in October, D'Estaing, pleading danger to his shipping, from Autumnal storms, as an excuse, suddenly resolved to depart, and the Americans were compelled to abandon the enterprise, and retire into South Carolina.

During the Spring of 1780, Lincoln, with a comparatively weak force, was besieged in Charleston by a strong land and naval armament, under General Sir Henry Clinton and Admiral Arbuthnot. After making a gallant defence for several weeks, he was compelled to capitulate, and the Southern Army, Charleston and its fortifications, and the inhabitants of the city, were surrendered, unconditionally, into the hands of British power. General Lincoln was permitted to return to his native town, on parole; and, in November following, he was exchanged. He remained in retirement until the Spring of 1781, when he joined the army under Washington, on the Hudson, and was very active in preparations to attack the British on Manhattan Island, the ensuing Summer. Toward Autumn he accompanied the army to Virginia, rendered efficient service in the siege of Yorktown, and had the honor of receiving the surrendered sword of Cornwallis, from the hands of General O'Hara.[1] A few days after that event, Lincoln was appointed, by Congress, Secretary of the War Department. He held the office until near the close of 1783, when he resigned and retired to his farm. In 1786-7, he was placed in command of troops called out to quell the insurrection in Massachusetts, known as *Shay's Rebellion.* He was immediately successful, and then again sought repose and pleasure in the pursuits of agriculture, science, and literature. There he remained until 1789, when President Washington appointed him collector of the port of Boston. He performed the duties of that office for about twenty years, when, on the 9th of May, 1810, his earthly career was closed by death. That event occurred at his residence, in Hingham, when he was about seventy-seven years of age.

General Lincoln was a ripe scholar and humble Christian, as well as a patriotic soldier and honest civilian. The Faculty of Harvard University conferred upon him the degree of Master of Arts. He was a member of the American Academy of Arts and Sciences; and he was president of the Massachusetts Society of the Cincinnati, from its organization, until his death.

RICHARD CLOUGH ANDERSON.

ONE of the earliest natives of Louisville, Kentucky, was Richard C. Anderson, in whose honor a county in that State is named. His father was a gallant soldier of the War for Independence, and his mother was a sister of the hero of the North-west, George Rogers Clarke. Louisville was a small village at the Falls of the Ohio, at the time of his birth, which occurred on the 4th of August, 1788. At an early age he was sent to Virginia to be educated, for the foot-prints of the schoolmaster were few west of the Alleghanies, at that time. Emigration was then pouring a vast tide into the Ohio valleys, and a few years afterward, villages began to dot its banks at every important point.

Young Anderson was graduated at William and Mary College, studied law under Judge Tucker, and commenced its practice in his native town, then rapidly swelling toward the proportions of a city. He soon stood in the front rank of his profession as an able counsellor and eloquent advocate. Political life presented a high road to fame, and friends and ambition urged him to travel it. For several years he was a member of the Kentucky legislature; and, in 1817, he was elected to a seat in the Federal Congress, where he continued four years. It was a period of great excitement in that body, for, during Mr. Anderson's membership, the admission of Missouri was the topic for long and angry debates.

---

[1]. Lincoln had been much mortified by the manner of his surrender at Charleston, imposed by the haughty Clinton, and he was now allowed to be the chief actor in a scene more humiliating to British pride than his own had experienced. It was a triumph and a punishment that pleased him.

In these Mr. Anderson took a prominent part, and was highly esteemed for his manly and conciliatory course. His constituents were anxious to reëlect him, in 1822, but he declined the honor, because he considered his services to be more valuable, at that juncture, in the legislature of his own State, to which he was elected. He was chosen Speaker of the Assembly, but did not preside in that body long, for, in 1823, President Monroe appointed him the first United States minister to the new Republic of Colombia, South America. There he was received with joy and great honor, and during his residence at Bogota, the capital, he won for himself and family the unaffected love and esteem of all classes. In 1824, he negotiated an important treaty. The following year death took his wife from him, and he returned to Kentucky to make provision for the education of his children. He was again in Bogota, in the Autumn of that year, and remained until the Spring of 1826, when President Adams appointed him envoy extraordinary and minister plenipotentiary to the diplomatic Congress held at Panama, to consider the welfare of the South American Republics. On his way thither he was taken ill at the village of Tubaco, where he died, on the 24th of July, 1826, at the age of thirty-eight years. He was succeeded in office by William Henry Harrison, afterward President of the United States.

MATHEW CAREY.

FEW men have exerted so wide and beneficial an influence, in the domain of letters, in the United States, as Mathew Carey, an eminent author and publisher, who was born in the city of Dublin, on the 28th of January, 1760. His early education was comparatively limited, but a love of knowledge when his faculties began to expand on the verge of youthhood, overcame all difficulties. Even while yet a mere child, books afforded him more pleasure than playmates; and before he was fifteen years of age, he had made great progress in the acquisition of the modern languages of Europe. He would have become a distinguished linguist, had opportunity for study been given him; but at the age of fifteen he was apprenticed to a printer and bookseller to learn the business which he had chosen as a life-vocation. His first effort in authorship was made when he was seventeen years of age. His topic was *Duelling*. Two years afterward (1779) he prepared and advertised a political pamphlet, which alarmed the Irish Parliament, and caused that body to suppress its publication. A prosecution was determined upon, and his friends judiciously advised him to leave the country. He escaped to Paris, where he became acquainted with Dr. Franklin, and learned much concerning America. The storm subsided; and, in the course of the following year, young Carey, then only twenty years of age, returned to Dublin, and became editor of the *Freeman's Journal*. In 1783, his father furnished him with means to establish a paper called the *Volunteer's Journal*. It exerted a wide and powerful political influence; and in consequence of the publication in its columns, in 1784, of a severe attack upon the British government, and an alleged libel upon the Prime Minister, Mr. Carey was arrested, taken to the bar of the House of Commons, and consigned to Newgate prison. The Lord Mayor of London released him in the course of a few weeks; and in the Autumn of 1784, he sailed for America. He landed at Philadelphia with a few guineas in his pocket, chose that city for a residence, and, in January, 1785, commenced the publication of the *Pennsylvania Herald*. That paper soon became famous for its legislative reports, prepared by Mr. Carey himself. Bold, and faithful to his convictions, in editorship, he often offended his opponents. Among these was

Colonel Oswald, of the artillery corps of the Revolution, who was then editing a newspaper. Their quarrel resulted in a duel, in which Mr. Carey was severely wounded.

In 1786, Mr. Carey commenced the publication of the *Columbian Magazine*. The following year he issued another publication, called the *American Museum*, which he continued for six years, when the prevalence of yellow fever, in Philadelphia, suspended it. During that season of pestilence the courage and benevolence of Mr. Carey, as an associate with Stephen Girard and others as health commissioners, were nobly exhibited. Their labors for the sick and orphans were incessant and beneficent. His experience led him to the publication of an able essay on the origin, character, and treatment of yellow fever, in 1794. At about the same time he was active in founding the *Hibernian Society*, for the relief of emigrants from Ireland. In 1796, he was zealously engaged, with others, in establishing a Sunday School Society in Philadelphia; and the same year he entered into a controversy with the celebrated William Cobbett, with so much logic and energy, that he silenced his antagonist.

The most important effort, made by Mr. Carey in publishing, was in 1802, when he put forth a handsome edition of the standard English Quarto Bible. His chief travelling agent for its sale was Reverend Mason L. Weems, who disposed of several thousand copies.[1] It was profitable and creditable to Mr. Carey. During the whole exciting period just previous to the breaking out of the war with Great Britain, in 1812, Mr. Carey's pen was continually busy on topics of public interest; and in the midst of the violent party excitement, in 1814, he published his famous *Olive Branch*. It was intended to soften the asperities of party spirit, create a thoroughly American sentiment among all classes, and produce peace and conciliation. It was eminently successful; and for this effort, Mathew Carey deserved a civic crown. Ten thousand copies were sold, and its salutary influence is incalculable.

In 1818, Mr. Carey commenced the preparation of his most important historical work, the *Vindiciæ Hiberniæ*. He soon afterward directed his attention especially to political economy, and wrote voluminously upon the subject of tariffs. No less than fifty-nine pamphlets upon that and cognate topics were written by him between the years 1819 and 1833, and comprising over twenty-three hundred octavo pages. Besides these, he wrote numerous essays for newspapers, memorials to Congress, &c. Internal improvements also engaged his mind and pen, and his efforts in that direction entitle him to the honor of a public benefactor. Indeed, throughout his whole life Mr. Carey was eminently a benefactor, public and private; and hundreds of widows and orphans have earnestly invoked Heaven's choicest blessings upon his head. Scores of young men, who had been profited by his generous helping hand, loved him as a father; and people of the city in which he lived regarded him with the highest reverential respect, for his many virtues. There was sincere mourning in many households, in Philadelphia, when, on the 17th of September, 1839, that good man's spirit left earth for a brighter sphere. He had lived to the ripe old age of almost eighty years; and, in addition to a large fortune, he left to his descendants the precious inheritance of an untarnished reputation.

DAVID PORTER.

THE motto "Free Trade and Sailors' Rights," which became the text for many a song and speech, some forty years ago, was first emblazoned upon the broad pennant of Commodore Porter, that floated from the mast-head of his flag-ship, the *Essex*, when he sailed on his famous cruise in the Pacific Ocean, toward the close of 1813. The author of that motto was one of the bravest of the American naval commanders during the last war between the United States and Great Britain. He was born in Boston, on the 1st of February, 1780. His parents were in moderate circumstances, and after receiving the rudiments of education, David was compelled to labor most of the time with his hands. He had early manifested a great desire to become a sailor; and, at the age of nineteen years, that ardent aspiration was fully gratified. His talent and general energy of character attracted the attention of some influential friends, who procured for him a midshipman's warrant; and at the time when war with France was yet a probability, he sailed in the frigate *Constellation*. His first experience in naval warfare was during that cruise, when the *Constellation*, in February, 1799, captured the French frigate, *L'Insurgente*. Young Porter's gallantry on that occasion was so conspicuous, that he was immediately promoted to lieutenant. He was also engaged in the severe action with *La Vengeance*, a year later; and, in the Autumn of 1803, he accompanied the first United States squadron to the Mediterranean, sent thither to protect American commerce against the Barbary pirates. He was on board the *Philadelphia*, when that vessel struck upon a rock in the harbor of Tripoli, and was among those who suffered a painful imprisonment in the hands of that barbarous people.[1] After that [1806] he was appointed to the command of the brig *Enterprise*, and cruised in the Mediterranean for six years. On his return to the United States, he was placed in command of the flotilla station in the vicinity of New Orleans, where he remained until war was declared against Great Britain, in 1812. Then he was promoted to captain; and, in the frigate *Essex*, he achieved, during the remainder of that year, and greater part of 1813, those brilliant deeds which made him so famous. From April to October, 1813, he captured twelve armed British whale-ships, with an aggregate of one hundred and seven guns, and three hundred men. He also took possession of an island of the Washington group, in the Pacific, and named it Madison, in honor of the then President of the United States. The English sent a number of heavy armed ships to capture or destroy Porter's little squadron; and near Valparaiso, on the coast of Chili, the *Essex* was captured, in February, 1814, after a hard-fought battle with immensely superior strength. Commodore Porter wrote to the Secretary of the Navy, "We have been unfortunate but not disgraced." When he came home he was every where received with the highest honors. Congress and the several States gave him thanks, and by universal acclamation he was called the Hero of the Pacific. He afterward aided in the defence of Baltimore. When peace came, he was appointed one of the naval commissioners to superintend national marine affairs. In 1817, he commanded a small fleet, sent to suppress the depredations of pirates and freebooters in the Gulf of Mexico, and along its shores.

Commodore Porter resigned his commission in the Summer of 1826, and was afterward appointed resident United States minister, in Turkey. He died near Constantinople on the 3d of March, 1843, at the age of sixty-three years.

ALEXANDER MACOMB.

AMONG the stirring scenes of a military post in time of war, Alexander Macomb was born, and afterward became a noted martial leader. His birth occurred in the British garrison at Detroit, on the 3d of April, 1782, just at the close of hostilities between Great Britain and her colonies. When peace came, his father settled in New York; and at eight years of age, Alexander was placed in a school at Newark, New Jersey, under the charge of Dr. Ogden. There his military genius and taste became manifest. He formed his playmates into a company, and commanded them with all possible juvenile dignity. At the age of sixteen years he joined a company of Rangers, whose services were offered to the government of the United States, then anticipating a war with France. The following year he was promoted to a cornetcy in the regular army, but the cloud of war passed away, and his services were not needed. He had resolved on a military life, and was among the few officers retained in the regular service, on the disbanding of the army. He was commissioned second-lieutenant, in February, 1801, and first-lieutenant, in October, 1802, when he was stationed at Philadelphia, in the recruiting service. On completing a corps, he marched to the Cherokee country to join General Wilkinson. After a year's service there, his troops were disbanded, and he was ordered to West Point to join a corps of

---

1. See sketches of Decatur and Bainbridge.

engineers. There he became adjutant, and also advocate-general. So highly were his services in the latter office esteemed, and his attainments admired, that he was employed by the government in completing a code of regulations for courts-martial.

Lieutenant Macomb was promoted to captain of a corps of engineers, in 1805; and, in 1808, he was raised to the rank of major. In the Summer of 1810, he was commissioned lieutenant-colonel; and, on the organization of the army, in April, 1812, he was appointed acting adjutant-general. After the declaration of war, a few weeks later, he was commissioned colonel of artillery, and joined Wilkinson on the Canada frontier. He shared in the mortifications of that campaign of 1813; but at Plattsburgh, in September, the following year, while bearing the office of brigadier, he nobly coöperated with Macdonough on the lake, in a victory so decided and important, as to almost obliterate the shame of former failures. For his gallant services on that occasion he received the thanks of Congress and a gold medal; and the President conferred on him the honor of a major-general's commission. At the close of the war he was retained in the service, and ordered to the command of the military fort at Detroit, his birth-place. In 1821, he was called to the head of the engineer department at Washington city; and on the death of Major-General Brown, in 1828, he was promoted to *General-in-Chief* of the army of the United States. He died at his head-quarters, Washington city, on the 25th of June, 1841, and was succeeded in office by Major-general Scott, now [1855] the highly honored incumbent.

JAMES MONROE.

THE fifth President of the United States, James Monroe, like four of his predecessors in office, was a native of Virginia. He was born in Westmoreland county, on the 2d of April, 1759. His early life was spent in the midst of the political excitements during the kindling of the War for Independence, and he imbibed a patriotic and martial spirit from the stirring scenes around him. He left the college of William and Mary, at the age of about eighteen years. His young soul was fired by the sentiments of the Declaration of Independence, then just promulgated, and he hastened to the head-quarters of Washington, at New York, and enrolled himself as a soldier for Freedom. The disastrous battle near Brooklyn had just terminated, but he tasted of war soon afterward in the skirmish at Harlem and the battle at White Plains. He accompanied Washington in his retreat across the Jerseys; and with a corps of young men, as lieutenant, he was in the van of the battle at Trenton, where he was severely wounded. For his gallant services there he was promoted to captain; and during the campaigns of 1777 and 1778, he was aid to Lord Stirling. In the battles of Brandywine, Germantown, and Monmouth, he was distinguished for bravery and skill; and desirous of official promotion, from which, as a staff officer, he was precluded, he made unsuccessful efforts to raise a regiment in Virginia. He soon afterward left the army, and commenced the study of law with Mr. Jefferson; but when Arnold and Cornwallis invaded his native State, in 1781, he was found among the volunteers for its defence. He had been sent to the South, the previous year, by the governor of Virginia, to collect information respecting the military strength of the patriots, after the fall of Charleston.

In 1782, Mr. Monroe was elected a member of the Virginia legislature, and that body soon afterward gave him a seat in the executive council. The following year, at the age of twenty-five, he was elected to the general Congress, and

JAMES MONROE.

was present at Annapolis when Washington resigned his military commission to that body. He originated the first movement, in 1785, which led to the constitutional convention, in 1787. He was a member of the Virginia legislature in 1787, and the following year he was a delegate in the State convention to consider the Federal Constitution. He took part with Patrick Henry and others in opposition to its ratification, yet he was elected one of the first United States Senators from Virginia, under that instrument, in 1789. He remained in that body until 1794, when he was appointed to succeed Gouverneur Morris as minister at the French court. Washington recalled him, in 1796; and two years afterward he was elected governor of Virginia. He served in that office for three years, when Mr. Jefferson appointed him envoy extraordinary to act with Mr. Livingston at the court of Napoleon. He assisted in the negotiations for the purchase of Louisiana, and then went to Spain to assist Mr. Pinckney in endeavors to settle some boundary questions. They were unsuccessful. In 1807, he and Mr. Pinckney negotiated a treaty with Great Britain, but it was unsatisfactory, and was never ratified. That year Mr. Monroe returned to the United States.

Mr. Monroe was again elected governor of Virginia, in 1811, and soon afterward President Madison called him to his cabinet as Secretary of State. He also performed the duties of Secretary of War, for awhile, and remained in Mr. Madison's cabinet during the residue of his administration. In 1816, he was elected President of the United States, and was reëlected, in 1820, with great unanimity, the Federal party, to which he had always been opposed, having become almost extinct, as a separate organization. At the end of his second term, in 1825, Mr. Monroe retired from office, and made his residence in Loudon county, Virginia, until early in 1831, when he accepted a home with his son-in-law, Samuel L. Gouverneur, in the city of New York. He was soon afterward attacked by severe illness, which terminated his life on the 4th of July, 1831, when he was in the seventy-second year of his age.

THADDEUS KOŚCIUSCZKO.

WHAT has been said of the American citizenship of La Fayette, Steuben, and De Kalb, is true of Kosciuszko. His deeds naturalized him, and we claim him as our own, though born in far-off Lithuania, the ancient Sarmatia. That event occurred in the year 1756. He was descended from one of the most ancient and noble families of Poland, and was educated for the profession of a soldier, first in the military school at Warsaw, and afterward in France. Love enticed him from Warsaw. He eloped with a young lady of rank and fortune, was pursued and overtaken by her proud father, and was driven to the alternative of killing the parent or abandoning the maid. He chose the latter, and went to Paris. There he became acquainted with Silas Deane, the accredited commissioner of the revolted American colonies, who filled the soul of the young Pole with intense zeal to fight for liberty in America, and win those honors which Deane promised. He came in the Summer of 1776, and presented himself to Washington. "What can you do?" asked the commander-in-chief. "Try me," was the laconic reply. Washington was pleased with the young man, made him his aid, and, in October of that year, the Continental Congress gave him the appointment of engineer in the army, with the rank of colonel. He was in the Continental service during the whole of the war, and was engaged in most of the important battles in which Washington in the North, or Greene in the South, commanded. He was greatly beloved by the American officers, and was cordially admitted to membership in the Society of the Cincinnati. At the close of the war he returned to Poland, whose sovereign had permitted him to draw his sword in America, and was made a major-general by Poniatowski, in 1789.

In the Polish campaign against Russia, in 1792, Kosciuszko greatly distinguished himself; and in the noble attempt of his countrymen, in 1794, to regain their lost liberty, he was chosen general-in-chief. Soon afterward, at the head of four thousand men, he defeated twelve thousand Russians. Invested with the powers of a military Dictator, he boldly defied the combined armies of Russia and Prussia, amounting to more than one hundred and fifty thousand men. At length success deserted him; and, in October, 1794, his troops were overpowered in a battle about fifty miles from Warsaw. He was wounded, fell from his horse, and was made prisoner, exclaiming, "The end of Poland!"

> "Hope for a season bade the world farewell,
> And Freedom shrieked when Kosciuszko fell."—CAMPBELL.

The hero was cast into prison, in St. Petersburg, by the Empress Catherine. When she died, the Emperor Paul liberated him, and presented him with his own sword. Kosciuszko courteously refused the blade, and then uttered that terrible rebuke for the destroyers of Poland—that noble sentiment of a Patriot's heart—: "I have no longer need of a sword, since I have no longer a country to defend." He never again wore a military weapon.

In the Summer of 1797, Kosciuszko visited America, and was received with distinguished honors. Congress awarded him a life-pension, and gave him a tract of land, for his revolutionary services. The following year he went to France, purchased an estate near Fontainebleau, and resided there until 1814. He went to Switzerland, and settled at Soleure, in 1816. Early the following year he abolished serfdom on his family estates in Poland. On the 16th of October, 1817, that noble patriot died, at the age of sixty-one years. His body was buried in the tomb of the ancient kings of Poland, at Cracow, with great pomp; and at Warsaw there was a public funeral in his honor. The Senate of Cracow decreed that a lofty mound should be erected to his memory, on the heights of Bronislawad; and for three years men of every class and age toiled in the erection of that magnificent cairn, three hundred feet in height. The cadets of the Military Academy, at West Point, on the Hudson, erected an imposing monument there to the memory of Kosciuszko, in 1829, at a cost of five thousand dollars. His most enduring monument is the record of his deeds on the pages of History.

CHARLES LEE.

"BOILING WATER" was the significant name which the Mohawk Indians gave to Charles Lee, when he resided among them, and bore the honors of a chief.[1] His character was indeed like boiling water—hot and restless. He was a native of Wales, where he was born in 1731. His father was an officer in the British army; and it is asserted that the fiery little Charles received a military commission from George the Second, when only eleven years of age. In all studies, and especially those pertaining to military services, he was very assiduous, and became master of several of the continental languages. Love of adventure brought him to America, in 1756, as an officer in the British army, and he remained in service here during a greater part of the French and Indian war. He then returned to England; and, in 1762, he bore a colonel's commission, and served under Burgoyne, in Portugal. After that he became a violent politician, in England; and, in 1770, he crossed the channel, and rambled all over Europe, like a knight-errant, for about three years. His energy of character and military skill made him a favorite at courts, and he became an aid to Poniatowski, King of Poland. With that monarch's embassador, he went to Constantinople as a sort of Polish Secretary of Legation, but, becoming tired of court inactivity and court etiquette, he left the service of his royal patron, went to Paris, came to America toward the close of 1773, and, at the solicitation of Colonel Horatio Gates, whom he had known in England, he was induced to buy an estate in Berkeley county, Virginia, and settle there. He resigned his commission in the British army, and became an American citizen.

When the Continental army was organized, in June, 1775, Charles Lee was appointed one of the four major-generals, and accompanied Washington to Cambridge. He was active there until the British were driven from Boston, in the Spring of 1776, when he marched, with a considerable force, to New York, and afterward proceeded southward to watch the movements of Sir Henry Clinton. He participated in the defence of Charleston, as commander-in-chief; and after the British were repulsed, he joined Washington, at New York. After the battle

---

1. His tarry among the Mohawk Indians was at near the close of the French and Indian war, or about the year 1762. They were greatly pleased with his martial and energetic character, adopted him as a son, according to custom, and made him a chief of the nation, with the title of *Boiling Water*.

at White Plains, and the withdrawal of a great portion of the American army to New Jersey, General Lee was left in command of a force on the east side of the Hudson. While Washington was retreating toward the Delaware, at the close of Autumn, Lee tardily obeyed his orders to reinforce the flying army, and was made a prisoner while tarrying in the interior of New Jersey. His services were lost to the country until May, 1778, when he was exchanged for General Prescott, captured in Rhode Island by Colonel Barton.[1] A month afterward he was in command at Monmouth, where, during the hot contest of battle, he was sternly rebuked by Washington, for a shameful and unnecessary retreat. That rebuke on the battle-field wounded Lee's pride, and he wrote insulting letters to the commander-in-chief. For this, and for misconduct before the enemy, he was suspended from command, pursuant to a verdict of a court-martial. Congress confirmed the sentence, and he left the army in disgrace.

It had been evident from the beginning, that General Lee was desirous of obtaining the chief command, in place of Washington, and it was generally believed that he desired to injure the commander-in-chief by causing the loss of the battle at Monmouth. The verdict gave general satisfaction. The event made his naturally morose temper exceedingly irascible, and Lee lived secluded on his estate in Berkeley, for awhile. Then he went to Philadelphia, took lodgings in a house yet [1855] standing, that once belonged to William Penn, and there died in neglect, at the age of fifty-one years. General Lee was a brilliant man in many respects, but he lacked sound moral principles, was rough and profane in language, and neither feared nor loved God or man. In his will, he bequeathed his "soul to the Almighty, and his body to the earth;" and then expressed a desire not to be buried within a mile of any Presbyterian or Anabaptist meeting-house, giving as a reason that he had "kept so much bad company in life, that he did not wish to continue the connection when dead." His remains lie in the burial-ground of Christ Church, Philadelphia.

HUGH SWINTON LEGARE.

ONE of the most promising men of the Palmetto State was Hugh S. Legaré, who was

> "Snatched all too early from that august fame
> That, on the serene heights of silvered age,
> Waited with laurelled hands."

He was born at Dorchester, near Charleston, South Carolina, about the year 1800. He was of Huguenot descent. His father died when he was an infant, and he was left to the charge of an excellent mother. At the age of nine years he was placed in the school of Mr. King (afterward promoted to the bench in South Carolina), in Charleston, and was finally prepared for college by the excellent Reverend Mr. Waddel. He learned rapidly, and at the age of fourteen years he entered the College of South Carolina, where he was graduated with the highest honors. The profession of the law became his choice, and for three years he studied assiduously under the direction of Judge King, his early tutor. He then went to Europe, where he remained between two and three years. Soon after his return, he was elected to a seat in the South Carolina legislature. While there, some of those measures which tended toward political disunion were commenced, but Mr. Legaré was always found on the Federal side of the question, for he regarded the UNION with the utmost reverence.

---

1. See sketch of William Barton.

In 1827, Mr. Legaré and other cultivated gentlemen in the South commenced the publication of the "Southern Review," a literary and political periodical, which soon acquired great influence. Mr. Legaré was one of the chief and most popular of the contributors. He was soon called to fill an important public station, by receiving the appointment of attorney-general of South Carolina. He performed the duties of that office with great ability, until 1832, when he was appointed minister to Belgium, by President Jackson. There he remained until early in 1837, when he returned to Charleston, and was almost immediately elected to a seat in Congress. He first appeared there at the extraordinary session called by President Van Buren to consider the financial affairs of the country. There he displayed great statesmanship and fine powers of oratory, and was regarded by friends and foes as a rising man. At the end of his congressional term, he resumed the practice of law in Charleston, and was pursuing his avocations with great energy and *eclat,* when President Harrison, in 1841, called him to his cabinet as attorney-general of the United States. He continued in that station, under President Tyler, until the Summer of 1843, when, on the occasion of a visit to Boston, with the chief magistrate, in June, he was seized with illness, and died there, on the 20th of that month, at the age of about forty-three years.

JOHN QUINCY ADAMS.

THOMSON truthfully says:

> "Whoe'er amidst the sons
> Of reason, valor, liberty, and virtue,
> Displays distinguished merit, is a noble
> Of nature's own creating."

Judged by such a book of heraldry, John Quincy Adams appears a true nobleman of nature, for, in the midst of many wise, and good, and great men, he stood preëminent in virtue. He was the worthy son of a worthy sire, the elder President Adams, and was born at the family mansion at Quincy, Massachusetts, on the 11th of July, 1767. At the age of eleven years he accompanied his father to Europe, who went thither as minister of the newly-declared independent United States of America. In Paris he was much in the society of Dr. Franklin and other distinguished men; and it may be truly said that he entered upon the duties of a long public life before he was twelve years of age, for then he learned the useful rudiments of diplomacy and statesmanship. He attended school in Paris and Amsterdam, and was in the University of Leyden, for awhile. In 1781, when only fourteen years of age, he accompanied Mr. Dana (United States minister) to St. Petersburg, as private secretary; and during the Winter of 1782–3, he traveled alone through Sweden and Denmark, and reached the Hague in safety, where his father was resident minister for the United States. When his father was appointed minister to England, he returned home, and entered Harvard University, as a student, where he was graduated, in July, 1787.

At the age of twenty years, young Adams commenced the study of law with Judge Parsons, at Newburyport,[1] and entered upon its practice in Boston. Politics engaged his attention, and he wrote much on topics of public interest, especially concerning the necessity of neutrality, on the part of the United States,

---

1. While Adams was a student, Judge Parsons was chosen to address President Washington on the occasion of his visit to New England. The judge asked each of his students to write an address. That of Adams was chosen and delivered by the tutor.

J. Q. Adams

in relation to the quarrels of other nations. On the recommendation of Mr. Jefferson, President Washington introduced him into the public service of his country, by appointing him resident minister in the Netherlands, in 1794. He was afterward sent to Portugal, in the same capacity, but on his way he was met by a new commission from his father (then President), as resident minister at Berlin. He was married in London, in 1797, to a young lady from Maryland, then residing there with her father. Mr. Adams returned to Boston, in 1801, and the following year he was elected to the Massachusetts Senate. In 1803, he was sent to the Federal Senate, where he uniformly supported the measures of Mr. Jefferson, the old political opponent of his father. Because of that act of obedience to the dictates of his conscience and judgment, the legislature of Massachusetts censured him, and he resigned his seat, in 1806. His republican sentiments increased with his age; and, in 1809, Mr. Madison appointed him minister plenipotentiary to the Russian court. There he was much caressed by the Emperor Alexander; and when, in 1812, war was declared between the United States and Great Britain, that monarch offered his mediation. It was rejected; and, in 1814, Mr. Adams was placed at the head of the American commission appointed to negotiate a treaty of peace with Great Britain. He also assisted in negotiating a commercial treaty with the same government; and, in 1815, he was appointed minister to the English court. There he remained until 1817, when President Monroe called him to his cabinet as Secretary of State. He filled that office with signal ability during eight years, and then succeeded Mr. Monroe as President of the United States.

Mr. Adams' administration of four years was remarkable for its calmness, and the general prosperity of the country. There was unbroken peace with foreign nations, and friendly domestic relations, until near the close of his term, when party spirit became rampant. He was succeeded in office by General Jackson, in the Spring of 1829, and retired to private life, more honored and respected by all parties than any retiring president since Washington left the chair of state. His countrymen would not allow him to remain in repose; and, in 1830, he was elected a representative in Congress. In December, 1831, he took his seat there, and from that time until his death he continued to be a member of the House of Representatives, by consecutive reëlections. There he was distinguished for wise, enlightened, and liberal statesmanship; and, like the Earl of Chatham, death came to him at his post of duty. He was suddenly prostrated by paralysis, while in his seat in the House of Representatives, at Washington, on the 22d of February, 1848, and expired in the Speaker's room, in the capitol, on the following day. His last words were, "This is the end of earth." He was in the eighty-first year of his age.

DAVID CROCKETT.

"BE sure you are right, then go ahead," is a wise maxim attributed to one whose life was a continual illustration of the sentiment. Every body has heard of "Davy Crockett," the immortal back-woodsman of Tennessee—the "crack shot" of the wilderness—eccentric but honest member of Congress—the "hero of the Alamo"—yet few know his origin, his early struggles, and the general current of his life. History has but few words concerning him, but tradition is garrulous over his many deeds.

David Crockett was born at the mouth of the Limestone river, Greene county, East Tennessee, on the 17th of August, 1786. His father was of Scotch-Irish descent, and took a prominent part in the War for Independence. It was all a wilderness around David's birth-place, and his soul communed with nature in its unbroken wildness, from the beginning. He grew to young manhood, without any education from books other than he received in his own rude home. When only seven years of age, David's father was stripped of most of his little property, by fire. He opened a tavern in Jefferson county, where David was his main "help" until the age of twelve years. Then he was hired to a Dutch cattle-trader, who collected herds in Tennessee and Kentucky, and drove them to the eastern markets. This vagrant life, full of incident and adventure, suited young Crockett, but, becoming dissatisfied with his employer, he deserted him, and made his way back to his father's home. After tarrying there a year, he ran away, joined another cattle-merchant, and at the end of the journey, in Virginia, he was dismissed, with precisely four dollars in his pocket. For three years he was "knocking about," as he expressed it, and then sought his father's home again. He now enjoyed the advantages of a school for a few weeks; and finally, after several unsuccessful love adventures, he married an excellent girl, and became a father, in 1810, when twenty-four years of age. He settled on the banks of the Elk river, and was pursuing the quiet avocation of a farmer, in Summer, and the more stirring one of hunter, in the Autumn, when war was commenced with Great Britain, in 1812. Crockett was among the first to respond to General Jackson's call for volunteers, and under that brave leader he was engaged in several skirmishes and battles. He received the commission of colonel, at the close of the war, as a testimonial of his worth. His wife had died while he was in the army, and several small children were left to his care. The widow of a deceased friend soon came to his aid, and in this second wife he found an excellent guardian for his children. Soon after his marriage, he removed to Laurens county, where he was made justice of the peace, and was chosen to represent the district in the State legislature. Generous, full of fun, possessing great shrewdness, and "honest to a fault,"[1] Crockett was very popular in the legislature and among his constituents. In the course of a few years he removed to Western Tennessee, where he became a famous hunter. With the rough backwoodsmen there he was a man after their own hearts, and he was elected to a seat in Congress, in 1828, and again in 1830.[2] When the Americans in Texas commenced their war for independence, toward the close of 1835, Crockett hastened thither to help them, and at the storming of the Alamo, at Bexar, on the 6th of March, 1836, that eccentric hero was killed. He was then fifty years of age.

NATHANIEL MACON.

JOHN RANDOLPH, of Roanoke, made his friend, Nathaniel Macon, one of the legatees of his estate, and in his Will, written with his own hand, in 1832, he said of him, "He is the best, and purest, and wisest man I ever knew." This was high praise from one who was always parsimonious in commendations, but it was eminently deserved. Mr. Macon was born in Warren county, North Carolina, in 1757. His early youth gave noble promise of excellent maturity, and it was fulfilled in ample measure. After a preparatory course of study, he entered Princeton College. The tempest of the Revolution swept over New Jersey, toward the close of 1776, and that institution was closed. Young Macon returned home, his heart glowing with sentiments of patriotism, which had ripened under the genial culture of President Witherspoon, and he entered the military service with his brother, as a volunteer and private soldier. While in the army the people elected him to a seat in the House of Commons of his native State. Then, as ever afterward, he was unambitious of office as well as of money, and it was with great difficulty that he was persuaded to leave his companions-in-arms, and become a legislator. He yielded, and then commenced his long and brilliant public career. He served as a State legislator for several years, when, in 1791, he was chosen to represent his district in the Federal Congress. In that body he took a high position at once; and so acceptable were his services to his constituents, that he was regularly reëlected to the same office until 1815, when, without his knowledge, the legislature of North Carolina gave him a seat in the Senate of the United States. During five years of his service in the House of Representatives [1801–1806], he was Speaker of that body. He continued in the Senate until 1828, when, in the seventy-first year of his age, he resigned, and retired to private life. At that time he was a trustee of the University of North Carolina, and justice of the peace for Warren county. These offices he also resigned, and sought repose upon his plantation.

---

1. Many anecdotes illustrative of Colonel Crockett's honesty and generosity have been related. During a season of scarcity, he bought a flat-boat load of corn, and offered it for sale cheap. "Have you got money to pay for it?" was his first question when a man came to buy. If he replied "yes," Crockett would say, "Then you can't have a kernel. I brought it here to sell to people who have *no money*."

2. He and the opposing candidate canvassed their district together, and made stump speeches. Crockett's opponent had written his speech, and delivered the same one at different places. David was always original, and he readily yielded to his friend's request to speak first. At a point where both wished to make a good impression, Crockett desired to speak first. His opponent could not refuse; but, to his dismay, he heard David repeat his own speech. The colonel had heard it so often that it was fixed in his memory. The other candidate was *speechless*, and lost his election.

Mr. Macon was called from his retirement, in 1835, to assist in revising the Constitution of North Carolina. He was chosen president of the convention assembled for that purpose; and the instrument then framed bears the marked impress of his genius and thoroughly democratic sentiments. The following year he was chosen a presidential elector, gave his vote in the Electoral College for Martin Van Buren, and then left the theatre of public life, forever. The sands of his existence were almost numbered. God mercifully spared him the pains of long sickness. He had been subject to occasional cramps in the stomach. On the morning of the 29th of June, 1837, he arose early, as usual, dressed, and shaved himself, and after breakfast was engaged in cheerful conversation. At ten o'clock he was seized with a spasm, and without a struggle after the first paroxysm, he expired. Peacefully his noble soul left its earth-tenement for its home in light ineffable. As he lived, so he died—a good man and a bright example.

Mr. Macon was a member of Congress thirty-seven consecutive years; a longer term of service than was ever given by one man. He was appropriately styled the Father of the House, and men of all creeds looked up to him as a Patriarch for counsel and guidance.

SAMUEL SLATER.

THE man who contributes to the comfort of a people and the real wealth of a nation by opening new and useful fields of industry, is a public benefactor. For such reasons, Samuel Slater, the father of the cotton manufacture in the United States, ought to be held in highest esteem. He was a native of England, and was born near Belper, in Derbyshire, on the 9th of June, 1768. After acquiring a good education, his father, who was a practical farmer, apprenticed Samuel to the celebrated Jedediah Strutt, an eminent mechanic,[1] and then a partner with Sir Richard Arkwright, in the cotton-spinning business. Samuel was then fourteen years of age, and being expert with the pen and at figures, he was much employed as a clerk in the counting-room. At about that time he lost his father, but found a good guardian in his master. He evinced an inventive genius and mechanical skill, at the beginning, and he soon became the "favorite apprentice." During the last four or five years of his apprenticeship he was Strutt and Arkwright's "right hand man," as general overseer both in the making of machinery and in the manufacturing department.

Before he had reached his majority, young Slater had formed a design of going to America, with models of all of Arkwright's machines. At that time the conveying of machinery from England to other countries was prohibited, and severe government restrictions were interposed. Slater knew that, but was not disheartened. He revealed his plans to no one, and when he left his mother, he gave her the impression that he was only going to London. With a little money, his models, and his indentures as an introduction, he sailed for New York on the 13th of September, 1789, and arrived in November.[2] There he was employed for a short time, when a better prospect appeared in a proposition from Messrs. Almy and Brown, of Providence, Rhode Island, to join with them in preparations for cotton-spinning. He went there, was taken to the little neighboring village of Pawtucket, by the venerable Moses Brown,[3] and there, on the 18th of January, 1790, he commenced making machinery with his own hands. Eleven

---
1. Mr. Strutt was the inventor of the Derby ribbed-stocking machine.
2. Just as the ship sailed, he intrusted a letter for his mother to the hands of a friend, in which he gave her information of his destination and his intentions. They never met again on earth.
3. See sketch of Moses Brown.

months afterward they "started three cards, drawing and roving, and seventy-two spindles, which were worked by an old fulling-mill water-wheel in a clothier's establishment." There they remained about twenty months, when they had several thousand pounds of yarn on hand, after making great efforts to weave it up and sell it. Such was the beginning of the successful manufacture of cotton in the United States. Tench Coxe and others had urged the establishment of that branch of industry; and several capitalists had attempted it, but with poor success with imperfect machinery.

In 1793, Mr. Slater was a business partner with Almy & Brown, and they built a factory yet [1855] standing, at Pawtucket. At about the same time he married Hannah Wilkinson, of a good Rhode Island family; and, in 1795, imitated Mr. Strutt by opening a Sabbath-school for children and youths, in his own house. The manufacturing business was gradually extended, and Mr. Slater took pride in sending to Mr. Strutt, specimens of cotton yarn, equal to any manufactured in Derbyshire. When war with Great Britain commenced, in 1812, and domestic manufactures felt a powerful impulse, there were seven thousand spindles in operation in Pawtucket alone; and within the little State of Rhode Island, there were over forty factories and about forty thousand spindles. A writer, in 1813, estimated the number of cotton factories built and in course of erection, eastward of the Delaware river, at five hundred.[1]

---

1. According to the census of 1870, the number of cotton establishments then in the United States, was 1,094, in which more than seventy-four millions of dollars were invested. These gave employment to

When President Jackson made his eastern tour, he visited Pawtucket, and, with the Vice-President, called on Mr. Slater and thanked him in the name of the nation, for what he had done. "You taught us how to spin," said the President, "so as to rival Great Britain in her manufactures; you set all these thousands of spindles at work, which I have been delighted in viewing, and which have made so many happy by lucrative employment." "Yes, sir," Mr. Slater replied; "I suppose that I gave out the psalm, and they have been singing to the tune ever since."

Mr. Slater died at Webster, Massachusetts, (where he had built a factory, and resided during the latter years of his life), on the 20th of April, 1834, at the age of about sixty-seven years.

LUCRETIA MARIA DAVIDSON.

"In the cold moist earth we laid her, when the forest cast the leaf,
And we wept that one so lovely should have a lot so brief;
Yet not unmeet it was, that one, like that young friend of ours,
So gentle and so beautiful, should perish with the flowers."—BRYANT.

"THERE is no record," says Dr. Sparks, "of a greater prematurity of intellect, or a more beautiful development of native delicacy, sensibility, and moral purity," than was exhibited by Miss Lucretia Maria Davidson, the wonderful child-poet. She was the daughter of Dr. Oliver Davidson, and a mother of the highest susceptibility of feeling and purity of taste. She was born at Plattsburg, New York, on the 27th of September, 1808. Her body was extremely fragile from earliest infancy until her death. The splendor and strength of her intellect appeared when language first gave expression to her ideas, and at the age of four years she was a thoughtful student at the Plattsburg Academy. She shrunk from playmates, found no pleasure in their sports, and began to commit her thoughts (which came in numbers) to paper, before she had learned to write. Before she was six years of age her mother found a large quantity of paper covered with rude characters and ruder drawings of objects, which Lucretia had made, and carefully hidden. She had secretly managed to make a record of her thoughts, in letters of printed form, as she could not write, and on deciphering them, her mother discovered that they were regular rhymes, and the rude drawings were intended as illustrative pictures. Here was an author illustrating her own writings before she was six years of age! The discovery gave the mother much joy, but the child was inconsolable. The key to the arcanum of her greatest happiness was in the possession of another.

Lucretia's thirst for knowledge increased with her years, and she would sometimes exclaim, "Oh that I could grasp all at once!" She wrote incessantly, when leisure from domestic employment would allow, but she destroyed all she wrote, for a long time. Her earliest preserved poem was an epitaph on a pet Robin, written in her ninth year. At the age of eleven her father took her to see a room which was decorated for the purpose of celebrating the birth-day of Washington in. The ornaments had no charms for her; the *character* of Washington occupied all her thoughts; and, on returning home, she wrote five excellent verses on that theme. An aunt ventured to express doubts of their originality. The truthful child was shocked at the hint of deception, and she immediately wrote a poetic epistle to her aunt, on the subject, which convinced her that Lucretia was the author.

---

over ninety-two thousand persons, male and female, and produced annually manufactured goods valued at more than sixty millions of dollars. The value of the raw material used was almost thirty-five millions of dollars.

Before she was twelve years of age Lucretia had read most of the works of the standard English poets; the whole of the writings of Shakspeare, Kotzebue, and Goldsmith; much history, and several romances of the better sort. She was passionately fond of Nature, and she would sit for hours watching the clouds, the stars, the storm, and the rainbow, and when opportunity offered, mused abstractedly in the fields and forests, as if in silent admiration. On such occasions her dark eye would light up with ethereal splendor, and she seemed really to commune with beings of angelic natures. At length her mother became an invalid, and the cares of the household devolved on Lucretia. The little maiden toiled on and hoped on; ever obedient, self-sacrificing, and thoughtful of her mother's happiness, while the wings of her spirit fluttered vehemently against the prison bars of circumstances, which kept it from soaring. "Oh," she said one day to her mother, "if *I* only possessed half the means of improvement which I see others slighting, I should be the happiest of the happy. I am now sixteen years old, and what do I know? Nothing!" Light soon beamed upon her darkened path. A generous stranger offered to give her every advantage of education. The boon was joyfully accepted, and Lucretia was placed in Mrs. Willard's school, in Troy. There she drank too deep and ardently at the fountain of knowledge—her application to study was too intense, and her fragile frame was too powerfully swayed by the energies of her spirit. During her first vacation she suffered severe illness. After her recovery she was placed in Miss Gilbert's school, in Albany, but soon another illness prostrated her. She rallied, and then went home to die. Like a flower when early frost hath touched it, that sweet creature faded and drooped; and on the 27th of August, 1825, the perfume of her mortal life was exhaled in the sunbeams of immortality, before she had completed her seventeenth year.

The last production of Miss Davidson's pen was written during her final illness, and was left unfinished.[1] She had a dread of insanity, and that poem was on the subject. She wrote,

> "That thought comes o'er me in the hour
> Of grief, of sickness, or of sadness;
> 'Tis not the dread of Death—'tis more:
> It is the dread of Madness!"

God mercifully spared her that affliction, and her intellect was clear as a sunbeam when death closed her eyelids.

JOHN ARMSTRONG.

WHILE the remnant of the Continental army was encamped near Newburgh, a few months before they were finally disbanded, and much dissatisfaction existed among the officers and soldiers because of the seeming injustice of Congress, anonymous addresses appeared, couched in strong language, and calculated to increase the discontents and to excite the sufferers to mutinous and rebellious measures. Those addresses, which exhibited great genius and power of expression, were written by John Armstrong, one of the aids to General Gates, and a young man then about twenty-five years of age. He was a son of General John Armstrong, of Pennsylvania, who was distinguished in the French and

---

1. In 1829, a collection of her writings was published, with the title of *Amir Khan and other Poems*, prefaced with a biographical sketch, by Professor S. F. B. Morse. That volume forms her appropriate

Indian war, and participated in the military events of the Revolution. John was born at Carlisle, Pennsylvania, on the 25th of November, 1758, and was educated in the college at Princeton. While a student there, in 1775, he joined the army as a volunteer in Potter's Pennsylvania regiment, and was soon afterward appointed aid-de-camp to General Mercer. He continued with that brave officer until his death, at Princeton, early in 1777, when he took the same position in the military family of General Gates, with the rank of major. He was with that officer until the capture of Burgoyne. In 1780, he was promoted to adjutant-general of the Southern army, when Gates took the command, but becoming ill on the banks of the Pedee, Colonel Otho H. Williams took his place, until just before the battle near Camden. Then he resumed it, and continued with General Gates until the close of the war. It seems to have been at the suggestion of General Gates and other distinguished officers, that Major Armstrong prepared the celebrated *Newburgh Addresses*.[1]

Under the administration of the government of Pennsylvania, by Dickenson and Franklin, Major Armstrong was Secretary of State and adjutant-general. These posts he occupied in 1787, when he was elected to a seat in Congress. In the Autumn of that year he was appointed one of three judges for the Western Territory, but he declined the honor. In 1789, he married a sister of Chancellor Livingston, of New York, and purchased a beautiful estate on the banks of the Hudson, in the upper part of Dutchess county, where he resided until his death, fifty-four years afterward. He continually refused public office until the year 1800, when, by an almost unanimous vote of the legislature of New York, he was chosen to represent the State in the Federal Senate. He resigned that office in 1802, but was reëlected, in 1803. A few months afterward, President Jefferson appointed him minister plenipotentiary to France, where he remained more than six years, a portion of the time performing the duties of a separate mission to Spain, with which he was charged.

In 1812, Major Armstrong was commissioned a brigadier-general in the army of the United States, and took command in the city of New York, until called to the cabinet of President Madison, the next year, as Secretary of War. He accepted the office with much reluctance, for he had many misgivings concerning the success of the Americans. He at once made some radical changes by substituting young for old officers, and thereby made many bitter enemies. The capture and conflagration of Washington, in 1814, led to his retirement from office.[2] Public opinion then held him chiefly responsible for that catastrophe, but documentary evidence proves the injustice of that opinion. No man ever took office with purer motives, or left it with a better claim to the praise of a faithful servant. He retired to private life, resumed agricultural pursuits, and lived almost thirty years after leaving public employment. He died at his seat at Red Hook, Dutchess county, on the 1st of April, 1843, in the eighty-fifth year of his age. General Armstrong was a pleasing writer. He is known to the public, as such, chiefly by his *Life of Montgomery*, *Life of Wayne*, and *Notices of the War of* 1812.

---

1. The first Address set forth the grievances of the army, evoked the use of power in their hands to redress them, and proposed a meeting of officers to take matters into their own hands, and *compel* Congress to be just. Washington defeated the movement by timely counter-measures. The attempt, however, aroused Congress and the whole country to a sense of duty toward the army, and a satisfactory result was accomplished. No doubt the Address and its bold propositions were put forth with patriotic intentions. Such was the opinion expressed to the author, by Washington, fourteen years afterward.

2. In August, 1814, a strong British force, under General Ross, penetrated Maryland by way of the Patuxent, and after a severe skirmish with the Americans at Bladensburg, pushed on to Washington city, burned the capitol, the President-house, and other public and private buildings, and then hastily retreated. Armstrong was censured for not making necessary preparations for the invasion, as was alleged.

HOSEA BALLOU.

THAT gifted and remarkable promulgator of the religious doctrine known as *Universalism,* Hosea Ballou, was the founder of the sect in this country, and for that reason, as well as for the patriarchal age to which he attained, as a minister, he was appropriately called by the affectionate and reverential name of Father Ballou. He was a native of Richmond, New Hampshire, where he was born on the 30th of April, 1771. His early years were passed among the beautiful and romantic scenery of Ballou's Dale, and in the groves, "God's first temples," his devotional feelings were early stirred and long nourished. His early education was utterly neglected; and it was when he was upon the verge of manhood that he first studied English grammar, and applied himself earnestly to the acquirement of knowledge from books. At the age of sixteen years he first managed to read and write fluently, after a great deal of unaided industry and perseverance. In those efforts, the family Bible became his chief instructor, and it was the instrument, under God, that made him what he was in after life. Farm labor was the daily occupation of his youth, and it gave him physical vigor for the severe labors of a long life.

At the age of eighteen years young Ballou became a member of the Baptist Church. His religious views soon changed. He became possessed of the idea that *all* would be finally happy, because "God is love, and his grace is impartial." The idea took the form of a creed, and an earnest longing to have others enjoy what he felt to be a great blessing, caused him to commence preaching, feebly yet effectively, at the age of twenty years. At a common school and an academy he studied intensely "night and day, slept little and ate little." Then he commenced school teaching for a livelihood, studying assiduously all the while, and preaching his new and startling doctrine, occasionally. At the age of twenty-four years he abandoned school teaching, and dedicated his life to the promulgation of his peculiar religious views, travelling from place to place, and subsisting upon the free bounties of increasing friends. His itinerant labors ceased in 1794, when he became pastor of a congregation, first in Dana, Massachusetts, and then in Barnard, Vermont. His warfare upon prevailing religious opinions produced many bitter opponents, yet meekly and firmly he labored on, spreading the circle of his influence with tongue and pen. Mr. Ballou was undoubtedly the first who, in this country, inculcated *Unitarianism;* and every where his doctrine was new, and "a strange thing in Israel."

In 1804, Mr. Ballou published *Notes on the Parables*, and soon afterward his *Treatise on the Atonement*, appeared. These were met by heartiest condemnation on the part of his opponents, while they were very highly esteemed by his religious adherents. In 1807, he was called to the pastoral charge of a congregation at Portsmouth, New Hampshire, where he continued to preach to crowded houses on the Sabbath, and teach a school during the week, until the war between the United States and Great Britain was kindled, in 1812. He was in the midst of those who violently opposed the war; and because he patriotically espoused the cause of his country, he made many bitter enemies, and impaired his usefulness. He accordingly left Portsmouth, in 1815, and accepted a call to Salem. While there he engaged in the celebrated controversy with Rev. Abner Kneeland, whose faith in Christianity had failed him. It ended happily in the avowed conviction of Mr. Kneeland of the truths of revealed religion. Mr. Ballou remained in Salem about two years, when he was invited to make Boston his field of labor. Near the close of 1817, he was installed pastor of the Second Universalist Church, in Boston, and that connection was only severed by his death. There his ministrations were attended by immense congregations, and he laid the foundations of *Unitarianism* and *Universalism* strong and deep in the New England metropolis.

In 1819, Mr. Ballou established the *Universalist Magazine*, which soon acquired high reputation for its literary merits and denominational value. The following year he compiled a collection of Hymns for the use of the sect; and soon afterward he made a professional visit to New York and Philadelphia, where great numbers of people listened to his eloquent and logical discourses. In Philadelphia, he preached in the *Washington Garden Saloon*, no meeting-house being large enough to hold the immense crowds that gathered to hear him. In 1831, he was associated with a nephew in publishing the *Universalist Expositor*, a quarterly periodical; and at about the same time volumes of his *Sermons* and *Lectures* were published. In 1834, he wrote and put forth *An Examination of the Doctrine of Future Retribution;* and in the meanwhile his pen was ever busy in contributions to denominational publications. Old age now whitened his locks, yet his "eye was not dim nor his natural forces abated," and at the age of seventy-two years [1843] he made a long journey to Akron, Ohio, to attend a national convention of *Universalists*. Thousands flocked thither to see and hear the far-famed Father Ballou, and were gratified. He was permitted to return to his beloved home and flock in safety, and continued his pastoral labors almost nine years longer. Finally, on the 7th of June, 1852, that eminently great and good man died, at the age of a little more than eighty years. He had been a distinguished preacher for the long period of sixty years. He was a vigorous yet generous polemic, a pleasing and voluminous writer, and an eloquent speaker. His thoughts, occasionally expressed in verse, exhibit many beautiful specimens of genuine poetry.

STEPHEN HOPKINS

NEXT to Doctor Franklin, Stephen Hopkins, of Rhode Island, was the oldest member of the Continental Congress, who signed the Declaration of Independence. He was born in that portion of the town of Providence now called Scituate, on the 7th of March, 1707. The opportunities at that time and place for acquiring an education were few and weak, and Hopkins became a self-taught man in the truest sense of the term. He was a farmer until the age of twenty-five years, when he commenced mercantile business in Providence. The following year he was chosen to represent Scituate in the Rhode Island legislature, and was annually reëlected until 1738. He resumed his seat there in 1741, and was made Speaker of the House. From that time until 1751, he was almost every year a member and the Speaker of the lower House. In the latter year he was chosen chief justice of the colony.

Mr. Hopkins was a delegate from Rhode Island in the first colonial convention, held at Albany, in 1754,[1] and two years afterward he was elected governor of Rhode Island. That position he held, with but a single interruption, until 1767; and he was very efficient in promoting the enlistment of volunteers in his province, for the expeditions against the French and Indians. He even took a captain's commission, and placed himself at the head of a volunteer corps, in 1757, but a change in events rendered their services unnecessary, and they were disbanded. When the quarrel with the mother country commenced, Governor Hopkins took a decided stand in favor of the colonists; and officially and unofficially he labored incessantly to promote a free and independent spirit among his countrymen. A proof of his love of justice, as well as a love of liberty, is found in the fact that he endeavored to procure legislative enactments in favor of the emancipation of slaves in Rhode Island, and he actually gave freedom to all owned by himself. When, in 1774, a general Congress was proposed, Governor Hopkins warmly advocated the measure, and was chosen one of the delegates for Rhode Island. At the same time he held the important offices of chief justice of the province and representative in its Assembly. In 1775, he was a member of the Committee of Public Safety, in Rhode Island, and was again elected to Congress. There he advocated political independence; and in the Summer of 1776, he affixed his remarkable signature[2] to the noble manifesto which declared it.

Mr. Hopkins was elected to Congress, for the last time, in 1778, and was one of the committee who perfected the *Articles of Confederation* for the government of the United States, then fighting under one banner, for independence. He was then more than seventy years of age, yet he was actively engaged in the duties of almost every important committee while he held his seat in Congress. He retired in 1780, and then withdrew from public life to enjoy repose and indulge in his favorite study of the exact sciences. He was a distinguished mathematician, and rendered efficient service to scientific men in observing the transit of Venus, in 1769.[3] But his season of earthly repose and happiness was short. The Patriot and Sage went down into the grave on the 19th of July, 1785, in the seventy-eighth year of his age. Through life he had been a constant attendant of the religious meetings of Friends, or Quakers, and was ever distinguished among men as a sincere Christian.

---

1. See sketch of Dr. Franklin.
2. It is remarkable because of its evidence that his hand trembled excessively. That tremulousness is not attributable, as might be suspected of a less bold man, to fear inspired by the occasion, but by a malady known as *shaking palsy*, with which he had been troubled many years. I have a document before me, signed by him in 1761. His signature at that time betrays the same unsteadiness of hand, though not in the same degree as in 1776.   3. See sketches of Winthrop and Rittenhouse.

ALBERT GALLATIN.

DURING the most important period in the progress of our Republic after its permanent organization, in 1789, Albert Gallatin, a native of Geneva, Switzerland, was an active, useful, and highly patriotic citizen and public officer. He was born on the 29th of January, 1761. His family connections were of the highest respectability. Among these was the celebrated M. Necker and his equally-distinguished daughter, Madame de Staël. His father, who died when Albert was four years of age, was then a councillor of state. At a proper age Albert was placed in the University of Geneva, where he was graduated in 1779. He had early felt and manifested a zeal for republican institutions, and declining the commission of a lieutenant-colonel in the service of one of the German sovereigns, he came to America, in 1780, when only nineteen years of age. In November of that year he entered the public service of his adopted country, by taking command of a small fort at Machias, Maine, which was garrisoned by volunteers and Indians. At the close of the war he taught the French language in Harvard University, for awhile. Having received his patrimony from Europe, in 1784, he purchased lands in Virginia. He afterward established himself on the banks of the Monongahela, in Pennsylvania, where his talents were soon brought into requisition. He was a member of the convention to revise the constitution of Pennsylvania, in 1789, and for two succeeding years he was representative of the State legislature. In that body those financial abilities, which afterward rendered him eminent in the administration of the national treasury, were manifested. In 1793, he was elected to a seat in the Senate of the United States, but, by a strictly party vote, he was excluded from it on the ground of ineligibility, because nine years had not elapsed since his naturalization in Virginia.[1] He was immediately elected a member of the House of Representatives, where he was confessedly the Republican leader, and was regarded as one of the most logical debaters and soundest statesmen in that body. In 1801, President Jefferson appointed Mr. Gallatin Secretary of the Treasury. He exercised the functions of that office with rare ability, during the whole of Jefferson's administration, and a part of Madison's, until 1813, when he went to St. Petersburg, as one of the envoys extraordinary of the United States, to negotiate with Great Britain under the mediation of Russia.[2] He was appointed one of the commissioners who negotiated a treaty of peace with Great Britain, at Ghent, in 1814; and early the following year he assisted in forming a commercial treaty with the same power. From 1816 until 1823, Mr. Gallatin was resident minister of the United States at the French court, and in the meanwhile had been employed on extraordinary missions to the Netherlands and to Great Britain. In these diplomatic services he was ever skilful, and always vigilant in guarding the true interests of his country. Other official stations had been proffered him, while he was abroad. President Madison invited him to become his Secretary of State, or Prime Minister; and President Monroe offered him a place in his cabinet, as Secretary of the Navy. He also declined the nomination of Vice-President of the United States which the Democratic party offered him, in 1824.

Mr. Gallatin returned home, in 1828, and became a resident of New York city, where he took an active interest in all matters pertaining to the public good. In 1831, he wrote the memorial to Congress of the Free-Trade Convention, and from that time until 1839, he gave a noble example of the true method of banking, while he was President of the National Bank. He was one of the founders,

---

1. See clause 3, section 3, article I. of the Constitution of the United States.
2. See sketches of John Quincy Adams and James A. Bayard.

and first president of the council of the New York University. At the time of his death he was President of the New York Historical Society, and also of the American Ethnological Society, of which he was chief founder. A few days before his death he was elected one of the first members of the Smithsonian Institute. His departure occurred at his residence at Astoria, Long Island, on the 12th of August, 1849, at the age of more than eighty-eight years.

DAVID WOOSTER.

FOR almost fourscore years the grave of one of America's best heroes was allowed to remain unhonored by a memorial-stone, until tradition had almost forgotten the hallowed spot. That hero was David Wooster, who lost his life in the defence of the soil of his native State against that ruthless invader, General Tryon. He was born at Stratford, Connecticut, on the 2d of March, 1710, and was graduated at Yale College, in 1738. When war between England and Spain broke out the following year, he entered the provincial army as a lieutenant, and was soon afterward promoted to the captaincy of a vessel built and armed by the colony as a *guarda costa*, or coast-guard. In 1740, he married Miss Clapp, daughter of the President of Yale College; and, in 1745, we observe his first movements in military life as a captain in Colonel Burr's regiment in the expedition against Louisburg. From Cape Breton he went to Europe in command of a cartel-ship.[1] But he was not permitted to land in France, and he sailed for England, where he was received with great honor. He was presented to the king, became a favorite at court, and was made a captain in the regular service, under Sir William Pepperell. When the French and Indian war in America broke out, he was commissioned a provincial colonel by the governor of Connecticut, and was finally promoted to brigadier-general. He was in service to the end of that war; and when, in 1775, the revolutionary fires kindled into a flame, he was found ready to battle manfully for his country in its struggle for freedom. He was with Arnold and Allen at the capture of Ticonderoga; and when the Continental army was organized, a few weeks later, he received the appointment of brigadier-general, third in rank. He was in command in Canada, in the Spring of 1776; and soon after his return to Connecticut, he was appointed first major-general of the militia of that State. In that capacity he was actively engaged when Tryon invaded the State, in the Spring of 1777, and penetrated to and burned Danbury. Near Ridgefield he led a body of militia in pursuit of the invader, and there, in a warm engagement, on Sunday, the 27th of April, he was fatally wounded by a musket-ball. He was conveyed to Danbury on a litter, where he lived long enough for his wife and children to arrive from New Haven, and soothe his dying hours. He expired on the 2d of May, 1777, at the age of sixty-seven years, and was interred in the village burying-ground. Congress ordered a monument to be erected to his memory, but that act of justice has never been accomplished by the Federal government. The legislature of Connecticut finally resolved to erect a memorial; and in April, 1854, the cornerstone of a monument was laid, with imposing ceremonies.[2] On opening the grave, the remains of the hero's epaulettes and plume, and the fatal *bullet*, were found among his bones.

---

[1]. A vessel commissioned in time of war to carry proposals between belligerent powers. It claims the same respect as a flag sent from one army to another.
[2]. On that occasion the Honorable Henry C. Deming pronounced an eloquent oration, which was subsequently published in pamphlet form.

THOMAS MACDONOUGH.

ON the very day when Washington resigned his military commission into the custody of Congress, from whom he had received it, a future American naval hero was born in Newcastle county, Delaware. It was on the 23d of December, 1783, and that germ of a hero was Thomas Macdonough. At the age of fifteen years he obtained a midshipman's warrant, and in the war with Tripoli he was distinguished for bravery. He was one of the daring men selected by Decatur to assist him in burning the *Philadelphia* frigate,[1] and he partook of the honors of that brilliant exploit. When war with Great Britain was proclaimed in 1812, Macdonough held a lieutenant's commission, having received it in February, 1807. He was ordered to service on Lake Champlain, and in July, 1813, he was promoted to master-commandant. There was very little for him to do, in that quarter, for some time, and he became restive in comparative idleness. But opportunity for action came at last, and he gladly accepted and nobly improved it. The war in Europe having been suspended, early in 1814, by the abdication of Napoleon and the capture of Paris by the allied armies, the British forces in America were largely augmented. Quite a strong army, under Sir

---

1. See sketch of Decatur.

George Prevost, invaded New York from the St. Lawrence; and a fleet, under Commodore Downie, sailed up Lake Champlain to coöperate with the land forces. They were called "the flower of Wellington's army, and the cream of Nelson's marines." General Macomb was in command of a small land force, composed chiefly of local militia, and Macdonough had a little squadron of four ships and ten galleys, with an aggregate of eighty-six guns. Such was the force which stood in the way of the sanguine invader. On the 11th of September, 1814, the British land and naval forces both approached. The conflict was short but decisive. Macdonough, by superior nautical skill and dexterity in the management of guns, soon caused the British flag to fall, when Prevost, in dismay, hastily retreated, leaving victory with the Americans on both land and water.[1] The victory was hailed with great joy throughout the country, and Macdonough's fame was proclaimed every where, in oration and in song. Congress awarded him a gold commemorative medal, and gave him the commission of a post captain. Other substantial rewards were bestowed. The State of New York gave him one thousand acres of land; that of Vermont, two hundred acres; and the cities of New York and Albany each gave him a lot of ground. At about the close of the war, Commodore Macdonough's health gave way, yet he lived for more than ten years with the tooth of consumption undermining his citadel of life. He died on the 10th of November, 1825, at the age of about forty-two years. He was exemplary in every relation of life, and had but few of the common faults of humanity. His bravery was born of true courage, not of mere intrepidity, and he never quailed in the face of most imminent danger.[2]

SAMUEL SMITH.

SAMUEL SMITH, the "hero of Fort Mifflin," lived more than sixty years after the achievements there, which won for him that appropriate title. He was a native of Lancaster county, Pennsylvania, where he was born on the 27th of January, 1752. His father was a distinguished public man, first in Pennsylvania and then in Maryland. Samuel's education commenced at Carlisle, Pennsylvania, and was completed at an academy in Elkton, Maryland, after his father made Baltimore his residence. At the age of fourteen years he entered his father's counting-house as a clerk, remained there five years, and then, in 1772, departed for Havre as supercargo in one of his father's vessels. After travelling extensively on the Continent, he returned home, and found his countrymen in the midst of the excitements of the opening of the revolutionary hostilities. The

---

1. When the British squadron appeared off Cumberland-head, Macdonough knelt on the deck of the *Saratoga* (his flag-ship), in the midst of his men, and prayed to the God of Battles for aid. A curious incident occurred during the engagement that soon followed. A British ball demolished a hen-coop on board the *Saratoga*. A cock, released from his prison, flew into the rigging, and crowed lustily, at the same time flapping his wings with triumphant vehemence. The seamen regarded the event as a good omen, and they fought like tigers, while the cock cheered them on with its crowings, until the British flag was struck and the firing ceased.

2. On one occasion, while first-lieutenant of a vessel, lying in the harbor of Gibraltar, an armed boat from a British man-of-war boarded an American brig anchored near, in the absence of the commander, and carried off a seaman. Macdonough manned a gig, and with an inferior force, made chase and recaptured the seaman. The captain of the man-of-war came aboard Macdonough's vessel, and in a great rage asked him how he dared to take the man from his majesty's boat. "He was an American seaman, and I did my duty," was the reply. "I'll bring my ship along side, and sink you," angrily cried the Briton. "That you can do," coolly responded Macdonough, "but while she swims, that man you will not have." The captain, roaring with rage, said, "Supposing *I* had been in that boat, would you have dared to commit such an act?" "I should have made the attempt, sir," was the calm reply. "What!" shouted the captain, "if I were to impress men from that brig, would you interfere?" "You have only to try it, sir," was Macdonough's tantalizing reply. The haughty Briton was over-matched, and he did not attempt to try the metal of such a brave young man. There were cannon balls in his coolness, full of danger.

battles at Lexington, Concord, and Breed's Hill, had been fought. Fired with patriotic zeal, young Smith sought to serve his country in the army; and in January, 1776, he obtained a captain's commission in Colonel Smallwood's regiment. He was soon afterward promoted to the rank of major; and early in 1777, he received a lieutenant-colonel's commission. In that capacity he served with distinction in the battle of Brandywine, and a few weeks later won unfading laurels for his gallant defence of Fort Mifflin, a little below Philadelphia, of which he was commander. There, for seven weeks, he sustained a siege by a greatly superior force, and abandoned the fort only when the defences were no longer tenable. For his services there, Congress voted him a sword, and the country rang with his praises. He afterward suffered with the army at Valley Forge, and fought on the plains of Monmouth.

At the close of the war, Colonel Smith was appointed a brigadier-general of militia, and commanded the Maryland troops under General Lee, in quelling the "Whiskey Insurrection" in Western Pennsylvania. He was active in support of Washington's administration throughout; and, in 1793, he was elected to represent the Baltimore district in the Federal Congress, where he remained for ten consecutive years. He held the commission of major-general of militia during the war of 1812-15, and was active in measures to repel invading Britons, at Baltimore, in 1814. Two years afterward he was again elected to Congress, and served in the House of Representatives for six years. He was also a member of the United States Senate for many years. In 1836, during a fearful riot in Baltimore, his military services were again brought into requisition, and by his prompt efforts the disturbance was soon quelled. The mob had defied the civil authority, and were wantonly destroying property, when the aged general appeared in their midst, bearing the American flag, and calling upon peaceably-disposed citizens to rally and assist him in sustaining law and order. That result was soon accomplished. In the Autumn of the same year, when at the age of more than eighty-four years, he was elected mayor of Baltimore, by an almost unanimous vote. He held that office by reëlection until his death, which occurred on the 22d of April, 1839, in the eighty-seventh year of his age.

JEHUDI ASHMUN.

THE first agent of the American Colonization Society, employed to plant a settlement of free negroes in the land of their fathers, was Jehudi Ashmun, the son of pious parents who resided near the western shore of Lake Champlain, in the State of New York. In the town of Champlain he was born, in April, 1794, and was graduated at Burlington College, in 1816. He commenced preparations for the ministry in the theological seminary at Bangor, in Maine, but soon made his residence in the District of Columbia, became attached to the Protestant Episcopal Church there, and took a zealous part in the early efforts to found a colony of free blacks in Africa. His zeal and usefulness were appreciated by the American Colonization Society; and, in 1822, he was appointed to take charge of a reënforcement for their infant settlement in Africa. He became the general agent there, and it was necessary for him to perform the duties of legislator, soldier, and engineer. Afflictions fell upon him at the beginning. His wife died; and within three months after his arrival, when the whole force of the colonists consisted of only thirty-five men and boys, he was attacked by armed savages. They were repulsed, but in December they returned with greatly increased numbers, and utter extermination of the little colony seemed certain. Again the savages were repulsed, and thoroughly defeated. For six years Mr. Ashmun labored faithfully there, with Lott Cary,[1] in laying the foundation of the Republic of Liberia, but the malaria of the lowlands made great inroads upon his health, month after month, until he was compelled to return to America to recruit. His departure was a great grief to the colonists, who now numbered twelve hundred souls. He felt that the hand of decay was upon him, and he expressed a belief that he should never return. Like the friends of Paul, they kissed him, "Sorrowing most of all for the words which he spake, that they should see his face no more. And they accompanied him to the ship."; Men, women, and children, parted with him at the shore, with tears. . His anticipations were realized, for on the 25th of August, 1828, only a fortnight after his arrival at New Haven, he departed for the "happy land," at the age of thirty-four years. There is a handsome monument to his memory in a cemetery in New Haven.

JOHN CALDWELL CALHOUN.

BY far the most profound, consistent, and popular statesman that South Carolina has ever produced, was John C. Calhoun, whose name will ever be associated in history with the institution of Slavery as its most cordial and honest defender. He will be remembered, too, as an uncorrupt patriot, and a statesman above reproach. That idol of the Carolinians was the son of Patrick Calhoun, an Irishman of great respectability, who took front rank among the patriots in Western Carolina during the War for Independence. John was born in Abbeville district, South Carolina, on the 18th of March, 1782. His mother was a Virginia lady of great worth, and to her care the moulding of the young mind and heart of the future statesman was chiefly intrusted. Although he was a great reader, from childhood, yet, until late in youthhood, he had acquired very little education from systematic instruction. Under the charge of his brother-in-law, Dr. Waddel, of Columbia county, Georgia, he was prepared for college, and entered Yale, as a student, in 1802. His progress there was exceedingly rapid. His genius beamed forth daily, more and more; and, in 1804, he was graduated with the highest honors of the institution. President Dwight admired him for his many manly virtues; and on one occasion he remarked, "That boy, Calhoun, has talent enough to be President of the United States, and will become one yet, I confidently predict."

For three years subsequent to his leaving college, Calhoun studied law, in Litchfield, Connecticut, and then entered upon its practice in his native district. He was elected to a seat in the legislature of South Carolina, the following year [1808], and after serving two terms there, he was chosen to represent his district in the Federal Congress. At that time a war spirit was kindling throughout the nation, and Mr. Calhoun entered Congress when his fine abilities were most needed. He was a staunch republican; and during his career of six years in the House of Representatives, he was an eloquent and consistent supporter of President Madison's administration. Mr. Monroe so highly appreciated his abilities, that when he took the presidential chair, in 1817, he called Mr. Calhoun to his cabinet as Secretary of War. In that capacity his great administrative abilities, so early discovered by President Dwight, were daily manifested, and he performed the duties of his office with signal fidelity and energy, during the whole eight years of Mr. Monroe's administration. He was elected Vice-President of

JOHN CALDWELL CALHOUN.

the United States, in 1825, and held that position more than six years, having been reëlected, with President Jackson, in 1828. In 1831, when Robert Y. Hayne left the Senate to become governor of South Carolina, Mr. Calhoun was chosen his successor, and resigned the vice-presidency. At the end of the term for which he was chosen, he retired to private life, and sought repose in the bosom of his family. In 1843, he was called to the cabinet of President Tyler, as Secretary of State; and, in 1845, he was again chosen United States Senator, by the legislature of South Carolina. He continued in that exalted position until his death, which occurred at Washington city, on the 31st of March, 1850, at the age of sixty-eight years.

Few men have exerted a more powerful and controlling sway over the opinions of vast masses of men, than Mr. Calhoun, for his views on several topics coincided with those of the great majority of the Southern people; and he was known to be inflexibly honest and true, and eminently reliable. No man of his faith ever doubted that leader any more than his creed. As a statesman, he was full of forecast, acute in judgment, and comprehensive in his general views. He was eminently conservative in many things, and by precept and example, recommended "masterly inactivity" as preferable to mere impulsive and effervescent movements. When intelligence came, in 1848, that Louis Philippe was driven from Paris and the French Republic had been proclaimed, it was proposed, in the United States Senate, that our government should acknowledge the new order of things. "Wait until it becomes a Republic," were the words of cautious wisdom uttered by Senator Calhoun. We *have* waited *many* years, and France is yet [1869] ruled by an usurper. Daniel Webster said of Mr. Calhoun, in the Senate of the United States, "We shall hereafter, I am sure, indulge in it as a grateful recollection, that we have lived in his age, that we have been his contemporaries, that we have seen him, and heard him, and known him."

HENRY DEARBORN.

WHEN the government of the United States declared war against Great Britain, in 1812, the chief command of the army then authorized to be raised, was given to Henry Dearborn, a meritorious soldier of the War for Independence. He was born in Hampton, New Hampshire, in March, 1751. He studied the science of medicine with Doctor Jackson, of Portsmouth, and commenced its practice there in 1772. As the storm-clouds of the impending Revolution gathered, he took an active part in politics on the side of the patriots, and gave much attention to military affairs. When, on the 20th of April, 1775, intelligence reached Portsmouth of the skirmishes at Lexington and Concord the preceding day, young Dearborn marched in haste to Cambridge, at the head of sixty volunteers. He soon returned to New Hampshire, was elected a captain in the regiment of Colonel Stark, enlisted his company, and was again at Cambridge on the 15th of May. In the memorable battle on Breed's Hill, on the 17th of June following, Captain Dearborn behaved gallantly; and in September ensuing, he accompanied General Arnold in his perilous march across the wilderness from the Kennebec to the St. Lawrence. Famine, with the keenness of a wolf's appetite, fell upon them, and a fine dog belonging to Captain Dearborn, that accompanied them, was used for food. Even moose-skin breeches were boiled: the extracted mucilage served as soup, and the hide was roasted and eaten. Many died from hunger and fatigue, and Captain Dearborn himself was left ill of a fever in the hut of a farmer, on the banks of the Chaudiere, without a physician. He slowly recovered, joined the army at Quebec, in December, participated in the siege and assault of that city, under Montgomery, and was made a prisoner. He was permitted to return home on parole the following May. His exchange was not effected until March, 1777, when he was appointed major in Scammell's regiment; and was at Ticonderoga, in May following. In the eventful conflicts at Saratoga, in the ensuing Autumn, he gallantly participated, and shared in the honors of the capture of Burgoyne. General Gates gave him special notice in his despatch to Congress. He was promoted to lieutenant-colonel in Cilley's regiment, and in that capacity he participated in the gallant charge at Monmouth, after Lee's retreat, that broke the power of the British force.

Lieutenant-colonel Dearborn accompanied General Sullivan in his expedition against the Senecas, in 1779. In 1780, he again became attached to Colonel Scammell's regiment, and on the death of that officer during the siege of Yorktown, Dearborn succeeded to his rank and command. After that event he was on duty at the frontier post of Saratoga, under the immediate command of Lord Stirling, and there, at the close of the war, his military services in the Continental army ended. He settled upon the banks of the Kennebec, in 1784, and engaged in agricultural pursuits. In 1789, Washington appointed him marshal of the District of Maine; and twice he was elected to a seat in Congress from that territory. Mr. Jefferson called him to his cabinet as Secretary of War, in 1801, and he discharged the duties of that office with great ability and fidelity, during Jefferson's entire administration of eight years. On retiring, in 1809, President Madison gave him the lucrative office of collector at the port of Boston. In February, 1812, when war with Great Britain appeared inevitable, Colonel Dearborn was commissioned senior major-general of the army; and the following Spring he was in chief command at the capture of York (now Toronto), in Canada, where General Pike was killed. He continued in command, for awhile longer, when the President recalled him on the ground of ill health, and he assumed command of the military district of New York city. He retired to private life, in 1815, where he remained until 1822, when President Monroe appointed him minister to Portugal. At his own request he was permitted to return home, after an absence of two years, and resided most of the time in Boston, until his death. That event occurred at the house of his son, in Roxbury, Massachusetts, on the 6th of June, 1829, at the age of seventy-eight years.

ABIEL HOLMES.

THE faithful annalist is a nation's benefactor; and it may be truthfully said to all such chroniclers; as the poet said to the historian of Rome—

> " And Rome shall owe
> For her memorial to your learned pen
> More than to all those fading monuments,
> Built with the riches of the spoiled world."

In this category of benefactors, Abiel Holmes, D.D., holds a conspicuous place, and Americans should cherish his memory with pride and deepest affection. His *Annals of America*, in two volumes, is one of the most valuable historical publications ever issued from the press, as a work of reference. And as an *Annalist* he is best known to the world.

Abiel Holmes was born at Woodstock, Connecticut, in December, 1763. He was graduated at Yale College at the age of twenty years, and went immediately to South Carolina as an instructor in a private family. He had received religious impressions at an early age, and these deepened with the lapse of years. The gospel ministry opened to his mind a field of great usefulness, and he entered upon it as a pastor of a church at Midway, Georgia, in the Autumn of 1785. There he remained until the Summer of 1791, when he visited New England, and accepted an invitation to become pastor of the first Congregational Church at Cambridge, Massachusetts. He was ever studious, and Biography and History had great charms for him. In 1798, he wrote and published a Life of President Stiles, of Yale College; and, in 1805, his *Annals of America* was first published. An edition was printed in England, in 1813; and, in 1829, a much-improved edition, in which the record is continued until 1827, was published at Cambridge. With this edition of *Holmes' Annals*, the *American Register* from 1826 to 1830 inclusive, and the *American Almanac* from 1830 to the present time, a library has an unbroken record of events in the United States from the earliest settlements. In addition to his works just mentioned, Dr. Holmes published about thirty pamphlets, consisting chiefly of sermons and historical disquisitions. He died at Cambridge, Massachusetts, on the 4th day of June, 1837, at the age of almost seventy-four years.

PHILIP SYNG PHYSIC.

PHILIP SYNG PHYSIC has been appropriately called the *Washington*—the Hero and Sage—of the medical profession, because, always cautious, he was nevertheless ready for any emergency, and his great mind never failed in its resources amidst the most complicated difficulties. That eminent physician was born in Philadelphia, on the 7th of July, 1768. His father had been keeper of the great seal of the colony of Pennsylvania; and, prior to the Revolution, he had charge of the estates of the Penn family, as confidential agent. At the age of eleven years, Philip was placed under the charge of Robert Proud, principal of an academy that belonged to the Society of Friends, and in due time entered the University of Pennsylvania, as a student. He was graduated in 1785, and immediately commenced the study of medicine with the distinguished Professor Kuhn. After attending a course of medical lectures at the university, he embarked for Europe, in the Autumn of 1788, in company with his father, who, through influential friends in England, procured the admission of Philip to the friendship and private instruction of the eminent Dr. John Hunter. No man ever had a better opportunity for acquiring a thorough knowledge of the healing art, and of practical surgery, than young Physic, and he nobly improved it to his own benefit and that of his race. His talents were so conspicuous, that on the earnest recommendation of Dr. Hunter, Physic was appointed house surgeon to St. George's Hospital, in 1790, to serve one year. At the close of the term he received a diploma from the Royal College of Surgeons, in London, and Dr. Hunter offered him a professional partnership. The young man had resolved to make his native city the chief theatre of his career, and after remaining with Hunter during 1791, he went to Edinburgh, studied and observed diligently there, in the University and in the Royal Infirmary, obtained the degree of M.D., in May, 1792, and in September, returned to America.

Thus prepared, Dr. Physic entered upon the practice of his profession, in Philadelphia. In 1793, the yellow fever tested his skill, moral courage, and benevolence, to the utmost, and all appeared eminently conspicuous. The following year he was chosen to be one of the surgeons of the Pennsylvania Hospital; and, when the yellow fever again prevailed, in 1798, his services were of the greatest importance. In 1801, he was appointed surgeon extraordinary to the Philadelphia Almshouse Infirmary. The following year, on the earnest request of a number of medical students, he delivered a course of lectures on Surgery. They were exceedingly popular, and students came from all parts of the country to enjoy his instructions. In 1805, a professorship of surgery, distinct from anatomy, was instituted in the University of Pennsylvania, and Dr. Physic was called to that chair. In fact it was created for him. He performed the duties of that station in a highly satisfactory manner, until 1819, when he was transferred to the chair of anatomy, in the same institution, on the death of its incumbent (his nephew), John Syng Dorsey. Year after year he continued his lectures to great numbers of medical students, notwithstanding his extensive practice and college duties made his labors very great.

In 1821, Dr. Physic was appointed consulting surgeon to the Philadelphia Institution for the Blind; and, in 1824, he was elected president of the Philadelphia Medical Society, a station which he filled with great dignity until his death. In 1825, the French Royal Academy of Medicine made him an honorary member of that institution, the first dignity of the kind ever received by an American. He was also made an honorary fellow of the Royal Medical and Chirurgical Society of London. In 1831, failing health caused Dr. Physic to resign his professorship in the University, when he was immediately elected

Emeritus Professor of Surgery and Anatomy, in that institution. His physical system gradually gave way under his incessant professional toil, and on the 15th of December, 1837, that eminent surgeon expired in Philadelphia, at the age of sixty-nine years. The immediate cause of his death was hydrothorax. Besides his lectures, Dr. Physic wrote but little. He labored intensely, in his profession, and left authorship to others.

JOHN SEVIER.

SOON after the return of peace when the War for Independence had ceased, the hardy mountaineers of the extreme western portions of North Carolina, established a separate government, and, in honor of Dr. Franklin, called the new State FRANKLAND. A brave militia officer of the Revolution was chosen governor, but his rule and the new State were of short duration. That officer was John Sevier, a descendant of an ancient French family, the original orthography of which was Xavier. He was born on the banks of the Shenandoah, in Virginia, about the year 1740. He was a bold and fearless youth, and was engaged much in athletic exercises during the earlier years of his manhood. In 1769, he accompanied an exploring party to East Tennessee, and settled on the Holston river, with his father and brother. There he assisted in erecting Fort Watauga, and was afterward made the commander of the little garrison, with the commission of captain. The Cherokees were then prowling around, with hostile intentions, British emissaries having excited them against the colonists. One pleasant morning in June, 1776, the gallant captain saw a young lady running with the speed of a doe, toward the fort, pursued by a party of Cherokees under "Old Abraham," one of their most noted chiefs. With a single bound she leaped the palisades, and fell into the arms of Captain Sevier. It was a lucky leap for Catherine Sherrill, for she was caught by a husband, unto whom she bore ten children.

Captain Sevier was with Evan Shelby at the battle of Point Pleasant, in 1774. During the first five years of the war he was an active Whig partisan on the mountain frontiers of the Carolinas; and, in 1780, when Cornwallis was penetrating toward the hills, he held the commission of colonel. He greatly distinguished himself at the battle on King's Mountain, in October of that year, and also at Musgrove's Mills. The following year he quieted hostile Indians among the mountains, by a severe chastisement. At the close of the war he was commissioned a brigadier; and he was so much beloved by the people, that on the formation of the State of FRANKLAND, above alluded to, he was elected governor by unanimous acclamation. He was so often engaged in conferences with the Indians, that they gave him a name which signified *treaty-maker*. When Tennessee was organized, and admitted into the Union as an independent State, Sevier was elected its first governor. In 1811, he was elected to a seat in Congress, and was reëlected in 1813. He was a firm supporter of President Madison's administration, and was appointed an Indian commissioner for his State and the adjoining territories. While engaged in the duties of his office near Fort Decatur, on the east side of the Tallapoosa river, he died, on the 24th of September, 1815, at the age of about seventy-five years. There he was buried with the honors of war, under the direction of the late General Gaines. No stone, it is said, identifies his grave; but in a cemetery at Nashville, a handsome marble cenotaph has been erected to his memory, by "An admirer of Patriotism and Merit unrequited."

ISABELLA GRAHAM.

EARTH hath its angels, bright and lovely. They often walk in the garden of humanity unobserved. Their foot-prints are pearly with Heaven's choicest blessings; fragrant flowers spring up and bloom continually in their presence, and the birds of paradise warble unceasingly in the branches beneath which they recline. They are born of true religion in the heart. Their creed comes down from heaven, and is as broad as humanity; their hope is a golden chain of promises suspended from the throne of infinite goodness; their example is a preacher of righteousness co-working with the Great Redeemer.

Of these blessed ones of earth, was Isabella Graham, a native of Lanarkshire, Scotland, where she was born on the 29th of July, 1742. Her maiden name was Marshall, and during her earlier years her father occupied the estate, once the residence of the renowned William Wallace. Isabella was early trained to physical activity, and was blessed with a superior education, which afterward became her life-dependence. Her moral and religious culture kept pace with her intellectual improvement, and under the teaching of Dr. Witherspoon (afterward president of the college at Princeton, New Jersey), she became a Christian professor at the age of seventeen years.

Miss Marshall was married to Dr. John Graham, an army surgeon, in 1765, and the following year accompanied him to Canada, whither he was ordered to join his regiment. She was a resident of a garrison at Fort Niagara for several years, and just before the American Revolution broke out, she accompanied her husband to the Island of Antigua. Then the furnace of affliction was prepared for her. First, intelligence came that her dear mother was buried. Soon after that two of her dear friends were removed by death; and in the Autumn of

1774, her excellent husband was taken from her, after a few days' illness, leaving her in a strange land, with three infant daughters. But she was not friendless. She had freely cast her bread of benevolence upon the waters, and it returned to her by corresponding benevolence, when it was most needed.

After giving birth to a son, Mrs. Graham returned to Scotland. Her aged father had become impoverished, and was added to the dependants upon her efforts for a livelihood. She opened a small school, and lived upon coarse and scanty food, made sweet by the thought that it was earned for those she loved. Old *acquaintances* among the rich and gay passed the humble widow by, but old *friends*, with hearts in their hands, assisted her in establishing a boarding-school in Edinburgh. God prospered her, and she distributed freely of her little abundance among the more needy. A tenth of all her earnings she regularly devoted to charity; and hour after hour, when the duties of her school had ceased, that good and gentle creature would walk among the poor and destitute, in the lanes and alleys of the Scottish capital, dispensing physical benefits and religious consolations. Thoroughly purified in the crucible of sorrow, her heart was ever alive with sympathy for suffering humanity, and that became the great controlling emotion that shaped her labors. She often lent small sums of money to young persons about entering upon business, and would never receive interest, for she considered the luxury of doing good sufficient usury. She encouraged poor laboring people to unite in creating a fund for mutual relief in case of sickness, by a small deposit each week, and thus she founded the "Penny Society," out of which grew that excellent institution, in Edinburgh, "The Society for the Relief of the Destitute Sick."

At the solicitation of Dr. Witherspoon, and of some friends in New York, Mrs. Graham came to America, in 1785; and in the Autumn of that year opened a school, with five pupils, in our commercial metropolis. Before the end of a month the number of her pupils had increased to fifty, and for thirteen years she continued that vocation with increasing prosperity. A great blessing came to her, in 1795, when her second daughter married the excellent Divie Bethune, an enterprising young merchant of New York, who became an earnest co-worker in the cause she had espoused.[1] Sorrow came at about the same time, for her oldest daughter was taken away by death. But the widow was not diverted from the path of Christian duty by prosperity nor adversity. She walked daily among the poor, like a sweet angel, dispensing with bountiful hand the blessing she had received from above. At her house, in 1796, a number of ladies formed that noble institution, the *Society for the Relief of Poor Widows with Children;* and two years afterward she gave up her school, went to reside with her daughters, and dedicated her time to the services of an abounding charity. We cannot follow her in all her ministrations public and private, for they were as manifold as the hours of the day. She was one of the promoters of the *Orphan Asylum* and the *Magdalene Society* She had printed and distributed several tracts, before any society for the purpose was formed, which were calculated to excite the public sympathy for the destitute and suffering. She was active in giving popularity to Lancasterian schools for the poor, and the Sabbath-school was her special delight. Every where, by light and by day, in the city of her

---

1. That eminent philanthropist (father of the late Rev. Dr. Bethune, of Brooklyn), was also a native of Scotland. Before any tract society was formed in this country, he printed 10,000 tracts at his own expense, and distributed them with his own hand. He also imported many Bibles for distribution, supported one or more Sunday-schools, and always devoted a tenth of his gains to charitable and religious purposes. He died in 1824.

adoption, that noble Sister of Charity might be met, dispensing her blessings, and rewarded by the benedictions of the aided.[1] Her last public labor was in forming a society for the promotion of industry among the poor. That was in the Spring of 1814, when the infirmities of health and age had shortened her journeys of love. On the 27th of July following, that faithful servant of the great Pattern of benevolence went home to receive her final reward, at the age of seventy-two years.

HENRY WHEATON.

THE most eminent American writer on International Law that has yet appeared, was Henry Wheaton, a native of Providence, Rhode Island, where he was born in November, 1785. He entered Brown University at the age of thirteen years, and was graduated there in 1802. The law was his chosen profession, and he commenced its study under the direction of Nathaniel Searle. After two years' close application, he went to France, became a welcome guest in the family of General Armstrong (then United States minister there), resided in Paris eighteen months in the earnest study of the French language, and then went to London and made himself thoroughly acquainted with the constitutional and international jurisprudence of Europe. On his return to Rhode Island he was admitted to the bar. In 1812, he made his residence in the city of New York, where he took a high position as a lawyer. The same year he assumed the editorial control of the *National Advocate*, and its columns abounded with able disquisitions on International Law, from his pen. The subject was of special current interest, for unsettled questions of that nature were some of the immediate causes of the war then in progress between the United States and Great Britain. Mr. Wheaton was also appointed a judge of the Marine Court, in the city of New York, the same year; and, in 1815, he relinquished his connection with the *National Advocate*. In May of that year he published his *Digest relative to Marine Captures*, which attracted much attention. The same year he was appointed reporter of the Supreme Court of the United States, and performed the duties of that important station with signal ability until 1827, when he was appointed *Chargé d'Affaires* to Denmark, by President Adams. His reports were published in twelve volumes, and form an invaluable library of legal decisions. He was engaged in public life but once during his long connection with the Supreme Court. That service was performed in 1821, as a member of the convention that revised the Constitution of the State of New York.

Mr. Wheaton was the first regular minister sent to Denmark by the United States. There he employed his leisure time in making diligent researches into Scandinavian literature; and he published the result of his investigations in a volume entitled *History of the Northmen*. No diplomatic duty was neglected, by these researches, and his mission was performed to the entire satisfaction of his government. In 1830, he visited Paris, and was highly esteemed in diplomatic circles there, as well as in London, the following year. In 1836, President Jackson transferred Mr. Wheaton from Copenhagen to Berlin, and a few months afterward he was raised to the rank of minister plenipotentiary at the court of

---

1. On one occasion, she was absent for some time on a visit to Boston, when, to the surprise of Mrs. Bethune, a great many people called to inquire about her mother. She asked the reason of their numerous inquiries, and was told that they lived in the suburbs of the city, where she visited and relieved the sick, and comforted the poor. "We had missed her so long," one of them said, "that we were afraid she was sick. When she walks in our streets," she continued, "it was customary with us to go to the door and bless her as she passed."

Prussia. There his services were of the greatest importance, and he stood, confessedly, at the head of American diplomacy in Europe. To him other American legations looked for counsel, and the various sovereigns of Europe held him in the highest esteem. In 1840, Mr. Wheaton made a treaty with Hanover; and the same year he attended the conference of representatives of twenty-seven German States, and there advanced the commercial interests of his country.

Mr. Wheaton is known as one of the best writers on the law of nations, and his works, on that topic, are held in the same estimation, in the cabinets of Europe, as were those of Grotius and Vattel before his day. He wrote a *Life of William Pinkney;* and in addition to his voluminous despatches on all sorts of subjects, he delivered many discourses, some of which have been published in pamphlet form. That skilful diplomatist, ripe scholar, accomplished author, and thorough gentleman, died at Roxbury, Massachusetts, on the 11th of March, 1848, at the age of sixty-three years.

JAMES KENT.

"I've scanned the actions of his daily life
With all the industrious malice of a foe;
And nothing meets mine eyes but deeds of honor."

THESE words of Hannah More may justly be applied to the character of that brilliant light of the American judiciary, Chancellor Kent, for no jurist ever laid aside a more spotless ermine than he. He was born in the Fredericksburg precinct of Dutchess county (now Putnam county), New York, on the 31st of July, 1763. At the age of five years he went to live with his maternal grandfather, at Norwalk, Connecticut, and remained there, engaged in preparatory studies, until 1777, when he entered Yale College, as a student. The war of the Revolution was then developing its worst features, for British, Hessians, and Tories were desolating various districts, by fire and plunder. For a time the students of the college were scattered; yet, with all the disadvantages produced by these interruptions, young Kent was graduated with distinguished honor, in 1781. The perusal of *Blackstone's Commentaries,* soon after he entered college, gave him a taste for law, and, on leaving Yale, he commenced its study with Egbert Benson, then attorney-general of the State of New York.

Mr. Kent was admitted to practice, in 1785, as attorney of the Supreme Court of his native State; and, in 1787, he was admitted as counsellor of the same court. He was then married and settled at Poughkeepsie, on the Hudson. He was exceedingly studious, and always methodical.[1] While his profession was his chief care, he did not escape the influence of the ambitious desire of a politician; and joining with Hamilton and other leading Federalists in his State, he soon became identified with the public measures of the day. In 1790, and again in 1792, he represented the Poughkeepsie district in the State legislature. Having failed as a candidate for the same office, in 1793, he removed to the city of New York, and became Professor of Law in Columbia College. In 1796, he was appointed master in Chancery, and the following year he was made recorder of the city of New York. At about this time the Faculty of Columbia College evinced their appreciation of his great legal learning, by conferring upon him the honorary degree of Doctor of Laws. Those of Harvard and Dartmouth after-

---

1. At that time he commenced a system of self-training, of great value. He divided the day into six portions. From dawn until eight o'clock, he devoted two hours to Latin; then two to Greek, and the remainder of the time before dinner to law. The afternoon was given to French and English authors, and the evening to friendship and recreation, in which he took special delight.

ward imitated their example. He was very highly esteemed by Governor Jay; and in 1797, that chief magistrate of the State of New York appointed Mr. Kent associate justice of the Supreme Court. Three years afterward, he and Judge Radcliffe were appointed to revise the legal code of the State, for which they received the highest encomiums of the best jurists in the country. Step by step Justice Kent went up the ladder of professional honor and distinction. In 1804, he was appointed chief justice of the State, and he filled that important office with great dignity and ability until February, 1814, when he accepted the office of chancellor. In that exalted station he labored on with fidelity, until 1823, when he had reached the age of sixty years, and was ineligible for service therein, according to the unwise provisions of the Constitution of 1821. He finished his labors as chancellor, by hearing and deciding every case that had been brought before him; and he left the office bearing the most sincere regrets of every member of his profession, and of the people at large. Soon after retiring from public life, he was again elected Law Professor in Columbia College. He revised his former lectures, added new ones to them, and then published the whole in four volumes, with the title of *Commentaries on American Law.* That great work is a text-book, and has given Chancellor Kent the palm, in the opinion of the best judges in this country and in Europe, as one of the first legal writers of his time.

Chancellor Kent possessed all those public and private virtues which constitute a true MAN. Industrious, temperate, social and religious, he was blessed with sound health, warm friends, devoted family affection, and an unclouded faith in Divine promises. He retained his robust health and activity until within a few weeks of his death,[1] which occurred at his residence on Union Square, New York, on the 12th of December, 1847, when at the age of eighty-four years.

WILLIAM DUNLAP.

AMONG the privileged few who had the honor of painting the portrait of Washington, from life, was William Dunlap, who is equally distinguished as artist and author. He was born at Perth Amboy, New Jersey, on the 19th of February, 1766, and at the house of a kind neighbor, his taste for pictures and reading was early developed by familiarity there with paintings and books. The storm of the Revolution produced great confusion in New Jersey, and young Dunlap's education was almost utterly neglected, until his father removed to the city of New York, in 1777, which was then in possession of the British. There, while at play, William lost an eye, by accident. He had become very expert in copying prints, in India ink, and this accident perilled all his future career as a painter, of which he now dreamed continually. The difficulty was soon overcome by habit, and he used his pencil almost incessantly, with occasionally a word of instruction from an artist. He commenced portrait-painting at the age of seventeen years, and at Rocky Hill, in New Jersey, he was allowed to paint the portrait of Washington.[2]

In 1784, young Dunlap went to England, and became a pupil of the great Benjamin West. His progress was slow, for he spent much of his time in the enjoyments of the amusements of London. After an absence of three years, he returned to New York, commenced portrait-painting, but being an indifferent artist, he found very little employment. Discouraged by his ill success, he abandoned the art, "took refuge," he says, "in literature," and afterward joined his father in mercantile business. He married a sister of the wife of Dr. Dwight, of Yale College, and he was much benefited by his connection with the family of one who proved a most excellent companion. That connection turned him from the paths that led to profligacy and ruin. He continued to be a thrifty merchant until 1805, when he unfortunately became the lessee of the New York theatre, and by losses was made a bankrupt. He immediately returned to portrait-painting for a livelihood, first in Albany, and then in Boston, but with his former ill success. Half-despairing, he again laid aside his pallette, and became general superintendent and occasional manager of the New York theatre. He continued in that business until 1812, when he again returned to his art. It failed to give him bread. He employed his pen in writing the *Memoirs of George Frederick Cooke*, the celebrated English actor, for the press; and he became editor of a magazine called *The Recorder*. In 1814, he was appointed paymaster-general of the militia of the State of New York, in the service of the United States. This employment took him from his pencil and pen, and continued until 1816. Then, at the age of fifty-one years, he first became permanently a painter, and his true artist-life began. He went from place to place in the United States and Canada, painting portraits with considerable success. He also turned his attention to the higher walks of art, and produced, in succession, three large pictures

---

1. The writer saw him often, during the Summer preceding his death, step from the city railway cars with the firmness and agility of a man of fifty.
2. It was at Rocky Hill, a little while before the disbanding of the Continental forces, in the Autumn of 1783, that Washington issued his *Farewell Address to the Army*. Congress was then in session at Princeton, a few miles distant.

—*Christ Rejected, Death on the Pale Horse,*[1] and *Calvary.* The exhibition of these in various parts of the Union, contributed materially to the support of his family, for many years. He painted other and smaller pieces, some of which, and especially *The Historic Muse,* were productions of great excellence.

In 1830, Mr. Dunlap commenced lecturing on Fine Art topics, and attracted much attention; and, in 1832, he published a *History of the American Theatre.* It was very favorably received, and was followed by his history of the *Arts of Design in the United States.* In the meanwhile [February, 1833], he received a complimentary benefit at the Park theatre, New York, which gave him over two thousand five hundred dollars. In 1839, he published the first volume of a *History of the State of New York.* The second volume was unfinished at the time of his death. Not long before that occurrence, his friends got up an exhibition of paintings for his benefit; and the last days of his life were made happy by plenty. He died in New York city, on the 28th of September, 1839, in the seventy-fourth year of his age. Mr. Dunlap was the author of several dramas; also a biography of Charles Brockden Brown.

JACOB BROWN.

GREAT events as often produce eminent men as eminent men produce great events. The heavings of the earthquake cast up lofty hills; so do the political and social convulsions of nations make dwarfs in quietude giants amid commotions. The war of the Revolution called a vast amount of latent genius into action, and great statesmen and warriors appeared, where even the germs were not suspected. The second War for Independence, commenced in 1812, had a like effect, and statesmen and military leaders came from the work-shop and the furrow. Of the latter was Jacob Brown, a native of Bucks county, Pennsylvania, and the son of Quaker parents. He was born on the 9th of May, 1775. He was well educated. At the age of sixteen years, Jacob's father lost his property, and the well-trained youth at once resolved to earn his own living. From eighteen to twenty-one years of age he taught a school at Crosswicks, in New Jersey, and at the same time he studied with great assiduity. Then, for about two years, he was employed as a surveyor in the vicinity of Cincinnati; and, in 1798, he was teaching school in the city of New York. There he commenced the study of law, but finding it not congenial to his taste, he abandoned it, purchased some wild land in the present Jefferson county, near the foot of Lake Ontario, and settled upon it, in 1799. He pursued the business of a farmer with skill and industry; and, in 1809, he was appointed to the command of a regiment of militia. The governor of New York commissioned him a brigadier, in 1811; and when, the following year, war with Great Britain commenced, he was intrusted with the command of the first detachment of New York militia, which was called into the service of the United States, and charged with the defence of the frontier, from Oswego to Lake St. Francis, a distance of almost two hundred miles. In October of that year, he gallantly defended Ogdensburg, with only about four hundred men, against eight hundred Britons. At the expiration of his term, the government offered him the commission of colonel in the regular army, but he declined it. In the Spring of 1813, he drove the enemy from Sackett's Harbor. In his operations there he displayed so much judgment and skill, that Congress gave him the commission of a brigadier-general in the

---

1. This composition he made from a printed description of West's great picture on the same subject.

Federal army. In the Autumn of that year he was active and efficient on the banks of the St. Lawrence; and after the retreat of the American troops from Canada, in November, the illness of General Wilkinson made the chief command devolve upon General Brown. Toward the close of January, 1814, he was promoted to major-general, and he was assiduous during the few weeks preceding the opening of the campaign for that year, in disciplining the troops and giving them encouragement. He was ordered to the command on the Niagara frontier, in the Spring of 1814, and during the succeeding Summer and Autumn he won imperishable honors for himself and country. For his gallantry and good conduct in the successive battles of Chippewa, Niagara Falls, and Fort Erie, he received the thanks of Congress and a gold commemorative medal, and the plaudits of the nation. He was twice severely wounded in the battle at Niagara Falls, but he was in service at Fort Erie, a few weeks later.

At the close of the war General Brown was retained in the army, and was appointed to the command of the northern division. In 1821, he was appointed general-in-chief of the armies of the United States, and held that office until his death, which occurred at his head-quarters, in Washington city, on the 24th of February, 1828, at the age of fifty-three years. His widow now [1855] resides at Brownsville, the place of their early settlement.

GEORGE CLINTON.

ENERGY, decision, courage, and purest patriotism, were the prominent features in the character of George Clinton, the first republican governor of New York, and afterward Vice-President of the United States. He was the youngest son of Colonel Charles Clinton, and was born in that portion of old Ulster county now called Orange, on the 26th of July, 1739. His education was intrusted to a private tutor, and at an early age his adventurous spirit yearned for the sea. He finally left his father's house clandestinely, and sailed in a privateer. On his return, he entered the military company of his brother James,[1] as lieutenant, and accompanied him in Bradstreet's expedition against Fort Frontenac, at the foot of Lake Ontario, in 1758. At the close of the French and Indian war, he studied law under Chief Justice Smith, and rose to distinction in that profession. The troubled sea of politics was consonant with his nature, and he embarked upon it with great zeal. He was a zealous Whig, and was a member of the Colonial Assembly of New York, in the Spring of 1775. In May of that year he took a seat in the Continental Congress, where he remained until the following Summer, and voted for the Declaration of Independence on the 4th of July. Having been appointed brigadier-general of the militia of New York, his new duties called him away from Congress before that instrument was signed by the members, and thus he was deprived of the immortal honor of an arch-rebel.

In March, 1777, General Clinton was commissioned a brigadier-general, by Congress, and a month afterward he was chosen both governor and lieutenant-governor of the State of New York, under its republican constitution. He accepted the former office, and the latter was filled by Mr. Van Cortlandt. Governor Clinton exercised the duties of chief magistrate for six consecutive terms,

---

1. James was born on the 9th of August, 1736. After the French and Indian war, he commanded four companies of provincial troops, in his native county, employed to bar the inroads of Indians. He accompanied Montgomery to Quebec, in 1775, and was an active officer, with the rank of brigadier, during a great portion of the Revolution. He returned to his estate near Newburgh, Orange county, New York, after the war, and there he died, on the 22d of December, 1812, at the age of seventy-five years. He was the father of DeWitt Clinton, the eminent governor of New York.

or eighteen years, when, in 1795, he was succeeded by John Jay. Acting in his civil and military capacity at the same time, the energetic governor and general performed the most essential service during the whole war. He was in command of Fort Montgomery, in the Hudson Highlands, when it was captured, with Fort Clinton, in the Autumn of 1777; and he did more than any other man not in service with the army, in preventing a communication between the British in Canada and the city of New York. In 1788, he presided over the convention held at Poughkeepsie to consider the Federal Constitution. After retiring from office, in 1795, he remained in private life about five years, when he was again chosen governor of his State. He was succeeded by Morgan Lewis, in 1804, and the same year he was elevated to the station of Vice-President of the United States. He was reëlected, with Mr. Madison, in 1808, and was acting in discharge of the duties of that office at the time of his death. That event occurred at Washington city, on the 20th of April, 1812, when in the seventy-third year of his age.

WILLIAM BAINBRIDGE.

THE first man who unfurled the American flag in the harbor of Constantinople, was Captain William Bainbridge, who was then in the unwilling service of the haughty Dey of Algiers, as bearer of that barbarian's ambassador to the court of the Turkish Sultan. That sovereign regarded the event as a happy omen of peace and good-will between his throne and the government of that far-off country (of which, perhaps, he had never heard), for there seemed an affinity between his own *crescent* flag and the *star*-spangled banner of the new empire in the West.

William Bainbridge was born at Princeton, New Jersey, on the 7th of May, 1774, and at the age of fifteen years went to sea as a common sailor. Three years afterward he was promoted to mate of a ship engaged in the Dutch trade, and at the age of nineteen he was its captain. He became very popular in the merchant service; and when an anticipated war with France caused the organization of an American navy, Captain Bainbridge was offered the commission of a lieutenant and the position of a commander. His first cruise was in the schooner *Retaliation*, which was captured by two French vessels and taken to Guadaloupe. The governor of the island, desiring to remain neutral, offered Captain Bainbridge his liberty and his schooner, if he would promise to return to the United States without molesting any French vessel that might fall in his way. Bainbridge peremptorily refused to make any stipulation concerning his own conduct, yet the governor gladly allowed him to depart. On returning home, his conduct was approved, and he was promoted to Master and Commander.

In 1799, Captain Bainbridge was appointed to the command of a small vessel to cruise off Cuba. He behaved so well that he was promoted to post captain, the following year. He soon afterward took command of the frigate *Washington*, and was ordered to proceed to Algiers with the annual tribute which the United States had agreed to pay that power. The Dey compelled him to carry an Algerine ambassador to the Sultan, and in the harbor of Constantinople Bainbridge received honors awarded only to the Lord High Admiral of the Turkish navy. On his return to Algiers, he was instrumental in saving the French residents there, for the Dey had declared war with France, and would have imprisoned or enslaved the few French people in his dominions. For this generous

act, Napoleon, then First Consul, thanked Captain Bainbridge, and his own government highly approved the act. In June, 1801, he was appointed to the command of the *Essex* frigate, and proceeded to the Mediterranean, to protect American commerce there against the piratical Tripolitans. He returned the following year; and in July, 1803, he sailed in the frigate *Philadelphia*, to join the squadron of Commodore Preble, in the Mediterranean. He captured a hostile Moorish vessel, and at once cooled the war spirit of the Emperor of Morocco. Under the directions of Preble, Captain Bainbridge proceeded to blockade the harbor of Tripoli, where the *Philadelphia*, on the morning of the last day of October, ran upon a reef of rocks, and was captured by the gun-boats of the Tripolitans.[1] Bainbridge and his crew were made captives, and suffered imprisonment and slavery until 1805, when they were liberated, by treaty. From that time until the commencement of war, in 1812, Captain Bainbridge was employed

---

1. See sketch of Decatur.

alternately in the public and the merchant service. Then he was appointed to the command of the *Constellation* frigate. He was transferred to the *Constitution*, after the destruction of the *Guerriere*, and off the coast of Brazil he captured the British frigate *Java*, late in December, 1812. In that action he was dangerously wounded. Among the prisoners was General Hislop, governor of Bombay, who was so pleased with the kind attentions which he received from Captain Bainbridge, that he presented him with a splendid gold-mounted sword. For his gallantry, Congress awarded him a gold medal. In 1813, he took command of the Navy Yard at Charlestown. After the war he went twice to the Mediterranean, in command of squadrons sent to protect American commerce. He was president of the Board of Navy Commissioners for three years; and he prepared the signals now in use in our navy. Commodore Bainbridge suffered from sickness, for several years, and his voyage of earthly life finally ended at Philadelphia, on the 27th of July, 1833, when he was about fifty-nine years of age.

ISAAC CHAUNCEY.

COMMODORE ISAAC CHAUNCEY ranks among the noblest of the naval heroes of the second War for Independence, notwithstanding his operations were confined during that war to the smallest of the great Lakes on our northern frontier. He was a native of Black Rock, Fairfield county, Connecticut, where he was born at about the commencement of the Revolution. His father was a wealthy farmer, and descendant of one of the earlier settlers of that colony. Isaac was well educated, and was designed for the profession of the law, but at an early age he ardently desired to try life on the sea, and was gratified by sailing with an excellent ship-master from the port of New York. He loved the occupation, very rapidly acquired a thorough knowledge of nautical affairs, and at the age of nineteen years was master of a vessel. He made several successful voyages to the East Indies in ships belonging to the late John Jacob Astor. In 1798, he entered the navy of the United States, with a lieutenant's commission, under Commodore Truxton. He behaved gallantly in the Mediterranean; and in actions off Tripoli he was acting captain of the frigate *Constitution*. For his gallantry and seamanship in that capacity, he received the highest praise from Commodore Preble, and Congress presented him with an elegant sword. He was also promoted to master commandant, in 1804; and, in 1806, he received the commission of captain.

When war with England commenced, in 1812, Commodore Chauncey was appointed to the highly-important post of commander of the naval forces to be created on Lake Ontario. A few months after his arrival at Sackett's Harbor, then in the midst of a wilderness, he had quite a fleet of merchant-vessels equipped for naval service; and in the following Spring he had a sloop-of-war and a frigate ready for duty. One was built in twenty-eight days, the other in forty-four, from the time of laying the keel. With these, and some other additions to his squadron, Commodore Chauncey performed very important services during the war, especially in the transportation of troops. He could never bring the British naval commander on the lake into action, and so failed of making any brilliant achievement.[1]

---

1. After the war, Commodore Chauncey and Commander Yeo were dining together, when the latter explained the reasons of his avoiding action. His government instructed him to do so, because all he would gain by a victory would be the destruction of the American fleet, while a defeat would be likely to lead to the entire loss of Canada.

At the close of the war, Commodore Chauncey was appointed to the command of the *Washington*, of seventy-four guns; and, in 1816, he commanded a small squadron in the Mediterranean. There he assisted the American consul-general at Algiers, in negotiating a treaty with that power,[1] which continued in force until the French conquest of the province, in 1830. In every Mediterranean port that he visited, Commodore Chauncey left a most favorable impression of the Americans. He returned to the United States in 1818, and after reposing awhile upon his estate on the East River, near the city of New York, he was called to Washington city to perform the duties of Navy Commissioner. He remained in the Federal city, in that capacity, until 1824, when he was appointed to the command of the naval station at Brooklyn, New York. In 1833, he was again chosen one of the Board of Navy Commissioners, and continued in that service until his death, when he was president of that body. He died at Washington city, on the 27th of January, 1840, at the age of about sixty-five years.

STEPHEN DECATUR.

AMONG the naval heroes whom the Americans delighted to honor, the memory of no one is cherished with more affection than that of the gallant Decatur, who, like Hamilton, "lived like a man, but died like a fool." He was of French lineage, and was born on the Eastern Shore of Maryland, on the 5th of January, 1779. His father was a naval officer, who, after the establishment of the United States navy, in 1798, had command first of the sloop-of-war *Delaware*, and afterward of the frigate *Philadelphia*, in connection with whose fate his son gained immortal honors.

Stephen Decatur was educated in Philadelphia, and at the age of nineteen years entered the navy as a midshipman, under Commodore Barry. He was promoted to lieutenant, in 1799. Three times he sailed to the Mediterranean, while holding that subordinate commission. Just before his third arrival there, the *Philadelphia* frigate had struck upon a rock in the harbor of Tripoli, and had fallen into the hands of the Tripolitans.[2] Lieutenant Decatur immediately conceived a plan for re-capturing or destroying the vessel. Commodore Preble gave him permission to execute it. At the head of seventy volunteers, in the ketch *Intrepid*, he entered the harbor of Tripoli at eight o'clock on a dark evening in February, 1804. The *Philadelphia* lay moored within half gun-shot of the bashaw's castle and the main battery, with her guns mounted and loaded, and watched by Tripolitan gun-boats. Nothing daunted, Decatur approached within two hundred yards of the frigate, at eleven o'clock, and was then discovered and hailed. His Maltese pilot misled the Tripolitans, and Decatur's intentions were unsuspected, until he was alongside. Decatur and Midshipman Morris sprang upon the deck of the frigate, followed by the volunteers, and soon the vessel was in complete possession of the Americans. She could not be borne away, so Decatur fired her in several places, and escaped without losing a man. Only four were wounded. For that daring achievement he was promoted to post-captain. During the remainder of the war with Tripoli he performed many bold exploits, which gave him rank among the noblest spirits of the age.

After his return home, Decatur was employed in the superintendence of gun-

---

1. The treaty which Commodore Decatur had previously negotiated had been violated immediately after that officer had left the Mediterranean.
2. See sketch of Bainbridge.

boats, until ordered to supersede Commodore Barron in command of the *Chesapeake*. During the war with Great Britain that soon followed, he was distinguished for his gallantry in action and generosity to the vanquished. In January, 1815, while in command of the *President*, he was made a prisoner, but was soon released by the treaty of peace. He was afterward despatched, with a squadron, to the Mediterranean, and in a very short time, during the Summer of 1815, he completely humbled the piratical Barbary Powers—Algiers, Tunis, and Tripoli—and compelled them to make restitution of money and prisoners. He did more: he compelled them to relinquish all claims to tribute hitherto given by the United States since 1795. Full security to American commerce in the Mediterranean was obtained, and the character of the government of the United States was greatly elevated in the opinion of Europe. Then was accomplished, during a single cruise, what the combined powers of Europe dared not to attempt.

On his return to the United States, Commodore Decatur was appointed one of the Board of Navy Commissioners, and resided at Kalorama, formerly the seat of Joel Barlow, near Washington city. For a long time unpleasant feelings had existed between Decatur and Barron; and, in 1819, a correspondence between them resulted in a duel at Bladensburg. Both were wounded; Decatur mortally. That event occurred on the 22d of March, 1820, and Decatur died that night, at the age of forty years. The first intimation that his wife had of the matter was the arrival at home of her dying husband, conveyed by his friends. Thirty-five years have since rolled away, and his "beloved Susan" yet [1855] remains the widow of Stephen Decatur.

JAMES FENIMORE COOPER.

THE name of James Fenimore Cooper, is first on the list of American novelists, and it will be long before one so gifted shall wear his mantle as an equal. "He was one of those frank and decided characters who make strong enemies and warm friends—who repel by the positiveness of their convictions, while they attract by the richness of their culture and the amiability of their lives." Mr. Cooper was born at Burlington, New Jersey, on the 15th of September, 1789. His father, an immigrant from England, had settled there some twenty years before. When James was two years of age, the family removed to the banks of Otsego Lake, and there founded the settlement and beautiful village of Cooperstown. The lad was prepared for college by Rev. Mr. Ellison, rector of St. Peter's Church, Albany; entered Yale as a student, in 1802, and was graduated there in 1805. He chose the navy as the theatre of action, and entered it as a midshipman, in 1806. After a service of six years, he was about to be promoted to lieutenant, when he loved and married Miss Delancey (sister of the present [1855] Bishop Delancey of the diocese of Western New York), and left the navy forever. It was a school in which he was trained for the special service of literature in a peculiar way; and to his nautical information and experience during that six years, we are indebted for those charming sea-stories from his pen, which gave him such great celebrity at home and abroad.

Mr. Cooper's first production, of any pretensions, was a novel entitled *Persecution*, a tale of English life. It was published anonymously, met with small success, and the author was inclined to abandon the pen that had so deceived him with false hopes. He resolved to try again, and *The Spy* was the result. His triumph was now greater than his previous failure. That work was a broad foundation of a brilliant superstructure, and Fame waited upon the author with

J. Fenimore Cooper

abundant laurels. In 1823, his *Pioneers* appeared; and as the series of Leather-Stocking Tales—*The Prairie, The Last of the Mohicans, The Pathfinder,* and *The Deerslayer*—were published, they were read with the greatest eagerness. His fame was fully established; and by the publication of his novels in Europe, American literature began to attract attention in quarters where it had been sneered at. His series of admirable sea-stories were equally successful; and as *The Pilot, The Red Rover, The Water Witch, The Two Admirals,* and *Wing and Wing,* were issued from the press, they were sought after and read with the greatest avidity.

In 1826, Mr. Cooper went to Europe, preceded by a fame that gave him a key to the best society there. On all occasions he was the noble and fearless champion of his country and democracy, and his pen was often employed in defence of these, even while his genius was receiving the homage of aristocracy. While abroad, he wrote *The Bravo, The Heidenmaur, The Headsman,* and one or two inferior tales; and on his return home, he wrote *Homeward Bound,* and *Home as Found.* These were preceded by a *Letter to his Countrymen.* The preparation and publication of these works were unfortunate for the reputation and personal ease of Mr. Cooper; and his sensitiveness to the lash of critics speedily involved him in law-suits with editors whom he prosecuted as libelers. His feuds increased his naturally irritable nature, and for several years they embittered his life. They finally ceased; his ruffled spirit became calm; the current of popular feeling which had been turned against him resumed its old channels of admiration, and the evening of his days were blessed with tranquillity. At his hospitable mansion on the banks of the Otsego, he enjoyed domestic peace and the society of intellectual friends; and there, on the 14th of September, 1851, his spirit went to its final rest, when he lacked but one day of being sixty-two years of age.

Mr. Cooper is best known to the world as a novelist, yet he was the author of several works of graver import. Among these may be named a *Naval History of the United States, Gleanings in Europe, Sketches of Switzerland,* and several smaller works, some of them controversial. "He still lives," says a pleasant writer, "in the hearts of grateful millions, whose spirits have been stirred within them by his touching pathos, and whose love of country has been warmed into new life by the patriotism of his eloquent pen."

NICHOLAS BIDDLE.

THE contest between President Jackson, chief magistrate of the Republic, and President Biddle, chief magistrate of the Bank of the United States, forms a most interesting chapter in our political and social history. The latter was a native of Philadelphia, the scene of that warfare, where he was born on the 8th of January, 1786. His ancestors were among the earlier settlers in that State, and came to America with William Penn. His father was distinguished for his patriotic services during the War for Independence; and while Dr. Franklin was chief magistrate of that commonwealth, he was vice-president. Nicholas was educated first in the academy at Philadelphia, then in the college department of the University of Pennsylvania, and completed his collegiate course in the college at Princeton, in September, 1801. He was unsurpassed in his class, for scholarship, when he was graduated. The law was his choice as a profession, and he was almost prepared to enter upon its practice, in 1804, when he accepted an invitation from General Armstrong (who had been appointed minister to France), to accompany him as his private secretary. He visited several countries on the Continent before his return, and was private secretary, for awhile, to Mr. Monroe, representative of the United States at the English court.

Mr. Biddle returned to America, in 1807, and commenced the practice of his profession in Philadelphia, where, in connection with Mr. Dennie, he edited the "Port-Folio," until the death of the latter. He also prepared a history of Lewis and Clarke's expedition to the Pacific Ocean, across the Continent, from material, placed in his hands. In the Autumn of 1810, he was elected to a seat in the lower house of the legislature of Pennsylvania, where he distinguished himself by efforts in favor of a common-school system; and also in favor of the re-charter of the Bank of the United States. He declined a reëlection, in 1811, but was a member of the State Senate, in 1814, where he evinced much sound statesmanship. He was afterward twice nominated for Congress, but his party (democratic) being in the minority, he was not elected. In 1819, he was appointed one of the government directors of the Bank of the United States, at which time Langdon Cheves became its president. That gentleman resigned, in 1823, and Mr. Biddle was chosen to succeed him, by an unanimous vote. For sixteen years he stood at the head of that great moneyed institution, and conducted its affairs with wonderful ability. When President Jackson brought all the influence of his position to bear against the re-charter of the bank, Mr. Biddle summoned the resources of his genius, and sustained the unequal contest for a long time. But he was obliged to yield. The bank expired by its charter-limitation, in 1836, when it was incorporated by the State of Pennsylvania. Mr. Biddle continued at the head of the institution until 1839, when he retired to private life, to enjoy repose at his beautiful estate of Andalusia, on the banks of the Delaware, above Philadelphia. There the great financier died, on the 27th of February, 1844, at the age of fifty-eight years. Among other papers of value prepared by Mr. Biddle, was a volume compiled at the request of Mr. Monroe, and published by Congress, entitled *Commercial Digest.*

JOHN SULLIVAN.

LIKE General St. Clair, General Sullivan was a meritorious but often unfortunate officer. His chief fault seemed to be a want of vigilance; and during the Revolution that weakness proved disastrous—first at Bedford, near Brooklyn, in 1776, and on the Brandywine a year later.[1] John Sullivan was of Irish descent, and was born in Berwick, Maine, on the 17th of February, 1740. His youth was spent chiefly in farm labor. At maturity he studied law, and established himself in its practice in Durham, New Hampshire, where he soon rose to considerable distinction as an advocate and politician. He was chosen a delegate to the Continental Congress, in 1774, and soon after his return from Philadelphia he was engaged, with John Langdon and others, in seizing Fort William and Mary, at Portsmouth.[2] When, the following year, the Continental army was organized, he was appointed one of the eight brigadiers first commissioned by Congress; and early in 1776, he was promoted to major-general. Early in the Spring of that year he superseded Arnold in command of the Continental troops in Canada; and later in the season he joined Washington at New York. General Greene commanded the chief forces at Brooklyn, designed to repel the invaders, then on Staten Island, but was taken sick, and the leadership of his division was assigned to Sullivan. In the disastrous battle that soon followed, he was made prisoner, but was soon afterward exchanged, and took command of Lee's division, in New Jersey, after that officer's capture, later in the season. In the Autumn of 1777, General Sullivan was in the battles of Brandywine and Germantown; and in the succeeding Winter, he was stationed in Rhode Island, preparatory to an attempted expulsion of the British therefrom. He besieged Newport, in August, 1778, but was unsuccessful, because the French Admiral D'Estaing would not coöperate with him, according to promise and arrangement. General Sullivan's military career closed after his memorable campaign against the Indians, in Western New York, early in the Autumn of 1779. He resigned his commission because he felt aggrieved at some action of the Board of War, and was afterward elected to a seat in Congress. From 1786 to 1789, he was president or governor of New Hampshire, when, under the provision of the new Federal Constitution, he was appointed district judge. That office he held until his death, which occurred on the 23d of January, 1795, when he was in the fifty-fifth year of his age.

---

1. The first was at the close of August, 1776. That conflict is generally known as the Battle of Long Island. On account of Sullivan's want of vigilance, Sir Henry Clinton, unobserved, got in his rear near Bedford, cut off his retreat to the American lines, and placed the Americans between the balls and bayonets of the British in the rear and the Hessians in front. Because of a lack of vigilance on the Brandywine, in September, 1777, Sullivan allowed Cornwallis to cross that stream, unobserved, and to fall upon the rear of the American army.
2. See sketch of Langdon.

JAMES BROWN.

ONE of the early enterprising Americans who sought and obtained wealth and renown in the newly-acquired Territory of Louisiana, was James Brown, a distinguished Senator and diplomist. He was born near Staunton, Virginia, on the 11th of September, 1766. He was one of a dozen children of a Presbyterian clergyman, and was educated at William and Mary College, at Williamsburg. After studying law under the eminent George Wythe, he went to Kentucky, and joined his elder brother, John, who represented that State in Congress for about twenty years. When that brother was called to political life, James succeeded him in his law practice, and soon rose to eminence. In 1791, he commanded a company of mounted riflemen, under General Charles Scott, in an expedition against the Indians in the Wabash Valley. When, in 1792, Kentucky was admitted into the Union as a sovereign commonwealth, Governor Shelby appointed Mr. Brown Secretary of State. He resided at Frankfort most of the time. He and Henry Clay married sisters, daughters of Colonel Thomas Hart, and were contemporaries at the bar.

After the purchase of Louisiana, Mr. Brown went to New Orleans, and at once entered into an extensive and lucrative practice, for there was an immense amount of valuable property requiring identification of ownership, through the medium of the new courts. He was associated with Mr. Livingston in the compilation of the civil code of Louisiana, and continued his lucrative law practice in New Orleans, until 1813, when he was elected one of the first Senators in Congress from the newly-organized State. He also held the office of United States District Attorney, by the appointment of President Jefferson. In Congress he ably sustained the administration, in its war measures. He left the Senate in 1817, but returned to it again, after a re-election, in 1819. President Monroe esteemed him very highly; and, in 1823, he appointed him minister plenipotentiary to France. He filled that station with great dignity and ability until the Autumn of 1829, when he obtained permission to return home. He then retired to private life, and could never be induced to leave its coveted repose afterward. He died of apoplexy, in the city of Philadelphia, on the 7th of April, 1835, in the sixty-ninth year of his age.

OLIVER HAZZARD PERRY.

THE laconic despatch of Commodore Perry—*We have met the enemy and they are ours*—and the *Veni vidi vici* of the old Roman, will ever stand as parallels on the page of History. The gallant author of that despatch was born in South Kingston, Rhode Island, on the 23d of August, 1785. His father was then in the naval service of the United States, and dedicated his infant son to that profession. He entered the navy as a midshipman, at the age of thirteen years, on board of the sloop-of-war, *General Greene*. At that time, war with France seemed inevitable; but young Perry was not permitted to see active service until the difficulties with Tripoli afforded him an opportunity, he being in the squadron of Commodore Preble. Always thoughtful, studious, and inquisitive on ship board, he soon became a skilful seaman and navigator, and an accomplished disciplinarian.

In 1810, Midshipman Perry was promoted to lieutenant, and placed in command of the schooner *Revenge*, attached to Commodore Rodger's squadron, then cruising in the vicinity of New London, in Long Island

Sound. In that vessel he was wrecked the following Spring, but was not only acquitted of all blame by a court of inquiry held at his request, but his conduct in saving guns and stores was highly applauded. Early in 1812, he was placed in command of a flotilla of gun-boats in New York harbor. He soon became disgusted with that service, and solicited and obtained, for himself and his men, permission to reinforce Commodore Chauncey on Lake Ontario. That officer immediately despatched Perry to Lake Erie, to superintend the building of a small squadron there to oppose a British naval force on those western waters. When ready, Perry cruised about the west end of the Lake, and on the 10th of September, 1813, he had a severe engagement with the enemy. In the *Lawrence*, which displayed at its mast-head the words of the hero after whom she was named—*Don't give up the ship*[1]—Perry led the squadron, and after many acts of great skill and courage, he achieved a complete victory. He was then only twenty-seven years of age. It was one of the most important events of the war. The victor was promoted to captain, received the thanks of Congress and State legislatures, and was honored by his government with a gold commemorative medal.

After the war, Cap. Perry was put in command of the *Java*, a first-class frigate, and sailed with Com. Decatur to the Mediterranean, to punish the piratical Dey of Algiers. On his return to the United States, he performed a

---

1. See sketch of James Lawrence.

deed of heroism equal to any achieved in the public service. His vessel was lying in Newport harbor, in mid-Winter. During a fearful storm, intelligence reached him that a merchant vessel was wrecked upon a reef, six miles distant. He immediately manned his barge, said to his crew, "Come, my boys, we are going to the relief of shipwrecked seamen; pull away!" and soon afterward he had rescued eleven half-exhausted men, who were clinging to the floating quarter-deck of their broken vessel. To Perry, it was an act of simple duty in the cause of humanity; to his countrymen, it appeared as holiest heroism, deserving of a civic crown.

The commerce of the United States was greatly annoyed and injured by swarms of pirates who infested the West India seas. A small American squadron was stationed there; and, in 1819, Commodore Perry was sent thither, in the *John Adams*, to take command of the little fleet, chastise the buccaneers, and exchange friendly courtesies with the new republics on the Caribbean coast. When he arrived, the yellow fever was prevailing in the squadron. The commodore was soon attacked by that terrible disease, and on his birth-day, the 23d of August, 1819, just as his vessel was entering the harbor of Port Spain, Trinidad, he expired, at the age of thirty-four years. He was buried with military honors, the following day. Seventeen years afterward, his remains were brought to his native land, in a vessel of war, and interred in the North burying-ground, at Newport, Rhode Island. Over his grave the State of Rhode Island erected a granite monument; and soon after his decease, Congress made a liberal provision for his aged mother, and his widow and children. That widow lived about forty years, the beloved relict of one of the most gallant and accomplished men whose deeds have honored our Republic.[1]

WILLIAM GASTON.

AMONG the more recent lights of the North Carolina bar, was William Gaston, the eminent statesman, the upright judge, and the profound scholar. He was born at Newbern, North Carolina, on the 19th of September, 1778. His family was greatly distinguished for patriotism during the War for Independence, and that moral quality occupied a large space in his character. His father died when he was only three years of age, and he was left to the care of his excellent mother, a member of the Roman Catholic Church. At the age of thirteen years he was sent to the college at Georgetown, District of Columbia,[2] where he took special delight in the study of the ancient classics. His health became impaired by excessive application to his studies, and he was called home. After some further preparation he entered the college at Princeton, as a student, in 1794, where he was graduated, two years afterward, with the highest honors. He studied law in his native town, with Francis Xavier Martin, and was admitted to practice in 1798. Before he was twenty-two years of age, he was a member of the Senate of North Carolina, where his talents soon became very conspicuous. In 1808, he was one of the electors of President and Vice-President of the United States; and from 1813 until 1817, he was a representative of his district in the Federal Congress. He was a warm opponent of Madison's administration, and

---

1. A brother of Commodore Perry, bearing the same title, was instrumental in gaining great commercial advantages for the United States. In command of a squadron, Commodore M. C. Perry made an official visit to Japan, and, by admirably-conducted negotiations, he succeeded in forming a treaty with the government of that empire in 1854, by which its long-sealed ports were opened to American vessels for ever.
2. See sketch of Archbishop Carroll.

ably battled against the war, with his Federal associates of New England. One of his most powerful speeches in Congress was in the early part of 1815, against the proposition for authorizing the President to contract a loan of twenty-five millions of dollars, for the purpose of carrying on the war. His learning and eloquence created great surprise, and he was regarded as one of the ablest and most useful men in Congress. His own State was enriched by his labors after 1817, where, for twenty-seven years longer, he was unremitting in active duties at the bar, in the legislature, in the convention to amend the Constitution of the State, and as a judge of the Supreme Court of North Carolina. He was chosen to the latter office in 1834, with the universal approbation of the people, notwithstanding a provision of the then existing State Constitution, prohibited all but *Protestant* Christians, holding a judicial station.

The memory of few men is so warmly cherished as that of Judge Gaston, by the North Carolinians. He was an elegant writer of both prose and poetry, pure in all his thoughts and acts, and a noble citizen in every particular. During all his life he cherished the memory of his mother with fondest affection, and uniformly attributed to her tender care and wise counsels, under Providence, all of the moral strength of his character, and his success in life.[1] Sweetly has Mrs. Sigourney sung—

> "This tells to mothers what a holy charge
> Is theirs ; with what a kingly power their love
> May rule the fountains of the new-born mind ;
> Warns them to wake at early dawn and sow
> Good seed before the world doth sow its tares."

Judge Gaston died on the 23d of January, 1844, in the sixty-sixth year of his age.

ZERAH COLBURN.

THE career of Zerah Colburn, who was remarkable for his extraordinary performances in mental arithmetic, exhibits the melancholy spectacle of a life made comparatively miserable by a dependence upon one precocious faculty, and the greed of a misguided parent. He was born at Cabot, Vermont, on the 1st of September, 1804, and until he was almost six years of age, he appeared the dullest of his father's children. At about that time he exhibited extraordinary powers of calculation, by a mental process wholly his own, and which he could not explain. His father was led to expect great achievements by his gifted boy, and at the same time, with the avowed purpose of procuring money to have him educated, he took him to different places in New England, to be examined, hoping to meet with some generous aid. It was offered by the president of Dartmouth College, who proposed to educate Zerah at his own expense. Hoping for a more favorable offer, his father took him to Boston, where his wonderful powers created a great sensation. They were indeed wonderful. The most difficult questions on the various arithmetical rules, were solved almost instantly, by a mental process, for the manual labor of making figures was altogether too tardy for his calculations.

---

1. When he was only seven or eight years of age, he was remarkable for his expertness in learning his lessons in school. A little boy said to him one day, "William, why is it that you are always at the head of the class, and I am always at the foot?" "There is a reason," William replied, "but if I tell you, you must promise to keep it a secret, and do as I do. Whenever I take up a book to study, I first say a little prayer my mother taught me, that I may be able to learn my lessons." And such was his practice through life. He never attempted any thing of moment, without first invoking Divine assistance.

Several gentlemen in Boston offered to educate the lad, but his father would not consent. He travelled with him through many of the Middle and Southern States, exhibiting him for money; and, in 1812, he went with him to England, for the same purpose. After travelling through much of Great Britain and Ireland, they went to France, and young Colburn became a student in the *Lycée Napoleon*, for a short time. But in all these wanderings the education of the boy was neglected, and tho unwise father had utterly failed in what appeared to be his main object—money-making—when, in 1816, they returned to England. There the lad found a generous patron in the Earl of Bristol, who placed him in Westminster school, and kept him there about three years. Young Colburn was making fine progress, and gave many promises of future success, when his father refused to comply with some wishes of the earl, and the patronage of that peer was lost. The foolish and greedy father then had his son prepared for the stage, but he was a poor actor, and was soon obliged to abandon that profession, and become an assistant teacher in a school in London, to procure bread. Zerah finally opened a school on his own account, and he earned some money by making astronomical calculations for Dr. Young, then Secretary of the Board of Longitude. The elder Colburn died in 1824, and the Earl of Bristol and others, assisted Zerah with means to return to his native country. He was then twenty years of age. After spending some time with his mother and sisters, he became assistant teacher in an academy connected with Hamilton College, in the State of New York. He soon afterward went to Burlington, Vermont, where he gained a precarious living by teaching the French language. There he united himself with the Methodist Society, and soon afterward became an itinerant preacher. He was an indifferent speaker. Finally, in 1835, he settled at Norwich, Connecticut, and became Professor of Latin, Greek, French, and Spanish languages, in the "Norwich University." Two years previously, he had written and published a memoir of himself, which contains a great deal of curious narrative. He died at Norwich, on the 2d of March, 1840, in the thirty-fifth year of his age. The moral of his life is, that the wonderful development of a single faculty, only, is no guaranty of success.

JAMES LAWRENCE.

A SINGLE act—a single expression—is sometimes sufficient to give a name an earthly immortality. The acts and words of Captain James Lawrence present an illustrative example. He was the son of a lawyer in Burlington, New Jersey, where he was born on the 1st of October, 1781. While yet a small boy he felt irrepressible longings for the sea; and at the age of sixteen years he was gratified by receiving the appointment of midshipman in the navy. He was schooled in the war against Tripoli. He acted as Decatur's first lieutenant in the daring achievement of burning the *Philadelphia* frigate under the guns of the Tripolitan batteries; and he remained for several years in the Mediterranean, in command successively of the *Vixen*, *Wasp*, *Argus*, and *Hornet*. With the latter he captured the *Peacock* off the coast of Demerara, in February, 1813; and on his return he was promoted to post captain, and placed in command of the frigate *Chesapeake*. While lying in Boston Harbor, at the close of May, the British frigate *Shannon* appeared, and signalled a challenge for the *Chesapeake* to come out and fight. It was accepted by Lawrence, and on the morning of the 1st of June, he went out to engage in that naval duel which proved so disastrous. They opened their guns upon each other, late in the afternoon. Early in the action Captain Lawrence was wounded in the leg. The vessels came so near each other, that the anchor of the *Chesapeake* caught in one of the ports of the *Shannon*, and her guns could not be brought to bear upon the enemy. While in that situation, Captain Lawrence received his death-wound, from a bullet, and when carried below, he cried out in those imperishable words— words which the brave Perry placed at his mast-head three months afterward— "*Don't give up the ship.*"[1] The *Chesapeake* was captured after an action of eleven minutes, and a loss of one hundred and forty-six men, in killed, and wounded. Captain Lawrence lived, in great pain, four days, when he died, on the 6th of June, 1813, at the age of thirty-one years. He was buried at Halifax, Nova Scotia, with military honors. His remains were afterward conveyed to New York, and interred in Trinity church-yard, where an appropriate monument was erected to his memory. It fell into decay, and a more beautiful one has since been reared.

ZACHARY TAYLOR.

THE people of the United States are professedly peace-loving, yet nowhere is a military hero more sincerely worshipped by vast masses than here, not, we may charitably hope, because of his vocation, but because of the good achieved for his country by his brave deeds. And when that worship is excessive because of some brilliant act, then the people desire to apotheosize the hero by crowning him with the highest honors of the nation—the civic wreath of chief magistrate. Of four already thus rewarded, General Zachary Taylor was the last. He was a native of Virginia, the "mother of Presidents," and was born in Orange county, on the 24th of September, 1784. His father removed to Kentucky the following year, and settled near the site of the present city of Louisville. At the age of about twenty-four years he entered the army of the United States as first lieutenant of infantry, and two years afterward he married Miss Margaret Smith, a young lady of good family in Maryland. When war was declared against Great Britain, in 1812, he held a captain's commission, and he was placed in command of Fort Harrison, a stockade on the Wabash river. There, in his gallant operations against the Indians, he gave promise of future renown, and for his heroic defence of his post he was breveted major. During the whole war he was an exceedingly useful officer in the North-west. At the close of the contest, when the army was reduced, he was deprived of his majority and re-commissioned a captain. His pride would not brook the measure, and he left the service. He was soon after reinstated as major, by President Madison.

In 1816, Major Taylor was placed in command of a post at Green Bay; and two years afterward he was promoted to lieutenant-colonel. In that position he remained until 1832, when President Jackson, who appreciated his great merits, gave him the commission of colonel. He served with distinction under General Scott in the "Black Hawk War," and remained in command of Fort Crawford, at Prairie du Chien, until 1836. Then he went to Florida, and in his operations against the Seminoles, he evinced generalship superior to any officer there. Because of his gallantry in the battle at Okeechobee swamp, at the close of 1837, he was breveted brigadier-general; and the following year the command of all the troops

---

1. A few years ago a newspaper paragraph asserted that a person then living, who was with Captain Lawrence when he uttered the expression attributed to him, says that his words were, instead of "*Don't give up the ship!*" the more probable ones, on such an occasion, *Fight her till she sinks.*"

in Florida was assigned to him. There he remained until 1840, when he was appointed to the command of the South-western division of the army. He took post at Fort Gibson, in 1841, and removed his family to Baton Rouge, Louisiana, the same year, where he had purchased an estate.

Pursuant to general expectation, the annexation of Texas to the United States, in 1845, caused a rupture with Mexico, and hostilities were threatened. General Taylor was ordered to take post in Texas, toward the Mexican frontier, and in August, he concentrated his troops, as an Army of Observation, at Corpus Christi. The following Spring he crossed the Colorado with about four thousand regular troops, and approached the Rio Grande. On the 8th and 9th of May he gained those brilliant victories at Palo Alto and Resaca de la Palma, which gave him imperishable renown as a military leader. Late in September following, he gained another great victory at Monterey, in Mexico; and on the 23d of February, 1847, at the head of only six thousand men, mostly volunteers, he achieved a great victory at Buena Vista, over Santa Anna, with an army of twenty thousand Mexicans. In all of his movements, from the first blow at Palo Alto until the last one at Buena Vista, Taylor displayed the highest order of generalship, the most daring intrepidity, and the most unwavering courage. On his return home, he was every where greeted with the wildest enthusiasm; and, in 1848, the

Whig party, governed by the applauding voice of the nation, regarded him as eminently "available," and nominated him for the office of President of the United States. In the Autumn of that year, he was elected by a very large majority, and was inaugurated chief magistrate of the Republic on the 4th of March following. The cares, the duties, the personal inaction incident to his station, bore heavily upon him; and when disease appeared, these aggravated it. After holding the reins of the Federal government for sixteen months, death came to the presidential mansion, and on the 9th of July, 1850, the brave hero died, at the age of sixty-five years. He was the second chief magistrate who had died while in office, and was succeeded by the Vice-President, Millard Fillmore.

SILAS WRIGHT.

THE origin and career of Silas Wright, presents a striking illustration of the fact that, under the fostering care of our free institutions, genius may lift its possessor to the pinnacle of fame and fortune, without the factitious aids of wealth and power which too frequently stand sponsors at the baptism of *great men*, so called, in the elder world. Silas Wright was born at Amherst, Massachusetts, on the 24th of May, 1795, and while he was an infant, his parents settled in Weybridge, Vermont. There he received his early education, entered Middlebury College, as a student, at a proper age, and was graduated in 1815. While yet a student, his active mind grasped the subject of politics. War with Great Britain was then progressing, and young Wright became quite distinguished as a democratic politician, in Middlebury. After leaving college, he studied law at Sandy Hill, New York, and commenced its practice, in 1819. The same year he was induced to settle at Canton, New York, and there he lived the remainder of his days, except when absent on public duty. His superior abilities were soon manifested, and he was successively chosen to fill several local offices. He also took pride in military matters, and rose to the rank of brigadier-general of militia. As a magistrate, he always endeavored to allay feuds and keep the people from litigation; and as a lawyer, he conscientiously pursued the same course.

In 1823, he was elected to the State Senate, from St. Lawrence county, that district then embracing that and eight others of the sparsely-settled counties of Northern New York.[1] He soon became a distinguished member of the Senate, as a sound logician, fluent speaker, and industrious laborer in the public cause.[2] He remained there about three years, when he was elected to a seat in Congress, in 1826. There he took an active part in the discussions concerning a tariff, and cognate measures. At the next election he was a candidate for Congress, but the omission of the word *junior*, in printing his name on the tickets, caused his defeat. In 1829, he was appointed comptroller of the State of New York, and was reëlected to the same office, by the legislature, in 1832. The following year that body chose him to represent New York in the Senate of the United States, which position he occupied with great honor to himself and his country until he was elected governor of that State, in 1844. The nomination for the

---

1. Saratoga, Montgomery, Hamilton, Washington, Warren, Clinton, Essex, and Franklin.
2. It is said that on one occasion, while a member of the Senate, he was indirectly offered the sum of fifty thousand dollars, if he would feign sickness the next day, be absent from his seat, and not oppose, with his great influence, a bill for chartering certain banks. He spurned the bribe with honest indignation, and he was so much agitated by the occurrence during that night, that he came very near being absent from his seat the next day, on account of *real* illness.

office of Vice-President of the United States was tendered to him by a national convention, the same year, but was declined. Two years before he had declined a nomination for governor, and also the appointment of judge of the Supreme Court of the United States. Governor Wright was again nominated for chief magistrate of his adopted State, in 1846, but lost his election. At the close of his official term he retired to private life, followed by the grateful appreciation of his countrymen. There he seemed to be gathering strength for greater and more brilliant achievements in the field of statesmanship, to which his countrymen desired to invite him, when death came suddenly, and laid him in the grave. He had consented to deliver the annual address at the State Agricultural Fair, to be held at Saratoga Springs. While preparing for that service, he was attacked by acute disease, and expired within two hours afterward. That event occurred on the 27th of August, 1847, when he was a little more than fifty-two years of age. The people of St. Lawrence county have erected a beautiful monument over his grave at Canton, composed of pure white marble, from the Dorset quarry. The citizens of Weybridge, where he spent his earlier years, have also erected a monument to his memory. It is a shaft of white marble, about thirty-eight feet in height, standing upon a pedestal.

JESSE BUEL.

IT has been justly said of Jesse Buel, one of the most eminent patrons of Agriculture, in this country, that "in example not less than in precept, he may be said to have conferred blessings upon the times in which he lived—blessings that will continue to fructify, and ripen into fruit, long after his body shall have mingled with his favorite earth." Mr. Buel was a native of Coventry, Connecticut, where he was born on the 4th of January, 1778, and was the youngest of fourteen children of the same mother. When Jesse was twelve years of age, his father made Rutland, Vermont, his residence; and there, two years afterward, the lad, at his own urgent request, was apprenticed to a printer. At the age of eighteen years he purchased from his employer, the unexpired term of his apprenticeship, worked as a journeyman first in the city of New York, and then in Lansingburg and Waterford, and, in 1797, commenced the publication of a political newspaper at Troy. He married in 1801, made Poughkeepsie, in Dutchess county, his residence, and established a newspaper there. It was an unsuccessful enterprise, and Mr. Buel lost sufficient by it to make him a bankrupt. He left the scene of his disaster, went to Kingston, in Ulster county, and there, in 1803, he established a weekly paper, and continued it for ten years. Success attended him there. His daily life was marked by great diligence in business, and uprightness in conduct. He obtained and deserved the public confidence, and, for awhile, filled the office of judge of the Court of Common Pleas of Ulster county.

In 1813, Judge Buel removed to Albany. He had accumulated some property, bore a high reputation, and with this capital, at the urgent solicitation of Judge Spencer and others, he assumed the editorial management of the *Albany Argus*. The following year he received the appointment of State printer, and held that lucrative office until 1820, when he sold out his interest in the *Argus*, disposed of his printing establishment, and upon a small farm near Albany commenced his eminent career as a practical agriculturist. There, for nineteen years, he was engaged in those experiments in Agriculture and Horticulture which have rendered his name famous throughout our Union, and in Europe. Desirous of inducing others to adopt his improvements, he commenced the publication of the *Cultivator*, in 1834, under the auspices of the New York State Agricultural Society, and conducted it with great ability and success, until his death. In addition to his contributions to that paper, he wrote and delivered many addresses before agricultural societies in his own State and elsewhere; and associations of cultivators delighted to honor him with tokens of their esteem. He was chosen honorary member of the *Lower Canada Agricultural Society;* the *London Horticultural Society;* the *Royal and Central Society of Agriculture* at Paris, and of the *Society of Universal Statistics* in the same city. For several years, at intervals, Judge Buel was a member of the New York legislature; and, in 1836, he was an unsuccessful candidate for the office of governor of the State. At the time of his death he was one of the regents of the University. His final departure occurred at Danbury, Connecticut, on the 6th of October, 1839, when he was in the sixty-second year of his age. He was then on a journey to New Haven, to address an Agricultural Society there, when death suddenly prostrated him.

OSCEOLA.

FADING, fading, fading! Such is the doom of the Aborigines of our Continent. Civilization is to them like the sunbeams upon snow or hoar-frost. They are fast melting in its presence; and the burden of many a sad heart among the tribes is expressed in the touching lines of Schoolcraft—

> I will go to my tent and lie down in despair;
> I will paint me with black and will sever my hair;
> I will sit on the shore when the hurricane blows,
> And reveal to the God of the Tempest, my woes.
> I will weep for a season, on bitterness fed,
> For my kindred are gone to the hills of the dead;
> But they died not of hunger, or ling'ring decay—
> The hand of the white man hath swept them away!"

From time to time, some daring spirit, bolder than his fellows, and fired with patriotic zeal and burning hatred, like Philip or Pontiac, have, in more recent times, made desperate efforts to retain the land of their fathers when the hand of the white man had grasped it. Among the latest of these gallant men was Osceola, a brave chief of the Seminoles. His people yet remain on their ancient domain, the everglades of Florida. They were a remnant of the once powerful Creek Confederacy; and while other tribes were emigrating to the wilderness beyond the Mississippi, they pertinaciously clung to the graves and the hunting-grounds of their ancestors. A treaty made by some of the chief men, which provided for their removal beyond the Father of Waters, was repudiated by the *nation*. Micanopy, as its representative, declared that the Indians had been deceived, and refused to go. The government of the United States resolved to remove them by force. A long and cruel war was kindled, in 1835; and at the beginning of the contest, a young chief of powerful frame, noble bearing, and keen sagacity, appeared as leader of the warriors. It was Osceola. By common consent the Seminoles regarded him as their general-in-chief and destined liberator. With all the cunning of a Tecumseh and bravery of a Philip, he was so successful in stratagem, skilful in manœuvres, and gallant in conflict, that he baffled the efforts of the United States' troops sent against him, for a long time. For more than two years the war was prosecuted vigorously amid the swamps of the great Southern Peninsula, and a vast amount of blood and treasure was wasted in vain attempts to subdue the Indians. Some of the most accomplished commanders in the army of the Republic—Scott, Taylor, Gaines, and Jesup—were there, but Osceola, in his way, out-generalled them all. At last he was subdued by treachery. He was invited to a conference in the camp of General Jesup, under the protection of a flag. Several chiefs, and about seventy warriors, accompanied him; and when they supposed themselves safe under the pledges of the white man's honor and the sacred flag, they were seized and confined. Osceola was sent in irons to Charleston, and immured in Fort Moultrie. This act of treachery was defended by General Jesup by the plea of Osceola's known infidelity to solemn promises, and a desire to put an end to blood-shed by whatever means he might be able to employ. It was the logic of mercy enforced by dishonor.

The misfortune of Osceola was too great, even for his mighty spirit. That spirit, chafed like a leashed tiger, would not bend until the physical frame of the chief gave way, and a fatal fever seized it. Gradually the stern warrior assumed the weakness of a little child; and on the 31st of January, 1839, Osceola died in his military prison. Since then a small monument to his memory has been erected near the entrance-gate to Fort Moultrie.[1] His capture and death was the severest blow yet felt by the Seminoles. The spirit of the nation was broken, yet they fought on with desperation. They did not finally yield until 1842. A remnant yet [1855] inhabit the everglades of Florida. They are quiet but defiant.

WILLIAM C. C. CLAIBORNE.

WHEN, early in the year 1804, intelligence reached the government of the United States, that the broad and beautiful territory of Louisiana had become a part of the Republic by actual cession, and the importance of appointing an extremely judicious man to govern the mixed population of Spaniards, Frenchmen, and Negroes, was palpable, President Jefferson, to the astonishment of many old and wise heads, sent thither a handsome young man of nine-and-twenty years, a descendant of one of the earliest settlers in Virginia. That young man was William Charles Cole Claiborne, who was born in 1775. He was nursed in the bosom of patriotic sentiment, and grew to manhood in the atmosphere of noble efforts in the founding of a new and glorious empire. He was a student in William and Mary College, for a while, but completed his education at an academy in Richmond. He inherited nothing but a good education and excellent character, and with these he entered upon the battle of life, confident of victories. With a determination to help himself, he went to New York, and sought employment under Mr. Beckley (with whom he was acquainted), then clerk to the Federal House of Representatives. He succeeded, and at the age of sixteen years the accomplished and resolute boy ate bread earned by his own industry. He became perfect master of the French language, and was very useful to his employer, in many ways. His talent and sprightliness attracted the attention of Jefferson, then Washington's Secretary of State, and that statesman gave the youthful Claiborne many of the encouragements which young men need. From General John Sevier, then a member of Congress, he received many kind attentions, and his young ambition grew apace. The profession of the law opened a high road to distinction, and he left New York, studied Blackstone, in Richmond, for three months, was then admitted to practice, and, bid-

---

1. See sketch of General Moultrie. The present fortress, near the site of the palmetto fort of the Revolution, is a strong, regular work; one of the finest belonging to the United States.

William C. C. Claiborne

ding adieu to the charms of society in the East, he went over the mountains, and established himself in the present Sullivan county, Tennessee. In eloquence, he exceeded every man west of the Blue Ridge, and in less than two years, he was at the head of his profession, and was called hundreds of miles to manage law-suits. A yearning for home took possession of his feelings, and he was about to return to Richmond, when Tennessee prepared to enter the Union as a sovereign State, and Claiborne was chosen a member of a convention to form a constitution. In that convention he began his political career; and he was regarded by all as a prodigy, for he was then only about twenty-one years of age. His friend, Sevier, was elected governor of the new State. One of his first acts was the appointment of young Claiborne as a judge of the Supreme Court of law and equity, of the budding commonwealth. He was not yet twenty-two years of age, yet he entered upon his duties with all the gravity and legal wisdom of many jurists of fifty. The ermine did not rest long upon his shoulders, for the people, by an immense majority, elected him their representative in Congress. He was again triumphantly reëlected, and there he repaid the kindness he had received from Mr. Jefferson, by giving him his vote for President of the United States. In that Congress Claiborne greatly distinguished himself by his learning, logic, and eloquence.

Soon after President Jefferson's accession, he appointed Mr. Claiborne governor of the Mississippi Territory, on the request of the people there; and on the 23d of November, 1801, he was enthusiastically received at Natchez, the seat of government. He found society heaving with the turbulence of faction; he poured the oil of conciliation upon the billows, and they soon became calm. He married a beautiful and wealthy girl in Nashville, and passed the two years that he was governor of Mississippi, in the greatest happiness. His duties of governor of Louisiana, to which office he was appointed early in 1804, were more arduous and perplexing, yet he performed them with signal ability and success. His justice and urbanity endeared him to all classes; and when, in 1812, Louisiana became an independent State, the people chose him for their governor, by an almost unanimous vote. He was in the executive chair during the memorable invasion of the British, and their repulse at New Orleans by General Jackson, early in 1815. On that occasion Governor Claiborne wisely and generously surrendered to Jackson all power and command, and, under that general's orders, the magistrate led a large body of the militia of his State. His long career as governor of Louisiana terminated in 1817, when he was chosen to represent that State in the Federal Senate. But his useful life closed too soon to allow him to serve his countrymen any more. He died of a disease of the liver, in the city of New Orleans, on the 23d of November, 1817, in the forty-second year of his age. The municipal authorities decreed a public funeral, and money was appriated to erect a marble monument to his memory.

JAMES MILNOR.

IT has been the privilege of few men, who have passed their lives in public labors, to be so warmly, tenderly, and universally loved, as the Rev. James Milnor, D. D., the rector of St. George's Church, New York, for almost thirty years. And it has been the privilege of very few men to be so eminently useful as he in all that pertains to the well-being of his fellow creatures. In the domestic circle, he was reverenced for his unalloyed goodness; in the legal profession he was called "the honest lawyer"; as a legislator he was beneficent and patriotic; as a Christian he was without guile; and in the Protestant Episcopal Church, he was one of the most prominent of all her evangelical clergy, yet in nothing wanting as one of her most loyal sons.

James Milnor was the son of Quaker parents, and was born in Philadelphia on the 20th of June, 1773. He was educated partly in the Philadelphia Academy, and partly in the University of Pennsylvania. To relieve his father of heavy expenses on his account, James left the University before taking his degree, and at the age of about sixteen years, commenced the study of law. He was admitted to the bar in 1794, before he was quite twenty-one years of age, and commenced practice in Norristown. There, among a preponderating German population, he was very successful, he having acquired a knowledge of the language at an early age. After remaining there about three years, he returned to Philadelphia, and, in 1799, married the lady who yet [1855] survives him. That ceremony having been performed by "a hireling priest," (the bride was an Episcopalian, by education) contrary to the discipline of Friends, Mr. Milnor was disowned, and his membership in the Society ceased forever.

In the year 1800, Mr. Milnor was chosen a member of the city council. He held the same position from 1805 until 1809; and during the latter year, he was its President. He was extremely popular among all classes; and in 1810, he was elected to a seat in Congress by the Federal vote in his district. There he remained until the Spring of 1813, and was a steady and consistent opponent of the war, and the belligerent measures of the Administration. He took a prominent part in the debates; and on account of a report of one of his speeches, which appeared in a Philadelphia paper, Henry Clay, then Speaker of the House, challenged him to fight a duel. Mr. Milnor bravely refused, first because Mr. Clay had no right to call him to account for his public acts, and secondly because he was opposed, in principle, to the cowardly practice of duelling. There the matter ended, and in after years, when Mr. Milnor was an eminent minister of the Gospel, he and the great statesman met on the most friendly terms.

It was during his Congressional career, that religious truths were pressed with greatest force upon his attention. He had been careless for many years; then he stood wavering between the doctrine of universal salvation and the orthodoxy of the day, but when his term of service in the national council had ended, his mind fully comprehended those great truths which he afterward so eloquently proclaimed, and he abandoned the legal profession and prepared for entrance upon the Gospel ministry.[1] He was admitted to the communion by Bishop White, and was ordained a deacon by that excellent prelate, in August, 1814. Twelve months afterward he was ordained a presbyter, and labored for about a year as an assistant minister in the Associated Churches, in Philadelphia. In 1816, he was called to the rectorship of St. George's Church, in New York, and commenced his long and useful labors there in September of that year. The Bishop of the diocese (Hobart) had been his play-fellow in boyhood, and Mr. Milnor anticipated pleasant pastoral relations with him. These anticipations were not realized. The rector of St. George's would indulge his heart and lips in the utterance of extemporaneous prayer at occasional religious meetings, and he also joined heartily with other denominations of Christians, immediately after his arrival in New York, in the formation of the Bible Society; and during the remainder of his life he was continually associated with disciples of every name, in other works of Christian benevolence. These were grave offences in the eyes of the Bishop, and a harmony of views, on these subjects, never existed between the prelate and the presbyter.[2]

Dr. Milnor was extremely active in the promotion of schemes of Christian benevolence. He was one of the founders of the American Tract Society, in 1824, and continued to be one of its most active members until his death. The Institution for the Deaf and Dumb; the Orphan Asylum; the Home for aged indigent Females, and many kindred institutions, felt his fostering care. In 1830 he went to England as a delegate of the American Bible Society to the British and Foreign Bible Society; and ever afterward his visit there was referred to with the greatest pleasure by all who enjoyed the privilege of his company and ministrations. He visited Paris, then the Isle of Wight, and then made a general tour through England, Wales, Scotland and Ireland, everywhere engaged in the duties of a Christian minister, and human benefactor. He returned home in the Autumn of the same year, bringing with him a vast amount of useful information for the various associations with which he was connected. In the excitements produced by Tractarianism, he was bold in the maintenance of evangelical truth, yet always kind and conciliatory. He labored on zealously until the Spring of 1845, when he was summoned away suddenly by a

---

[1] On one of his visits home, during his term in Congress, his little daughter, Anna, met him as he entered the house, and said, "Papa, do you know I can read?" "No, let me hear you," he replied. She selected the words, "Thou shalt love the Lord thy God with all thy heart." This incident made a great impression on his mind.

[2] Bishop Hobart objected to the prayer meetings, which the members of St. George's Church were in the habit of holding, and which Dr. Milnor warmly encouraged, though he did not always attend them. On one of those evenings, the Bishop was in the rectory, and requested Dr. Milnor to go and dismiss the assembly. "Bishop," he said firmly, "I dare not prevent my parishioners from meeting for prayer; but if you are willing to take the responsibility of dismissing them, you have my permission." The praying members remained undisturbed.

disease which had twice brought him to death's door. On the evening of the 8th of April, 1845, a meeting of the Directors of the Deaf and Dumb Institution was held at his study. Five hours afterward his spirit was in the immediate presence of his divine Master.

RETURN JONATHAN MEIGS.

A BRIGHT-EYED Connecticut girl was disposed to coquette with her lover, Jonathan Meigs; and on one occasion, when he had pressed his suit with great earnestness, and asked for a positive answer, she feigned coolness, and would give him no satisfaction. The lover resolved to be trifled with no longer, and bade her farewell, for ever. She perceived her error, but he was allowed to go far down the lane before her pride would yield to the more tender emotions of her heart. Then she ran to the gate and cried, "Return, Jonathan! Return, Jonathan!" He did return, they were joined in wedlock, and in commemoration of these happy words of the sorrowing girl, they named their first child, Return Jonathan. That child, afterward a hero in our War for Independence, a noble Western pioneer, and a devoted friend of the Cherokees, was born at Middletown, Connecticut, in December, 1740. He received a good common education, and learned the trade of a hatter. Of his earlier life we have no important information; and he first appears in public at the opening of the Revolution. He was then thirty-five years of age; and one of the companies of minute-men, in his native town, had chosen him their captain. When intelligence of bloodshed at Lexington reached him, he marched his company to Cambridge, and soon received the appointment of major, from Governor Trumbull. In the ensuing Autumn, he accompanied Arnold in his memorable expedition from the Kennebec to the St. Lawrence. He participated in the attack on Quebec, at the close of the year, and was made a prisoner there. His fellow-captives were much indebted to him for comforts during the remainder of the dreary Winter. In the course of the following year he was exchanged, and, receiving the commission of colonel from the Continental Congress, he raised a regiment in Connecticut, which was known as The Leather-cap Battalion. With a part of his force (seventy in number), he made a bold attack upon the British post at Sag Harbor, east end of Long Island, in May, 1777, where he destroyed a good deal of property, and carried off almost a hundred prisoners, without losing a man. Congress gave him thanks and an elegant sword, for that exploit.

In the capture of Stony Point, on the Hudson, in 1779, Colonel Meigs and his regiment, under the direction of General Wayne, performed a gallant part. He was one of the first to mount the parapet and enter the fort. He remained in active service until the close of the war, and then sat down quietly in his native town, to enjoy the honors he had so bravely won. His knowledge of surveying, acquired in early life, was now called into practice. He was appointed one of the surveyors of the Ohio Land Company,[1] and in the Spring of 1778, he went over the mountains, and halted at Marietta, the head-quarters of emigrants to that region. He at once became a prominent man among the settlers; and soon after the arrival of General St. Clair, as governor of the newly-organized Northwestern Territory, Colonel Meigs was appointed one of the judges of the Court of Quarter Sessions. He was also appointed clerk of the same court, and prothonotary of the Court of Common Pleas. He was much engaged in surveying, until interrupted by the Indian war. At the time of the treaty at Greenville, in

---

1. See sketch of Rufus Putnam.

1795, Colonel Meigs was commissary of clothing; and in all his duties, public and private, he exhibited such a kindly heart, perfect justice, and unselfish benevolence, that he won the esteem of the white people and the Indians.

In 1798, Colonel Meigs was elected a member of the Territorial legislature; and, in 1801, President Jefferson appointed him Indian agent, among the Cherokees, where he resided until his death, which occurred at the Cherokee agency, on the 28th of January, 1823, at the age of eighty-three years. The Indians with whom he lived so long, loved and revered him as a father. Even until the last week of his life, he engaged with them in their athletic sports.

BENJAMIN WRIGHT.

THERE is an unwritten, early, and secret history of the great Erie Canal, which, if brought to the light of to-day, would give to men a title to true renown, on whom eulogium has bestowed only a passing remark. Among these, the names of Hawley, Brooks, M'Neil, Ellicott, Watson, Eddy, and Wright, would appear conspicuous. The latter was a native of Weathersfield, Connecticut, where he was born on the 10th of October, 1770. His parents were humble, and his opportunities for early education were very limited. At the age of sixteen years he went to live with an uncle, in Litchfield county, where he acquired a knowledge of surveying. When in his nineteenth year, he accompanied his father and family to the wilderness of central New York, and settled at Fort Stanwix, now Rome. All beyond was the "Indian country." Settlers were locating rapidly in that region, and young Wright was constantly employed in surveying lands. Within four years [1792–1796], he surveyed over five hundred thousand acres of land in the counties of Oneida and Oswego. His fame for speed and accuracy in his occupation became wide spread, and his services were constantly sought, in all directions. He was employed by the *Western Inland Lock Navigation Company*, in their efforts to connect Lake Ontario and the Hudson river, by a canal between Oneida Lake and the Mohawk. He became the general agent of the proprietors of extensive tracts of land, in that region; and, in 1801, and again in 1807, he represented the district in the State legislature. During the latter year, Mr. Wright, Jesse Hawley, General M'Neil, and Judge Forman, discussed the feasibility of making a canal through the Mohawk Valley, and westward, so as to connect Lake Erie with the Hudson. The legislature, at the suggestion of Forman and Wright, appropriated six hundred dollars for a preliminary survey. It was accomplished; and, in 1810, a board of Canal Commissioners was appointed. Such were the incipient measures which led to a great result. Mr. Wright was very active, until operations were suspended by the war with Great Britain. They were resumed, with vigor, in 1816, when Judge Geddes and Mr. Wright were charged with the construction of the Erie Canal. Under their direction the work went steadily on, until 1825, when the stupendous undertaking was completed.[1]

In 1814, Mr. Wright was appointed one of the judges for Oneida county; and during the remainder of his life, he was either a consulting or chief engineer in the construction of almost every important work of internal improvement throughout the country. In 1835, he went to Cuba, by invitation of the authorities and capitalists there, to consult respecting a railroad from Havana to the interior of the island. After that he did not engage much in active life; and on the 24th of August, 1842, he died, in the city of New York, when in the seventy-second year of his age.

1. See sketch of Dewitt Clinton.

ADONIRAM JUDSON.

IN the little parlor of the late Professor Stuart, at Andover, Massachusetts, on a sultry day in June, 1810, a few grave men consulted upon the expediency of forming a Foreign Missionary Society. A few pious and zealous young men, students in the Andover Theological Seminary, who ardently desired employment in the missionary field of far-off India, had urged the propriety of such a measure. That consultation was favorable, and at the meeting of the General Association, the following day, at Bradford, an earnest memorial was presented, signed by four of those young men. The *American Board of Commissioners for Foreign Missions*, was then established;[1] and in February, 1812, three of the signers of that memorial sailed for India, the pioneer American missionaries to the heathen in distant lands. The three were Adoniram Judson, jr. (author of the memorial), Jamuel Nott, jr., and Samuel Newell.

Adoniram Judson was born at Malden, Massachusetts, on the 9th of August, 1788. His father was a Congregational clergyman, and cultivated the mind and heart of his promising boy with great care. He was graduated with highest honors at Brown University, in 1807, and after lingering, for a while, in great doubt upon the borders of the dank marsh of infidelity, the light of Christian

---

1. The following gentlemen composed that first Board: John Treadwell (governor of Connecticut), Rev. Timothy Dwight, D.D., General Jedediah Huntington, Rev. Calvin Chapin, Rev. Joseph Lyman, D.D., Rev. Samuel Spring, D.D., William Bartlett, Rev. Samuel Worcester, and Deacon Samuel H. Walley.

truth beckoned him away to the beautiful land of gospel blessings. He entered the Andover Theological Seminary, as a student. There he experienced a desire to preach the gospel to the heathen, and was about to offer his services to the London Missionary Society, when, after much effort, the formation of the American Board, above mentioned, opened the way for him. He married the lovely Ann Hasseltine, early in February, 1812, and, on the 19th of that month, sailed with her and other companions, for Calcutta. They reached that port in June following, and were lodged, for a short time, at the house of the eminent Baptist missionary, Dr. Carey, at Serampore. Compelled to leave the British East Indies, they fled to the Isle of France,[1] and from thence went to Rangoon, in Burmah. Mr. and Mrs. Judson had embraced Dr. Carey's views of baptism, were immersed by him, and were afterward sustained by the Baptist Board of Foreign Missions, which was established in 1814.

At Rangoon the missionaries employed themselves diligently in studying the Burmese language, and in otherwise preparing for labor in the great missionary field before them. They translated portions of Scripture and other words of instruction concerning Christianity, into the Burmese language; and the first fruit of their labors appeared in March, 1817, when an intelligent native came to them with an earnest desire for spiritual knowledge. A month later, Mr. Judson was allowed to preach to the people, publicly; and, in June following, the first convert was baptized. Then the heart of the missionary was filled with gladness, for he saw the dawning of a glorious morning for the pagans of Burmah. He labored on hopefully, and now and then a disciple would appear. He prepared a small dictionary and a grammar, and many were taught but few seemed profited. At the beginning of 1820, there were only ten converts, yet these were prepared to be each at the head of a cohort of disciples in after years, if Providence should call them to act. A printing-press, sent from Serampore, was erected at Rangoon, and a translation of the Gospel of St. Matthew, and some tracts, were printed and distributed among the people. In the sketch of Mrs. Judson, events from this period, until her return from America, and the close of the Burmese war with the English, have been glanced at, and need not be repeated here. After that, in a new town named Amherst, within territory ceded by the King of Ava to the British, Mr. Judson and his missionary family resumed their labors, in 1826. There Mrs. Judson died; and soon afterward their little daughter was laid by her side under the hope-tree. Eight years afterward, Mrs. Sarah Boardman, the widow of a missionary, became Mr. Judson's wife, and they labored on together with great zeal, at Rangoon, Amherst, and Maulmain. Dr. Judson had then just completed his wonderful task of translating the Holy Scriptures into the Burmese language. He was also employed in forming a complete Burmese and English Dictionary, for the use of those who desired to learn the language, as well as for the natives. At length the health of his second wife failed; and, in 1845, Dr. Judson started with her to visit his native land, after an absence of two and thirty years. Bereavement smote him on the voyage. In the harbor of St. Helena, his excellent wife died, and the sorrowing husband left her body upon that lonely spot in the ocean. He reached Boston, with his children, in the Autumn of 1845, and was every where greeted with the most affectionate reverence by Christians of every name. He remained in America until July, the following year, when he departed for his chosen field of labor in Burmah, accompanied by a third wife,[2] whom he had married a few weeks previously. But the day of his pilgrimage was drawing to a close. The tooth of disease began its work in the Autumn of 1849, and in

---
1. See sketch of Mrs. Newell.
2. The accomplished Miss Emily Chubbuck, better known in the literary world as Fanny Forester. She and Dr. Judson accidentally met in Philadelphia, and were soon afterward married.

April following, he sailed for the isle of Bourbon, for the benefit of his health, leaving his wife and infants at Maulmain. They never met again on earth. Nine days after he left them, being the 12th of April, 1850, that eminent servant of the Most High expired on ship-board, and his grave was made in the depths of the Indian Seas. His widow returned to America, and died in the arms of her mother, at Hamilton, New York, on the 1st of June, 1854.

FELIX GRUNDY.

THE Great West, including the broad valleys between the Alleghany Mountains and the Mississippi River, has ever been remarkable, since its redemption from the wilderness state, for its redundancy of powerful men, physically and intellectually. The free air and the virgin soil; the simple aliment and daily dangers of that region, seemed congenial to the birth and growth of true men. Among these, Felix Grundy, a distinguished member of Congress, was long eminent. He was born in Virginia, but nurtured in the wilderness, at a time when, to use his own forcible expression, "death was in almost every bush, and when every thicket concealed an ambuscade." His nativity occurred in Berkeley county, Virginia, on the 11th of September, 1777. Three years later, his father went, with his family, to Kentucky, then "the dark and bloody ground." There the opportunities for education were small, but Felix was favored above the rest of his family, for, being the seventh son, he was destined, according to the superstitious notion of the times, to become a physician. His father died when he was a lad, and his mother, a believer in omens, had him educated for the purpose of preparing for the medical profession. He finished his studies under Dr. Priestly, at Bardstown, Kentucky, when, preferring law, he disregarded the oracles, and prepared himself for the legal profession, under the charge of Colonel George Nichols, then one of the ablest counsellors west of the mountains.

Grundy was admitted to practice, in 1798, soon rose to eminence, and, in 1799, was chosen a member of the committee called to revise the constitution of Kentucky. He was elected to a seat in the legislature, the same year, and served in that body with distinction until 1806, when he was appointed one of the judges of Supreme Court of Errors and Appeals. He was soon afterward appointed chief justice of Kentucky, on the resignation of Judge Todd. The salary was insufficient for the wants of a growing family, and he resigned the office, in 1808, and removed to Nashville, Tennessee, where he prosecuted his vocation with industry and great success. He ranked highest among the criminal lawyers of the West, and practiced in the courts of several of the States. His eloquence was pure and forcible; and he took the proud position, by general consent, as the head of the Tennessee bar.

Mr. Grundy was elected to a seat in the Federal Congress, in 1811. The tempest of war was then brooding in the horizon, and Mr. Grundy was placed upon the Committee of Foreign Relations—the most important section of the House, at that time. He remained in that body until 1814, and was always a hearty, consistent, and sincere supporter of the administration of President Madison. At the close of the contest he returned to Nashville, and resumed the practice of his profession, but was soon called to duty in the State legislature, where he served for six years. In 1829, he was elected a Federal Senator, and by reëlection he held a seat there during the whole eight years of Jackson's administration. From first to last, he was that chief magistrate's firm and cordial adherent and supporter. In 1839, he was called to the cabinet of Mr. Van Buren, as attorney-general of the United States; and, in 1840, he was again elected to a seat in the Federal Senate. He was not permitted to occupy that exalted position again, for, in December following, at about the time when he would have presented his credentials there, death removed him to another sphere. He was then a little more than sixty-three years of age.

RICHARD M. JOHNSON.

KENTUCKY is justly proud of her noble son, Richard M. Johnson; and throughout the Union his memory is cherished as one of the most enlightened, industrious, and honest of the servants of the Republic, whose zeal and valor have been tried in the legislative council and on the field of battle. That distinguished man was born at Bryant's station,[1] five miles north-east of Lexington, Kentucky, on the 17th of October, 1781. He received very little instruction from books during boyhood, but at the age of fifteen years he acquired the rudiments of the Latin language. He then entered Transylvania University, as a student, and on leaving that institution, he studied law under the directions of the eminent James Brown.[2] He possessed great mental and physical energy, and these, acting in concert with perseverance and industry, soon placed him high in his profession. Before he was twenty years of age the foundation of his future popularity and fame was laid, and his patriotism and military genius were developed by circumstances which seemed to menace the peace then existing between the United States and its Spanish neighbor in Louisiana. In violation of then existing treaties, the Spanish authorities closed the port of New Orleans against vessels of the United States, in 1802. The people of the Southwest were greatly excited, and nothing but a resort to arms seemed likely to be the result. Young Johnson took an active part in the public proceedings, in his section, and volunteered, with others, to make a descent upon New Orleans, in the event of a war. The difficulty was speedily settled by negotiations, the cloud passed by, and Johnson's military ardor was allowed to cool before other and more important events again awakened it.

Before he was twenty-two years of age, young Johnson was elected to a seat in the Kentucky legislature, where he served two years, to the great satisfaction of his constituents. In 1807, he was elected a representative in the Federal Congress, and took his seat there when he was just twenty-five years of age. There he took a prominent position at the beginning, and was continually re-elected during the whole of that momentous period of our history, from 1807 until 1819. In the meanwhile, he acquired that military distinction in the service of his country, for which he is better known to the people, than as a sound and judicious legislator. He was a firm supporter of President Madison's war measures; and when Congress adjourned, after the declaration of war against Great Britain, in 1812, he hastened home, raised a battalion of volunteers, and pushed forward toward the Canada frontier in the West, bearing the commission of colonel, given to him by Governor Shelby. At the close of Autumn, he laid aside his sword, took his seat in Congress, worked faithfully in the prosecution of measures for the public defence, and when the adjournment came, he went

---

1. That station was settled in 1779, by four brothers, named Bryant, one of whom married a sister of the renowned Daniel Boone. These stations were usually palisaded log-houses, arranged for protection against the Indians.
2. See sketch of James Brown.

home and called another regiment of volunteers to the field. Under the command of General Harrison, he was the chief actor in the sanguinary battle on the Thames, in Canada West, in October, 1813, when the Americans gained such a decisive victory over the combined forces of British regulars, under Proctor, and fifteen hundred Indians, under the renowned Tecumseh, that it ended the war in the West. Colonel Johnson led the division against the Indians, and he was in the thickest of the fight during the whole contest. Even when his bridle-arm was shattered, and his horse was reeling from the loss of blood, he fought on, encouraged his men, and put the Indians to flight. When he was borne from the field, there were twenty-five bullet-holes in his person, his clothing, and his horse. He was taken to Detroit, and from thence was borne home, in great pain. In February following, though not able to walk, he took his seat in Congress. He was every where greeted by the people with wildest enthusiasm as the Hero of the West.

Colonel Johnson retired from Congress, in 1819, and was immediately elected a member of his State legislature. He had just taken his seat in that body, when it chose him to represent Kentucky in the Federal Senate. He entered that assembly, as a member, in December, 1819, and served his constituents and the country faithfully until 1829, when he was again elected to a seat in the Lower House. There he remained until March, 1837, when he became president of the Senate, having been elected Vice-President of the United States in the preceding Autumn. After four years of dignified service in the Senate, he retired from public life, and passed the remainder of his days on his farm in Scott county, Kentucky, except a brief period of service in his State legislature.[1] He was engaged in that service, at Frankfort, when he was prostrated by paralysis, and expired on the 15th of November, 1850. His State has erected a beautiful marble monument to his memory, in the cemetery at Frankfort.

ANN HASSELTINE JUDSON.

WHEN we glance retrospectively over the field of modern missionary labor, we see no form more lovely in all that constitutes loveliness; no heart more heroic, and no hand more active in the service of the Great Master, than that of the first wife of Adoniram Judson, the eminent American missionary in Burmah. She appears upon the page of missionary history like an illuminated initial letter, for she was the pioneer in the service—the first American woman who volunteered to carry the Gospel to the pagans of the old world.

Ann Hasseltine was born in Bradford, Massachusetts, on the 22d of December, 1789. She was a gay and active girl, full of enterprise, eager in the pursuit of knowledge, extremely beautiful in person, and lovely in all her ways. She was educated at the Bradford Academy, where she always bore off the palm of superior scholarship. On the 5th of February, 1812, she was married to Adoniram Judson, who had been appointed one of the first American missionaries to India; and twelve days afterward she sailed, with Harriet Newell and others, for Calcutta. On the passage, she and her husband embraced the principles of the Baptists, and were baptized on their arrival at Calcutta, in September following. When, as has been observed in the sketch of Harriet Newell, the American

---

[1]. Colonel Johnson was the author of the laws which abolished imprisonment for debt, in Kentucky; and of the famous report in Congress, against the discontinuance of the mail on Sunday. He is greatly revered for his unwearied efforts in behalf of the soldiers of the Revolution, and of the war of 1812, who asked Congress for pensions or relief.

missionaries were ordered to quit India, Mr. and Mrs. Judson sailed to the Isle of France, and there they heard of the death of their beloved female friend. They remained there until the following July, when they went to Rangoon, in Burmah, and there began to cultivate the missionary field in earnest. Other missionaries joined them there, but death took them away, and in 1820 Mr. and Mrs. Judson alone remained in the vineyard. Disease, incident to the climate, now began to manifest its power upon Mrs. Judson, and at the close of the Summer of 1821, she went first to Calcutta, then to England, and finally returned to America in September, 1822. After remaining a few weeks with her friends at Bradford, she accepted an invitation to pass the Winter in Baltimore, in the family of her husband's brother. There she wrote an interesting *History of the Burman Mission*, in a series of letters to Mr. Butterworth, a member of Parliament, in whose family she had tarried while in England.

In June, 1823, Mrs. Judson again sailed for the field of missionary labor, with renewed bodily strength and increased earnestness of purpose, and joined her husband in December following. A few days afterward they started for Ava, the capital of Burmah, and had just completed their preparations for missionary effort there, when war between the Burmese and the British government of Bengal, broke out. Mr. Judson was seized, cruelly treated, and kept a prisoner by the Burman government for more than eighteen months, half of the time in triple fetters, and two months in five pair. The labors of Mrs. Judson, during that time, form one of the most wonderful chapters in the record of female heroism. Day after day she made intercessions before government officers for the liberation of her husband and other prisoners, but to no purpose; and every day she walked two miles to carry them food prepared with her own hands. Without her ministrations they must have perished. She had readily learned the language; and finally her appeals, written in elegant Burmese, were given to the Emperor, when no officer dared mention the subject to him. The sagacious monarch, trembling for the fate of his kingdom, (for a victorious English army was marching toward his capital,) saw safety in employing her, and he appointed her his embassadress to General Sir Archibald Campbell, the British leader, to prepare the way for a treaty. She was received by the British commander with all the ceremony of an envoy extraordinary. She managed the affairs of the Emperor with perfect fidelity, and a treaty was made through her influence, for which the proud monarch gave her great praise. She secured the release of her husband and his fellow-prisoners, and they all recommenced their missionary work.

When the intense excitement which she had so long experienced, was over, Mrs. Judson felt the reaction with terrible force. This, added to her great sufferings, prostrated her strength, and in the course of a few months, while Mr. Judson was absent at another post of duty, that noble disciple of Jesus fell asleep and entered upon her blessed rest. Her spirit departed on the 24th of October, 1826, when she was almost thirty-seven years of age. A few months afterward her only surviving child died. They both lie buried beneath a spreading *hope-tree*, near the banks of the Salween river. She is one of the most beloved in memory of the laborers during the earliest missionary seed time, and she will have her full reward of sheaves at the harvest.

JOSEPH HOPKINSON.

THE author of our spirited national song, *Hail Columbia*, was highly distinguished for other intellectual achievements. But that production was sufficient to confer upon him the crown of earthly immortality.[1] He was a son of Francis Hopkinson, one of the signers of the Declaration of Independence, and was born in Philadelphia, on the 12th of November, 1770. He was educated in the University of Pennsylvania, and then studied law, first with Judge Wilson, and afterward with William Rawle. He was admitted to the bar, at the close of 1791, and commenced its practice at Easton, on the Delaware. He was beginning to be quite successful there, when he returned to Philadelphia, and there took a high rank in his profession. He was the leading counsel of Dr. Rush in

---

1. That song was produced almost impromptu, for a special occasion. A young man named Fox, attached to the Philadelphia theatre, chiefly as a singer, was about to have a benefit. At that time [1798] there was a prospect of war between the United States and France, and Fox, anxious to produce some novelty for his benefit, conceived the idea of having an original song that should arouse the national spirit. The theatrical poets tried to produce one, but failed. The benefit was to take place on Monday, and on the previous Saturday afternoon, Fox called on Judge Hopkinson (who had known him from a school-boy), and asked him to write a song for him, adapted to the popular air of *The President's March*. Hopkinson consented, and with the object of awakening a truly *American spirit*, without offence to either of the violent political parties of the day, he wrote *Hail Columbia*. It was received by the audience at the theatre with the wildest applause, and was encored again and again. The words flashed all over the land, as soon as the press could conduct them, and were every where electrical in their effect. By common consent, *Hail Columbia* became, and remains, a national anthem. It is an interesting fact in this connection, that *The President's March* was composed, in 1789, by a German, named Feyles, leader of the orchestra of the old theatre in John Street, New York; and was first performed there on the occasion of President Washington's first visit at that play-house, by invitation of the managers. This fact was mentioned to the writer, by Mr. Custis, the adopted son of Washington, who was then a lad, and was present on the occasion.

his famous suit against William Cobbett, in 1799, and also in the insurgent trials before Judge Chase, in 1800. The legal knowledge, acute logic, and eloquent advocacy which he displayed on those occasions, caused Judge Chase to employ Mr. Hopkinson as his counsel, when, afterward, he was impeached before the Senate of the United States. His efforts in behalf of Judge Chase before that august tribunal, drew forth the warmest voluntary eulogiums from Aaron Burr, and other distinguished men.

In 1815, and again in 1817, Mr. Hopkinson was elected a representative of Philadelphia in the Federal Congress, and ranked among the first of the many sound statesmen who graced that body at that interesting period of our political history. His speeches against re-chartering the Bank of the United States, and on the Seminole war and other topics of interest, were regarded as exceedingly able. His constituents would gladly have reëlected him, in 1819, but he preferred the retirement of private life.

At the close of his second term in Congress, Mr. Hopkinson made his residence at Bordentown, in New Jersey, and was soon elected to a seat in the legislature of that State. After an absence of three years, he resumed the practice of his profession, in Philadelphia, in which he continued until 1828, when President Adams appointed him a judge of the United States Court, for the Eastern District of Pennsylvania. That office had been filled by his father and grandfather; and he performed its duties with dignity and marked ability, until his death. Judge Hopkinson was a member of the convention which met at Harrisburg, in May, 1837, to revise the constitution of Pennsylvania. He was chairman of the judiciary committee in that body, and eloquently sustained a report which he submitted, in a long and brilliant speech. Judge Hopkinson was very public-spirited, and took part in many movements intended for the moral and intellectual advancement of his fellow-citizens. At the time of his death he was one of the vice-presidents of the American Philosophical Society; a trustee of the University of Pennsylvania; and the president of the Pennsylvania Academy of Fine Arts, of which he was the chief founder. For more than twenty years he was the intimate and confidential friend of Joseph Bonaparte, who owned, and lived upon, a fine estate at Bordentown. During the ex-king's absence, Judge Hopkinson always managed his affairs; and he was one of the two executors of his will. Judge Hopkinson died at Philadelphia, on the 15th of January, 1842, at the age of a little more than seventy-one years.

MOSES BROWN.

AN eminently good man was lost to earth when the spirit of Moses Brown, one of the founders of the Rhode Island College (afterward called Brown University), departed for its home. He was the youngest of four brothers, who were all remarkable for public spirit, generous enterprise, and practical benevolence. He was born at Providence, Rhode Island, in 1738. Having lost his father while he was yet a small boy, he left school at the age of thirteen years, and made his residence with a paternal uncle, an eminent and wealthy merchant of Providence. There he was trained to useful habits and a mercantile profession; and in the bosom of that excellent home he found a treasure in a pretty cousin, the daughter of his patron, whom he married, in 1764. Young Brown had commenced mercantile business on his own account the previous year, in connection with his three brothers. After ten years' close application, he retired from business, chiefly on account of feeble health, and passed much of his time in those intellectual pursuits to which his taste led him.

Mr. Brown was a Baptist until 1773 (about the time when he left business), when he became a member of the Society of Friends. and remained a shining light in that connection until his death. He had accumulated wealth by his business, and inherited a large property through his wife. These possessions he used as means for carrying on an active and practical philanthropy during a long life. He manumitted all his slaves, in 1773, and was ever a consistent and zealous opponent of all systems of human servitude. He was a munificent patron of a Friends' Boarding-school at Providence; founded the Rhode Island Abolition Society, and was an active member and supporter of the Rhode Island Peace Society. When Slater, the father of the cotton manufactures in this country, went to Providence, Moses Brown was the first to give him encouragement and substantial friendship; and it was in his carriage that the enterprising Englishman was conveyed to Pawtucket, to commence the preparation of a cotton-mill.[1] Though always in feeble health, Mr. Brown never suffered severe illness. His correspondence was very extensive, yet he seldom employed any one to write for him. Even his Will, prepared when he was ninety-six years of age, was drawn by his own hand. That eminent servant of goodness died at Providence, on the 6th of September, 1836, in the ninety-eighth year of his age.

JOHN RODGERS.

MORE than a year before the American Congress declared war against Great Britain, a naval engagement took place near our coast between vessels of the two nations, being partly, it was alleged, the result of accident. The issue of the engagement was a foreshadow of what occurred during the succeeding few years. The American vessel alluded to was in command of Captain John Rodgers, a gallant American officer, who was born in the present Harford County, Maryland, on the 11th of July, 1771. His passion for the sea was very early manifested, and at the age of thirteen years it was gratified by a voyage. He loved the occupation, prepared himself for it as a profession, and at the age of nineteen years he was intrusted with the command of a ship, which made trading voyages between Baltimore and the north of Europe. Captain Rodgers continued in the merchant service until the organization of the American navy, in 1797, when he entered it as a first lieutenant on board the frigate *Constellation*, under Commodore Truxton. He commanded the prize crew that took charge of the captured French ship, *L'Insurgente*, in February, 1798, and in that capacity he behaved with great coolness and ability in times of imminent danger. On his return home, during the terrible massacre of the white people there, in 1804, was instrumental in saving many lives.

In the Spring of 1799, Lieutenant Rodgers was promoted to Post-Captain in the navy, and ordered to the command of the Sloop-of-War *Maryland*. He cruised on the "Surinam Station" until the Autumn of 1800, when he returned home, and the following Spring was sent with dispatches to France. He served gallantly in the war with the Barbary Powers; and in conjunction with Colonel Lear, the American consul-general, he signed a treaty with the Bey of Tripoli, in June, 1805, which put an end to the contest with that State. Captain Rodgers

---

1. See sketch of Slater.

had command of the flotilla of gun-boats, in the harbor of New York, in 1807, where he remained until 1809, when he put to sea in the frigate *Constitution*. In 1811 he was in command of the *President*, cruising off the coasts of Maryland and Virginia. English ships of war were then hovering upon our shores, engaged in the nefarious business of kidnapping seamen from American vessels. With that vessel he compelled the commander of the British Sloop, *Little Belt*, to be frank and courteous, when he had met her under suspicious circumstances in the waters of Chesapeake Bay. These were the vessels alluded to at the commencement of this memoir. The event created a great sensation, and the two governments fully sustained the conduct of their respective commanders. War was finally declared, and within an hour after receiving his orders from the Secretary of the Navy, Commodore Rodgers sailed from the port of New York, with a small squadron, to cruise on the broad Atlantic. He made successful cruises in the *President* until 1814, when he was engaged on the Potomac in operations against the British, who burned Washington City in August of that year. He soon afterward participated with gallantry in the defence of Baltimore.

Commodore Rodgers twice refused the proffered office of the Secretaryship of the Navy, first by President Madison, and then by President Monroe. During almost twenty-one years he was President of the Board of Naval Commissioners, except for about two years, from 1825 to 1827, when he commanded the American squadron in the Mediterranean, having the *North Carolina* for his flag-ship. There he won the highest respect from the naval officers of all nations, whom he met. In the Summer of 1832 he was prostrated by cholera, but recovered. His constitution, however, was permanently shattered. A voyage to England for the improvement of his health, was of no avail, and he lingered until 1838, when, on the first day of August, he expired at Philadelphia, in the sixty-seventh year of his age.

WILLIAM ELLERY CHANNING.

RHODE ISLAND has produced some of the noblest specimens of the true American, in almost every department of life. Of these, there was never a mind and heart more truly noble in emotion and expression, than that of William Ellery Channing. He was born at Newport, Rhode Island, on the 7th of April, 1780. He was a lovely child in person and disposition—"an open, brave, and generous boy." William Ellery, one of the signers of the Declaration of Independence, was his maternal grandfather, and he inherited that statesman's strength of character and honest patriotism. At twelve years of age he was placed in the family of an uncle, at New London, where he prepared for college, and entered Harvard, as a student, in 1794. He bore the highest honors of the institution at his graduation, in 1798, and then went to Virginia, as tutor in the family of David M. Randolph, Esq., of Richmond. Ill health compelled him to return home, and be prepared for the gospel ministry. He was made regent in Harvard University, in 1801, was licensed to preach, in 1802, and was ordained pastor of the Federal Street Unitarian Society, in Boston, in 1803. Then commenced his noble labors in the cause of Christianity, whose doctrines he so eloquently enforced by precept and example. He continued to discharge the duties of pastor, without aid, until 1824, when the great increase of his congregation, and the multiplication of his labors, caused his people, who loved him as a father, to employ a colleague for him. He visited Europe, held communion with some

of the best minds there, and he returned home with larger views, and more ennobling thoughts and purposes. For almost forty years, Dr. Channing (the title of D.D. was conferred by the Faculty of Harvard University) was connected with the same society; and during all that time he was afflicted with ill health, sometimes in only a slight degree. His fervid eloquence made his permanent congregation a large one, and crowds of strangers attended his ministrations. He wrote much and nobly, for the honor of God and the good of humanity. He was an uncompromising advocate for freedom in all its relations and conditions, and yet he urged his plea for humanity with so much gentleness and affectionate persuasion, that no one could be offended, however unpalatable his truths or his doctrines might be. In the Christian world he moved as a peace-maker, laboring incessantly to break down the hedges of creeds, and to unite all who loved righteousness, under the broad and beautiful banner of a pure practical CHRISTIANITY. He was a man of the purest nature and most guileless life; and he moved like the gentle spirit of love among his fellow-men, scattering roses and sunshine upon every lonely pathway of life's weary pilgrims, and always telling the care-worn and afflicted travellers of the sweet resting-places by the side of the still waters of a better sphere. His spirit yet breathes out his noble humanities in his writings; and he is to-day a powerful preacher of love and justice, though his voice was hushed into eternal silence, long years ago. His spirit was called home on the 2d of October, 1842, when he was tarrying at Bennington, in Vermont, while on a journey for the benefit of his health.

ANDREW JACKSON DOWNING.

NO American ever contributed so much toward the creation and cultivation of a taste for beautiful rural architecture, landscape gardening, and the arrangement of fruit and ornamental trees, as A. J. Downing, who was drowned on the occasion of the destruction of the steamer *Henry Clay*, near Yonkers, in July, 1852. An extensive traveller in the Atlantic States said, soon after the sad event, "Much of the improvement that has taken place in this country during the last twelve years, in Rural Architecture, and in Ornamental Gardening and Planting, may be ascribed to him;" and another, speaking of suburban cottages in the West, said, "I asked the origin of so much taste, and was told it might principally be traced to Downing's *Cottage Residences*, and his *Horticulturist*."

Mr. Downing was born in Newburgh, Orange County, New York, in 1815. From early boyhood he delighted to commune with nature, and loved flowers with a passionate delight. The beautiful was worshipped by him long before his acute logical and analytical mind could give a reason for his devotion; and his dislike of everything that wanted symmetry and fitness, was an early manifestation of his pure taste. When he grew to manhood, those tastes and faculties were nobly developed and actively employed; and at the age of twenty-six years he published the results of his practice, observations and reflections, in a valuable book on *Landscape Gardening*. It was a work eminently original, for he had few precedents, either in personal example or in books, as guides in his peculiar method of treating the subject. He seized upon the great principles of the science as developed in the works of Repton, Loudon, and others; and then, bringing the great powers of his mind to bear upon the topic, produced a book which caused an eminent British writer on the subject to say of him, "no English landscape gardener has written so clearly, or with so much real intensity."

Mr. Downing next turned his attention to the kindred art of Architecture, and soon produced a volume on *Cottage Residences*. Then appeared his *Architecture of Country Houses*, in which he gave designs for Cottages, Farm Houses and Villas, exterior and interior, with valuable suggestions respecting furniture, ventilation, &c. In 1845 his large work on *Fruit and Fruit Trees of America*, was published in New York and London, which has passed through many editions. His mind and hands were ever actively employed in his favorite pursuit; and through the *Horticulturist*, a monthly repository of practical knowledge on the subject of cultivation of every kind, which he edited, Mr. Downing communicated the results of his observations and personal experiences. Every movement having for its object the promotion of the science of cultivation, received his ardent support, and by lectures, essays, reports of societies and other vehicles of information, he was continually pouring a flood of influence that is seen and felt on every side. In addition to his large works, he had published *Rules of American Pomonology*, and edited the productions of others.

Mr. Downing was eminently practical in all his efforts. His beautiful residence and grounds around it, at Newburgh, formed the central point of his labors. He was continually called upon for plans for buildings, and pleasure grounds, public and private; and at the time of his death he was on his way to Washington City, in the prosecution of his professional engagements there, in laying out and adorning the public grounds around the Smithsonian Institute. A part of his plan for beautifying that public square was to make a great central avenue, and to border it with trees and shrubs which should exhibit every variety produced in America, that would flourish in the climate of Washington city. But, alas! this labor, as well as all of his other numerous professional engagements, was suddenly arrested by a fearful calamity in which he was involved. On a beautiful afternoon, the 31st of July, 1852, he was a passenger, for New York, in the steamer *Henry Clay*. When opposite Forrest Point, a little below Yonkers, it was discovered that the vessel was on fire. Her bow was turned toward the shore, when the smoke and flames rushed over that part of the boat where most of the passengers were collected. Just as she struck the beach these were compelled by the heat to leap into the water, and fifty-six persons perished by being either drowned or burned. In attempting to save the life of his mother-in-law, Mr. Downing lost his own, although he was an expert swimmer. That last act of his life reflected a prominent trait in his daily intercourse with society—*unselfish goodness*. He was not yet thirty-eight years of age, when he was stopped in the midst of a useful career.

JONATHAN HARRINGTON.

ON a lovely afternoon in the Autumn of 1848, the writer reined up his horse at a little picket-gate in front of a neat residence in East Lexington, Massachusetts. A slender old man, apparently not more than seventy years of age, was splitting fire-wood in the yard near by, and plied the axe with a vigorous hand. The residence belonged to Jonathan Harrington, who, when a lad not eighteen years of age, played the fife for the minute-men upon the green at Lexington, on the morning of the memorable 19th of April, 1775. The vigorous axe-man in the yard was the patriot himself. I had journeyed from Boston, a dozen miles or more, to visit him; and when he sat down in his rocking-chair, and related the events of that historic morning, the very spirit of Liberty seemed to burn in every word from those lips that touched that little instrument of music at the gray dawn. He kindly allowed me to sketch his features for my portfolio; and then, writing his name beneath the picture—"Jonathan Harrington, aged 90, the 8th of July, 1848 "—he apologized for the rough appearance of his signature, and charged the unsteadiness of his hand to his labor with the axe. His younger brother, who sat near him, appeared more feeble than he.

Mr. Harrington was born on the 8th of July, 1757, in the town of Lexington; and though a mere youth when the train-bands were formed, in 1774, he enrolled himself as one of the militia of his district, who, because they were bound to appear in arms at a moment's warning, were called *minute-men*. When the few patriots gathered upon the green at Lexington to oppose the invading march of British troops from Boston, young Harrington was there with his fife, and with its martial music he opened the ball of the Revolution, where

> "—— Yankees skilled in martial rule,
> First put the British troops to school;
> Instructed them in warlike trade,
> And new manœuvres of parade;
> The true war-dance of Yankee reels,
> And *manual exercise* of heels;
> Made them give up, like saints complete,
> The *arm* of flesh and trust the *feet*,
> And work, like Christians undissembling,
> Salvation out with fear and trembling."—TRUMBULL.

After performing that prelude, he retired. He was not a soldier during the war; nor was his life afterward remarkable for any thing except as the career of a good citizen. He lived on in the quiet enjoyment of rural pursuits, not specially noticed by his fellow-men, until the survivors of the Revolution began to be few and cherished. Then the hearts of the generation around him began to be moved with reverence for him. On the seventy-fifth anniversary of the skirmishes at Lexington and Concord, the event was celebrated at the latter place. In the procession was a carriage, bearing the venerable Harrington and his brother; Amos Baker, of Lincoln; Thomas Hill, of Danvers; and Dr. Preston, of Billerica—the assembled survivors of those first bloody struggles for American Independence. Edward Everett made an eloquent speech on the occasion; and, when alluding to the venerated fifer, he repeated the words of David to the good son of Saul, "Very pleasant art thou to me, my brother Jonathan." Mr. Harrington lived almost four years longer, and by the death of his compatriots just mentioned, he became the last survivor of the *minute-men* of Lexington.[1] He died on the 28th of March, 1854, in the ninety-sixth year of his age. His funeral was attended by the governor and legislature of Massachusetts, and at least six thousand other citizens.

HARMAN BLENNERHASSETT.

IN the bosom of the Ohio river, about fourteen miles below the mouth of the Muskingum, is a beautiful island, around which cluster memories and associations, and the elements of many legends; and these increase in interest with the flight of years. Those memories, and associations, and legends, are connected with the name and destiny of a family whose history illustrates the wonderful vicissitudes of human life, and the uncertainty of earthly possessions. It was that of Blennerhassett, whose name, radiant with light, will ever be associated with that of Aaron Burr, clouded in darkness.

Harman Blennerhassett was descended from an ancient Irish family of the county of Kerry, whose residence was Castle Conway. While his mother was visiting in Hampshire, England, 1767, he was born. His father, belonging to one of the oldest aristocratic families of Ireland, gave his son every educational advantage that wealth could afford, first at Westminster School, and then in Trinity College, Dublin. He and his friend and relation, the late Thomas Addis Emmett, of New York, were graduated at the same time; and after young Blennerhassett had made a tour of the Continent, he and Emmett were admitted to the practice of the law, on the same day. Mr. Blennerhassett had a great fondness for science and literature, and being an expectant of a large fortune, he paid more attention to those attractive pursuits than to business in his profession. That fortune was possessed by him, on the death of his father, in 1796. At that time he had become a popular politician, of the liberal stamp, and having involved himself in some difficulties, he sold his estate, went to England, and there married Miss Agnew, a young lady possessed of great beauty and varied accomplishments.[2] Each appeared worthy of the other, and the at-

---

1. Early in 1856, one of the British soldiers who followed Pitcairn to Lexington, eighty years before, died in England, at the age of 107 years. He was a Wesleyan minister, named George Fletcher. For eighty-three years he was in active life; twenty-six of which he was a soldier in the royal army. He is supposed to have been the last survivor of that detachment sent out by General Gage, on the night of the 18th of April, 1775, to capture or destroy the American stores at Concord.
2. She was a granddaughter of Brigadier-General James Agnew, of the British army, who was killed in the battle at Germantown, in the Autumn of 1777.

mosphere of their future was all rose-tinted. Charmed by the free institutions of the United States, Mr. Blennerhassett resolved to make his home in the bosom of the Republic of the West. With a fine library and philosophical apparatus, and a competent fortune, he came hither toward the close of the Summer of 1797. After spending a few weeks in New York, the reports of the beauty, fertility, and salubrious climate of the Ohio country beckoned him thither, and early in Autumn he reached Marietta. In March, following, he purchased a fine plantation upon an island in the Ohio (above alluded to), and at once commenced transforming that luxuriant wilderness into a paradise for himself and family. A spacious and elegant mansion was erected; the grounds were tastefully laid out and planted, and that island soon became the resort of some of the best minds west of the mountains. Science, music, painting, farm culture and social pleasures, made up a great portion of the sum of daily life in that elegant retreat. For almost five years that gifted family enjoyed unalloyed happiness, and they regarded their dwelling as their home for life. One day in the Spring of 1805, a small man, about fifty years of age, elegantly attired, landed from a boat and sauntered about the grounds. With his usual frankness, Mr. Blennerhassett invited him to partake of his hospitality, though a stranger to him in name and person. It was Aaron Burr, the wily serpent, that beguiled the unsuspecting Blennerhassett from his books, his family and home, to feed on the dangerous fruit of political ambition and avaricious desires. Burr was then weaving his scheme of conquest in the far south-west, and fired the imagination of Blennerhassett with dreams of wealth and power. When he had departed, Blennerhassett was a changed man, and clouds began to gather around the bright star of his destiny. He placed his wealth and reputation in the keeping of an unprincipled demagogue, and lost both. For a year and a half the scheme was ripening, when the Federal government, suspecting Burr of treason, put forth its arm and crushed the viper in the egg.[1] Burr and Blennerhassett were arrested on a charge of treason. The former was tried and acquitted, when proceedings against the latter were suspended. From that time poor Blennerhassett was a doomed man. His paradise was laid waste, and with a sad heart he went to Mississippi and became a cotton planter. There he struggled against losses, which were more depressing because, from time to time, he was called upon with Burr's notes endorsed by himself, and was compelled to pay them. At the end of ten years his fortune was almost exhausted, and with the promise of a judgeship in Lower Canada, he went to Montreal in 1819. Disappointment awaited him, and he returned to England in expectation of public employment there. That hope, too, was blighted; and after residing awhile at Bath with a maiden sister, he went, with his family, to the island of Guernsey. There that highly-gifted and unfortunate man died in 1831, at the age of sixty-three years. In 1842 his widow came to America, with her two invalid sons, for the purpose of seeking remuneration from Congress for losses of property sustained at the time of her husband's arrest. She petitioned Congress, and her suit was eloquently sustained by Henry Clay and others. While the matter was pending, Mrs. Blennerhassett sickened. She was in absolute want, and her necessities were relieved by some benevolent Irish females of New York, where she resided. Death soon removed her, and that beautiful and accomplished woman, the child of social honor and of opulence, was buried by the kind hands of the Sisters of Charity, in August, 1842.

---

1 See sketch of Aaron Burr.

JOHN JACOB ASTOR.

NOT far from lovely Heidelberg, on the Rhine, in the grand-duchy of Baden, is the picturesque little village of Walldorf, nestled among quiet hills, away from the din of commerce and the vexations of promiscuous intercourse with the great world of business and politics. Near that little village, in the mid-summer of 1763, an infant was born of humble parents, who, in after years, became a "merchant prince," and died a Crœsus among an opulent people. His name was John Jacob Astor. He was nurtured in the simplicity of rural life, yet he manifested ambition for travel and traffic, at an early age. While a mere stripling, he left home for London. He started for a sea-port, on foot, with all his worldly wealth in a bundle hanging over his shoulder; and beneath a linden tree, in whose shadow he sought repose, he resolved *to be honest, to be industrious, and to avoid gambling.* Upon this solid moral basis he built the superstructure of his fame, and secured his great wealth.

Mr. Astor left London for America, in the same month when the British troops left New York, at the close of the War for Independence, bringing with him some merchandize for traffic. His elder brother had been in this country several years, and had often written to him concerning its advantages for a young man of enterprise. Mr. Astor soon became acquainted with a furrier (one of his countrymen), and, having obtained from him all necessary information concerning the business, he resolved to employ the proceeds of his merchandize in the fur traffic. He commenced the business in New York, and was successful from the beginning. His enterprise, guided by great sagacity, always kept in advance of his capital; and year after year his business limits expanded. He made regular visits to Montreal, where he purchased furs of the Hudson's Bay Company, and shipped them for London. When commercial treaties permitted, after 1794, he sent his furs to all parts of the United States, and for many years carried on a very lucrative trade with Canton, in China. Success was always at his right hand. After spending many years as a second-hand operator in furs, and having accumulated a large fortune, he resolved to do business on his own account entirely, by trading with the Indians directly, who were supplying a new corporation, known as the North-western Company, with the choicest furs, from the Mississippi and its tributaries. The general government approved of his plan for securing that vast trade of the interior; and, in 1809, the State of New York incorporated The American Fur Company, with a capital of one million of dollars and the privilege of extending it to two millions. The president and directors were merely nominal officers, for the capital, management, and profits, all belonged to Mr. Astor.

In 1811, Mr. Astor bought out the North-western Company, and, with some associates, formed a system of operations by which the immense trade in furs of the middle regions of North America might be controlled by him. Under the name of the South-western Fur Company, their operations were commenced, but the war between the United States and England, kindled in 1812, suspended their movements, for a while. In the meanwhile, the mind of Mr. Astor had grasped a more extensive enterprise. The Pacific coast was a rich field for carrying on the fur trade with China. Already the country of the Columbia river had been made known by the visits of Boston merchant-ships, and the expedition of Lewis and Clarke, across the Continent, in 1804. Mr. Astor conceived the idea of making himself "sole master" of that immense trade. In 1810, the Pacific Fur Company was chartered, with Mr. Astor at its head. His plan was to have a line of trading posts across the Continent to the mouth of the Columbia river, and a fortified post there to be supplied with necessaries by a ship passing around Cape Horn once a year. The post at the mouth of the Columbia was established, and named Astoria. It was the germ of the budding State of Oregon. Then commenced a series of operations on a scale altogether beyond any thing hitherto attempted by individual enterprise. The history is full of wildest romance; and the chaste pen of Irving has woven the wonderful incidents into a charming narrative that fills two volumes. We cannot even glance at it, in this brief memoir. The whole scheme was the offspring of a capacious mind; and had the plans of Mr. Astor been faithfully carried out by his associates, it would, no doubt, have been eminently successful. But the enterprise soon failed. During the war, a British armed sloop captured Astoria, and the British fur traders entered upon the rich field which Mr. Astor had planted, and reaped the golden harvest. When the war had ended, and Astoria was left within the domain of the United States, by treaty, Mr. Astor solicited the government to aid him in recovering his lost possessions. Aid was withheld, and the grand scheme of opening a high-way across the continent, with a continuous chain of military and trading posts, which Mr. Astor had laid before President Jefferson, became a mere figment of history, over which sound statesmen soon lamented. His dream of an empire beyond the mountains, "peopled by free and independent Americans, and linked to us by ties of blood and interest," vanished like the morning dew! It has since become a reality.

After the failure of this great enterprise, Mr. Astor gradually withdrew from commercial life. He was the owner of much real estate, especially in the city of New York and vicinity, and held a large amount of public stocks. The remainder of his days was chiefly spent in the management of his accumulated and rapidly-appreciating property. He died in the city of New York, in the month of March, 1848, at the age of almost eighty-five years. The great bulk of his immense property, amounting to several millions of dollars, was left to his family. Before his death, he provided ample funds for the establishment and support of a splendid public library in the city of New York; and he also gave a large sum of money to his native town, for the purpose of founding an institution for the education of the young, and as a retreat for indigent aged persons. The *Astor Library* in New York, and the *Astor House* in Walldorf, were both opened in 1854. They are noble monuments to the memory of the "merchant prince."

THOMAS H. GALLAUDET.

"THE cause of humanity is primarily indebted to him for the introduction of deaf mute instruction into the United States, and for the spread of the information necessary for prosecuting it successfully in public institutions, of which all in the country are experiencing the benefits." What greater eulogium need any man covet than this expression of the Board of Directors of the American Asylum for the Deaf and Dumb, at Hartford, when they accepted the resignation of the Rev. Thomas H. Gallaudet, as president of that institution? The winning of such laurels in the field of active philanthropy, is a result more noble than any achieved upon Marathon or Waterloo.

Thomas H. Gallaudet was a native of Philadelphia, where he was born on the 10th of December, 1787. He acquired a good Academic education in his native city, and soon after his parents removed to Hartford, in Connecticut, in 1800, he entered Yale College. There he was graduated in 1805, and commenced the study of law. The profession had but few charms for him, and on being chosen a tutor in Yale College, in 1808, he abandoned it. He continued his connection with Yale until 1810, and then engaged in commercial business. That employment was also uncongenial to his taste, and he abandoned it after a trial of a few months. In the meanwhile his mind had received deep religious convictions, and he felt called to the Gospel ministry. He entered the Andover Theological Seminary in 1811, completed his studies there in 1814, and was then licensed to preach. Again he was diverted from a chosen pursuit, and he was led by Providence into a field for useful labor, far above what he had aspired to. His attention had been drawn to the instruction of the Deaf and Dumb, while at Andover, and when he left that institution Dr. Mason Coggswell, of Hartford, invited him to instruct his little daughter, who was a deaf mute. Mr. Gallaudet's experiments were eminently successful, and Dr. Coggswell felt an irrepressible desire to extend the blessings of his instruction to others similarly afflicted. An association of gentlemen was formed for the purpose; and in the Spring of 1815, they sent Mr. Gallaudet to Europe to visit institutions for the Deaf and Dumb, already established there. The selfishness and jealousy of the managers of those in England prevented his learning much that was new or useful there; but at the Royal Institution in Paris, under the care of the Abbé Sicard, every facility was given to him. He returned in 1816, accompanied by Lawrence Le Clerc to be his assistant. Measures had been taken, in the meanwhile, to found a public institution; and on the 15th of April, 1817, the first Asylum for the Deaf and Dumb, established in America, was opened at Hartford, under the charge of Mr. Gallaudet.[1] It prospered greatly, and became the centre of abundant blessings. There he labored with intense and increasing zeal until 1830, when impaired health compelled him to resign his charge as principal, though he remained a director, and always felt a lively interest in its welfare. After a brief cessation from labor, he commenced the preparation of several works designed for educational purposes; and wherever a field of Christian philanthropy called for a laborer, there he was found, a willing worker.

In the Summer of 1838, Mr. Gallaudet became chaplain of the Connecticut Retreat for the Insane, at Hartford, and in that important duty he labored with abundant useful results, until the last. He died at Hartford on the 9th of September, 1851, at the age of about sixty-four years. His name is a synonym of goodness and benevolence. A handsome monument to his memory was erected near the Asylum building, at Hartford, in 1854, wholly by contributions of deaf mutes in the United States. The designer and architect were both deaf mutes.

ELIJAH HEDDING.

ONE of the most useful and beloved of the ministers of the Methodist Episcopal Church, in America, was Elijah Hedding, D.D., who, for almost thirty years, was one of its chief pastors, and at the time of his death the senior bishop of that church. He was born in the town of Pine Plains, Dutchess county, New York, on the 7th of June, 1780. His good mother taught him to know and love God, and at the age of four years he could pray understandingly. During his boyhood, the celebrated Benjamin Abbott was on the Dutchess Circuit, and under his powerful preaching the zeal of Elijah's mother was fired, and she became an earnest Methodist.[2] She loved the communion of that people, and her heart was greatly rejoiced when her son took delight in her Christian way of life.

In 1791, the family removed to Vermont, and at the age of eighteen years, young Hedding made an open profession of Christianity, and joined the Methodist

---

1. It soon became the asylum for all New England; and the several legislatures, except that of Rhode Island, made appropriations for its support. The second institution of the kind was established in the city of New York, in 1818. The American system, as that of Mr. Gallaudet (an improvement on the French) was called, was not adopted there until Dr. Harvey P. Peet, a teacher at Hartford, became a tutor in that institution. Dr. Peet has been at the head of the New York Asylum many years, and has managed its affairs with eminent success. There are now about a dozen institutions for the Instruction of the Deaf and Dumb, in the United States, and all employ the system introduced by Mr. Gallaudet. There are now [1855] full ten thousand Deaf and Dumb persons in the United States. There is one in the Asylum at Hartford (Julia Brace) who is also *blind*. She lost these several senses by sickness, when she was four years of age. She continued to talk some for about a year, and the word she was longest permitted to speak, was the tender one of *mother*. In the Blind and Deaf Asylum in Boston, is now a woman (Laura Bridgman) whose history possesses the most thrilling interest. She was born puny and sickly, in Hanover, New Hampshire, in 1829, and by severe disease she lost both *sight* and *hearing* before she was two years of age. When her health was restored, she had almost entirely lost the senses of *taste* and *smell!* As she grew to girlhood she evinced a strong mind, but oh! in what silence and darkness was she enveloped! In 1837, Dr. Howe took her to his Asylum in Boston, and successfully attempted the developement of her intellect, at the age of eight years. We have not space to speak of her acquirements. They are wonderful indeed; and she seems to live in an atmosphere of exquisite enjoyment. Her moral faculties have full play, and she is a loving and lovely creature at 52 years of age.

2. The mother of the writer once mentioned a circumstance that occurred in the ministry of Mr. Abbott, which was witnessed by herself. On a sultry afternoon, a heavy thunder-shower occurred while Mr. Abbott was preaching at the little hamlet of Beekmanville. When his discourse was about half finished, lightning struck the building with a terrible crash. The preacher stopped, and, with a calm voice, said, "When God speaks, let man hold his peace," and then sat down.

Church. In the Summer of 1799, he became a local preacher, as those who are licensed to exhort are called, and labored partly in Vermont and partly in Canada, on a circuit just vacated by the eccentric Lorenzo Dow. In the Spring of 1800, he was licensed to preach; and in June, the following year, he was admitted to the New York annual conference as a travelling preacher, on probation. His itinerant labors were very great. The circuits often embraced almost a wilderness, requiring journeys from two hundred to five hundred miles, to be made in the space of from two to six weeks, while every day a sermon was to be preached and a class met. Mountains were climbed; swamps and rivers were forded; tangled forests were thridded; and in sunshine or in storm, the travelling preacher went on in his round of duty. Privations were cheerfully suffered; and as those messengers of glad tidings went on their way, the forests were made vocal with their hymns. In severe and earnest labors for the real good of souls, the Methodist Church is preëminent.

For a time Mr. Hedding was stationed on the Plattsburg circuit, which extended along the western shore of Lake Champlain, far into Canada. Then he took a circuit on the east side of the lake, extending back to the Green Mountains. After two years of hard service, in this way, he was ordained a Deacon, in 1803, and was sent to a circuit in New Hampshire. There he labored intensely until his health gave way. He arose from the borders of the grave, after being ill eight months, with a constitution much shattered, but a soul burning with more intense zeal for the Gospel, than before. His labors were highly esteemed; and, in 1805, he was ordained an Elder, by Bishop Asbury. Two years afterward he became a presiding elder; and he performed the duties of that office with great ability and dignity. Plain in speech and earnest in manner, his preaching always seemed accompanied with the demonstrations of the spirit, and revivals every where attended his ministrations. Yet in all his labors he won no earthly gain. During ten years, his average cash receipts were only *forty-five dollars a year!* Yet he says the sisters were kind to him, for they put patches upon the knees of his pantaloons, and often turned an old coat for him.

From 1810 until 1824, Mr. Hedding's field of ministerial labor was in New England. At the general conference, in 1824, he was elevated to the office of Bishop of the Methodist Episcopal Church, and was ordained, by the imposition of hands, on the 28th of May, of that year. With great humility, but with unwavering faith in the sustaining grace of God, he entered with zeal upon the responsible duties of the prelacy; and during the first eight years of his episcopal life, he presided over fifty-two conferences, extending over the whole Union. That was a most interesting period in the history of Methodism in America, and no man contributed more to its growth and respectability, than Bishop Hedding. When he commenced his ministerial labors, in the year 1800, the Methodist Church in the United States and Canada numbered less than seventy-three thousand members; when he left the field, in 1852, that membership had swollen to over a million and a quarter.

In 1832, Bishop Hedding was at the door of death; but he was spared to the church twenty years longer. After 1844, his bodily infirmities abridged his sphere of active labor, yet he continued to be the oracle of wisdom when advice was needed. His last episcopal services were performed in 1850. Then he sat down in his pleasant residence at Poughkeepsie, and in the midst of much bodily suffering, he waited to be called home. The message came on the 9th of April, 1852, and his spirit went joyfully to the presence of the great Head of the Church in earth and heaven.

STEPHEN OLIN.

WE have few records in human history more touching and instructive than that of the ministerial labors of the Rev. Dr. Olin, one of the brightest luminaries of the Methodist Episcopal Church, who was continually struggling with great bodily infirmity while engaged in arduous toils. The possessor of a huge frame more than six feet in height, he had all the appearance of an iron man, outwardly, but from earliest years that frame was weak and deceptive.

Stephen Olin was born in Leicester, Vermont, on the 2d of March, 1797. His father, a descendant of one of the earlier settlers of Rhode Island, was successively a State legislator, Judge of the Supreme Court of Vermont, Member of Congress and Lieutenant Governor. Stephen was carefully educated, chiefly at home under the direction of his father, and at the age of fifteen years he commenced teaching a village school. His father designed him for the profession of the law, and he was placed under legal instruction in Middlebury, Vermont. He yearned to enter the College there, for he soon perceived that his education was not sufficient for success in professional life. He finally told his father that he was willing to return to labor on the farm, but he was unwilling to be "half a lawyer." The hint was sufficient, and Judge Olin placed his son in Middlebury College, at the age of nineteen years. He was an apt scholar, and was graduated with highest honors.

Although he was of large frame, he felt much physical weakness on leaving College. The South presenting a field for its recovery, he went thither in 1820, and became a teacher in a Seminary in Abbeville District, South Carolina, which was located in a rude log-cabin. He boarded in the family of an exemplary "local" Methodist preacher, and became a converted man. With the joy of religious impressions came a desire to spread the glad tidings of Christianity, and abandoning all idea of becoming a lawyer, he assumed the duties and privations of a Methodist preacher, in 1822. He was soon afterward invited to a professorship in the college at Middlebury, but declined it, because, notwithstanding his feeble health would not allow him to enter upon the itinerancy, he could not give up his devotion to Methodism and its ministry. In 1824, he was stationed in Charleston, in the travelling connection, where he labored zealously. Ill health demanded relaxation, and he visited his friends in Vermont, after an absence of four years. In the Autumn of 1824, he travelled back to Charleston on horseback.

In 1825, Mr. Olin became editor of the *Wesleyan Journal*, assisted by the late Bishop Capers, but his health would not allow him to conduct it as he desired, and he became only an occasional contributor. In 1826, he was chosen Professor of belles-lettres in Franklin College, at Athens, Georgia, and soon after entering upon his duties there he was married to a beautiful and exemplary young lady. At about the same time, he was ordained an elder in the Methodist Episcopal Church. He soon afterward made another visit to his native State, and then resided in Virginia for some time, all the while suffering from disease. In 1834, he attended the conference at Charleston, where he was greeted with much love; and the same year three Colleges conferred upon him the honorary degree of Doctor of Divinity.

Dr. Olin was active for the benefit of Randolph Macon College in Georgia, and was chosen its president; but ill health compelled him to relinquish that field of useful endeavor. In the Summer of 1837, he went to Europe with his wife, and after spending some time on the continent and in the British Isles, he went to Greece, Egypt, and the Holy Land. During his journeyings, he suffered several attacks of severe illness, and finally he returned home in the Autumn of 1840. He had been elected President of the Wesleyan University at Middletown, Connecticut, to fill the place of the deceased Dr. Fiske, but his feeble health would not permit him to accept the appointment. In 1842, his strength seemed to warrant him in accepting an urgent call to that institution, and he became its President. He suffered much; and in the Winter of 1842-3, he withdrew from active duty there, and passed the time in the house of his friend, Fletcher Harper, of New York, where he revised the proof-sheets of his *Travels in the East*. That interesting work was published in two volumes the ensuing season.

In the troubles between the Methodists North and South, occasioned by the slavery question, Dr. Olin was eminently a peace-maker, and commanded the highest respect of both parties. Gladly would his brethren have honored him with the office of Bishop, but his feeble health denied to him the privilege of such hard labor. He worked on and suffered on; and in the Autumn of 1845, he made another trip to Europe, but of short duration. On his return he became a zealous member of the Evangelical Alliance, but his feebleness now became more and more general. Yet he travelled, and preached, and wrote much, until the Summer of 1851, when at Middletown, he was compelled to put off the armor of a brave soldier in the Church militant, and prepare for communion with the Church triumphant. His spirit departed for that blessed community on the morning of the 16th of August, 1851, when he was in the fifty-fifth year of his age.

HENRY INMAN.

ART, literature, and social life, were all widowed by the death of Henry Inman, one of the most gifted men of our century. Wordsworth pronounced him the most decided man of genius, he had ever seen from America; and our own Bryant has said of him that "he was no less beloved as a friend, than admired as a painter; that his social qualities were of the richest order, and although he seldom indulged in rhyme, his conversation and letters were often instinct with the spirit of poetry." That child of genius was born in Utica, New York, then a beautiful little village in the upper valley of the Mohawk, on the 20th of October, 1801. His talent for drawing was evinced at a very early age, and his father, who had a taste for the beautiful in nature or in art, warmly encouraged it. An itinerant teacher of drawing gave the lad some lessons in the science, but he did not enter even the vestibule of the great temple in which he was afterward such a distinguished worshipper, until the removal of his family to the city of New York, in 1812. While under the care of an elementary teacher there, his superior talent attracted the attention of John Wesley Jarvis, then in the zenith of his fame as the best living portrait painter in America, except Stuart. Young Inman was then about thirteen years of age, and his father had just obtained a warrant for his entrance to the Military Academy at West Point. Jarvis invited him to become his pupil. The father left the choice to his son, and fortunately for art he chose to be a painter. A bargain for a seven years' apprenticeship was soon concluded, and both parties faithfully fulfilled their engagements during that time.

Mr. Inman erected his easel in New York, in 1822, as a portrait and miniature painter, and in both departments of the art he was eminently successful, from the beginning. Miniatures pleased him best, and he devoted himself almost exclusively to that branch of art, until his pupil, Thomas S. Cummings, (now [1855] one of the best miniature painters in America), displayed such superior merit in that line, that Inman left the field to him. Life-sized portraits, and sketches on Bristol board, now occupied his attention, and he labored with great zeal and assiduity. In 1825, when the National Academy of Design was established in New York, Mr. Inman was elected its Vice-President, and held that office until he made Philadelphia his residence. After prosecuting his vocation there for awhile, with great success, he purchased a small rural-estate in the neighborhood of Mount Holly, New Jersey, where he was continually engaged in his delightful art. There he produced many beautiful compositions in landscape and historical painting, copies of which have since been scattered broadcast over the land by engraving. In 1834 Mr. Inman returned to New York, His health was now becoming delicate, yet he labored incessantly, and with the highest remuneration ever received by any painter in this country. The gorgeous bubble of speculation, glowing with rainbow hues, fascinated him, and in an evil hour he grasped at its beauties. Its promises all vanished in thin air, and in 1836 he found himself a hopeless bankrupt. He had received a commission from Congress to paint a picture for one of the vacant panels in the Rotunda of the Federal Capitol, but this terrible blow deferred his labor upon it, for he was obliged to work hard for bread for his growing family. He had already received some money in part payment for the work. Because he did not go forward with that public commission as a man in full health and prosperity might have done, slander began to cast its venom upon his spotless fame. His noble nature was deeply wounded, and his disease (an enlargement of the heart) was aggravated. Finally, in 1844, he went to England, hoping to regain health and to paint his promised picture there. But his hopes were soon clouded, and he returned home to die, bringing with him the finest of all the trophies of his genius—the portraits of Wordsworth and Dr. Chalmers. He continued the practice of his art with great zeal until within a few weeks of his death. That event occurred on the 17th of January, 1846, at the age of about forty-four years. He was, at that time, President of the Academy of Design, and after his death, a large collection of his works was exhibited for the benefit of his family. In that collection there were one hundred and twenty-seven paintings.

WILLIAM MILLER.

IN all ages of the world credulity has produced strange shapes in society. The most absurd notions, honestly entertained by deluded persons, or artfully promulgated by wicked impostors, for personal benefit, have found ardent supporters, fired with martyr zeal, especially when the dogma was arrayed in the mysterious garb of a religious necessity. Time and again the broad mantle of Christianity has been used to cover up the deformities of these parasitical systems; and, apparently under the awful sanctions of divine revelation, multitudes have "believed a lie." In our day, the peculiar doctrines concerning the second personal appearance of Jesus upon earth, known as *Millerism*, have had a more wide-spread and disastrous influence than any other, except that of the wicked and obscene system of Mormonism. The author of *Millerism*, familiarly known, like the founder of Mormonism, as *The Prophet*, was William Miller, a plain, uneducated, religious zealot, who was born in Pittsfield, Massachusetts, in 1771. Of his early life we have no important record. He seems not to have been distinguished from his fellow-men by anything remarkable, except that he was an honest man and good citizen.

When war between the United States and Great Britain was kindled in 1812, Mr. Miller was captain of a company of volunteers on the northern frontier, and did good service at Sacketts Harbor, Williamsburg and Plattsburg. When peace came he resumed his farm labors, and we hear nothing more of him until about 1826, when, almost simultaneously with Joe Smith's annunciation of his pretended visions, Mr. Miller began to promulgate his peculiar views concerning prophecy. It was not until 1833, that he commenced his public ministry on the subject of the approaching Millennium. Then he went forth from place to place throughout the Northern and Middle States, boldly proclaiming the new interpretation of Scripture, and declaring that Christ would descend in clouds, the true saints would be caught up into the air, and the earth would be purified by fire, in 1843. No doubt the aged zealot was sincere. He labored with great fervor; and during the ten years of his ministry he averaged a sermon every two days. As the time for the predicted consummation of all prophecy approached, his disciples rapidly increased. Hundreds and thousands embraced his doctrine, withdrew from church-fellowship, and banded together as *The Church of Latter Day Saints*. Other preachers appeared in the field. The press was diligently employed; and an alarming paper, called *The Midnight Cry*, was published in New York, embellished, sometimes, with pictures of hideous beasts, and the image seen by the Babylonian Emperor in his dream; at others with representations of benignant angels. The office of that publication was the head-quarters of the deluded sect, and the receptacle of a large amount of money continually and bountifully contributed by the disciples, even up to the very evening before "the last day," in the Autum of 1843.[1] The excitement became intense. Many gave up business weeks before. Some gave away their property to the managers of the solemn drama. Families were beggared, and scores of weak men and women were made insane by excitement, and became inmates of mad houses. The appointed day passed by. The earth moved on in its accustomed course upon the great highway of the ecliptic. The faith of thousands gave way, and infidelity poured its slimy flood over the wrecks. And these were many—very many. Full thirty thousand people embraced the doctrine of Miller, and had unbounded faith in his interpretation of all prophecy. Alas! who shall estimate the desolation of true religion in the hearts of that multitude, when the delusion vanished like a dream at dawn? In the course of a few weeks the excitement subsided, and soon the rushing torrent of delusion dwindled into an almost imperceptible rill. Mr. Miller acknowledged his error, and seldom preached about the Millennium. He died at Hampton, Washington County, New York, on the 29th of December, 1849, at the age of seventy-eight years.

JAMES KNOX POLK.

MECKLENBURG COUNTY, in North Carolina, was settled chiefly by Scotch-Irish and their descendants, and when the War for Independence broke out, the people of that section were so zealous and active in the cause of popular liberty, that Mecklenburg was called *The Hornet's Nest.* Among the energetic patriots who led the rebellion there, were the relatives of James Knox Polk, the eleventh President of the United States. He was born in that *Hornet's Nest,* on the 2d of November, 1795, and was the eldest of ten children. His father was an enterprising farmer, and a warm supporter of Jefferson. When James was eleven years of age, his family removed from Mecklenburg to the wilderness, on the banks of a branch of the Cumberland river, in Tennessee, and there the future President passed the greater portion of his life. The wilderness disappeared before the hand of cultivation, and that portion of Tennessee became famous for its productiveness.

After acquiring a fair English education, James was placed with a merchant to be fitted for commercial life. The pursuit was not congenial to his taste, and after some preparatory studies, he entered the University of North Carolina, in the Autumn of 1815, to be educated for a professional life. He was one of the most remarkable students in that institution, and, at the end of three years, he was graduated with the highest honors. His character in after life was foreshadowed there; for he never missed a recitation, nor omitted the punctilious performance of his duty. At the beginning of 1819, he commenced the study of law with Felix Grundy; and, in 1820, was admitted to the bar. He had suffered feeble health from childhood, but the energies of his mind overcame the infirmities of his body, and he soon arose to the front rank in his profession. His talent and urbanity won him many friends; and, in 1823, he was elected to

---

[1]. During the Summer and early Autumn of 1843, the pencil and graver of the writer were frequently brought into requisition in making illustrative pictures for the Arch Saints of the new faith, who employed the press. At sunset, on the evening previous to "the last day" a person connected with *The Midnight Cry,* came rushing into my studio in hot haste, and anxiously implored me to draw and engrave two flying angels with trumpets, before eleven o'clock that night, for the last hours for doing good on earth were rapidly passing away. The "commission" was executed in time. I shall never forget the appearance of the dozen men in the office of the *Cry,* when I handed the little pictures to the publisher, and received my pay without being asked for a "bill of particulars." It was a "serious family" indeed; yet there appeared to be one or two Aminadab Sleek's among them, who, like Judas, had charge of the treasury bag, and evidently expected to have a place in the next census.

a seat in the legislature of Tennessee. As a warm personal and political friend of General Jackson, he was chiefly instrumental in drawing him from his retirement, and electing him a United States Senator. In August, 1825, Mr. Polk, then thirty years of age, was chosen a representative in the Federal Congress, where he was distinguished for his faithfulness in every thing, and as a democratic republican of the strictest stamp. He took a position of highest respect, at once, and was one of the most efficient opposers of the administration of President Adams. Year after year he was continued a member of the House of Representatives by the suffrage of his admiring constituents. As chairman of important committees, he was indefatigable in labor and careful in the preparation of reports. He took sides with President Jackson against the Bank of the United States, at the beginning, and was one of its most powerful enemies in the popular branch of the Federal legislature. His course arrayed against him the friends of the Bank, and efforts were made to defeat his reëlection. But he was always triumphant. In 1835, he was elected Speaker of the House of Representatives, and was reëlected in 1837. Never was the presiding officer of that body more vigorously assailed and annoyed than Mr. Polk, yet with dignified equanimity he kept on consistently in his course of duty, and the House thanked him for his services.

After a service in Congress of fourteen years, Mr. Polk declined a reëlection, in 1839, and the same year he was elected governor of Tennessee by a very large majority. He was nominated for Vice-President of the United States, with Mr. Van Buren, by the Legislature of Tennessee, and in other States, but received only one electoral vote. He was an unsuccessful candidate for governor of Tennessee, in 1841, and also in 1843; and from that time until his elevation to the Presidency of the United States, in 1845, he remained in private life. His administration of four years was a stormy one, and included the period of the Mexican war, the excitements incident to the Oregon boundary question, and the finding of gold in California. His administration will be looked back to as a brilliant one. It is yet too early to judge of its permanent effects upon the commonwealth. The verdict must be awarded by another generation.

President Polk retired from office in March, 1849, and died at his residence at Nashville, Tennessee, on the 15th of June following, at the age of fifty-four years.

LEONARD WOODS.

"BLESSED are the peace-makers, for they shall be called the children of God." So spake the Head of the Church; and the fulfilment of that promise was eminently exemplified in the person of Leonard Woods, D.D., the father of the Andover Theological Seminary. In the history of the Presbyterian Church, in New England, he appears prominent as a peace-maker, at a time when contention about unessential points of doctrine and discipline menaced their unity; and all over the Union he was intimately known and loved as a "child of God."

Leonard Woods was born in Princeton, Massachusetts, on the 19th of June, 1774, and, like the infant Franklin, he was baptized on the day of his birth. He was educated at Harvard University, where he was graduated in 1796. He taught school at Medford, for a while; and after studying theology under Dr. Backus, of Connecticut, for three months, he entered the Christian ministry, by ordination at West Newbury, in 1798. At that time there was a warm contention between Dr. Morse,[1] of Charlestown, and Dr. Spring,[2] of Newburyport, the former planting his foot firmly upon the Westminster catechism as a basis of faith for individuals as well as for the General Association, and the latter willing to be more latitudinarian in both faith and polity. Dr. Morse promulgated his views in the *Panoplist*, and Dr. Spring gave his arguments through the *Missionary Magazine*. Mr. Woods was known as a vigorous writer, and both divines endeavored to secure the services of his pen. He wrote for the *Panoplist*, and then commenced his long career as a theologian.

Mr. Woods soon discovered that Drs. Morse and Spring had each projected a theological seminary, without the knowledge of the other, and that each had selected the same locality. The comprehensive and benevolent mind of Mr. Woods immediately devised a plan to fraternize the belligerents, and to prevent the great evil that would flow from the establishment of two seminaries holding conflicting views. He applied to men of both parties, and after a series of negotiations for six months, carried on with great skill, he broke down the partition, and had the pleasure of seeing those men unite in founding one sem-

---

[1] Rev. Jedediah Morse, D.D., the father of Professor S. F. B. Morse, the inventor of the electromagnetic telegraph. Dr. Morse was pastor of a church at Charlestown about thirty-two years, and died at New Haven, in June, 1826, at the age of sixty-five years. He was the first American author of a Geography. He also wrote a History of the American Revolution, and prepared a Gazetteer.

[2] Rev. Samuel Spring, D.D., was some sixteen years older than Dr. Morse. He was the chaplain of Arnold's regiment, in the expedition from the Kennebec to the St. Lawrence, in 1775. He was the father of the Rev. Gardiner Spring, D.D., pastor of the church fronting the City Hall Park, New York. He died in March, 1819, aged seventy-three years.

inary, their respective publications merged into one, and the General Association placed upon a firmer basis than ever. Andover was chosen as the locality for the seminary, and, by common consent, the person who had secured the happy union, was chosen the first professor in the new institution. The seminary was founded in 1808, and the same year he was inaugurated Abbott Professor of Christian Theology. In that position he labored until 1846, a period of thirty-eight years, when he resigned its duties into younger hands, and was made Emeritus Professor in the same institution.

Dr. Woods was distinguished for his zealous encouragement of every effort directed to the promotion of morality and the spread of the Gospel. Within the sphere of his influence, several of the noblest societies of our day had their germination and early culture, among which the *American Board of Commissioners for Foreign Missions*, and the *American Tract Society*, are the most prominent. The cause of Temperance, Education, Human Freedom, all found in Dr. Woods a warm and judicious friend. After his retirement from the seminary, he carefully revised his theological lectures and miscellaneous works, and superintended their publication, in five volumes. During the last few years of his life he was engaged in writing a history of the seminary over which he had presided so long. It was almost completed at the time of his death, when, according to his expressed desire, it was placed in the hands of his son, to be completed from materials that he had left, and then published. Dr. Woods died at Andover, on the 24th of August, 1854, at the age of little more than eighty years. The simple inscription for the stone that should mark his grave was found in his will.

TIMOTHY FLINT.

VERY few men in private life have engaged so large a share of public attention and cordial esteem as Timothy Flint, especially in the Great West, beyond the Alleghanies. Though bearing the heavy burden of ill health for many weary years, he labored incessantly in the inviting fields of science, literature, and history. He was a native of North Reading, Massachusetts, where he was born in July, 1780. He was graduated at Harvard University, in 1800, and entered immediately upon the study of theology, preparatory to assuming the labors of a gospel minister. He became pastor of a Congregational church at Lunenburg, in his native State, in 1802, where he performed his responsible duties with fidelity for twelve years. In the meanwhile, he enriched his mind with much scientific knowledge, and was very fond of philosophical experiments. Some ignorant neighbors, seeing him at work with his alembic and crucibles, in chemical experiments, charged him with the crime of counterfeiting coin. In defence of his character he prosecuted the slanderer. Unpleasant feelings grew into bitterness, and as Mr. Flint differed in politics from most of his congregation, who were Federalists and opposed to the war then in progress, he thought it expedient to resign his pastoral charge, in 1814. After preaching in several parishes in Massachusetts and New Hampshire, he accepted, from a missionary society in Connecticut, the appointment of a Gospel laborer in the Ohio and Mississippi valleys. In the pleasant month of September, 1815, he started for the Far West, with his wife and three children, in a two-horse wagon. For several years he spread the glad tidings of Christianity over Ohio, Indiana, Kentucky, and Missouri, when he resigned his mission, tried farming, and, with the assistance of his wife, taught several pupils, who became inmates of his family.

In 1822, Mr. Flint and his family went down the Mississippi to New Orleans.

After a short residence near the borders of Lake Pontchartrain, he went to Alexandria, on the Red River, and there took charge of a collegiate school. His health gave way; and, in 1825, he went to the North, and on reaching the house of a friend at Salem, Massachusetts, greatly emaciated, he told him he had come there to die. The change of climate was beneficial, and while under the roof of that friend he wrote the first part of his *Recollections of Ten Years' Residence and Travels in the Mississippi Valley.* It was published in 1826, and attracted much attention throughout the United States and Europe. It was republished in London, and parts of it were translated and published in Paris. With renewed health he joined his family at Alexandria, in the Autumn of 1826, and then commenced writing his first novel—*Francis Berrian, or the Mexican Patriot.* He again went to New England, the following Spring, published his new work, and returned to Alexandria, in the Autumn. In 1828, he removed to Cincinnati, Ohio, where he remained engaged chiefly in literary pursuits, for almost seven years. During that time he wrote and published *Arthur Clavering; History and Geography of the Western States; George Mason, or the Backwoodsman;* and *Shoshonee Valley.* He edited a monthly magazine, entitled *The Western Review,* for three years. He also wrote a sketch of the *Life of Daniel Boone;* a narrative of the adventures and explorations of a pioneer named Pattie; and compiled a *History of the Indian Wars of the West.* In 1833, Mr. Flint removed to New York city, and became editor of the *Knickerbocker Magazine,* but ill health compelled him to relinquish it before the end of that year. He soon afterward went to Alexandria, where a son and daughter were living, and there he spent a greater part of the remainder of his days. His Summers were passed in New England. On the last visit to his friends there, he took with him the manuscript of the second part of his *Recollections of the Mississippi Valley.* He died at the house of one of his friends in Salem, on the 16th of August, 1840, at the age of sixty years. "Of a genius highly imaginative and poetical, he united with a vigorous intellect and discriminating judgment a quick sensibility, and warm affections, a vivid perception and enjoyment, a deep-felt and ever grateful recognition of the Author of the beautiful, grand and lovely in nature, of the true and good, the elevated and pure, the brilliant and divinely-gifted in human endowments and character."

AMBROSE SPENCER.

ONE of the most active and influential of the jurists and politicians of the State of New York, was Ambrose Spencer, a native of Salisbury, Connecticut, where he was born on the 13th of December, 1765. His father was a farmer and mechanic, yet his limited pecuniary means did not prevent his exercise of a wise discretion, in giving his two sons, Ambrose and Philip, a good education. They both entered Yale College, as students, in the Autumn of 1779, where they remained three years, and after studying twelve months longer at Harvard University, they were graduated there in July, 1783. Ambrose was then only seventeen years and six months old. He commenced the study of law with John Canfield, of Sharon, and completed his course with Mr. Gilbert, of Hudson, New York. Before he was nineteen years of age, he married a daughter of his earliest law preceptor, settled at Hudson, and commenced the practice of his profession there. The clerkship of that city was given to him, in 1786; and, in 1793, he was elected a representative of Columbia county in the State legislature. Two years afterward he was elected to the State Senate, for three years; and, in 1798, was reëlected to the same office, for four years. In the meanwhile he had been chosen assistant attorney-general of the State, for the counties of Columbia and Rensselaer; and, in 1802, he was appointed attorney-general. At that time he was confessedly at the head of the bar in the State of New York, as an advocate, counsellor, and jurist. His talents were appreciated; and, in 1804, he was appointed one of the justices of the Supreme Court of that State. Although he was always remarkable for his strict attention to his judicial business, he became an active and widely potential politician of the democratic school. He had been a Federalist, but joined the Republican party at an early day in its history. He and Dewitt Clinton were warm personal and political friends for many years, and acted in concert in the Republican party until 1812, when they took different views of the question of war with Great Britain. Judge Spencer warmly supported President Madison, in his hostile measures, and in his own State he labored shoulder to shoulder with Governor Tompkins in opposition to a great moneyed scheme. At that time he wielded immense political influence in his State, and his support was considered so important by President Madison, that Judge Spencer might have received any office asked for, in the gift of the chief magistrate.

In 1819, Judge Spencer was raised to the seat of chief justice of the State of New York, but retired from the bench in 1823, and resumed the practice of his profession in the city of Albany. In 1821, he was a representative in the convention to amend the constitution of the State. He took great interest in its proceedings, and many sections of the new instrument bear the impress of his strong practical mind. After retiring from the bench, Judge Spencer was mayor of Albany, filled several public stations in his own State; and, in 1829, was elected to a seat in the Federal Congress, where he served two years.

For many years toward the close of his life Judge Spencer was deeply engaged in agricultural pursuits, in the vicinity of Albany. He left these, in 1839, and made his residence in the pleasant village of Lyons, in Wayne county. In 1844, he presided at the Whig National Convention, held at Baltimore, when Henry Clay was nominated for the chief magistracy of the Republic. His last public act was the issuing of a letter to his fellow-citizens, in which he opposed the provision of the new constitution of the State, by which judges were made elective by the people. His sands of life were now almost run out; and on the 13th of March, 1848, his spirit went home, when he was in the eighty-third year of his age.

HORATIO GREENOUGH.

"ART, though a grand and beautiful, is not a universal language, and when her gifted votaries are also priests at the altar of humanity, they are doubly mourned and honored." Such was the just reflection of the intimate personal friend[1] of Greenough, the Sculptor, expressed in closing a brief memoir of that gifted and earth-lost artist. Throughout life, Greenough was, indeed, a "priest at the altar of humanity," for his noble soul was the eager recipient of all good impressions, and his heart and hand were the almoners of a multitude of

---

1. Henry T. Tuckerman, Esq., whose *Memorial of Greenough*, published by Putnam in a small volume, is a most beautiful tribute of a warm heart to the memory of a beloved friend and brilliant genius. That little volume also contains many of the literary productions of the artist, and tributes of others to his genius, in prose and verse. I am indebted to Mr. Tuckerman for the accompanying portrait, which is a copy of a fine daguerreotype from life, in his possession; and to his *Memorial* for the principal facts in this sketch.

bounties. Superior to all jealousies, he recognized no rivals in art, for all who loved the Good, the Beautiful and the True, were loved by him and reciprocated that love.

Horatio Greenough was born in Boston, on the 6th of September, 1805. His father was one of those enterprising merchants who, at the commencement of our century, held highest social position in the New England metropolis. The home of the gifted child of whom we are writing, was a model of excellent influences, and his education was entrusted to the most eminent instructors. His genius, and his taste for art, were developed simultaneously in his early childhood; and hours devoted by other boys in romping play, were employed by him in carving toys for his companions, the implements of his *atelier* being a pencil, knife and scissors. One day he sat upon the doorstep of a neighbor, and with his pen-knife and a nail, he fashioned from plaster, in miniature form, the head of a Roman, copied from a coin. He was watched by the lady of the house, who became the possessor of that earliest of his works of art, and in after years gave him his first commission. For her he produced that beautiful ideal bust, of the *Genius of Love*. His boyish efforts were appreciated, and artists and artisans gave him aid and encouragement. Librarians lent him books, and he studied and wrought, and wrought and studied, for he felt irrepressible desires to express his ideas in tangible art. Yet he did not neglect learning, the companion of all true art; and in the Academy and in the College, he was always a thoughtful, assiduous and successful student. His perceptions were active, his memory remarkably attentive,[1] and his thirst for knowledge was ardent. His physical developement kept pace with his mental activity, and he excelled in all manly exercises. He was the intimate and loving friend of Allston the poet-painter, and they became as one in sentiment and feeling, for their souls affiliated by mutual attraction.

Sometimes Greenough would express his thoughts in Painting; sometimes in Poetry, but most frequently in Sculpture. To the latter art he dedicated his genius; and soon after the close of his collegiate studies, he went to Italy as a pupil of art and nature there. He took up his residence in Rome, and was the first American student of art who made the Eternal City his permanent abiding place. There he studied and wrought in a far higher sphere of influence and effort, than when in his college days. There he enjoyed the friendship of Thorwalsden, the great Danish Sculptor; and with the purest of our living painters, Mr. Weir, he occupied rooms in the house of Claude, on the Pincian Hill. The sky bent in beauty over them, but from the Pontine Marshes came a deadly malaria that menaced the life of the young sculptor, and with his friend and brother artist, he returned home. His health was soon restored, and he again sailed for Europe. While tarrying in Paris, the generous Cooper was his friend; and there he executed a bust of La Fayette, more truthful, in the estimation of judges, than that of the same subject produced by the eminent David. He did not remain long in Paris, but hastened across the Alps, and took up his abode in a somewhat dreary "palace" near the Pinti Gate. For a long time he waited there for a commission. Cooper was again the encouraging friend, and, at his request, Greenough produced for him that exquisite group, *The Chanting Cherubs*. That work, in the hands of such a zealous possessor, introduced the Sculptor to his countrymen, and his successful career then commenced.

We cannot, in this brief memoir, follow the artist in all his pleasant, laborious life, from the modelling of his *Abel*, in 1826, until the completion of *The Rescue*, in 1851.[2] The work in which he took the greatest pride, because of the subject, was his collossal statue of *Washington*, completed in 1843, and now occupying the public square eastward of the Federal Capitol. He executed more than twenty other ideal groups or single statues, and a great many busts of living men, but that will be his chief memorial in the public mind. For many years in Florence—beautiful, classic Florence—his studio, a model of its class, was on the Piazza Maria Antonia; and there he dispensed a generous but unostentatious hospitality. Finally, in the Autumn of 1851, he returned to his native land, ostensibly to erect his group of *The Rescue*, but really to breathe again the free air of the Republic. He chose Newport as his place of residence, and there he resolved to erect a studio, and leave his country no more. He had become acclimated in Italy, and the changeful seasons here disturbed him. Here he lacked the quiet social routine of Florence. All around him was activity to which he had not been accustomed, and his whole being became excited. A brain fever ensued, and after a few days' illness, he expired in the bosom of his loving family, at the age of little more than forty-seven years. That sad event occurred at Newport, on the 18th of December, 1852. So perished in the meridian of his life and fame, a noble, kindly and generous man; and an artist whose works form a part of the rising glory of our country.

---

1. While yet a mere boy, he could repeat two thousand lines of English verse, without error or hesitation.
2. This is a colossal group ordered by Congress for the Federal Capitol. It consists of four figures, a mother and child, an American Indian and the father. It is intended to illustrate the unavoidable conflict between the Anglo-Saxon and the aboriginal races.

HUGH MERCER.

ON the first day of December, 1853, Colonel Hugh Mercer, the foster-child of the Republic, died at the "Sentry-Box," his pleasant residence, near Fredericksburg, Virginia, at the age of little more than seventy-seven years. He was a son of the brave General Hugh Mercer, who was mortally wounded in the battle at Princeton, on the morning of the 3d of January, 1777, and who is revered as one of the eminent martyrs of liberty, who fought for American Independence. That brave soldier was a native of Scotland, and was a surgeon on the bloody field of Culloden, in 1745. Ten years later he was the companion-in-arms of Washington, in the sanguinary conflict on the Monongahela, where Braddock was killed; and when another ten years had elapsed, he left his apothecary shop, his medical practice, and his beloved family, and drew his sword for the liberties of his adopted country. Sixty-three days after he had fallen on the battle-field, the Continental Congress resolved to erect a monument to his memory, in Fredericksburg, with a suitable inscription; and also resolved, "That the eldest son of General Warren,[1] and the youngest son of General Mercer, be educated, from this time, at the expense of the United States."

That "youngest son of General Mercer" was the subject of our brief memoir.[2] He was born at Fredericksburg, Virginia, in July, 1776. His mother was Isabella Gordon, who survived her martyred husband about ten years, and during that time made an indelible impression of her own excellence of character upon that of her son. He was educated at William and Mary College, in Virginia, during its palmiest days, while under the charge of the good Bishop Madison. For a long series of years he was colonel of the militia of his native county (Spottsylvania), and for twenty years he was an active magistrate. For five consecutive years he represented his district in the Virginia legislature, when, preferring the sweets of domestic life, to the turmoils of politics and public office, he declined a reëlection. He was soon afterward chosen president of the branch bank of Virginia, located at Fredericksburg, and held that situation until his death. Throughout his long life, Colonel Mercer enjoyed almost uninterrupted health until a short time before his departure. He was greatly beloved by those who were related to him by ties of consanguinity or friendship, and was universally esteemed for his solid worth as an honorable, energetic, and methodical business man and superior citizen. He was one of the few noble specimens of the Virginia gentleman of the old school; and was the last survivor of the martyr's family, which consisted of four sons and a daughter.

ROBERT M. PATTERSON.

ONE of the most illustrious scientific men of our age and country, was Dr. Robert M. Patterson, of Philadelphia, who is better known to the public in general as the accomplished Director of the United States Mint, during many of the latter years of his life. He was a son of Dr. Robert Patterson, a distinguished professor in the University of Pennsylvania, Director of the Mint, and President of the American Philosophical Society, all of which stations his eminent

---

1. See sketch of Joseph Warren.
2. A portrait of Colonel Mercer may be found in Lossing's *Pictorial Field-Book of the Revolution*, page 668 of the second edition.

son afterward filled. That son was born in Philadelphia, in 1787, was educated at the University of Pennsylvania, and at an early age was graduated there, as a physician. He pursued medical studies in Europe, for several years, and returned to his native city in 1812, with the intention of engaging in his profession there. Being immediately appointed Professor of Natural Philosophy in the medical department of the University, and soon afterward of Mathematics and Natural Philosophy in the classical department, he was diverted from practice. At the age of twenty-seven years he was elected Vice-Provost of that institution. Having paid much attention to the science of engineering, he was invited by the Committee of Safety of Baltimore, in 1813, to lay out and superintend the construction of fortifications there, the city being menaced by the British. He performed the duty so satisfactorily, that he won a public vote of thanks.

For fourteen years Dr. Patterson remained a professor in the University, and was always distinguished for extensive and varied scientific attainments. Other objects of taste and refinement occupied his attention. He was one of the founders and most efficient officers of the Franklin Institute, of Philadelphia, the pioneer association, of its kind, in this country. In 1820, he joined, with others, in establishing the Musical Fund Society, which was also the first of its class, and is still [1855] a rich and prosperous institution. He was its president for many years, and its most efficient member, from the beginning. The American Philosophical Society, of which he became a member at the age of twenty-one years, was his favorite institution, and after the death of the eminent Dr. Chapman, he was elected its president. That chair, so worthily filled by Dr. Franklin, Rittenhouse, Duponceau, and others, was as worthily occupied by Dr. Patterson.

In 1828, Dr. Patterson accepted an invitation to occupy the chair of Natural Philosophy in the University of Virginia. After seven years' service there, President Jackson appointed him Director of the United States Mint. He held that responsible station during several administrations, until 1851, when rapidly declining health compelled him to resign. He was then President of the American Philosophical Society, and of the Pennsylvania Life Annuity Company; also Vice-President of the Pennsylvania Institution for the Instruction of the Blind. His was a liberal heart, and it was ever devising liberal things. Every impulse of his nature was pure and benevolent, and every scheme having for its object the good of humanity always enlisted his sympathy, and his hearty cooperation. His intercourse with society was exemplary in the highest degree, and he imparted a charm to every social circle which was favored by his presence. His death, which occurred in Philadelphia, on the 5th of September, 1854, was regarded as a public calamity, for a man of great usefulness had departed.

SARGEANT S. PRENTISS.

AN intellectual luminary of great and increasing splendor went out and faded from the political and social firmament, when Sargeant S. Prentiss disappeared from earth, on the 1st of July, 1850, at the age of about forty years. The brilliancy of his genius as a statesman of the highest order had just begun to excite the admiration of the nation, when the dark clouds of broken health veiled it, and its light soon waned into invisibility. He was a native of Portland, Maine, where he was born in 1810. He received an excellent classical education, and at the age of about eighteen years he went to Mississippi.

where, in the vicinity of Natchez, he spent about two years as tutor in a private family, and in the pursuit of legal studies, under the instruction of General Felix Houston. Mr. Prentiss was always remarkable, from boyhood, for fluency of language and ready wit; and his first speech to a jury, after being admitted to the bar, won for him the highest applause from judges, colleagues, and opponents. He made Vicksburg (then a small village) his residence, in 1830, and he soon became the acknowledged head of his profession in that region. His eloquence was of that popular order which always charms and overpowers; and, like O'Connell, he could adapt his words and figures to his particular audience, with wonderful facility. His practice became very lucrative, and the payment of his fee, in land, for his successful management of a suit which involved the most valuable portion of Vicksburg, made him, in a short time, one of the wealthiest men in the State.

Mr. Prentiss entered the field of politics with great enthusiasm, and was a brilliant and successful stump orator; but at about the time when his fellow-citizens called him to service in the national councils, he became embarrassed during the financial troubles of 1836, and removed to New Orleans to retrieve his fortune by professional labor. He first became known to the people of the United States, in general, when, in 1837, he appeared in the House of Representatives as the claimant of a disputed seat there. His speech in favor of his claim was listened to with the most profound attention, and it was admitted by all, that he had no superior in the country as an eloquent and logical parliamentary debater. His claim was rejected by the casting-vote of the Speaker, Mr. Polk, and he was sent back to the people. He at once canvassed the State, and was reëlected by an overwhelming vote. His services in the Hall of Representatives were brief, but brilliant in the extreme. Private engagements, and a distaste for political life, produced by his discovery of its hollowness and its dangers, caused him to refuse office, and with great industry he applied himself to his profession, in New Orleans. He was eminently successful. No man ever possessed greater powers of fascination by his forensic oratory than he, and few jurors could withstand that power. Nor was he entirely absorbed in professional duties. He was distinguished for his love and knowledge of literature, and he was always prominent in philanthropic movements in the chosen city of his residence. His social qualities were of the highest order, and the attachment of his friends was exceedingly strong. In the midst of his active career, and bearing the blossoms of greatest promise, he was suddenly cut down by disease, and died at Longwood, near Natchez, in the pleasant Summer time.

"What made more sad, the outward form's decay,
A soul of genius glimmered through the clay;
Genius has so much youth, no care can kill,
Death seems unnatural when it sighs, 'Be still.'"

HENRY CLAY.

A FEW miles from the old Hanover court-house, in Virginia, where the splendors of Patrick Henry's genius first beamed forth, is a humble dwelling by the road-side, in the midst of a poor region, technically called *slashes*. There, on the 12th of April, 1777, Henry Clay, the great American statesman, was born, and from the poor district schools of his neighborhood, he derived his education. His father was a clergyman with slender worldly means, and at an early age Henry became a copyist in the office of the clerk of the Court of Chancery, at

Richmond. There the extraordinary powers of his intellect began to develope, and at the age of nineteen years he commenced the study of law. Close application and a remarkably retentive memory overcame many difficulties, and he was admitted to practice at the age of twenty. At that time emigration was pouring steady streams of population over the mountains into the fertile valleys of Kentucky, and thither Henry Clay went, early in 1799, and settled at Lexington. He was admitted to the bar there, in the Autumn of that year, and commenced the practice of law and politics at about the same time, and with equal success. A convention was called to revise the constitution of Kentucky, and young Clay worked manfully in efforts to elect such delegates as would favor the emancipation of the slaves. Thus early that subject assumed great importance in his mind; and throughout his long life he earnestly desired the abolition of the slave system. His course offended many, and he was unpopular for a time; but his noble opposition to the Alien and Sedition laws restored him to favor; and, in 1803, he was elected a member of the Kentucky legislature, by a large majority. With fluent speech, sound logic, and bold assurance, he soon took front rank in that body, as well as in his profession; and, in 1806, he was chosen to fill a seat in the Senate of the United States, for one year, made vacant by the resignation of General Adair. There he left an impression of that statesmanship, then budding, which afterward gave glory and dignity to that highest legislative council of the Republic.

On his return from the Federal city, Mr. Clay was again elected to a seat in the Kentucky legislature, and was chosen Speaker of the Assembly, by a large majority. That station he held during two consecutive sessions. In 1809, he was again sent to the Senate of the United States, for two years, to fill a vacancy, and there he became distinguished by several brilliant speeches on important occasions. A crisis in the affairs of the nation was then approaching. Men of the highest character for talent and integrity were needed in the national councils. Perceiving this, the Kentuckians wisely elected Henry Clay to a seat in the House of Representatives, at Washington, where he first appeared in 1811. Almost immediately afterward, he was elected Speaker, by a large majority, and he performed the very important duties of that station with great ability until 1814, when he was appointed one of the commissioners to negotiate a treaty of peace with Great Britain. In that service he exhibited the skill of a good diplomatist; and when, in 1815, he returned to his constituents, they immediately reëlected him to a seat in Congress. Now commenced his series of important services in the Federal legislature, which have distinguished him as one of the first statesmen of his age. There he triumphantly pleaded the cause of the South American Republics; and, in 1818, he put forth his giant strength in behalf of a national system of internal improvements. A grateful people commemorated his services in that direction, by placing a monument on the margin of the great Cumberland road, inscribed with his name.

In 1819 and 1820, Mr. Clay entered upon the great work, in Congress, of establishing tariffs for the protection of American industry. At the same time, he rendered signal services in the adjustment of the question known as the Missouri compromise. Then he retired from Congress, to attend to his embarrassed private affairs. Three years of professional services retrieved his pecuniary losses; and in 1823, he returned to Congress, and was elected Speaker, by an immense majority. During that session Daniel Webster presented his famous resolutions in behalf of the suffering Greeks, and Mr. Clay warmly seconded the benevolent movement of the great New England statesman. After the election of John Quincy Adams to the presidency of the United States, Mr. Clay was appointed his Secretary of State, and held the office until the accession of General Jackson to the chief magistracy, in 1829. He remained in retirement a short time; and, in 1831, he was elected to the Senate of the United States, for six years. He was soon afterward nominated for the office of President of the United States, and was the candidate opposed to the successful Jackson, in 1832. At about that time he was instrumental, by the proposition of a compromise measure in Congress, in saving the country from civil war. He was reëlected to the Senate, in 1836; and, in 1842, he took, as he supposed, a final leave of that body. He had earnestly labored for his favorite protective policy; and, in 1844, the Whig party nominated him for the office of President of the United States. He was defeated by Mr. Polk, and he remained in retirement until 1849, when he was again elected to the Federal Senate. There he put forth his energies in securing that series of measures known as the Compromise Act of 1850. His health was now greatly impaired; and in the Winter of 1850 and 1851, he sought relief by a visit to Havana and New Orleans. The effort was of no avail. Notwithstanding his feeble health, he repaired to Washington city at the commencement of the session, but was unable to participate in active duties. His system gradually gave way, and he resigned his seat, the act to take effect on the 6th of September, 1852. He did not live to see that day. He died at Washington city, on the 29th of June, 1852, at the age of about seventy-five years.

ROBERT BURNET.

ON a cold, frosty, but clear and brilliant morning in November, 1783, the remnant of the American Continental army, led by General Knox, and accompanied by civil officers of the State, crossed King's bridge, at the upper end of Manhattan Island, and marched triumphantly into the city of New York, just as the British troops, who had occupied that city for seven long years, embarked in the harbor, to return no more. Great rejoicings and feastings were had in the emancipated city; and nine days afterward, the principal officers of the army, yet remaining in the service, assembled at the public-house of Samuel Fraunce, on the corner of Broad and Pearl Streets, to take a final leave of their beloved commander-in-chief. When Washington entered the room where they were waiting, he took a glass of wine in his hand, and said, "With a full heart of love and gratitude, I now take leave of you. I most devoutly wish that your latter days may be as prosperous and happy as your former ones have been glorious and honorable." After the usual salutation, by drinking, he continued, "I cannot come to each of you to take my leave, but shall be obliged to you if each will come and take me by the hand." Knox stood by the side of the Great Leader, and as he turned, with eyes brimming with tears, to grasp his hand, Washington affectionately kissed him. This he did to all of his officers in turn, and then, without uttering a word, he left the room, passed through a flanking corps of infantry to a barge at Whitehall, and proceeded on his journey to Annapolis, to surrender his commission into the hands of Congress.

Of all the officers who participated in that tender scene, Major Robert Burnet, of Little Britain, Orange county, was, for many years, the sole survivor. His father was a Scotchman, and his mother was a native of Ireland. She was one of those who accompanied the first members of the Clinton family, who settled in the vicinity of Newburgh. Major Burnet was born in Little Britain, on the 22d of February, 1762, and was engaged in agricultural pursuits until about 1779, when he entered the revolutionary army, in the artillery branch of the service, under Captain Ebenezer Stevens.[1] He was a lieutenant in Stevens' company, and commanded Redoubt No. 3, at West Point, at the time of Arnold's defection, in September, 1780. He was afterward promoted to the rank of major,[2] and was one of the delegates who attended a meeting of the officers, convened by Washington, on account of the seditious tendency of the anonymous Address put forth by Major Armstrong, at Newburgh, in the Spring of 1783.[3] He continued in the army, under the immediate command of the chief, until it was disbanded. In the march into the city of New York, on the day when the British evacuated it, Major Burnet commanded the rear-guard. When I visited the veteran, in the Summer of 1850, and he was then in his nintieth year, he gave me a very interesting account of the scenes of that memorable Autumn morning. Major Burnet was the last to grasp the hand of Washington at that solemn parting at Fraunce's; and then he returned to his rural pursuits in the town of his nativity. There he lived in the enjoyment of great domestic happiness, until called to his final home. He lived to see, what few men in modern times have beheld—the living representatives of seven generations of his kin-

---

1. See sketch of Ebenezer Stevens.
2. Washington, in a letter to Greene, dated "Newburgh, 6th February, 1782," refers to Major Burnet as follows: "I intended to write you a long letter on sundry matters; but Major Burnet came unexpectedly, at a time when I was preparing for the celebration of the day, and was just going to a review of the troops previous to the *feu de joie.* As he is impatient, from an apprehension that the sleighing may fail, and as he can give you the occurrences of this quarter more in detail, than I have time to do, I will refer you to him." The celebration spoken of was that of the anniversary of the signing of the treaty of alliance between the United States and France, four years before,
3. See sketch of John Armstrong.

dred. These were his great-grandfather of the ancestral part of the connection, and the great-grandchildren of his own posterity. Major Burnet died at his residence, in Little Britain, on the 1st of December, 1854, when almost ninety-three years of age. His funeral was attended by his neighbor, Uzal Knapp, who was almost three years his senior. Mr. Knapp, the last survivor of *Washington's Life-Guard*,[1] died about a year afterward.

HARRISON GRAY OTIS.

OF the New England "gentlemen of the old school," who have graced our generation, and illustrated by their deportment the dignified simplicity of the earlier years of our Republic, the late Harrison Gray Otis was one of the finest examples in person, intellectual acquirements, and amenity of manners. He was a son of Samuel A. Otis, who, for about twenty-five years, was clerk of the Senate of the United States. Harrison was born in 1765, the memorable year when patriots of his name were manfully battling the odious Stamp Act. And the same year when, by definitive treaty, the independence of the United States was acknowledged by Great Britain, he was graduated at Harvard University, at the age of eighteen years. He had been a successful student, and he then entered upon the study of law with a preparation possessed by few young men. Before he was twenty-one years of age he had commenced his successful career as a practitioner, with promises which were all redeemed in his maturity. He soon stood foremost at the bar with such men as Parsons, Lowell, Gore, Cushing, Paine, Ames, Cabot, and other distinguished lawyers of New England, and was excelled by none of them in acuteness as an attorney, and in impressive and graceful oratory as an advocate. His political and literary acquirements were as extensive as his legal knowledge, and he often employed them with great success before the bench, or an intelligent jury.

In 1797, Mr. Otis represented the Suffolk (Boston) district in the Federal Congress, as the successor of Fisher Ames; and he held that station until 1801, when the Republicans came into power under the leadership of Mr. Jefferson. For many years he was a member, alternately, of both branches of the Massachusetts legislature, and, at different times he was the presiding officer of both Houses. Although firm and unflinching in his political faith, and exceedingly strict as a disciplinarian in official station, his urbanity and rare consistency commanded the respect of his opponents and the warmest affections of his adherents. He was eminently reliable, heartily disliked concealment, and despised stratagem. His constituents always felt their interests perfectly safe in his hands.

Mr. Otis was chosen United States Senator, in 1817, and his course in that body during the exciting scenes preceding the admission of Missouri into the Union as a sovereign State, won for him the highest applause of his constituents. After five years' service there he retired, and contemplated repose in private life; but his fellow-citizens of the Federal faith, for which he had contended manfully against the growing Democratic party, in his State, begged him to continue his leadership. They nominated him for governor, in 1823, but the Federal party, as an efficient organization, was then just expiring, and he was defeated. After filling several local offices (judge of the Court of Common Pleas, mayor of Boston, and others of less note), Mr. Otis withdrew from public life, in the full enjoyment of his intellectual vigor and his rare capacities for social pleasures. That vigor he retained until his death, which occurred in the city of Boston, on the 28th of October, 1848, at the age of about eighty-three years.

---

1. Portraits of Major Burnet and Mr. Knapp are published in Lossing's *Pictorial Field-Book of the Revolution*.

DAVID KINNISON.

THE latest survivor of the notable band of patriots, in 1773, known as *The Boston Tea Party*,[1] was David Kinnison, who lived to the remarkable age of more than one hundred and fifteen years. The facts of this brief memoir were obtained from his own lips, by the writer, in August, 1848, together with a daguerreotype likeness. He was then one hundred and eleven years of age. He was born in Old Kingston, Maine, on the 17th of November, 1736, and was employed in farming until the tempest of the Revolution began to lower. He was a member of a secret club, who were pledged to destroy the obnoxious article of TEA, wheresoever it might be found; and when the East India Company's ships had arrived at Boston, Kinnison and others hastened thither, were among the "Mohawks"[2] in the gallery of the Old South Church, and assisted in casting the two cargoes of tea into the waters of Boston harbor, on the evening of the 16th of December, 1773. Kinnison remained in the vicinity of the New England capital, working on a farm, until the Spring of 1775, when, as a minute-man, he participated in the events at Lexington and Concord. With his father and two brothers, he fought in the battle of Bunker's Hill; and after the British were driven from Boston, he accompanied the American army to New York. From that time until the Autumn of 1781, he led the life of a Continental soldier, under the immediate command of Washington most of the time. Then, while engaged as a scout in Saratoga, he was captured by some Mohawk Indians, and did not regain his liberty until peace came, after a captivity of more than eighteen months.

At the close of the Revolution, Mr. Kinnison resumed the labors of agriculture, at Danville, Vermont, where he resided about eight years, and then removed to Wells, in Maine. There he lived until the commencement of the war with Great Britain, in 1812, when he again went to the field as a private soldier. He was under General Brown at Sackett's harbor; and in the battle at Williamsburg, on the St. Lawrence, he was badly wounded in the hand by a grape-shot. That was the first and only injury he had ever received in battle, but by accidents afterward, his skull had been fractured; his collar bone and both legs, below the knees, had been broken; the heel of a horse had left a deep scar on his forehead, and rheumatism had dislocated one of his hip joints. As he forcibly expressed it, he had been "completely bunged up and stove in."

Mr. Kinnison was an illiterate man, and possessed none of the elements of greatness. He was eminent because of the peculiar associations of his life, his long experience, and his remarkable longevity. He learned to write his name when in the revolutionary camp; and he was sixty-two years of age when his granddaughter taught him to read. He had married and buried four wives, who had borne him twenty-two children. When he related this narrative, he had lost all trace of his relatives, and supposed himself childless.[3] His pension of eight dollars a month was insufficient for his wants, and until his one hundred and tenth year, he added sufficient for a livelihood, by the labor of his hands. Then a benevolent stranger, in Chicago, gave him a home. He was little less than six feet in height, with powerful arms, shoulders, and chest; and at the

---

1. See note 3, page 148.
2. Many of those who cast the tea into Boston harbor were disguised as Mohawk Indians. After a harangue in the Old South Church, Boston, just at twilight, some of them gave a war-whoop in the gallery, and all started for Griffin's wharf, where the ships lay.
3. About a year before his death, his daughter, living in Oswego, New York, saw the portrait and biographical sketch of her long-lost father, in *Lossing's Pictorial Field-Book of the Revolution*. She at once hastened to Chicago to see him. Until then, she had no idea that he was among the living. She remained with him, and smoothed the pillow of his death-bed.

age of one hundred and two years, he was seen to lift a barrel of cider into a wagon, with ease. When one hundred and ten, he walked twenty miles in one day. At eighty, his sight and hearing failed. Both were restored at ninety-five, and remained quite perfect until his death. That venerable man died at Chicago, Illinois, on the 24th of February, 1852, in the one hundred and sixteenth year of his age.

CATHERINE FERGUSON.

"THIS poor widow hath cast in more than they all; for they did cast in of their abundance, but she, of her penury, hath cast in all the living that she had." Such was the estimate of good works by the Great Pattern of benevolence. The motive and the sacrifice alone are considered; the person and the condition are but "dust in the balance." Thus judged, Katy Ferguson seems entitled to the plaudit from men, angels, and her God, "Well done, good and faithful servant." Katy was a colored woman, born a slave while her mother was on her passage from Virginia to New York. For almost fifty years she was known in that city as a professional cake-maker, for weddings and other parties, and was held in the highest esteem.

When Katy was eight years of age her mother was sold, and they never met again. Her own anguish at parting taught her to sympathize with desolate children, and they became the great care of her life. Her mistress was kind and indulgent, and Katy was allowed to attend Divine service, and hear the instructions of the good Dr. John M. Mason, the elder. She never learned to read, but her retentive memory treasured up a vast amount of Scripture knowledge, which she dispensed as opportunity allowed. When she approached womanhood her mind became agitated respecting her soul and its destiny, and she ventured to call on Dr. Mason for advice and consolation. She went with trembling, and was met by the kind pastor with an inquiry whether she had come to talk to him about her soul. The question took a burden from her feelings, and she left the presence of the good man with a heart full of joy.

A benevolent lady purchased Katy's freedom for two hundred dollars, when she was sixteen years of age, and allowed her one hundred of it, for eleven months' service. The excellent Divie Bethune raised the other hundred, and Katy became free. She married at eighteen, had two children, and lost them, and from that time she put forth pious efforts for the good of bereaved and desolate little ones. At her humble dwelling in Warren Street, she collected the poor and neglected children of the neighborhood, white and black, every Sunday, to be instructed in religious things by herself, and such white people as she could get to help her. Sometimes the sainted Isabella Graham would invite Katy and her scholars to her house, and there hear them recite the catechism, and give them instruction. Finally, Dr. Mason[1] heard of her school, and visited it one Sunday morning. "What are you about here, Katy?" he asked. "Keeping school on the Sabbath!" Katy was troubled, for she thought his question a rebuke. "This must not be, Katy; you must not be allowed to do all this work alone," he continued; and then he invited her to transfer her school to the basement of his new church in Murray Street, where he procured assistants for her. Such was the origin of the Murray Street Sabbath-school; and it is

---

1. This was the son and pulpit successor of Dr. Mason, the elder, under whom Katy became converted. That excellent pastor died soon after the interview named in the text, at the age of fifty-seven years.

believed that Katy Ferguson's was the first school of the kind established in the city of New York.[1]

Katy's benevolent labors did not end with her Sunday-school duties. Every Friday evening and Sunday afternoon she gathered the poor and outcast of her neighborhood, children and adults, white and black, into her little dwelling, and always secured some good man to conduct the services of a prayer-meeting there. Such was her habit for forty years, wherever in the great city she dwelt. Her good influence was always palpable; and tract distributors uniformly testified that wherever Katy resided, the neighborhood improved. Nor was this all. Though laboring for daily bread at small remuneration, she cheerfully divided her pittance with unsparing generosity. She always found some more needy than herself; and during her life, she took FORTY-EIGHT CHILDREN (twenty of them white) from the almshouse or from dissolute parents, and *brought them up or kept them until she could find good homes for them!* Who shall estimate the social blessings which have flowed from those labors of love by a poor, uneducated colored woman! Do not those labors rebuke, as with a tongue of fire, the cold selfishness of society? Ought they not to make our cheeks tingle with the blush of shame for our remissness in duty? The example of such a life ought not to be lost; and I have endeavored thus to perpetuate the memory of Katy Ferguson and her deeds for the benefit of posterity.[2] She was a philanthropist of truest stamp. Her earthly labors have ceased. She died of cholera, in New York, on the 11th of July, 1854, at the age of about seventy-five years. Her last words were, "All is well." Who can doubt it?

---
1. The Rev. Dr. Ferris, sometime chancellor of the New York University, informed the writer that his first extemporary expositions of the Scriptures, while he was yet a theological student, were made in Katy's Sunday-school, in the Murray Street Church.
2. The accompanying portrait is from a daguerreotype taken in 1850, at the instance of Lewis Tappan, Esq., of New York, and now in the possession of Rev. Henry Ward Beecher, of Brooklyn.

BENJAMIN BANNEKER.

THE germ of genius is often hidden in very common mold, and springs up into glorious efflorescence, at a time, and in a place, least expected by the common observer. The African race, so inferior in condition everywhere, seldom presents the world with any thing startling in the way of intellectual achievements. This is the rule, while the exceptions are sometimes very remarkable. Of these exceptions, there are few characters more prominent than that of Benjamin Banneker, of Maryland, the descendant from a fair-complexioned English woman, and a native of Africa. His grandmother came from England, purchased a small plantation in Maryland, and also two negro slaves from a ship just from Africa. She finally liberated and married one of them. Her daughter, Benjamin's mother, married an African, who assumed her surname. Benjamin was their only son, and he was born on the 9th of November, 1731. His grandmother taught him to read, and instructed him in religious things. He became fond of books, and devoted much of the time which he could spare from farm labors to studies of various kinds. At maturity he was possessed of a farm left by his father, and he cultivated it with care and thrift. Arithmetic, and mathematics in general, were his delight, and extraordinary mechanical abilities were early displayed by him in the construction of a wooden clock. This instrument was long a wonder among the settlers upon the banks of the Patapsco river, where Banneker resided.

When, in 1773, Ellicott & Co. built their mills in that deep valley, crossed by the railway from Baltimore to Washington, Banneker was an earnest spectator of the process, not only of construction, but of continued operation. At about that time he had become noted for expertness in the solution of mathematical problems, and scholars in different parts of the country frequently sent him questions to test his capacity. The answers were always correct, and sometimes he would propose questions in return, expressed in verse. On the suggestion of George Ellicott, who appreciated his genius, Banneker made astronomical calculations for almanacs; and, in the spring of 1789, he accurately calculated an eclipse. He was now almost sixty years of age, and, though industrious with his hands, he panted for leisure to pursue scientific studies. He finally disposed of his little farm for a competent annuity, and lived alone. Wrapped in his cloak, he lay many a night upon his back on the bare earth, in contemplation of the heavenly bodies. In 1790 he was employed, by commissioners, to assist them in surveying the lines of the District of Columbia, then called the *Federal Territory*. This was the only time that he was ever far from his little dwelling; and, on his return, speaking of the good treatment he had received, he said, "I feared to trust myself, even with wine, lest it should steal away the little sense I have."

Banneker's first almanac was published in 1792. He sent a copy of it, in his own hand-writing, to Thomas Jefferson, then Secretary of State. It excited the warmest approbation of Jefferson, who wrote him a noble letter in reply, assuring him that he had sent the almanac to M. Condorcet, Secretary of the Academy of Sciences at Paris. There it commanded universal admiration, and the "African Astronomer" became well known in the scientific circles of Europe. He kept a common-place book, in which he recorded the events of his daily life. That book is preserved, and in it is the memorandum, "Sold on the 2d of April, 1795, to Butler, Edwards, and Kiddy, the right of an almanac for the year 1796, for the sum of eighty dollars, equal to £30." His last recorded astronomical observations appear under date of the month of January, 1804, Banneker died in October, 1806, aged seventy-five years. It was a brilliant day, when, having been upon the neighboring hills, for fresh air, he returned to his cottage, complained of feeling ill, and, lying down, soon afterwad expired, at the age of about seventy-three years. The following question, submitted by Banneker to George Ellicott, will give the reader some idea of his poetic, as well as mathematical talent:

"A Cooper and Vintner sat down for to talk,
Both being so groggy that neither could walk;
Says Cooper to Vintner, 'I'm the first of my trade,
There's no kind of vessel but what I have made,
And of anyshape, sir,—just what you will,
And of any size, sir,—from a tun to a gill!'
'Then,' said the Vintner, 'you're the man for me—
Make me a vessel if we can agree.
The top and the bottom's diameter define,
To bear that proportion as fifteen to nine;
Thirty-five inches are just what I crave,
No more and no less, in the depth will I have;
Just thirty-nine gallons this vessel must hold,—
Then I will reward you with silver or gold—
Give me your promise, my honest old friend!'
'I'll make it to-morrow, that you may depend!'
So the next day the Cooper, his work to discharge,
Soon made the new vessel, but made it too large;
He took out some staves, which made it too small,
And then cursed the vessel, the Vintner and all.
He beat on his breast—'By the Powers!' he swore,
He never would work at his trade any more.
Now, my worthy friend, find out, if you can,
The vessel's dimensions, and comfort the man."

"BENJAMIN BANNEKER."

JOHN W. FRANCIS, JR.

IN the roseate petal bursting from the calyx in Spring-time, we see sure promises of the fruit of Autumn; and if the frost or the canker withers it, we mourn as reasonably as when the frost or the canker blights at full fruition. So with the soul in its calyx of humanity. In its budding promises,

"Ere fame ordained or genius had achieved,"

we often behold greatness, and goodness, and all else that ennobles man, benefits the world, and honors the Creator, as clearly manifested as in the fruit of full consummation. When one, like our young friend of whom we write, is taken from among men, at the full bursting of the buds of promise which prophesy of a brilliant and useful career, society is bereaved, indeed, for it is denied the benefits of great achievements.

John W. Francis, jr., was the eldest son of Dr. John W. Francis, the well-known, well-beloved, and eminent physician and scholar. He was born in the city of New York, on the 5th of July, 1832. From the dawn of life he lived in the midst of intellectual influences of the highest and purest kind. His father's house was the welcome resort of men distinguished in science, art, and literature; and in the domestic circle his heart and mind were the daily and hourly recipients of the noblest culture. His wise father watched his physical development with great care, and he grew to manhood with robust health. With such preparations he entered upon the tasks and pleasures of the school-room. He sought knowledge with a miser's greed, but not with a miser's sordid aim; for, like his father, he delighted as much in distributing as in gathering. Habituated from infancy to the society of the mature, he was always manly beyond his years. His love of reading, and his free personal intercourse with the dis-

tinguished associates and visitors of his father, intensified his thirst for knowledge, and made its acquisition easy. He was an ardent lover of nature, and to him the sea-shore seemed like the presence of God. When, in 1848, he entered Columbia College as a student, he was remarkable for general information. He was already familiar with the works and thoughts of the best English writers, and was an adept in the critic's difficult art. His collegiate course was in the highest degree honorable, and he completed it with a thoroughness of discipline and culture, possessed by few. He was the favorite of his classmates, as well as his tutors, and to all he was known by the name of "the young doctor." He had become proficient in the classics and other regular studies in the usual course, and wrote and spoke fluently several modern languages. "He had," said his favorite preceptor, "the soul of a classical scholar." Humor was a marked trait in his character, and it had a beneficent effect upon his too earnest intellect. Fully equipped for the great battle of life, he chose the medical profession as his chief theater of action. He was led to it by his preference, and by intense filial devotion; for he loved his father as such a father deserves to be loved, and earnestly desired to relieve that good man's professional toil. He made thorough preparations for the duties he was about to assume, by attendance upon medical lectures, and extensive practical study in the Hospital. There he assumed duties of great responsibility. He took special delight in treating poor patients, for whom he always had the balm of kind words, and often relieved their immediate necessities by contributions from his own purse.[1] Thus, in intense study and important practice, he was preparing for the reception of his degree and diploma as a physician, with all the zeal of an ardent worshiper. The labor was too great for even his strong mind and vigorous body. Both were overwrought, and he fell in the harness. A typhoid fever bore him rapidly to the grave. On the 20th of January, 1855, his spirit returned to the bosom of its Creator, while the stricken parents—

> "Two—whose gray hairs with daily joy he crowned,"

mourned in the midst of sympathizing friends, but not as those without hope. His body was followed to the temple and the tomb by many of the most distinguished citizens of New York; his class-mates of Columbia College and of the University Medical School; and by almost every member of the New York Academy of Medicine. The press testified its sense of the public loss by his departure; his associates gathered and expressed their approbation of his worth, by appropriate resolutions; distinguished friends from various parts of the Union, sent letters of tender condolence to his parents; a beautiful commemorative poem flowed from the graceful pen of his friend, Henry T. Tuckerman; and our Lyric Poet, George P. Morris, wrote for his epitaph—

> "The pulse-beat of true hearts!
> The love-light of fond eyes!
> When such a man departs,
> 'Tis the survivor dies."

Few young men are endowed with such intellectual beauty of face as was young Francis. While yet a child, Miss Hall painted a miniature of him. The publisher of the *Magnolia* had it engraved as "Oberon;" and the editor, one of our most honored literary men, "declared of this ideal of infant strength and loveliness, that he could

> "'In every speaking feature trace
> A brilliant destiny.'"

THEODORIC ROMEYN BECK.

AS a model of industry and disinterestedness, T. Romeyn Beck, M.D., LL.D., appears prominent among the truly great men of our day. "He never lost a minute," says his friend, co-laborer and pastor,[2] "and we all know how

---

[1]. Mr. Tuckerman, who has since prepared an admirable Memoir of young Francis, mentions the case of an old lame beggar, who for years had daily taken his station in front of the New York Hospital. So constant was young Francis's kindness to this poor fellow, that the mendicant watched regularly for his benefactor; and when he was so far off as not to be recognized by less devoted eyes, he took off his hat to welcome "Master Francis," as he called him even when grown to young manhood.

[2]. Rev. Dr. Campbell of Albany.

much he accomplished; yet he never appeared, in any thing he did, to be seeking to acquire position or honor for himself. He was a remarkably pure-minded man—of true honor, above all meanness, and of the sternest integrity."

Dr. Beck was born at Schenectady, in the State of New York, on the 11th of August, 1791. He was of English and Dutch descent, and inherited the virtues of both. At an early age he was left to the care of a widowed mother, who had four other sons in charge. After attending the Common Schools of his native town, he entered Union College, in Schenectady, as a student, in 1803. He was graduated at the age of sixteen years, and at once commenced the study of medicine in the city of Albany. His professional education was completed in New York, under the eminent Dr. David Hosack. On the occasion of receiving his degree, as Doctor of Medicine, in 1811, the subject of his inaugural thesis was "Insanity," a topic which, in after life, occupied much of his attention. He commenced the practice of medicine and surgery, in Albany, and the same year he was appointed physician to the Almshouse. In 1812 he became a member of "The Society for the Promotion of Useful Arts," at the head of which was Chancelor Livingston. At the second meeting after his election he was made chairman of a committee appointed for "the purpose of collecting and arranging such minerals as our State affords;" and less than two months after his admission, when in the twenty-first year of his age, he was appointed to deliver the annual address at the following meeting of the Society. From that period he was an active promoter of agriculture and manufactures, and a great portion of his useful life was spent in their advancement. In 1815 Dr. Beck received the appointment of Professor of the Institutes of Medicine, and of lecturer on Medical Jurisprudence in the newly established College of Physicians and Surgeons at Fairfield, in Herkimer County. He withdrew from the practice of medicine in 1817, when he was appointed Principal of the Albany Academy. The sufferings he was compelled to witness had a powerful effect upon his sensitive organization, and he left the practice willingly, while he always delighted in the study of the healing art. From that time he became devoted to Science and Literature, and in those fields he always sustained an exalted position.

In 1823, Dr. Beck was elected vice-president of the Albany Lyceum of Natural History; and the same year he published his popular work, in two volumes, on the *Elements of Medical Jurisprudence.* This production attracted great attention, and gave the author substantial fame. Dr. John W. Francis, who was long Professor of Medical Jurisprudence in the University of the State of New York, speaking of this work, remarks, "I have various editions, in various languages, which the foreign press has issued for enlightened Europe. This, of itself, is eulogium enough concerning this work." He then forcibly adds, "The thought has sometimes crossed my mind of the peculiar circumstances, that the Empire State, which was so long rendered famous by the high decisions of the great Chancelor Kent and Chief Justice Spencer, should cotemporaneously have had its renown in legal authority still further augmented by the elaborate work on Medical Jurisprudence, with which the name of Professor Beck will ever be identified." [1]

In 1829, Dr. Beck was elected president of the Medical Society of the State of New York; and, in 1836, he was appointed Professor of Materia Medica in the College at Fairfield, which position he held until the final closing of the institution in 1840, when he was elected to the same chair in the Albany Medical College. That professorship he held until 1854, when declining health caused him to resign it. From 1841, until his death, he occupied the important post-

---

1. Anniversary Discourse before the New York Academy of Medicine, 1847.

tion of Secretary of the Board of Regents of the State of New York. In February, 1855, Dr. Beck became seriously ill, and from that time he gradually wasted away, until the 19th of November following, when the spirit of this great and good man departed for its home. His death was a public calamity, and was mourned as such by those numerous societies of which he was a member,[1] as well as by all who appreciated private worth and eminent public services. The papers from his pen, read before various societies, and his contributions to the scientific periodicals of his day, form remarkable and most valuable gifts to the common fund of American literature. The time is near when Dr. Beck will be regarded as one of the noblest, wisest, and best of the sons of the State of New York.

ABBOTT LAWRENCE.

THE wise man in Holy Writ said, "Seest thou a man diligent in his business? he shall stand before kings; he shall not stand before mean men." Nobly was this assertion vindicated in the life of Abbott Lawrence, one of the "merchant princes" of New England, and a philanthropist of truest stamp. He was a practically useful man, and while, in business operations, he helped himself, he was continually helping others. Mr. Lawrence could trace his pedigree back to the reign of Richard Cœur de Lion, toward the close of the twelfth century; and he was lineally descended from Sir Robert Lawrence of that period, whose family, in subsequent years, intermarried with the noble family of Washington. Abbott Lawrence was born at Groton, Massachusetts, on the 16th of December, 1792, and received his education at the local school in the place of his nativity. At the age of sixteen years young Lawrence entered the store of his brother Amos, in Boston, as clerk. He took with him his bundle under his arm, with less than three dollars in his pocket, and these composed his whole fortune. After five years of faithful service, his brother took him into partnership. Soon the business horizon was clouded by the gathering storm of war between the United States and England, and Abbott became a bankrupt. He applied to the War Department for a commission in the army, but before his application was acted upon, peace was proclaimed. With the generous aid of his brother Amos, the two commenced business again, after the war, and Abbott went to England to purchase goods, and forward them to Boston. Through his skill, industry, and prudence, he greatly benefited the firm, and they were rewarded by large profits. He made several other voyages to England on business errands: and when in the 27th year of his age [June 28, 1819], he was married to the eldest daughter of Timothy Bigelow, an eminent lawyer in Boston. At about this time his mind was much occupied with the subject of domestic manufactures, and with uncommon foresight, Amos and Abbott Lawrence ceased importing British goods, and employed their energies and capital in the establishment of home manufactures. They associated themselves with the Lowells and others; and the most ennobling monuments in commemoration of these men of business, are the great manufacturing towns of Lowell and Lawrence.

From the period of the establishment of cotton manufactures, that subject occupied much of the thought and labors of Abbott Lawrence; and in 1827,

---

1. Dr. Beck was an honorary member of no less than twenty-one learned societies, at home and abroad, and was a member of many others. He was also presented with the honorary degree of LL.D. by two colleges.

he was a delegate in a convention held at Harrisburg, in Pennsylvania, whose memorial to Congress resulted in the tariff act of 1828, that so aroused the violent opposition of the cotton-producing States. In 1834 Mr. Lawrence was elected a member of the Federal House of Representatives, and served on the important Committee of Ways and Means. Having no desire for official station, other than a willingness to serve the public when absolutely necessary, he declined a re-election; but, four years later, he yielded to the importunities of friends, and was again sent to Congress. At Washington city he suffered long sickness from fever, and was compelled to resign his seat, and return home. There he was efficient in quieting the public feeling aroused by the suspension of specie payments by the banks. In his judgment the people had implicit confidence; and Daniel Webster showed great sagacity when he suggested Mr. Lawrence as the proper person to negotiate with the British Commissioner upon the settlement of the North-eastern boundary question.

In 1843, Mr. Lawrence, with his family, embarked for England, in quest of health. The vessel in which they departed was wrecked, but Mr. Lawrence and his family arrived safely at Halifax, and from there continued their voyage. President Taylor afterward invited him to a seat in his cabinet, but he declined the honor. Then the mission to England was offered him, and this he accepted. The duties of the station he performed with great credit to himself, and the honor of his country. After three years' service as a diplomat, he resigned, and returned home, followed by the warmest expressions of regard from the best men of England. At the funeral of Daniel Webster he met several of his Boston friends, for the first time, after his return, and this solemn occasion prevented his acceptance of a public dinner, tendered to him. This truly great and good man (for he was a Christian philanthropist)[1] died on the 18th of August, 1855, at the age of almost sixty-three years. On that occasion it may be truly said, that Boston was in mourning. Many closed their places of business; the bells of the churches were tolled; the military companies were out on solemn parade; the flags of ships were placed at half-mast, and minute guns were fired. So passed away one of the merchant princes of New England.

JAMES G. PERCIVAL.

"The world is full of Poetry—the air
Is living with its spirit ; and the waves
Dance to the music of its melodies,
And sparkle in its brightness—earth is veiled,
And mantled with its beauty ; and the walls,
That close the Universe, with crystal, in,
Are eloquent with voices, that proclaim
The unseen glories of immensity,
In harmonies, too perfect, and too high
For ought but beings of celestial mold,
And speak to man, in one eternal hymn,
Unfading beauty, and unyielding power."

THUS, in his happier years, warbled one of our sweet poets, James Gates Percival, but who, in the vale of elder manhood, was frequently so overshadowed by a cloud of melancholy, that he could not discern that upper air which was "living with the Spirit" of Poetry, and glorious promises. He was born in Kensington, Connecticut, on the 15th of September, 1795. His father was an eminent physician in that town, and died while his three sons were quite young, leaving all of them to the care of an excellent mother. James was a precocious child, and with the first dawnings of his genius in infantile years, he gave promises of a brilliant future. He accomplished his academic course of study in brief time, entered Yale College, at the age of sixteen years, and was at the head of his class in 1815, when his tragedy of *Zamor* formed part of the commencement exercises. Previous to this he had written fugitive pieces of poetry of considerable merit. Even as early as his fourteenth year, he wrote a satire in verse, that commanded much attention. In 1820 his first volume of poems was published. It contained the first part of *Prometheus*, a poem in the Spenserian stanza, and was received with favor. He was admitted to the practice of medicine the same year, and went to Charleston, South Carolina, to enter upon the duties of that profession. He found literature far more alluring, and yielded to its temptations. There, in 1822, he published

---

1. Mr. Lawrence gave freely of his wealth for religious and charitable purposes. He gave fifty thousand dollars for the establishment of a scientific school in connection with Harvard College; and when it was in operation, he gave an additional sum of fifty thousand dollars for its use in the way of endowments of professorships, etc. He also bequeathed, in his will, fifty thousand dollars for the establishment of model houses for the poor in Boston. For charitable purposes he left, in all, one hundred and fifty thousand dollars, of which the Public Library of Boston received ten thousand. His brother Amos was still more remarkable for his liberal benefactions. He died in December, 1852, at the age of sixty years. It was found, on an examination of his papers, that during his life he had given away about seven hundred thousand dollars! He was blessed with wealth, and he gladly shared with the needy.

the first number of *Clio*, from which the above epigraph was taken. It was a pamphlet of a hundred pages, in prose and verse. Another number, entirely in verse, appeared soon afterward.

In 1824, Dr. Percival was appointed assistant surgeon in the United States army, and Professor of Chemistry at the Military Academy at West Point. In the course of a few months he resigned his situation there, and became connected, as surgeon, with the recruiting service at Boston. In 1827, he published the third part of *Clio*, in New York; and about that time he was engaged in assisting Dr. Webster in the preparation of the first quarto edition of his great Dictionary. He then translated and edited Malte Brun's Geography, the publication of which was completed in three quarto volumes, in 1843. Fond of nature, he investigated her secrets and her beauties with great zeal, and became a skillful geologist. On account of his extensive knowledge of the sciences, he was appointed in 1835, in conjunction with Professor Shepard, to make a survey of the Mineralogy and Geology of Connecticut; and in 1842 he published a report on the subject, embraced in nearly five hundred pages. In the summer of 1854 he was commissioned State Geologist of Wisconsin, and entered upon the work at once. His first annual report, in a volume of one hundred octavo pages, was published at Madison, Wisconsin, early in 1855. At the time of his death, on the second day of May, of that year, he held the office of State Geologist of Illinois.

Dr. Percival was a man of scholarly tastes and habits, quite eccentric at times, and frequently misanthropic. He was excessively fond of literature and science; and, as a linguistic scholar, he had few superiors. "As a specimen of his readiness," says Duyckinck,[1] "it may be mentioned, that when Ole Bull was in New Haven, in 1844 or 1845, he addressed to him a poem of four or five stanzas in the Danish language." The following is one of the stanzas, with the translation, as given by Duyckinck—

> "Norge, dit Svœrd bler en Lire :
> Himmelen gav hendes Toner,
> Hiertet og Sielen at atyre,
> Fuld som af Kummerens Moner."

Translation—"Norway, thy Sword has become a Lyre—Heaven gave its tones, to lead heart and soul, filled as with grief's longings."

Dr. Percival died at Hazelgreen, Illinois, when at the age of almost sixty years.

JOHN C. SPENCER.

THE Revised Statutes of the State of New York bear evidence of the learning, talent, acumen, and industry of John C. Spencer, one of the most honored sons of the State of New York. He was the son of Chief Justice Ambrose Spencer, and was born at Hudson, New York, on the 8th of January, 1788. He was educated chiefly at Union College, Schenectady, and was admitted to the bar, as a practising lawyer, in 1809, at Canandaigua, where he resided until 1845. At the age of nineteen years he became connected with public affairs, as Secretary to Governor Daniel D. Tompkins. He held various offices, connected with his profession, during the war of 1812-'15, and in the latter

---

1. Cyclopedia of American Literature, Vol II., p. 213.   2. See page 93.

year he was appointed Assistant Attorney General for the western part of New York. He was elected to Congress in 1816, and as chairman of a committee of that body, he drew up a report concerning the affairs of the United States Bank.

In 1820, Mr. Spencer was elected to the New York Assembly, and was chosen speaker. In 1824 he was elected to the State Senate, where he served four years. He joined the Anti-masonic party, and was appointed by Governor Van Buren, special Attorney-General, under the law passed for that purpose, to prosecute the persons connected with the alleged abduction of Morgan. He was again elected to the Assembly in 1832; and in 1839 he was chosen Secretary of State, and became, ex-officio, Superintendent of Common Schools. In that office he rendered important public service, by perfecting the Common School System of the State of New York. In 1841 he was appointed one of the Regents of the University; and the same year President Tyler called him to his cabinet as Secretary of War. He was made Secretary of the Treasury in 1843, but resigned that office the following year, chiefly because of his opposition to the admission of Texas.

Eminent as was Mr. Spencer in every field of labor upon which he entered, his chief fame will ever rest upon his services in revising the Statutes of the State of New York, and his published essays upon that subject, explaining the purposes of the Statutes. So perfect was the confidence in his ability, that he was selected to revise the whole body of the Law of his native State, but he declined the task, on account of his age and growing infirmities. He died at Albany, his residence from the year 1845, on the 18th of May, 1855, at the age of sixty-seven years.

ROBERT L. STEVENS.

THE history of successful steam navigation forms a wonderful chapter in the record of inventions and human progress; and the first, as well as the greatest achievements by its means, have been won by Americans. Next to the name of Fulton, as one of the pioneers in the progress of this great industrial agent, stands the name of Stevens, father and son, of Hoboken, New Jersey. The father was John Stevens, a man of inventive genius, and owner of the territory now known as Hoboken, opposite New York city. He was engaged with John Fitch [2] in some of his experiments in steam navigation; and thus, in earliest life, his son, Robert L. (who was born at Hoboken in 1788), became familiar with the subject. The inventive and mechanical abilities of Robert were early developed; and several years before Fulton made the first exhibition of his steam-boat, he and his father had succeeded in propelling a small paddle-wheel vessel, by steam, upon a broad ditch near Hoboken. This little craft they named the *Mary Ann*. They also built a screw-propeller at Hoboken, similar in form and principle to that of Captain Ericsson's of our day.

The greater portion of Robert L. Stevens's life was spent in business connected with steam navigation, and many of the most useful inventions pertaining thereto are the productions of his genius. He was the first to discover a method for saving the power lost in the working of machinery by steam. The remedy which he first applied was the contrivance known as the *Eccentric Wheel*. Subsequently he produced a better invention for that purpose known as the *Patent Steam Cut Off*, which was long in general use, but which has since been superseded by improvements upon his valuable hints. He was the first to devise a plan for passing the exhaust steam from bow to stern, under flat-bottomed boats, by which they may be raised some six inches, thereby allowing them greater speed, and adapting them, in a peculiar manner, to shallow water. Mr. Stevens was also the first to use steam in propelling ferry-boats, it having been applied to a boat on the Barclay-street ferry, as early as 1817.

Soon after the war of 1812, Mr. Stevens invented a bomb, but declined applying for a patent. The government, perceiving its value, secured a right to its exclusive use, by granting Mr. Stevens an annuity equivalent to five dollars a day during his life. When railways and locomotives came into use in 1828, the subject instantly attracted the earnest attention of Mr. Stevens. Several of the best of the earlier machines in use in this country were invented by him, and many of the improvements now used are of his suggestion.

Several years ago Mr. Stevens's attention was turned to the art of gunnery, and for nearly twelve months he experimented, near Hoboken, for the purpose of testing the powers of a cannon-shot upon plates of iron. He erected a target, upon which he fastened iron plates of different thicknesses, in compact order, and fired balls against them. He then fixed plates of the same thickness, a little distance apart, and found the latter mode much the best for resisting the balls. By that arrangement, the force of the heaviest shot might be broken and spent, without perforating more than four or five of such plates. When satisfied with his experiments, he called the attention of our government to them, and proposed the erection of an immense floating battery, with such guards, to be ball and bomb-proof, for the defense of the harbor of New York. The government authorized him to construct one, and he was busily engaged upon it at the time of his death. It is to be seven hundred feet in length, of six thousand tons' burden, to be propelled by engines, without masts, to bear thirty heavy guns upon each side, and four Paixhan guns upon its deck, and to be so constructed that its ends, being driven into an ordinary ship, would cut it in two. It is intended to have this monster of destruction moored in the harbor of New York, midway between the Battery and the Narrows. The work upon it is carried on in secret, within an inclosure. Already more than a million and a quarter of dollars have been spent on it, and yet it is not completed.

Mr. Stevens was actively engaged in business until a month before his death, which occurred at his residence, at River Terrace, Hoboken, on Sunday morning, the 20th of April, 1865, when he was about sixty-eight years of age.

WASHINGTON IRVING.

AT the close of the Indian Summer in 1859, the writer dined at "Sunnyside," on the Hudson, at the table of Washington Irving. He was then suffering from difficult breathing, which was an exception to his usual good health and spirits. A fortnight afterwards the mortal remains of the master of "Sunnyside" was laid by the side of those of his mother, in the burial-ground on the borders of that "Sleepy Hollow" so immortalized in Irving's legendary story.

That sweetest of humorists and story-tellers was born in the city of New York, on the 3d of April, 1783. His father was a descendant of one of the oldest families of the Orkney Islands, who had emigrated to America about twenty years before. Books were favorites in his family; and at an early age Washington delighted in reading the poems of Chaucer and Spenser. Out of their wells of wisdom, fancy and imagination he drew much of the inspiration which served him and his generation so nobly afterward. Fond of novelty, he was in the

habit, while yet a little child, of strolling alone out of town to observe the varied aspects of nature, and to wander along the wharves or into the bye-places of the city, studying the peculiarities of men. In this habit may be found the germ of many of his literary productions.

At the age of sixteen years young Irving left the common school in which he had been educated, and began the study of law. He loved literature better, and at nineteen he began to write for the "Morning Chronicle," edited by his elder brother, Peter, over the signature of "Jonathan Old Style." A little later (1804) his health failed and he went to the South of Europe to seek its recovery. He loitered along the shores of the Mediterranean Sea, and among its islands, for several months; and in the Spring of 1805, he found himself in Rome, where he met Washington Allston[1] and resolved to become a painter. He soon changed his mind, and wandering through Italy, Switzerland, France, a part of Germany, and Holland, he reached London after an absence from home of eighteen months.

Mr. Irving returned to New York in March, 1806, and resumed his law studies. He was soon admitted to the bar, but sooner left it for literary pursuits. With his brother, William, and James K. Paulding, he produced a series of periodical publications entitled "Salmagundi: or the Whim Whams and Opinions of Launcelot Langstaff and Others." They were full of satire, wit and good humor, and made a great local sensation. Not long afterward appeared the inimitable burlesque "History of New York," by Diedrich Knickerbocker, which attracted attention at home and abroad.

---

1. See page 262.

Mr. Irving now engaged with two of his brothers, in mercantile pursuits, he being a silent partner and left free to spend his time as he pleased. He edited the "Analectic Magazine" during the War of 1812, and wrote for it many charming biographies of naval heroes. For awhile he was on the staff of Governor Tompkins. At the close of the war he revisited England, and while there a commercial revulsion swept away his business house and reduced him to poverty. He turned to literature for a subsistence. Mr. (afterward Sir Walter) Scott was his friend in need. "The Sketch Book" laid the foundation of his fame and fortune; and during seventeen years that he remained abroad, he wrote a large portion of his books.

In 1829, Louis M'Lane, American Minister at the British Court, chose him to be his Secretary of Legation. In 1831, the University of Oxford conferred upon him the degree of LL. D.; and in May, 1832, he returned to his native country. Ten years afterward he was appointed Minister to Spain, which position he filled for four years. Soon after he returned home (1848–'50,) Mr. Putnam published a revised edition of his works in fifteen volumes. Meanwhile he had resumed labor upon a "Life of Washington," which he had begun several years before, and laid aside. It was finished in five volumes, early in 1859. This was his longest, most laborious, and last work. He had suffered from unsuspected disease of the heart for some time. He supposed his difficult breathing, at times, to be the effect of some other cause. "I am suffering," he said in a letter to the writer, a few months before his death, "from a nervous affection, caused by asthma." A sudden paroxysm of his disease terminated his life soon after he had retired to his room on the night of the 28th of November, 1859. A more gentle human spirit never inhabited the form of man. Every body loved him. For more than a year after his burial, the hands of his fair neighbors laid fresh flowers, every morning, upon his modest grave, at whose head is a small white slab bearing only the words—WASHINGTON IRVING.

FRANCIS WAYLAND.

AMONG the enlightened and progressive educators of our time, the name of Francis Wayland appears conspicuous; and his successful presidency over an important seminary of learning for the space of thirty years, marks him as a man of eminence. He was born in the city of New York, on the 11th of March, 1796. His father was a popular Baptist clergyman, a native of England. He was settled as pastor of a Baptist congregation, in Poughkeepsie, on the Hudson, and afterward at Saratoga Springs. At Poughkeepsie Francis commenced his academic studies under Daniel A. Barnes, and at the age of seventeen years, he was graduated at Union College with honor. In that institution he was noted for his love of metaphysical and economic studies.

Young Wayland prepared himself for the practice of medicine, in the office of Eli Burritt, in Troy, New York; but he was drawn from that vocation by a conviction that it was his duty to engage in the work of the Christian ministry. He spent a year at Andover, and then entered Union College as a tutor, while pursuing his theological studies, and others connected with literature and science.

In 1821, Mr. Wayland was ordained pastor of the first Baptist church in Boston. He left that pulpit in 1826, to take the chair of Professor of Mathematics and Natural Philosophy in Union College. He was soon called from that post to preside over Brown University, at Providence, Rhode Island, into which important office he was installed in February, 1827. That institution was then in a low condition. He soon brought order out of the comparative chaos in which he found it, and for several years the instruction and discipline of the school were entirely in his hands. He managed both with great ability. He obtained a liberal endowment for the college, yet it did not flourish. He was satisfied that its stagnation was owing chiefly to the vicious system of college education which Americans had borrowed from the English, and made worse. He investigated the subject closely, and gave his views in a little work entitled "Thoughts on the College System of the United States." He finally consented to remain President of the University on condition that the institution should be reorganized upon a plan he had proposed, and be liberally endowed. The change was agreed upon, and in the course of four months, an endowment fund of $125,000 was raised by subscription. After settling the University upon a solid foundation, under the new system which was inaugurated in 1850–'51, and seeing its catalogue of students and its usefulness constantly increasing, he resigned the presidency of it on account of impaired health. That act took place in August, 1855. From that time until his death at Providence, Rhode Island, on the 26th of September, 1865, he was engaged in literary pursuits, and in a multitude of services for the good of his fellow men.

President Wayland was honored by Harvard University with the degree of LL. D. in recognition of his services as instructor, orally and by writings. His "Elements of Moral Science," "Elements of Political Economy," and "Elements of Intellectual Philosophy," have maintained their position as text-books. Besides these, he published several volumes, comprising letters and discourses on moral and religious subjects, memoirs, etc. He was greatly beloved by all; and he was so popular in Rhode Island that he might have received any official honors in the gift of the people, had he consented to accept them.

GEO. P. MORRIS.

THE most genuine lyric poet who has yet honored American literature, was George P. Morris. His songs are almost as familiar to American and English households as the music of birds, and they are ever welcome guests, for they are chaste in language and sentiment. They are magnetic because of their sympathy with the finer feelings of human nature. The author's genial humor, and kindliness of heart were ever manifest in his writings; and these qualities gave him hosts of friends even among those who never looked upon his ruddy face and sparkling black eyes.

George P. Morris was a native of Philadelphia, where he was born on the 10th of October, 1802. He became a resident of New York city when a small child; and at the age of fifteen years he commenced his literary life by writing verses for the "New York Gazette" and "American" newspapers. In the Summer of 1823 he formed a partnership with Samuel Woodworth, a brother poet, in the publication of a quarto literary periodical, called "The New York Mirror," which was the first of its class, and was exceedingly popular during a career of nineteen years. It was discontinued at the close of 1842. The "Mirror" was the chosen vehicle of some of their best communications with the public, by Bryant, Halleck, Paulding, Leggett, Fay, Hoffman, Willis, and others of lesser note. The latter was associated with Morris in 1843, in the publication of the "New Mirror." This was superseded in 1844 by the "Evening Mirror." These publications were not very successful, and in 1845, Morris commenced publishing, alone, a paper called the "National Press." That title was soon changed to that of "Home Journal." Willis joined Morris in the publication of this paper, and it became very popular. Their partnership and warm personal friendship continued until Morris's death, which occurred in the city of New York, on the 6th of July, 1864.

It was not as a journalist that General (he held the office of brigadier) Morris won his widest popularity. It was chiefly and most substantially by his songs. These were ever sought after; and Balfe, Sir John Stephenson, Sir Henry Bishop and other English composers wedded them to sweet melodies, when they were sung by Malibran, Braham, Russell, Dempster, Anna Bishop and other noted vocalists, at public concerts. Millions of copies of "Woodman Spare that Tree" were sold; and other songs, such as "We were Boys together," "My Mother's Bible," "Origin of Yankee Doodle," "Long Time Ago," were sources of great profit to author and publisher, because of their popularity.

General Morris's poems have been published in volumes at different times. He also published a volume of humorous prose, entitled "The Little Frenchman and his Water Lots." He published a volume in 1853, entitled "The Deserted Bride and other Poems." He also produced a drama called "Briercliff," its incidents drawn from events of the American Revolution. He also wrote an opera entitled "The Maid of Saxony," which was set to music by Charles E. Horn. He edited a volume of "American Melodies," and he and Willis jointly prepared a large volume entitled "The Prose and Poetry of Europe and America."

On a picturesque plateau at the foot of a precipitous mountain in the Hudson Highlands near the village of Cold Spring, was the Summer residence of General Morris, which he called "Undercliff." There he ever dispensed an open-handed and open-hearted hospitality to friends and strangers.

EDWARD EVERETT.

AMONG the more eminent scholars and statesmen of our land no one has ever been more deservedly honored for intellectual power, purity of character, public and private, and for clearness of perception and judgment, than Edward Everett. He was born in Dorchester, close by the New England capital, on the 11th of April, 1794. He entered Harvard College as a student at the age of thirteen years; and when he was a little more than seventeen years old he was graduated with the highest honors of his class of uncommonly able students. While he was yet an undergraduate, he was the chief conductor of a magazine called the "Harvard Lyceum."

Young Everett remained in the college as a tutor for awhile, and was at the same time a divinity student. He entered the ministry (Unitarian) in 1813, in the city of Boston, and was eminent from the beginning as a polished pulpit orator and logician. In 1814 he was appointed to fill the Eliot chair of Greek literature then recently created in Harvard College, but before entering upon his duties there, he thoroughly qualified himself by travel and study in Europe for about four years. During that time he acquired that solid information concerning the history and principles of law, and of the political systems of Europe, which formed the foundation of that broad statesmanship for which he was distinguished.

Mr. Everett exalted and commended classical studies by his class instruction, and by a series of brilliant lectures on Greek literature and Ancient Art. At about the same time he became the conductor of "The North American Review."

In the course of a few years, Mr. Everett had so well prepared himself for popular oratory, that ever after he entered upon its practice in 1824, he held the first rank among American public speakers. His life as a statesman began at the same time, for he was, that year, elected to a seat in the National Congress. He was a member of that body ten years, and during all that period he was one

of the Committee on Foreign Relations, a part of the time as Chairman. He was a laborious and most valuable worker in the public service; and on nearly every occasion he was chosen by the Standing or Select Committee of which he was a member, to draw up their report. These papers were models in every sense. His essays on public affairs, in the form of letters or otherwise, were extensively read at home and abroad.

In 1834, Mr. Everett was chosen Governor of his native State, and was three times reëlected. In that position as well as in all others, his speeches, prepared with great care, were always most perfect of their kind.

In June, 1840, Mr. Everett again visited Europe, accompanied by his family. The same year he was appointed resident Minister of his government at the British Court. It was an important mission, for the relations of his country with Great Britain then wore a grave aspect. His official career in London was eminently successful. Pacific relations were preserved and the interests of his countrymen were secured. His personal accomplishments made him a favorite with the leading men and families of England; and his departure, in 1843, to enter upon a new field of duty as Commissioner to China, was regretted by all.

On his return from China in 1845, Mr. Everett was chosen President of Harvard University. Ill health compelled him to resign the place at the end of three years. On the death of Mr. Webster, in 1852, President Fillmore called Mr. Everett to fill the thus vacated position in his Cabinet as Secretary of State. He performed the arduous and delicate duties of that office, at a trying time, with signal ability and success. Meanwhile the Legislature of Massachusetts had elected him to the National Senate, in which he took his seat in March, 1853. Ill health compelled him to resign his seat in the Spring of 1854. Rest restored him, and he entered upon the patriotic task of assisting the Ladies' Mount Vernon Association in raising funds for the purchase of the Home of Washington. He delivered a lecture on the character of that great man, more than a hundred times, and applied the proceeds to the good purpose. His efforts placed over sixty thousand dollars in the treasury. He delivered other addresses in aid of benevolent institutions; and it is probable that his oratory won for such purposes at least one hundred thousand dollars.

In 1860, Mr. Everett was nominated for Vice President of the United States by the so-called "Union Party," with John Bell, of Tennessee, who was nominated for President. The ticket did not succeed. The late Civil War broke out, and Mr. Everett took strong ground, with great zeal, against the insurgents. The last act of his political life was the casting of his vote for Abraham Lincoln in 1864, in the Massachusetts Electoral College, of which he was a member.

Mr. Everett's death was very sudden. On the 9th of January, 1865, he spoke at Faneuil Hall, in Boston, in favor of sending provisions to the destitute inhabitants of Savannah. He was affected by a severe cold for a few days afterward. He went to his bed on the evening of the 14th without any apprehensions of serious difficulty, but was found in a dying state early the next morning. Before his physician arrived he was dead. The Secretary of State at Washington (Mr. Seward) announced the sad tidings to the people of the United States on the same day.

N. P. WILLIS.

WHEN, about the year 1822, the late Rembrant Peale was painting in Boston, he met a youth in the street, about sixteen years of age, whose beauty of features, and especially his exquisite complexion, impelled him to invite the lad to his studio for the purpose of painting his portrait. That youth was Nathaniel Parker Willis, the son of a publisher, who was born in Portland, Maine, on the 20th of January, 1807. His family removed to Boston when he was about six years of age; and at the Latin School in that city, and the Phillips Academy at Andover, he was prepared for a collegiate course. He was graduated at Yale College at the age of twenty years, with the reputation of a good scholar and poet of much promise. He wrote and published a series of Scripture sketches in rhyme while he was a student; and he won a prize of fifty dollars offered by a publisher for the best poem.

Immediately after his graduation, young Willis was employed in editorial labors by Samuel G. Goodrich (Peter Parley,) and at the same time he established the "American Monthly Magazine." This was afterward merged into the "New York Mirror," in which, a few years later, appeared a series of brilliant sketches of travel, entitled "Pencilings by the Way," from Mr. Willis's pen. These were spirited and picturesque descriptions of scenes and incidents of the author's experience during a long tour in the countries bordering on the Mediterranean, Levant and Black seas. He went to England, and there, in 1835, he married a daughter of General Stace, commander of Woolwich Arsenal. In England, as well as on the Continent, he enjoyed society in the higher circles.

On his return to America, with his bride, in 1837, Mr. Willis purchased a small estate near Owego, New York, which he called "Glenmary." There he resided until 1839, when he revisited England, and there wrote the letter-press for Bartlett's "Views of the Scenery of the United States and Canada." In 1844, he was in New York, where he associated himself with General Morris in the publication of the "Evening Mirror." The death of his wife and his own ill-health caused him to revisit England in 1845. The following year he returned to New York, and was married to a daughter of Joseph Grinnell of New Bedford. With that accomplished woman he lived in a delightful home in a picturesque spot on the western border of Newburgh Bay, near Cornwall (which he named "Idlewild,") until his death, which occurred there on the 20th of January, 1867. He had then been associated for many years with General Morris in editing and publishing the "Home Journal," a popular weekly paper, devoted much to a record of the doings of society in general, and the literary world.

Mr. Willis was a prolific writer of prose and poetry. His published works are comprised in about thirty volumes. We can not enumerate them here. Most of them are familiar to American readers. His writings are mostly discursive. He was possessed of those rare gifts which constitute a great and solid thinker—a philosopher; and he was capable of producing works that might have been eminent standards in literature. But he spent his wonderful powers in such a way—diffusive—that he has left a false impression of his real intellectual character. He is generally regarded as an accomplished poet, and an essayist of great brilliancy employed upon unimportant themes; as a journalist who was more fascinated with the frivolties of fashion, dress and the gay and idle world, than with the higher topics of human thought. Mr. Willis was practically untrue to himself.

HENRY R. SCHOOLCRAFT.

TO Henry Rowe Schoolcraft the world is more indebted for a variety of knowledge of Indian history, ethnology, archæology, character, customs and costumes, than to any other man. He was a native of Watervliet, Albany country, New York, where he was born on the 28th of March, 1793. His ancestral name was Calcraft. The first immigrant of that name, to this country, taught school in Albany, and he was called *School*-craft.

Young Schoolcraft entered Union College as a student at the age of fifteen years, and obtained a knowledge of the natural sciences and some foreign languages from other sources also. He learned the business of glass-making from his father, but loved scientific pursuits better. He explored mineral regions in Missouri and other parts of the then "West," and published an account of his adventures there, in 1825.

Mr. Schoolcraft became much interested in the Indians, with whom he had lived much during his travels; and in 1822 he was appointed Indian Agent on the Northwest frontier, with his headquarters at the Saut St. Marie. He was afterward stationed at Michillimackinac, where he married the grand-daughter of an Indian chief, who had been well educated in Europe, and was a girl of remarkable beauty. For a long period he devoted a greater part of the time to a study of the Indians. Meanwhile, from 1828 to 1832, he was a member of the State Legislature of Michigan, and founded the Historical Society of Michigan. He also founded the Algic Society of Detroit. Two of his lectures on the grammatical construction of the Indian languages were translated by Mr. Duponceau, of Philadelphia, and won for the author the gold medal of the French Institute. His mind and pen worked most industriously, and he published poems, essays and addresses.

At the head of an exploring party in 1832, Mr. Schoolcraft was the first to discover the real chief source of the Mississippi River, in Lake Itasca. He was engaged successfully in making treaties with the Indians for the cession of lands to the United States; and was, for some time, chief superintendent of Indian affairs and disbursing agent for the northern department. He visited Europe in 1842, and on his return he made a tour in Western Virginia, Ohio and Canada, and communicated what he had discovered of Indian Antiquities to the Royal Antiquarian Society of Denmark, of which he was an honorary member.

In 1845, Mr. Schoolcraft, by authority of the Legislature of New York, made a census of and gathered a large amount of statistics concerning the Six Nations, which was published in a condensed form, in 1848. Early in 1847, the National Congress, appreciating the importance of his labors, passed a resolution under which he was engaged in the preparation of an elaborate work on the Indians. Six large quarto volumes of this work had appeared at the time of his death, with the title of "Historical and Statistical Information respecting the History, Condition and Prospects of the Indian Tribes of the United States." He resided in the city of Washington while engaged upon this great work, and there he died, after suffering sometime from partial paralysis, on the 10th of December, 1864.

JOSIAH QUINCY.

"KING Josiah the First" was the title given to a caricature of Josiah Quincy, of Boston, while he was the leader of the Federal party in the National Congress. It was in allusion to his almost regal sway over that body, his party, and the majority of the people of New England at the beginning of our last war with Great Britain. Mr. Quincy was then in the full vigor of mature manhood. He was born in Boston on the 4th of February, 1772, and was the only child of Josiah Quincy, Jr., the eloquent orator and zealous patriot when the old war for independence was a-kindling.

Josiah Quincy was graduated at Harvard College in 1790, at the age of eighteen years, with the highest honors of his class. Three years later he commenced the practice of law in Boston, but was more enamored with politics and public life, than with his profession. It was at the period of the formation of the two great political parties known respectively as Federal and Republican. He associated with the former party, took an active part in all its operations in his section, and in the year 1800 was its candidate for a seat in the national House of Representatives. He was defeated, but won the honor in 1804, and took his seat in Congress in December, 1805. There he was kept by successive elections until 1813, when he retired to private life with the intention of devoting his time chiefly to agricultural pursuits at his country seat in Quincy, Massachusetts.

In Congress Mr. Quincy's fiery eloquence and commanding force of character made him a conspicuous leader. He denounced the war declared against Great Britain, in 1812, as unnecessary and unjustifiable; but when it was begun, he patriotically laid aside all prejudices and opinions of his own, and voted for supplies of men and money.

Mr. Quincy's abilities were of too high an order to allow him to withhold them altogether from the public service. He was soon drawn out from his quiet retreat to engage in the turmoil of politics. In 1814, he was elected to a seat in the Massachusetts Senate, and he continued to occupy it until 1820. Then he was elected a member of his State's House of Representatives, and chosen to be its Speaker. In 1821, he was made Judge of the municipal court of Boston, in which capacity he was the first to declare, in the face of prevailing ideas and the common practice, that the publication of the truth with good motives is not libelous. In 1823 he was elected Mayor of Boston. He held that office until

1828, when he was chosen President of Harvard University, and entered upon its duties in June, 1829. These duties he continued to perform with signal ability until the summer of 1845, when he was seventy-three years of age. Then he made a final withdrawal from public life.

Mr. Quincy's remaining years, which were many, were happily spent in literary employment, and in rare social enjoyments. A Memoir of his Father; a "History of Harvard University," in two volumes; "Municipal History of Boston during Two Centuries," and a "Life of John Quincy Adams," comprise his most conspicuous writings. He always took a lively interest in public affairs; and when he was eighty-two years of age (1856,) he wrote and spoke in public in behalf of the Republican party, then just formed, and of its candidate for President, Colonel Fremont.

Mr. Quincy was a firm supporter of the government when the late civil war broke out, in 1861; and at the age of ninety years, he made a public harangue, in which he said that he regarded the war as a most hopeful sign of the future prosperity of the Republic, and predicted that the date of its close would be the commencement of a new and more glorious era of our national greatness. To-day that prediction is evidently fulfilled.

Mr. Quincy was the last survivor of the members of Congress during the war of 1812. He had outlived the political cotemporaries of his earlier years. He, too, died when he was some months more than ninety-two years of age. That event occurred on the first day of July, 1864, at his ancestral home, in Quincy.

NATHANIEL HAWTHORNE.

IN Salem—quaint and curious to the apprehension of the student of our social, religious and political history—the theatre of events which form some of the most remarkable episodes in the chronicles of New England, Nathaniel Hawthorne was born, on "Independence Day," in the year 1804. He was the product of the genuine Puritan seed planted there when John Endicot set out the pear-tree yet flourishing in green old age.

Living on the borders of the sea, Hawthorne's ancestors, for several generations, were mariners. The last of that profession, in direct line, was his father, who died of fever in Calcutta, in 1810. Nathaniel was a delicate boy, yet he went well through preparations for higher studies, and entered Bowdoin College, in Maine, where he was graduated at the age of twenty years, with Longfellow, the poet, and other men who have become eminent. The habits of his early life were peculiar. He was a recluse, seldom walking out excepting at night, and passing the day in his room indulging his imagination in writing wild stories and burning many of them when finished. Some were saved and anonymously published; and in 1837 he made a collection of them and issued them in a volume with the title of "Twice-told Tales." These were recognized by the appreciating few as the fruits of rare genius, and they gradually won their way to popular favor. In the following year, Mr. Bancroft, the historian, then collector of customs at Boston, gave Mr. Hawthorne the office of weigher and gauger. He was displaced by a new collector in 1841, when he joined a community known as the Brook Farm Fraternity, then organizing at Roxbury. In the course of a year he left it, married, made his residence at the old parsonage at Concord, and there hid in seclusion for about three years, when Mr. Bancroft, then Secretary of the Navy, appointed him collector of the port of Salem.

In 1849 there was a change of administration, and Mr. Hawthorne was again displaced. He moved to a cottage in Lennox, where he wrote his remarkable romance, "The House with Seven Gables." This was followed by "The Scarlet Letter" and "Blithedale Romance;" and in 1852, by a "Life of Franklin Pierce," his intimate college friend, then a candidate for the Presidency of the Republic. Mr. Pierce was elected, and appointed Mr. Hawthorne consul at Liverpool. He resigned that office in 1857, traveled on the Continent, and returning home resumed the labors of his pen. He wrote "The Marble Faun," and a collection of sketches of English scenery and character which he called "Our Old Home." He wrote several pleasing books for the young; and until a few weeks before his death he was engaged upon a novel which was to have been published in the "Atlantic Monthly" magazine. It was never finished. Journeying with his friend, Mr. Pierce, to the White Mountains, in search of recreation of body and mind, he was a lodger at the Pemigewasset House, in Plymouth, New Hampshire, on the night of the 18th of May, 1864, and there he died, alone, early on the morning of the 19th. He was a great and original thinker and writer, yet not so well known and admired by the multitude as many men of less genius.

JOHN TYLER.

THE tenth President of the Republic was John Tyler, a native of Charles City county, Virginia, where he was born on the 29th of March, 1790. He was graduated at William and Mary College in 1807, and was admitted to the bar at the age of nineteen years. He was a young man of more than ordinary ability, and soon rose to distinction in his profession. In 1811 he was elected to a seat in the Virginia Legislature, and continued in that position about five years. He was elected to Congress to fill a vacancy, in 1816, where he served, after reëlection, until 1819. He was elected governor of Virginia in 1825, and after serving two years, was chosen to represent his State in the National Senate. He continued in that office until 1836. In 1840 he was elected Vice President of the United States, when General Harrison was elected President.[1] The latter died a month after his inauguration, in the Spring of 1841, when Tyler became President. At the close of his administration he retired to private life, from which he emerged in the winter of 1861, when he espoused the cause of the conspirators against the life of the Republic. He was president of the so-called "Peace Convention" held in Washington, and was one of the committee who, in April following, transferred the control of all the military forces of Virginia to the so-called Confederate Government, at Montgomery, of which Jefferson Davis was chief. Mr. Tyler took an active part against his country, and was rewarded with the office of "Senator" in the "Confederate Congress" at Richmond. He was acting in that capacity when he died, at Richmond, on the 18th of January, 1862.

MARTIN VAN BUREN.

IN the quiet little village of Kinderhook, in Columbia county, New York, there was an indifferent tavern at the close of the Revolution, kept by a Dutchman named Van Buren. There his distinguished son, Martin, was born on the 5th of December, 1782. He was educated at the Academy in that village, and at the age of fourteen years commenced the study of law. In 1803 he was admitted to the bar. He had a fondness for politics, and attached himself to the Democratic party. In 1808 he was appointed Surrogate of Columbia county; and in 1812 he was elected to a seat in the State Senate. In 1815 he was appointed attorney-general of the State, and the following year he was again elected State Senator. With a few others he now formed a political organization which controlled the politics of the State for twenty years.

In 1821 Mr. Van Buren was chosen by his State Legislature to a seat in the National Senate. He was reëlected to the Senate in 1827, but resigned that office on being chosen governor of New York to fill the vacancy caused by the death of Dewitt Clinton. While in that office he proposed the admirable "Safety Fund" system of banking, which was set in motion. In 1829 he was called into the cabinet of President Jackson as Secretary of State. He resigned the office in April, 1831, and in September following he arrived in England as American Minister at the British Court. His nomination was rejected by the Senate three months afterward, and he returned home. He was on the ticket with Jackson, as a candidate for the Vice-presidency of the republic, in 1832, and was elected; and in 1836 he was elected President of the United States, the eighth incumbent of that office. His term was marked by much excitement, growing out of financial embarrassments throughout the country. He called an extraordinary session of Congress, when the financial measure known as the Independent Treasury System was adopted, on his earnest recommendation.

For several years the Democratic party had been largely in the majority.

---

1. See page 240.

Now came a change, and Mr. Van Buren, who was the Democratic nominee for President, in 1840, was overwhelmingly defeated by General Harrison. In 1844 he was a candidate for another nomination, at Baltimore, but was rejected by the slave-holding interest, and Mr. Polk was chosen in his stead. Four years later he was nominated for the presidency by the "Free-soil Democracy," or that portion of the party who were opposed to the extension of slavery. The Democratic party was divided on that issue, and General Taylor, the Whig candidate, was elected. From that time until his death Mr. Van Buren remained in private life, living most of the time at his home in the village of his birth, excepting when he made a tour in Europe in 1853, 1854 and 1855. When the civil war broke out in 1861, Mr. Van Buren expressed himself decidedly in favor of the maintenance of the Union. He did not live to see the end of the conflict. He died at his fine mansion, in Kinderhook, on the 24th of July, 1862, at the age of eighty years.

EDWARD ROBINSON.

THERE are few biblical scholars and writers on the sacred books to whom the world is so much indebted for accurate knowledge of Palestine and its neighborhood, which Jews and Christians fondly call the "Holy Land," as to Edward Robinson, whose learning and patience achieved great things in the field of research. He was a native of Southington, Connecticut, where he was born on the 10th of April, 1794. He was graduated at Hamilton College, in New York, at the age of twenty-two, and remained there as tutor until 1821, when he removed to Andover, Massachusetts. At the theological seminary there he studied the Hebrew language; and he engaged with Professor Stuart in the translation of some text-books in German.

In 1826, Mr. Robinson went to Europe, where he spent four years in studying and traveling. At Halle, in Germany, he married the daughter of Professor von Jakob, who afterward became widely known in both hemispheres by her writings over the signature of "Talvi." On his return to America in 1830, he was appointed Professor of Sacred Literature and Librarian, at the Andover Seminary, in which position he remained until 1833, when he removed to Boston. Four years afterward he was appointed Professor of Biblical Literature in Union Theological Seminary, in the city of New York. Before entering upon the duties of that office, he visited Palestine, and spent more than a year there, with Dr. Eli Smith, in making a careful geographical survey of that interesting country. At Berlin he prepared an account of their operations, for the press, and his celebrated work entitled "Biblical Researches in Palestine, and in the Adjacent Countries: a Journal of Travels in the year 1838," was published simultaneously in Europe and in America. He made his residence in New York in 1840, and from that time until the year of his death, he held the professorship in the theological seminary there, already mentioned.

The honorary titles of D. D. and LL. D. were conferred upon Mr. Robinson, the latter by Yale College; and he was always an honor to the title and the institution. In 1852, he revisited Palestine, with Dr. Smith, and made many important discoveries, especially among the ruins of Jerusalem. He published a volume embodying a narrative of new discoveries, in 1856. At the time of his death he was engaged in the preparation of a physical and historical geography of the Holy Land. He did not live to complete it. His death occurred in the city of New York on the 27th of January, 1863.

Dr. Robinson was not only a most profound biblical scholar, but a philologist and linguist of rare repute. He translated several Greek and Hebrew text-books, as well as other standard works in the Greek language; also Calmet's "Biblical Dictionary." He edited, for several years, the "Biblical Repository," and "Bibliotheca Sacra;" and was a prominent member of the New York Historical Society, and of the American Geographical, Ethnological and Oriental Societies.

ELIPHALET NOTT.

HISTORY furnishes no other example of longevity in a single public position, like that of Eliphalet Nott, who was, for the space of sixty-two years, President of Union College, at Schenectada, in the State of New York. He was a native of Ashton, Windham county, Connecticut, where he was born on the 25th of June, 1773. His father had been a merchant, but by a series of misfortunes, he was reduced to poverty and rendered unable to give his son the college education he had intended for him. His mother, a woman of culture, aided him much in the difficult search for knowledge; and his uncle, Rev. Samuel Nott, taught him Latin and Greek. He was so well home-educated, that at the age of sixteen years he was a school teacher in Plainfield, Connecticut. There he studied mathematics and the "dead languages" under the Rev. Dr. Benedict, whose daughter he afterward married. He spent a year at Brown University, and was graduated out of the regular course, in 1795. He studied theology, and entered upon the duties of a minister of the gospel, as a missionary in Central New York, then almost a wilderness. He accepted an invitation to take charge of a congregation at Cherry Valley, where he was also the successful head of an academy for boys. In 1798 he accepted a call to the pastorate of a Presbyterian church in Albany, and there he remained preaching to large and admiring congregations until 1804, when he was chosen President of Union College, at Schenectada: an institution then in its infancy. It was without suitable buildings, library and apparatus, and involved in debt. Mr. Nott gave it the help of his energies of body and mind, without stint; and in 1814 he procured a legislative act for raising money by lottery, which gave it funds and a permanent foundation. The management of the lottery and investment of the funds were left entirely with Mr. Nott; and an investigation of the pecuniary affairs of the institution, made at his request after forty years of his management, showed that every thing had been done wisely and well. He not only made the property of the college valuable, but he added to it a large sum from his own private fortune, at the close of that investigation. He had taken the institution in his arms in its infancy and poverty, and lifted it to honor and wealth.

In 1854, the semi-centennial anniversary of his presidency was celebrated, when nearly seven hundred men, some of the most distinguished in the land, who had been graduated at Union College, came together to do him honor. During his Presidency, over four thousand graduates left the institution.

Dr. Nott (he had received the degrees of D. D. and LL. D.) paid much attention to the subject of heating apartments, and was the inventor of a celebrated stove that bore his name. He was a life-long advocate of temperance, and spoke and wrote much on that subject. Many of his discourses were published. Of these, the most celebrated was a sermon preached before the General Assembly of the Presbyterian Church in 1804, on the occasion of the death of Alexander Hamilton.

Dr. Nott was President of Union College at the time of his death, which occurred at Schenectada, on the 29th of January, 1866, when he was almost ninety-three years of age. He had lived to see the government of his country which was established in his youth, settled upon a solid foundation of justice and wisdom; and the fact demonstrated by the results of a great civil war, that of all forms of government for an enlightened people, the republican is the strongest and most stable.

DAVID L. SWAIN.

OF David Lowry Swain it might be justly written as Hannah More wrote of another, saying,

"I've scanned the actions of his daily life
With all the industrious malice of a foe;
And nothing meets my eyes but deeds of honor."

Mr. Swain was an honored statesman and beloved educator. He was born near Asheville, Buncombe county, North Carolina, on the 4th of January, 1801. His earlier education was obtained at the Asheville Academy; and his studies were completed at the University of North Carolina, at Chapel Hill. He was admitted to the practice of the law as a life vocation, in 1823. His rare abilities and excellent deportment soon won for him a lucrative business in his profession.

Mr. Swain began his public career in 1824, when he was elected a representative of his native county in the legislature of North Carolina. He served therein three consecutive years. In 1827 he was solicitor of the Edenton District. He was again in the Legislature in 1828 and 1829; and in 1830 he was elected one of the Board of Internal Improvements. The same year he was chosen to be a judge of the Superior Court of his State. In 1832, he was elected Governor of North Carolina. While holding that office in 1835, he was chosen to a seat in the convention that revised the Constitution of his native State. His influence was potential in that body. In December, that year, he was chosen to fill the important position of President of the University of North Carolina wherein he had been educated. It had been established at Chapel Hill, a few miles from Raleigh, the capital of the State, soon after the old War for Independence. He was the immediate successor of the eminent Dr. Caldwell, its first President.

The most useful part of Governor Swain's life was spent in the conduct of that University. When he was called to assume its control, he was only thirty-four years of age. Nine years before, he had married Eleanor White, a grand-daughter of the eminent patriot, Governor Richard Caswell, who yet (1869) survives him. His administration of the affairs of the University, financial and educational, was eminently successful. When he took charge of it in 1835, the number of its students was eighty. Just before the breaking out of the late civil war, its catalogue contained over four hundred and fifty names. His government was parental, and his influence upon the students was that of "the highest style of man,"—a Christian gentleman.

President Swain was an ardent delver in the rich mines of American history. No man ever worked those of his native State so industriously, patriotically and wisely as he; and when he was summoned to a higher sphere of life, he was about to arrange his collected treasures in proper form for use. "He knew more of North Carolina and of her public men," said a cotemporary, at his death, "than any living man. Perhaps it is not going too far to say that his knowledge upon these two points was more extensive than the combined knowledge of every man in the State." It may be added that at the time of his death, a very large number of the most distinguished men of North Carolina had been his pupils at Chapel Hill. More than a thousand living men had listened to his instruction in that school.

When the late civil war was impending, and after it was kindled, President

Swain did all in his power to calm the troubled waters. He was a Patriot and a Christian, in the highest sense of the terms. He enjoyed the confidence of all; and when Sherman's victorious army was approaching Raleigh in the Spring of 1865, he was at the head of a commission appointed to wait upon that leader and make arrangements for staying bloodshed and devastation in that region. In the heat of passion that everywhere prevailed then, and immediately after the war, President Swain's wise conduct was misinterpreted and misrepresented; and so bitter was the feeling because his daughter, at the close of the war, married General Atkins of the National army, that all support was withdrawn from the University at Chapel Hill, and it was allowed to fall asleep.[1] Its property, excepting its land and buildings, had been wasted by the operations of the war, and it now (1869) seems dead. It will doubtless one day awake from its slumbers with increased vigor, and enter upon a new career of usefulness. And on the tomb of David L. Swain, the good, the wise, the generous benefactor of his race, posterity will write, in spirit,

"He was the noblest Roman of them all."

President Swain was thrown from his light carriage on the 11th of August, 1868. He lingered until the 27th of the same month, when he died at the age of little more than sixty-eight years.

JOHN W. FRANCIS.

ON a chilly day in February, 1861, there was a large concourse of the most noted inhabitants of the city of New York at old St Thomas' church, on the corner of Broadway and Houston street, to pay the last tribute of respect to the remains of an eminent and beloved physician and distinguished citizen. The physician so beloved, and the citizen so esteemed, was John Wakefield Francis, a native of New York city, where he was born on the 17th of November, 1789. He was a printer's apprentice when a small lad, but was afterward prepared for a professional life. He entered Columbia College, in New York, as member of an advanced class, in 1807. At about the same time he began the study of medicine with Dr. Hosack. He was graduated with the degree of Bachelor of Arts in 1809, and received a diploma as Medical Doctor from the College of Physicians and Surgeons, in 1811. He was the first person on whom the degree was conferred by that institution. Soon afterward the medical school of Columbia College was consolidated with that of Physicians and Surgeons, and to young Francis was assigned the chair of materia medica in the united body. He had been associated with Dr. Hosack, as a business partner, soon after his medical graduation, and was a co-laborer with that distinguished physician in the editing and publishing of the "American Medical and Philosophical Register."

Soon after his appointment to the chair of materia medica, in 1813, he went to Europe for the purpose of increasing his knowledge of his profession. There he became acquainted with most of the living men distinguished in science and

---

1. General Atkins' advanced guard entered Chapel Hill on Sunday, the 16th of April, 1865. On the following day the General himself entered with four thousand cavalry, and took possession. He had orders to protect the University buildings and the village, in consequence of President Swain's services on the commission mentioned in the text. He visited at Governor Swain's house, became acquainted with his daughter, who was, being of lawful age, mistress of her own actions, and they were engaged to be married before the Governor suspected the fact. It was not known until after General Atkins' departure, when the affianced informed her father. They were married. Because of this, a noble institution of learning was smitten to death. The folly was soon repented of, when reason and not passion finally bore.

literature; among them Dr. Rees, to whose Cyclopedia he contributed several papers. On his return to New York, he became professor in the College of Physicians and Surgeons, first of the institutes of medicine, and in 1817, of medical jurisprudence. Two years later he was appointed professor of obstetrics, which position he filled until 1826, when, with others, he founded the short-lived institution known as the Rutgers' Medical School, and held in it the professorship of obstetrics and forensic medicine.

While Dr. Francis held these professional positions and filled them with marked industry and ability, he was engaged in an extensive and increasing practice. In addition to his arduous professional duties, he was also continually engaged in literary pursuits. He was a ready and eloquent writer upon whatever subject employed his pen. He was particularly eminent as a biographer, especially of distinguished men with whom he was acquainted; and no one man ever made so many and excellent contributions to the treasury of American biography as he. His essays and discourses on a great variety of topics, occupy a large space in our literature. He was an ardent lover and patron of art; and the deserving man of genius, however humble, always found in him a benefactor and friend. He was honored and beloved by all of the literary men and artists of his day; and men of science esteemed him highly for his genial sympathy in their labors.

Dr. Francis was an active worker in all efforts around him for the promotion of the good of his fellow men; and his influence and services were continually sought, for both were powerful. He took great interest in the New York Typographical Society; the New York Historical Society; the Lyceum of Natural History; the New York Academy of Medicine; the American Academy of Design, and other institutions. He was the first president of the New York Academy of Medicine, which was organized in 1847. He was active in the promotion of the objects of the Woman's Hospital in New York, and the Inebriate Asylum at Binghampton, N. Y.; and he was an honorary member of several foreign and domestic associations. In 1850, Trinity College, at Hartford, conferred upon him the honorary degree of LL. D. In knowledge of the men and things of his native city, he was regarded as an almost unerring oracle. His house was the pleasant resort of intellectual men of every kind, and in their entertainment he was happy in the companionship of his wife, one of the best of women. The social gatherings at his house were kept up until a very short time before his death, which occurred in the city of New York on the 8th of February, 1861. In the death of his promising son, J. W. Francis, Jr.,[1] a few years before, his nervous system received a shock from which he never recovered. His affection for relatives and friends was very strong. His genial good nature made him a delightful companion, and his skill in medicine won for him the profound reverence of his professional cotemporaries. Dr. Francis was "the beloved physician" of his native city.

ABRAHAM LINCOLN.

"WITH malice toward none, with charity for all, with firmness in the right as God gives us to see the right, let us strive to finish the work we are in, to bind up the Nation's wounds, to care for him who shall have borne the battle and for his widow and orphan, to do all which may achieve and cherish a just and lasting peace among ourselves and with all nations." These were the

---

1. See page 407.

closing words of the second inaugural address of Abraham Lincoln, the sixteenth president of the Republic, just before the end of the great Civil War. They are illustrations of the character of the man, who was always patient, kind, forgiving, trusting, wise and patriotic.

Mr. Lincoln was born in Hardin county, Kentucky, on the 12th of February, 1809. His father was an early settler, and struggled hard for a livelihood. When Abraham was in the eighth year of his age, the whole family embarked on a raft on Salt river, went down the Ohio, and settled in the then wilderness of Spencer county, Indiana. There, in a log cabin built by the elder Lincoln's own hands, Abraham's mother taught him to read and write. When he was ten years of age she died. Two years later a kind step-mother took her place. At twelve the boy was taught arithmetic and some other branches of a common school education. But few books fell in his way, and these he read with avidity.

Young Lincoln labored with his father in the solitudes, until, at the age of nineteen, when he was a very tall lad, he made a voyage to New Orleans on a flat-boat, with the son of the owner of it. It bore a valuable cargo, and at one place they were compelled to fight for its preservation from a band of plunderers.

In 1830, the Lincoln family removed to Decatur, Illinois, where young Lincoln assisted his father in clearing and fencing a farm. He was also a clerk in a store a part of the time. In 1832, the conflict known as the "Black Hawk War" broke out on the borders of the Mississippi. Abraham Lincoln enlisted as a volunteer, and as Captain of a company went to the seat of war, but had no fighting. On his return he received a heavy vote for a seat in the Illinois Legislature, but was defeated. Then he opened a store on his own account; was appointed postmaster; studied hard all the time; became a good surveyor, and for about two years made surveying his chief business. He served a term in the Illinois Legislature, in 1834, and then studied law. He was admitted to the bar in 1837, when he was twenty-eight years of age. He soon won reputation and a lucrative practice. He served again in the legislature, ranking as a Whig of the Henry Clay school. He was a ready pleader at the bar, and speaker at public gatherings. In 1846 he was elected to Congress, and was the only Whig Representative from Illinois. There he was marked for soundness of judgment and attachment to the principles of justice and right. He was uniformly a decided but conservative anti-slavery man; and when the Nebraska bill was passed and the "Missouri" compromise was violated, in 1854, he greatly assisted in revolutionizing Illinois politically. Judge Douglas originated the Nebraska bill in the National Senate, and his party (Democratic) suffered in consequence. The Whigs carried the State, and Mr. Lincoln, who was a prominent candidate for the National Senate, generously withdrew in favor of Mr. Trumbull, a rival candidate, who he knew would receive many Democratic votes. Trumbull was chosen.

In 1856, Mr. Lincoln took an active part in favor of the Republicans, and he was a prominent candidate for the Vice-presidency. In 1858, he was a candidate for the National Senate, in opposition to Stephen A. Douglas. They ably canvassed the State together. It was one of the most interesting and able conflicts of oratory ever known in this country. Their speeches were afterward published from phonographic reports. It was generally conceded that Mr. Lincoln was the victor.

Between 1856 and 1860 Mr. Lincoln made several powerful speeches. In May, the latter year, he was nominated for the presidency of the Republic, and elected in November. Leading slaveholders made his election a pretext for an open rebellion which they had long contemplated; and he was inaugurated President on the 4th of March, 1861, when insurrection and rebellion had begun in the Slave-labor States. He met the crisis calmly, generously and firmly; and during the four years of terrible civil war that ensued, he controlled the helm of the ship of State with eminent wisdom and steadiness. At the moment when peace for the saved Republic and rest for himself was near, he was mortally wounded by a ball from a pistol in the hands of an assassin, at a place of public entertainment in Washington city, whither he had been invited. The wound was received on the evening of the 14th of April, 1865, and early the next morning the victim died. The event produced a profound sensation throughout the civilized world. Among the many impressive testimonials of love, esteem and admiration of the martyred President that were given, was a gold medal sent from France to his widow, for the cost of which forty thousand "French Democrats," as they called themselves, made contributions, mostly one sous, each.

JAMES BUCHANAN.

MANY of the strong men, physically and intellectually, who have appeared conspicuously in the annals of our country, have been the children of Scotch-Irish parents. Of such lineage was James Buchanan, the fifteenth President of our Republic. He was born at a place called Stony Batter, in Franklin county, Pennsylvania, on the 23d of April, 1791. He was prepared, at home, for admission to Dickinson College, at Carlisle, as a student, where he was graduated with high honors at the age of eighteen years. He was admitted to the practice of law at the Lancaster bar, in 1812; and toward the close of the war with Great Britain which was declared that year, he went as a volunteer soldier to the defense of Baltimore, but had no occasion for fighting.

Young Buchanan rose rapidly in his profession and won an extensive and lucrative practice. He was always fond of public life. In 1814 he was elected to the Pennsylvania Legislature by the Federalists. In 1820 he was sent to Congress as a representative of the Lancaster District; and he was kept there, by reëlection, until 1831. During that long service he was ranked among the leading members for ability and industry. During the last two years of his service there, he was chairman of the Judiciary Committee. He was appointed by President Jackson, in 1831, American minister to the Russian Court, where he remained only two years. On his return in 1833, he was chosen by the Pennsylvania Legislature to represent that State in the National Congress. Twelve years he was a member of the Senate, and was regarded as the leader of the Democratic party in that body. There he ever strenuously opposed all agitation of the subject of slavery; and during his whole political life he was a zealous and consistent supporter of the policy of the slaveholders.

In 1845, Mr. Buchanan was called to the cabinet of President Polk, as Secretary of State, and was influential in shaping that officer's policy concerning a war with Mexico. From the close of Polk's administration until the accession of President Pierce in 1853, he remained in private life. Then he was sent, as minister, to England. It was during his residence at that court, that a conference of American ministers in Europe, held, at his suggestion, at Ostend, issued that "manifesto" concerning the purchase or seizure of Cuba, which forms one of the most disgraceful records in American diplomacy.

Mr. Buchanan returned home early in 1856, and in July, of that year, he was nominated for the chief magistracy of the Republic, by the Democratic party. He was elected. His administration was marked by an intense agitation of the slavery question, which culminated in civil war in Kansas. Finally, in 1860, the last year of his term of office, when Abraham Lincoln, the nominee of the Republican party was elected President, leaders of the slave interest made earnest preparations for a general insurrection and rebellion. It broke out fiercely in the winter of 1860–'61, before the close of Mr. Buchanan's administration. He took no efficient measures to suppress it; and gladly left the grave responsibilities of his office at that perilous hour, for the quiet of private life at "Wheatland," his seat near Lancaster, Pennsylvania, where he died on the first of June, 1868. Mr. Buchanan was never married. In private life he was a courteous gentleman and an excellent citizen.

JAMES HARPER.

THE sacred Proverbialist says, "Seest thou a man diligent in his business? he shall stand before kings; he shall not stand before mean men." The truth involved in this was illustrated by James Harper, the eldest of four brothers who composed the great publishing house of Harper and Brothers, in New York, which was in existence during fifty years previous to his death.

James Harper was the eldest son of an estimable farmer near Newtown, Long Island, where he was born on the 11th of April, 1795. At the close of 1810, he was apprenticed to Messrs. Paul and Thomas, printers in the city of New York, He was "diligent in his business;" became a perfect master of his trade, and won the respect and confidence of all who knew him. His next brother, John, learned the same business, and the terms of their apprenticeship ended at about the same time. By saving the earnings of overwork, they had, jointly, a few hundred dollars, and with this capital they commenced business on their own account, in 1818. James was a strong young man and one of the best pressmen in the city. John was a very correct compositor and proof-reader. Prompt and skillful in business, they never lacked employment in printing books for others. It was not long before they began to print books for themselves, and selling them to "the trade," as the business of retail bookselling is called. Their first venture was a reprint of "Locke on the Understanding," and it was successful. Others followed. Their younger brothers, Joseph Wesley and Fletcher, were apprenticed to them, and in time became business partners, under the name of Harper and Brothers. Mutual confidence, industry and application to business made the four as one man. They ranked and acted as equals in all things; and mutual agreement was their rule of life in business and in social relations. It was also an element of power. James was once asked, "Which is the 'Harper,' and who are the 'Brothers?'" He replied, "Either of us is 'Harper,' and the rest are the 'Brothers.'" This was precisely their practical relationship.

The history of the house of Harper and Brothers for a long series of years was the history of James Harper, excepting in his private relations. He was reared under the direct influence of the Methodist Episcopal Church, and of that denomination he was a life-long and consistent member. In him the religious sentiment was a controlling power, yet it was never ostentatiously displayed. In his domestic relations he was an excellent exemplar. In the church he was faithful and generous. In the community in which he lived he was deservedly held in the highest esteem.[1] This fact was shown in 1844, when he was elected Mayor of the city of New York by a very large majority, while the party by whom he was nominated was in a decided minority. He had no political ambition, nor a

---

1. Mr. Harper was an active member of religious and benevolent institutions in the city of New York, and a trustee of literary establishments of a high character; among them the Wesleyan University of Middletown, Connecticut, and Vassar College for Young Women, at Poughkeepsie, New York.

thirst for office; and on that occasion he yielded to the importunities of his friends rather than to any suggestions of his own inclinations. He filled the office with ability and general satisfaction.

It was as the head of the leading publishing house in America that James Harper was best and most widely known, and will be chiefly remembered. He dispensed the cheerful hospitality of the establishment; and for each visitor he had a cheery welcome, a kind word, a pleasant anecdote, some sly wit or telling repartee, and a constant flow of good humor, notwithstanding he was often plagued with dull and burdensome people.[1] "He carried the highest principles into the conduct of business," said a leading newspaper[2] at the time of his death, "and he never willingly gave the sanction of his name to unworthy or mischievous productions in literature. No prospects of gain or popular success could tempt him to publish a book which he believed to be injurious to the interests of society. .... Our national literature will reap the benefit of his example in this respect after his kindly face shall no more be seen in our busy haunts, and his personal traits shall fade away from the memory of a new generation."

While riding in his carriage, with his daughter, on Fifth Avenue, New York, his vehicle came in collision with another. He was thrown to the pavement, taken up in an insensible condition and carried to St. Luke's Hospital near by, where he lingered about fifty hours, and then died, on Saturday evening, the 27th of March, 1869. His funeral was attended by the city authorities; the great body of the publishers and booksellers of the city, who closed their places of business; a large number of literary men, and a crowd of other friends, and his relatives. By none, excepting his immediate family, was he so sincerely mourned as by the six hundred men, women and boys employed in the establishment of Harper and Brothers, for he was like a father to them all. Some had been in his employment between forty and fifty years.

WINFIELD SCOTT.

THE military genius of our countrymen was wonderfully developed during the late civil war. Its most distinguished exemplar previous to that was Winfield Scott, who was born in Petersburg, Virginia, on the 13th of June, 1786. He was a grandson of a Scotch soldier who fought for the Young Pretender on the field of Culloden.

Young Scott was a student of William and Mary College for two years, where he studied law and was admitted to the bar at the age of twenty years. He was a very tall and powerful young man, of fine personal appearance. He had a taste for the military profession, and finding an opportunity to enter the army, he procured the commission of captain of artillery. After recruiting a company he reported to General Wilkinson, at Baton Rouge, Louisiana. After Wilkinson left the command there, Captain Scott freely expressed what was generally believed, that his late commander was implicated with Aaron Burr in a conspiracy against the Union.[3] For this he was suspended from rank and pay for a year, by recommendation of a court martial. During that time he studied the

---

1. On one occasion a very prosy clerical friend, who had consumed an hour of his time in small talk, said, "Brother Harper, I am curious to know how you four men distribute the duties of the establishment between you." "John," said Mr. Harper good humoredly, "attends to the finances; Wesley to the correspondence; Fletcher to the general bargaining with authors and others; and—don't you tell anybody," he said, lowering the tone of his voice—"I entertain the bores."
2. The *New York Daily Tribune*, March 29, 1869.
3. See page 253.

military art diligently; and when, in June, 1812, war was declared by our government against Great Britain, he was appointed a lieutenant-colonel.

After the gallant Captain Wool was disabled by wounds at the battle of Queenston, Scott took command there, and first won and then lost the field. He was made a prisoner; with a greater part of the army; and his personal courage and kindness of heart saved a number of his fellow soldiers, who were natives of Ireland, from the vengeance of the British government.

Scott was exchanged in January, 1813, and joined General Dearborn on the frontier as his adjutant. He was very active in the capture of Fort George, where he pulled down the British flag. He served with Wilkinson several months, and was commissioned a brigadier general in March, 1814. During that year he was the hero of many gallant exploits, under General Brown, on the Niagara frontier, where he was twice seriously wounded. For his gallant conduct in the battle of Niagara, he was brevetted a major-general, and received a gold medal from Congress. After the war he went to Europe in the service of the government and for the restoration of his health. He returned in 1816, and was soon afterward married to Miss Mayo of Richmond, Virginia. For several years afterward there were no military movements of much importance.

In 1832, General Scott led in the Black Hawk war, and then went to Charleston to look after the insurrectionary movements of certain Southern politicians. He was conspicuous in hostilities with the Southern Indians. Afterward he was a good peacemaker when the rebellion in Canada and troubles on the eastern frontier threatened his country with hostile relations with Great Britain. In 1838 he had charge of the removal of the Cherokees to new lands west of the Mississippi.

General Scott was presented as the Whig candidate for the Presidency, in 1840, but he declined in favor of General Harrison. On the death of General Macomb the following year, he was appointed general-in-chief of the armies of the Republic, and as such, he conducted military affairs in the war with Mexico, in which he was conspicuously engaged. He was at the head of the victorious American army when it entered the city of Mexico in triumph in September, 1847. He was highly honored by Congress and the people, for his conduct in that war. In 1852, he was nominated for the Presidency, but was defeated. In 1855, he was brevetted lieutenant-general, to take rank from 1847, the close of his services in Mexico.

When the leaders of the slave interest had resolved on rebellion, every inducement was held out to General Scott, as a Virginian, to espouse their cause. He rejected all, and did all in his power first to avert the rebellion, and afterward to crush it. But his infirmities were too great to allow him to act efficiently, and he resigned his position as the chief of the army, in the autumn of 1861, when he made a voyage to Europe and a brief stay there. He lived to see the war end and the authority of the government vindicated. His character was unstained. His honor was perfect. His career was brilliant and untarnished. His patriotism was pure and exalted. At the time when he left the command of the army, he was regarded as one of the greatest military men of the age. His physical powers gradually declined, and on the 29th of May, 1866, he died at West Point, on the Hudson, near the Military Academy, at the age of eighty years.

JOHN ELLIS WOOL.

NO man ever had a purer record of his public life than Major General John Ellis Wool, who held a commission in the regular army of the Republic for the period of fifty-seven years. Fifty-three of those years he was in active service, in peace or war.

General Wool was the son of a soldier of the Revolution, and was born in the village of Newburgh, on the Hudson River, in the year 1788. On the death of his father, when he was only four years of age, he went to live with his grandfather, in Rensselaer County, N. Y., where he received a common school education. At the age of twelve years he was taken from school and apprenticed as clerk to a merchant, in Troy. At the age of eighteen years he opened a bookstore in that place. A fire swept away all his worldly goods, and he commenced the study of law. War with Great Britain commenced soon afterward. In the spring of 1812, before it was declared, he was commissioned a captain in the Thirteenth Regiment of Infantry. In September following, his regiment, under Lieutenant Colonel Chrystie, was ordered to the Niagara frontier, and there, in the battle at Queenston, the following month, he performed gallant service as leader of the troops after Colonel Van Rensselaer was disabled by a wound. Captain Wool was shot through both thighs, but fought on until a superior officer took command. For his gallant conduct there, he was promoted to Major in the Twenty-ninth Infantry, in the spring of 1813. For bravery and skill at and near Plattsburg in September, 1814, he was promoted to Lieutenant Colonel in December.

At the close of the war, Lieutenant Colonel Wool was retained in the army. When peace was declared, he obtained a furlough for a fortnight, during which time he was married to a charming young woman, who survived him after a wedlock of more than fifty-three years. That was the only furlough he ever asked for, during his long military service.

In September, 1816, he was appointed inspector-general of division; and in 1821, inspector-general of the Army of the United States, with the rank of Colonel. Five years later he was made Brigadier General by brevet, "for ten years' faithful service." He was a thorough disciplinarian; sleepless in vigilance, and always one of the most trusted officers in the service. His reports were always models of their kind.

In 1832, General Wool was sent to Europe to collect information connected with military science. He received great attention, especially in France, where he formed one of the suite of King Louis Philippe in a grand review of 70,000 men. In November, the same year, he accompanied the King of Belgium in a review of 100,000 men, and was in Antwerp during its siege. On his return, and when difficulties with France were anticipated, he made a thorough inspection of our sea-coast defences. In 1836, he assisted in measures for removing the Cherokee Indians from Georgia, and displayed in that business the higher traits of a soldier and statesman. Two years later, when trouble was anticipated on account of insurrection in Canada, he was sent to the then wilds of Maine to look after the border defenses.

In the war with Mexico, General Wool's services as a tactician were of great value. He drilled a large portion of the volunteers, and was chiefly instrumental in securing victory at Buena Vista. For his gallant conduct in that war he was breveted a Major General. His grateful countrymen bestowed upon him many tokens of their approval and regard.

Toward the close of 1853, when fillibustering expeditions were fitted out on the Western coast, General Wool was appointed to the command of the *Department of the Pacific.* * It was a laborious and delicate trust, involving some international questions, and dealings with Indian tribes. He performed the complex duties of his station with wonderful energy, wisdom and skill. In the spring of 1855 he made a tour of inspection in the Territories of Oregon and Washington, and afterward was efficient in ending hostilities between the white people and the Indians in that region. He was soon afterward appointed to the command of the *Eastern Department,* which comprised the whole country eastward of the Mississippi River. He was engaged in the quiet routine of his duties as such, with his head-quarters at his home in Troy, when the great Civil War broke out. With his wonted energy he warned and intreated the national government to use its powers in crushing the rebellion in the bud. When the blow was struck, he put forth all his energies in his Department; and it is conceded that to General Wool, more than to any other man, the country is indebted for the salvation of, its capital from seizure by the insurgents. He did excellent service early in the war that ensued, and in 1863 he retired to private life. He had been commissioned a full Major General in the Army of the Republic, the year before.

General Wool died at his residence in Troy early on the morning of the 10th of November, in the eighty-second year of his age. The General-in-chief of the Army ordered public honors to be paid to the memory of the deceased soldier; and on the 13th he was buried with military honors. In accordance with his request, the bands played the air of "Home, Sweet Home," as the funeral procession moved. It was estimated that full fifty thousand persons were in the streets. General Wool was greatly esteemed by the inhabitants of Troy, who sincerely mourned his death.

CHARLES STEWART.

FOR many years the oldest living officer in the service of the United States, and whose commission was given in the last century, was Charles Stewart, one of the prominent American heroes of the war with England in 1812–'15. His parents were natives of Ireland. His father was a mariner in the merchant service, and came to America at an early age. His son Charles was born in the city of Philadelphia on the 28th of July, 1778. He was the youngest of eight children, and lost his father when he was only ten years old. At the age of thirteen years he entered the merchant service as a cabin-boy, and gradually rose to the office of captain. His home was on the ocean, and his pursuit was delightful to him. In March, 1798, when his government was strengthening its naval force in anticipation of hostilities with France, he was commissioned a Lieutenant in the Navy, and made his first cruise under Commodore Barney. In the year 1800 he was appointed to the command of the armed schooner *Experiment.* In the early autumn of that year, he fought and captured the French schooner *Two Friends,* after an action of ten minutes, without incurring loss on his part. He was conspicuous in the war with Tripoli, and was greatly beloved by Decatur for his services there and his generous friendship ever afterward.

In the month of May, 1804, Lieutenant Stewart was promoted to Master-Commandant, and to that of Captain, in 1806. During that and the following year, he was employed in the construction of gun-boats. In 1812, he was appointed to the command of the frigate *Constitution,* with which he achieved great victories for his country and won immortal honors for himself. He was with her in Hampton Roads early in 1813, when, by skillful management, he eluded the enemy, and took his ship safely to Norfolk. He was always a skillful sailor, and when he was too weak to fight, he managed to retreat or flee in safety. His great victory over the British frigates *Cyane* and *Levant*, in one engagement, early in 1815, was considered a most valiant exploit by both nations, and his countrymen lavished honors upon him when he returned after peace had been proclaimed. The authorities of New York gave him the freedom of the city, in a gold box, and tendered to him and his officers the hospitalities of a public banquet. Pennsylvania gave him thanks and a gold-hilted sword; and Congress voted him thanks and a gold medal. His exploits and that of his ship became the theme for oratory and song; and she, always a "lucky" vessel, was called "Old Ironsides;" a name by which her brave commander was known in later years. The *Constitution* is yet (1869) in the public service, as a school-ship.

After the war, Commodore Stewart was placed in command of the *Franklin*, 74, which conveyed the Honorable Richard Rush, American Minister, to England, and then cruised with a squadron in the Mediterranean Sea. He was afterward in command of the Pacific squadron. After his return, Stewart was constantly employed in active service, afloat and ashore, until the breaking out of the late Civil War, when he retired to his beautiful estate on the banks of the Delaware, near Bordentown, New Jersey. There the writer visited him a few days after the battle of Gettysburg, in July, 1863, and listened with great interest to his fluent speech in the recital of some of the most stirring incidents in his long and eventful life. He was then eighty-five years of age, but was a hale, compactly-built and active man, with mental powers very little abated. Under the new arrangement of official titles in the navy, he was bearing that of Vice-Admiral. We left him with a feeling similar to that expressed by an anonymous poet, who wrote,

> "O, oft may you meet with brave Stewart
> The tar with the free and the true heart;
> A bright welcome smile, and a soul free from guile
> You'll find in the hero, Charles Stewart.
> A commander both generous and brave, too,
> Who risked his life others to save, too,
> And thousands who roam by his neat Jersey home
> Bless the kind heart of gallant Charles Stewart."

Rear-Admiral Stewart died at his residence near Bordentown, on Sunday, the 9th of November, 1869, in the ninety-second year of his age. In his native city (Philadelphia) imposing funeral honors were awarded him. His body lay in state in Independence Hall, and thousands of citizens looked for the last time on the face of the hero. For five hours there was a continued stream of persons passing the casket in which the body lay. There was an immense funeral procession—naval, military, and civic; the city was draped in mourning, and minute guns were fired.

ROBERT TREAT PAINE.

> "Ne'er was a nobler spirit born,
> A loftier soul, a gentler heart;
> Above the world's ignoble scorn,
> Above the reach of venal art."

THUS sung a genial friend, at the tomb of Robert Treat Paine, a New England bard. He was born at Taunton, Massachusetts, on the 9th of December, 1773, and was the second son of Robert Treat Paine, one of the signers of the Declaration of Independence. He

was named Thomas,[1] but on the death of his eldest and unmarried brother, Robert Treat, in 1798, he assumed his name, and had his choice legally confirmed by an act of the legislature, in 1801. Paine was educated at Harvard, where his poetic genius was early developed.[2] He was intended for the profession of the law, but soon after leaving college he became a merchant's clerk. He was quite irregular in his habits, and became greatly enamored of the theater. He obtained a medal for a prologue, spoken at the opening of the new theater in Boston, in 1793;[3] and the following year he assumed the editorial control of a newspaper called the *Federal Orerry*. It was an unsuccessful enterprise, for the editor was idle, and it expired for want of proper food, in 1796. Paine had married the

---

1. I have given his signature, written before the death of his brother.
2. A class-mate abused him, in rhyme, upon the college wall. Young Paine had never written a line of poetry, but instantly resolved to answer his antagonist in meter, and did so. To that circumstance he attributed his attention to rhyme. When he was graduated, in 1792, he delivered a poem.
3. The Federal Street Theater, yet (1855) devoted to the drama. It was destroyed by fire, in 1798, and rebuilt on a larger scale, in the autumn of that year.

beautiful daughter of an actor, the year before, which offended his father, and an alienation ensued. The young lady proved an excellent wife, and was an angel at his side when intemperance clouded his mind and beggared his family.

In 1795, Mr. Paine delivered a poem at Cambridge, entitled *Invention of Letters*, for which he received from the book-seller $1500. Two years afterward, his *Ruling Passion* brought him $1200; and his *Adams and Liberty*, written in 1798, at the request of the Massachusetts Charitable Fire Society, yielded him $750, or more than $11 a line.[1] Mr. Paine was appointed master of ceremonies at the theater, with a salary, and that connection threatened his health and reputation with shipwreck. A happy change soon occurred. 'He abandoned dissipation, and, on the solicitation of friends, he left the theater, moved, with his family, to Newburyport, entered the law-office of Judge Parsons, became a practitioner, enjoyed reconciliation with his father, and gave his friends great hopes. In 1803, when fortune and bright character were within his grasp, he was again allured to the theater, its associations and its habits, and he fell to rise no more. He neglected business, became intemperate, and died in wretchedness, on the 14th of November, 1811, when in the thirty-eighth year of his age. It was a sad evening of life, in contrast with the promises of the brilliant morning. His career is a warning to the gifted to avoid the perils of inordinate indulgence of passions and pleasures, for no intellect is so strong that it may not be bowed in degradation.

BENJAMIN SILLIMAN.

THE founder of The American Journal of Science and Art (better known in America and Europe as *Silliman's Journal*), and one of the first American lecturers before miscellaneous audiences on scientific subjects, was Benjamin Silliman, a native of North Stratford (near Trumbull), Conn., where he was born August 8, 1779. He graduated at Yale College in 1796, was appointed a tutor there in 1779, and having prepared himself by study, was admitted to the bar in 1802. The same year he accepted the new chair of chemistry in Yale College, and studied two years with Dr. Woodhouse, in Philadelphia. His first full course of lectures were given at Yale in 1805. Then he sailed for Europe, and was gone fourteen months. On his return he made a partial geological survey of Connecticut. In 1810

---

1. Never was a political song more popular, or more widely sung, than this. Paine showed the verses to Mr. Russell, editor of the *Boston Centinel*. It was in the midst of company at Mr. Russell's house. Paine was about to take a glass of wine, when his host said, "You have said nothing about Washington; you cannot drink until you have added a verse in his honor." The poet paced the room a few moments, and then, calling for pen and ink, wrote with great rapidity:

"Should the tempest of war overshadow our land,
Its bolts would ne'er rend Freedom's temple asunder;
For, unmoved, at its portal would Washington stand,
And repulse, with his breast, the assaults of the thunder!
His sword from the sleep
Of its scabbard would leap,
And conduct, with its point, every flash to the deep!"

he published a *Journal of Travels in England, Holland, and Scotland* in 1805–6. He examined a meteorite lately fallen in Connecticut, made a chemical analysis of it, and published the earliest and best authenticated account of the fall of a meteorite in America. In 1813 Prof. Silliman published an account of the compound blowpipe of Dr. Robert Hare, and experiments with it, by which the list of known fusible bodies was greatly extended. In 1818 he founded the *American Journal of Science and Arts*, of which he was twenty years sole editor, and for eight years longer senior editor. His account of a Journey from Hartford to Quebec, published in 1828, is an interesting and valuable book of travel by a keen observer. It was between 1831 and 1840 that Prof. Silliman gave his scientific lectures to miscellaneous audiences in most of the principal cities of the United States; and in 1851 he made a second visit to Europe. At the age of seventy-four years he resigned his position in Yale College, having filled the chair of chemistry fifty-one consecutive years. Then he was made emeritus professor, and by request of his colleagues continued his lectures in geology until June, 1855, when he closed his active professional life. He was pre-eminent as a leader, and he had few equals as an interesting lecturer, for his soul was filled with his subject. A late writer speaks of Prof. Silliman as "a finished gentleman, and a social favorite; his person was commanding, his manner dignified and affable, and his general traits of character such as to win universal respect and admiration." Prof. Silliman died on Thanksgiving Day (Nov. 24), 1864, at the age of eighty-five years.

JARED SPARKS.

ONE of the most accomplished, painstaking, and industrious American scholars was Jared Sparks, whose carefully arranged collections of historical and biographical materials for the use of historians of the American people, has won for him the grateful benedictions of his countrymen. He was born at Willington, Conn., May 10, 1789. He graduated at Harvard College in 1815, studied theology at Cambridge two years, and was a tutor in the college awhile, teaching mathematics and natural philosophy. Soon after his graduation he became one of an association that conducted the *North American Review*. In 1819 Mr. Sparks was ordained as minister of a Unitarian congregation in Baltimore, and in 1821 was chosen chaplain of the United States House of Representatives. The same year he established *The Unitarian Miscellany*, which he conducted for about two years. Having prescribed for himself a course of historical study and labor, he made extensive researches in this country, and in 1828 he went to Europe, where, in the public offices in London and Paris, he transcribed a large number of documents relating to American history. On his return he undertook the editing of the writings of George Washington, the materials having been placed in his hands by the family of Judge Bushrod Washington (to whom the Mount Vernon estate had descended) and others. These, with a life of the patriot, and fully annotated, were published in twelve octavo volumes in 1834-37. He had resigned his pastoral charge on account of impaired health in 1823, returned to Boston, and purchased the *North American Review*, of which he was editor seven years.

During his preparation of the Washington writings, Mr. Sparks edited and published (1829–30) *The Diplomatic Correspondence of the Revolution*, in twelve octavo volumes. In 1832 appeared his Life of Gouverneur Morris, in three volumes. He had established *The American Almanac* in 1830, and edited the first volume. From 1834 to 1838 he edited ten volumes, 18mo, of the *Library of American Biography*, and from 1844 to 1848 he edited a second series of such biographies in fifteen volumes, same size. In 1840 he completed the publication of *The Life and Writings of Benjamin Franklin*, in ten volumes. He afterward made a second visit to Europe.

In the task of editing the writings of Washington, Mr. Sparks took the liberty of making a few alterations in phrases which had been used by Washington in his private correspondence not intended for the public eye, such as "General Putnam" for "Old Put," a common appellation of the veteran officer. This was severely criticised by Lord Mahon, which drew from Mr. Sparks, in 1852, two pamphlets in defense of his mode of editing the writings of Washington. In 1854 he edited and published *Correspondence of the American Revolution*, consisting of letters written to Washington from the time of his taking command of the Continental army, in July, 1775, until the end of his presidency, in the spring of 1797. They were edited from original manuscripts, and published in four volumes octavo. Mr. Sparks was McLean professor of history at Harvard college for ten years from 1839, and from 1849 to 1853 he was president of that institution. Mr. Sparks's first literary venture was the publication of *Letters on the Ministry, Ritual, and Doctrine of the Protestant Episcopal Church*, in 1820, when he was twenty-one years of age.

STEPHEN ARNOLD DOUGLAS.

SHORT, thickset, and muscular in person, and strong in intellect, Stephen A. Douglas received the familiar appellation of "The Little Giant." For many years he held a very conspicuous place in the political history of the republic. His family were of Scotch descent. His grandfather was a soldier in the old war for American independence, and his father was a skillful physician, who died suddenly of heart disease while holding his infant son (the subject of the sketch), then only two months old, in his arms. Stephen was born in Brandon, Rutland county, Vt., on April 23, 1813; received a common-school education, and desired to enter college, but the pecuniary condition of his family would not permit it. At the age of fifteen years he apprenticed himself to a cabinet-maker. At the end of eighteen months his health became impaired, and he began the study of law, and at the same time pursued his academic studies. In 1833 he settled in Jacksonville, Ill., where he taught school and continued his legal studies. Admitted to the bar in 1834, he soon acquired a lucrative practice; and he was elected attorney-general of the state before he was twenty-two years of age. In 1837 President Van Buren appointed him register of the land office at Springfield, Ill., and he was a democratic candidate for congress the same year. In 1840 he was chosen secretary of the state of Illinois, and the following year, at the age of twenty-eight years, he was elected a judge of the supreme court. From 1842 to 1848 he occupied a seat in congress by successive elections. In the latter years he was chosen United States Senator, and was twice re-elected, and he held the office until his death. In both houses of congress, Mr. Douglas was an acknowledged democratic leader, being a sound, ready, and fluent debater. In 1854 he introduced the Kansas-Nebraska bill, which would violate the Missouri compromise, and he strongly advocated leaving the question of slavery in these territories to the expressed will of the people, a doctrine called "squatter sovereignty." The bill was carried through in the face of strong opposition.

Mr. Douglas was a rival candidate to Mr. Buchanan for the democratic nomination for president of the United States in 1856. The latter was nominated. He was a prominent candidate before the democratic convention held in Charleston in 1860. There were two candidates before the convention. John C. Breckenridge was the choice of the southern democrats, and Mr. Douglas of the northern democrats. There was a split in the convention—many of the southern members seceding and forming a separate convention. The southern democrats opposed Mr. Douglas because he would not coalesce with them in efforts to maintain slavery. Douglas and Breckenridge were both defeated by Abraham Lincoln, the republican candidate for president, though Douglas received a large popular vote—within about 500,000 as many as Mr. Lincoln. Soon after that election the southern politicians led the people of several slave-labor states into open insurrection against the national government. Then the voice of Mr. Douglas was heard in earnest pleas for the union, and this was the burden of his last words at his death, which occurred on June 3, 1861, when insurrection had assumed the dignity of civil war.

MATTHEW VASSAR.

ON the 28th of February, 1861, twenty-eight gentlemen were assembled in the parlor of the (then) "Gregory House," at Poughkeepsie on the Hudson, and received from Matthew Vassar, a resident of that city from his youth, a casket containing securities of various kinds, to the value of $408,000, in trust, for the establishment of a college for the higher education of women. Standing by a table on which was placed the casket, and with the key in his open palm, he thus concluded a brief address: "And now, gentlemen of the board of trustees, I transfer to your possession and ownership the real and personal property which I have set apart for the accomplishment of my designs." Who shall estimate the importance or measure the significance of that act?

Matthew Vassar was born in Norfolk county, England, on April 29, 1792, and came to America with his parents and uncle when he was five years of age. They bought a farm near Poughkeepsie, where they planted the first barley ever cultivated in that region. With this they made excellent home-brewed ale for family use and for sale. James, the father of Matthew, afterwards became a brewer in Poughkeepsie, for which the son had no taste. He was about to be apprenticed to a tanner, when the lad, adverse to the arrangement, started out in the world clandestinely to find employment. After an absence of four years, he entered his father's establishment as a clerk. James Vassar was unfortunate in business, when Matthew began brewing ale on his own account, at first making three barrels at a time and peddling it in Poughkeepsie. It finally expanded into a large and profitable business, and after pursuing it for about fifty years, and accumulating a large fortune, he retired.

In 1845 Mr. Vassar and his wife spent several months traveling in Europe. Visiting Guy's Hospital, in London, an institution founded by a kinsman of his, Mr. Vassar, who was childless, resolved to devote a large portion of his fortune, in his life-time, to some benevolent object. In the course of a few years his wife died, and he resolved in his mind several projects for the disposition of his large estate. Finally, at the suggestion of his niece, Miss Lydia Booth, then principal of a young ladies' seminary at Poughkeepsie, he concluded to erect buildings and endow a college for young women. He obtained an act of incorporation in January, 1861, and in February following, a board of trustees, consisting of twenty-eight gentlemen of different religious denominations, was organized, and the sum of $408,000 was placed in their hands to carry on the work. The site was selected, and on the 4th of June, the same year, Mr. Vassar, with his own hands, cut out the first spadeful of earth in preparation for the foundation of the building. It was completed in the early summer of 1865, a president and faculty were selected, and it was first opened on the 20th of September, the same year, with nearly three hundred and fifty students. Mr. Vassar spent $20,000 in furnishing an art gallery for educational purposes, and in his will bequeathed to the institution $150,000 in three separate and equal sums, the interest of each to be appropriated for a special purpose, namely, for assisting deserving pupils who may have become pecuniarily disabled, to complete the college course; for the increase of the library and to advance the usefulness of the philosophical cabinets and apparatus; and for an annual course of lectures. Mr. Vassar's entire gifts to the institution amounted to about $800,000. He lived to see his great enterprise pass beyond the boundaries of an experiment, to a position of assured success. Up to the last moment of his life, he labored incessantly in its behalf. At the annual meeting of the board of trustees, on June 26, 1868, while he was reading, as usual, his annual address to that body, his manuscript was seen to drop suddenly from his hands, for a stroke of paralysis with which he had been for some time menaced had violently deprived him of life, and his inanimate form was caught in the arms of the writer of this article, a member of the board of trustees.

Vassar College, with its buildings in the midst of a farm of 200 acres, on which is a spring lake that furnishes the institution with an abundance of pure water the year round, and a means for skating in the winter and boating in the summer; its competent faculty, and its ample supply of pupils, who have the advantages of an art school, rich cabinets of natural history, a chemical laboratory, presented by the two nephews of the founder, and a library of about 12,000 volumes, is Matthew Vassar's best and most enduring monument. It is the first college for the higher education of women established on the earth. In every particular Vassar College has remained absolutely unsectarian, but thoroughly religious in its moral teachings and political influence. This character it was the earnest desire of the founder should be maintained. In one of his annual communications he said: "All sectarian influences should be carefully excluded; but the training of our students should never be intrusted to the skeptical, the irreligious or immoral."

FRANKLIN PIERCE.

IN another part of this work (page 283) may be found a sketch of the life of Gen. Benjamin Pierce, a soldier of the revolution, and father of the fourteenth president of the United States. That distinguished son was born at Hillsborough, N. H., on the 23d of November, 1804, and graduated at Bowdoin College in Maine in 1824. Choosing the profession of the law as a life vocation, he studied under Levi Woodbury, a distinguished statesman and cabinet officer under president Jackson. He was admitted to the bar in 1827, and began the practice of his profession in his native town. His father was an earnest democratic politician, and young Pierce, imbibing from him a taste for political life, became active in local politics and was elected to a seat in the New Hampshire legislature, where he served four years with so much ability that, in 1833, he was chosen to represent his district in congress. He was then twenty-nine years of age. The following year he married a daughter of the Rev. Jesse Appleton. Mr. Pierce remained in the house of representatives until 1837, when, by the choice of his legislature, he was transferred to the senate of the United States, at the beginning of the administration of Martin Van Buren. He there found himself among the ablest statesmen of the country—Clay, Webster, Calhoun, Benton, and Wright.

In 1838 Senator Pierce removed to Concord, N. H., where he rose to high rank as a lawyer. He remained in congress until 1842, when, on the accession of President Polk, he was offered the position of attorney-general of the United States, which Mr. Pierce declined, as well as the nomination by the democratic party for governor of New

Hampshire at about the same time. Mr. Pierce was a warm supporter of the measure of the annexation of Texas; and when, in consequence, a war with Mexico occurred, he was made colonel of United States infantry, but was soon appointed brigadier-general, leading a large reinforcement for Gen. Scott. In August, 1847, just before the battle of Churubusco, he was severely injured by the falling of his horse upon his leg. When he returned to Concord at the close of the war, Gen. Pierce was received with enthusiasm by his neighbors and friends, and in recognition of his public services in the field, the legislature of New Hampshire presented to him a sword. Chosen a member of the New Hampshire constitutional convention in 1850–51, he was made its president, and at the democratic national committee which convened at Baltimore in June, 1852, he was nominated for the presidency of the United States. Gen. Winfield Scott was his whig competitor in the ensuing canvass. Gen. Pierce received 250 electoral votes, and Gen. Scott only 42. In the midst of a storm of sleet, he was inaugurated at the east front of the Capitol in the presence of a vast concourse of people, on March 4, 1853. In his inaugural address he denounced the agitation of the slavery question; and it was during his administration that the agitation became more exciting than ever because of the violation of the Missouri compromise by the Kansas-Nebraska act, which permitted slaves to be held in those territories, provided a popular vote should sanction it. The efforts to make Kansas a slave-labor state ensued, and a civil war there during a part of Pierce's and Buchanan's administration was the consequence.

President Pierce exerted his influence to promote the interests and designs of the slave power in Kansas and elsewhere. He ordered the conference of United States ministers in Europe upon the subject of the annexation of Cuba to the United States, which resulted in the promulgation of the infamous "Ostend Manifesto." Late in January, 1856, President Pierce sent a message to congress representing the formation of a free-state government in Kansas as rebellious. The contest in Kansas between the pro-slavery and anti-slavery settlers in Kansas was raging fiercely when his term of office expired, and he was succeeded by James Buchanan, who "followed in the footsteps of his illustrious predecessor." Soon after he left the presidential chair Gen. Pierce made quite an extended tour in Europe. When the late civil war broke out, he sympathized with the enemies of his country, by which he lost the esteem of his loyal personal friends. These were many, for Gen. Pierce was one of the most genial of companions and kindest of neighbors. He died at his home in Concord on the 8th of October, 1869.

THOMAS HART BENTON.

FOR thirty years Thomas H. Benton occupied a seat in the senate of the United States, where his indomitable energy, iron will, industry, and self-reliance placed him in the front rank with Webster,

Calhoun, Clay, and Cass. He was born near Hillsborough, N. C., March 14, 1782; began his education at a grammar school, and was completing it at Chapel Hill university, when he removed to Tennessee. There he studied law and soon rose to eminence in his profession, after beginning its practice at Nashville in 1811. He was elected a member of the legislature, where he procured the passage of a law which gave the slaves the right of trial by jury. At about that time Andrew Jackson was major-general of the state militia, and Benton, becoming his aid-de-camp, a close intimacy was formed between them. This was terminated by a personal encounter with pistols and daggers in the streets of Nashville, in which Jackson was severely wounded.

When the war of 1812 had fairly begun, Benton was made colonel of a Tennessee regiment, and afterwards became lieutenant-colonel of United States infantry, with which he served until the close of the war. He had then made his residence in St. Louis, Mo. (1813); and at the close of the war established the Missouri Inquirer. He took an active part in the struggle for the admission of Missouri into the union, and was one of that new state's first representatives in the United States Senate, at which post he remained, by successive re-election for thirty years consecutively, much of the time an acknowledged leader. He was opposed to the administration of John Quincy Adams, but warmly supported that of Jackson, with whom he had long been on friendly terms. He was also a political friend of Van Buren. He was among the foremost who advocated the construction of a railroad across the continent to the Pacific. The untiring guardian of the west, he did much to open and protect the trade with New Mexico, to establish military stations on the Missouri river, to establish friendly relations with the Indians, and to build up the commerce on the great lakes. His persistent advocacy of a specie currency obtained for him the nickname of "Old Bullion." The senate having passed a resolution censuring President Jackson for his removal of the government money from the United States bank, Mr. Benton procured the passage of a resolution ordering the expunging of that record from the journal of the senate. Mr. Benton took an active part in the debates in the senate concerning the disputed boundary between the United States and British possessions, and caused the adoption of the 49th parallel as the boundary. He gave his influence in support of the war with Mexico. The compromise acts of 1850, which, it was supposed, would settle the slavery agitation, he opposed, especially the fugitive slave law. Mr. Benton warmly opposed "nullification" sentiments whenever expressed, for he was an earnest supporter of the national government as supreme, and his known opposition to the extension of the slave system caused his defeat in the Missouri legislature as a candidate for the United States Senate. Thus in defense of human rights ended his thirty years' career in the upper house of the national legislature by the frown of an increasing and overbearing oligarchy. But two years later he was elected by the people of Missouri to a seat in the house of representatives, where he was an able opposer of the Kansas-Nebraska act as a violation of the Missouri compromise. This course arrayed against him the pro-slavery leaders in Missouri, and being a candidate for re-election in 1854, he was defeated. In 1856 he was a candidate for the office of governor of Missouri, and made a strong personal canvass, but was defeated, when he finally retired from the public service. He gave his support to James Buchanan, the democratic candidate for president in 1856, against John C. Fremont, his son-in-law.

The short remainder of Mr. Benton's life, after he retired from the public service, was devoted to literary pursuits. In two bulky volumes, entitled *Thirty Years' View; or a History of the Working of the American Government for Thirty Years, from* 1820 *to* 1850, he gave an account of his political experiences and of the most prominent proceedings of the national legislature during that period; a task which his personal connection with the events noticed specially qualified him for. It contained his best speeches, and much matter which displayed the warmth of his attachment to political and personal friends. The work was exceedingly popular, more than 60,000 volumes being sold as soon as published. When the first volume was completed, and while he was preparing the second volume, his books and manuscripts were destroyed by fire. He immediately reproduced the lost manuscript, and when this work was completed he began another, entitled *Abridgment of the Debates of Congress from* 1789 *to* 1850, which, when completed, composed fifteen octavo volumes. On this work he labored incessantly during the last years of his life. The latter portions of it he dictated while on his death-bed, when he could not speak above a whisper. It was completed down to the close of the debate in the compromise bill in the autumn of 1850. His work finished, Mr. Benton's spirit calmly passed into the world of immortals on the 10th of April, 1858. He died in Washington city. In person Mr. Benton was short and stout, his head was large and grandly proportioned; he had a Roman nose, and his gray eyes were expressive of remarkable intelligence.

FITZ-GREENE HALLECK.

THE author of *Marco Bozzaris* (the best known of his poems among the people) cannot rank with the great American poets, but he is a conspicuous figure among the minor poets of the republic. He was born at Guilford, Conn., July 8, 1790, and was a lineal descendant of John Eliot, the "Apostle to the Indians." In his native town he received a good academic education, and at the age of twenty-one he entered the service of Jacob Barker, a banker in New York. Afterwards he became bookkeeper in John Jacob Astor's private office, and was associated with him in his business affairs as confidential clerk about sixteen years.

Mr. Halleck began to write verses in his boyhood, but his first poem, in the collected edition to "Twilight," appeared in the New York *Evening Post* in 1819. The next year he formed a literary partnership with Joseph Rodman Drake, in the production of the *Croaker* papers—poetical squibs—published in the *Evening Post;*

and in the same year appeared his *Fanny*, a satire on the fashions, follies, and public characters of the day. It was his longest poem. Drake died in 1820, and Halleck commemorated the event in a touching poem, in which appeared the often quoted lines—

> "Green be the turf above thee,
> Friend of my better days!
> None knew thee but to love thee,
> None named thee but to praise."

A second and enlarged edition of *Fanny* appeared in 1821. The original was written in the space of three weeks from its commencement and was very popular. Mr. Halleck made a tour in Europe in 1822-23, and in 1827 he published a collection of his poems, anonymously, in which were embodied his *Alnwick Castle* and *Burns*, which had been inspired by a visit to the home of the Scotch poet. They had first appeared in the New York Review and United States Review, edited by Mr. Bryant. His *Marco Bozarris* first appeared in the latter.

Mr. Halleck was one of the original trustees of the Astor Library. Having "been made rich with forty pounds a year," or an annuity of $200, secured to him by the will of the wealthy merchant (Mr. Astor) whom he served so long and faithfully at a very moderate salary, Mr. Halleck retired to Guilford, and resided with a sister who, like himself, remained unmarried. Devotion to business seemed to have subordinated to it literary compositions, and for many years nothing appeared from his pen in the form of a poem. In 1832 he prepared an edition of Byron's works with notes and a memoir, and in 1840 he compiled two volumes of *Selections from the British Poets*. He was silent until January, 1864, when he published in the *New York Ledger* a poem of about three hundred lines on *Young America*.

Mr. Halleck died at Guilford, Nov. 17, 1867, and at the head of his grave a handsome obelisk was erected to his memory. There is also a statue of him, in bronze, in the Central Park, New York.

WILLIAM GILMORE SIMMS.

AMONG the literary men of our country no one was a more industrious and prolific writer than William Gilmore Simms, of South Carolina. He was born in Charleston, on April 17, 1806. In youth he was a clerk in a drug-store in that city, but very early exhibited a taste and genius for literature. He began the study of law at the age of eighteen, and was admitted to the bar in 1827. He never practiced his profession much, but devoted himself almost wholly to literary pursuits. In 1828 he became editor and part proprietor of the *Charleston City Gazette*, and continued in that position until 1832, opposing "nullification" with vigor. This opposition, in face of the general public opinion in South Carolina, reduced him to poverty, when he gave his whole time to writing books. He wrote prose and poetry with equal facility. His first publications were volumes of poems; his prose writings were mostly works of fiction, of which the first that appeared was *The Book of my Lady*, issued in 1833. In 1864 a collected edition of his poems was published; and in 1867 he edited a collection of war poems by southern writers. Mr. Simms also wrote dramas, biographies, and histories. Among the biographies were lives of General Marion, Captain John Smith, General Greene, and the Chevalier Bayard. He wrote a small *History of South Carolina* for the use of schools, also a *Geography of South Carolina*. He also edited, with notes, the seven dramas ascribed to Shakespeare but not published among his works. He called the collection *A Supplement to Shakespeare's Plays*.

Mr. Simms, while devoted to the Union, was an advocate of the slave system, and while the agitation in the public mind both north and south was constantly increasing, he, as a distinguished literary man, received invitations from northern lyceums to lecture, sufficient to insure him a profitable winter course; but so offended the cultivated citizens of New York city, where he gave his discourse first, by his strictures on the anti-slavery sentiment of the northern people, that he was compelled to abandon the lecture campaign and return home. The people showed their indignation, not by any violent act or speech, but by quietly staying away from his lectures. After repeating it two or three times, he perceived the drift of public sentiment, and retired. During the civil war that soon afterwards ensued, Mr. Simms appeared somewhat conspicuous in public life in South Carolina, fully sympathizing with the revolutionists of his state.

Mr. Simms was possessed of a kindly nature, but was somewhat imperious in his deportment. When the war was over he was cordially received by his old friends in the north. A selected edition of his novels was published in New York in 1865 in seventeen volumes. He died in Charleston, June 11, 1870.

SAMUEL HOUSTON.

THE commander-in-chief of troops in Texas which gained the independence of that territory, and was the first president of that commonwealth, was a remarkable man, whose life was marked by a series of adventures almost romantic. Samuel Houston was born near Lexington, Va., March 2, 1793. He received a good common-school education. On the death of his father when he was fourteen years of age, his mother, with six sons and three daughters, removed to East Tennessee, on the borders of the Cherokee country. Dissatisfied with the situation of clerk in a country store, he absconded to the Cherokees and dwelt among them about three years. Returning he opened a school, and in 1813 enlisted as a private soldier in the contest of the war of 1812-15. He served under Gen. Jackson against the Creek Indians and in the battle of New Orleans, rising to the grade of lieutenant. In 1818 he resigned his commission, studied law in Nashville, and, after six months, was admitted to the bar, and entered upon practice in a country town. After holding some minor offices he was elected to congress in 1823. He served two terms and was chosen governor of Tennessee in 1827. Two years later he was married, and three months afterwards he separated from his wife, resigned his office, and joined the Cherokees, then in the region west of Arkansas, where he became a citizen among them and was chosen to be a chief.

Houston took measures to defend the Cherokees against frauds practiced by government agents, and these men and their friends became his bitter enemies, which led to a series of legal and personal conflicts. After gaining a victory for his cause at Washington, he returned to his wigwam, and in Dec., 1832, went to Texas, where a revolutionary movement was organizing against Mexico. A member of a constitutional convention in that province in 1833, which was rejected by Santa Anna, president of Mexico, Houston was chosen commander-in-chief of the revolutionary forces. He ably conducted the war for independence which ensued, and gained a final victory at the battle of San Jacinto in April, 1836, when the Mexican army, led by Santa Anna in person, was completely routed and its leader made prisoner. Houston was severely wounded in the battle.

The Republic of Texas was organized in the fall of 1836, by the inauguration of Houston as president. He was re-elected in 1841 and favored the scheme of annexing Texas to the United States. After the annexation in 1845, Houston was one of the first United States senators, and, true to his early friends the Indians, he was ever their advocate and defender. He remained in the senate until 1859, when he was elected governor of Texas. He persistently opposed secession in 1861. Finding opposition to be useless, and wearied with the popular clamor for an extraordinary session of the Texas legislature, which he steadily refused to call, Governor Houston retired to private life, refusing to take the oath required by the secession convention of Texas.

Governor Houston was six feet in height and perfectly proportioned; slow of speech and always kindly in manner; his face was expressive of great intelligence and firmness of will, and he was a ready and impressive debater. The writer remembers seeing him when he first appeared in Washington as senator, attracting the attention of everybody as his commanding figure appeared in Pennsylvania avenue, moving with military precision, while a bright scarlet Mexican light blanket cast jauntily over his shoulders made him a conspicuous object in the street.

WILLIAM HICKLING PRESCOTT.

THE accomplished historian, William H. Prescott, "was tall and slender, with a fresh and florid complexion, and lively, graceful manners," says a late writer. He rose early, clothed himself according to the weather indicated by the thermometer, his clothes being marked with their weight in pounds and ounces, and walked five miles each day in the open air, or, if the weather was stormy, in his house. Mr. Prescott was born in Salem, Mass., May 4, 1796, and graduated at Harvard College in 1814. He had removed with his family to Boston when he was twelve years of age. In the last year of his life at Harvard, a classmate playfully threw a crust of bread which struck one of his eyes, and nearly deprived it of sight. Excessive use of the other eye produced an inflammation which deprived him of sight several weeks. Then he could read for several hours at a time, but finally was compelled to give up reading more than a few moments at a time. During the last half of his life this was the case. He employed a reader, and wrote with an instrument used by the totally blind.

Mr. Prescott traveled in Europe, lingering some time in Italy, and at the end of two years returned to Boston, married, and settled in his father's family. He determined to devote ten years to the study of ancient and modern history, and to give the next ten years to the composition of a history. He studied the French and Italian literature for the purpose of writing a history of Italian literature. This design he abandoned, began to study Spanish in 1825, and selected as a subject for his first historical work the reign of Ferdinand and

Isabella. At a very great expense he made a large collection of materials, much of it unedited manuscripts. With a patient reader and the use of the writing contrivance for the blind, his *History of Ferdinand and Isabella* was made ready for the press and was published in 1837 in Boston and London. It was immediately translated into the Spanish, German, and French languages, and the Royal Academy of History at Madrid elected Mr. Prescott a corresponding member. He devoted six years of labor to the *History of the Conquest of Mexico*, three volumes, and four to the *Conquest of Peru*, two volumes. The latter was published in 1847. These works were received with the greatest favor in all civilized countries. Mr. Prescott was made a corresponding member of the Institute of France. In 1840 Columbia College, New York, conferred on him the degree of LL.D., and in 1843 Harvard College gave him the same degree. After his return from a short visit in Europe in 1850, he began the preparation of a history of the reign of Philip II., intending to make the entire work comprise six volumes. The first two volumes appeared in 1855, and the third in 1868. Early in Feb. that year he experienced a slight shock of paralysis. He soon recovered, and resumed his literary labors. Within a few days of a year afterwards, Jan. 28, 1859, while at work with his secretary in his study, he suddenly became speechless, and died about an hour afterwards, leaving his last great historical work unfinished. He resided part of the year in Boston and part in the country. He kept the account of his daily expenditures with great exactness, and one tenth of his income was always devoted to charity. At his residence in Boston he had collected one of the finest private libraries in the country.

GEORGE PEABODY.

A NOTABLE moral phenomenon appeared in the history of the world toward the close of 1869. It was public homage paid by royalty to a private citizen because of his practical sympathy with the poor of his race. The occasion was the funeral of George Peabody, a banker in London of American birth.

Mr. Peabody was born in Danvers, Mass., Feb. 18, 1795. After serving as a merchant's clerk in New England, he joined his uncle, Elisha Riggs, in carrying on a dry-goods house in Georgetown, D. C. The house was transferred to Baltimore, where, at the age of about twenty years, young Peabody and his uncle began the business of draper, under the firm name of Riggs & Peabody, the latter, even at that time, being recognized as a most sagacious business man. They were wonderfully successful, and established branch houses in Philadelphia and New York. Mr. Riggs retired in 1829, and Mr. Peabody continued the business under a new firm name. In 1837 he settled permanently in London, where, in 1843, he established the banking-house of George Peabody & Co. At the time of the great commercial revulsion in America in 1837, Mr. Peabody, with great

boldness and sagacity, patriotically sustained American credit by the free purchase of American securities, at a risk of losing his fortune. He was successful, and had performed an important public service for his country. Known in private life as a generous man, it was not until 1851, when his fortune was counted by millions, that he began to dispense public benefactions. He supplied the sum needed to arrange and display the contributions to the World's Fair in London. In 1852 he gave $10,000 toward the second Grinnell arctic expedition under Dr. Kane. The same year the citizens of his native town celebrated the two hundredth anniversary of its birth. Mr. Peabody could not accept an invitation to be present in person, but inclosed a "sentiment" in an envelope which should not be opened until the name of George Peabody should be called at the banquet, among those of the invited guests. It was: "Education—a debt due from the present to future generations." In an accompanying note he said: "In acknowledgment of the payment of that debt by the generation that preceded me in my native town of Danvers, and to aid in its prompt future discharge, I give to the inhabitants of that town the sum of $20,000 for the promotion of knowledge and morality among them."

Mr. Peabody visited his native country in 1857. Soon after his arrival he gave to the city of Baltimore $300,000 for the founding of an institution of learning in that city. To this sum he afterwards added $200,000, and in 1866 $500,000 more. On visiting this country again in 1866 he gave the institution $400,000 more, making his total gifts for the endowment of the *Peabody Institute* $1,400,000.

On his return to London in 1858, after his first visit, he set about the execution of a plan he had devised for the benefit of the poor of that city, and he gave first the munificent sum of $750,000 for the purpose of erecting comfortable houses in which indigent deserving families might dwell at a very small rent. The queen acknowledged his generosity in an autograph letter, and sent him her portrait painted on ivory and set in jewels, valued at $25,000. Mr. Peabody's entire gifts for this noble purpose amounted to nearly $2,000,000. With this sum buildings have been erected sufficient to accommodate more than 6,000 persons. On his return to London in 1867, the queen offered Mr. Peabody a baronetcy, which he declined. While in this country in 1866, he gave to Harvard College for a specific purpose $150,000; to Yale College $150,000; and gave for the purpose of promoting education in the southern states $2,100,000, increased in 1869 to $3,500,000, besides $200,000 for other purposes. He endowed an art school in Rome in 1868, and in 1869 he again visited the United States, when he distributed, in various benefactions among the educational institutions of the republic, $315,000. He left, at his death, mostly to his relatives, $5,000,000. Mr. Peabody died within a month after his return to England. His death occurred on Nov. 4, 1869. His obsequies were celebrated in Westminster Abbey, and his remains were brought to the United States in the royal turret ship *Monarch* and buried at Danvers, since named Peabody.

CHARLES SUMNER.

ON the very day when Henry Clay left the senate of the United States forever, Charles Sumner, of Massachusetts, took his seat in that body. The relative positions of these two statesmen in our national history show a marked difference between them. Clay is known in our history as the great compromiser; Sumner is known as one of the most uncompromising of men when dealing with great national, moral, and political subjects. Mr. Sumner was born at Boston, Jan. 6, 1811, and after graduating at Hartford in 1830, he entered the law school of that university and was favored with instruction by Judge Story. After entering upon the practice of his profession in 1834, he rose to eminence rapidly. He was appointed reporter of the circuit court, and lectured to the Cambridge law school until 1837, when he went to Europe and studied and traveled three years. On his return he resumed the practice of law, and first took an active part in politics in opposition to the annexation of Texas. He delivered a most eloquent and able speech against the measure on July 4, 1845, in Faneuil hall, which was published under the title of the "True Grandeur of

Nations." This great speech gave him a national, and even international reputation. He warmly supported Van Buren for president in 1848, who was the nominee of the free-soil party, and from that time he was closely identified with the anti-slavery movements.

When in 1851, Daniel Webster resigned his seat in the senate, Mr. Sumner was chosen to fill his place. He opposed the fugitive slave law, declaring that "Freedom is national, and slavery is sectional." In 1856 he delivered a most effective speech in the senate, entitled "The Crime against Kansas." In that speech he did not spare the slave oligarchy. For this speech he was felled to the floor by a bludgeon wielded by Preston S. Brooks, a member of congress from South Carolina, who approached him stealthily from behind while writing at his desk, and alone, in the senate chamber, and struck him on the head. Mr. Sumner was so severely injured that he was unable to resume his duties in the senate for three or four years, and never fairly recovered from the shock. On resuming his seat in 1860, his first speech was on the barbarism of slavery. He labored incessantly for the salvation of the republic during the civil war which began in South Carolina at the close of 1860. He early proposed the emancipation of the slaves as the readiest means for ending the civil war. His proposition to treat each state in which insurrection and rebellion had reigned supreme during the civil war, as an unorganized domain, and to reconstruct those states by organizing them as territories, and afterwards re-admitting them as states, as other territories had been admitted into the union, conceded all that the secessionists claimed, namely, their power to secede. He soon abandoned that position as untenable.

Mr. Sumner remained a member of the senate, by re-election, until his death, which occurred on Mar. 11, 1874. From 1861 to 1870 he was chairman of the senate committee on foreign affairs. Although his health was feeble for some time, Mr. Sumner's death was quite sudden. He appeared in the senate only the day before that sad event. He was buried in Mount Auburn cemetery, near Boston. "It is a pleasant spot on a little path just to one side of the main road which runs from the chapel to the town," says a recent writer. "A great oak rises a little before you get to the grave, and throws a kindly shade over the statesman's resting-place. No magnificent monumental shaft with elaborate epitaphs marks the spot where the great senator sleeps, but a plain white tablet, only a foot or so in height, with the brief inscription: '*Charles Sumner*, born Jan. 6, 1811—died March 11, 1874,' informs the stranger that he stands before the grave of a giant."

Mr. Sumner, in his writings and speeches, exhibited great power of condensation. So early as 1831 he was the chief editor of *The American Jurist*. He edited *Dunlap on Admiralty*, and prepared *Circuit Court Reports* for ten years, in three volumes, and with J. C. Perkins edited Vesey's *Chancery Reports*, twenty volumes. It is said he suggested to Mr. Wheaton his work on the Law of Nations; and wrote for Galignani's Messenger a defense of our north-east boundary claim. Many of his orations and speeches have been published and widely read.

WILLIAM HENRY SEWARD.

" THERE is an irrepressible conflict between opposing and enduring forces, and it means that the United States must and will, sooner or later, become either entirely a slave-holding nation or entirely a free-labor nation." Thus spake William H. Seward at Rochester in 1858, after alluding to the constant collision between the systems of free and slave labor in the United States. Mr. Seward was then a ripe statesman. He was born in Florida, Orange county, N. Y., May 16, 1801, and there in after-years he endowed a seminary which bears the name of "Seward Institute." He was graduated with distinction at Union College, Schenectady, in 1820. He taught school in Georgia six months, and then entered the law office of John Duer, of New York, as a student. He studied law under him, John Anthon, and Ogden Hoffman. Admitted to the bar, he began the practice of law at Auburn, in association with Judge Miller, whose daughter he married.

Mr. Seward began public official life in 1830, when he was twenty-nine years of age, as a state senator. From that time until his death he was conspicuous in the politics of New York and of the nation. He was a champion of the United States bank, and made an able speech in the New York Senate in favor of that institution. In 1833 he made a short tour in Europe, and the next year he was an unsuccessful whig candidate for governor of the state of New York; but he was elected to that office in 1838, and re-elected in 1840. During his official career in New York state, Mr. Seward was an advocate of all judicious progressive measures. In 1842 he resumed the practice of his profession, which soon became extensive and lucrative. Yet he took a lively interest in the politics of the day; was an earnest supporter of Henry Clay for president in 1844, and of Gen. Taylor in 1848. He had opposed the annexation of Texas as a scheme for the extension of the area of slavery.

The field of Mr. Seward's work as a statesman was enlarged in 1849, when he was elected United States Senator by the legislature of New York, and opposed the compromise measures in 1850. He was re-elected in 1855, and held that position until 1861, when he was called to the cabinet of Mr. Lincoln, as secretary of state, in which he conducted the delicate and arduous duties connected with foreign affairs, during the whole of the civil war, with admirable ability and sagacity. He had been identified for many years with the opponents of slavery, and was regarded as one of the ablest champions for freedom. The civil war had been begun for the purpose of establishing an empire of which the corner-stone was to be slavery—an empire built of the ruins of the republic. Upon this great and exciting topic Mr. Lincoln and Mr. Seward were united, and it was fortunate for the president and the country that such an able prime minister was at the head of the cabinet. Mr. Seward continued in that position through President Johnson's administration.

In the spring of 1865 Mr. Seward was thrown from his carriage, and while lying in his bed in a crippled state, he was attacked by a would-be assassin, and very severely wounded. It was on the same night when the president was murdered (April 14, 1865). The shock given by the accident and this murderous attack impaired the able secretary's intellectual force, and, in dissonance with nearly the whole of the republican party, he sustained President Johnson in his opposition to the reorganization measures adopted by congress. Late in the summer of 1870 he began a tour around the world, which he accomplished, notwithstanding his feeble health. He was everywhere received with demonstrations of profound respect throughout his journey, and after his return home he superintended the preparation of a work entitled *William H. Seward's Travels Around the World*. The venerable statesman died at his home in Auburn, N. Y., Oct. 10, 1872.

SAMUEL FINLEY BREESE MORSE.

" CANST thou send lightnings, that they may go, and say unto thee, Here we are?" said the Almighty to afflicted Job, who remained dumb, for he could not answer. The question has been answered in the affirmative in our day by the perfecter of the electro-magnetic telegraph, the late Prof. Morse, by whose invention Puck's promise, "I'll put a girdle 'round the earth in forty minutes," has been performed. Mr. Morse was born in Charlestown, Mass., April 27, 1791, and was the first-born son of Rev. Jedediah Morse, the first American author of a geography. He graduated at Yale College in 1810, and in 1811 went to England under the care of Washington Allston, the painter, and became a pupil in art of Benjamin West. During his college course he had discovered a strong predilection for science, but his love of art was stronger. He made such progress in art that, in 1813, he exhibited at the Royal Academy a picture of the dying Hercules, which won much praise. He first modeled the figure in plaster, and with this he had won the prize of a gold medal from a London Adelphi Society of Arts. The following year he exhibited "The Judgment of Jupiter," a painting praised by West. Young Morse returned home in 1815, and, after a brief sojourn in Boston, painted portraits, at very moderate prices, in New Hampshire, and in Charleston, S. C., where his paintings were appreciated and he prospered. In 1822 he made his residence in New York city, where, commended by the corporation, he painted a full-length portrait of Lafayette in 1824. Chiefly through Morse's instrumentality, the artists of New York, dissatisfied with the "American Academy of Fine Arts" in that city, founded a new association, with the title of the "National Academy of Design," which is still a flourishing institution. He was the first president of the institution.

In 1829 Mr. Morse again visited Europe, and remained there about three years. During his absence he was chosen Professor of the Literature of the Arts of Design in the University of the City of New York. On his return voyage in the fall of 1832, through a casual conversation with the late Dr. Jackson, of Boston, one of the passengers, his mind was turned to the subject of electricity, and he conceived the idea of an electro-magnetic *recording* telegraph, Prof. Henry having already invented an electric telegraph, with mechanical power. Within three months after his return home Prof. Morse began the construction of a recording telegraph. He demonstrated the practical utility of his machine in the New York University in 1835, and in 1838 he applied for a patent. After persistent efforts Prof. Morse procured from congress an appropriation of $30,000, to enable him to construct an experimental line between Washington and Baltimore. It was successful, and the first public message transmitted between the two cities was the announcement of the nomination, by the democratic convention sitting in Baltimore in the spring of 1844, of James K. Polk for the presidency. Then appeared rival claimants to the invention, infringements of his patent, and long, expensive, and vexatious litigations; but Morse finally triumphed, and he was everywhere acknowledged and honored as the inventor of the recording electro-magnetic telegraph. The representatives of the principal European powers, assembled at Paris in 1857, at the suggestion of the emperor of the French, presented Prof. Morse with the sum of $80,000 in gold, in testimony of their appreciation of his great service to the world; and European monarchs bestowed upon him tokens of their regard. In 1843 he suggested, in a letter to the secretary of the U. S. treasury, the project of a telegraphic communication between America and Europe, which he lived to assist in establishing, in 1858. He also lived to see his invention used and appreciated nearly all over the civilized world. Only a few weeks before his death, was realized his dream that dispatches might be sent each way over the same wire at the same instant of time. Possessed of an ample fortune derived from his invention, Prof. Morse lived on the banks of the Hudson, near Poughkeepsie, in winter, and in New York in the summer, until April 2, 1872, on which day he died at his home in New York.

HORACE GREELEY.

A PALE, flaxen-haired, delicate, precocious boy about fifteen years of age, son of a poor farmer, was a printer's apprentice at Poultney, Vt., in 1826. He was very studious, very faithful, very honest, and besides performing the drudgery of "printer's devil" and setting type, he soon became an assistant in editing the newspaper, the *Northern Spectator*. This was Horace Greeley's introduction into the realm of journalism, in which he played such a conspicuous part. He was born at Amherst, N. H., Feb. 3, 1811, went to Vermont with his parents ten years later, and while serving as a printer's apprentice they removed to a farm near Erie, Penn. Horace made them two visits there, walking a greater part of the way. In Aug., 1831, he was in New York city seeking work, without a friend, and only ten dollars in his pocket. He soon found employment as a journeyman printer. Ability, faithfulness, and honesty soon caused his advancement, and he was successively editor and proprietor of the *Morning Post*, the *New Yorker*, the *Jeffersonian*, and the *Log Cabin*. In the publication of the first named, Francis Story was his partner, and in the second, Jonas Winchester. The *Post*, a "penny paper," soon died; the *New Yorker*, a weekly literary paper, neutral in politics, was successful in establishing Mr. Greeley's character as an editor, but was a failure financially, while the *Log Cabin*, a paper devoted to the election of Gen. Harrison to the presidency of the United States, had a large circulation, and brought him fame and emolument. Finally, in the spring of 1841, Mr. Greeley began the publication of the *New York Tribune*, which became the theater of his great exploits in journalism during the remainder of his life, a period of more than twenty years. Henry J. Raymond was his assistant editor. From the beginning, the paper attracted the favorable notice of the public for its independence and public spirit.

Mr. Greeley advocated the election of Henry Clay to the presidency in 1844, and soon afterwards the *Tribune* assumed the position of an active foe of the slave system in our country. In congress in 1848-49 he attacked the abuses of the mileage system, and was instrumental in effecting a reform, for to this end he lent the powerful influence of his newspaper. Mr. Greeley visited Europe in 1851, and was chairman of one of the juries of the world's fair in London. He supported in successive campaigns, for the office of president of the United States, Gen. Scott in 1852, John C. Fremont in 1856, and Abraham Lincoln in 1860. In 1859 he went to California, delivered lectures, and was honored with public receptions, for his fame as a journalist and publicist was then at its culminating point. When the civil war was a-kindling he favored at first a peaceable division of the republic, but when it began by flagrant attacks upon the government he urged a vigorous prosecution of the war. His attempts to bring about peace during the war were almost ludicrous failures, and at its conclusion he advocated conciliatory measures, and universal amnesty and universal suffrage. In May, 1867, he signed his name as surety on the bail bond of Jefferson Davis, which effected his release from prison in Fortress Monroe, and by this act alienated some of his friends at the north who desired to see treason punished, not condoned. Disaffection toward the administration of President Grant caused a partial secession from the republican party. The secessionists called themselves the "liberal republicans," and they nominated Mr. Greeley for president in 1872. The democratic convention also nominated him, but he was defeated by Grant, who was elected for a second term. The excitement of the canvass, the desertion of a large number of his old and most valued political friends, and the death of his wife, combined to almost overthrow his reason and to completely prostrate his physical strength, and he died, Nov. 29, 1872, less than a month after the election. Mr. Greeley was fond of agricultural pursuits, and spent much time on his farm at Chappaqua, in Westchester county, in his later years. He wrote much on the subject. He was one of the busiest of men, sleeping, on an average, little more than four hours out of the twenty-hour. His chief published productions are *Hints about Reform*, 1850; *Glances at Europe; History of the Struggle for Slavery Extension*, 1856; *Over-*

land *Journey from New York to San Francisco; The American Conflict,* 1864-'66, a history of the civil war, in two volumes; *Recollections of a Busy Life,* 1868; *Essays on Political Economy,* and *What I Know about Farming,* published a year before his death. One who knew Mr. Greeley well, wrote of him: "Pure, simple, and conscientious in character. He had a peculiar disregard for dress, and neglected many of the customs of society, but was a true gentleman at heart, and possessed rare gifts in conversation."

HENRY WILSON.

"AN honest man's the noblest work of God," wrote Pope. Henry Wilson, who, in his youth, was a farmer's apprentice, possessed of the most slender rudiments of education, and at his death was vice-president of the United States, was one of those noble productions of his Creator, for he was, in every position in life, an eminently honest man. Born in Farmington, N. H., on the 16th of Feb., 1812, his early education was almost nothing, for his father was very poor. At the age of fourteen he was apprenticed to a well-to-do neighbor, a farmer, for seven years, his compensation being his food and clothing, and at his majority six sheep and a yoke of oxen. His apprenticeship expired on a stormy Saturday. He sold his sheep that day for $9, but could not dispose of his oxen until Monday, when the man he had served faithfully as long as Jacob did for his wife, charged him for the hay his cattle had eaten over Sunday! During that apprenticeship his evenings had been spent in reading useful books lent to him, and when he was twenty-one he was well versed in English and American history.

Wilson began business life as a shoe-maker at Natick, Mass., and earned money enough to pay for his tuition in an academy, at the same time reading and studying the legislative history of his country. In 1838 he visited Washington, when the sight of slaves sold at auction so impressed him with abhorrence for the great Wrong, that he resolved to wage unceasing war upon those institutions. Returning, he found his funds gone in consequence of the failure of a friend, and he resumed shoe-making at Natick, where, for ten years, he manufactured shoes for the southern market. He entered the arena of politics in 1840, and he made eighty speeches in favor of Gen. Harrison for president of the United States. That year he married, and was elected to the state legislature, and became one of the ablest speakers in the house. In 1843 he was elected to the state senate; at the same time he carried on the manufacture of shoes at Natick. In 1848 he published the *Boston Republican,* a whig newspaper, which he edited with ability for two years. In 1850-52 he was president of the state senate, and, in the latter year presided at the national convention of the free-soil party at Pittsburg, as a pronounced and outspoken enemy of slavery. He was the free-soil candidate for governor of Massachusetts in 1853, but was defeated; and in 1855 was elected United States Senator, in which body he was an active, conspicuous, and indefatigable worker in the cause of human rights and good government. His speeches during the Kansas excitement were numerous and remarkable. In March, 1859, he made his celebrated speech in favor of northern labor. He had taken an active part in the organization of the republican party, and was one of its acknowledged leaders. He continued to occupy a seat in the national senate until 1872, when he was elected vice-president of the United States. During the civil war his labors were arduous and wise. The secretary of war declared that "no man, in my opinion, has done more to aid the war department in preparing the mighty army now under arms." He introduced acts for providing men and money for the war. He enlisted 2,300 men in Massachusetts, organized a regiment, and, as its colonel, conducted it to Washington. He was the author of the bill for abolishing slavery in the District of Columbia, and for employing colored soldiers. In 1867 he instituted the congressional temperance society at Washington, and in 1871 spent the summer in Europe. In 1872 he was elected vice-president of the United States, by a large majority. He died of apoplexy in the vice-president's room in the Capitol at Washington, on Nov. 22, 1875. Mr. Wilson wrote a *History of the Anti-Slavery Measures in the Thirty-seventh and Thirty-eighth Congresses; History of the Reconstruction Measures of the Thirty-ninth and Fortieth Congresses;* and *History of the Rise and Fall of the Slave-Power in America*, three volumes. The last volume of this work was nearly completed when he died, and was finished by another hand.

LEWIS CASS.

WHEN President Buchanan hesitated in the exercise of national authority to suppress rising rebellion at the close of 1860, his patriotic secretary of state, Lewis Cass, retired from that office in disgust. He approved the president's denial of the existence of a constitutional power to coerce a state, and so gave passive aid to the secessionists, but when war had begun he was found stoutly supporting the national government. Lewis Cass was born at Exeter, N. H., Oct. 9, 1782, and was a school-fellow with Daniel Webster at the academy there. His family moved to Ohio, near Zanesville, while Lewis was teaching school at Wilmington, Del. The young pedagogue went over the Alleghany mountains on foot, rested at Marietta, where he studied law, and began its practice at Zanesville, Ohio. In 1806 he was a member of the Ohio legislature, and as chairman of a committee to investigate the movements of Aaron Burr he reported a bill which resulted in the arrest of the supposed conspirator. Cass was appointed United States marshal for Ohio in 1807, and in 1811 he resigned and engaged in repelling attacks of Indians on the northern frontier. At the beginning of the war of 1812 he was commissioned colonel of volunteers, served under Hull

in the vicinity of Detroit, and was included in the capitulation in Aug., 1812. Admitted to parole, he hastened to Washington, and so represented the affairs at Detroit that Hull was arrested on a charge of cowardice and treason. Cass was exchanged in Jan., 1813, was made colonel in the regular army, and served as volunteer aid to Gen. Harrison in the battle of the Thames. Cass was appointed civil and military governor of Michigan in the autumn of 1813, and as superintendent of Indian affairs in the north-west he negotiated no less than nineteen treaties with the barbarians.

In 1819-20, Governor Cass organized and conducted a scientific expedition in the exploration of the region of the upper Mississippi river. He held the responsible position of governor until the summer of 1831, when President Jackson called him to his cabinet as secretary of war. His advocacy of the policy of removing all the Indians west of the Mississippi led to war with the Seminoles in Florida. Jackson sent him to France as United States resident minister, where he remained from 1836 to 1842. Opposed to some of the measures of the government, he was recalled by his own request, and in 1845 chosen United States Senator by the legislature of Michigan. He retained the office until 1848, when he resigned and became a nominee for the presidency of the United States. He was defeated at the election in the autumn of that year by Gen.

Zachary Taylor, when he was re-elected to the senate. He was re-elected in 1851, for the full term of six years, and supported measures favorable to the slave power. He and Mr. Buchanan were in accord concerning these measures, and when the latter became president of the United States in 1857, he called Senator Cass to his cabinet as secretary of state. The active secessionists counted upon Cass's support, for he had vigorously opposed the "quintuple treaty" for the suppression of the slave trade, had warmly supported the compromise measures of 1850, including Mason's fugitive slave law, and argued against the proposition that the national government possessed the constitutional right to coerce a state in insurrection into submission. He had opposed the Wilmot Proviso and other measures for restricting the spread of slavery. But when the secessionists resorted to arms, he was found among the supporters of the government. He resigned his position as secretary of state and retired to his home in Detroit, where he died on the 17th of June, 1866. He edited and published an interesting work entitled *France, its King, Court, and Government.*

SAMUEL GRISWOLD GOODRICH.

"I STAND before the public," wrote Mr. Goodrich in his *Recollections of a Lifetime,* "as the author and editor of about 170 volumes, 116 bearing the name of Peter Parley. Of all these, over seven million of volumes have been sold." Like Jacob Abbott, "Peter Parley" (the assumed name of Mr. Goodrich) labored chiefly for the amusement and instruction of the young. He was born in Ridgefield, Conn., Aug. 19, 1793. Having received a good common-school education, he began the publishing business at Hartford, on attaining his majority. In 1824 he visited Europe, and, on his return, established himself as a publisher in Boston. From 1828 to 1842 he edited and published *The Token,* an illustrated annual, to which he contributed several tales and poems, and in which first appeared the finest of Hawthorne's *Twice-Told Tales,* without attracting much attention. The entire annual, literary and artistic, was composed of the work of Americans.

It was soon after Mr. Goodrich removed to Boston that he began his popular series of "Peter Parley's" juvenile books. The 116 volumes comprised geographies, histories, travels, stories, and various illustrations of the arts and sciences. In 1841 he established *Merry's Museum and Parley's Magazine,* a juvenile periodical, which he edited until 1854. Mr. Goodrich was appointed United States consul at Paris in 1851. While there he published a work in French on the geography and history of the United States of America. On his return to his native country he published a kind of autobiography entitled *Recollections of a Lifetime; or Men and Things I have Seen: in a series of Familiar Letters to a Friend, historical, biographical, anecdotal and descriptive.* In that work he gives the names of the books of which he was the author, the recital of which fills six closely printed pages. His latest production was an *Illustrated Natural History of the Animal Kingdom*, completed in 1859. Mr. Goodrich died suddenly in the city of New York, May 9, 1860. On May 8 he called upon the writer of this sketch, and appointed another interview at 11 o'clock the next day. At 9 o'clock that morning his life ended. In person Mr. Goodrich was commanding in appearance, and was singularly vigorous in mind and body for one of his age. In deportment he was courteous and polite on all occasions, and was a charming companion with men of cultivation.

MILLARD FILLMORE.

ON the death of President Zachary Taylor, in July, 1850, the vice-president—Millard Fillmore—according to the provisions of the constitution in such cases, became president of the United States. He had worked his way up to eminence from poverty and obscurity by patient perseverance. He was born at Summer Hill, Cayuga county, N. Y., Jan. 7, 1800. In his youth he was apprenticed to a wool-carder and fuller, and during the four years that he worked at his trade he assiduously cultivated his mind to the extent of his opportunities, for his school education had been very meager. He conceived the idea of studying law when he was nineteen years old, and by contracting to pay his master $30 for the remainder of his time (two years) he was released. He studied with a retired lawyer for a while, and then he went, on foot, to Buffalo, having, on his arrival, only $4 in his pocket. He was then twenty-one years old. There he supported himself by severe drudgery in teaching school and assisting the postmaster, while he studied, by permission, in a lawyer's office. At the end of two years he was admitted to the bar of Erie county as an attorney in the court of common pleas, and commenced the practice of law at Aurora, N. Y. He soon acquired an extensive business, and took rank, in the course of a few years, among the foremost lawyers of the state. He was admitted to practice in the supreme court of the state. Removing to Buffalo in 1830, he pursued his profession there until 1847, when he was elected comptroller of the state.

Mr. Fillmore's political life began in 1828. He was elected to the state legislature by the anti-masonic party, where he served three terms in succession, and was active in efforts for the repeal of the law for imprisonment for debt, which was accomplished in 1831. Mr. Fillmore drafted most of the bill repealing that barbarous law. He was elected to congress in 1832, and again in 1836, when he remained there by successive elections for six years. Mr. Fillmore was a whig, and supported John Quincy Adams in his assertion of the right of petition on the subject of slavery. He opposed the annexation of Texas because it would extend the area of slave territory, and advocated the immediate abolition of the inter-state slave-trade and slavery in the District of Columbia. In the famous contest of New Jerseymen for seats in congress, in 1839, Mr. Fillmore took a prominent part as one of the committee to which the subject was referred. In the next congress, in which the whigs had a majority, Mr. Fillmore was chairman of the committee of ways and means, and, as such, performed valuable public services.

In 1843 Mr. Fillmore retired from congress. Defeated as a candidate for the governorship of his state in 1844, he was elected comptroller in 1847, and, in that capacity, he proposed a system of state banking substantially like that of our national banking system. Mr. Fillmore was elected vice-president with Mr. Taylor in 1848, and, on the death of the president in 1850, he succeeded to that office. During the acrimonious debates in congress in 1849-50 on the subject of slavery, Mr. Fillmore declared to the senate that he should exercise the power of calling senators to order. His course was unanimously approved by a vote of the senate. On becoming president, Mr. Fillmore called Daniel Webster to his cabinet as secretary of state. During his administration, measures were taken for opening commercial intercourse with Japan, and other notable treaties were made. Mr. Fillmore retired to private life in March, 1853, leaving the country at peace at home and abroad. He had been a candidate for nomination by the whig party for president, in 1852, but failed. In 1854 he made an extensive tour of the southern and western states, and, in the spring of 1855, after an excursion in New England, he sailed for Europe, where he remained until the next summer. While he was in Rome he received information that he had been nominated for president by the native American party. He accepted it, but Maryland, alone, gave him its electoral votes. Mr. Fillmore died in Buffalo, March 8, 1874.

JOHN LOTHROP MOTLEY.

ONE of the most eminent historians of our time was John Lothrop Motley, who was born in Dorchester, Mass., April 15, 1814, and graduated at Harvard University in 1831. He spent a year at each of the universities of Göttingen and Berlin, and then traveled in Europe. On his return home he studied law, and was admitted to the bar in 1836. He practiced little, for he loved literature better than law. He published a novel in 1839, and the next year went to Russia as secretary of legation to the American embassy, where he remained about eight months, when he resigned and returned to the United States. In 1849 he published a romance called *Merry Mount*. He had already begun to collect materials for a history of Holland, and had written enough to make two volumes, when, unable to find material needful to complete the work, he embarked for Europe with his family in 1851. Dissatisfied with his previous labors on the history of Holland, he threw the manuscript aside and began anew, using original materials found in Holland and elsewhere. He spent five years abroad, and produced his famous work entitled *The Rise of the Dutch Republic*, in three volumes. It was reprinted at Amsterdam, with an introduction by the historian Bakhuysen Van den Brink. It was also translated into French (with an introduction by Guizot), German, and Russian. The second portion of Motley's history of Holland was published in 1860, entitled *The History of the United Netherlands from the Death of William the Silent to the Twelve Years' Truce*, 1609. It was completed in 1867 in two additional volumes. This work was followed in 1874 by *The Life and Death of John of Barneveld, Advocate of Holland, with a View of the Primary Causes of the Thirty Years' War*, in two volumes. Mr. Motley was engaged in writing a *History of the Thirty Years' War* at the time of his death, which occurred in England on May 29, 1877.

Mr. Motley was appointed minister to Austria late in 1861, and resigned in 1867. On the accession of Gen. Grant to the presidency in 1869 he was appointed minister to England, but was recalled a year later, when he revisited Holland and afterward went to England. Mr. Motley was elected a member of many learned societies in Europe and America, among them the Institute of France, in place of W. H. Prescott, deceased. In 1860 he received the degree of D.C.L. from the University of Oxford, Eng., and LL.D. from Harvard University; also the same degree from the University of Cambridge. The next year he published an able paper in the London Times on "The Causes of the American Civil War." In 1868 he delivered an address before the New York Historical Society on "Historical Progress and American Democracy." His daughter was married to a distinguished gentleman in England, and Mr. Motley was residing with her at the time of his death.

ANDREW JOHNSON.

THE life-career of the seventeenth president of the United States illustrates the spirit and genius of our free institutions. Andrew Johnson was born at Raleigh, N. C., on Dec. 29, 1808. His parents were very poor, and he was so little educated that he was first taught to write and cipher by his wife. He learned the trade of a tailor. He had settled in Greenville, East Tennessee, just before his marriage, taking with him his mother, who depended upon him. Endowed with great physical and mental energy, and taking an interest in local politics, he soon acquired the name of a skillful leader and the position of alderman of the town. He was chosen its mayor when he was less than twenty-three years of age. In 1825 he became a member of the Tennessee legislature, and again in 1839; and in 1840 was chosen a presidential elector. In 1841 he was in the state senate, and from 1843 to 1853 held a seat in the national congress, where he was a conspicuous advocate, as a ready debater, of the annexation of Texas. In 1853 he was elected governor of Tennessee, and re-elected in 1855. He took his seat in the United States

Senate in 1857 for a term of six years. He was then a member of the Democratic party; but when the civil war broke out he took sides with the government and was made military governor of Tennessee in 1862, and in the fall of 1864 was elected vice-president of the United States, with Mr. Lincoln as president. The promise of the inaugural scenes on March 4, 1865, was not auspicious. On the death of Mr. Lincoln he became, constitutionally, president of the United States. At first he was very zealous, in words, against the enemies of the government, but very soon he not only favored them, but made war, as far as he was able by his personal acts, upon congress, trying to foil their measures for the reorganization of the disorganized states, and every act for the benefit of the freedmen. So revolutionary became his words and his efforts that he was finally impeached. There was a lack of only one vote of two thirds of the senate to convict him, and he was acquitted. It was sad to see a man, late in life, destroying, in a few months, by giving way to passion, a good character as a citizen and statesman which he had been years building up. His vetoes of wholesome measures adopted by congress were universally overruled by a two thirds vote, and he went out of the unseemly conflict thoroughly vanquished. Mr. Johnson returned to his home in Tennessee in March, 1869, and died in Clarke county in that state on the 31st of July, 1875. In 1866 the University of North Carolina conferred upon President Johnson the honorary degree of LL.D.

JACOB ABBOTT.

THE young people of America, and, indeed, wherever the English language is spoken, have reason to cherish with reverence and affection the name of Jacob Abbott, because of the delight and instruction he has given them in his numerous stories for youths and which include in their scope almost every department of human activity. His brother—John S. C.—was also a pleasing writer for the young. Together they wrote a series of short histories from which President Lincoln once said he had learned more of history than from any other sources.

Jacob Abbott was born at Hallowell, Maine, Nov. 14, 1803. He graduated at Bowdoin College in 1820, and at Andover Theological Seminary studied divinity. From 1825 to 1829 Mr. Abbott was professor of mathematics and natural philosophy in Amherst College, whence he removed to Boston, where he took charge of the Mt. Vernon School for girls in that city, which had then been lately established. In 1834 he assisted in the organization of a new Congregational church in Roxbury—the Eliot Church—of which he was installed pastor. About 1838 he relinquished the pastoral charge to his brother—John S. C. Abbott—and settled in Farmington, Maine, which place, an old homestead of the family, continued to be his residence until his death, which occurred there Oct. 31, 1879. From that time (1838) forward he devoted his life to literary pursuits, chiefly in the preparation of books for the instruction and amusement of the young. These comprise about two hundred volumes. One of the earliest of his volumes was "The Young Christian," issued the year of his graduation at Amherst. His interest in young people never abated. His books are remarkable for their wealth of information, their absolute purity of tone and expression, and for their wonderful attractiveness for the young of both sexes. Few men have done so much for the intellectual and moral training of youth as Jacob Abbott.

Mr. Abbott spent much time during his active life in New York, where much of his literary labor was performed; but his summers were usually passed at his home in Farmington, which he appropriately named "Few Acres," only a few, which he cultivated with care and assiduity. His personal character was as lovely as his most ardent admirers among his millions of readers could imagine.

WILLIAM LLOYD GARRISON.

"MY country is the world; my countrymen are all mankind," declared William Lloyd Garrison, in the first number of his famous *Liberator*, issued in Boston, Jan. 1, 1831. And he said in his salutatory, on the subject of slavery, "I am in earnest. I will not equivocate; I will not excuse; I will not retreat a single inch, and I will be heard." Mr. Garrison had then suffered much for conscience sake, but his spirit was not even bent.

Mr. Garrison was born in Newburyport, Mass., Dec. 12, 1804. His parents were from the British province of New Brunswick. On account of poverty, his excellent mother became a professional nurse, and William, at an early age, was apprenticed to a shoemaker. He was afterwards sent to school, and partly supported himself by aiding a wood-sawyer. In 1815 he went to Baltimore with his mother, and on his return in 1818, he was apprenticed to a newspaper printer. He soon began to write acceptable articles for the paper, but always anonymously. He wrote for other journals, and his political articles attracted much attention. His first venture as a publisher, in Newburyport—the *Free Press*—was unsuccessful, and he labored a while in Boston as a journeyman printer. In that city he became editor of the *National Philanthropist* in 1827. It was the first journal ever established to advocate the cause of "total abstinence from intoxicating liquors." Afterwards Mr. Garrison, with another, published a paper at Bennington, Vt., devoted to politics, general reform, and especially to the cause of anti-slavery. His course on the latter subject was so decided and effective, that Benjamin Lundy, a Quaker, was then publishing the *Genius of Universal Emancipation* at Baltimore, engaged Mr. Garrison to assist him. Before going to Baltimore, he delivered an address in the Park Street Church, Boston, on July 4, 1829, which, by its bold denunciation of slavery, startled all thoughtful people. In the fall he began his career in Baltimore, and advocated immediate emancipation as the right of the slave and the duty of the master. He also derided the Colonization Society. Mr. Garrison very soon incurred the enmity of all who were interested in the perpetuation of the slave system. He was fined and imprisoned as the result of libel-suits. The northern press, the Manumission Society of North Carolina, and Henry Clay condemned his imprisonment as a direct blow at the liberty of the press, and Arthur Tappan, a New York merchant, paid his fine and he was set at liberty.

Mr. Garrison now prepared a course of lectures on slavery, which he delivered in Philadelphia, New York, and Boston, under great opposition. He was unable to procure a public place to lecture in at Boston until he advertised that unless some church or hall should be offered in which he might make his plea for humanity, he should address the people on the common. An association of men whom society called infidels offered him the use of their hall. A large audience attended, and he declared that in Christianity alone rested the hopes of the slave. He gave the system of slavery and its abettors hard blows. His fervid and logical appeals were listened to with great attention, and there were many

"Who came to scoff remained to pray."

At the beginning of 1831 Mr. Garrison issued the first number of the *Liberator*, with the words quoted at the beginning of this sketch. Under the severe pressure of poverty and public odium he persevered, working in the printing-office all day, and writing half the night. The *Liberator* attracted great attention, north and south. The mayor of Boston having been appealed to by a magistrate in a southern state to suppress the paper, replied, "I have ferreted out the paper and its editor, whose office was in an obscure hole, his only visible auxiliary a negro boy, his supporters a very few insignificant persons of all colors." What a testimony is this to the power of faith animating a courageous spirit, which subsequent events in the history of our country demonstrate. Almost every mail brought to Mr. Garrison threats of assassination if he did not discontinue the *Liberator*. At near the close of 1831 the legislature of Georgia passed an act offering a reward of $5,000 to any person who should arrest and prosecute to conviction the obnoxious editor and publisher. This was answered by Mr. Garrison by the immediate formation of an anti-slavery society in New England. He went to England as its agent, where he found powerful support of the cause, and soon after his return the American Anti-slavery Society was formed in Philadelphia. In all subsequent movements in opposition to the slave system, until it was destroyed, by the rebellion of its adherents, in 1863, Mr. Garrison was the acknowledged leader. His name was continually on the lips of mobs who assailed the meetings of abolitionists everywhere. These meetings were broken up by violence in Boston by persons described by the press at that day as "gentlemen of property and standing." In 1843 Mr. Garrison was chosen president of the American Anti-slavery Society, and held the office until the dissolution of the society in 1865. He saw the full triumph of the cause in which he had so long and so fearlessly labored. By invitation of the secretary of war in April, 1865, he accompanied a party from the north who proceeded to Charleston harbor and assisted at the raising of the flag of our emancipated country over the ruins of Fort Sumter. A writer in Appleton's *Cyclopædia* says: "The first number of the *Liberator*, issued in 1831, found the whole nation asleep over the wrongs and dangers of slavery; the last number, issued on the last of December, 1865, after thirty-five years of conflict with the slave power, recorded the ratification of an amendment to the constitution of the United States forever prohibiting the existence of slavery." Soon after the close of the war, many distinguished citizens of our country united in presenting to Mr. Garrison the sum of $30,000 as a testimonial of their appreciation of his great services to the republic. He visited England in 1867, where he was cordially welcomed by distinguished citizens and statesmen. Mr. Garrison died May 24, 1879.

BAYARD TAYLOR.

ONE of the most persevering, extensive, and enlightened of the world's travelers was Bayard Taylor, as he was one of the most charming and prolific of American writers of prose and poetry. He was born at Kenneth Square, Chester County, Penn., Jan. 11, 1825. At the age of seventeen he became an apprentice in a printing-office in West Chester, and he employed his leisure hours in studying and writing verses. In 1844 a collection of them was published under the title of Ximena. The same year he began a pedestrian tour in Europe after securing employment as a contributor during his absence to a number of American newspapers. On his return, after two years of travel, he published a volume entitled *Views Afoot*. In 1848 Mr. Taylor became permanently connected with the *New York Tribune*, having edited a newspaper in Phœnixville, Penn., for a year, and writing for the *Literary World*. It was in the *Tribune* that his subsequent books of travel first appeared. In 1850 he visited California and Mexico, and describes his experiences there in his *Eldorado ; or Adventures in the Path of Empire*. His *Book of Romauces, Lyrics, and Songs* appeared in 1851, and that year he began a long tour in the eastern hemisphere—Europe, Asia, and Africa. While in China, he was attached to the American legation a short time, and then joined Commodore Perry on his mission to Japan. He returned home at the close of 1853, having traveled about 50,000 miles during his absence. He continued to travel, and published his notes in the *Tribune* and in book form, until 1862, when he was appointed secretary to the American legation at St. Petersburg, where, for a time, he acted as Chargé d'affaires. He left that position the next year, and during the next two or three years produced two novels. He also wrote and published poems and brief sketches of travel; and in 1871 he completed and published a translation of Goethe's

Faust, which is accepted as the best in the English language. He assumed the editorship of the *Illustrated Library of Travel, Exploration, and Adventure* in 1872, in a series of small volumes.

For a while Mr. Taylor occupied a conspicuous place in the lecture field, and was a constant contributor to serial publications. He was appointed American minister to the court of the emperor of Germany, and in April sailed for Europe with his family. The German people gave him a hearty welcome, for his name was well known throughout the empire. He had long contemplated writing a full biography of Goethe, and he expected his position as minister at Berlin would give him many advantages for such a task, but death cut short his career in the course of a few months after his arrival at his diplomatic post. He died in Berlin on Dec. 19, 1878. Mr. Taylor visited Iceland in 1874, on the occasion of the one-thousandth anniversary of its settlement by the Norwegians. His remains were brought to New York in March, 1879, where they were received with appropriate public respect. They were buried near his home at Cedar Croft, Penn.

ROBERT EDMUND LEE.

THE most distinguished but not the most skillful of the military leaders of the Confederate forces during the late civil war, was Robert E. Lee. He was born at Stafford, Westmoreland County, Va., on June 19, 1807. He was a son of Col. Henry Lee of the Revolution, known as "Legion Harry." He became a cadet at West Point in 1825, where he was distinguished for his good behavior, and graduated in 1829, second in his class. During the whole four years of his cadetship he was never reprimanded or received a demerit mark. He entered the corps of engineers, was engaged as assistant engineer, from 1829 until 1834, in the construction of Fortress Monroe. In 1839 he was assistant astronomer in determining the boundary between Ohio and Michigan. In 1838 he was promoted to captain, and when the war with Mexico began, he was appointed chief engineer of the army under Gen. Scott, and was distinguished for important services during the contest. For his gallantry he received successive brevets, the last that of colonel. From 1852 to 1855 he was superintendent of the military academy at West Point. In the latter year he was made lieutenant-colonel of one of two new regiments of cavalry, of which Albert Sidney Johnston was colonel, Hardee and Thomas majors, and Van Dorn and Kirby Smith captains. All of these officers excepting George H. Thomas deserted their flag in 1861, and fought against their country. Through his wife, Mary Custis, a great-granddaughter of Mrs. Washington, and daughter of Washington's adopted son, G. W. P. Custis, he came into possession of the Arlington estate, near the national capital, and the "White House" on the Pamunkey.

In the fall of 1859 Lee was placed in command of United States

ROBERT EDMUND LEE.

forces to suppress the invasion of John Brown, at Harper's Ferry, and was soon afterward sent to take command of the Department of Texas. Seduced from his allegiance to the national government by the champions of the doctrine of state supremacy, he obtained leave of absence in Dec., 1860, and came home. When, in April, 1861, a Virginia convention issued an ordinance of secession, he resigned his commission, saying: "Save in defense of my native state, I never desire again to draw my sword." Lee at once repaired to Richmond and was appointed major-general of the forces of Virginia. In accepting the position, he said: "Trusting in Almighty God, an approving conscience, and the aid of my fellow-citizens, I devote myself to the service of my native state, in whose behalf alone will I ever again draw my sword." Circumstances led him to draw his sword in the service of several confederated states whose people were in arms against his country. He was not successful at first, in command in western Virginia, and he was sent to perform engineering service on the Savannah river. He also acted as military adviser of Jefferson Davis. In June, 1862, he was appointed to the command of the army of Northern Virginia, and with that army he fought the national forces until he was compelled to surrender at Appomattox Court-house, April 9, 1865. Early in that year he was made general-in-chief of the confederate forces. After the war he returned to private life. In Nov., 1865, he accepted the position of president of Washington and Lee College, at Lexington, Va., to which his popularity in the south soon drew nearly 500 students. On the 28th of Sept., 1870, while apparently in his usual health, Gen. Lee was struck with paralysis and died a fortnight afterwards (Oct., 12). His three sons were officers in the Confederate service.

WILLIAM CULLEN BRYANT.

AMONG the hills of Hampshire County, Mass., at the village of Cummington, William Cullen Bryant was born on Nov. 3, 1794. He was a son of a distinguished local physician, whose mind was richly cultivated by study and travel, and who spent much time in the intellectual culture of his children, and particularly of William, whose poetic genius was early made manifest. In his boyhood he communicated rhymes to the country newspapers, and when in his thirteenth year he wrote a political poem entitled "The Embargo," which evinced great precocity of intellect. He entered Williams College in 1810, but did not graduate. Choosing the profession of law, he was admitted to the bar at the age of twenty-one. Meanwhile he had written several meritorious poems. The most remarkable literary production of his life was "Thanatopsis," written when he was nineteen years of age. Mr. Bryant began the practice of law first at Plainfield. He soon removed to Great Barrington, and rose very rapidly in reputation as a pleader in the local courts. His tastes inclined him to the pursuit of literature, and it was not long before he abandoned law as a profession. "Thanatopsis" was published in the *North American Review*, and introduced him to the late Richard H. Dana, who was one of the club which then conducted the *Review*. It was published anonymously, and excited the curiosity and admiration of the literati of that day. He contributed some prose articles to the *Review*. In 1821 he delivered a didactic poem on "The Ages," before the Phi Beta Kappa Society at Harvard College, and the same year he published a collection of his poems in a volume.

In 1825 Mr. Bryant became associate editor of the *New York Review*, and in 1826 he formed an editorial connection with the New York *Evening Post*, which continued until his death. When, some years after he became associate editor of the *Post*, and he had become editor-in-chief, Mr. Bryant made it a decided democratic newspaper, taking ground in favor of freedom for all and free trade, a position which he consistently maintained, with an independent spirit, until the end of his life. In 1834 Mr. Bryant sailed, with his family, to Europe, where he was already familiarly known, and traveled through France, Italy, and Germany, continually studying the language and literature of those countries. He visited Europe again in 1845, 1849, and 1858, and in the intervals had visited much of his native country from Maine to Florida; also Cuba. In 1863 he published a small volume of new poems, entitled *Thirty Poems*, and the next year, on the completion of his seventieth year, his birthday was celebrated by a festival at the Century Club, nearly all the prominent literary men of the country being present, or sending complimentary letters. He translated the poems of Homer after he was seventy years of age. He began that of the *Iliad* in 1865, and finished the last book of the *Odyssey* in Dec. 1871. Mr. Bryant's occasional speeches and more formal orations are models of stately style, sometimes enlivened by quiet humor. He was equally happy in the composition—prose and poetry. His translation from Homer into blank verse is universally conceded to be the best English version of the great epics. His last poem, on the subject of Washington, was published in the *Sunday School Times*, Philadelphia, on Feb. 22, 1878. At the time of his death, June 12, 1878, he was engaged with Mr. Sidney Howard Gay in the preparation of a *History of the United States*. He had also completed, with the assistance of the late Evert A. Duyckinck, a new and carefully annotated edition of Shakespeare's Works, yet (1881) unpublished.

JOSEPH HENRY.

ABOUT fifty years ago (1831–32), the minds of two Americans were occupied in efforts to solve the problem of the transmission of intelligence by means of electricity. These two men, who became famous in scientific annals, were Joseph Henry and Samuel F. B. Morse. The first named may fairly claim the honor of being the inventor of the electro-magnetic telegraph; the latter performed a greater work for the public good by the invention of a method for making the telegraph useful by giving it a voice.

Joseph Henry was a native of the city of Albany, N. Y., where he was born, Dec. 1797. Educated in the common schools and the academy of his native city, young Henry early evinced a taste and genius for mathematics and scientific research. He was apprenticed to a watchmaker and jeweler, and bent all his energies to the acquirement of knowledge. Such was his success in intellectual attainments, that in 1826 he was appointed professor of mathematics in the academy at which he had graduated. The next year he began a series of investigations and experiments in electricity, and in 1828 he made his first communication on the subject to Silliman's *American Journal of Science*. These experiments and reports continued for about twelve years. The electro-magnet had long been known as a scientific toy; but, until Henry's investigations, no attempt had been made to develop its capacity as a philosophical instrument. He was the first to prove, by actual experiment, that, in order to develop magnetic power at a distance, a galvanic battery of intensity must be employed to project the current; and that a magnet surrounded by many coils of one long wire must be used to receive this current. In

1831 he placed a wire more than a mile in length in circles around a room in the Albany academy through which he transmitted signals by means of an electro-magnet which caused a lever to impinge upon a bell. In his report of this experiment published in the *American Journal of Science*, the professor pointed out the possibility of instantaneous conveyance of intelligence between distant points. This was as far as his investigations carried him in the way of telegraphy. Had he discovered a method of giving intellectual signs or (figuratively) a voice to his invention, he would have gained the crown won and worn by Prof. Morse. During the same year (1831) Henry exhibited the first contrivance ever invented for producing and maintaining continuous motion with electricity as a motor. He invented, and exhibited in 1861, the first telephone ever constructed, but, as with his other inventions, he failed to give it practical utility.

Professor Henry's communications in the *American Journal of Science* having given him a great reputation, he was invited to Yale College in 1831, and while there he constructed a magnet capable of sustaining a weight of two thousand pounds. Another was constructed a few weeks later for the College of New Jersey, at Princeton, which sustained a weight of three thousand pounds. In 1832 Mr. Henry was elected professor in that institution. At the end of five years he was overworked, took leave of the college and made a tour in Europe, where his brilliant reputation had preceded him. We know but little concerning the intellectual activities of Prof. Henry during the succeeding years until 1846, when, upon the organization of the Smithsonian Institution, he was made its secretary, which responsible and very important position he held until his death, on the 13th of May, 1878, a period of thirty-two years. In 1849 he was chosen president of the American Association for the Advancement of Science, and in 1868 he became president of the National Academy of Science. He was placed at the head of the Lighthouse Board of the United States in 1871. This is one of the most laborious posts in the gift of the Navy Department. So early as 1829, at the age of thirty-two years, while yet a mere professor *à grace*, in the Albany Academy, Union College conferred upon him the honorary degree of LL.D., and in 1851 Harvard University conferred the same degree upon him. His literary work is scattered through many publications. As secretary of the Smithsonian Institution at Washington, he had the principal control of its publications, which involved much critical labor, and he was the chief person in making selections for the *Transactions*. In this labor his intellectual grasp was made manifest, for these papers treated upon the whole subject of physical scientific research, including that of his specialty —electricity. The influence of Prof. Henry in stimulating original researches in the domain of the physical sciences cannot well be overestimated. His last illness was caused by a severe cold taken on a trip north in connection with the fog signal service, which developed into a severe attack of Bright's disease of the kidneys. It ran its course rapidly and ended the life of the great scientist. His remains were interred in Rock Creek cemetery, near Georgetown, D. C.

REVERDY JOHNSON.

ONE of the most active members of the "Peace Convention," held at Washington at the beginning of the late civil war, was Reverdy Johnson, an eminent lawyer of Baltimore. He was born in Annapolis, Md., May 21, 1796, and died there on the 10th of Feb., 1876. His father was, at different times, attorney-general, judge of the court of appeals, and chancellor of Maryland. Reverdy entered the primary department of St. John's College, at Annapolis, when he was six years of age, and remained there ten years. He studied law with his father, and was admitted to the bar in 1815, and for fifty years was engaged in the practice of his profession. In 1814 he enlisted in the military service to defend his state against the invading British, and took part in the battle of Bladensburg. Returning to Baltimore in 1817, he began the study of law. Three years later he was appointed chief commissioner of insolvent debtors, which office he held until 1821, when he was elected to a seat in the state senate. He was re-elected, but soon resigned to devote himself entirely to his profession. He reported and edited the judicial decisions in the court of appeals in Maryland, in seven volumes, known as *Harris's and Johnson's Reports*. Active in the whig party after it assumed that name, he did good service as a private, never accepting office until 1845, when he was chosen United States Senator. He remained in congress ten years, when, in 1849, he was called to the cabinet of President Taylor as attorney-general. Soon after the president's death the next year he resigned, and for the next ten years was engaged unremittingly in his profession, chiefly in the Supreme Court of the United States.

When the turmoil of preparation for secession and civil war was heard in the southern states in 1860, Mr. Johnson viewed the situation with great anxiety. His sympathies were on the side of his country and the union, but on every side, socially, there was a severe pressure upon him in the direction of secession. He was a member of the "Peace Convention" at Washington, early in 1861, where he took a leading part in endeavors to bring about a reconciliation. Soon afterwards he was chosen to represent Baltimore County in the Maryland Assembly, and in 1862 was chosen United States Senator for six years from March, 1863. There he was a firm supporter of the union, and was one of the most industrious and active members of the senate during his entire term, and a member of various important committees. Mr. Johnson was a delegate to the "National Union Convention" held at Philadelphia in 1866, in the interest of President Andrew Johnson, and was nominated by that functionary to the English mission in the summer of 1868. His special business was to procure a settlement of the "*Alabama* claims," but he failed to effect anything. On his return, he resumed the practice of his profession, and was engaged in it at Annapolis at the time of his sudden demise. His lifeless body was found in the evening lying upon the stone pavement of the carriage-way leading under the porch of the governor's mansion, where Mr. Johnson was a guest. It was supposed he fell, on account of defective vision, in passing down the stone steps leading to the carriage-way, and was killed. Mr. Johnson was of medium height, of a grave countenance, courteous and pleasing manners, and was a favorite in society.

RUFUS CHOATE.

"HE fairly fought his way to eminence, created the taste which gratified, and demonstrated the possibility of almost a new variety of eloquence," wrote Prof. Brown, concerning Rufus Choate, the celebrated lawyer and orator of Massachusetts. He was

born Oct. 1, 1799, in the old Massachusetts town of Ipswich, and was descended from a race of thrifty farmers. The training of Rufus devolved upon his mother after he was nine years of age, at which time his father died. With the parish clergyman and teachers of the district schools he studied Latin, beginning in his tenth year, and in 1855 entered Dartmouth College, at which he graduated with highest honors. For a year afterward he was a tutor in the college, when he entered the Dane law school at Cambridge. He afterwards studied under the celebrated William Wirt, of Washington, completing his legal studies at Salem. Mr Choate entered upon the practice of law at Danvers, soon removed to Salem, and in 1825 was elected to a seat in the Massachusetts legislature. Two years later he occupied a seat in the senate, and acquired a wide spread reputation for eloquence, logical ability, and sagacity. From 1832 to 1835 he represented the Essex district in congress, and then went to Boston, where he devoted himself to the practice of his profession. He rapidly attained the highest place as a lawyer and forensic orator, and took the position of one of the leaders of the bar in his native state. When, in 1841, Daniel Webster retired from the senate, Mr. Choate was chosen to fill his place, where he took a conspicuous part in several important debates on momentous public questions; and when the Smithsonian Institution was established, he was chosen one of the regents. He warmly opposed the annexation of Texas, because he regarded it as a scheme of southern politicians for the extension of the dominion of slavery. At the close of his senatorial term, in 1846, he gave himself up entirely to the practice of his profession, and never entered the public service again excepting as attorney-general of his state in 1853. After the death of Webster, he was the acknowledged leader of the Massachusetts bar, and his services were sought for by litigants in other states.

In 1855 Mr. Choate suffered from an accident so severely that his health was seriously impaired, and in 1858 he was compelled to retire from professional labor. In search of restoration he sailed for Europe in the summer of 1859, but proceeded no further than Halifax, Nova Scotia, where he died on July 13, when he was about sixty years of age. In person Mr. Choate was tall and commanding. His face had a remarkable expression of intellectual vigor; his voice was rich, musical, and sympathetic, and he was probably the most persuasive pleader of his time. His utterances were exuberant and brilliant, at the same time powerful in carrying conviction to the minds of others. He possessed consummate tact and unerring judgment in the management of causes, and never made a mistake himself nor overlooked one in his opponent in the examination of witnesses. The leading men of the bar regarded with respect and admiration the great mind they saw beneath some peculiarities of manner.

DAVID GLASCOE FARRAGUT.

"I HAVE no volition in the matter; your duty is to give me orders, mine to obey." So wrote commandant Farragut to the secretary of the navy, in 1856, on receiving an intimation from him that if he would indicate his preference for a station, it would be granted. This sentence is a key to his whole public character, from his entrance into the navy as midshipman before he was ten years of age. He was born near Knoxville, Tenn., July 5, 1801. His father was a native of Minorca, and came to America in 1776, when he became an active soldier in the continental army. His early life was passed on the frontier. Capt. David Porter took charge of him when he was between nine and ten years of age, and on Dec. 17, 1810 he was appointed a midshipman. He first served on the *Essex*, under Porter, and was with him on his long cruise to the Pacific ocean in 1812–13. Porter intrusted him with the command of a prize to be taken into Valparaiso, while he was yet a little boy. "I was sent as prize-master to the *Barclay*," wrote Farragut in after-years. "This was an important event in my life, and when it was decided that I was to take the ship to Valparaiso, I felt no little pride at finding myself in command at twelve years of age." He was engaged in the battle between the *Essex* and the *Phœbe* and *Cherub*, off Valparaiso.

Young Farragut was commissioned lieutenant in 1825, having been recommended for promotion three years before. Meanwhile he had distinguished himself by a cruise against pirates in the West Indies. In the sloop-of-war *Vandalia* he joined the American squadron on the Brazilian station, when he was executive officer of the *Natchez* in 1833. He rose to commander in 1841, and was ordered to the sloop-of-war *Decatur* off the coast of Brazil. In 1847 he was placed in command of the sloop-of-war *Saratoga*. From 1851 to 1853 he was assistant-inspector of ordnance, and was placed in command of the navy-yard at Mare Island, near San Francisco, in 1854. Farragut was commissioned captain in the navy in 1855, and was placed in command of the steamship *Brooklyn* of the home squadron.

Capt. Farragut was put in a very delicate position on the breaking out of the civil war. By nativity and by marriage of two wives in succession, he was identified with the slave-labor states. When his country was assailed by its recreant children in the southern states, and scores of southern-born naval officers deserted the old flag and joined the enemies of the republic, Farragut did not hesitate a moment in choosing to defend the union, for he was a true patriot, owing his allegiance to the national government, not to the pretended petty sovereignty of a state. He took his family to a village on the Hudson river, and then went forth to give mighty blows against the dragon of rebellion. All through the four years' war that ensued he was the model commander wherever his flag was seen, whether on the Mississippi river or the gulf of Mexico, in his good wooden ship *Hartford*. He led in the expedition against and capture of New Orleans, and in efforts to make the Mississippi free for the navigation of national vessels. He attempted to reduce Vicksburg, and took a conspicuous part in the attack on Port Hudson, the following year. For his services at New Orleans, and on the Mississippi above and below, he was thanked by Congress, and placed first on the list of rear-admirals soon afterwards created. He did gallant service on the coast of Texas, as commander of the Gulf squadron. His most brilliant achievement during the war was in Mobile bay at near the close of the summer of 1864. Lashed to a position among the shrouds of the *Hartford*, where he could oversee and command his whole squadron, he boldly sailed into the bay, fighting a fort, gun-boats, and a powerful ram, and every moment in danger of destruction by torpedoes. One of these destroyed an iron-clad gun-boat just in front of the *Hartford*. She filled and sunk in a few seconds, carrying down her commander and nearly all of her men. At that moment he felt that all was lost, but his first impulse was to appeal to heaven for guidance, and he prayed: "O God, who created man and gave him reason, direct me what to do. Shall I go on?" And it seemed as if a voice in answer commanded him to "Go on!" and he cried out: "Four bells! Capt. Drayton, go ahead! Jouett, full speed!" and victory was the result.

In Dec., 1864, he received the thanks of congress and was promoted to the rank of vice-admiral, which was created expressly for him. He was afterward commissioned admiral, which placed him at the head of the navy. In 1867-68, Admiral Farragut visited stations in Europe, Asia, and Africa, and was everywhere received with highest honors. He died at Portsmouth, N. H., on Aug. 14, 1870, having served sixty years in the navy. A memorial monument to his memory modeled by Launt Thompson was placed on the left of the chancel in the Church of the Incarnation, in New York; and a monument was erected by his family over his remains which rest in Woodlawn cemetery, in Westchester county, N. Y. Congress appropriated $20,000 for the erection of a colossal bronze statue, and gave the commission to Miss Vinnie Ream. A commission was also given by citizens of New York to Mr. St. Gauden to produce a statue of the admiral to be set up in that city.

BENJAMIN PEIRCE.

THE domain of science lost one of its most efficient laborers and brightest scholars when Prof. Benjamin Peirce died at Cambridge, Mass., Oct. 6, 1880. He was born at Salem, in that state, April 4, 1809; and graduated at Harvard College, at the age of twenty years. He became a tutor there in 1831; university professor in mathematics and natural philosophy in 1833; and Perkins professor of astronomy and mathematics in 1842, in which position he continued until his death, a period of thirty-eight years. No person, excepting tutor Henry Flynt, of the class of 1693, was ever so long connected with Harvard, professionally. In 1849 Prof. Peirce was appointed consulting astronomer to the *American Ephemeris and Nautical Almanac*. He was one of the scientific council to which was intrusted the organization of the Dudley Observatory, at Albany, in 1855. He assisted Prof. Bache in the coast Survey and rendered valuable aid in this great national work for several years. In 1867 he succeeded Prof. Bache as superintendent of the coast survey, but resigned the office in 1874.

Prof. Peirce's labors in the realm of science have been incessant and most valuable. While he was a pupil of Dr. Bowditch, he read the proof-sheets of the translation of La Place's *Mecanique Celeste*.

He undertook the publication of the "Cambridge Miscellany of Mathematics, Physics, and Astronomy," of which only five numbers appeared. Between 1836 and 1846 he prepared a series of mathematical text-books which are used in Harvard College. His Boston lectures on the comet of 1843 aroused an interest which led to the foundation of the observatory at Cambridge; and his investigations relating to the discovery of Nepture by Leverrier, in 1846, attracted the attention of astronomers in Europe and America, and proved him to be a thinker of extraordinary power. In that paper, while he did not intimate that Leverrier's calculations had been erroneous, he assumed that both the French mathematician and the English astronomer Adams had arrived at erroneous conclusions concerning the perturbations of Uranus, and demonstrated that the mass, the distance from the sun, and other characteristics of the real planet were entirely different from those assumed by them. He declared that the discovery of the planet by Galle nearly in the position pointed out by Leverrier was due to a happy accident rather than the necessary result of the mathematician's calculations. He discussed with great ability other astronomical questions, such as the nature of Saturn's rings. All his writings are characterized by singular directness, and his intellectual nature was most vigorous. He loved all that was beautiful in the world and revered everything of God's works, from the delicate flower to the ponderous planet. His latest productions were a course of Lowell lectures, on "Ideality in Science."

LUCRETIA MOTT.

"TRUTH for Authority; not Authority for Truth," was the form of a favorite aphorism which Lucretia Mott wrote, in a fair round hand, on the back of a photographed portrait which she sent to the writer of this volume when she was eighty-six years of age. By the principle formulated in this aphorism the career of this noble woman was always governed. It was a predominating element in her character. It was the light she followed: the inspirer of her courage to walk fearlessly in the path of duty prescribed by the light within—the conscience—Emmanuel, God with us. Her name was a synonym for a rare combination of Christian graces. Hers was a strong, sweet, and noble soul, ever guided by unswerving loyalty to truth and righteousness.

Lucretia Mott's maiden name was Coffin, a descendant of one of the earliest settlers on Nantucket, where she was born on the 3d of Jan., 1793. Her parents removed to Boston, and when she was thirteen years of age, she was sent to the "Nine Partners'" boarding-school, an institution established by the Friends, in Duchess county, N. Y., a few years before. There she was under the instruction of Deborah Rodgers (afterwards Mrs. Jacob Willetts), who died in 1879 at the age of above ninety years. During her absence at that time, her parents removed to Philadelphia. She returned

home in 1809, and two years afterwards, when in her nineteenth year, she was married to James Mott, a young merchant, and a member of the Society of Friends, who formed a business partnership with his father-in-law. Anxious to be as useful as possible, Lucretia took charge of a school in Philadelphia in 1817, and the next year she began to preach in the religious society to which she belonged. She was then twenty-five years of age. Her sweet voice, her fervid manner, her persuasive eloquence, and her words of wisdom always charmed and edified her hearers. She soon extended her labors, journeying through New England, Pennsylvania, Maryland, and parts of Virginia on religious visits, and preaching whenever opportunity to do so was afforded. Everywhere and on all occasions she advocated the peaceable and benevolent principles of the Society of Friends or Quakers. She waged incessant battle against slavery, intemperance, and war with material weapons. When, by the ministrations of Elias Hicks, who became a unitarian in theology, the Society of Friends became separated into two parts, the "Orthodox" and the "Hicksites," in 1827, Lucretia adhered to the latter, and was a very able minister of the gospel among them through the remainder of her life.

Mrs. Mott took an active part in the organization of the American Anti-Slavery Society at Philadelphia, in 1833, and was one of its ablest supporters. In 1840 she was chosen a delegate to the World's Anti-Slavery Convention held in London. Men had not then reached the happy era in modern civilization, now dawning, when women are admitted to an equality with men in human efforts of every kind, and Lucretia Mott was excluded from the seat of a delegate in that convention! But she was invited to a breakfast of which many persons of high rank partook, some of whom had voted to exclude her from the convention. She thought it a good opportunity to say what she intended to in the convention, had she been admitted. Rising before the company, she gave a most fervid and eloquent address. At the beginning of her speech the high-toned guests were amazed at her presumption in giving utterance to her thoughts in that manner in such a presence; but before she had concluded, that amazement was changed to admiration, and her mission was then fulfilled.

Mrs. Mott was always an earnest and consistent advocate of the rights of woman to participate in the duties and privileges of American citizenship. She was an active member of the national convention of women seeking to secure these rights for their sex, from the first one held at Genesee Falls in 1848 (at which her husband presided), until the last year of her life. She was permitted to live until some of her most earnest aspirations were gratified—the bonds stricken from the limbs of four million slaves; noble victories achieved by the champions of temperance; and to witness the opalescent glow of the dawning of the day when woman in society as in nature shall be recognized as the peer of man. She could say with abounding gratitude when the messenger came, "Now lettest thou thy servant depart in peace according to thy word, for mine eyes have seen thy salvation."

Mrs. Mott died on Nov. 11, 1880, at her home in Philadelphia. Husband and children had departed before, but no funereal gloom shadowed her spirit, for she was in sympathy with all sufferers, and a bright, beckoning hope always made her cheerful. During all her public ministrations, Lucretia Mott never neglected her home duties. She was an exemplary old-fashioned housekeeper, and her four daughters were brought up to be the same. The atmosphere of her home was almost ideal in its peace and harmony. She leaned trustingly upon her husband as the stronger being. His was a nature similar to her own, but he was a very silent man. She was fond of all domestic occupations, and at the age of eighty-six she could thread her own needle with ease. She labored much for the poor; distributing comforts among them with a lavish hand, while she bestowed very little upon herself. She was fond of bright things, and had a piano, paintings, and warm colors in the carpets and curtains of her home.

Mrs. Mott was of small and slight stature and figure, and her face had the charm of delicate and regular features, combined with great strength of character. Her eyes were very bright, and expressive of great intelligence, appearing gray ordinarily, but when animated in conversation or by some strong emotion, their color deepened and appeared almost black.

EDWIN HUBBELL CHAPIN.

ONE of the most accomplished scholars and earnest, studious, and eloquent pulpit orators of our time died in the city of New York on Sunday evening, Dec. 26th, 1880. That eminent divine was Edwin H. Chapin, D.D., LL.D., a lineal descendant of the first of that name who emigrated to America, and who settled in Massachusetts in 1636. The family is a ministerial one, there having been no less than sixteen clergymen among the descendants of the emigrant. Mr. Chapin was born at Union Village, Washington county, N. Y., Dec. 29, 1814. He began the study of law, but soon abandoned it for a pursuit more consonant with his tastes. When he was about twenty-one years of age, he was one of the editors of the "Magazine and Advocate," at Utica, N. Y., and there began to preach. At the age of twenty-three he was ordained a minister in the Universalist church. His eloquence attracted large audiences, and his fame as a speaker went abroad. Soon after his ordination he was called to the pastorate of the Independent Christian church in Richmond, Va., which was composed of Universalists and Unitarians. Mr. Chapin was so successful there, that, in 1840, the Universalists of Charlestown, Mass., called him to take charge of their growing church there. He labored with great success in that position six years, having among his hearers many of the leading men of intellect in Charlestown. Social reforms of every kind found in him a powerful advocate, and when the lyceum lecture system was springing into vigorous life, Mr. Chapin was the most popular platform speaker of the day. Crowds flocked to the lectures of the eloquent divine, and he, more than any other speaker, made the lyceum popular among all classes.

In 1842 Mr. Chapin was chosen a member of the Massachusetts State Board of Education; and before he was thirty years of age, he was selected to preach the annual election sermon before the legislature. In 1846 he was called to share the pulpit, in Boston, with Rev. Hosea Ballou, the founder of the Universalist church in America. Two years later he received a call to the pastorate of the Church of the Divine Paternity in the city of New York. He accepted the call, and preached his first sermon there, before a crowded congregation, in May, 1848, and remained the beloved shepherd of that flock until his death, a period of more than thirty years. His relations with his people, official and social, ripened into an attachment that has few parallels in the history of religious organizations.

In 1849 Dr. Chapin attended the peace convention at Frankfort-on-the-Main, where he gained the reputation of the wisest and most eloquent speaker in that assembly of able men. During his long ministerial labor in New York he was an ardent and most efficient sympathetic worker in any field of labor for the good of his fellow-men. He was ever ready to grapple fearlessly with wrong in every form; and when the encroachments of the slave power upon the rights of human nature became intolerable, no man's voice was louder or more certain than his in denunciation of the entire slave system. When the flames of civil war were bursting forth in 1860-61, and the insurgents at the south and their sympathizers at the north attempted to muzzle the press and the pulpit, Dr. Chapin's pulpit was a citadel of defiance, and the very few members of his congregation who resented his denunciations with rude demonstrations soon became quiet and ultimately loyal. His fervid patriotism and his rare eloquence drew to his church every Sunday a congregation composed of representatives of the best, the freest, and most progressive elements of metropolitan life in the north. Persons living at a distance timed their visits to New York so as to include a Sunday at the Church of the Divine Paternity, listening to the eloquent divine. To his arduous pulpit labors Dr. Chapin, for many years, added the exhausting toils of a public lecturer during the winter months.

In 1866 Dr. Chapin's church first occupied their new edifice at Fifth avenue and Forty-fifth street, when the pastor's salary was fixed at ten thousand dollars a year. Under his auspices the Chapin Home for the Aged was erected in 1869, at a cost of over eighty thousand dollars. Dr. Chapin was one of the most industrious of men. He prepared his sermons with great care, and they were models of English composition. They were scholarly, rich in original thought and expression, and were always delivered by a voice of rare power. Few clergymen were so well versed in English literature and theology. He was a profound student and an exhaustive reader. He fairly devoured books, and wherever he was, at home or on the wing of travel, he was seldom seen without a book in his hand. His library of about eighteen thousand volumes is regarded as one of the most valuable private collections of books in the English language in our country. By his unceasing mental labor a robust physical constitution was undermined, and he died of asthenia. For two years he declined in strength of mind and body, and finally died suddenly. Dr. Chapin received the honorary degree of D.D. from Harvard College, and of LL.D. from Tufft's College. The list of his public works is long, for he was an able and ready writer as well as a great preacher. His writings are chiefly on religious and benevolent subjects.

Many ministers of other denominations were present at Dr. Chapin's funeral, and addresses were delivered by Rev. Henry Ward Beecher, Dr. Armitage, and Robert Collyer.

www.ingramcontent.com/pod-product-compliance
Lightning Source LLC
Chambersburg PA
CBHW021427300426
44114CB00010B/685